ACHIEVEMENTS
THROUGH
THE
AGES

A History of Our World

D1299698

ACKNOWLEDGMENTS

Grateful acknowledgment is made to the following persons for their consultation and review of the manuscript:

Stanley Spector
Director, Office of International Studies
Washington University
St. Louis, Missouri

Josephine M. Moikobu
Consultant, International
Business and Trade
Trenton, New Jersey

Editorial Staff

Project Director Kenneth A. Kruse / *Supervising Editor* David P. Morton / *Staff Editors* James E. Diestler, Darrell J. Kozlowski, Thomas R. Prehn, Stephen A. Waldron / *Production Director* LaVergne G. Niequist / *Production Supervisor* Susan Mills / *Production Associates* James E. Colao, Annette Dudley, Mary Ann Newnam / *Photo Researcher* William A. Cassin / *Indexer* Joyce Goldenstern / *Art Director* Gloria J. Muczynski / *Designer* Dennis Horan / *Artists* Lee Ames & Zak Ltd., John D. Firestone & Associates, Inc., Paul Hazelrigg, Joanna Adamska Koperska/John Walter and Associates, Frank Larocco, Joseph LeMonnier/Craven Design, Tek Nēk Inc.

Photography Credits   Credit for each photograph in this book is given where the photograph appears, except for the following: Page 28: "Crown Copyright: reproduced by permission of Scottish Development Department."/Page 68: *The Siege of Lanka from the Ramayana*, Pahari, Jamu, early seventeenth century painting in gold and colors; .825 x .580m.; 17.2749, The Ross-Coomaraswamy Collection. Courtesy, Museum of Fine Arts, Boston./Page 82: Details from Han Dynasty stone rubbing. Courtesy of Holt, Rinehart & Winston. Photo by Eileen Tweedy.

Special Acknowledgments and Credits   For excerpts and quotations that appear on pages indicated: Page 82: from Dun J. Li, *The Civilization of China from the Formative Period to the Coming of the West.* Copyright © 1975 by Dun J. Li. (New York: Charles Scribner's Sons, 1975). Reprinted with the permission of Charles Scribner's Sons./Page 109: from *Daily Life in Greece at the Time of Pericles* by Robert Flacelière and translated by P. Green. Macmillan Publishing Co., Inc., 1965. Reprinted by permission of Georges Borchardt, Inc./Page 112: from *Life of Greece* by Will Durant. Simon and Schuster, 1939./Page 144: from pp. 326–327 of *A History of Rome Through the Fifth Century* by A.H.M. Jones. Published by Walker and Co./Page 147: from *Tacitus: On Britain and Germany*, translated by H. Mattingly (Penguin Classics 1958). Copyright © H. Mattingly, 1958./Page 154: from *India: A Short Cultural History* by H.G. Rawlinson. Praeger Publishers, 1952./Page 176: from *The African Past: Chronicles from Antiquity to Modern Times* by Basil Davidson. Copyright © 1964 by Basil Davidson. By permission of Little, Brown and Company in association with Atlantic Monthly Press./Page 205: from *The Birth of Europe* by Robert Lopez. Copyright © 1962 by Max Leclerc et Cie, Proprietors of Librairie Armand Colin. Copyright © 1966; translation by J.M. Dent and Sons, Ltd. Reprinted by permission of the publisher, M. Evans and Company, Inc., New York, New York 10017./Page 229: from *The European Peasantry From the Fifteenth to the Nineteenth Century* by Jerome Blum. Reprinted by permission of the author and the American

(Acknowledgments continued on page 736.)

ISBN 0–8445–6820–1

Copyright © 1985 by Laidlaw Brothers, Publishers

A Division of Doubleday & Company, Inc.

4

CONTENTS

Bjorn Klingwall

The Bettmann Archive

The Bettmann Archive

The Bettmann Archive

The Granger Collection

Mary Evans Picture Library

Hugo Jaeger/Life. © Time Inc.

Photri

MAPS, CHARTS, AND GRAPHS

Political Map of the World

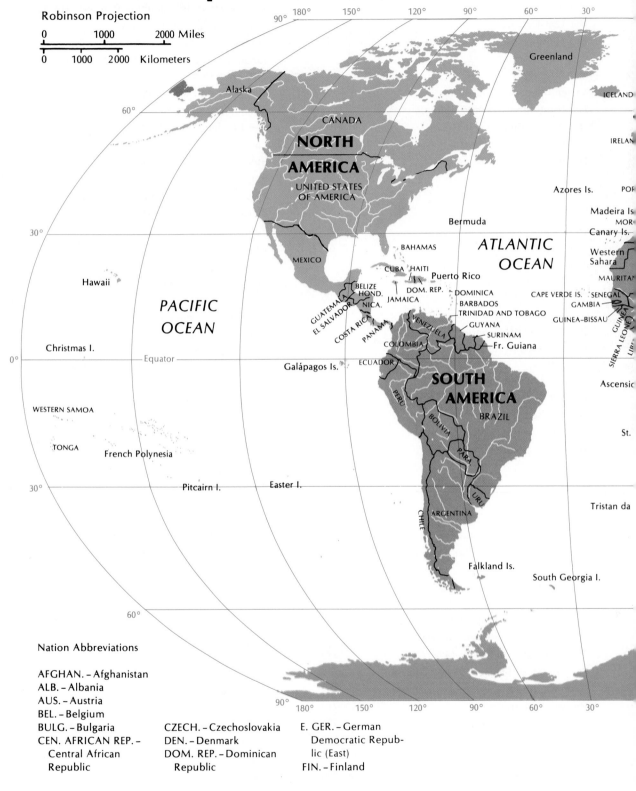

Robinson Projection

0   1000   2000 Miles

0   1000   2000   Kilometers

Greenland

ICELAND

Alaska

IRELAN

CANADA

NORTH

AMERICA

UNITED STATES
OF AMERICA

Azores Is.

POR

Madeira Is

Bermuda

MOR

Canary Is.

BAHAMAS

ATLANTIC

OCEAN

Western
Sahara

MEXICO

CUBA   HAITI

Puerto Rico

MAURITAN

Hawaii

BELIZE
HOND.

DOM. REP.

DOMINICA

CAPE VERDE IS.

SENEGAL

PACIFIC

GUATEMALA

NICA.

JAMAICA

BARBADOS

TRINIDAD AND TOBAGO

GAMBIA

GUINEA-BISSAU

OCEAN

EL SALVADOR

COSTA RICA

PANAMA

VENEZUELA

GUYANA

SURINAM

Fr. Guiana

SIERRA LEONE

LIB

Christmas I.

COLOMBIA

Galápagos Is.

ECUADOR

Equator

Ascensic

SOUTH

AMERICA

PERU

BRAZIL

St.

WESTERN SAMOA

BOLIVIA

TONGA

French Polynesia

PARA

Pitcairn I.

Easter I.

URU

Tristan da

ARGENTINA

CHILE

Falkland Is.

South Georgia I.

Nation Abbreviations

AFGHAN. – Afghanistan
ALB. – Albania
AUS. – Austria
BEL. – Belgium
BULG. – Bulgaria
CEN. AFRICAN REP. –
 Central African
 Republic

CZECH. – Czechoslovakia
DEN. – Denmark
DOM. REP. – Dominican
 Republic

E. GER. – German
 Democratic Repub-
 lic (East)
FIN. – Finland

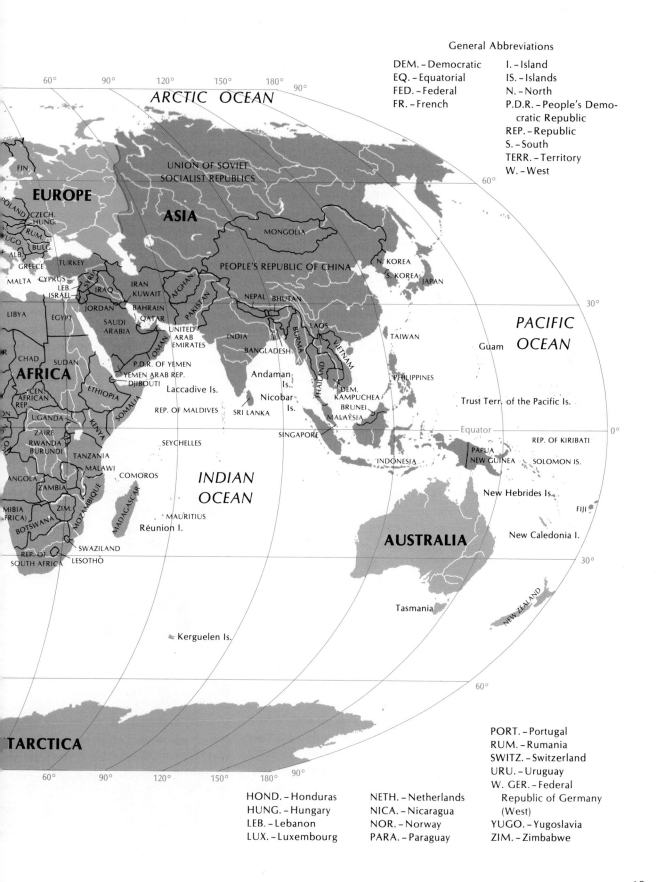

General Abbreviations

DEM. – Democratic	I. – Island
EQ. – Equatorial	IS. – Islands
FED. – Federal	N. – North
FR. – French	P.D.R. – People's Democratic Republic
	REP. – Republic
	S. – South
	TERR. – Territory
	W. – West

ARCTIC OCEAN

EUROPE

FIN.

POLAND
CZECH.
HUNG.
YUGO.
RUM.
BULG.
ALB.
GREECE
MALTA
CYPRUS
LEB.
ISRAEL
JORDAN
LIBYA
EGYPT

UNION OF SOVIET
SOCIALIST REPUBLICS

ASIA

MONGOLIA

PEOPLE'S REPUBLIC OF CHINA

N. KOREA
S. KOREA
JAPAN

TURKEY
SYRIA
IRAQ
IRAN
KUWAIT
BAHRAIN
QATAR
AFGHAN.
PAKISTAN
NEPAL
BHUTAN
INDIA
BANGLADESH
BURMA
LAOS
VIETNAM
THAILAND
DEM. KAMPUCHEA

SAUDI ARABIA
UNITED ARAB EMIRATES
OMAN
P.D.R. OF YEMEN
YEMEN ARAB REP.
DJIBOUTI

CHAD
SUDAN

AFRICA

CEN. AFRICAN REP.
ETHIOPIA
SOMALIA
UGANDA
KENYA
ZAIRE
RWANDA
BURUNDI
TANZANIA
MALAWI
ANGOLA
ZAMBIA
NAMIBIA
(S.W. AFRICA)
ZIM.
BOTSWANA
MOZAMBIQUE
REP. OF SOUTH AFRICA
SWAZILAND
LESOTHO

TAIWAN

PACIFIC OCEAN

Guam

PHILIPPINES

BRUNEI
MALAYSIA
SINGAPORE

Trust Terr. of the Pacific Is.

Andaman Is.
Nicobar Is.
Laccadive Is.
REP. OF MALDIVES
SRI LANKA

SEYCHELLES

COMOROS

MADAGASCAR

MAURITIUS
Réunion I.

INDIAN OCEAN

Equator

INDONESIA

PAPUA NEW GUINEA

REP. OF KIRIBATI

SOLOMON IS.

New Hebrides Is.

FIJI

New Caledonia I.

AUSTRALIA

Tasmania

NEW ZEALAND

Kerguelen Is.

ANTARCTICA

60° 90° 120° 150° 180° 90°

60°
30°
0°
30°
60°

HOND. – Honduras	NETH. – Netherlands	PORT. – Portugal
HUNG. – Hungary	NICA. – Nicaragua	RUM. – Rumania
LEB. – Lebanon	NOR. – Norway	SWITZ. – Switzerland
LUX. – Luxembourg	PARA. – Paraguay	URU. – Uruguay
		W. GER. – Federal Republic of Germany (West)
		YUGO. – Yugoslavia
		ZIM. – Zimbabwe

GEOGRAPHY HANDBOOK

This geography handbook is designed to provide a reference tool for reviewing some of the basic geographic terms and concepts that are relevant to history. The geography handbook will be valuable to understanding and interpreting the more than 100 maps that appear throughout the text. Frequent reference to the geography handbook will provide a review of the geographic concepts that are presented on many of these maps. In addition, the geography handbook will prove useful for answering the various skills features that are presented in the text.

An understanding of *geography*—the science that studies the earth and its life—is essential to developing a firm grasp of many of the events that have shaped world history. From prehistoric times, geography has affected the life-style and the culture developed by society. For example, climate and landforms dictated the location of early farming villages as well as the types of crops that could be grown there. Throughout the centuries, the adaptability of people has been tested time and time again by the earth's environment. Geography has, in many instances, swayed the events of history.

The use of terrace farming is dictated by the geography and the climate of this area of Indonesia. The geography of a region often has a profound effect on the life-style of the people living there.

Geography Influences History Geography has played an important part in history. For example, mountains and highland regions have usually limited the development of widespread communication, trade, and economic growth. Often, these regions are not suited for extensive farming, and the number of people in these regions tends to be small. Thus, the bulk of the population of countries such as China or India is found in the lower plains. In lands such as Greece, the mountainous nature of the area led, in ancient times, to the growth of independent city-states (see map on page 99). In addition, mountains have often formed natural boundaries between peoples. The Pyrenees separate France and Spain, and the Alps serve as the northern border of Italy (see map on page 166).

The presence of water has also played a key role in the history of many areas. Rivers tend to aid transportation as well as provide the water necessary for farming. The role of the Nile River in ancient Egypt is one example of the geography of a region's influencing its history (see map on page 175). Because of the importance of rivers to commerce and transportation, most major cities developed near rivers.

Oceans have also influenced history. It was natural for many

Dr. E.R. Degginger

14

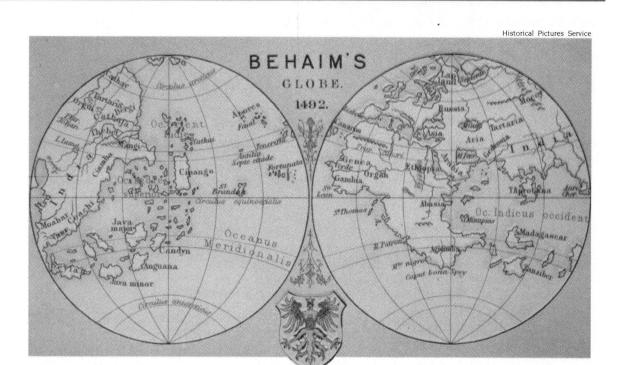

Advances in technology have improved our ability to illustrate the earth's surface. Behaim's globe of 1492 (above) fails to show North America and South America. The modern globe (below) is an extremely accurate representation of the earth's surface.

countries with ocean ports to engage in long-distance trade. Oceans have also affected history by influencing climate. For example, the climate of the northwestern coast of Europe is milder because of the nearby ocean currents, and the growing season of the region is extended (see map on page 300).

The history of countries such as Great Britain and Japan has been influenced by their island location. Britain has not been successfully invaded since 1066, when William of Normandy conquered the island. Japan was not successfully occupied by outsiders for nearly 2,000 years, until the Americans occupied the islands after World War II. Thus, the geographical characteristics of a particular region have often made a lasting impact upon that region's history.

REPRESENTATIONS OF THE EARTH

Globes   A *globe*—a three-dimensional model of the earth—is the most accurate representation of the earth's surface. A globe is an important reference tool because it correctly shows the relationship between land and water on the earth's surface. Only on a globe can the true shape, area, and location of all the parts of the earth be accurately represented.

Although globes are very exact representations of the earth, they are awkward to handle and difficult to store. In addition, it would be impractical to make a globe large enough to show local details. For most purposes, flat maps are more useful tools of geographers and historians than are globes.

Maps A *map* is a representation of all or part of the earth's curved surface on a flat sheet of paper. Most maps exhibit some distortion, or misrepresentation. This is because the earth's surface is curved, but the paper is flat. In general, the larger the area shown on the map, the more the map will be distorted. Thus, world maps usually exhibit more distortion than city maps because smaller areas such as cities are not as greatly affected by the curvature of the earth's surface.

A map projection is a way of showing the round earth on a flat sheet of paper. *Cartographers*—mapmakers—have invented many different projections, each of which has certain advantages and disadvantages. One of the most familiar map projections is the Mercator map, developed by Gerhardus Mercator in the 1500's. The Mercator projection (see Figure 1) keeps shapes reasonably accurate, but not size or distance. Distortion is greatest in the polar regions. Thus, Greenland appears larger than South America on a Mercator map, even though Greenland is less than one eighth the size of South America. An advantage of the Mercator projection is that it keeps directions true. The Mercator map greatly aided sea travel in the 1500's and 1600's and is still used for sea travel today.

Another common map projection is the polar projection. On a polar projection (see Figure 2), either the North Pole or the South

Figure 1   Mercator Projection

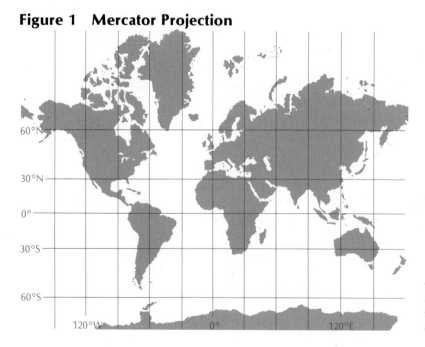

Figure 1 *The Mercator projection makes areas near the poles much larger than they really are, but it is ideal for sea travel because it keeps directions true.*

Figure 2   Polar Projection

Figure 2 *The polar projection is an equal-area projection; that is, all the land areas are shown in their correct relative proportions.*

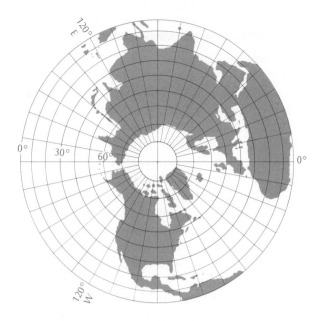

Pole is the focal point of the map. The greatest distortion on a polar projection occurs near the edges of the map. Polar projections are often used for flight navigation.

Equal-area projections (see Figure 3) show the true sizes of places on the earth's surface, but the shapes of the land and water areas are not true. Distance and direction are also somewhat distorted. Often, equal-area projections are cut up, or interrupted. The interruptions place each continent in the center part of a projection, resulting in more accurate shapes. However, the interruptions distort distance on the map.

Figure 3 *This equal-area projection, which uses interruptions, minimizes the distortion of the shapes of the land masses.*

Figure 3   Equal-Area Projection

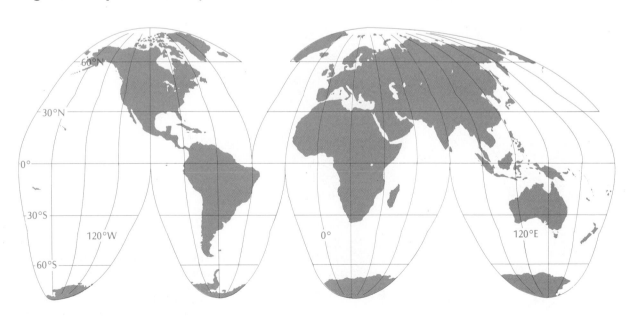

Latitude and Longitude Geographers can locate any place on a globe by using the grid system that is formed by two sets of imaginary lines—latitude lines and longitude lines. Latitude lines, or parallels, are the east-west lines of the global grid. The starting point for measuring latitude is the equator. The equator is an imaginary line that divides the earth into the Northern Hemisphere and the Southern Hemisphere. It is the midpoint between the North and South poles. The equator is 0 degrees latitude (see Figure 4). Places north of the equator, in the Northern Hemisphere, are said to be located in the north latitudes. For example, New Orleans is said to be located at 30 degrees north latitude (30°N). Similarly, places south of the equator, in the Southern Hemisphere, are said to be in the south latitudes.

Lines of longitude, or meridians, are the north-south lines of the global grid (see Figure 4). They are numbered from 0° to 180°. The *prime meridian,* or 0° longitude, runs through Greenwich, England. On the other side of the globe is the meridian that marks 180° longitude. The part of the globe east of the prime meridian up to 180° is east longitude. The part of the globe west of the prime meridian up to 180° is west longitude.

Any place on the earth's surface can be located on a line of latitude. The latitude of a particular place indicates its distance and direction from the equator. Similarly, any place on the earth's surface can be located on a line of longitude. The longitude of a particular place indicates its distance and direction from the prime

Figure 4 Longitude and Latitude

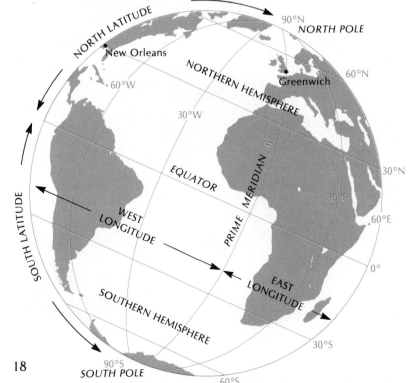

Figure 4 *The use of latitude and longitude enables geographers to accurately locate any point on the earth's surface.*

Figure 5 Annual Rainfall

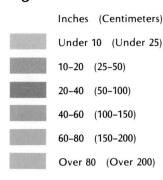

Inches   (Centimeters)

Under 10   (Under 25)

10–20   (25–50)

20–40   (50–100)

40–60   (100–150)

60–80   (150–200)

Over 80   (Over 200)

Figure 5 *The map key, or map legend, enables map users to read and understand a map. This sample map key indicates annual rainfall.*

Figure 6 *The colors shown on this sample map key indicate elevation.*

Figure 6 Elevation

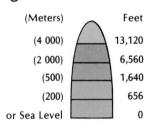

(Meters)		Feet
(4 000)		13,120
(2 000)		6,560
(500)		1,640
(200)		656
or Sea Level		0

Accurate map reading is an important skill in many occupations, such as that of a ship's navigator.

meridian. Thus, the latitude and the longitude of a particular place mark its exact location on the earth's surface.

Reading Maps   Reading a map is made easier through the use of symbols, map keys, and map scales. Information on a map is usually represented with symbols. The map key, or map legend, explains the meaning of the symbols and the colors used on a map (see Figure 5). The map scale, which is often part of the map key, indicates the relationship between the size of the map and the size of the area it represents. The map scale is the number of miles or kilometers each inch or centimeter on the map represents. The map scale is often indicated by a ruled line or bar known as a line scale or a distance scale. The line scale helps in measuring distances on a map. On maps with little distortion, the line scale shows fairly accurate distance on all parts of the map. However, on maps that show large areas, the scale often varies on different parts of the map. Thus, the line scale may indicate distance accurately only for places near the equator or near the center of the map.

The map keys of some maps provide information about the *elevation*—the height above or below sea level—of the land. Relief maps use color and/or contour lines to indicate the elevation of the land shown on the map (see Figure 6).

Kinds of Maps   Maps often have specialized purposes. For example, a political map may show current international boundaries,

and a physical map may show geographical features. A historical map may show important trade routes at a particular time in history (see map on page 158). A weather map may indicate various atmospheric conditions. Other common types of maps are highway maps and street maps.

THE EARTH'S SURFACE

Water   Over 70 percent of the earth's surface is water, most of which is ocean salt water. Because no boundaries actually divide the oceans, there is really one world ocean. It is customary, however, to separate this one large ocean into four bodies of water—the Pacific, Atlantic, Indian, and Arctic oceans. The oceans are connected by straits. Smaller parts of the oceans are called seas, bays, or gulfs.

Rivers are usually formed in mountain or highland regions by melting snow and ice, by runoff from rain, and by water from underground springs. A river and its branches, or tributaries, form a river system. River systems eventually empty into the sea. The place where a river starts is called its source; the place where a river empties into another body of water is called its mouth (see Figure 7).

Land   The total land area of the earth is approximately 57,280,000 square miles (148 355 200 square kilometers). The land on the earth's surface is divided into seven large landmasses called continents—Asia, Africa, North America, South America, Europe, Australia, and Antarctica (see map on pages 12–13). Islands are bodies of land that are smaller than continents and are completely surrounded by water. Greenland is the largest island. Peninsulas are tracts of land that are nearly surrounded by water and are connected to a larger body of land, usually a continent (see map on page 131). The Iberian Peninsula, the Italian Peninsula, and the Balkan Peninsula are three large peninsulas in Europe.

The surfaces of continents and islands have different landforms. Geographers use elevation and *relief*—the changes in elevation from one point to another—to distinguish one landform from another. Four major types of landforms are mountains, hills, plains, and plateaus.

Major Landforms   Landforms with a high elevation—usually 6,600 feet (2 000 meters) or more above sea level—are mountains. Mountains have a high relief—that is, within a very short distance, the elevation from one point to another may rise or drop very greatly. Hills differ from mountains in that hills have an elevation of 1,650 to 6,600 feet (500 to 2 000 meters). Hills have

Figure 7　Landforms

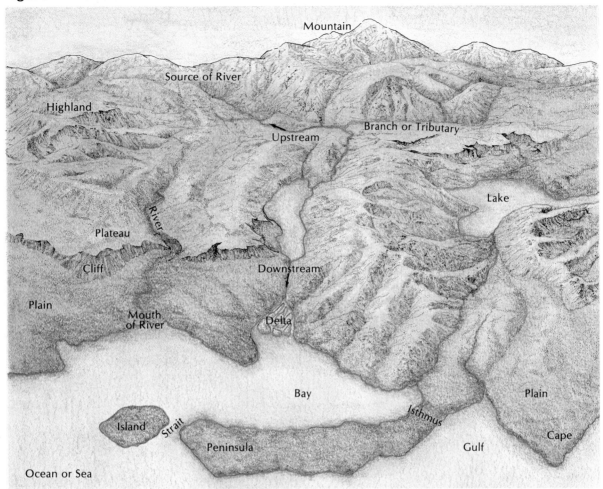

Figure 7　*The vast differences in the earth's surface are indicated by these bodies of water and these varied types of landforms.*

a moderate relief (see map on page 36). Many hills are the remnants of mountains that have been diminished by *erosion*—the process by which water, wind, or ice slowly wears down landforms.

Plains are relatively flat or gently rolling lands. Their elevation and their relief are usually less than 500 feet (150 meters). Plateaus are also flat-surfaced lands, but plateaus have a higher elevation than do plains—usually 1,650 feet (500 meters) or more. Like plains, plateaus generally have relatively low relief (see Figure 7).

CLIMATE

Weather and Climate　*Weather* may be described as the temperature and precipitation of a particular place at a particular time. The weather of a place often changes from day to day. *Climate*, however, may be described as the average weather conditions of an area over a long period of time.

The climate of a particular region has often had a significant influence upon the history and the development of the area. For example, in prehistoric times, climate affected the migration of people. Later, as early people settled in farming villages, they discovered that they could not grow the same crops in all climates. In time, people discovered ways—irrigation, for example—that enabled them to adapt their life-styles to the particular climate in which they lived.

An area's climate depends upon many factors, including latitude, height above sea level, and ocean currents. An area's location in relation to landforms and large bodies of water also affects its climate. Geographers have divided the world's climates into several different types, based upon average annual temperature and precipitation (see Figure 8).

Types of Climate   Hot, or tropical, climates are found near the equator. There are two types of tropical climates—tropical rain-forest climate and savanna climate. Both of these climates are hot all year long, but the tropical rain-forest climate receives a great

Figure 8 *In general, colder climates are located near the polar regions, and warmer climates are located near the equator.*

Tropical Rain Forest

Tropical Savanna

Steppe

Desert

Mediterranean

Humid Subtropical

Marine West Coast

Continental, Warm Summer

Continental, Cool Summer

Subarctic

Tundra

Highlands

Figure 8   Climatic Regions

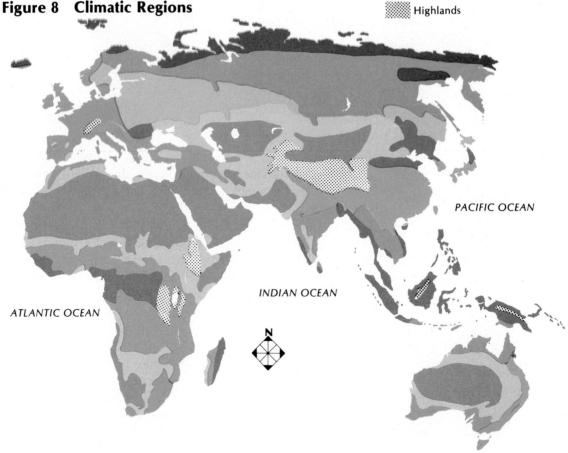

PACIFIC OCEAN

INDIAN OCEAN

ATLANTIC OCEAN

N

amount of rainfall throughout the year. The savanna climate, however, generally has six dry months and six wet months each year.

Dry climates—desert areas and steppe areas—can be found in the low and middle latitudes. Steppe areas are semiarid; that is, they get more rainfall than do desert areas. Desert areas average less than 10 inches (25 centimeters) of rainfall per year, and sometimes deserts receive no rainfall for many years (see map on page 171).

Mild climates are generally found in the middle latitudes—between 30° and 60° north or south of the equator. Marine-west-coast climate, or maritime climate, has moderate temperatures and adequate amounts of rainfall. Humid subtropical climate regions are characterized by very warm summers and mild winters. Rainfall is heavier during the summer than during the winter. Mediterranean climate regions have warm dry summers and mild winters. This type of climate region receives most of its rainfall during the winter months.

Continental climates are generally found in the middle and high latitudes. Warm summer continental climate is characterized by a warm summer, a cold winter, and dependable annual precipitation. Cool summer continental climate is characterized by a

Climate is a primary influence upon the growth of the dense vegetation of the tropical rain forest (left) and the sparse plant growth of the desert (right).

V Englebert/ZEFA

Scott Ransom/Taurus

warm but short summer, a cold winter, and moderate annual precipitation.

Cold climates are found in the high latitudes. Subarctic climate regions have short summers and long cold winters. Precipitation in subarctic regions tends to be light. Polar climates are divided into two types—tundra and ice cap. The tundra has a short, cool summer during which some plant life grows. However, virtually nothing grows on the ice cap, where the temperature never gets above freezing. Both areas receive little precipitation.

Highlands climate regions are characterized by several different types of climate. Since temperatures become colder as altitude increases, climates change at different levels of a mountain range. These various small climate areas cannot accurately be shown on a map and are called highlands.

THE WORLD'S POPULATION

Population Distribution and Density The earth's geography and climate have, in large part, determined the distribution of the world's population. *Population density*—the average number of persons living on a square unit of land—is usually greater in plains areas and in coastal regions (see Figure 9). This is because these areas are generally well suited to farming and trade. Natural resources also influence population density because large amounts of resources often can support significant numbers of people.

Figure 9   Population Density

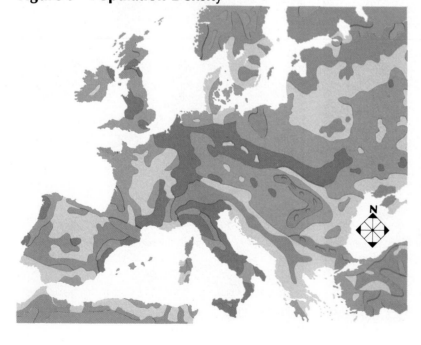

Figure 9 *Population density varies greatly, even within relatively short distances, as this map of Europe shows.*

Inhabitants per Square Mile   (Kilometer)

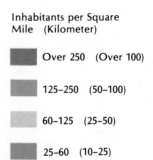

Over 250   (Over 100)

125–250   (50–100)

60–125   (25–50)

25–60   (10–25)

2–25   (1–10)

Under 2   (Under 1)

Immigration may be a significant factor in the growth rate of a country, as it was for the United States around the turn of the century.

Figure 10 *The number of years it takes for a nation's population to double at certain rates of growth is shown below. Many nations face social and economic problems because of rapid population growth.*

Figure 10 Population Doubling Time

Population Growth Rate	Years to Double Population
0.5%	139
1.0	69
1.5	46
2.0	35
2.5	28
3.0	23
3.5	20
4.0	17

Population Growth   The world's population stands at over 4.5 billion people. Recently, the world's population has increased by about 1.7 percent—approximately 80 million people—each year (see Figure 10).

Demographers—people who study the characteristics of human populations—measure the increase in population by the rate of natural growth (see map on page 708). To determine this figure, demographers first calculate the birth rate and the death rate of a country or area. The birth rate is the number of births each year per 1,000 people. The death rate is the number of deaths each year per 1,000 people. The difference between the death rate and the birth rate, per 1,000 people, is the rate of natural growth. If the rate of natural growth of the world's population remains at 1.7 percent, the world's population will double every 41 years.

Another factor that determines the total population growth rate of a country is *migration*—the movement of people from place to place. Migration has played an important part in the history of many nations. For example, in the nineteenth century, millions of people emigrated from Europe to other parts of the world.

Geography has played an important role in both the prehistory and the history of the world. Throughout the centuries, geography has affected migration, settlement, commerce, transportation, and warfare. A knowledge of geography and maps is important to developing an understanding of history. This geography handbook will help you understand and interpret the more than 100 maps that are presented throughout the text.

UNIT 1

THE RISE OF EARLY CIVILIZATIONS

c. 10,000 B.C. to 200 B.C.

1 The Growth of Early Societies 2 The Earliest Civilizations
3 Civilization in Ancient India 4 Early Civilization in China

Grant Heilman

Valley glacier in the Harding Ice Field, Alaska

Detail, Egyptian wall painting, *c.* 1200 B.C.

The earliest civilizations were formed as human cultures gradually learned to adapt to and to use the environment. As early cultures grew and changed, many important developments took place. Among the most important of these was farming. Farming enabled early societies to slowly build a more settled way of life in permanent villages and towns.

A settled way of life led to additional changes in early cultures. The first governments arose as the need to control resources, such as water for crop irrigation, became important. Organized religions developed. And systems of writing were invented to keep records and to communicate ideas, thoughts, and feelings.

The earliest civilizations emerged independently in a number of regions throughout the world. Nearly 5,500 years ago, the first civilization developed in the Middle East. Later, civilizations grew up in the Nile, Indus, and Yellow river valleys and in Central and South America. In time, contacts between some early civilizations resulted in the spread of ideas from one region to another.

Jonathan T. Wright/Liaison

Ruins of a Sumerian ziggurat at Uruk, *c.* 4000 B.C.

CHAPTER 1 THE GROWTH OF EARLY SOCIETIES

1 Early Cultures   2 The Agricultural Revolution   3 The Foundations of Civilization

The story of early people is one of slow but steady development. In part, it describes the continual attempt by early people to adapt to changes in the environment. The record tells of the ways in which early people learned to live and to work together to survive and to improve their way of life.

Because the prehistoric record is still being pieced together, much remains unknown about early people and their way of life. Even the origin of human life is open to question. Today, most scientists believe that human development was a product of slow change over vast stretches of time—a process called evolution. However, not all people agree with this view of human development.

In any case, the development of early cultures, and the forces and events that helped to shape them, are a fascinating story. And as we learn more about the record of human change and achievement, we will be better able to understand the nature of civilization.

British Crown Copyright/Department of Environment

The 4,000-year-old Neolithic village of Skara Brae lies on an island in the Orkney chain off the coast of Scotland.

1 EARLY CULTURES

Writing, invented more than 5,000 years ago, is a relatively recent development in human history. Thus, only a tiny portion of human existence has been recorded in written accounts. Early people, however, have left a record of their progress in the tools that they made and used and in the places where they lived and died. Scientists have uncovered just a small part of that record. They have discovered that early people constantly developed new ways to meet changing conditions. Evidence indicates that by 12,000 years ago, early people had developed the skills necessary to thrive in many different environments.

DISCOVERING PREHISTORY The story of people who lived before written records were kept—that is, during *prehistoric* times— has puzzled experts for many years. Historians often use the findings of *archaeologists* [AHR-kee-AHL-uh-juhsts]—scientists who study the remains of early people—to learn more about prehistoric life. Archaeologists work to carefully piece together information gathered from *artifacts*—objects made by early people—and from *fossils*—remains of plants, animals, and people. For example, stone tools and weapons have been found that give some clues about the *technology*— the way tools, weapons, and other objects are made and used—of early hunters. Animal bones found in caves help to show the kinds of food eaten by early people. Other remains give experts some understanding of the beliefs and the way of life of early people.

One problem facing archaeologists is that of determining the age of ancient remains. One of the most widely used methods today is *radiocarbon dating*. Using this method, scientists measure the rate at which atoms of radioactive carbon 14—an element present in all living things—decay. Generally, radiocarbon dating can only be used to find the age of things that existed after about 50,000 B.C.—that is, 50,000 years before the birth of Christ. Years following Christ's birth are identified with the initials A.D., which stand for the Latin phrase *anno Domini*—"in the year of the Lord."

Some scientists question the accuracy of radiocarbon dating for finding the age of remains that date before 4000 B.C., that is, that are more than 6,000 years old. However, other methods of dating estimate the age of the layers of rock and soil in which the objects are found. When the results are compared, the age of many early remains can be estimated rather accurately.

THE SEARCH FOR HUMAN ORIGINS Recent discoveries by archaeologists and *anthropologists*—scientists who study the origins and behavior of people—have radically changed many of scientists' earlier ideas about the origins of human life. In a remote area of Ethiopia, fossils have been found that indicate that early *hominids*—humanlike life forms—may have existed at least 3.5 million years ago. However, the world's earliest known tools go back about 2 million years.

The first major discovery that has led scientists to reevaluate their theories about the origins of humans occurred in 1974. Anthropologist Donald Johanson, while searching for fossils in the Afar Triangle region of Ethiopia, found the remains of an early female hominid that has come to be known as Lucy. Nearly one half of Lucy's skeleton remained. After using accepted dating procedures, scientists believe Lucy to be about 3.5 million years old. Slightly over 3.5 feet (1.1 meters) tall, Lucy, when she was alive, probably weighed about 60 pounds (27 kilograms). Her brain was no larger than a chimpanzee's, but evidence shows that she walked upright. Since the discovery of Lucy, other hominid fossils have been found in the same area that may be as much as 4 million years old. These

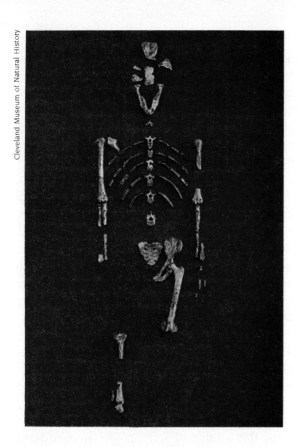

The skeleton of an early hominid—estimated to be 3.5 million years old and known as Lucy—has changed what some scientists believe about human origins.

fossils also show that these early hominids with chimpanzee-sized brains walked upright and stood less than 5 feet (1.5 meters) tall. These discoveries have led some scientists to a new theory. The hominid fossils from Ethiopia, they believe, belong to a newly discovered species, which they call *Australopithecus afarensis* [aw-STRAY-loh-PITH-i-kuhs uh-fahr-EN-sis]. It is theorized that these hominids, who had small brains, walked upright at least 1.5 million years before tools began to be used. Before the discovery of Lucy, it was assumed that the ability to walk upright was coupled with a large brain and the use of tools.

THE EMERGENCE OF MODERN PEOPLE Based on the new fossil record, a new theory of human origins has been proposed by Donald Johanson and others. This new theory suggests that *Australopithecus afaren-sis*—though neither human nor ape—was an early ancestor of the first human genus—*Homo*—which fully emerged about 2 million years ago. The first of this truly human genus is generally agreed to have been *Homo habilis*, or handyman. *Homo habilis* is considered to have been the first early human to use tools.

Not all scientists accept this new theory. However, most of them do agree that the fossil record indicates that human beings evolved from *Homo habilis* to *Homo erectus*—upright man—to *Homo sapiens*—thinking or modern man.

Fossils of *Homo erectus* have been found in Asia (Peking man and Java man) and in Europe (Heidelberg man). Other remains of *Homo erectus* have been found in Africa. It is believed that *Homo erectus* appeared on the earth about 1.5 million years ago. The fossil record seems to show that by about 500,000 years ago these early humans hunted, were able to make fire, and probably were able to communicate with one another. In contrast, *Homo sapiens*—the group that modern people belong to—emerged rather recently, probably within the last 300,000 years.

Even today, scientists are not sure exactly where or when modern people first appeared on the earth. Some of the oldest fossils of *Homo sapiens* have been found in Europe. These fossils are the remains of an early modern people called *Neanderthals* [nee-AN-duhr-TAWLZ]. It is believed that by at least 100,000 years ago Neanderthals were living in Asia, Africa, and Europe. As you will read, these early modern people were able to adapt and to survive during a period in which the earth's environment was undergoing dramatic changes.

THE CHANGING EARTH Anthropologists use information gathered by archaeologists to study early cultures. A *culture* is the way of life of a people, which includes the peoples' traditions and beliefs, their habits of behavior, and their technology. Many experts believe that an important factor in the development of early cultures was *adaptation*—the ways that people change to meet the needs and demands of new environments.

Early people found that as their environment changed, they were forced to develop new technologies and life-styles in order to survive. Nearly 100,000 years ago, the earth's climate slowly began to change, as it had several times before. In many areas, the weather became more harsh. As a result, new cultures emerged to meet the changing environment.

During the last 1,500,000 years, the earth's climate has undergone several cooling and warming cycles. During the cooling cycles, the earth's polar ice caps expanded. As a result, *glaciers*—large ice sheets—formed over large parts of the globe. During the *Ice Age*—period of glacial formation—the weight of the ice caused the expanding polar caps to inch slowly outward. The movement of the ice sheets caused great changes in the earth's surface. In what is now the United States, for example, important changes in the land surface were caused by glacial movement. The stony soil of New England and the Great Lakes of the Midwest were only two results of glacial action. During this time, glaciers in some areas of the world reached a thickness of nearly 2 miles (3.3 kilometers).

During the last period of the Ice Age, about 20,000 years ago, more than 30 percent of the earth's surface was covered by ice, compared to only about 10 percent today (see map on page 32). The levels of the world's oceans dropped several hundred feet because so much water, in the form of ice, was trapped in the enormous glacial sheets. As a result, land bridges formed, connecting areas of land that today are separated by large stretches of water.

The last period of the Ice Age ended about 10,000 years ago. But the climatic changes brought about by the Ice Age had lasting effects. For example, vegetation in many areas of the world changed drastically.

SOCIAL		ECONOMIC AND TECHNOLOGICAL
	B.C.	
Neanderthal culture flourished	*c.* 100,000	Use of fire, stone tools, and storage pits for food
Cro-Magnon culture appeared	*c.* 35,000	
	c. 20,000	Cave paintings Bow and arrow developed
Ice Age ended	*c.* 10,000	
Neolithic Age began	*c.* 8000	Earliest domestication of grain and animals
	c. 7000	Southeast Asian root-farming developed Agriculture began in Americas
	c. 6000	Use of copper widespread in Middle East and Balkan Peninsula
Shrines built at Çatal Hüyük	*c.* 5500	
	c. 4000	Irrigation in Middle East began Millet grown in Yellow River Valley
Early civilization developed in Mesopotamia	*c.* 3500	
Egyptian civilization arose in Nile Valley	*c.* 3100	Rice domesticated in Yangtze River region
	c. 2750	Stonehenge constructed
Indus Valley and Yellow River civilizations appeared	*c.* 2200	
	c. 1500	Maize cultivated in the Americas
Early civilization arose in Mexico	*c.* 1300	

c. = *circa* (approximate date)

31

The Last Ice Age

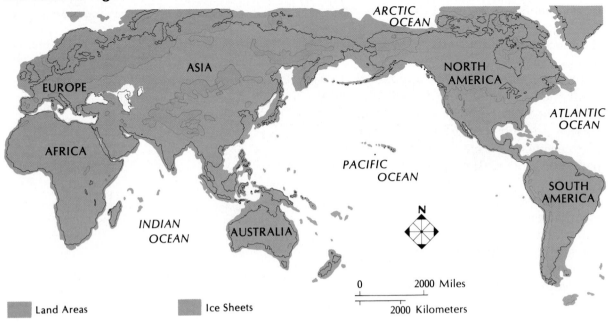

As recently as 20,000 years ago, great ice sheets covered vast areas of the world and caused many once-submerged land areas to be exposed. After the ice melted, these land areas were again covered by water.

Woodlands were slowly changed into vast grasslands because of the cold. In the northernmost regions, areas of *tundra* — treeless plains where the subsoil is frozen year round—were created by the extreme cold.

Early people were forced to adapt to the changing climatic conditions brought about by the Ice Age. As a result, they developed new and different cultures. Two major cultures that developed during prehistoric times were the Neanderthal culture and the *Cro-Magnon* [kroh-MAG-nuhn] culture.

THE NEANDERTHALS The Neanderthal culture began to develop about 100,000 B.C. Remains of this culture were first unearthed in a cave in the Neander Valley of Germany in 1856. Since that time, Neanderthal skeletons and artifacts have been found in many parts of Europe, Asia, and Africa. Experts believe that Neanderthals lived in small bands generally numbering no more than about 25 people. Neanderthals were hunters and food gatherers. That is, they met their food needs by hunting and by gathering fruits, nuts, berries, and other edible items.

A major factor in the development of the Neanderthal culture was adaptation. Archaeologists point out that Neanderthal tools and weapons steadily improved in design and in effectiveness. Primarily, these early hunters of the *Paleolithic* [PAY-lee-uh-LITH-ik] *Period*—Old Stone Age—used crude stone tools and weapons. The earliest tools used by Neanderthals were made by striking pieces of stone together to shape a rough cutting edge. Later, tools were made by sharply striking large pieces of stone several times, breaking off long chips. The chips were further trimmed to produce many different kinds of tools. Hand axes, scrapers, and stone knives were the tools most commonly formed and used by these early people.

Improvements in technology enabled the Neanderthals to adapt to their harsh environment. Neanderthals used fire for cooking, for protection, and for warmth. Some experts believe that fire may also have been

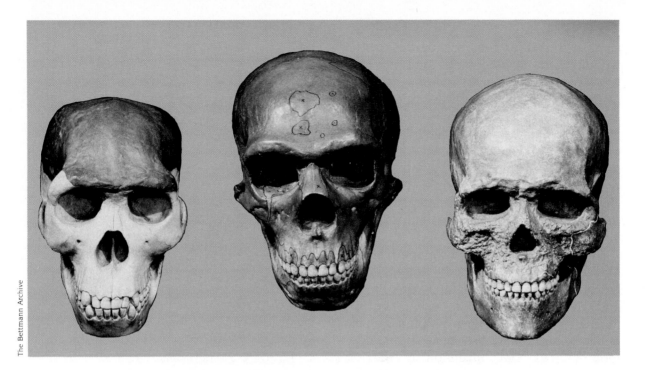

Java man (left)—a type of *Homo erectus*—probably lived 500,000 years ago. Neanderthal man (center) and Cro-Magnon man (right) were *Homo sapiens.* Neanderthals probably lived until about 30,000 B.C.

used by Neanderthals to dry and to harden wood to make spearpoints, digging sticks, and other tools and weapons. Neanderthals probably used animal skins to make clothing and also used the skins as a covering for primitive shelters. Some archaeological evidence points to the Neanderthals' use of storage pits for food that was to be shared by the entire hunting band.

Recent findings by archaeologists are significant because of what they reveal about the beliefs and the ideas of the Neanderthals. After studying fossils from Neanderthal burial sites, experts concluded that these early people may have had some concern for sick or disabled members of their group. It appears that people who were unable to hunt were allowed to share in the band's supply of food and were able to reach old age. Moreover, remains of food, weapons, and other items have been found in many Neanderthal burial grounds. For example, a Neanderthal grave found in present-day Iraq contained the remains of several types of flowers. These flowers—

bachelor's button, grape hyacinth, and hollyhock—may have been used as burial flowers. Some experts feel that evidence of such elaborate burials suggests that Neanderthals believed in a life after death.

Around 35,000 B.C., the Neanderthal culture slowly disappeared. Scientists are unsure of what became of these people. Some believe that the Neanderthals developed into a new culture—the Cro-Magnon. Others feel that the Neanderthals could not compete with the developing Cro-Magnon culture. For whatever reason, the Neanderthal culture died out and the Cro-Magnon culture took its place.

THE CRO-MAGNON CULTURE Archaeologists believe that the Cro-Magnon culture emerged about 35,000 B.C. The skeletal remains of Cro-Magnon people seem to show that the physical differences between these people and modern-day humans are very small. Tools made of bone, ivory, antler, and stone also show that the knowledge and skill of this new culture far surpassed that of the Neanderthal culture. Working with new methods and materials, Cro-Magnon toolmakers improved their technology and, as a result, gained more control over their environment. Primitive chisels, hammered-stone spearheads, scrapers, and sewing needles made from bone were some of the developments that improved life for these people. Animal-skin clothing with tightly sewn seams helped the Cro-Magnon people conquer their frigid environment.

New ways of hunting developed as Cro-Magnon hunters devised better, more-efficient weapons, such as the spear-thrower and the harpoon. As a result, the Cro-Magnon diet became more varied as small animals, birds, and fish became important food sources. One invention of the Cro-Magnon culture—the bow and arrow—has remained an important weapon of many different cultures for nearly 20,000 years. Moreover, the Cro-Magnons had mastered the use of fire. They were the first people to leave evidence that they could kindle a fire whenever they wanted.

One of the most important developments of the Cro-Magnon culture was art. Vividly realistic paintings found in caves throughout Europe show many of the animals that lived during the time of the Cro-Magnon painters. Cave painters used many colors—shades of black, red, yellow, and brown—which came from natural materials found in the earth. The Cro-Magnon artists painted directly on the cave walls. Gradually, they learned to use the cave walls' rocky contours to give a sense of action and dimension to their animal subjects.

Experts are unsure of the meanings of these cave paintings. Many believe that the paintings may have had a ceremonial or magical meaning and were used by Cro-Magnon hunters to improve their hunting. In any case, the cave paintings help to show that Cro-Magnon people lived in close harmony with their environment.

Cro-Magnon artists also were the first to

Cave art, such as this painting found in Lascaux Cave near Montignac, France, shows that the Cro-Magnons' artistic skills were highly developed.

bake clay. Small clay figurines believed to be nearly 25,000 years old have been found. The meaning of these mysterious figurines is unclear, but many scientists believe that the clay figures were used for religious ceremonies.

By about 12,000 years ago—10,000 B.C. —the Cro-Magnon culture had gradually adapted to a wide variety of environments. Cro-Magnons lived in nearly every climate. As a result of their improved tools, weapons, and knowledge, these people began to live in permanent shelters and to lead a settled way of life.

QUESTIONS FOR REVIEW

1 *What is one of the most widely used methods of dating artifacts and fossils?*

2 *How did toolmaking methods improve during the last period of the Ice Age?*

3 *Why is the Cro-Magnon culture considered to be more advanced than that of Neanderthal people?*

2 THE AGRICULTURAL REVOLUTION

Roughly 10,000 years ago, some of the Cro-Magnon cultures scattered throughout the world began to undergo a gradual but steady change. This change—from a hunting-and-gathering life-style to a way of life based upon farming—did not occur everywhere at the same time. Nor did it take place among all Cro-Magnon cultures.

By learning to raise their own food, early people were able to more fully control their environment. In turn, the invention of farming led to the establishment of permanent settlements and to the development of new, more-advanced technologies. The changes brought about by the discovery of agriculture were so great, in fact, that they ushered in a new period of cultural achievement.

ADAPTING TO A NEW ENVIRONMENT At the end of the Ice Age, early people gradually settled in certain areas year round and depended upon the plants and the animals of each area for food. The transition from a wandering, hunting and food-gathering way of life into a more settled life-style took place over a period of several thousand years. Although scientists disagree as to the exact causes, many point out that two factors were probably important. These factors were a warmer climate and a steadily growing population.

Nearly 20,000 years ago, the earth's climate underwent a warming trend. As a result, the glaciers that covered many parts of the earth began to melt. By about 10,000 B.C., the ice sheets had shrunk to their present size. In addition, the level of the world's seas rose in some places by as much as 450 feet (137 meters). In some areas of the world—including parts of southwestern Asia, Europe, and the Americas—slowly expanding forests replaced open grasslands. Large animals that had once roamed the open plains slowly disap-

peared. Over the centuries, people gradually adapted to the warmer environment.

At the same time that the environment was changing, the world's population, although still small by today's standards, was increasing. By about 10,000 B.C., the world's population was large enough to cause overcrowding in some areas and competition for the richest hunting land.

To meet the demands for increased food supplies, people turned to other sources of food, such as wild grain. Such sources had been largely ignored by the earlier hunting cultures. As people concentrated on the gathering of wild plants for food, they also began to settle in places where the plants could more easily be found, collected, and stored. One such area was the grassy hills of the Zagros Mountains in present-day Iraq (see map on page 36). More than 10,000 years ago, people in this area began to use underground pits for storing grain and to use stone knives for harvesting it. Heavy, flat stones were used to grind the harvested grain into meal. Permanent villages of mud-and-straw buildings began to be built. An improved method of making stone tools was developed. Instead of chipping stones to make tools, toolmakers learned to grind and to polish stone tools with volcanic rock and other materials. This time of change is known as the *Neolithic* [NEE-uh-LITH-ik] *Period*—New Stone Age—and lasted from about 8000 B.C. to about 3000 B.C.

Gradually, Neolithic farmers began to plant and to raise their own crops from the seeds of wild wheat and barley that they collected. As a result, they were no longer dependent upon areas where wild grain grew in abundance. Thus, the first farmers were able to settle new lands and to more effectively provide the food needed by a growing population.

THE BEGINNING OF FOOD PRODUCTION Farming—the raising of crops and the domestication of animals—began independently in many parts of the world between about 9000 B.C. and about 4000 B.C. Evidence of ancient farming *societies*—groups of people who lived together and who shared the same culture—has been found in the regions of the Middle East, eastern Asia, Southeast Asia, and the Americas. Discoveries in the Zagros Mountains and in the hills of present-day Israel and Jordan show that nearly 10,000 years ago the people of these areas first settled in permanent communities and began to produce their own food. This area later became part of the *Fertile Crescent*, which gave birth to several early civilizations (see map on this page).

The earliest evidence of the domestication of grain comes from the Middle East and is thought by experts to be about 11,000 years old. About 1,000 years later, early Neolithic farmers began to regularly prepare the soil for planting. By about 5000 B.C., farming villages existed throughout the Middle East, and crops of domesticated wheat and barley had become a principal source of food.

Remains of domesticated animals have been dated to about the same time as the domestication of grain. Over a period of many centuries, goats, sheep, pigs, and cattle were tamed by Neolithic farmers. As a result, herds of these animals provided farming societies with steady supplies of meat and other products, such as milk and wool.

The development of *agriculture*—the science of growing and harvesting crops and of raising animals for food—led to tremendous change in many early societies. Early farmers no longer needed to hunt animals or to search for wild stands of grain. Agriculture enabled them to control and to change the environment in which they lived. As a result, the discovery of agriculture led to many basic cultural changes. One important change was the rapid development of technology in early farming societies.

ADVANCES IN TECHNOLOGY The basic cultural transformation from a food-gathering way of life to a food-producing life-style prompted Neolithic farmers to gradually improve their technologies. One of the first of these improvements was in the way that stone tools were made. New techniques of grinding and polishing stones resulted in the production of tools made of hard, fine-grained stone that had keen, even cutting edges. Such tools could also be resharpened many times.

Improved tools enabled early farmers to cut down trees and to clear woodlands for

The geography and the climate of the ancient Middle East encouraged the growth of wild barley and wheat, which were domesticated by the first farmers.

The Middle East

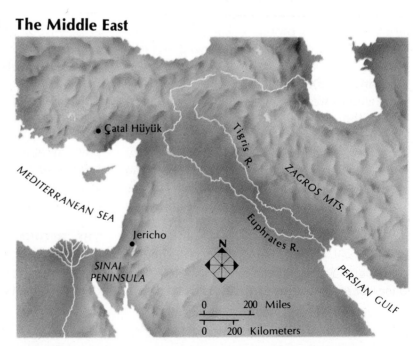

planting crops. Moreover, Neolithic farmers learned to use fire to remove timber and brush from their fields. This method of farming—called *slash-and-burn farming*—has the added effect of renewing important elements in the soil and thus of fertilizing the land.

The development of farming resulted in many other technological advances. For example, clay pottery enabled Neolithic people to carry and to store food and water. Molded, sun-dried mud bricks were used for building. Wool was spun and woven into cloth. Neolithic farmers also developed many kinds of tools, such as spades and hoes with blades made of stone or bone, for cultivating crops.

The first evidence of metalworking also comes from the Neolithic Period. At first, metal—primarily native copper—was used only for ornaments and decoration. It was easily hammered into shape and by about 6000 B.C., copper tools were common in many areas of the Middle East and the Balkan Peninsula. However, copper tools did not completely replace stone tools because they were generally too soft. Around 4000 B.C., metalworkers on the continent of Europe and in the Middle East learned to extract metal from ore by smelting.

By 5000 B.C., Middle Eastern agriculture had spread from the areas of the first farmers to the region of the Tigris and the Euphrates rivers, the area of present-day Turkey, and as far west as the Balkan Peninsula. Only a few centuries later, agricultural societies emerged in the region of central Europe and in the lower Nile River valley. In all likelihood, however, agriculture also began independently in several other parts of the world during the Neolithic Period. Early farmers in each region had to adapt their farming methods to different environments.

EARLY FARMING AROUND THE WORLD
The earliest farmers of tropical Southeast Asia probably cultivated root crops—such

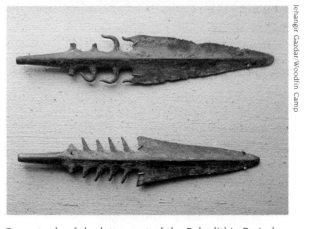

Stone tools of the latter part of the Paleolithic Period were made by striking a stone and producing flakes that were trimmed. Later stone-tool makers improved this method (center). Bronze weapons (bottom) and tools were used about 5,000 years ago.

The agricultural methods used in some countries have changed little over the span of centuries.

as cassavas, yams, manioc, and taro—as important sources of food. The beginnings of root farming are unclear, but many experts believe that it began nearly 9,000 years ago. This type of farming can survive only in an area where there is little change in temperature and in the amount of rainfall from one season to the next. Unlike grain cultivation, root farming probably did not provide the basic food supplies for the early farmers of Southeast Asia. Experts point out that root farming was probably less productive than grain farming. Also, large-scale root farming was impractical in tropical areas where the land was difficult to clear. Some scientists believe that as a result, large, permanent settlements did not develop in Southeast Asia for several centuries after the discovery of farming.

Experts are unsure when farming began in eastern Asia. Remains found in what is now China show that a kind of grain called millet was grown along the Yellow River around 4000 B.C. In addition, early farming villages were established by this time throughout the area. Neolithic farming tools made of stone—axes, hoes, spades, and reaping knives—have been found at several early sites in present-day China. By 3000 B.C., rice was domesticated in the region of the Yangtze River. Soybeans were a principal food source of early Asian farmers by about 1600 B.C. This protein-rich food was an important addition to the diet of the ancient Chinese.

Agriculture also developed among the early people who settled in the Americas. The first domesticated plant in the region of modern-day Mexico and Central America was a kind of squash. It was grown nearly 9,000 years ago. About 2,000 years later, several different kinds of beans were also being grown by early farmers in the Americas. Maize—an early ancestor of corn—was a major source of food in the Americas by about 1500 B.C. Moreover, early farmers in parts of the Americas domesticated the guinea pig, the llama, and the alpaca. The guinea pig was raised for food and the alpaca was raised for its wool. The llama was used mainly as a pack animal.

Agriculture thus evolved independently in many places around the globe. Although the process of agricultural development was gradual and took place over thousands of years, the results were revolutionary. New life-styles and new and more complex social and political organizations were developed. Within only a few centuries of the discovery of farming, many early agricultural societies had successfully adapted to the new way of life.

QUESTIONS FOR REVIEW

1 *Where was grain probably first domesticated?*

2 *In what way did Neolithic toolmakers improve the way that stone tools were made?*

3 *Why did agriculture lead to a more settled life-style among early Neolithic farming cultures?*

Myths and Realities

Dating the Mysterious Past

Scattered throughout modern-day Western Europe are nearly 50,000 mysterious stone structures that have recently been dated by a new method to between 4000 B.C. and 1500 B.C. Using giant boulders that weighed between a few tons and nearly 385 tons (346 metric tons), Neolithic builders hammered and shaped the huge stones—called *megaliths*—with tools made of stone, wood, and bone. The stones were often moved great distances without the use of wheeled vehicles. Many scholars have held that the megalithic structures of Europe were proof that early Middle Eastern cultures gradually spread throughout the European continent. To many experts, it did not seem likely that the Stone Age "barbarians" of early Europe could develop advanced cultures capable of building megalithic structures independently. Most experts believed that the enormous Middle Eastern stone structures, such as the Pyramids of Egypt, were the basis for the European megaliths. However, recent discoveries may change this view.

Using a new way of dating ancient remains—tree-ring dating—some archaeologists today believe that many of the technological developments of Europe may not have been directly influenced by outside cultures. In fact, some feel that the developments may have taken place before, or perhaps about the same time as, similar developments in more-advanced societies.

When tree-ring dating is used to date an object, the rings of the oldest living tree—the bristlecone pine—are counted. Scientists know that one ring grows every year. Then, after the number of rings are counted, the tree-ring sample is radiocarbon dated. The results of the two techniques are compared. This comparison helps to show the age of artifacts less than about 6,000 years old. This method has produced some interesting results. For example, the stone temples on the Mediterranean island of Malta were once believed to have been built around 1800 B.C. Today, however, some experts have shown by using the tree-ring dating technique that the temples may have been built about 3100 B.C. This date is clearly too early to support the idea that the temples' designs were influenced by eastern Mediterranean cultures. Furthermore, the most well-known European megalithic structure, Stonehenge, is believed by many today to have been begun about 2750 B.C., several centuries earlier than was once thought. A few scientists even feel that Stonehenge may have been an observatory for recording the movements of the sun and the moon. Moreover, some technological developments, such as metalworking, are believed to have begun independently in both Europe and the Middle East.

No one is sure exactly why the megalithic structures were built—as temples, monuments, tombs, meeting places, or observatories. However, it seems clear that the prehistoric people of the European continent had remarkable engineering and mathematical skills that were once believed to belong only to more-advanced societies.

This aerial view of Stonehenge, in the south of England, shows the traces of earlier concentric stone rings that once circled the mysterious monument.

Photo Researchers

3 THE FOUNDATIONS OF CIVILIZATION

The development of farming during the Neolithic Period led to the growth of complex societies. As more people relied on farming, decisions about food production—what crops to plant, when to plant them, which fields to use, and who would plant the crops—had to be made. Moreover, ways of defending the society's resources from attack had to be found. In areas of low rainfall, water supplies for growing crops and for grazing animals had to be provided. As a result, many societies began to develop organized ways of making these decisions and of dealing with these problems.

REVOLUTIONARY DEVELOPMENTS IN AGRICULTURE Irrigation —bringing water to crops by using ditches, canals, basins, and other systems—was important to the growth of societies throughout the world. The irrigation of crops led to great increases in food production among many early farming societies. Eventually, irrigation in some areas enabled farmers to grow and to harvest two or three crops from the same field each year. As a result, people who specialized in occupations other than farming could be supported on a limited amount of land. This, in part, led to the growth of the first towns and cities. In addition, some experts believe that the social organization and the cooperation needed to build large irrigation systems helped to promote the growth of governments.

Irrigation was first used in the region of the Middle East—the area between the eastern end of the Mediterranean Sea and the Arabian Sea. More than 7,000 years ago, as early farmers began to move onto the dry plains of the region, irrigation was necessary to provide water for farming. In Mesopotamia—the area between the Tigris and Euphrates rivers—many centuries of flooding had deposited layers of silt. The enriched soil came to life with the use of irrigation. Not long before 4000 B.C., early Mesopotamian farmers dug simple ditches along the riverbanks to divert water to their fields. At roughly the same time, early farmers of the Nile River valley in Egypt irrigated their crops. Later, these farmers created an extensive system of irrigation by trapping the Nile floodwaters in clay-lined lakes, called basins. During times of little rainfall, water from the basins could be drained off and used to irrigate crops.

Irrigation was also developed independently in several other parts of the world. Early farmers in the regions of Peru, Mexico, China, and India discovered ways to irrigate their crops. Many of the world's early societies depended upon irrigation to feed large populations.

THE GROWTH OF COMPLEX SOCIETIES The earliest evidence of the increasingly complicated nature of societies comes from the Middle East. For example, more than 9,000 years ago, some agricultural settlements in this region gradually developed into small trade centers. Jericho, an early city located in the Jordan River valley, carried on a local trade in salt, sulfur, and bitumen [buh-TOO-muhn]—a natural asphalt used to waterproof materials. By about 7350 B.C., Jericho's population had grown to more than 2,000 people. Stone walls used for defense encircled the city. They reached more than 11 feet (3.5 meters) high and were nearly 5 feet (1.5 meters) thick. At Çatal Hüyük [CHAH-tuhl hoo-YUK], in present-day southern Turkey, archaeologists have found what may have been the shrines of an early religion. At other sites throughout the Middle East, temples have also been discovered. These buildings are believed to be more than 7,000 years old.

Between 5500 B.C. and 4000 B.C., Middle Eastern societies grew more complex. Methods of food production became more efficient. As a result, food surpluses that could support many nonfarmers were produced.

This enabled many *artisans*—potters, stonecutters, leatherworkers, and others—to develop their skills. By about 4000 B.C., some cities with populations of more than 10,000 people began to appear. Massive public buildings that needed long-range planning and the organization of many people were built. As a result of growing trade, contact between different cultures increased. This led to exchanges of ideas among cultures.

Shortly after 4000 B.C., the cultural and technological development of some societies reached a relatively high level. As these societies grew, and as their achievements and their influence became more widespread, the first civilizations began to appear.

CIVILIZATIONS Between about 3500 B.C. and about 1300 B.C., *civilizations*—societies that developed governments, religions, writing, cities, specialized occupations, and social classes—arose in many parts of the world. While early civilizations developed in many different ways, they all shared several characteristics. One of the most common characteristics was the growth of governments. Increasingly, decisions about food production and distribution, defense, and the building of public projects—temples, fortifications, and irrigation systems—were made by a few powerful members of society.

Another characteristic of many early civilizations was the development of organized religions. Moreover, many people no longer farmed. Instead, these people began to specialize in different occupations. Commerce grew as early trade routes were extended. Social classes were usually formed as people began to be ranked in society by their wealth, power, and prestige.

Beginning around 3000 B.C., early civilizations emerged in many parts of the world, particularly in or around fertile river valleys.

Early Civilizations

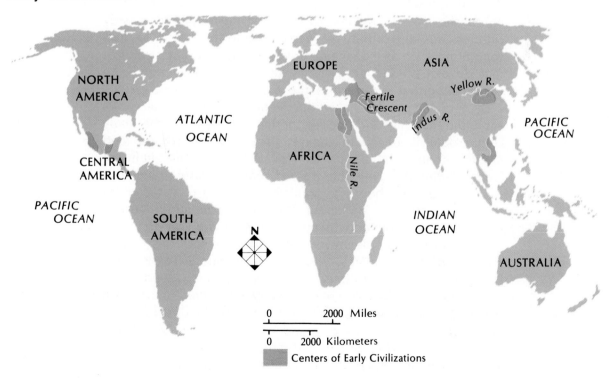

0   2000 Miles
0   2000 Kilometers
Centers of Early Civilizations

In Mesopotamia between about 3500 B.C. and 3100 B.C., writing was invented and the first written records were kept. Advanced technologies—including new ways of farming, building, toolmaking, and metalworking—were developed.

Shortly before 3000 B.C., an early civilization appeared along the Nile River in Egypt. Several centuries earlier, civilization had arisen between the Tigris and the Euphrates rivers in Mesopotamia (see map on page 39). By about 2200 B.C., an early civilization had emerged in the Indus Valley of India. Only a few centuries later, a civilization arose along the Yellow River in China. And around 1300 B.C., an early civilization appeared in the area of present-day Mexico.

The emergence of civilizations was a gradual process. Beginning in the areas settled by the first farmers, early civilizations spread over vast territories. Most flourished for many centuries. As people gained more control over their environments, civilizations became the centers for accomplishments in art, government, religion, and technology.

QUESTIONS FOR REVIEW

1 *What technological development led to an increase in the food production of early agricultural societies?*

2 *How did Egyptian farmers irrigate their crops?*

3 *Why were many artisans of early civilizations able to specialize in particular occupations?*

CHAPTER SUMMARY

By studying the artifacts and the fossil remains of early cultures, experts are able to uncover the way that people lived thousands of years ago. Scholars have discovered that one of the most important factors in the development of early cultures was the ability of early people to adapt to new conditions, such as a changing environment. Two early cultures that developed and grew during the Paleolithic Period were the Neanderthal culture and the Cro-Magnon culture.

By the end of the Paleolithic Period—about 10,000 years ago—the hunting and food-gathering life-style of the early cultures slowly began to change. Faced with increased food needs, Stone Age hunters learned to gather wild grain for food. During the Neolithic Period, early people in various parts of the world began to plant the seeds of the wild grains that they gathered. By about 3000 B.C., farm crops were a principal source of food in many parts of the world.

The growing complexity of early farming societies led to many important changes. New developments in agriculture, such as irrigation, enabled early societies to feed large populations. Gradually, the first civilizations were born as a few societies reached a high level of cultural development. The earliest civilizations emerged in the Middle East. Later, civilizations developed along the Indus River in India, the Yellow River in China, and in Central and South America.

CHAPTER 1 IN REVIEW

IMPORTANT WORDS, NAMES, AND TERMS

1 Explain, define, or identify each of the following:

archaeologist	adaptation	agriculture
fossil	Paleolithic Period	slash-and-burn farming
technology	Neolithic Period	irrigation
culture	society	civilization

FACTS AND IDEAS

2 What is radiocarbon dating?

3 How did Cro-Magnon artists make their cave paintings seem more realistic?

4 What two types of grain were domesticated in the region of the Middle East?

5 Approximately when did the last period of the Ice Age end?

6 List several characteristics that were common to many of the world's first civilizations.

ANALYZING VISUAL MATERIAL

7 Based on the map on page 32, in what ways might the great ice sheets have affected the movement of early peoples from one continent to another?

8 Study the illustration on page 33 carefully. What major differences can you observe among Java man, Neanderthal man, and Cro-Magnon man?

CONCEPTS AND UNDERSTANDINGS

9 How did adaptation affect the growth of early cultures?

10 Why do some archaeologists believe that people of the Neanderthal culture probably valued life more highly than did earlier cultures?

11 What factors were important in the change among some cultures from hunting and gathering to food producing?

12 In what ways did root farming slow the development of large-scale agricultural communities in Southeast Asia?

13 Why was irrigation important to the growth of early agricultural societies?

PROJECTS AND ACTIVITIES

14 Prepare a bulletin board showing the different stages of development in the making of stone tools from the early Neanderthal culture to the end of the Stone Age around 3000 B.C.

15 Based on library research, prepare a report to the class, comparing the geography and climate of any two of the world's early centers of agriculture.

CHAPTER 2 THE EARLIEST CIVILIZATIONS

More than 5,500 years ago, about 3500 B.C., the first civilizations emerged in the region of the Middle East. Geography, religion, trade, and farming were some of the factors that were most important to the development and the spread of early civilization. And because these early people left written records, much is known about their social, political, and economic development.

Early Middle Eastern civilizations achieved many cultural advances. These civilizations also suffered times of decline, constant warfare, and foreign rule. However, the contributions made by the earliest civilizations have remained an important part of civilization to the present time.

Artstreet

Reminders of a once-great civilization loom over Egypt's Nile River.

1 EARLY CIVILIZATION ALONG THE NILE

One of the earliest civilizations arose in the Nile River valley of Egypt around 3100 B.C. The Nile Valley was especially well suited for the development of an early farming civilization. The annual flooding of the river continually renewed the soil of the valley and was the basis for Egyptian agricultural life.

Egyptians experienced long periods of peace and great prosperity. At one point in their long history, the Egyptians dominated much of the Middle East. At other times, however, Egypt suffered civil wars and rule by foreign invaders. Thus, Egyptian civilization slowly but steadily evolved to meet changing political conditions.

THE NILE VALLEY For thousands of years under a blazing sun, the Nile River has flowed from the mountains of eastern Africa northward to the Mediterranean Sea (see map on this page). Every spring, melting snows and heavy rainfall from the highlands washed the fertile black soil of the region into the river. In an unchanging cycle, the swollen Nile rose and overflowed its banks about the same time each year. The flooding occurred during each summer through early autumn and receded each winter. As a result, a rich layer of topsoil was deposited along the banks of the lower river in an area between 2 miles (3.2 kilometers) and 15 miles (24 kilometers) wide. Thus, by about 5000 B.C., early Egyptians were able to farm an area along the river from the First *Cataract*—steep rapids—north to the Mediterranean Sea.

In a region of sparse rainfall, the Nile's annual flooding was essential. The yearly flood provided needed water for irrigation and also left a layer of rich soil for farming. Egyptian farmers divided the year into three seasons. These seasons were based on the annual flood. The first season began

Ancient Egypt

Egyptian civilization began along the fertile banks of the Nile and eventually extended southward from the Mediterranean Sea to the Fourth Cataract.

with the first rise of the Nile River in June. The second season began with the planting that started after the river began to recede in October. The third season came in late spring, when crops were quickly harvested before the river began to rise again.

The fertile soil and the climate of the Nile Valley and of the river's *delta*—land at the mouth of a river—resulted in rich harvests. The major crops of Egypt were wheat, barley, flax, vegetables, and fruits. Between about 5000 B.C. and about 4000 B.C., irrigation became an important part of Egyptian farming. Shortly after 3000 B.C., the Egyptians built a system of canals and basins to evenly distribute the Nile flood waters.

POLITICAL	B.C.	SOCIAL AND ECONOMIC
	c. 4000	Complex irrigation developed in Mesopotamia and in Egypt
	c. 3500	Cities developed in Mesopotamia
Kingdoms of Upper and Lower Egypt united	c. 3000	Plow invented in Mesopotamia / Writing developed in Mesopotamia and in Egypt
Egyptian Old Kingdom began	2686	Great Pyramids constructed in Egypt
Sargon I united Sumerian city-states	c. 2500	
Egyptian Middle Kingdom began	2040	Hebrews reached Canaan; ideas of ethical monotheism began to develop
	c. 2000	
	c. 1900	Faiyūm irrigation project completed along Nile
Hammurabi's code of law written	c. 1790	
Hyksos gained control of Egypt	1674	Hyksos introduced horse-drawn chariot and use of bronze to Egypt
New Kingdom began in Egypt	1570	
Thutmose III enlarged Egyptian Empire	c. 1480	
	c. 1370	Akhenaten attempted to establish monotheistic beliefs in Egypt
Tutankhamen died	1351	
	c. 1300	Hittites developed process of hardening iron
Hebrew kingdom established in Palestine	1025	
King Solomon died and Hebrew kingdom divided	922	
End of Assyrian Empire / Persian Empire established	c. 600	Hebrew Babylonian captivity began
	586	First Temple in Jerusalem destroyed
Conquests of Alexander the Great began	332	Trade routes opened between Mediterranean and western Asia

Throughout their history, the Egyptians have traveled on the Nile River. They have used the current to float their boats downstream toward the Mediterranean Sea. Prevailing winds from the north also have enabled them to sail upstream toward the south. This unique two-way travel made transportation and contact between river communities relatively easy along the Nile.

Geography helped to shape early Egyptian development in another important way. Deserts lay to the west, south, and east. To the north was the Mediterranean Sea (see map on page 45). Thus, for many centuries, ancient Egypt was protected from foreign invasions and was left almost untouched by outside influences. As a result, a stable and prosperous civilization arose in the Nile River valley.

UNIFICATION AND THE OLD KINGDOM
Traditionally, Egypt was divided into two distinct regions. The Nile Valley—the upstream portion of the river—came to be known as Upper Egypt. The Nile's delta, through which the river flowed downstream to empty into the Mediterranean, was known as Lower Egypt. But about 3100 B.C., the lands of Upper and Lower Egypt were united in a single large kingdom by a ruler named Menes [MEE-neez]. To emphasize unity, Menes established the capital of Egypt at the city of Memphis, on the frontier between the two regions. Throughout history, Egyptian kings worked to maintain political unity between Upper and Lower Egypt. Menes and his successors established a strong central government led by monarchs who founded *dynasties*—successions of rulers from the same family or group. During more than 2,500 years, leaders from 30 separate dynasties governed Egypt.

During this Early Dynastic Period—about 3100 B.C. to about 2686 B.C.—the rulers of Egypt gained absolute control of the government. By the beginning of the Old Kingdom—about 2686 B.C. to about 2160 B.C.

Photri

The Great Pyramids, built near the modern city of Cairo, are a spectacular monument to the engineering skills of Egyptians who lived 45 centuries ago.

—the rulers were considered by their subjects to be divine and to have descended from the gods. The Egyptians also believed that the world belonged to their gods. Thus, they felt that their rulers—gods on earth—were the rightful owners of all the land and of the farmers' surplus crops. In addition, the Egyptians believed that their rulers made the Nile rise and fertilize the fields. Egyptian rulers also controlled the resources of the entire country and directed the people in tremendous public building projects.

During the earliest periods of Egyptian history, local and foreign trade flourished. African merchants brought ebony, ivory, incense, oil, and animal skins into Egypt. Trade between ports along the eastern Mediterranean coast and Egypt enabled the Egyptians to gain scarce resources, such as wood and minerals. Expeditions were sent to the Eastern Desert and to the Sinai Peninsula to mine copper and gold (see map on page 45).

By the end of the Old Kingdom an increase in the power and the influence of Egyptian nobles and priests gradually led to the breakdown of the rulers' authority in Egypt. For about 100 years, powerful local leaders struggled for control of a land divided by civil war. Around 2040 B.C., Egypt was finally reunited by Mentuhotep II [MEN-too-HOH-tep]. A new capital was built at Thebes in Upper Egypt. Egyptian civilization entered another period of stability and prosperity known as the Middle Kingdom, which lasted until about 1786 B.C.

THE MIDDLE KINGDOM At the beginning of the Middle Kingdom, the rulers of unified Egypt worked to bring more land under their control. They accomplished this goal by annexing new territories and by extending the boundary of Egypt to the south. In addition, the Egyptians built military outposts and patrolled extensively along the frontiers. Military expeditions were undertaken into Nubia and into the deserts that surrounded the Nile Valley.

During this period, seagoing Egyptian traders opened markets for their goods in many lands around the eastern Mediterranean Sea. Egyptian artifacts of this period have been uncovered by archaeologists on the island of Crete and in many locations throughout the Middle East. Moreover, a huge irrigation project was completed shortly after 1900 B.C. About 40 square miles (103.6 square kilometers) of rich farmland was reclaimed in a marshy area known as the Faiyūm [fay-OOM] (see map on page 45). Nearly 1,500 years later, these canals were still in operation.

During the period of the Middle Kingdom, Egypt's rulers placed new and more effective limits on the power of the nobles. A new system of government was begun in which the central government reorganized the provinces to gain greater control of the country.

By about 1800 B.C., several groups of Asiatic people—together known as the Hyksos [HIK-SAHS]—had lived in the eastern Nile Delta for many generations. A series of weak Egyptian leaders slowly undermined

King Tutankhamen's tomb held many treasures for modern archaeologists, including a painted wooden chest that shows that young pharaoh in battle.

the stability of Egypt and allowed the Hyksos to gain control of territory within Egypt. In 1674 B.C., the Hyksos captured Memphis and installed their own leader as the king of Egypt. For the first time, Egypt was ruled by outsiders. However, the Hyksos did not bring about great cultural change. Generally, they adopted Egyptian customs and ways of living.

The Hyksos brought many Asian innovations to Egypt, including the use of bronze and the spoked wheel. Moreover, new weapons, such as body armor and the horse-drawn chariot, were brought into use. About 1570 B.C., the Egyptians managed to unite and expel the Hyksos. Egypt was once again united under one dynasty. To prevent being ruled again by foreigners, the new rulers of Egypt felt the need to expand and to protect their kingdom by establishing an Egyptian Empire.

IMPERIAL EGYPT AND DECLINE Following the expulsion of the Hyksos, Egypt entered a period known as the New Kingdom—which lasted from about 1570 B.C.

to about 1085 B.C. Egypt's power reached great heights as a succession of *pharaohs* [FER-ohz]—a title by which the Egyptian rulers became known during this period —conquered new lands.

The greatest New Kingdom pharaoh, Thutmose III [thoot-MOH-suh], extended Egypt's influence northward to the mountains of Anatolia and eastward as far as the Euphrates River (see map on page 45). Many Middle Eastern states accepted Egypt's power and paid tribute to the pharaoh. To the south, Egyptian armies reached the Fourth Cataract of the Nile River and gained control of Nubia. By the end of the reign of Thutmose III, seaborne trading expeditions were making visits to the Aegean Islands, Crete, and Phoenicia.

The traditional religious ideas of Egypt were also challenged during the New Kingdom. Akhenaten [AHK-NAHT-uhn], pharaoh from 1379 B.C. to 1362 B.C., rejected Egyptian *polytheism* [PAHL-i-thee-IZ-uhm]—the worshiping of many gods. Instead, he favored the worship of one god, Aten—the life-giving sun. This religious revolution, however, was short-lived. Only seven years after Akhenaten's death in 1362 B.C., the old polytheistic traditions were restored under the pharaoh Tutankhamen [TOO-TANG-KAHM-uhn].

During the later period of Egyptian history, ineffective rulers helped to weaken the power of the once-mighty Egyptian empire. Once again, Egypt entered a period of gradual decline. Between about 950 B.C. and 332 B.C., Egypt was invaded and ruled by foreigners several times. During this period, African armies and invaders from the Middle East and Asia conquered the Nile Valley. Throughout these centuries of foreign domination the proud and ancient culture of Egypt remained largely unchanged. Then, in 332 B.C., Alexander the Great marched his Greek soldiers across the land along the Nile, bringing values and ideas that eventually reshaped the character of Egyptian culture (see Chapter 6). Thus, after nearly 3,000 years of development and progress, the civilization of ancient Egypt came to an unexpected end.

QUESTIONS FOR REVIEW

1 *During which period of ancient Egyptian history was the government reorganized to lessen the power of the nobles?*

2 *In what way was traditional Egyptian religion challenged during the New Kingdom?*

3 *Why was geography important to the stability of ancient Egypt?*

2 CULTURE AND SOCIETY IN ANCIENT EGYPT

The protection offered by the Nile River valley helped, in part, to produce the unique character of Egyptian civilization. The Egyptians' religious beliefs shaped their way of life and helped to promote many advances in the arts and the sciences. The Egyptians also developed one of the first systems of writing. And, although Egyptian society was highly structured, many opportunities for social improvement were provided through education.

THE ROLE OF RELIGION Throughout the Egyptians' history, religion was central to their way of life. Local gods who were thought to protect the fortunes of a city or of a district abounded. Some gods were worshiped by nearly all ancient Egyptians. It was believed that Ra, the sun-god, made the daily journey across the sky. According to Egyptian mythology, he was also the divine father of the Egyptian kings. Osiris [oh-SY-ruhs], one of the leading gods of later Egyptian history, judged the souls of the dead. The Nile—known as Hapi—was also considered to be a deity.

There were two basic forms of religious practice in Egypt—public and private. Public religious practices were based upon the religious traditions and ceremonies in which all Egyptians took part. Huge temples where many ceremonies were performed were built as homes for many of Egypt's gods. Powerful priesthoods evolved to serve these gods. The priests performed temple ceremonies and led the people in celebrating public festivals dedicated to the gods.

The second form of religious practice was based upon individual Egyptians' personal religious beliefs and private rituals. Small shrines to personal gods have been found in many early Egyptian homes. Moreover, ancient Egyptians frequently used magical charms, amulets, and religious spells in everyday life.

Most Egyptians believed that death was another stage of life. During the Old Kingdom, it was believed that only the souls of the rulers joined the gods in an afterlife. Eventually, however, these early religious beliefs gave way to the belief that most Egyptians could achieve a life after death.

The temple of Nefertari, one of the wives of Ramses II, is guarded by giant rock-cut statues of the queen and the New Kingdom pharaoh.

Jethro Plummer/Cyr Color Photo Agency

The gold burial mask of Tutankhamen carried a vulture and a cobra, symbols of a unified Egypt.

In addition, the Egyptians believed that the souls of the dead could only survive in an afterlife if the physical body was preserved. Because of this belief, early Egyptians felt that it was vital to preserve and to protect the remains of the dead through elaborate funeral preparations and burial customs.

At first, these customs were reserved for the rulers. By the time of the Fourth Dynasty—about 4,500 years ago—large monuments were used for royal tombs. The Pyramids of Egypt are the best examples of the monuments built during this period. Offerings of great value and large quantities of food and drink to be used by the dead in an afterlife were also placed in the tombs. In time, elaborate burials were given to most Egyptians who could afford such rituals.

EGYPTIAN SOCIETY The society of the Egyptians was headed by the ruler, or pharoah, and was divided into several so-cial classes. The highest social class was made up of the nobility, the most important government officials, the priesthood, and the largest landholders. Craft workers, merchants, *scribes*—educated government workers—and small landholders made up the next class. Most Egyptians belonged to the class of peasant farmers who tilled the land of the Nile Valley. They also provided most of the labor for the building of irrigation systems, temples, and pyramids. The lowest social class was made up of slaves, who were usually foreigners captured in war.

Egyptian society changed little over more than 25 centuries. However, it was possible to move from one class to another during many periods of early Egyptian history. Scholars have found many examples of Egyptians who came from humble households and who rose to important positions in Egyptian society. Probably the key to social advancement in early Egypt was education. Only a small part of Egyptian society was *literate*—able to read and to write. Many important government officials were first trained as scribes. Moreover, members of the upper class, including many women, were educated.

Most occupations in ancient Egypt were highly specialized and were usually held by men. Egyptian craft workers included sandal makers, bakers, beekeepers, mat makers, brewers, pottery makers, and metalworkers, among many others.

Egyptian women had many rights and were considered equal under the law. They could own property and will it to their heirs. Women could also bring lawsuits in the Egyptian system of justice. As late as the Middle Kingdom, the Egyptian language even had a word for female scribe, though experts have not yet discovered any examples of what life as a female scribe was like.

Some women gained great power in Egyptian society. However, only one woman, Hatshepsut [hat-SHEP-soot], sat on the throne of Egypt and claimed the title of pharaoh. Beginning around 1500 B.C., Hatshepsut ruled Egypt for nearly 20 years. Some of the finest examples of Egyptian architecture were constructed during her reign.

EGYPTIAN ACHIEVEMENTS Egyptian history between about 3000 B.C. and 1200 B.C. was a time of great cultural achievement. During this time, long periods of stability and prosperity allowed Egyptians to develop unique styles of art and architecture. Many advances were also made in science. An early document discovered by historians described medical practices in Egypt. Nearly 50 different cases of surgery were listed in the document.

One of the outstanding accomplishments of the Old Kingdom rulers was the building of huge stone monuments. The largest and finest of these stone buildings, the Great Pyramid at Giza, was built more than 4,500 years ago. It is an example of efficient planning and organization and of great engineering skill. Experts have estimated that about 2,300,000 hand-hewn stone blocks, weighing an average of 2.5 tons (2.3 metric tons) each, were used for its construction. For about 20 years an estimated 80,000 people worked on the monument during the Nile flood season. They worked without pulleys, wheeled vehicles, or other mechanical devices.

Another important development in early Egypt was the invention of writing, which took place shortly before 3000 B.C. (see feature on page 55). Egyptian *hieroglyphic* [HIY-ruh-GLIF-ik] writing consisted of picture symbols. It was often inscribed on tombs and other buildings. Egyptian scribes also used hieroglyphs, and later a script known as hieratic, for such purposes as record keeping. The Egyptians also made a writing material, known as *papyrus* [puh-PIY-ruhs], from a kind of reed that grew along the Nile. Papyrus—the origin of the word *paper* —enabled Egyptians to keep and transport records more easily.

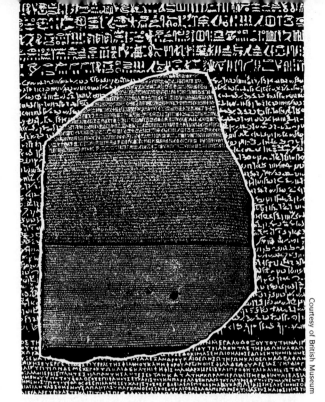

Courtesy of British Museum

The Rosetta Stone (inset) is a broken basalt rock. An enlargement of the writing shows the inscriptions in Egyptian and in Greek that enabled scholars to decipher the ancient Egyptian language.

Egyptian hieroglyphs remained a mystery until their meaning was unraveled less than 200 years ago. The signs were deciphered using a tablet—known as the *Rosetta Stone*— that was inscribed with hieroglyphics, hieratic writing, and Greek. By comparing the three inscriptions and guessing that they carried the same message, a French expert was able to decode the Egyptian picture symbols. As a result, many things have been discovered about Egyptian history.

QUESTIONS FOR REVIEW

1 *To what social class did most Egyptians belong?*

2 *In what way was education important to social advancement in ancient Egypt?*

3 *Why did Egyptians believe that it was necessary to preserve the remains of the dead?*

3 MESOPOTAMIA: AN EARLY CIVILIZATION

The land between the Tigris and the Euphrates Rivers—the region of present-day Iraq—was the scene of another early civilization. The land, known as Mesopotamia, was extremely hot and dry. As a result of yearly flooding by the rivers, however, the descendants of the first farmers who moved into the region found the soil amazingly productive.

The first people to create a civilization in Mesopotamia were the Sumerians. As civilization spread throughout Mesopotamia, the rich culture of the Sumerians formed the basis for later societies.

THE LAND BETWEEN TWO RIVERS Flowing southward from the Anatolian highlands, the Tigris and the Euphrates rivers enter a broad plain more than 500 miles (800 kilometers) from the Persian Gulf (see map on this page). From the foothills of the nearby mountains, early farmers gradually spread onto this fertile plain and

The Fertile Crescent nourished several Middle Eastern civilizations for thousands of years.

Ancient Mesopotamia

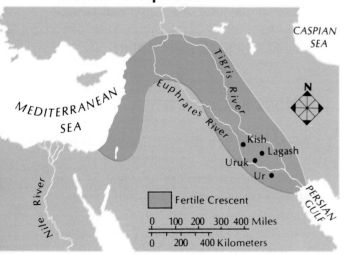

built thriving farming villages nearly 7,700 years ago. Eventually, part of the Fertile Crescent, the land between the Tigris and the Euphrates that became known as Mesopotamia, nourished several ancient civilizations.

The annual flooding of the Tigris and the Euphrates came earlier each year than did the flood of the Nile River and was often more violent. The Euphrates River rose to a peak in April and May and receded in June. The Tigris River generally flooded one month earlier. Because the floods came when the winter crops were ripening and after the summer crops had been planted, a system of dikes had to be built to protect the fields. The courses of the two rivers also frequently shifted and new riverbeds were cut in the flat land. These changes often destroyed villages and croplands.

Unlike the Nile River, which flooded gradually from June to October, the Tigris and the Euphrates had short flood seasons. As a result, early farmers of the region had to develop irrigation methods to conserve water supplies for the very hot, dry summer months.

Mesopotamia also lacked natural geographic barriers. As a result, Mesopotamian history is a record of warfare and conquest, as one group of invaders gave way to the next.

Despite problems of geography and of climate, early Mesopotamian farmers grew abundant crops of barley, wheat, and date palms. Many varieties of vegetables were also grown. In addition, early Mesopotamian farmers domesticated cattle, sheep, goats, and pigs for food. Fish and waterfowl were also important sources of food.

By about 3500 B.C., Mesopotamian life had become increasingly complex. Villages and towns had grown into cities, and a centralized form of government had begun to develop. Social classes based upon wealth and prestige had started to form. Occupations became more highly specialized. And the first steps toward the development of a written language were taken. Thus, by about 3500 B.C., the people of the land between the rivers had reached the threshold of civilization.

THE SUMERIANS Nearly 5,000 years ago, the Sumerians were the first people to develop a civilization in Mesopotamia. Although little is known about the origins of these people, experts believe that they settled the land between the Tigris and the Euphrates before 3500 B.C. Many historians point out that the arrival of the Sumerians provided the final push toward civilization in this region. In addition, the civilization created by the Sumerians served as the foundation of later civilizations throughout Mesopotamia.

Between about 4000 B.C. and 3000 B.C., several cities grew up along the lower Tigris and Euphrates rivers. These cities became the centers of Sumerian civilization. Among the earliest and largest of these cities was Uruk [OO-ruk]. Uruk was first settled around 4000 B.C. and reached a population of about 50,000 people about a thousand years later. Other major cities included Ur, Kish, and Lagash (see map on page 52). These Sumerian cities were surrounded by smaller, dependent rural villages and towns. The cities and their surrounding districts are known as *city-states*. Unlike Egypt, which was unified early in its history, the Sumerian city-states remained fiercely independent and were not united for several centuries. Although they shared a common culture, the city-states often fought one another for control of water rights and for land.

The Sumerian city-states were briefly united under Sargon I of Akkad, ruler of a land to the north of Sumer. His empire stretched from the Persian Gulf to the Mediterranean Sea. Akkadian rule was overthrown during the reign of Sargon's grandson, and the Sumerian city-states were once again divided.

Between 2050 B.C. and 1950 B.C., Mesopotamia was ruled by a Sumerian dynasty from the city of Ur. The rulers of Ur built a complex system of government. Under this system, officials were appointed by the king to carry out his powers. In this way, the central government could more effectively govern lands far from the capital.

The Sumerians achieved many technological advances. A type of plow, pulled by oxen, was developed around 3000 B.C. At about the same time, the wheel was invented. This invention proved to be one of the most important achievements in human history. The Sumerians also developed the potter's wheel—a small, rapidly turning wheel held horizontally—which enabled pottery makers to make large quantities of their wares. In addition, the concepts of the 60-second minute, the 60-minute hour, and the 360-degree circle used today grew out of the Sumerians' number system.

SUMERIAN SOCIETY In early Sumer, the city was the center of civilization. City life centered on the temple, which was often made up of several buildings. An imposing stepped pyramid of whitewashed mud brick called a *ziggurat* [ZIG-uh-RAT] rose above the temple buildings. Ziggurats reached from 85 feet (26 meters) to 200 feet (60 meters) or more high. Originally built for religious ceremonies, the temple buildings also served other purposes in Sumerian life. Because the religious leaders often controlled much of the cropland around the cities, the temple buildings were used as storage and distribution centers for surplus crops. This meant that the temple storehouses helped to support many nonfarmers—craft workers and priests—who worked for the religious leaders.

Early Sumerian society was headed by the priests. Gradually, however, the nobles and the highest government officials, as well as the priests, began to form an upper class. Most landowners and merchants made up the next social class. Craft workers, dependents of the temples and the estates of the nobility, and the peasants formed the

Sumerian stone sculpture often portrayed distinctive figures thought to be worshipers or deities.

largest class. At the bottom of society were the slaves.

Women enjoyed many rights and privileges in Sumerian society. They could own property and operate businesses. Women could serve as witnesses at trials. They could also divorce their husbands. Moreover, experts have found references in Sumerian writings to female physicians and scribes.

One of the greatest accomplishments of the Sumerians was the development of the world's first system of writing more than 5,000 years ago (see feature on page 55). Writing brought early people out of prehistory into historical times. Writing enabled people to keep accurate records and, in time, to communicate with others and to record thoughts, feelings, and experiences.

In Sumer, as in Egypt, the road to success often began in the schools. Young scribes often worked from dawn until dusk studying the Sumerians' difficult written language and acquiring other skills, such as mathematics. Nearly all important officials and many of the nobles were educated. Most professions, including government administration,

the priesthood, medicine, and the management of estates, were open to the scribes.

THE SPREAD OF MESOPOTAMIAN CIVILIZATION Throughout its history, Mesopotamia suffered long periods of warfare. Because of a lack of natural barriers, the region was conquered and ruled by many foreign invaders. Some historians explain this constant conflict as a struggle between the "civilized people" of Mesopotamia and the "less-civilized" people of the surrounding lands.

In many cases, less-civilized people first came into contact with more-advanced societies through trade. For example, Mesopotamia had few resources. As a result, the Sumerians traded widely for such things as stone, wood, and metals. In exchange, their less-civilized trading partners received many Sumerian goods, such as cloth, finished metal products, and grain. In time, these less-civilized people came to depend upon such goods. And in a pattern that continued for centuries, conquerors from less-civilized lands fought for control of the centers of Sumerian civilization. Moreover, the cultures of less-civilized people were often absorbed by the cultures that they conquered. The result of this intermingling was a Mesopotamian civilization that mirrored the cultural patterns of many different peoples. In part, conquest and trade shaped Mesopotamian civilization and helped to spread it throughout the Middle East.

QUESTIONS FOR REVIEW

1 *What group of people first developed civilization in Mesopotamia?*

2 *How did geography and climate affect agriculture in Mesopotamia?*

3 *Why do some historians consider trade to have been important to the spread of Mesopotamian civilization?*

Contributions

Development of Writing

Writing was one of the most distinctive characteristics of the first civilizations. Between about 3100 B.C. and about 1300 B.C., writing was invented in many places around the world, often independently. The first system of writing was developed in ancient Sumer. Not long after, the Egyptians were using hieroglyphs. Several centuries later, the people of the Indus River valley possessed a writing method of their own. By about 1300 B.C., writing had also appeared in China.

Many early written languages evolved in much the same way as the language of Sumer. However, the development of writing was a slow process, and it often followed a course of trial and error. Several thousand years before writing appeared, people had discovered that one of the easiest ways to record an object or an event was to draw a picture of it. Very early, the Sumerians took this idea one step further by using a drawing to represent a word in their spoken language. This kind of symbol is known as a *logogram*. Moreover, symbols were also used to represent ideas or concepts, such as time, day, night, strong, and weak. In its early stages, the written Sumerian language had more than 2,000 signs or symbols.

Between about 2900 B.C. and about 1900 B.C., the Sumerians gradually created a more complete system of writing. They invented signs that represented many of the sounds of their spoken language. For example, in our language a picture of a bee might be used to represent the sound of *B*, or an eye might be used to represent the sound of *I*. This kind of symbol, called a *phonogram*, was a major advance in development of writing. Phonograms greatly simplified Sumerian writing, and the number of signs that were used for writing was reduced to about 500.

Another important step in written Sumerian was the emergence of *cuneiform* [kyu-NEE-uh-FAWRM]. Writing Sumerian cuneiform consisted of making wedge-shaped marks on a wet clay tablet with the end of a reed. Complicated pictures that had been used as symbols were gradually replaced by a series of marks. Cuneiform developed as Sumerians searched for a way to write their language more quickly.

Although the Sumerians created a very complex system of writing, they did not invent an alphabet. Eventually, alphabets were developed to express the single sounds of a spoken language. The Phoenicians, who lived along the eastern coast of the Mediterranean Sea, made an early attempt at an alphabet. It was not until about 800 B.C., however, that the Greeks formed an alphabet and established the principles that underlie all modern alphabetic writing.

The picture symbols that formed the earliest Sumerian writing were eventually rotated horizontally and changed so that they could be written more quickly.

Original Meaning	Pictograph 3000 B.C.	Pictograph Rotated on Side	Cuneiform Sign 1900 B.C.	Later Meanings
bowl of food				food *or* to place
stream of water				water *or* in
head and mouth				to speak *or* word
mouth and water				to drink *or* thirst
fish				fish *or* may

4 LATER MIDDLE EASTERN CIVILIZATIONS

Several civilizations rose and fell in the region of the Middle East—including Mesopotamia—between about 2000 B.C. and 330 B.C. Large empires and small kingdoms were formed and later reorganized as conquering armies swept through the region.

Despite the turmoil caused by these events, several important developments took place in the Middle East. The first recorded law code was devised. Iron was developed and became an important metal, essential in the making of tools and weapons. Finally, religious developments that ultimately had a great impact on cultures throughout the world took place during this time.

HAMMURABI Shortly after 1900 B.C., a nomadic people—the Amorites—established a dynasty at Babylon on the Euphrates River (see map on page 57). These people became known as Babylonians. In 1792 B.C., the Babylonian king, Hammurabi [HAM-uh-RAHB-ee], began to build a large empire. By 1763 B.C., Hammurabi's kingdom stretched from northern Mesopotamia to the Persian Gulf.

Hammurabi is probably best known for the organized and written code of laws that was composed during his reign. This written code was based upon the customs and practices of Hammurabi's Amorite people as well as on those of the Sumerians. The code covered many areas of law and established severe penalties for many criminal acts. The code defined the position of women in Babylonian society and established marriage, divorce, and adoption laws.

Two important features of Hammurabi's code were the severity of the penalties and the inequality of the social classes under the law. Many penalties of the law code were based on the principle of "an eye for an eye." For example, one part of the code

stated that "if a man strike his father, they shall cut off his hand." Another part of the code declared that "if he break a man's bone, they shall break his bone." This harsh system of justice, however, was not applied equally to all. The punishment for a crime committed by a member of the upper class against a member of a lower class was usually less severe.

The lasting effect of Hammurabi's law code was that everyone, regardless of social position, was subject to the law in some way. The code, one of the earliest bodies of recorded law, has contributed to many legal systems throughout history.

About 150 years after Hammurabi's death, new invaders conquered Mesopotamia and new kingdoms were formed. However, the cultural foundation of Mesopotamia, established more than 1,500 years before, continued to survive.

MESOPOTAMIA UNDER NEW RULERS Beginning around 1600 B.C. and continuing for several centuries, the region of Mesopotamia was conquered by a succession of invading armies. One of the first of these groups, the Hittites, formed a powerful kingdom north of Mesopotamia in Anatolia —the region of present-day Turkey.

Although the Hittites attacked and plundered Babylon in 1530 B.C., they did not reach the peak of their power for another 200 years. During that time, the Hittites developed a unique smelting process for hardening iron by using small amounts of charcoal. Hardened iron weapons and horse-drawn chariots enabled Hittite leaders in the 1300's B.C. to establish an empire that stretched into northern Syria and along the eastern coast of the Mediterranean Sea (see map on page 57). By 1200 B.C., however, revolts and pressure from outside invaders had led to the fall of the Hittite Empire.

Between about 900 B.C. and about 700 B.C., the highly organized military kingdom of Assyria rose to power in northern Mesopotamia. Using iron weapons, chariots, and cavalry—an Assyrian innovation—the Assyrian Empire rapidly expanded. By 650 B.C., ruthless Assyrian commanders had conquered nearly all of the ancient Middle East and had extended their control into Egypt (see map on this page). Their large empire was soon weakened by repeated revolts of conquered subjects and by the decline of their military power. As a result, the Assyrian Empire collapsed around 600 B.C..

During the next century, the Persians—a people who lived to the east of Mesopotamia in the region of present-day Iran—built one of the largest empires of ancient times. Persian kings ruled over an area from the Indus River in the east to the Balkan Peninsula and Egypt in the west (see map on this page). For more than 200 years, the mighty empire withstood internal revolts and attacks from outsiders. But in 330 B.C., the armies of Alexander the Great marched through Persia and the empire crumbled (see Chapter 6).

One important development during the time of the Persian empire was the rise of a religion based upon the teachings of a Persian prophet named Zoroaster [ZOHR-uh-WAS-tuhr]. Zoroastrianism, as the religion became known, was *monotheistic*—based upon a belief in one god. Zoroaster believed that the universe was a scene of continual struggle between good and evil. Those who chose to follow the path of goodness and truth during their earthly life would be rewarded after death. Moreover, this reward would be open to all people, regardless of social rank. Zoroastrianism was generally not accepted by other cultures and remained a Persian religion. But the beliefs of Zoroastrianism were similar to some of the beliefs of another ancient Middle Eastern religion—that of the early Hebrews.

THE EARLY HEBREWS Between about the time of Hammurabi and the time of Alexander the Great, an important religious development took place in the Middle East.

The Hittite and Assyrian Empires

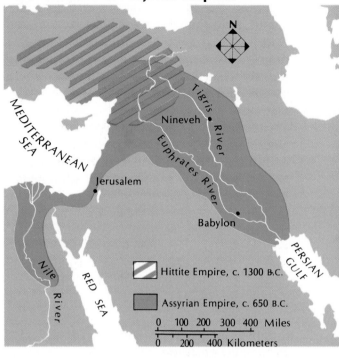

The Hittites and the Assyrians built advanced and powerful civilizations in the Middle East between 1300 B.C. and 600 B.C.

The Persian Empire

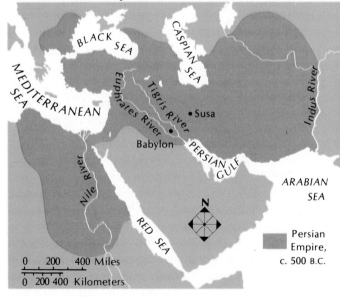

By 500 B.C., the Persian Empire stretched from the Indus Valley to the Mediterranean Sea.

57

The people known originally as Hebrews accepted the idea of *ethical monotheism*. This meant that the Hebrews believed in one God, who required people to follow a proper and moral way of life. The religion of the Hebrews eventually became known as *Judaism* and had a major influence on later history.

The Hebrews appear to have come originally from southern Mesopotamia. According to biblical accounts, the first Hebrews journeyed from Ur to the land of Canaan, between the Jordan River and the Mediterranean Sea. Early Hebrews may have settled in Canaan as long ago as 2000 B.C. Sometime later, according to Hebrew tradition, a famine caused many Hebrews to cross the Sinai Peninsula into Egypt in search of a better life.

Although their life in Egypt was comfortable for a time, the Hebrews were eventually enslaved and forced to work for the pharaoh. At this time, a leader named Moses arose among the Hebrews and showed them a way to freedom. In the biblical account, Moses led his people back into Sinai. At Mount Sinai, Moses received the Ten Commandments. A *covenant*—agreement—was made between the Hebrews and their God at Mount Sinai. Under this covenant, the Hebrews promised to accept and to obey God's law. These events formed the basis of Judaism. Today, the Commandments represent the highest laws of Judaism and are the source of all Jewish teachings.

Following their return from Egypt, the Hebrews gained control of Canaan—which became known as Israel. Eventually, a kingdom was formed and around 1025 B.C. the first Hebrew king, Saul, took the throne. Saul was followed by David, who was followed by his son Solomon.

During this time, the kingdom of Israel prospered greatly. Solomon built the first great Hebrew Temple at the city of Jerusalem. After Solomon's death in about 922 B.C., the Hebrew kingdom was divided into Israel in the north and Judah, along the Dead Sea, in the south. About two centuries later, the Assyrians conquered Israel. In 586 B.C., Judah was defeated by the Babylonians, the Temple was destroyed, and many of the remaining Hebrews were captured and taken back to Babylon.

THE HEBREW TRADITION   Strong religious faith enabled the Hebrews—who at this time became known as Jews—to preserve their customs and practices during the Babylonian captivity. A primary development was the *synagogue*—a meeting place that became a house of worship for the Jews. Here the Jews could study and interpret their religious writings. The synagogue became the center of Jewish religious life. Over the centuries it helped the Jews to maintain their sense of unity and of cultural identity wherever they lived. No longer was the survival of the religion tied entirely to the land of their ancestors or to the Temple. Throughout history, this has meant that Judaism has been able to survive nearly anywhere in the world.

Judaism has maintained a sacred written tradition from the time of the first Hebrew Scriptures, which are believed to have been written 3,000 years ago.

After the Persians conquered Babylonia, the Jews were permitted to return to their homeland. Shortly before 500 B.C., the second Temple was built in Jerusalem. A part of this temple still stands today. During the next two centuries, the *Hebrew Scriptures* were brought together to preserve the customs, the traditions, and the religious beliefs of the Jews. The Scriptures contained writings that were later included in the Jewish Bible, which was known among the Jews as the *Tanach* [tah-NAHK]. Many of these sacred writings are known to Christians as the Old Testament of the *Bible*.

The basic ideas of Judaism and of ethical monotheism have been major influences on many world cultures up to the present time. The belief in one God and in a moral life based upon the Commandments underlies many modern societies. Many of the deep concerns of Judaism, such as peace and social justice, are also basic concerns of modern civilization.

QUESTIONS FOR REVIEW

1 *What was probably the greatest contribution of Hammurabi's reign?*

2 *In what way was the development of the synagogue important to Judaism?*

3 *Why, in your opinion, might the development of ethical monotheism be considered an important achievement of Middle Eastern civilization?*

CHAPTER SUMMARY

The earliest civilizations arose in the Middle East. The Egyptians created an advanced society in the Nile Valley. At about the same time, the Sumerians developed a rich, advanced culture in Mesopotamia, the land between the Tigris and the Euphrates rivers.

Geography greatly influenced the development of the earliest civilizations. Although the Nile Valley and Mesopotamia received little rainfall, yearly flooding by the rivers renewed the soil. Irrigation enabled the fertile lands of the Middle East to support early civilizations. Natural boundaries were also important to the development of civilization in the Middle East. In Egypt, the deserts and the sea isolated the Nile Valley. As a result, a unique and stable culture took root and grew. Mesopotamia had few natural boundaries. This resulted in long periods of warfare, as one group of invaders gave way to the next.

Early civilizations in the Middle East were characterized by great cultural achievements. Writing was one of the most important of these accomplishments. Religion played a major role in all Middle Eastern civilizations. The ideas of ethical monotheism were developed by the early Hebrews. By about 330 B.C., the conquests of Alexander the Great and, eventually, the challenge of Greek ideas changed the nature of civilization throughout the Middle East.

CHAPTER 2 IN REVIEW

IMPORTANT WORDS, NAMES, AND TERMS

1 Explain, define, or identify each of the following:

dynasties	hieroglyphs	Zoroaster
pharaoh	papyrus	ethical monotheism
polytheism	city-states	synagogue
literate	ziggurat	Hebrew Scriptures

FACTS AND IDEAS

2 By the beginning of the Old Kingdom, what beliefs did the Egyptians hold about their rulers?

3 What major technological innovations were brought to Egypt by the Hyksos?

4 What is the Rosetta Stone?

5 What two rivers were important to the development of Mesopotamian agriculture?

6 Upon which early civilization were most Mesopotamian civilizations based?

7 What was Hammurabi's code?

ANALYZING VISUAL MATERIAL

8 Compare the maps on pages 45, 52, and 57. What empires were part of the Fertile Crescent?

9 What significant invention, shown in the illustration on page 48, is believed to have been brought to Egypt by the Hyksos?

CONCEPTS AND UNDERSTANDINGS

10 In what ways did the building of the Great Pyramid reflect the planning, organization, and skill of the early Egyptians?

11 How did the religious beliefs of the Egyptians affect the burial of their rulers?

12 How did the flood cycle of the Nile River differ from the flood cycle of the Tigris and the Euphrates rivers in ancient times?

13 How did trade and warfare help to spread civilization throughout Mesopotamia?

PROJECTS AND ACTIVITIES

14 Make a chart or a bulletin-board display on how papyrus was made by early Egyptians.

15 Gather information from the library on the Egyptian technique of preserving the remains of the dead by a process known as mummification. Make a report to the class.

CHAPTER 3 CIVILIZATION IN ANCIENT INDIA

1 Early Civilization in the Indus Valley 2 The Indo-Aryans
3 Society and Religion in Ancient India 4 Conquest and
Collapse: The Maurya Empire

Around 2500 B.C., several centuries after civilization emerged in Egypt and in Mesopotamia, civilization arose in the Indus River valley in the northwestern region of the Indian subcontinent. The Indus Valley culture achieved remarkable advances. By about 1500 B.C., however, the civilization had disappeared.

Following the decline of the Indus Valley culture, another civilization began forming in early India. For more than a thousand years, the cultures of people who had migrated from central Asia blended with the cultures of the first inhabitants of the Indian subcontinent. Together, these cultures created a new civilization that was the basis for modern Indian culture.

Nearly all that remains today of the Indus civilization are the ruins of the once-great cities of Mohenjo-Daro (shown here) and Harappa.

1 EARLY CIVILIZATION IN THE INDUS VALLEY

Civilization developed on the Indian subcontinent nearly 4,500 years ago. Archaeologists have pieced together a picture of a complex society in the Indus River valley. The cities of the Indus Valley were well planned and well fortified. City-wide sanitation systems were built. Indus Valley merchants exchanged goods with Sumerian traders. However, beginning about 1700 B.C. the Indus Valley civilization began to decline. And by about 1500 B.C., it had come to an end.

THE INDIAN SUBCONTINENT The southernmost region of Asia is known as the Indian subcontinent. Today, the countries of India, Pakistan, Nepal, Bangladesh, Bhutan, and Sri Lanka make up this region.

The Indian subcontinent is bordered to the north by towering mountain ranges and to the east and west by the Indian Ocean (see map on this page). These geographic features formed barriers that helped isolate ancient India. In addition, the mountains were the source of three great river systems —the Indus, the Ganges [GAN-JEEZ], and the Brahmaputra [BRAHM-uh-POO-truh]. These river systems formed a fertile plain of rich farmland in northern India that has provided much of India's food for centuries.

The river plain receives between 40 and 60 inches (102 and 152 centimeters) of rain each year. Nearly all of the rain is brought between June and September by the *monsoons*—winds that blow across southern Asia, bringing moist air and torrential thunderstorms. Because of the extremely hot climate, the monsoons have always been essential to life in India. Even today, monsoon rainwater must be carefully collected and stored for use during the dry season. In this way, two crops of rice can be harvested annually in this region.

Another rich agricultural area lies along the coast of the Indian subcontinent. The

The Indian subcontinent is dominated by large river systems and is separated from Asia by immense mountain ranges.

The Indian Subcontinent

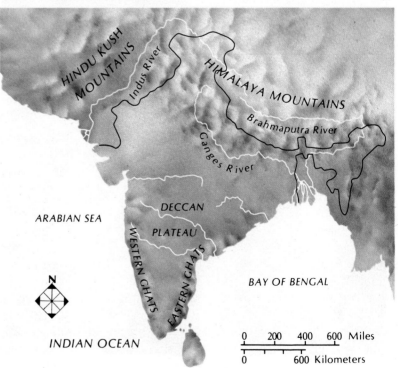

coastal plains are subtropical and receive heavy rainfall during the monsoon season. Rice and spices are major crops. In the south, the dry and hilly Deccan plateau covers much of the lower subcontinent. The Eastern Ghats and the Western Ghats rise along each side of the plateau (see map on page 62). These mountains prevent the monsoon rains from reaching the plateau. For this reason, farming is not as productive on the plateau as it is on the northern river plain or on the subtropical coastal plains. Today, the principal crop of the plateau is wheat.

THE INDUS VALLEY The Indus River rises in the world's highest mountains—the Himalaya. The river flows nearly 1,800 miles (2 900 kilometers) through mountains and across wide, flat plains to the Arabian Sea (see map on page 62). Annual flooding of the Indus River created and renewed a fertile valley. The barren Thar Desert bordered the valley's eastern edge, while the towering Himalaya Mountains and the snow-capped Hindu Kush Mountains lay to the north and west. Thus, the Indus Valley, like Egypt's Nile Valley, was sheltered and protected by natural barriers from early invaders.

The first steps toward civilization in the Indus Valley were taken when Neolithic farmers settled in the region. The earliest Neolithic farming settlement in the Indus River valley recently has been dated to about 3700 B.C. Several centuries later—about 3000 B.C.—permanent agricultural villages were scattered throughout the Sind and Punjab plains. Around 2500 B.C., the growth of a strong central government, of large cities, and of extensive overseas trade transformed the Indus Valley into the site of a flourishing civilization.

Little is known about early civilization in the Indus Valley. Thus far, experts have been unable to decode the written language of the Indus Valley people. We know that writing was developed in the Indus

POLITICAL		SOCIAL AND ECONOMIC
	B.C.	
	c. 3700	First Neolithic farming settlements established on Indus plain
Strong central government developed in Indus Valley	c. 2500	Large planned cities built in Indus Valley
	c. 2000	Indo-Aryan migrations began / Cotton first used for textiles
	c. 1700	Decline of Indus civilization began
	c. 1500	Mohenjo-Daro destroyed / Vedic Age of India began / Harappan culture disappeared
	c. 1000	Sacred Hindu *Vedas* written
	c. 900	*Mahabharata* and *Ramayana* composed / Epic Age began
Darius the Great of Persia invaded north-western India	563 / 516	Gautama Siddhartha—the Buddha—was born
	c. 500	Essential ideas of Hinduism and Buddhism had been formed
Alexander the Great crossed Indus River	326	*Mahabharata* and *Ramayana* took written form
	c. 300	
Asoka became Maurya ruler	273	
End of Maurya Empire	184	
	c. 150	Trade flourished between India and the Mediterranean world
	A.D.	
Kanishka ruled Kushan Empire	c. 100	
Kushan Empire ended India divided	225	
Gupta Empire began in northern India	320	

Valley only a few centuries after its invention in the Middle East. However, scholars have not found bilingual writings—such as the Egyptian Rosetta Stone—with which to compare and to decode the ancient Indus Valley language. Moreover, experts are unsure how much could be learned if the writing is deciphered because so few inscriptions of this early language exist.

The lack of written records has made it difficult for experts to study the origins of the earliest Indus people. Also, floods and the valley's rising water table have probably destroyed buried evidence that might help to trace the beginnings of Indus civilization. Thus, there are gaps in our knowledge of this early civilization and of the people who built it. The archaeological evidence that does exist, however, reveals much about the Indus civilization and its rich and varied culture.

THE HARAPPAN CULTURE Civilization appeared in the Indus River valley around 2500 B.C. Eventually, the Indus civilization covered an area along the river and the coast of the Arabian Sea more than twice the size of Egypt or Mesopotamia (see map on page 66). The remains of two great cities have been discovered in the river valley that show, in part, the uniform nature of this early civilization. One city, Harappa, gave its name to the culture and the people of the region. The other city is called Mohenjo-Daro [moh-HEN-joh-DAHR-oh] by modern historians.

The remains of these two cities indicate that the Harappan culture was highly organized and that the people were probably ruled by a strong, central government. Both cities were early examples of efficient city planning and were laid out according to a definite pattern. Blocks of buildings were divided by streets of standard widths that intersected at right angles. For the most part, the buildings were of similar design and were built of fire-hardened clay bricks of a uniform size.

In addition, a remarkably complex sanitation system has been uncovered at

Wheeled clay toys and fine clay sculpture have been uncovered in the ruins of Indus Valley cities. The large number of toys that have been found by archaeologists may indicate that the objects were exported as trade goods.

Clay seals, believed to have been used by merchants to mark their goods, are the only examples of the still-undeciphered Indus language.

Mohenjo-Daro. Houses had separate bathrooms with brick-lined drains that were connected to public drains beneath the streets. A few houses even had chutes that were connected to outside rubbish bins. Many homes had private wells.

Other discoveries made at Harappa and at Mohenjo-Daro point to a great degree of government control and organization. Both cities had large *granaries*—buildings used for storing grain. These granaries may have been used as government storehouses. Moreover, rows of small, two-room houses were found. Many historians believe that these buildings housed government workers. In Harappa, these dwellings were found near a mill where it is believed that the workers may have pounded grain into flour. Each city also had a *citadel*—a fortress. The citadels rose above the level of the surrounding land and had thick walls that were more than 25 feet (7.6 meters) tall. A large bath or pool was also found at Mohenjo-Daro that may have been used for religious ceremonies. These findings suggest that the Indus Valley cities may have been both military and religious centers.

AGRICULTURE AND TRADE The *economic system*—the ways in which a society produces and uses goods and services—of the Indus Valley was based on agriculture and on trade. Indus Valley farmers grew crops of wheat and barley, a part of which was probably delivered to the granaries as a form of tax. Dates, peas, melons, and sesame were also grown. Moreover, rice was probably used for food. However, experts are unsure whether this rice was domesticated rice or wild rice. In addition, the people of the Indus Valley raised cattle, sheep, goats, horses, camels, and elephants.

The Harappans seem to have been the first people to grow cotton. A piece of dyed cotton cloth was found at Mohenjo-Daro, which shows that cotton was spun and woven into textiles more than 4,000 years ago. Some scholars believe that cotton was a major export to Mesopotamia.

Uniform weights and measures that were essential to trade between two different cultures have been uncovered in the Indus Valley. Archaeologists have also unearthed structures that are believed to have been docks for seagoing trading ships. These discoveries indicate that trade, particularly foreign trade, helped to support the Harappan farming economy.

Traders in the Indus Valley probably exchanged goods by sea and by land with merchants in the Sumerian city-states and in the Persian Gulf. This trade began at least as early as the reign of Sargon I, who united Mesopotamia around 2300 B.C. Trade routes between the two civilizations remained active for more than 300 years. Evidence of this trade comes from the remains of the Sumerian city of Ur, where seals used in the Indus Valley to mark the ownership of goods have been found.

Experts can only guess at what types of goods were exchanged between these two civilizations. It seems likely that exports from the Indus Valley might have included small luxury items, cotton, and perhaps grain. Imports may have included precious stones, copper, and tin. But as the Indus civilization declined, its trade with other parts of the world came to an end.

THE END OF THE INDUS CIVILIZATION

Around 1700 B.C., the once-great Harappan culture began to decline. Cities were no longer carefully planned and homes became smaller and were more poorly made than before. New but less advanced pottery styles were also found among artifacts uncovered from this period. By about 1500 B.C., the Indus Valley civilization had disappeared. No written records survive from this period to indicate the reasons for this decline and disappearance. However, experts have suggested several reasons to explain the end of the Harappan culture.

Perhaps the most widely accepted explanation of the mysterious disappearance of the Indus civilization is the result of recent geographical studies of the river valley. Many experts today feel that several Indus towns and cities, including Mohenjo-Daro, were the victims of flooding. This flooding began around 1700 B.C. and was the result of a natural disaster.

Many scientists believe that the earth's crust rose suddenly along the seacoast near the delta of the Indus River. This was probably the result of an earthquake or a series of earthquakes. This sudden occurrence caused the course of the Indus River and of some of its tributaries to change (see map on this page). Moreover, the coastline in this region also shifted dramatically. As a result, a large lake was created that slowly covered the river valley. For more than 200 years, the Harappans battled the rising water. Exhausted, they gave up and either gradually left the region or were victims of foreign invaders. At about this time, people

The Indus Valley

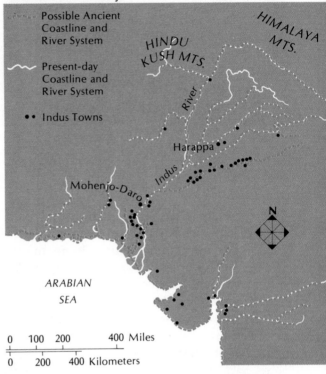

The decline of the Indus Valley civilization may have been speeded by a natural disaster—possibly an earthquake—that permanently altered the river system and the coastline.

from central Asia—known to modern historians as Indo-Aryans—migrated through the mountain passes and invaded the Indus Valley. Around 1500 B.C., for reasons that are still unclear, the Harappan civilization gave way to the culture of the Indo-Aryans.

QUESTIONS FOR REVIEW

1 What evidence exists of trade between Mesopotamia and the Indus Valley?

2 How were streets laid out in ancient Mohenjo-Daro?

3 Why do experts know little about the decline and disappearance of the Indus civilization?

2 THE INDO–ARYANS

The earliest seeds of civilization on the Indian subcontinent lay in the Indus Valley. However, following the end of the Indus Valley civilization around 1500 B.C., a people known as the Indo-Aryans gradually migrated eastward across the Indian subcontinent. Unfortunately, few historical sources exist that provide experts with information about the early Indo-Aryans. Therefore, religious writings of the period must be used to learn more about the development of the Indo-Aryan culture.

THE COMING OF THE INDO–ARYANS The Indo-Aryans were a group of Indo-European-speaking peoples, probably from central Asia. Around 2000 B.C., they began to migrate to western and southern Asia. Historians still know very little about this mysterious migration. However, it seems to have been part of a vast movement of Indo-European-speaking peoples to many parts of Europe and the Middle East. The Hittites were among the first of these peoples to reach southwestern Asia. There, they established a powerful empire in the region of modern-day Turkey (see Chapter 2).

The Indo-Aryans, on the other hand, migrated to the Indus River valley. By about 1500 B.C., early groups of Indo-Aryan nomads had crossed the Hindu Kush Mountains from central Asia into India. The Indo-Aryans, however, did not come as an invading army. Instead, they formed part of a gradual eastward migration. Eventually, they conquered the native people of northern India—the Dravidians. As they took control of the region, the Indo-Aryans developed a distinctive culture and a well-organized society. This period of formation is known as the Vedic Age.

THE VEDIC AGE For several generations, the Indo-Aryans continued to pass through the mountains and settle in India. The only information that historians have regarding the first centuries of Indo-Aryan settlement in northwestern India comes from the *Vedas* [VAYD-uhz]—a word meaning "books of knowledge." These writings are in the form of hymns to the Indo-Aryan gods and are considered sacred today by many people in India. The oldest and most sacred of these writings is the *Rig-Veda*.

Many historians believe that these works were not written down until shortly after 1000 B.C. However, the *Vedas* describe many elements of earlier Indo-Aryan life. For example, the warlike people of the Vedic hymns were nomadic herders who raised cattle, sheep, goats, and horses. They also worshiped nature gods. These early people had knowledge of farming and grew crops, such as barley. They enjoyed music, dancing, gambling with dice, and racing chariots. Vedic Age metalsmiths worked with gold and bronze. Other crafts included carpentry, leather tanning, blacksmithing, and weaving.

Early Indo-Aryans were organized into tribes and were led by rulers called *rajas* [RAHJ-uhz]. A council of elders was chosen to advise the raja.

According to the *Vedas*, early Indo-Aryan society was divided into three major social classes—priests, warriors, and commoners. These classes became the basis for the more rigidly divided society that developed in India shortly after 1000 B.C.

By the end of the Vedic Age, the Indo-Aryans had slowly moved eastward and had settled on the Ganges River plain. To study what life was like after the Vedic Age, historians rely mainly upon two long epic poems.

THE EPICS Between about 900 B.C. and 500 B.C., many changes took place in India. As the Indo-Aryans moved slowly across northern India, new ideas challenged and changed their ancient religion and way of life. Two great epic poems began to take shape during this time and reflected these changes. The poems were the *Mahabharata*

A colorful scene from an Indian epic, the *Ramayana*, is depicted in this seventeenth-century painting. The poem describes the adventure-filled rescue of Prince Rama's wife from Ravana, a demon king. The prince is shown attacking Ravana's stronghold of Lanka at the head of an army of gods and sacred monkeys.

[muh-HAH-BAH-ruh-tuh] and the *Ramayana* [rah-MAH-YAH-nuh].

The *Mahabharata* deals with the secret plots and the wars involved in the struggle for a kingdom. One of this poem's best-known parts is the *Bhagavad Gita* [BAHG-uh-VAHD-GEET-uh]—"The Lord's Song." The story of the *Bhagavad Gita* takes place before a great battle. It teaches that people should fulfill their moral duties and that they should not fear death. The *Ramayana* retells the adventures of a king and his battle to rescue his wife, who had been kidnapped by a demon king. Some scholars believe that this poem may symbolize the conquering of southern India by the Indo-Aryans. Today, the *Mahabharata* and the *Ramayana* are believed to be sacred by most of the people of India.

LIFE DURING THE EPIC AGE While the great epic poems of India are regarded as great literature, they are not considered historical fact. However, they present a clear and fascinating picture of life at the time. The epic poems enable historians to gain a better understanding of the changing Indo-Aryan culture.

By the end of the Epic Age—approximately 500 B.C.—northern India was divided into several kingdoms. Also, many of the ancestors of the nomadic herders of earlier times became city dwellers. Rice was a major crop and was grown on the Ganges River floodplain. And although the economy of northern India was still based upon agriculture, a class of successful merchants was forming in the cities.

During the Epic Age, Indo-Aryan civilization developed many of the characteristics that continue to affect life in present-day India. Among these, social and religious developments have done much to shape Indian civilization.

QUESTIONS FOR REVIEW

1 *What is the* Bhagavad Gita?

2 *How was early Indo-Aryan society organized?*

3 *Why are the* Vedas *important to modern historians?*

3 SOCIETY AND RELIGION IN ANCIENT INDIA

For more than 3,000 years, two important characteristics of India's civilization were its rigid social order and the role of the family. Unable to move upward or downward in society, most people in ancient India accepted their place in the social order. The family provided a stable base on which to build this system.

Another characteristic of the development of civilization in India was religion. From the time of the Indo-Aryans, religion had a great impact on the culture, the society, and the government of India. Two of the world's great religions developed in India. These were Hinduism and Buddhism.

THE CASTE SYSTEM Near the end of the Vedic Age—about 1000 B.C.—a strict social order based upon four *varnas*—social classes —arose in India. These classes included the *Brahmans*—priests and scholars; the *Kshatriyas* [SHA-tree-uhz]—warriors and government officials; the *Vaisyas* [VIYSH-uhz]—farmers, shop owners, traders, and craft workers; and the *Sudras*—servants and workers. A fifth group—the *Untouchables*—were considered to be socially unacceptable and had to remain outside the social system. These people performed the lowest jobs in society.

The idea of rigid social classes was based on the belief that all people had certain duties to perform. These duties determined a person's life-style and thus the social class to which the person belonged. The origins of this social system are unknown. However, many experts believe that the Indo-Aryans first formed this class system to remain separate from the original inhabitants of India, the Dravidians. Thus, most Dravidians became Sudras—members of the lowest varna—while some Dravidians were placed outside the system entirely.

By about 500 B.C., a more rigid social order had developed in India. This became known as the *caste system*, and it developed within the four orders of varna. During this time, all people in India belonged to a caste and it became their hereditary place in society. Castes were formed according to marriage, occupations, and even different religious beliefs. Members of the caste could not change their jobs or improve their place in society.

Each caste formed rules to govern its members. People were required to marry within their caste. Generally, they could not move out of the caste. Each caste also had its own rules about diet and social behavior. Breaking a caste's rules led to a number of penalties that also included expulsion from a caste. *Outcastes*—persons who did not belong to a caste—were left without a place in an extremely structured society.

Experts have often criticized the caste system because it divided the people. Moreover, this system did not allow for rapid social and economic changes within Indian civilization. However, the caste system gave the people of India a sense of identity and stability. People knew their place in society and knew what was expected of them. In addition to the caste system, the family played an important role in Indian society.

THE FAMILY IN ANCIENT INDIA The family was probably the most important, stable, and influential unit of ancient Indian society. The family unit in early India was an example of an *extended family*. This means that many generations of family members lived together. Extended families shared possessions and worshiped together in the home. The extended family's interests were considered to be more important than the wishes of an individual family member.

The head of the extended family was the oldest male member of the household. He led religious worship and controlled the family's property. In addition, he made all the important decisions that affected family members. The duty of women family members was to run the household. The laws and customs of ancient India often put women in an inferior legal position. However, they were honored by society and by their husbands and their sons.

Marriage was arranged by a young couple's parents after the social and economic interests of each family were taken into consideration. After marriage, a son and his wife came to live in his father's house. Marriage was a permanent bond, and divorce and remarriage were unknown. A dutiful wife was also expected to join her husband in death.

The importance of the family, the role of women, the caste system, and many other aspects of Indian society were reinforced by religious beliefs. These beliefs became known as Hinduism. The roots of Hinduism can be found in the many cultures and civilizations of ancient India. By the end of the Epic Age—about 500 B.C.—Hinduism had been gradually developing for more than a thousand years.

HINDUISM The ideas of Hinduism had been formed by about 500 B.C. Hindu beliefs were described in the epic poems and in religious writings known as the *Upanishads* [oo-PAHN-i-SHAHDZ]. The three great Hindu gods—Brahma, the Creator; Vishnu, the Preserver; and Siva, the Destroyer—took the place of many of the earlier gods. Moreover, changes in religious belief placed less emphasis on the priests, the rituals, and the ceremonies of earlier times. Instead, a more-personal religion emerged.

Hinduism taught that all living things had a soul that was part of a universal spirit. However, the soul was caught in a cycle of life, death, and rebirth. The goal of Hinduism was release of the soul from the cycle of rebirth. This achievement, Hinduism believed, would lead to a union between the soul and the universal spirit.

Hindus believed that the soul was continually reborn in another human body or in another form of life. Rebirth depended, however, upon *karma*. Karma was the sum total of an individual's actions—good and evil—in this life and in previous lives. Thus, karma determined a person's present life, occupation, and caste.

These beliefs enabled the Hindus to uphold the caste system. It was believed that if individuals of a low caste led a good life, their soul would be reborn into a higher caste. Hindus also felt that the present life must be dutifully accepted. Only then could they hope for a better life to come.

Hinduism became a flexible set of beliefs that accommodated people who believed many different things. For example, Hinduism did not require a belief either in one god or in many gods. There was room in the beliefs of Hinduism for people who cherished established rituals and for people who meditated alone. In part, this flexibility has enabled Hinduism to remain the major

A many-armed copper statue of the Hindu god Siva shows a symbolic crushing of ignorance.

Ritual bathing in India's sacred Ganges River has been practiced by Hindus for many centuries.

religion of India to the present day. Hinduism's influence upon Indian art, literature, and philosophy has given Indian civilization its distinctive quality.

Around 500 B.C., another religion that challenged the popularity and the ideas of Hinduism was born in India. It came about, in part, as a reaction to Hinduism. This religion is known as Buddhism.

BUDDHISM   About 563 B.C., Siddhartha Gautama [sid-DAHR-tuh GOW-tuh-muh] was born to a royal family in northern India near the present-day country of Nepal. At the age of twenty-nine, the prince left his wife and child and began a search for an answer to the suffering and pain that he saw all around him. One day, more than six years later, he suddenly gained insight into the meaning of life. Thereafter, he was known as *Buddha*—"the enlightened one." Buddha traveled widely and spread his ideas about becoming free from suffering and pain.

Buddha accepted the Hindu beliefs of rebirth and of karma. Although he probably disagreed with the caste system, he chose simply to ignore it. Buddha taught that a person could escape from the cycle of rebirth and of constant suffering and enter a state of great calm and happiness known as *nirvana*. Buddhism required a belief in and an understanding of the Four Noble Truths. These truths were (1) everyone suffers, (2) the cause of suffering is desire for worldly things, (3) suffering and pain can end by removing desire, and (4) the way to remove desire is to follow the Eightfold Path.

The Eightfold Path began by gaining an understanding of the cause and the end of suffering. Followers of Buddha's teachings sought to resist evil in everyday life. They had to say things about others that were truthful yet kind. They had to respect life, respect the property of others, and hold an occupation that did not injure living things. Buddhists tried to control their thoughts and feelings. Many even practiced trancelike meditation to achieve inner peace.

After Buddha's death around 483 B.C., his ideas spread throughout India and other Asian lands. Buddhism became a major religion in China, Japan, and many of the countries of Southeast Asia. Buddhism also influenced India and its culture for nearly a thousand years. However, by about A.D. 600 the popularity of Buddhism declined in India. Hinduism again became the major religion of the land.

QUESTIONS FOR REVIEW

1 *What was karma?*

2 *In what ways did Hinduism uphold the caste system?*

3 *Why do you think Buddhism is often characterized as being nonviolent?*

Biography

The Buddha

According to Buddhist legends, greatness was predicted for Siddhartha Gautama by several Brahman priests at the time of his birth. The priests foresaw that the prince would reach greatness either as an emperor or as a sage. The possibility that Siddhartha might not choose to inherit the kingdom greatly upset his father, the king. From then on, the king commanded that Siddhartha lead a privileged and totally isolated life.

Buddhist legends recount that the prince eventually became restless with his sheltered way of life. One day, he ventured out from the palace, attended by a servant. Along the road they met an extremely old man, bent and disabled with age. The prince, who had been protected from seeing people who were old and feeble, was shocked by the man's condition. Siddhartha asked his servant why the old man looked like that. The servant explained that everyone, even princes, grew old.

The legend goes on to recount how sometime later, the prince again took a trip into the countryside. This time he met a sick man who could not stand and was writhing with pain. Again the prince asked his servant why this man was suffering. He was told that it was not uncommon for people to become ill and that it was possible for any-

one to suffer in this way. The prince returned to the palace deeply troubled.

Then, according to the legend, the prince made a third trip and this time he saw a dead man. The servant explained to the prince that all living things eventually die. He said that death was as much a part of life as was birth and that there was nothing anyone could do to change this. The prince slowly began to realize that life was full of pain and suffering.

The prince made yet another trip and met on the road a man who seemed to be filled with calm and inner peace. The prince asked his servant why this was so. The servant replied that the man had rejected all worldly desire. The servant said that the man wandered, homeless, eating and living simply. Also, the man tried to be pure in his thoughts and in the things that he did, telling others of how he found happiness.

Following this fourth meeting, the prince realized that he, too, must reject the world and its surface pleasures and search for a deeper meaning to life. Siddhartha Gautama left the palace and his wife and newborn son, and began his quest. For nearly six years, he sought wisdom by punishing his body through pain and hunger. Eventually, Siddhartha rejected this way of finding wisdom because he felt that it did not lead anywhere.

Soon after, during a deep meditative trance, Siddhartha gained enlightenment as to the cause and the elimination of suffering. Siddhartha became known as *Buddha*—"the enlightened one"—and spent the next 45 years teaching throughout northern India. At the age of 80, around 483 B.C., he died and left a system of thought that has persisted to present times.

A serene Buddha, deep in meditation, has been a traditional subject of Indian art.

Enrico Mariani

4 CONQUEST AND COLLAPSE: THE MAURYA EMPIRE

Throughout much of its early history, India was divided into numerous small kingdoms. But about 320 B.C., many of these kingdoms were united for the first time by the Maurya dynasty. The Maurya family also produced Asoka—one of the most enlightened leaders in history. Asoka attempted to build his government around Buddhist ideals. Following the collapse of the Maurya Empire, however, India was again divided and many regions were ruled by foreign invaders.

THE RISE OF THE MAURYA EMPIRE Between about 500 B.C. and 325 B.C., parts of northwestern India were ruled by invaders from the west. In 516 B.C., Darius the Great extended Persia's control eastward to the Indus Valley. This was the first time that India came into close contact with the advanced cultures of the Middle East and of the eastern Mediterranean coast. For the next two centuries, ties between these cultures remained close, as merchants from India made many voyages to the Middle East.

In 330 B.C., the Greek armies of Alexander the Great destroyed the Persian Empire and marched across the Hindu Kush Mountains (see Chapter 6). Alexander crossed the Indus River during the spring of 326 B.C. By the next year, he had begun the long journey home and had left behind only a few small Greek colonies.

Following his death in 323 B.C., Alexander's vast empire broke up. Shortly after, a new leader, Chandragupta Maurya [CHUHN-druh-GUP-tuh MAH-ur-yuh], began to unite many of the small kingdoms of northern India into a new Indian empire.

The Maurya dynasty founded by Chandragupta ruled for about 140 years over a territory that stretched from the Bay of Bengal westward to the towering Hindu Kush Mountains. The highly centralized government was located in Pataliputra, a city along the Ganges River. Chandragupta's rule was harsh and was supported by a large army and an efficient *bureaucracy*—a group of appointed government workers. All land belonged to the government. The tax on crops was between one quarter and one half of a farmer's yearly production.

Goods were traded between the Maurya Empire and merchants of Mesopotamia and other parts of the Middle East, and China. Although foreign trade flourished, it was strictly controlled by the government.

According to legend, Chandragupta *abdicated*—gave up—his throne around 300 B.C. and retired to a religious life. Under his son, the southern boundary of the empire was extended while relations with Middle Eastern civilizations remained friendly. However, it was under Chandragupta's grandson, Asoka [uh-SOH-kuh], that the Maurya Empire reached its greatest heights.

ASOKA Asoka came to the throne of the Maurya Empire in 273 B.C. During the first decade of his reign, he ruthlessly expanded his power. In addition, he conquered Kalinga, a kingdom along the eastern coast of the subcontinent. The Kalinga War was a turning point in Asoka's career. Shortly after, he publicly declared his sadness and remorse at the slaughter in Kalinga. From then until the end of his rule thirty years later, Asoka governed according to the moral and ethical principles of Buddhism. As a result, the Maurya Empire was no longer controlled by harsh military power and ruled by terror. Instead, gentleness and nonviolence prevailed.

Asoka became a compassionate leader who thought first of his subjects. The main roads were lined with shade trees, wells were dug, and rest houses were built for weary travelers. Moreover, Asoka frequently traveled, visiting the most-remote corners of the empire. Proclamations were carved in rocks and in stone pillars to teach his subjects what was expected of them under

The stone columns of Asoka were carved with the Maurya ruler's proclamations and laws and were frequently capped with magnificent sculpture.

In the common Western style of historical dating, the century immediately before the birth of Christ is referred to as the first century B.C. ("before Christ"). The century following the birth of Christ is called the first century A.D. (from the Latin *anno Domini*—"in the year of the Lord").

METHOD OF DATING BY CENTURIES

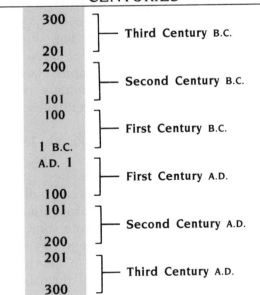

300 — 201	Third Century B.C.
200 — 101	Second Century B.C.
100 — 1 B.C.	First Century B.C.
A.D. 1 — 100	First Century A.D.
101 — 200	Second Century A.D.
201 — 300	Third Century A.D.

his new program. Modern experts conclude that these proclamations indicate that education was widespread at that time, even though there are no records of schools.

Asoka sought the love and respect of his subjects so that they might willingly obey the government, rather than fear it. Although the bases of Asoka's ideas were the teachings of Buddha, he did not require the people to become Buddhists. He realized that societies often became divided because people did not respect the ideas and views of others. As a result, all religions were tolerated during his reign. Buddhist missionaries were sent, however, to other lands, and their influence is still strongly felt today throughout Asia.

Asoka's ideals did not survive long after his death in 232 B.C. Only fifty years later, internal revolts led to the downfall of the Maurya Empire. India was again divided into several small kingdoms.

INDIA AFTER THE MAURYA EMPIRE Between the second century B.C. and the fourth century A.D., a divided India suffered many foreign invasions (see time line on this page for an explanation of dating by centuries). During this period, Greeks from Bactria, a kingdom north of the Hindu Kush Mountains, invaded the subcontinent. The Greeks reached the walls of Pataliputra, the former capital of the Maurya Empire, around 150 B.C.

One result of Greek influence was the opening of major sea and land trade-routes between the Mediterranean and India. This pattern of trade lasted until the eighteenth century A.D. In addition, contact with the Mediterranean world resulted in the establishment of Christianity in India by the third century A.D. The Greeks also profoundly influenced the art—especially the sculpture—of India.

During the second and first centuries B.C., northwestern India was invaded first by the Parthians and later by nomads from central Asia called Scythians. By the end of the first century A.D., another nomadic people—the Kushans—had established a vast empire across northern India. The Kushans carried on a prosperous trade with the Roman Empire. By that time, the Romans had expanded into the region of present-day Turkey, about 600 miles (960 kilometers) from the boundary of the Kushan Empire (see Chapter 7).

The greatest Kushan ruler was Kanishka, who reigned around A.D. 100. He is well-known because of his conversion to Buddhism. This event ignited a rich period of literary and cultural activity in India. Kanishka's kingdom became the center of Buddhist learning and culture.

The Kushan Empire gradually broke up and disappeared completely around A.D. 225. During the next century India remained divided. In A.D. 320, another powerful dynasty—the Gupta—emerged. The Guptas built an empire that reached from the Indus Valley in the west, to the mouth of the Ganges River in the east. For the next several centuries, India flourished under the Guptas.

QUESTIONS FOR REVIEW

1 *What leader began to unite northern India after 323 B.C.?*

2 *In what ways did Asoka provide comfort for travelers?*

3 *Why were all religions tolerated during Asoka's rule?*

CHAPTER SUMMARY

An early civilization arose in the Indus River valley around 2500 B.C. The Indus Valley culture included planned cities, a complex sanitation system, writing, and trade with Mesopotamia. The Indus civilization disappeared around 1500 B.C.

At about the same time, nomadic people from central Asia—known as Indo-Aryans—had settled in the Indus Valley and eventually moved across northern India. Today, few historical sources exist that recount the development of Indo-Aryan civilization in India. As a result, historians must rely on the *Vedas*, religious writings that became the foundation of the Hindu religion.

India's culture has been strongly influenced by religious ideas, particularly those of Hinduism and Buddhism. Hinduism developed over a period of a thousand years and can be traced to the early ideas of the Indo-Aryans. The beliefs of Buddhism were formed around 500 B.C.

India was united near the end of the fourth century B.C. by Chandragupta Maurya. His grandson, Asoka, was one of the world's first great rulers. Asoka worked to bring compassion and moral principles to his government. However, following Asoka's death, the Maurya Empire collapsed. Over the next four hundred years, India was ruled by a series of foreign invaders and by several small kingdoms.

CHAPTER 3 IN REVIEW

IMPORTANT WORDS, NAMES, AND TERMS

1 Explain, define, or identify each of the following:

monsoons	export	extended family
Harappa	import	karma
granaries	Dravidians	nirvana
economic system	caste system	bureaucracy

FACTS AND IDEAS

2 What type of economic activity supported the Harappan farming economy?

3 What discoveries indicate that the Harappan culture was in decline after 1700 B.C.?

4 About when were the sacred Hindu texts known as the *Vedas* written?

5 Who were the Brahmans?

6 Who was Siddhartha Gautama?

ANALYZING VISUAL MATERIAL

7 What important economic characteristic of the Indus civilization can be inferred from the illustrations on pages 64 and 65?

8 Why do you think a ruler of ancient India would use stone columns for proclamations of new laws and policies, as shown in the illustration on page 74?

CONCEPTS AND UNDERSTANDINGS

9 What were the characteristics of a planned city of the Indus Valley civilization?

10 How did the *Vedas* divide early Indo-Aryan society?

11 In what ways did the caste system stabilize society in ancient India?

12 How did the leadership of the Maurya ruler Asoka differ from that of his grandfather?

PROJECTS AND ACTIVITIES

13 The trade routes between India and the Middle East and the Roman Empire produced an effective exchange of ideas and goods. Gather information from the library on these trade routes and draw a map to be displayed in the classroom.

14 Based on library research, prepare a report to the class on the contributions made by Indian culture to modern civilization in areas such as math and science. Make a chart of modern English terms that can be traced to ancient India.

CHAPTER 4 EARLY CIVILIZATION IN CHINA

1 The Beginnings of Chinese Civilization 2 The Chou
Dynasty 3 The Development of Chinese Thought
4 The Ch'in Dynasty

The development of farming along the Yellow River more
than 8,000 years ago slowly nurtured an advanced culture in
China. About 4,000 years later, an early farming civilization
appeared in the region of the Yellow River valley. Between
about 1800 B.C. and 210 B.C., this civilization underwent many
changes. As a result, a unique Chinese culture was gradually
formed. The stable civilization that arose persisted throughout
Chinese history to the present century.

This life-size clay statue was one of thousands that were buried in the tomb of
China's first emperor, Shih Huang-ti.

1 THE BEGINNINGS OF CHINESE CIVILIZATION

The first advanced society in China arose along the Yellow River about 1800 B.C. Under the first rulers of the region—the Shang dynasty—many characteristic features of Chinese culture emerged. These included the development of writing, extensive trade, ancestor worship, and unsurpassed skill in working in bronze. Seven centuries after its formation, the Shang dynasty came to an end.

THE GEOGRAPHY OF CHINA Throughout much of its history, China has been isolated from the rest of the world by its geography. To the west and southwest of China lie the nearly impassable Himalaya mountains (see map on this page). To the north are deserts. Jungles and low mountains form another barrier to the south. In addition, the Yellow,

East China, and South China seas—all part of the Pacific Ocean—border China to the east and southeast.

China can be divided into three geographic regions. The first geographic region is the Yellow River valley, which was the birthplace of Chinese civilization. The Yellow River flows from central Asia to the Yellow Sea through a broad plain of rich, yellowish soil called *loess* [LEHS]. The loess is washed into the river and clogs its course, making travel along much of the river nearly impossible. Throughout much of its history, the Yellow River has periodically overflowed its banks, causing devastating floods that have destroyed homes and crops. The floods have given the Yellow River the name China's Sorrow.

The second geographic region of China consists of the Yangtze [YANG-SEE] River valley. Generally, the Yangtze River runs swiftly, carries little sediment, and does not often flood. As the river nears the ocean, it passes through a fertile agricultural region

Throughout Chinese history, deserts, mountains, and vast plains have isolated China from the West.

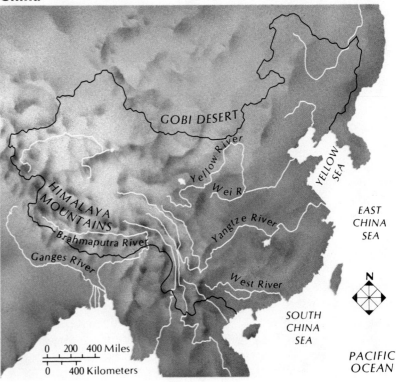

China

that, during China's early history, became the center of Chinese rice production.

China's third geographic region includes the hilly coastal region south of the Yangtze River and the West River valley. This region receives an abundance of rain and produces two or three harvests on the same land each year.

During the earliest part of China's history, the Yangtze Valley was heavily wooded. In addition, tropical forests covered southern China. As a result, early Chinese farmers in this region had to clear the land before it was ready for planting. Probably for this reason, agriculture first began in northern China, on the plains of the Yellow River valley.

EARLY AGRICULTURE ALONG THE YELLOW RIVER Many experts believe that farming developed on the rich loess plains of northern China more than 8,000 years ago. Roughly 2,100 years later—approximately 3900 B.C.—small farming villages dotted the plains along the Yellow River.

Heavy seasonal rains—called *monsoons*—are typical of China's yearly weather pattern. Between May and September, moist air from the Pacific Ocean sweeps northward across China. As a result, the rainfall is greatest in southeastern China and least in the extreme northwestern part of the country. Thus, the earliest farmers along the Yellow River, unlike those in Egypt and Mesopotamia, probably relied more upon seasonal rains than upon irrigation to water their crops.

Beginning around 6000 B.C., *millet*—a type of grain—was the major crop grown on the plains of northern China by early Chinese farmers. Millet was a very versatile crop. The grain provided food for the early Chinese. Moreover, the stems of the plants could be used as fuel and as food for animals. In addition to growing grain, early farmers along the Yellow River hunted, fished, and raised pigs, fowl, cattle, and sheep. Archaeologists have also found that

POLITICAL		SOCIAL AND ECONOMIC
	B.C.	
	c. 6000	Farming began on the loess plains of Yellow River valley
Legendary Hsia dynasty flourished	*c.* 2000	Permanent farming settlements emerged in Yellow River valley Raising of silkworms began
Shang dynasty established	*c.* 1800	
Chou dynasty came to power in Wei River valley Chou monarch ruled by Mandate of Heaven	1122	
Seat of Chou government was moved eastward Chou influence began to decline	771	Chou capital in Wei River valley destroyed by barbarians
	c. 500	Confucius began teaching ideas of his philosophy Ideas of Taoism developed
Period of Warring States began	403	
	c. 300	Iron tools introduced into Chinese agriculture
Establishment of first Chinese empire by leaders of Ch'in	221	
	214	Great Wall completed
Shih Huang-ti, first Chinese emperor, died	210	Private landownership had become common throughout China
Han dynasty began	202	

79

about 4,000 years ago the Chinese began to raise silkworms. This is the earliest evidence of silk production in China.

By about 2000 B.C., an advanced agricultural society had developed in northern China. Permanent farming villages that included specialized craft workers—such as potters, carpenters, leatherworkers, and weavers—were already well established.

According to ancient legends, China's first dynasty—the Hsia [shee-AH]—was formed about this time. Because evidence of this dynasty is sketchy, many experts believe that it was, in part, a mythical creation of later Chinese writers. Shortly after 1800 B.C., Chinese civilization began to emerge under the next dynasty—the Shang.

THE SHANG DYNASTY The first widespread advanced culture in China was the culture of the Shang kingdom that lasted from about 1800 B.C. to about 1100 B.C. The Shang kingdom eventually controlled an area from the Yellow Sea in the east to the province of Shensi [SHEN-SHEE] in the west. The kingdom also extended north to the mouth of the Yellow River and south to the Yangtze River (see map on this page).

The earliest Chinese civilization flourished in the Yellow River valley under the Shang dynasty.

The Shang Kingdom

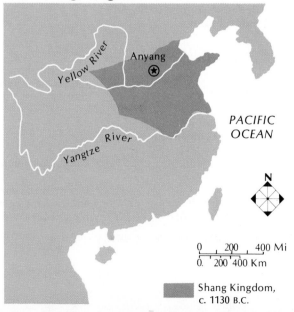

Shang Kingdom, c. 1130 B.C.

The Shang *dynasty*—or ruling family—dominated a union of small states. These states were ruled, in turn, by a class of warrior-nobles. The nobles were required to provide legions of workers for public building projects, such as dikes, temples, and palaces. They were also expected to provide soldiers for the kingdom's armies. Moreover, the nobles were required to pay taxes to the Shang kings.

Agriculture was the main economic activity of the lands ruled by the Shang. As in earlier times, the major crop was millet. However, Chinese farmers also grew wheat, barley, rice, and vegetables. Silkworms were raised and their cocoons were unraveled for the silk. The thread made from the raw silk was then used to weave clothes, curtains, kerchiefs, and many other goods. In addition, hemp was grown and was also used for textiles.

During the Shang dynasty, the Chinese developed an accurate lunar calendar of 360 days. Periodically, the calendar was brought into line with the solar year of 365 ¼ days by adding a thirteenth month. The Shang calendar helped farmers to know when to prepare their fields for planting.

Trade between villages, towns, and cities flourished during the Shang dynasty. Many of the objects uncovered by archaeologists at the Shang capital of Anyang [AHN-YAHNG] came from other parts of the kingdom. Archaeological finds show that jade, tin, copper, and salt were among the trade goods that reached Anyang from other parts of Shang China. These discoveries prove that many Shang cities and towns enjoyed close contact with one another as a result of their trade ties. This contact, in turn, helped to spread the brilliant culture that grew during the Shang dynasty.

SHANG CULTURE AND RELIGION Archaeologists have discovered that many crafts were highly developed under the Shang. Carvings of marble, ivory, jade, and wood—many inlaid with turquoise—have been

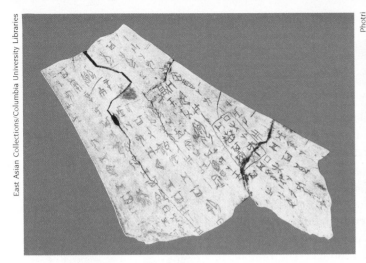

The bronze elephant (right) is typical of the expertly crafted art of the Shang dynasty. The cracks in the oracle bones (above) were used by the early Chinese to foretell the future. Oracle bones are the earliest examples of Chinese writing.

found. Glazed pottery and pottery made of fine white clay—known as *porcelain*—were also made at this time.

The period of the Shang dynasty is well-known for beautiful works in bronze—an alloy of copper and tin. The superb Shang artistry in bronze weapons, religious artifacts, and household utensils has rarely been matched.

Religion was an important feature of Shang civilization. Heavenly gods and gods of nature were worshiped by the early Chinese. More importantly, ancestor worship became well established during this time. Many Shang people believed that the spirits of their ancestors could be called upon for advice and protection. For this reason, many Shang people worshiped the spirits of their ancestors.

Kings often questioned the gods and the spirits about such things as the weather, the next harvest, and the possible outcome of a military expedition. Answers to these questions were sought by priests, who consulted objects known as *oracle bones*. Thousands of these oracle bones have been found at Anyang and at other Shang sites.

Oracle bones were made by priests who heated ox bones until cracks appeared on their surface. The priests would then foretell the future by interpreting the patterns of cracks on the oracle bones. Often the questions and answers were carved on the surface of the bones. Similar prophecies were made from heated tortoise shells. These carvings—dating from about 1200 B.C.—are the first evidence of a written Chinese language. This language used more than 3,000 pictographic symbols and nearly 2,000 of these characters have been identified. The origins of modern written Chinese can be traced to this shell-bone script.

During the twelfth century B.C., Shang leadership grew steadily weaker and more cruel. According to traditional accounts, the Shang dynasty was overthrown in 1122 B.C., and a new dynasty—the Chou [JOH]—came to power.

QUESTIONS FOR REVIEW

1 What are the three geographic regions of China?

2 In what way did the early Chinese farmers use millet?

3 Why are oracle bones and tortoise shells important to the study of ancient China?

81

Life at the Time

Legends of China

Little is known about the beginnings of Chinese culture. During this early period, however, many myths and legends that sought to explain the beginnings of Chinese culture were created. Many of these myths and legends were passed along orally from generation to generation until, with the birth of writing, they were recorded in written accounts.

Many of the early mythological accounts of China's cultural origins were probably no more than highly imaginative stories. Other legends, however, were apparently based upon fact and were passed along with surprisingly little variation for many lifetimes. In their later written form, these legends have helped to improve our understanding of China's past.

Several legendary rulers, for example, were said to have governed China during the prehistoric times before the Hsia and the Shang dynasties. According to legend, these rulers taught the early people of China ideas and skills that, over the years, became characteristic of Chinese life-styles.

The following passage is an example of an early Chinese legend that was passed orally for many generations before the birth of Chinese writing. Experts believe that the account was written by an unknown author and may date from sometime after 1200 B.C. The remote time described by the account, however, was a much earlier era—probably before 2000 B.C. Thus, the excerpt gives some valuable details about life in prehistoric China.

". . . These rulers taught people to fashion wood to make boats and oars, so goods could be exchanged between different parts of China. They also taught people to harness horses and oxen,

so men and goods could be transported to distant areas. They instructed people to strengthen their doors and to hire watchmen to beat rattles at night, in order to ward off thieves and robbers. . . . They also taught people to use wood to make bow and arrows, so they would be feared by those who intended to harm them.

"In remote times people lived in caves in the wilderness. The sages [wise rulers] of a later period taught them to build houses, complete with beams

and pillars, so they could protect themselves from the harsh elements.

"In remote times people wrapped their dead with straw before burying them in the wilderness. The dead body was not sealed in a casket; nor was a tree planted on the grave site.

They did not even observe a mourning period. The sages changed all this in a later period. Not only was a coffin required, but the coffin with the dead man in it also had to be housed in a brick vault.

"In remote times people made knots with ropes as a means of communication. [This refers to an ancient system of recording amounts of trade goods by knotting ropes or cords; each knot represented a specific quantity of goods.] The sages of a later period taught people to communicate with one another through the use of written words. As a result of the invention of a written language, not only did the government become more efficient, but the people also became better governed."

2 THE CHOU DYNASTY

A new ruling family—the Chou—came to power in China at the end of the Shang dynasty. The early years of the Chou dynasty were characterized by a stable, agricultural society. However, later Chou rule was plagued by wars that resulted from the rising power of many nobles.

The period of the Chou dynasty was also the time of China's Classical Age, a time when a truly classical Chinese culture was formed. Chou rule ended in 256 B.C., and a new state—Ch'in—rose to leadership.

RISE OF THE CHOU DYNASTY In 1122 B.C., the ruling Shang dynasty was overthrown by the leaders of Chou, a powerful state in the Wei River valley to the west. The new Chou dynasty continued to rule for nearly 9 centuries, the longest dynastic reign in Chinese history. For the last 500 years of their rule, however, the Chou kings were little more than figureheads as several states led by ambitious nobles rose to power and fell in succession.

The early Chou rulers spread Chinese culture to new areas. Shantung in the east, Szechwan [SECH-WAHN] in the west, and the lower Yangtze Valley came under the influence of the Chou (see map on this page). During this time, the Chou monarch became known as the Son of Heaven. The ruler was believed to be the link between the people and their gods. Moreover, the monarch claimed to rule by the *Mandate of Heaven*. This meant that the king had the right to rule as long as he did so justly and the people were contented. Throughout Chinese history, this reasoning was used to explain the coming to power of each new dynasty.

During the early centuries of Chou rule, much of the kingdom was governed directly by the king. Later, an efficient bureaucracy developed to deal with the increasingly

The Chou Kingdom

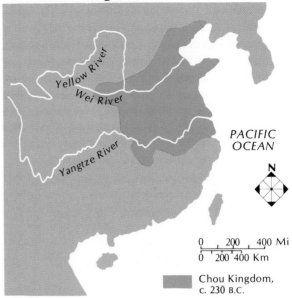

The Chou dynasty ruled over an area that stretched eastward from the Wei River valley to the Pacific Ocean and southward to the Yangtze River valley.

complex problems of governing a large territory.

LAND AND SOCIETY An important idea introduced by the Chou kings was that all land was owned by the monarch. Therefore, land could be granted by the king to whomever he wished. As a result, many large and small states were formed as the rulers gave large grants of land to nobles and to members of the royal family. Generally, those given land grants appointed lesser nobles to rule smaller areas within the overlord's domain.

In return for the land and the authority to govern it, overlords owed loyalty to the king. And lesser nobles, who received land from the overlords, owed loyalty and military aid to the overlords in return. The king was obligated to protect the nobles from barbarian attacks and also from each other. Moreover, the overlords and lesser nobles owed taxes to the king. These taxes were collected from the peasant farmers who worked the lands of the overlords and of

83

the lesser nobles. Ownership of land by peasants did not exist in China at this time.

Ideally, peasant farmers worked a 15-acre (6-hectare) section of land. Another section of land the same size was worked in common by several families. The produce of this section went to the noble who actually held the land. Sometimes, farmers contributed a share of their production to the lord rather than work the common land.

This system of land usage and of social and political organization was similar to the system of feudalism that developed in Europe during the Middle Ages (see Chapter 11). However, in practice the system varied widely throughout China. During the fourth and third centuries B.C., it slowly disappeared. In its place, private landownership by merchants, peasants, and others who were not part of the nobility became common and was eventually legalized. This was the result of a rapidly changing Chinese society during the later years of the Chou dynasty.

SHIFT OF POWER TO THE EAST By the eighth century B.C., China was divided into several states. Some of these states were controlled by the king, while others were controlled by powerful princes. The style of Chou government—that is, giving the nobility sovereignty over large territories—contributed greatly to this division. Moreover, the nobles continually fought one another to gain more land for themselves. This situation was further complicated by the consistently poor leadership of the later Chou rulers.

In 771 B.C., the Chou capital was attacked and destroyed by barbarian raiders from the fringes of the kingdom. The capital was then moved further east to Loyang. As a result, Chou influence declined as other Chinese states vied with one another for power. By about 400 B.C., after more than 300 years of warfare and expansion, the number of major Chinese states was reduced to 7.

As territory was conquered and reconquered, Chinese society also changed. Some of the most important changes occurred in the social and political organization of Chou China. By the end of the third century B.C., much of the land once controlled by the Chou monarchy or by powerful nobles was privately owned. The old landownership system—based upon the idea that the king owned all the land and disposed of it at will—had disappeared. Land could be bought and sold by nearly anyone. As a result, landownership became common among peasant farmers for the first time. However, large landowners frequently became landlords. They rented farmland to peasants who had previously worked it for the overlord.

After about 400 B.C., China faced many more problems. This was the beginning of a time known by modern historians as the Period of Warring States. For the next 200 years, China was in constant turmoil as

Elaborate jade carvings, such as this ceremonial jade ax, are characteristic of Chou art.

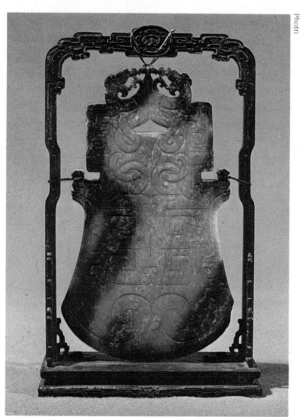

Photri

Photos by Photri

The art of bronze casting in early China flourished under the careful craft workers of the Chou dynasty.

powerful nobles continuously fought among themselves.

CHANGING CHINESE CULTURE   During the last centuries of Chou rule—about 771 B.C. to 256 B.C.—many changes took place in China. This time, which included the Period of Warring States, is called China's *Classical Age*. During these years, many lasting characteristics of Chinese civilization were formed.

During the Classical Age, towns and cities grew up throughout China. By about 300 B.C., several Chinese cities had populations of more than 100,000. Urban growth, the expansion of trade, and growing prosperity created a demand for more luxury goods. As a result, a class of successful and wealthy merchants arose. Moreover, education and individual ability—rather than birthright—became important ways to gain a better standard of living.

Many technological changes led to improvements in farming in classical China. Because of a limited amount of fertile land and an ever-growing population, Chinese agriculture became more *intensive*. That is, farmers worked small plots of land and

raised as many crops as possible. In order to accomplish this, Chinese farmers developed large-scale methods of irrigation. Also, swamps were drained to increase farmland. Fertilizers were used to increase crop production. The idea of rotating crops from one field to another to prevent the soil from wearing out became widespread. Ox-drawn plows also came into use at this time.

The earliest iron artifacts found in China were made around the fourth century B.C. The first iron tools, including iron plows that enabled farmers to open new fields, were introduced. These tools were cast from molten iron, a process not generally used in the region of Europe for another 2,000 years.

QUESTIONS FOR REVIEW

1   *What was the Mandate of Heaven?*

2   *How did the style of Chou government help to divide early China?*

3   *Why did Chinese agriculture become more intensive in the later centuries of Chou rule?*

85

3 THE DEVELOPMENT OF CHINESE THOUGHT

One of the most important developments in classical China took place in philosophy. Many philosophers offered explanations and proposed solutions for the confusion brought about by the constant struggles for power among the Chinese states. Two philosophies—*Confucianism* and *Taoism*—established traditions of Chinese thought that continued until present times. These and other philosophies had a major influence upon the development of China.

CONFUCIANISM During the later years of China's Classical Age, the influence of the Chou dynasty had declined across much of China. The various independent Chinese states were constantly at war with one another. Thus, the late Classical Age was a time of violence and of widespread social upheaval. During these years, a number of Chinese thinkers, hoping to restore peace and order, worked to spread their ideas about how people should live. These ideas and ways of looking at life—called *philosophies*—had a major impact upon Chinese life.

The great Chinese philosopher, K'ung Fu-tzu—better known as Confucius [kuhn-FYOO-shuhs]—began his teaching about the year 500 B.C. Confucius firmly believed that the world could become a better place to live. He felt that people were basically good. If people worked to improve themselves and their government, Confucius thought, they could bring harmony, order, and peace to society.

The essence of Confucian teaching was that people should play their proper role in society in relation to other people. One of Confucius' best-known proverbs was "What you do not want done to yourself, do not do to others." By this, Confucius meant that every time a person acts, someone else is affected.

Confucius taught that there were five kinds of social relationships. These were the relationships between father and son, elder brother and younger brother, husband and wife, elder friend and younger friend, and ruler and subject. Each of these relationships had its own special duties. For example, a father was to be loving and to set a good example for his son. A son was to obey and respect his father. A ruler must be kind, and a subject must be loyal. Only in this way could society achieve harmony and order.

Confucius lived his life according to his beliefs and provided a model for others. He sincerely believed that the world would be improved if his ideas were put into practice. Nearly 400 years after his death in 479 B.C., his beliefs had become part of every Chinese scholar's learning. Confucian ideas helped to shape Chinese thoughts and life-styles for almost 2,000 years.

THE IMPACT OF CONFUCIANISM The philosophy of Confucius has endured throughout Chinese history. By 100 B.C., it had become the official state philosophy of China and remained so until recent times.

The reasons for the tremendous impact of Confucianism are many. It was a system of thought that dealt with the way people should act in society. It provided an orderly way by which people could conduct their lives. But Confucius did not ask people to do the impossible. Rather, people could reach the reasonable goals of behavior that he had set if they tried. As a result, Confucianism became a way of life in China.

Confucius taught that one's life-style should be governed by an understanding of the *Mean*—the middle way of action. People should live between life's extremes, and nothing in life should be done to excess. Confucius also believed that people who lived according to the Mean would be more willing to compromise with one another. Thus, violence should no longer be used to settle arguments. Compromise and nego-

The foundation of Confucian society—the family—was depicted in a twelfth-century A.D. painting from the Confucian classic *Book of Filial Piety*, in which children were taught to honor their parents.

tiation were important in the settlement of public disputes as well.

Confucius loved the "arts of peace"—music, art, and poetry. He believed that a country that developed these arts to the highest degree would be admired by all other countries. This idea led to many periods of great artistic achievement in Chinese history.

Confucian thought also relied upon tradition. Because tradition was so important to this philosophy, however, new ideas and change became less acceptable in China. As a result, Chinese culture and the Chinese view of people and of society remained basically unchanged for more than 2,000 years. But Confucianism was not the only system of ideas to influence China. The teachings of another great Chinese philosopher, Lao-tzu [LOWD-ZUH], were also important to the development of Chinese culture.

TAOISM Lao-tzu is thought to have lived in China around the sixth century B.C. His ideas—known as Taoism [DOW-iz-uhm]—

were written in a short, 5,000-word book called the *Tao Te Ching*. Taoism became popular around 200 B.C. and was accepted, in part, as an alternative to the rituals, ceremonies, and traditions of Confucianism.

Like Confucianism, Taoism stressed the goodness of all people. However, Taoism was a personal philosophy that emphasized the simple life and a closeness to nature. Taoism did not agree with the Confucianist relationship between people and society. Instead, Taoists wanted to isolate themselves from society. They believed that only then could people return to a simple life, unspoiled by society. In addition, Taoists also emphasized the need to achieve harmony with nature. In this way, they believed that they could find the *tao*—the "way."

Taoism had a great impact on Chinese culture and was second in influence only to Confucianism. The Taoist concern with nature became an important part of Chinese painting and poetry. Moreover, Taoism became one of many philosophies that the Chinese used to mold their beliefs and their views of life.

Lao-tzu, the founder of Taoism, personified the serenity and the simplicity of his philosophy, which developed in China at about the same time as Confucianism.

OTHER CURRENTS OF CHINESE THOUGHT

During the fourth century B.C., a new Chinese philosophy challenged the importance of Confucianism. Mo Ti, later known as Mo Tzu [MOHD-ZUH], preached a doctrine of universal love that became extremely popular for a short time with many Chinese.

The goal of Moism was the fulfillment of the immediate needs—food, clothing, and housing—of each member of society. Mo Ti strongly believed that all people must be provided by society with a decent standard of living. Mo Ti also condemned offensive warfare during a time when war was a constant threat to every Chinese state. However, because of the chaotic conditions of the time, Mo Ti and his followers were sometimes forced to help defend weaker states from outside attack.

Another school of thought developed in China during the third century B.C. and provided the underlying principles for the foundation of the first Chinese empire. These ideas were known as Legalism.

Legalists felt that human nature was basically evil. Thus, the Legalist philosophy differed from other Chinese philosophies, which emphasized human goodness. However, the Legalists also believed that society could be improved through a system of laws.

The Legalist philosophy maintained that the strong enforcement of laws was absolutely necessary to keep society orderly. The laws must be detailed, exact, and clear. The punishments for breaking the laws must be severe. A central government was also needed to ensure that the laws were strictly followed.

During the mid-200's B.C., the ideas of Legalism were used by the rulers of Ch'in [CHIN]—a state in western China—to justify their military aims. Within about 30 years, the Ch'in had built the first Chinese empire—an empire based upon Legalist ideas of government.

QUESTIONS FOR REVIEW

1 *What were the five social relationships of Confucianism?*

2 *How did Taoism differ from Confucianism?*

3 *Why did Legalist thinkers believe in the strong enforcement of laws?*

4 THE CH'IN DYNASTY

In 221 B.C., the first Chinese empire was established by the Ch'in dynasty. Thus, China was united under one strong central government for the first time in its history. Because of the emperor's oppressive rule, however, the dynasty did not long survive his death in 210 B.C. Only 8 years later, the Ch'in dynasty collapsed. But the empire that had been created continued for more than 2,100 years.

THE RISE OF THE CH'IN DYNASTY After the Chou capital was moved eastward in 771 B.C., the leaders of the small state of Ch'in were able to occupy the lands once held by the Chou kings. These lands lay in the fertile Wei River valley in the present-day province of Shensi (see map on this page). The rich lands became the basis for a growing and prosperous Ch'in economy. Moreover, the mountains to the east and south of the state provided natural barriers. They enabled the Ch'in to defend themselves against attack during the Period of Warring States—403 B.C. to 221 B.C.

The Ch'in state was located on the northwestern frontier of China. For centuries, Ch'in was considered to be culturally backward by the older, more civilized states to the east. This was because the Ch'in rulers constantly fought barbarian tribes from the *steppes*—dry, treeless plains—that bordered Ch'in to the north. As a result, the Ch'in adopted many barbarian customs. Among these customs were many methods of fighting, including the use of cavalry and foot soldiers, that helped the Ch'in to eventually conquer China.

In 249 B.C., the state of Ch'in began a campaign to defeat each of its major rivals. In 221 B.C., the last Ch'in opponent—the state of Ch'i—was beaten and China was finally united under one government. The influence of the Ch'in was felt as far south

The Ch'in Empire

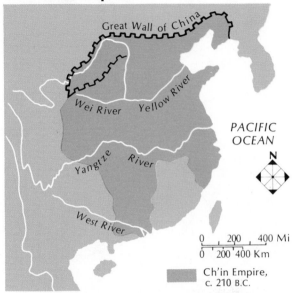

By 221 B.C., the leaders of the small state of Ch'in had united China under a single strong government.

Chinese archaeologists recently uncovered huge bronze castings of horse-drawn carriages and their drivers that were made during the Ch'in dynasty.

Many early Chinese writings were destroyed in the book burnings ordered by the emperor Shih Huang-ti, who, in 213 B.C. feared that the books contained ideas that were dangerous to his firm rule.

as Vietnam, in southeastern Asia. To the north, Ch'in leadership was recognized in Korea. The province of Szechwan marked the westernmost expansion of the Ch'in (see map on page 89). The leader of the Ch'in called himself Shih Huang-ti [SHIR-HWAHNG-TEE]—the "first sovereign emperor" of China.

THE REIGN OF SHIH HUANG-TI China was ruled by Shih Huang-ti for only 11 years. In that time, he established a system of government that united China for 2,000 years. The new emperor believed that the empire could be more easily governed if control of the country was centralized. As a result, local governments called counties were formed. These, in turn, became part of 36 provinces that were under the direct control of the emperor. Officials were also appointed by the emperor to oversee the operation of each province.

Shih Huang-ti attempted to prevent rebellions through harsh rule. Metal weapons were collected, melted down, and recast into bells and statues. The most wealthy and powerful local leaders were required to move with their families to the capital, where their activities could be watched. To prevent criticism of his rule, the emperor prohibited scholars from speaking out against the government. In some cases, those who continued to criticize the emperor's rule were killed.

Shih Huang-ti completed several public building projects during his short reign. Irrigation and canal systems were built. Huge palaces were constructed. An extensive system of roads was completed. This system resulted in better communications within the empire and also enabled the army to be sent quickly anywhere in the realm.

Weights, measures, and currency were all

90

Bibliotheque Nationale, Paris

The Great Wall of China, much of it built over beautiful but rugged terrain, was completed in 214 B.C. and linked many previously existing walls. The purpose of the wall was to defend the Chinese against northern barbarians.

standardized by the government in order to encourage trade. A standard style of Chinese writing was also adopted throughout the empire.

During his reign, Shih Huang-ti completed the Great Wall of China. The wall stretched about 1,500 miles (2 414 kilometers) across the northern frontier of China (see map on page 89). It was used mainly to defend the empire against northern barbarians. Using hundreds of thousands of forced workers, the wall was completed in only 7 years by connecting many already-existing walls. Because of repeated repairs over many centuries, however, little of the emperor's original wall remains today. In 210 B.C., Shih Huang-ti died, and shortly thereafter his dynasty came to an end.

COLLAPSE OF THE CH'IN DYNASTY The Chinese people paid a bitter price in lost lives and property for the unification of

China. Shih Huang-ti's harsh laws, heavy taxes, and costly building projects placed severe burdens upon the people. Moreover, the emperor's efforts to permanently unify the Chinese states were cut short by his death in 210 B.C.

Thus, the social and political organization of the empire was only partly completed when Shih Huang-ti died. The Ch'in dynasty was further weakened when the emperor's successor proved to be a poor leader. As a result, the dynasty collapsed in 202 B.C., only eight years after Shih Huang-ti's death. A new dynasty—the Han [HAHN]—replaced the Ch'in as China's imperial rulers.

The Han dynasty ruled China for more than 400 years—from 202 B.C. to A.D. 200. During that time, Han emperors completed many of the social and political changes begun by Shih Huang-ti. Even after the Han dynasty ended these changes continued to influence Chinese civilization. It was not

Photri

The tradition of finely-crafted jade carving continued in China into the Han dynasty. This fierce, winged beast roared defiantly to ward off evil spirits.

until the last imperial ruler of China was overthrown in A.D. 1912 that many of the traditions begun during the Han dynasty began to change (see Chapter 25). Thus, Shih Huang-ti's social and political ideas continued to shape Chinese life-styles for more than 2,100 years after his death.

QUESTIONS FOR REVIEW

1 *What was the basis for the prosperous Ch'in economy?*

2 *How did Shih Huang-ti centralize government control of his new empire?*

3 *Why do you think Shih Huang-ti probably feared rebellion during his reign?*

CHAPTER SUMMARY

Agriculture developed in the Yellow River valley of northern China more than 8,000 years ago—about 6000 B.C. Around 1800 B.C., an early civilization was formed in northern China under the leadership of the Shang dynasty. Many important developments in Chinese culture took place at this time. Silk became an important product, and various forms of art were highly developed. Ancestor worship, an element of Chinese culture that lasted for more than 4,000 years, became established. The first Chinese writing also appeared.

In 1122 B.C., the Shang dynasty was overthrown by the Chou. Under Chou rule, China experienced its Classical Age. Many features of Chinese civilization that have endured to modern times were formed under the Chou. During this time, many philosophers, including Confucius, developed their ideas. The philosophy known as Taoism also had an important impact on Chinese culture.

After 771 B.C., several states grew in power. These states frequently fought one another. As a result, China suffered nearly constant warfare and turmoil. In 221 B.C., the leader of the northern state of Ch'in finally unified China under a single government.

CHAPTER 4 IN REVIEW

IMPORTANT WORDS, NAMES, AND TERMS

1 Explain, define, or identify each of the following:

loess	philosophy	Ch'in
Anyang	*Tao Te Ching*	steppe
oracle bones	Mo Ti	Shih Huang-ti
Mandate of Heaven	Legalism	Great Wall

FACTS AND IDEAS

2 What was the major crop of early Chinese civilization?

3 What was shell-bone script?

4 About when were the first iron tools used in China?

5 About when did Confucianism become the official Chinese state philosophy?

6 What was the basic belief of Moism?

ANALYZING VISUAL MATERIAL

7 Compare the illustration on page 77, which shows Chinese sculpture of the late third century B.C., with the illustration of a bronze casting of the Shang dynasty on page 81. What similarities or differences in Chinese art over a 900-year span can you find?

8 Study the map on page 78 carefully. What major river systems drain the vast area of China?

CONCEPTS AND UNDERSTANDINGS

9 How was silk made?

10 In what ways did Chinese peasants in classical times intensify their crop production?

11 In what way did Shih Huang-ti centralize the government of China?

12 What were some of the reasons for the collapse of the Ch'in dynasty?

PROJECTS AND ACTIVITES

13 Prepare a chart or a bulletin-board display showing the emphasis upon nature in Chinese painting and poetry.

14 The government of the People's Republic of China has recently made many attempts to systematically study and explore the remains of early China. Prepare a research report for the class on archaeological discoveries in present-day China. Consult library sources for information on these discoveries.

Using Geography Skills

Early farming societies were greatly influenced by geographic factors. We know, for example, that patterns of settlement and of land use were often similar among early farming societies. We also know that these patterns were strongly affected by similar geographic conditions.

The physical map below illustrates the surface features of a particular geographic area. It also uses symbols to depict an important concept or theme.

By analyzing such a map, we can better understand the many ways in which geography has helped to shape the course of human history.

This map represents a hypothetical region of the ancient Middle East. It shows the relationship between geography and the patterns of settlement typical of many early farming societies. Study the map carefully. Then answer the following questions:

1 How can the areas in which wild cereal grains grew be most accurately described?

2 Within what geographic environment did the earliest farming villages develop?

3 How did farming villages of the period 6000 B.C. – 5000 B.C. differ from those of the period 8000 B.C. – 6000 B.C.?

4 What general trends may be seen in the development of early Middle Eastern farming societies?

5 What factors may have caused early farming societies to move from their original upland sites into more arid, semidesert regions between 8000 B.C. and 3000 B.C.?

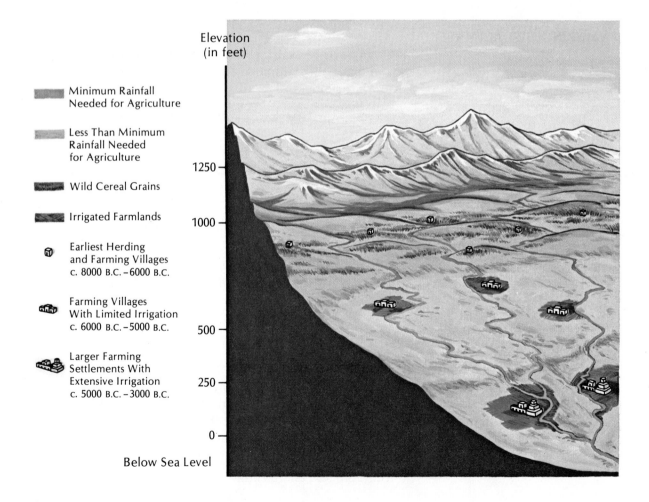

Elevation (in feet)

Minimum Rainfall Needed for Agriculture

Less Than Minimum Rainfall Needed for Agriculture

Wild Cereal Grains

Irrigated Farmlands

Earliest Herding and Farming Villages c. 8000 B.C. – 6000 B.C.

Farming Villages With Limited Irrigation c. 6000 B.C. – 5000 B.C.

Larger Farming Settlements With Extensive Irrigation c. 5000 B.C. – 3000 B.C.

1250

1000

500

250

0

Below Sea Level

94

UNIT 1 IN REVIEW

CONCEPTS AND UNDERSTANDINGS

1 How were Neanderthal and Cro-Magnon cultures a result of adaptation to their environment?
2 In what ways was the Neolithic Period important to the development of early civilizations?
3 In what ways was irrigation important to the development of early agricultural societies?
4 In what ways were the religious ideas of Judaism, Hinduism, and Buddhism similar? How were they different?
5 What cultural and technological characteristics were shared by the earliest civilizations?

QUESTIONS FOR DISCUSSIONS

6 To what extent would you agree or disagree with the following statement? "The environments in which early civilizations flourished affected the type of government that developed in each civilization." Explain your answer.
7 Why, in your opinion, were early civilizations characterized by sharp social divisions based upon wealth, family, power, and prestige?
8 In what ways do you think that the caste system slowed social and economic changes in ancient India?

SUGGESTED READING

Asimov, Isaac. *Land of Canaan.* Boston: Houghton Mifflin Company, 1971.

Baumann, Hans. *In the Land of Ur: The Discovery of Ancient Mesopotamia.* New York: Pantheon Books, 1969.

Buck, Pearl S. *China Past and Present.* New York: The John Day Company, 1972.

Clymer, Eleanor. *The Second Greatest Invention: Search for the First Farmers.* New York: Holt, Rinehart and Winston, 1969.

Hamilton-Peterson, James, and Carol Andrews. *Mummies: Death and Life in Ancient Egypt.* New York: The Viking Press, 1979.

Hay, John. *Ancient China.* New York: Henry Z. Walck, Inc., 1973.

Higham, Charles. *The Earliest Farmer and the First Cities.* Minneapolis: Lerner Publications Company, 1977.

Kerwin, Carlotta, series ed. *The Emergence of Man Series.* New York: Time-Life Books Inc., 1972–74.

Nancarrow, Peter. *Early China and the Wall.* Minneapolis: Lerner Publications Company, 1980.

Saddhatissa, H. *The Life of the Buddha.* New York: Harper and Row, Publishers, 1976.

Swinburne, Laurence, and Irene Swinburne. *Behind the Sealed Door: The Discovery of the Tomb and Treasures of Tutankhamun.* New York: Sniffen Court Books, 1978.

UNIT 2

THE CLASSICAL WORLD

c. 500 B.C. to A.D. 500

5 The Rise of Greece   6 The Hellenistic Age   7 The Roman World
8 The Classical Age in India and China

Archers from the palace at Susa in ancient Persia   Rock-cut Buddhist statues, Lung-men, China, c. A.D. 600

Between about 500 B.C. and A.D. 500, civilizations in the Mediterranean and in Asia formed classical cultures. This "classical age" helped set many of the patterns of culture for later civilizations in these regions. Achievements in philosophy, religion, science, and art during classical times were rarely matched by later civilizations. Government also gradually changed in the Mediterranean world during this time and helped to develop Western political institutions. For example, the Greeks developed an early form of democracy. And the Romans established the workings of a republic and later, of a vast empire. In Asia, Hindu and Chinese civilizations flourished.

More importantly, however, the classical world was brought together through trade and the exchange of ideas. The eastern exploits of Mediterranean conquerors and the westward expansion of the Chinese brought the cultures of the East and the West more closely into contact. As a result, these cultures were greatly enriched.

By about A.D. 500, the classical world had changed dramatically. However, many of the achievements of the classical age survived and had an important influence on the development of later cultures.

Bjorn Klingwall

The Granger Collection

Fragment of a Minoan fresco, *c.* 1500 B.C., from the island of Thera

CHAPTER 5 THE RISE OF GREECE

1 The Foundations of Greek Civilization   2 The Hellenic Age
3 The Way of Life in Hellenic Greece   4 The Legacy of
Classical Greece

The civilization of classical Greece reached its peak during the fifth and fourth centuries B.C. Its beginnings can be found in the cultures of the eastern Mediterranean Sea and in the civilizations of Egypt and the Middle East.

The achievements of the classical Greeks have shaped the development of Western civilization to present times. Greek civilization developed one of Western society's most important cultural institutions—democracy. Many other characteristics of Western culture—in the fields of philosophy, science, mathematics, literature, and history—were formed by the Greeks. The Greeks were the first to shape a thoughtful, systematic approach to each of these subjects.

Despite the advancements of Greek civilization, Greek society remained divided along class lines. Human slavery was tolerated. Women had no political rights. The city-states of Greece, unable to unite under a single government, fell to invaders in 338 B.C. Little more than 150 years after it had begun, the Golden Age of Greece ended.

Camerique

The ruins of the Parthenon, which was built during Greece's golden age, stand atop the Acropolis in modern-day Athens.

1 THE FOUNDATIONS OF GREEK CIVILIZATION

The origins of Greek civilization can be traced to many sources. The early inhabitants of the Balkan Peninsula were first influenced by the Minoan civilization. In turn, the Mycenaean civilization and the cultural patterns brought by invading barbarians made a mark on the evolution of Greek society. Trade between these early peoples and the civilizations of Egypt and the Middle East added new ideas and life-styles. By about 800 B.C., the contributions of many cultures and peoples were brought together in the creation of a classical Greek civilization.

GREECE AND THE AEGEAN Civilization began to emerge along the rim of the Aegean [i-JEE-uhn] Sea more than 3,500 years ago. In this region, geography and climate have played important roles in forming a distinctive culture. The steep mountains and narrow valleys that dominate the region begin far to the north. They continue through the Aegean Sea to Asia Minor (see map on this page). Thousands of years ago, geologic upheavals resulted in the sinking of many of these mountains into the sea. These sunken mountains, many of which are old volcanoes, form the islands that lie in the Aegean Sea, from the Balkan Peninsula to Asia Minor.

Ancient Greek civilization flourished in an area that included the central part of modern-day Greece and the *Peloponnesus* [PEL-uh-puh-NEE-suhs]—the southernmost region of Greece. The Peloponnesus was separated from central Greece by the Gulf of Corinth but could be reached by a narrow isthmus (see map on this page). In addition, the inhabitants of central and southern Greece were no more than about 40 miles (68 kilometers)—roughly a day's journey on foot—from the sea. As a result, a seafaring and trading culture developed more than 4,000 years ago.

Although trade was important to the earliest Greeks, agriculture was the basis of the early Greek economy. Only about one fifth of the soil of ancient Greece could be cultivated, however, and farmers also depended entirely on the rain that fell from the autumn planting to the spring harvest. Crops could not be grown under the hot, dry summer skies. Irrigation was not widely used in ancient Greece because of the rugged and rocky terrain and the small, narrow streams. Despite the many problems created by geography and climate, farming remained the basic economic activity of Greece for several centuries. In addition, the widely separated valleys and small plains eventually led to the growth of independent farming settlements throughout the Peloponnesus.

The rugged terrain of Greece encouraged the growth of widely-scattered, independent city-states.

The Aegean World

POLITICAL		SOCIAL AND ECONOMIC
	B.C.	
Minoan civilization arose on island of Crete	c. 2000	
	c. 1600	Minoans traded extensively with Egyptians
Mycenaean civilization began to flourish	c. 1400	
Trojan War fought	c. 1200	Greek dark age began
	c. 750	Greek traders ventured into Mediterranean
	c. 650	First coins used in Hellenic state of Lydia
Solon reformed Athenian laws	594	
Cleisthenes formed one of the first direct democracies in Athens	508	
	c. 500	Pythagoras developed concepts of geometry
Darius invaded Greece	490	
Persians under Xerxes invaded Greece	480	
	461	Golden Age of Hellenic culture began
War between Sparta and Athens began	431	
Spartans defeated Athenians	404	
	399	Socrates executed
	387	Plato established Academy in Athens
Philip I of Macedonia conquered Greece	338	

THE MINOAN CIVILIZATION An important influence on the development of Greek culture was an early civilization that arose on the island of Crete in the Mediterranean Sea about 4,000 years ago. This culture is known today as *Minoan* [muh-NOH-uhn] after the legendary king Minos.

Neolithic people are believed to have first settled the island of Crete nearly 8,000 years ago—about 6000 B.C. (see map on page 99). By about 2700 B.C., new settlers from more-civilized areas of the Aegean had come to Crete. They introduced new styles of pottery and most important, they brought metalworking to the island. By 2200 B.C., an early Minoan civilization had emerged on Crete.

The Minoan civilization reached its peak between about 1700 B.C. and 1400 B.C. Large cities with splendid palaces were built for the Minoan rulers. The Minoan capital of Knossos [NAHS-uhs] had an estimated population of 80,000 people. The Minoan rulers paved the city's streets and built a covered drainage system.

The influence of Minoan civilization was felt throughout the region of the Aegean. Adventurous Minoan sailors and merchants established trade routes to many parts of the eastern Mediterranean. Minoan trading colonies were built on several Aegean islands, and on the coasts of the Balkan Peninsula and of Asia Minor. Evidence also shows that there was an extensive trade with Egypt between about 1700 B.C. and 1400 B.C.

Around 1400 B.C., the Minoan civilization began to decline. Many scholars believe that invaders from the Balkan Peninsula attacked and defeated the Minoans. However, not all experts agree that invasion was the only reason for the decline of Minoan culture. Some archaeologists believe that Crete also suffered tremendous destruction caused by the explosion of a volcano on the island of Thera (present-day Santorin—see map on page 99). This disaster so weakened Minoan society, some experts believe, that

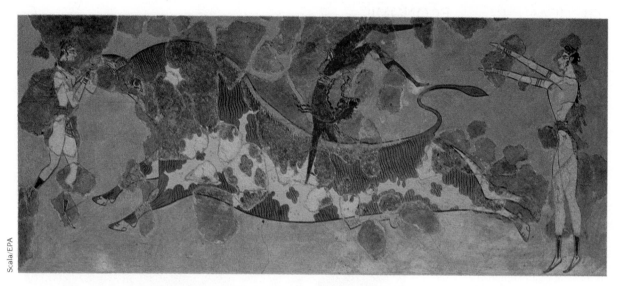

Grabbing a charging bull's horns and somersaulting over its back was a dangerous Minoan feat that required great skill.

the *Mycenaeans* [MIY-suh-NEE-uhnz]—invaders from the north—were able to bring Crete under their control.

THE MYCENAEANS—THE FIRST GREEKS

Shortly after 2000 B.C., groups of nomadic herders from the north began to filter slowly southward into the Balkan Peninsula. This gradual migration took place over a period of many centuries. About 1600 B.C., these warlike people began to build a civilization that was greatly influenced by the advanced Minoan culture. Today, this early Greek culture is known as Mycenaean, after the fortress and trade city of Mycenae.

By about 1400 B.C., the Mycenaeans had become a major sea-trading power in the Aegean Sea. Their influence quickly spread across the eastern Mediterranean Sea. The Minoans probably came completely under the control of the Mycenaeans sometime after 1400 B.C. The island of Cyprus, 300 miles (482 kilometers) to the east of Crete, was also settled by the Mycenaeans. Mycenaean traders exchanged goods with Egyptian merchants and with the merchants of other cultures along the eastern Mediterranean coast.

In addition to their Mediterranean trade routes, the Mycenaeans traded along the coast of Asia Minor and eventually ventured into the Black Sea. However, the ancient city of Troy, on the coast of Asia Minor, controlled the narrow strait that connected the Mediterranean and Black seas (see map on page 99). This channel was known as the Hellespont [HEL-uh-SPAHNT] and is known today as the Dardanelles [DAHRD-uhn-ELZ].

Later Greek legends told of a war between the Mycenaeans and the Trojans shortly before 1200 B.C. The war—known as the Trojan War—resulted in the destruction of Troy. Around the ninth century B.C., these legends were used as the basis for two epic poems—the *Iliad* and the *Odyssey*—by the Greek poet Homer. The Homeric poems were long thought to be only legends until the historic city of Troy was unearthed by archaeologists about 100 years ago. The discovery of Troy and of Mycenaean cities on the Peloponnesus showed that Homeric epics were based, in part, on historical fact.

The period of Mycenaean power came to an end sometime after 1200 B.C. Barbarians from the north—called Dorians—invaded central Greece and the Peloponnesus and savagely destroyed Mycenaean civilization.

A gold mask that may show the likeness of Agamemnon, a king of Homer's epics, was discovered in the 1880's at Mycenae by Heinrich Schliemann, a German archaeologist. Schliemann also helped to substantiate the Homeric epics by uncovering the site of ancient Troy.

As the less advanced culture of the Dorians blended with the Mycenaean civilization, Greece entered a period of conflict and uncertainty that lasted for nearly four centuries.

A DARK AGE Historians know little about the reasons for the Dorian invasions of the twelfth century B.C. However, experts believe that the Dorians were Greek-speaking people from the northernmost regions of Greece. The Dorians were less civilized than people to the south and lacked such important cultural developments as writing. They did possess, however, an important technological advance—iron making—that had not yet reached the south. The Mycenaeans and other Greek peoples in central and southern Greece still made weapons and other metal goods with bronze. Because iron was stronger than bronze, warriors who used iron weapons had an advantage over those who used bronze weapons. Iron swords could split bronze shields, and iron shields could easily protect warriors from bronze weapons. In part, the Dorians' use of iron enabled them to disrupt and eventually to conquer the Mycenaean civilization.

As a result of the Dorian invasions, Greece fell into a long period of cultural decline. Archaeological remains that date from this time show that the production of finely tooled gold and silver artifacts nearly stopped. Moreover, houses were poorly built, and pottery was badly crafted and copied older styles.

Many basic changes in the development of Greece also took place during this time. Among the most important of these changes was the political reorganization of the region. The Dorian invasions broke up the old Mycenaean kingdoms. Many experts believe that the chaos and the uncertainty of the times, coupled with the mountainous geography of Greece, forced many people to seek refuge in the Greek cities. These widely scattered and independent cities became the foundation for the Greek city-states.

The period between about 1200 B.C. and 800 B.C. is often considered a dark age of Greek history. However, this was also a time of slow cultural development and advance. By the end of this period of decline and of change, a genuinely Greek civilization had taken shape on the Balkan Peninsula, throughout much of the Aegean, and on the coast of Asia Minor.

QUESTIONS FOR REVIEW

1 *What two reasons do some archaeologists give for the collapse of the Minoan civilization?*

2 *How did archaeologists provide some evidence for the historical accuracy of the* Iliad *and the* Odyssey?

3 *Why do many scholars believe that the "dark age" in Greece was a period of cultural decline?*

2 THE HELLENIC AGE

During the Hellenic Age—from about 800 B.C. to 338 B.C.—Greek civilization was centered in numerous city-states. As these city-states gradually evolved, many lasting cultural institutions were formed. Most important, government by the people—*democracy*—slowly emerged in Athens and in other city-states during this time.

Throughout the Hellenic Age, intense rivalries prevented the city-states from uniting under a single government. Frequently, Greece was a battlefield as the city-states went to war to settle their disputes. Years of warfare weakened Greece and pushed Hellenic culture into a period of slow decline. By 338 B.C., Greece was finally united, but under a foreign invader.

THE RISE OF THE GREEK CITY–STATES Originally, the Greek *polis* [PAHL-uhs]—city-state—was little more than a small fortified town. Between about 1200 B.C. and 800 B.C., these towns offered refuge from the in-

vasions of the barbarians. These early city-states, ruled by hereditary kings, generally controlled relatively small areas. Typically, the boundaries of each city-state incorporated only the city itself and the nearby lands. These lands, used for growing crops and for grazing goats and sheep, helped to support the city. The society of these fiercely independent city-states was most often organized according to old tribal customs and traditions.

Around 800 B.C., Greece entered the *Hellenic Age*, a name that comes from "Hellene," the Greeks' term for themselves. During the first century of the Hellenic Age, groups of landowning nobles gained power in several city-states. These nobles formed *oligarchies*—governments controlled by a few powerful individuals. Many of these oligarchies remained powerful for nearly two centuries.

Between 800 B.C. and 650 B.C., many city-states faced the problems of a growing population and a lack of fertile farmland. As a result, many city-states sought new lands. Colonies were set up along the Mediterranean and Black seas (see map on page 104). Among these colonies were settlements at Massilia (the modern French city of Marseilles), at Neapolis (today's Italian city of Naples), and on the island of Sicily.

In addition to providing the lands and opportunities necessary for a growing population, colonization also led to a tremendous increase in trade. Greek colonies exported raw materials and grain to Greece and became very prosperous. In turn, the merchants of the Greek city-states sent wine, olive oil, silver, and finished products —such as weapons and pottery—to the colonies.

THE GREEK TYRANTS The steadily increasing prosperity of the Greek economy was not shared by all Greeks. Generally, the gap between the rich and the poor became wider. As a result, the lower classes became bitter and rebellious.

During the seventh century B.C., increases

Greek Colonies and Sea-Trade Routes, c. Sixth Century B.C.

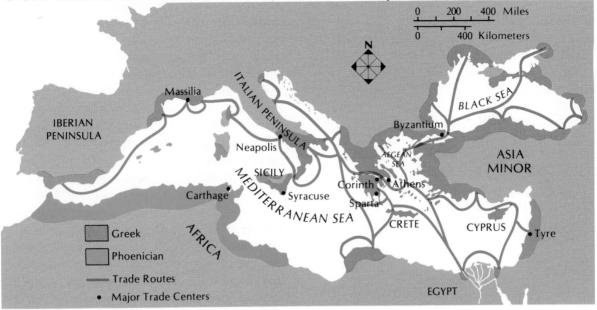

By the sixth century B.C., Greek traders in their many-oared ships had established trade routes throughout the Mediterranean world.

in the export of goods from the Greek city-states encouraged the growth of large farms. Small farmers found that they could not compete with large landowners and were gradually forced to sell their lands. As a result, many small landholders became tenant farmers, who rented farmland from others. Moreover, some small farmers and their families became slaves because they were unable to pay their growing debts.

As this situation worsened, the growing class of wealthy merchants and artisans began to demand a role in the government of the city-states. This led to the overthrow of the ruling nobles of many Greek city-states between 650 B.C. and 500 B.C. In place of the fallen oligarchies, strong leaders—called *tyrants*—began to rule. The Greek tyrants generally gained power from the nobles by force. Today, we use the term "tyrant" to mean a harsh and unpopular dictator. However, the Greek tyrants were often popular with the common people of the city-states, and many were fair and just rulers. A few tyrants ruled cruelly and

ruthlessly and took away the rights of the people. Some tyrants sought to maintain their power by reforming the government of the city-states.

REFORM AND THE DEVELOPMENT OF DEMOCRACY By about 600 B.C., the oligarchy of the eastern Greek city-state of Athens faced growing unrest among the people. The ruling nobility feared that this would weaken their control. In 594 B.C., Solon [SOH-luhn] was appointed to the leadership of Athens and began to reform the laws of the city-state to quiet the discontent.

Solon's major achievements included the first written code of laws for Athens. The new law code made it illegal to force debtors, usually small farmers, into slavery. Courts were established on which common citizens—rather than just the nobles—could serve. Moreover, because wealth, instead of birth, became a requirement for holding public office, Solon helped more citizens to participate in government. These reforms became a permanent part of Athenian government, and even today, Solon's name stands for "wise lawmaker."

Solon's reforms, however, did not completely satisfy all Athenians. In 560 B.C., Pisistratus [piy-SIS-truht-uhs] overthrew the oligarchy and became the tyrant of Athens. He further weakened the Athenian nobles by taking their large estates and dividing them among the small farmers.

In 508 B.C., Cleisthenes [KLIYS-thuh-NEEZ] came to power in Athens. During his rule, many more reforms were undertaken. Cleisthenes broke the remaining power of the nobility by reorganizing the political system of Athens. The old system of tribes and clans—from which Athens' political leaders had traditionally been drawn—was abolished. In its place, ten *demes* were formed. These new divisions classified Athenian citizens according to where they lived, not according to their family. This resulted in the breakdown in the influence of traditional tribes and clans.

Cleisthenes also established the Council of Five Hundred, a body that enforced laws made by the General Assembly, to which every Athenian male citizen belonged. Fifty representatives from each of ten demes were chosen for the council. At first, members of the council were elected. Later, they were chosen by lot. In this way, many Athenian citizens were able to participate in the governing of Athens. Athenian citizenship, however, was limited to adult males, who made up a small percentage of the total population of Athens. Women, slaves, and foreigners were excluded from citizenship.

Cleisthenes' reforms helped to create one of the first examples of a *direct democracy*—government by the people. Although Athenian citizenship was limited, the development of democracy was the most important and precious accomplishment of the early Greeks.

Shortly after 500 B.C., other Greek city-states began to follow the reforms of Cleisthenes. However, one city-state—Sparta—resisted these changes.

SPARTA—A CONTRAST Unlike Athens, the Peloponnesian city-state of Sparta did not develop a democratic form of government. Around 600 B.C., the Spartans established a government dominated by a military way of life. As a result, Sparta remained unchanged for many generations.

The Spartans rejected the trend in Greece toward trade and colonization during the eighth and seventh centuries B.C. Instead, Sparta relied upon farming and became entirely self-sufficient. To ease problems of overpopulation, the Spartans conquered surrounding peoples and seized their lands. Because the Spartans were vastly outnumbered by the people they conquered, they were constantly fearful of revolts. To guard against rebellion, they turned their city-state into an armed camp.

Spartan society was made up of three social classes. The members of the highest class, which included only men, were Spartan citizens. Spartan women were not considered citizens. They had no political rights and could not participate in Spartan life. Women, however, received some formal military and physical training at a young age.

The next social class was made up of Peloponnesian craft workers and merchants who willingly submitted to Spartan rule. They were allowed to keep their freedom and their livelihoods, but they did not hold Spartan citizenship. The members of the lowest—and also the largest—class were the *helots*. They farmed the land of the Spartan citizens and were treated as slaves. The helots were largely made up of the peoples conquered by the Spartans.

The warlike Spartan way of life was very harsh. At the age of 7, Spartan boys were taken from their homes in order to begin their military training. Generally, older Spartan men who had been successful warriors were responsible for overseeing the physical and military training of these youths. At age 12, the boys' education was broadened slightly to include music and poetry, as well as the required physical training. The training received by Spartan boys was purposely harsh and cruel. This was because the Spartans believed that each citizen should be able to endure cold, hunger, and pain.

Between the ages of 20 and 30, Spartan soldiers lived together in military barracks and were constantly ready for war. At age 30, Spartan citizens could live with their wives and families and become involved in public affairs. But they also had to remain on alert for war.

By about 500 B.C., Spartan influence extended across the Peloponnesus. Despite Sparta's dominating position in Greece, Spartan culture added little to the development of Greek civilization.

THE PERSIAN WARS AND THE RISE OF ATHENS During the sixth century B.C., the mighty Persian Empire arose to the east of Greece. The once-great empires of Egypt, Assyria, and Babylonia all came under Persian control. Moreover, the Greek cities of Ionia—the region along the coast of Asia Minor—were conquered by Persia. In 500 B.C., the Greek cities of Ionia, with the support of Athens, rebelled against Persian rule. The rebellion was ruthlessly put down by the Persian king Darius I [duh-RIY-uhs].

To seek revenge for Athens' role in the uprising, Darius invaded the Greek mainland in 490 B.C. (see map on this page). Although they were outnumbered by about two to one, the Athenians, led by Miltiades [mil-TIY-uh-DEEZ], soundly defeated the Persian army on the plain of Marathon, about 25 miles (40 kilometers) from Athens.

Ten years later, Darius' successor, Xerxes [ZUHRK-SEEZ], invaded Greece from the north (see map on this page). Xerxes' huge army crushed a small detachment of valiant Spartans who sought to delay the Persians' conquest at Thermopylae [thuhr-MAHP-uh-lee]. Xerxes then marched to Athens and burned the city. A few days later, however, the entire Persian fleet was destroyed off the Greek coast near the island of Salamis by a combined Greek fleet. The Persian army retreated to the north. The next year,

In 490 B.C. and again in 480 B.C., Persian kings attempted to conquer Greece. Each time, however, the Greeks united to repel the powerful invaders.

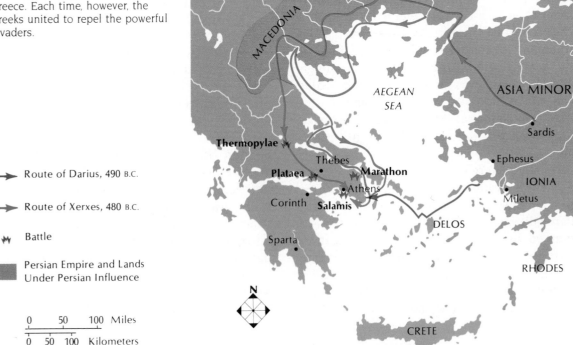

The Invasions of Darius and Xerxes

→ Route of Darius, 490 B.C.

→ Route of Xerxes, 480 B.C.

⚔ Battle

▮ Persian Empire and Lands Under Persian Influence

0   50   100 Miles

0   50   100   Kilometers

N

the Persians again invaded Greece. At Plataea [pluh-TEE-uh], the Greeks, led by a large unit of Spartans, defeated the Persians and drove them out of Greece.

Following the Persian Wars, Athens formed an alliance with other Greek city-states in Ionia and on islands in the Aegean. This alliance was known as the League of Delos, or the Delian League. It was established for the mutual defense of its members against Persia. However, because of its military and naval power, Athens was soon able to control the league and with it, to control trade in the Aegean.

Athens reached new heights of influence and power during the mid-fifth century B.C. In addition, Athens experienced a period of great cultural achievement as Athenian art, literature, sculpture, and architecture flourished. Historians refer to this time as the Golden Age of Hellenic culture. Athenian democracy was also broadened under the democratically minded Pericles [PER-uh-KLEEZ], who led Athens from 461 B.C. to 429 B.C.

DISUNION AND WAR The growing power of Athens alarmed many Greek city-states, including Athens' chief rival, Sparta. Athens had continued to expand its influence to the Gulf of Corinth, and to the northern Aegean as well as to Sicily and southern Italy in the western Mediterranean. These actions threatened the trade of the Peloponnesian city-states. Sparta, supported by several allies, went to war against Athens in 431 B.C. This struggle, known as the Peloponnesian War, lasted for 28 years. The Spartans were finally able to defeat the Athenians in 404 B.C. This marked the end of Athens' Golden Age.

In the years that followed the Peloponnesian War, no strong ruler or city-state emerged in Greece. Bitter rivalries touched off nearly constant warfare between Sparta, Thebes—another powerful Greek city-state—and Athens, as each city-state struggled for leadership. By 338 B.C., more than

This statue of a charioteer dates from about 470 B.C. and shows the ideal representation of the human body that was characteristic of Greek art.

60 years of fighting among themselves had made the Greeks vulnerable to outside invaders. In that year, a new power from the north—Macedonia, led by King Philip—defeated the combined forces of Thebes and Athens. A new era in Greek history had begun.

QUESTIONS FOR REVIEW

1 *What problems led many Greek city-states to set up colonies along the Mediterranean and Black seas during the eighth and seventh centuries B.C.?*

2 *In what ways did Solon reform the laws of Athens?*

3 *Why might Athenian democracy not be considered a government of all the people?*

3 THE WAY OF LIFE IN HELLENIC GREECE

Although democracy was an important development of Hellenic Greece, only the citizens of democratic city-states could enjoy full political freedom. The existence of slavery provided an important work force for Greece. Women and foreign-born residents of many city-states were considered free but did not have political rights. Many foreigners, however, were prosperous and often gained some social prestige.

Two important characteristics of the Hellenic way of life were education and religion. In Athens, for example, many people from the highest social classes were able to read and to write during the fifth century B.C. Moreover, their religious beliefs provided a common cultural heritage among all Greeks.

SOCIETY During the fifth century B.C., Greek society in many city-states was divided into several social classes. The upper class consisted of the citizens who devoted much of their time to public affairs. These citizens participated in the Assembly, performed jury duties, and held public office when called upon to do so. Moreover, in Athens during the time of Pericles, the payment of public officials for their service became customary. As a result, poorer citizens were able to participate in the governing of their city-state.

In Athens, citizenship could be gained by any 18-year-old male of Athenian-born parents. Between the ages of 18 and 20, however, citizens were required to serve in the military. Therefore, most citizens did not enter the Assembly—where laws were passed or rejected directly by all citizens—until after they reached the age of 20. Modern historians have estimated that Athens had a population of about 300,000 during the fifth century B.C. Of this total, about 43,000 were citizens.

The idea of democratic government was one of the greatest legacies left by the classical Greeks. Athena is depicted in this cup painting, c. 490 B.C., watching Athenians casting their ballots.

The second social class was made up of the foreign-born residents of the city-states. In Athens, this class numbered about 30,000. Although foreigners were considered free, they could not own land and had no political rights. Most foreigners were craft workers, such as tanners, weavers, potters, and metalworkers. Trade and commerce were not considered worthy occupations for a citizen. As a result, the major merchants and bankers of Athens during this time were foreigners. Many of these people acquired great wealth and enjoyed social and economic equality with the citizen class.

The lowest social class was that of the slaves. Slaves were general laborers and household or personal servants. For the most part, slaves were prisoners of war. Many experts believe that the slaves made up more than one third of the population of Athens during the time of Pericles.

WOMEN Women possessed no political rights in many Greek city-states. Their main responsibility was managing the household. Athenian women, for example, rarely left their homes except to attend festivals or to shop in the marketplace. Some of the main responsibilities of women were listed by a classical Greek writer named Xenophon [ZEN-uh-fuhn]:

> You are also responsible for supervising those [servants] who remain [in the house], and who perform their duties in the house itself. You must personally take charge of all goods brought into the house, and issue what is needed for necessary outgoings— budgeting in advance for a reserve, and taking care not to squander [waste] in a month what should last a full year. When your slaves bring you spun wool, you must see to it that this wool is used to make clothes for those who need them. You must keep a constant eye on the grain in the store-room, and make sure it remains fit to eat . . . When a servant falls ill, you must always ensure that he is receiving proper care and attention.

In many Greek city-states, a girl's education was very limited and took place entirely in the home. The skills needed at home, such as cooking and spinning and weaving, were taught girls by their mothers and grandmothers or by servants. According to custom, many girls married around the age of 16. Men usually did not marry until well after their education ended.

THE EDUCATION OF ATHENIAN CITIZENS

Unlike Sparta, some Greek city-states did not have compulsory education. In Athens, for example, education was not required by law. But tradition demanded that the children of Athenian citizens receive some formal schooling. It was believed that educated citizens ensured the future of the city-state.

Athenian citizens were responsible for the cost of their children's education. Parents hired tutors, who used their own homes to give instruction to a number of pupils. Children of wealthy citizens often continued their education to the age of 18. Children of poorer citizens were forced to end their schooling much earlier.

The aim of Athenian education was to produce well-rounded citizens who were trained in many areas. Most Athenian children were taught reading, writing, spelling, mathematics, and music. Classic epic poetry —particularly Homer's *Iliad* and *Odyssey*— was also studied. In addition, physical training was part of a child's education. The Greeks valued physical exercise and athletic competition as much as they valued an educated mind.

RELIGION The religion of the ancient Greeks, like many other early religions, was based upon *polytheism*—a belief in many gods. The Greeks believed that the world of the gods was similar to the human world. Thus, to the Greeks, the gods at times took on a human form. Although these gods possessed special powers and were believed to be immortal, they also had many human characteristics, such as jealousy and pettiness. They often quarreled among themselves and were, by no means, all-powerful.

The Greeks believed that their gods inhabited Mount Olympus in northern Greece (see map on page 99). Experts agree that many of the Greek gods may have originated as gods of nature. As the beliefs of the early Greeks changed, the gods gained other responsibilities, and more gods were added.

Chief among the gods was Zeus, the thunder god, who was "lord of the sky." Others on Mount Olympus included Poseidon [puh-SIYD-uhn], god of the sea; Aphrodite [AF-ruh-DIYT-ee], goddess of love and beauty; Artemis, goddess of hunting; Ares, god of war; Demeter, goddess of the earth and of fertility; and Athena, goddess of wisdom and war.

The Greeks celebrated many festivals in

honor of their gods. One of the most important of these festivals began in 776 B.C. and was held every four years at the temple of Zeus. The temple was located near the Peloponnesian city of Olympia (see map on page 99). This festival included athletic, literary, and musical competition. During the festival, warfare was temporarily halted between the city-states. Today, an international athletic competition known as the Olympic Games has grown out of this festival and is celebrated every four years in the spirit of ancient Greek competition.

Greek religion, unlike many other ancient religions, was unorganized and lacked a strong priesthood. However, the human qualities of the gods enabled early Greeks to more easily understand their religion in human terms.

QUESTIONS FOR REVIEW

1 *What were the three social classes of fifth century B.C. Athenian society?*

2 *In what ways did the education of Athenian boys differ from that of girls?*

3 *Why do you think ancient Greeks may have believed that the problems of the gods were similar to their own problems?*

Contributions

The Development of Coins

The regular use of coins made from precious metals, such as gold and silver, appeared in the Aegean world more than 2,600 years ago. Prior to that time, the earliest Greeks had relied upon a system of *barter*—that is, trading one type of goods for another. Later Greek traders came to depend upon a system in which quantities of goods were traded for gold and silver. However, as trade increased throughout the Greek world after 800 B.C., this system became very awkward. This was because the metals had to be weighed during each transaction. Often it was difficult for one merchant to trust another merchant's scales.

During the seventh century B.C., the ruler of Lydia, a Hellenic state in Asia Minor, issued the first coins and guaranteed their value. These coins were also stamped to mark either the purity of the metal or its weight (see picture below). Following the development of coinage in Lydia, Greek city-states began to issue coins of their own.

Coinage led to several important developments. First, coins made trade easier within a country and also among countries. Because of the guaranteed value of the money, people found that they could put their trust in it. In effect, money was valuable because people believed in its value and because they knew others accepted it as valuable, too. Coins also enabled many people to acquire a great deal of wealth without owning property, which was the traditional measure of wealth. This eventually led to important changes in many societies because control of government by landowning nobles was weakened.

The Greek coins shown are a gold Lydian coin, c. 550 B.C. (near right); a silver coin from Syracuse, c. 480 B.C. (center); and an Athenian coin, c. 460 B.C. (far right), with the symbol of Athena.

Photos by The Granger Collection

4 THE LEGACY OF CLASSICAL GREECE

Hellenic civilization reached its greatest heights during the fifth and fourth centuries B.C. From Greece, it spread northward and westward into the European world and became the foundation of Western civilization. More than 2,000 years later, the influence of Hellenic culture is still felt in the modern world. Classical Greek philosophy established the Western tradition of logic. The curiosity and the reasoned thinking of the Greeks during this time formed the basis for modern science. Greek literature also developed many forms that present-day audiences take for granted, such as epic and lyric poetry, tragic and comic drama, and history. Moreover, throughout the centuries, Greek art and architecture have inspired Western artists and builders.

GREEK THOUGHT During the fifth and fourth centuries B.C., the Greeks' ways of thinking underwent tremendous change. The Greek philosophers of this period formed a system of thought that has greatly influenced much of the world for more than 2,000 years. The first philosopher to shake the Greek mind loose from the ideas of the past was an Athenian citizen, Socrates [SAHK-ruh-TEEZ].

Socrates sought to understand the world by constantly asking questions. He believed that when people were guided by careful questioning, they could find truth, knowledge, and justice. Socrates declared that "an unexamined life is not worth living." He encouraged all people to study their own thoughts, actions, and ideas.

Athenian leaders felt that the ideas of Socrates were dangerous and were destroying young people's beliefs in the gods and also in the city's rulers. In 399 B.C., Socrates was condemned to die for his teachings by a jury of 501 Athenian citizens. Socrates did not leave any written record of his ideas. Most of what we know about him comes from the writings of one of his students, a man named Plato [PLAYT-oh].

The French painter Jacques Louis David's idealized picture "The Death of Socrates" was painted more than 2,000 years after the Greek philosopher's death.

The Granger Collection

The concepts of Plato were based on the belief that all things in this world are imperfect representations of eternal, pure, and unchanging forms, which he called *ideas*. Essentially, Plato believed that because humans are less than perfect, they should be guided by an ideal form, or idea, of what a human ought to be. Plato set down many of his theories in a book entitled *The Republic*. In this book, Plato also outlined his plan for a highly structured society based upon his beliefs. Among the unchanging ideas that he believed should guide the citizens of his planned society were truth, justice, goodness, and knowledge.

Among Plato's students was Aristotle [AR-uh-STAHT-uhl], who formed a system of step-by-step reasoned thinking known as *logic*. Aristotle also developed the practice of careful experimentation in seeking explanations for natural forces, such as the movement of the stars. This marked the beginning of the modern scientific method.

Aristotle wrote on many subjects, including science, politics, history, literary criticism, and philosophy. His clear thinking and insight have influenced scientists and philosophers for more than 2,000 years.

SCIENCE During the Classical Age, science was generally studied by philosophers who searched for a way to explain the forces of nature. Many great strides were made by these early Greeks. By careful reasoning, they came to realize that nature was ruled by fixed natural laws, not by the gods. They also believed that these laws could be discovered and systematically studied.

Pythagoras [puh-THAG-uh-ruhs], who lived at the end of the sixth century B.C., and his followers helped to develop concepts of geometry and astronomy. Pythagoras believed that the earth and the planets were round. In addition, his pupils developed one of the most lasting theories of ancient Greek science—that is, that all things are made of atoms. Other Greeks also attempted to explain such things as weather,

eclipses of the sun, and the formation of the planets.

Other important developments of the fifth century B.C. were in the field of medicine. Hippocrates [hip-AHK-ruh-TEEZ] and the physicians who followed him succeeded in bringing reasoned thinking to medical practice. No longer did medicine rely upon religion or the supernatural. Hippocrates believed that diseases had natural causes. He emphasized that physicians should carefully observe diseases and apply appropriate remedies. Hippocrates expressed his ideas on medicine in his writings when he wrote:

> Men continue to believe in its [a disease's] divine origin because they are at a loss to understand it. . . . [Q]uacks, having no treatment that would help, concealed and sheltered themselves behind superstition . . . in order that their complete ignorance might not be revealed.

Hippocrates also composed an oath regarding the moral and ethical principles that should be followed by physicians. The oath is still recited today by many new physicians.

Early Greek physicians included many women. Physicians had a knowledge of simple surgical methods and of the functions of the heart and the importance of the pulse. They also knew that the brain was the center of human thought. The discoveries of the Greeks in medicine remained unmatched in the Western world for more than 2,000 years.

GREEK LITERATURE The literature of the ancient Greeks was rich and varied. The epic poems of Homer—the *Iliad* and the *Odyssey*—not only provided the Greeks with entertainment but were important sources of historical and religious information. These masterpieces are still read and enjoyed today.

Lyric poems were the next development in Greek literature. These were rythmic verses sung to the *lyre*—a harplike instrument—or to the flute. The best-known lyric poet was Pindar. Lyric poems dealt with human emotions and were often produced with elaborate choral arrangements.

During the fifth century B.C., another form of Greek literature—drama—reached maturity. Drama began in Athens, where competing playwrights staged two kinds of dramas—tragedies and comedies—during a yearly spring festival. The authors of tragedies used masked and costumed actors, a chorus, poetry, music, and dance to examine the struggle of people against their fate. The major Greek tragedians were Sophocles [SAHF-uh-KLEEZ], Aeschylus [ES-kuh-luhs], and Euripides [yu-RIP-uh-DEEZ]. Aristophanes [AR-uh-STAHF-uh-NEEZ] used biting satire and endless wit in his comedies to ridicule nearly every aspect of Athenian life.

The writing of history also began during this time. The two greatest Greek historians were Herodotus [hi-RAHD-uh-tuhs] and Thucydides [thoo-SID-uh-DEEZ]. They were the first writers to recount historical events in an organized manner. Herodotus set about writing a popular history of the Persian Wars many years after the wars had ended. He relied upon the memories both of those who had survived and those who had heard the tales of the wars. Thucydides wrote a scholarly history of the Peloponnesian War, in which he himself had participated. Using many factual details, he hoped to lead his readers to a clearer understanding of past events. These two great historians are still widely read by scholars today.

ART AND ARCHITECTURE During the fifth century B.C., Greek art and architecture reached a peak rarely equaled by any civilization. The imagination, beauty, and harmony of Greek art can be seen in many kinds of works. These include Greek pottery paintings, sculptures of stone and bronze, and monuments built to the Greek gods. In various ways, the art and architecture that

Greek theaters, some of which seated thousands of spectators, were built outdoors. Male actors used masks to play every role. A chorus was often used to narrate the dramatic action.

flourished during this period, particularly in Athens, brought together the Greek ideas of logic and visual balance.

Following the destruction of Athens by the Persians in 480 B.C., the Athenians rebuilt their city. From 447 B.C. to 431 B.C., their artists decorated the *acropolis*—originally a fortified hill—with beautiful temples, statues, and paintings. Probably the best-known example of Greek architecture—the *Parthenon*—was built at this time. Constructed atop the acropolis as a temple to the goddess Athena, the Parthenon stands in ruin today. Yet the balance and beauty of the original building are still very much in evidence.

For the most part, Greek art was displayed in public for all Greeks to enjoy. Statues that were carved from marble and other kinds of stone or cast in bronze decorated the city. It was the Greeks' love of beauty and form and their study of anatomy that produced these graceful works.

Since the fifth century B.C., Greek art and architecture has continued to influence artists and to shape artistic ideals. In this way, the Greeks have made an invaluable contribution to Western civilization up to the present time.

QUESTIONS FOR REVIEW

1 Which Greek philosopher encouraged all people to examine their own thoughts, actions, and ideas?

2 In what way did Aristotle contribute to the development of modern science?

3 Why do you think Hippocrates criticized the early Greeks who believed in the supernatural causes of disease?

CHAPTER SUMMARY

The beginnings of Greek civilization can be traced to two early advanced cultures in the eastern Mediterranean—the Minoan and the Mycenaean. Between about 1700 B.C. and about 1200 B.C., these two civilizations built sea-trading empires. Many historians believe that the Mycenaean civilization was conquered by invading barbarians from the north, called Dorians. These invasions plunged Greece into a chaotic "dark age" between about 1200 B.C. and 800 B.C.

An advanced Greek culture—known as Hellenic culture—emerged from this dark age and flourished for nearly 500 years. During that time, the achievements of the Golden Age of Greece laid the foundation of Western civilization. Among the most important of these accomplishments was the development of democracy in Athens.

The Greeks also evolved a unique outlook on many aspects of life, based upon logical and reasoned thinking. As a result, great achievements were made in philosophy, science, mathematics, literature, and history. By the mid-fourth century B.C., the Golden Age of Hellenic culture had ended. However, the achievements of the classical Greeks continue to live on in modern times.

CHAPTER 5 IN REVIEW

IMPORTANT WORDS, NAMES, AND TERMS

1 Explain, define, or identify each of the following:

Peloponnesus	oligarchy	Zeus
Mycenaeans	tyrant	Socrates
Troy	Cleisthenes	*The Republic*
Dorians	democracy	Hippocrates

FACTS AND IDEAS

2 Who was Homer?

3 What technological advance did the Dorians possess in the twelfth century B.C.?

4 What were Solon's major reforms?

5 What was the Council of Five Hundred?

6 Which early Greek city-state was dominated by a strict military way of life?

7 Who was Pythagoras?

ANALYZING VISUAL MATERIAL

8 According to the map on page 106, what was the major difference between the invasions of the Greek peninsula by the Persian rulers Darius and Xerxes?

9 Study the illustrations on pages 102 and 107 carefully. How did the artistry of the sixth-century-B.C. Greeks differ from that of the much earlier Mycenaeans?

CONCEPTS AND UNDERSTANDINGS

10 In way ways did the use of iron help the Dorians to conquer southern Greece?

11 Give several reasons why many Greek oligarchies were overthrown between about 650 B.C. and 500 B.C.

12 When the structure of ancient Greek society is considered, why might the early Greek democracies be considered "limited democracies"?

13 Why might some of the discoveries of the classical Greek philosopher Aristotle be considered the beginning of modern science?

PROJECTS AND ACTIVITIES

14 Prepare a bulletin board showing the different stages of development in Greek shipbuilding between 800 B.C. and 300 B.C.

15 Some historians believe that the Greek army's development of a military formation known as the *phalanx* was an important contribution to democracy. They point out that the phalanx relied upon the shared responsibility and the cooperation of its members. Prepare a report to the class in which you agree or disagree with this theory. Give several reasons for your opinion.

CHAPTER **6** THE
HELLENISTIC AGE

1 The Rise of Macedonia   2 The Hellenistic World
3 Hellenistic Civilization

As the Greek city-states declined throughout the fourth century B.C., the northern kingdom of Macedonia gained strength. The Macedonians defeated the Greeks and united them under one ruler in the 330's B.C. Soon after, the Macedonian king Alexander began an invasion of the Persian Empire. Within a decade, Alexander had conquered Persia and Egypt and had reached India. As one of history's greatest conquerors, he ruled the largest empire of the ancient world.

The upper classes of these conquered lands introduced Greek civilization into their ancient cultures. This period produced many great cultural achievements and scientific discoveries. But the years following Alexander's conquests were also times of turmoil and warfare. By about 30 B.C., the influence of Greek civilization had reshaped and molded much of the early Mediterranean world.

Ancient Delphi, the site of the famous oracle, reflects the rugged beauty of Greece. Alexander the Great visited Delphi in 336 B.C.

1 THE RISE OF MACEDONIA

Throughout the first 60 years of the fourth century B.C., the Greek city-states constantly fought one another for control of Greece. Weakened by the steady drain on their resources, the Greeks were no match for a new power—Macedonia—that arose to the north. Patiently building the best fighting force in the Mediterranean world, Macedonia's ruler, Philip II, gradually expanded his kingdom. He defeated the Greeks convincingly in 338 B.C. and imposed his rule on the once proud and independent city-states.

Philip's son and successor, Alexander, was one of the greatest conquerors of history. Spurred on by a dream of crushing Persia and spreading Greek culture to Asia, Alexander led his army on an 11-year campaign of conquest. As a result, Greek civilization was introduced into nearly every corner of the classical world.

GREECE DURING THE FOURTH CENTURY
The Spartan's victory over the Athenians in 404 B.C. brought an end to the Peloponnesian War, which had divided Greece for nearly 30 years. The war, however, led to a steady decline of Greek power. Athens, in particular, was nearly drained of its financial and human resources. The victorious Spartans hoped to unite Greece under their leadership by establishing loyal oligarchies in many Greek cities. The classical Greek ideals of personal freedom and of democracy gave way to the harsh ways of the Spartan rulers. In addition, Sparta collected tribute from many of the Greek city-states. As a result, Spartan rule was resented by nearly all Greeks. And instead of unifying Greece, Spartan leadership led to the beginning of more warfare among the major Greek cities.

During these years of bitter conflict—404 B.C. to 371 B.C.—a Persian ruler re-

This Greek vase painting shows the familiar sight of families seeing their sons off to the nearly constant wars between the Greek city-states.

marked that he did not need to fear the Greeks because their hatred for one another would soon lead to their own destruction. The Persians were well aware that without a single military campaign they had regained land lost in Ionia to the Greeks a century earlier.

In 371 B.C., the city-state of Thebes shocked the Greek world by achieving an unexpected victory over the powerful Spartan infantry. For a time, Thebes dreamed of controlling Greece. However, for the next decade the Theban generals and their allies were occupied fighting an alliance of other Greek cities. Thebes was never able to completely control Greece. A short time later, Athens lost control of several islands and cities along the northern coast of the Aegean Sea that had long been under its influence. Finally, exhausted by constant warfare, the Greeks settled into an uneasy peace. During these same years, however, a powerful threat to Greek independence was growing in the north.

PHILIP OF MACEDONIA
Philip II came to the throne of Macedonia [MAS-uh-DOH-nyuh], a small kingdom in the northernmost part of the Greek peninsula, in 359 B.C. (see map on page 119). The Macedonians

POLITICAL		SOCIAL AND ECONOMIC
	B.C.	
Sparta defeated Athens to end Peloponnesian War	404	
	343	Aristotle became tutor of Alexander of Macedonia
Philip II united Greece	338	
Invasion of Persia	334	
	332	City of Alexandria founded
Alexander died in Babylon	323	Hellenistic Age began
Seleucid, Ptolemaic, and Antigonid empires established	c. 300	Euclid wrote *Elements* on geometry
	c. 250	Hebrew Scriptures translated into Greek at Library of Alexandria
Archimedes defended Syracuse from Roman attack	212	
	c. 200	Population of Alexandria reached 500,000; trade with Asia flourished
Macedonia became Roman province	149	
	c. 130	Hipparchus cataloged known stars
	c. 120	Monsoons used for sea travel to India
Egypt came under Roman domination	30	Hellenistic Age ended

were seen as barbarians by their Greek neighbors to the south. But over many generations, the Macedonians had been strongly influenced by Greek traditions. King Philip himself greatly admired Hellenic culture and tried to pattern the Macedonian society along Greek lines. Thus, by the 350's B.C., Macedonia had become relatively hellenized.

Philip had two goals when he took power in Macedonia. First, he wanted to unite all of Greece under his rule, a feat the Greeks themselves had failed to accomplish. Second, Philip wanted to invade the Greeks' traditional enemy, Persia, with the help of Greek military power.

Philip was a shrewd and patient leader and spent many years putting his plans into action. He began by organizing and training a powerful army that became the best fighting force in the Mediterranean world. Philip then gained control of the Greek cities along the northern coast of the Aegean Sea. As a result, the Macedonians won an outlet to the sea and also controlled the rich gold mines of Thrace. Next, Philip gained control of Thessaly, to the south (see map on page 119). Although these moves threatened the security of the Greek city-states, the Greeks failed to unite against Philip.

By 339 B.C., the city-states of Thebes and Athens had recognized the danger that Macedonia presented to southern Greece. But Philip's army could not be stopped. At Chaeronea [KER-uh-NEE-uh], the Macedonians defeated the combined armies of Thebes and Athens in the spring of 338 B.C. (see map on page 119). Philip entered the Peloponnesus unchallenged and brought most of the region under his control. With Philip as leader, the League of Corinth—an alliance between Macedonia and the conquered Greek city-states—was formed. But Philip did not live long enough to carry out his planned invasion of Persia. In 336 B.C., he was assassinated and Alexander, Philip's 20-year-old son, became king.

Greece and Macedonia, c. 338 B.C.

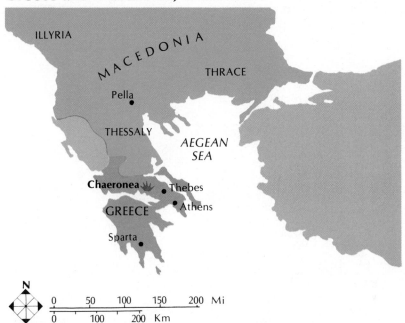

Philip of Macedonia, with his powerful army, had conquered and unified the Greek city-states by the time of his death in 336 B.C.

THE MACEDONIAN ARMY Perhaps the greatest legacy left by King Philip to his son Alexander was the awesome Macedonian Army. During his 23-year reign, Philip carefully shaped his army into a well-balanced and disciplined force. By the time of his death, the Macedonian Army was probably the best fighting force in the Mediterranean world.

King Philip's success as a leader was largely the result of his organization and preparation. Philip introduced many new tactics and weapons that increased the speed and the striking power of his soldiers. He was one of the first classical generals to use cavalry. Philip also trained his soldiers to use catapults and other siege weapons to more easily capture fortified towns and cities.

Philip perfected the *phalanx*—a close formation of foot soldiers many ranks deep. Soldiers of the Macedonian phalanx were armed with long, heavy spears called *sarissas*. These spears, longer than the spears possessed by the Greeks and the Persians, measured between 14 and 16 feet (4.3 and 4.8 meters) long and had to be held with 2

hands. With the sarissa, the Macedonian phalanx formed a bristling, almost impenetrable wall. Moreover, the *flanks*—the sides —of the main force formed by the phalanxes were protected by more-mobile troops not equipped with the sarissa. These were the finest soldiers in the Macedonian Army and were the decisive factor in many battles.

Philip also introduced compulsory military service in Macedonia. All fit Macedonian men could be called to serve in the army during wartime, giving Philip a large, well-trained reserve of soldiers. This meant that the king did not have to depend upon costly, unreliable hired soldiers to make up his army.

When Alexander took the Macedonian throne in 336 B.C., he inherited both his father's kingdom and his father's dream of ruling Persia. But without Philip's most valuable gift—the mighty Macedonian Army— Alexander could not have achieved his dreams of conquest.

THE CONQUESTS OF ALEXANDER After Philip's death, Alexander moved swiftly to

The Battle of Issus was portrayed in an ancient mosaic. Alexander personally led his troops into battle against Darius, who is shown fleeing in his chariot.

put down an uprising in Thrace, to the north of Greece. A short time later, Thebes rose against its Macedonian governors. Alexander totally destroyed the city as an example to the Greeks. He was never again bothered by disloyalty in Greece.

Like his father, Alexander greatly admired and respected Greek civilization. In his youth, Alexander had been tutored by the Greek philosopher Aristotle. The young monarch shared his father's dream of crushing Persia and of spreading Greek culture eastward. In 334 B.C., Alexander began the invasion that his father had long planned. Easily defeating the Persians in Asia Minor, Alexander freed the Greek cities of Ionia from Persian rule (see map on page 121). At Issus [IS-uhs], Alexander's army routed the Persians, who were led by their king, Darius III. Alexander marched through Syria and along the Mediterranean coast to Egypt, where he was hailed as a god-king.

Alexander wisely chose to be lenient and generous to many of the cities through which his army passed. Because the inhabitants of many of these cities had little to fear from Alexander, they often welcomed him as a hero. The few cities that resisted Alexander, such as Tyre and Gaza on the Mediterranean coast, were completely destroyed.

In the spring of 331 B.C., Alexander struck at the heart of the Persian Empire. Near Arbela [ahr-BEE-luh], Alexander again crushed Darius' forces. The Persian king fled and was later murdered by one of his generals. Alexander's army reached the city of Babylon in triumph. Soon after, the Persian cities of Susa and Persepolis fell to the invaders.

At last, Alexander had realized his dream of defeating Persia. However, following his victory, he turned his army eastward. Conquest had come easily, but Alexander was not content with the throne of Persia. The urge to explore, to open new trade routes,

The Empire of Alexander, c. 323 B.C.

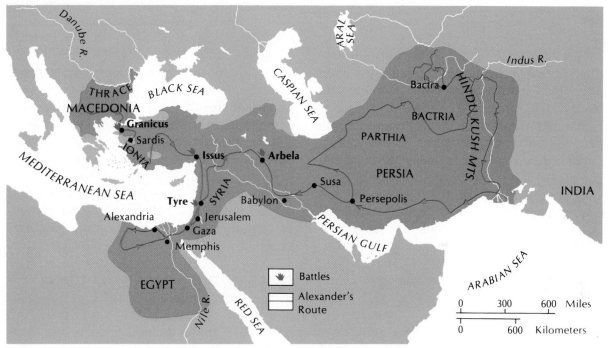

By 323 B.C., the lands conquered by Alexander the Great stretched from the Mediterranean eastward to the Indus Valley.

and to spread Hellenic culture pushed Alexander and his army toward the vast and populous lands of western Asia.

ALEXANDER'S EMPIRE In 327 B.C., Alexander led his Macedonians across the mighty Hindu Kush Mountains and into the Indus Valley. The Ganges plain, with its rich and cultured cities, lay ahead. But at this point, after 11 years of hard fighting and thousands of miles of marching, Alexander's soldiers refused to go farther. Bitterly disappointed, Alexander had no choice but to begin the long march back through his conquered lands. In 323 B.C., the 32-year-old Alexander died an untimely death in Babylon, probably of a fever. At the time of his death, the great conqueror ruled over much of the classical world.

At its height, the empire of Alexander the Great stretched from the Black Sea in the north to Egypt in the south and from Greece eastward to India (see map on this page). Alexander founded nearly 70 cities, including Alexandria, in the Nile delta, which soon became the commercial and the cultural center of the Mediterranean world. New trade routes were opened between East and West. Greek ideas flourished in this new environment. The blending of Greek and Asian cultures led to a new period in history—the *Hellenistic Age*—which lasted nearly 300 years.

QUESTIONS FOR REVIEW

1 *What two goals did Philip II of Macedonia set for himself as king?*

2 *In what ways did Philip put his plans for uniting Greece into action?*

3 *Do you think Alexander's generosity toward many of the cities he conquered might be considered a wise policy? Explain your answer.*

2 THE HELLENISTIC WORLD

The empire formed by the conquests of Alexander was divided into three parts soon after the conqueror's death. Greece and Macedonia formed a separate kingdom. Egypt and the rest of the conquered Asian lands formed two empires. As a result, Greek culture spread to many parts of the conquered lands, and trade flourished. However, the empires of the Hellenistic Age were plagued by almost constant political upheaval. Slowly, the power of these empires withered away.

THE DIVIDED EMPIRE Alexander's death in 323 B.C. threw the newly established empire into turmoil. Two decades of conflict between Alexander's leading generals—Antigonus, Seleucus [suh-LOO-kuhs], and Ptolemy [TAHL-uh-mee]—followed. Eventually, the empire was divided into three parts. Antigonus and his descendants ruled Macedonia and Greece. Seleucus and his heirs governed a vast area that stretched from the eastern Mediterranean Sea to the Indus Valley. Ptolemy and his descendants established control of Egypt. For the next 300 years—until about 30 B.C.—Alexander's successors ruled these far-flung lands and Greek culture gradually spread throughout the ancient world.

The rulers of the Seleucid and Ptolemaic empires set up absolute monarchies to control their subjects. This meant that the kings were the sole source of law and ruled their kingdoms with absolute power. Moreover, ruler worship—a concept new to the Greeks but quite common in the conquered lands of Asia and the Middle East—was established. The kings of the Hellenistic world soon demanded to be worshiped as gods everywhere but in their native Macedonia.

Large bureaucracies were also formed to help govern these new lands. Greek became the official language of the new governments. Government officials were generally Greeks and Macedonians who had been encouraged to settle in the growing cities of the new empires.

The establishment of Greek governments and the founding of Greek cities led to important results in the Hellenistic Age. Immigration to the new centers of Greek culture brought many Greeks and Macedonians into the conquered lands. In addition, the trade that developed between these cities and the Mediterranean world carried Hellenistic culture to the far corners of territories once part of Alexander's empire.

TRADE IN THE HELLENISTIC WORLD One of the most important results of the conquests of Alexander the Great was the opening of trade routes between the Mediterranean world and Asia. Land routes through the old Persian Empire became roads upon which new ideas and goods flowed. Moreover, part of Alexander's army had returned by sea from the Indus Valley. Alexander's fleet helped to open up a sea route between the Persian Gulf and India. As a result of this growing trade, the center of Mediterranean commerce moved from Greece to Egypt, Rhodes, and Asia Minor during the third century B.C.

Caravans of goods from as far east as India streamed through the Seleucid and Ptolemaic empires and were tightly controlled by these governments. Sea traders from India traveled through the Persian Gulf and up the Tigris River to Seleucia. From there, overland caravans transported trade goods further west, to such places as Antioch and beyond to Alexandria (see map on page 123). The old Royal Road of the Persian kings, which ran from Tarsus to Ephesus on the coast of Asia Minor, was also used. Both the Ptolemaic and the Seleucid kings coveted this route and each controlled it at different times during the Hellenistic Age.

Trade Routes in the Hellenistic World, c. 100 B.C.

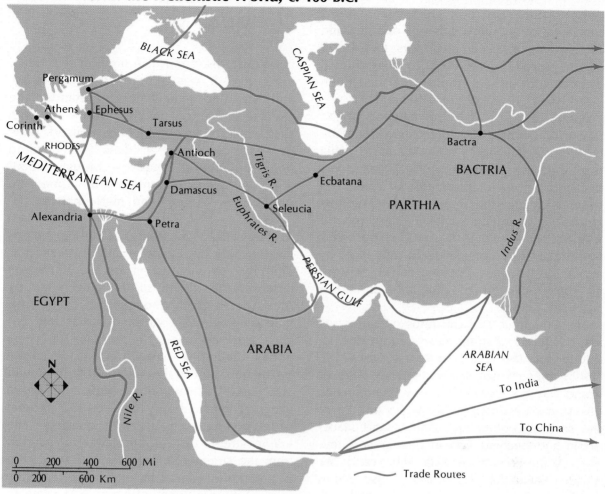

The seasonal monsoons that powered merchant vessels between Arabia and India helped trade to flourish during the Hellenistic Age.

The Red Sea was also often used by Egyptian traders as a direct trade link to the East. Around 120 B.C., sea travel between India and points west was greatly speeded. Sailors learned to navigate across the open sea, instead of hugging the coastline. In addition, the discovery of strong east-west monsoon winds enabled ships to cross quickly to India between May and October. The shift in the monsoons between November and March allowed a direct crossing from India to southern Arabia during the winter months (see map on this page).

Goods traded during the Hellenistic Age included raw materials as well as exotic luxury goods. Timber, metals, farm products, olive oil, honey, cloth, wool, and cinnamon and other spices found markets throughout the Hellenistic world. Later, silk was brought from China. Papyrus from Egypt and parchment from the Asia Minor kingdom of Pergamum were sought by the growing number of educated people in the Hellenistic world.

DECLINE OF THE HELLENISTIC EMPIRES

Almost from their formation, the empires of the Hellenistic world were torn apart by internal and external struggles. The highly

123

organized governments and large bureaucracies could not hold together empires consisting of so many different peoples and cultures. As a result, civil wars and bitter competition for lands led to the gradual disintegration of the empires that had been established by Alexander's generals.

Barely 65 years after the creation of the Seleucid Empire, its rulers had lost the easternmost kingdoms of Bactria and Parthia (see map on page 123). These kingdoms became important crossroads for trade between Asia and the region of the Mediterranean. In addition, smaller kingdoms in Asia Minor and along the coast of the Black Sea broke away from Seleucid influence. By about 140 B.C., Mesopotamia and Syria were all that remained of the once immense Seleucid Empire.

The Ptolemaic and the Antigonid empires also suffered revolts and steady decline throughout the 200's and the 100's B.C. During these years, the Italian city-state of Rome was gradually extending its influence eastward (see Chapter 7). By the middle of the second century B.C., Greece and Macedonia had become Roman provinces. Rome also claimed lands in Asia Minor and the Middle East. The absorption of the Hellenistic world by Rome was not completed, however, until about 30 B.C. This year is traditionally thought to be the end of the Hellenistic Age, because Ptolemaic Egypt became a Roman province then.

QUESTIONS FOR REVIEW

1 *Who were the Ptolemies?*

2 *In what ways did sailing habits change during the second century B.C.?*

3 *Why were the lands of Mesopotamia and Syria all that remained of the Seleucid Empire in 140 B.C.?*

3 HELLENISTIC CIVILIZATION

Despite the political turmoil of the Hellenistic Age, it was a time of great cultural and scientific achievement. Alexander the Great's dream of unifying the world with Greek culture was never fully realized. However, the exchange of ideas that resulted from Alexander's conquests brought about important developments in literature, art, philosophy, science, and mathematics.

ALEXANDRIA The center of Hellenistic civilization was the Egyptian city of Alexandria. The city was founded on the Mediterranean coast at the mouth of the Nile River by Alexander after he conquered Egypt (see map on page 121). Alexandria was laid out as a large rectangle. More than 300 years after its founding, Alexandria was described as being 3 miles (5 kilometers) in length and 1 mile (1.6 kilometers) wide. Two broad avenues, each about 100 feet (30 meters) wide, divided the city into quarters. The major streets of Alexandria were shaded from the summer sun. By about 200 B.C., the population of Alexandria had reached nearly 500,000 people, many of whom had come to the city from throughout the Hellenistic world.

During the reign of Ptolemy I, the idea of a large government-supported library grew. Under Ptolemy II and Ptolemy III, the Library of Alexandria was completed and books from throughout the world were gathered. By the end of the first century B.C., the Library may have contained as many as 700,000 rolls of papyrus and parchment manuscripts.

Under a chief librarian and the scholars of the Museum—an institution for advanced studies in Alexandria—many subjects were discussed and written about, and many writings were translated and eventually passed on to later generations. Today, much of our information dealing with the Med-

The Library of Alexandria contained more than half a million scrolls written by scholars throughout the Hellenistic world.

iterranean world and its civilizations has come to us through the Alexandrian scholars. Alexandria attracted outstanding Hellenistic scholars, some of whom produced important advances in mathematics, science, geography, literature, and philosophy.

SCIENCE IN THE HELLENISTIC WORLD

The accomplishments of the Hellenistic Age advanced many fields of scientific study. In the tradition of Aristotle, Hellenistic scholars used experimentation to search for practical uses for their discoveries. Many of their brilliant and unique achievements stood unchallenged for centuries.

During the Hellenistic Age, great strides were made in astronomy. The solar year was calculated to within about 6 minutes of modern calculations. The lunar month was computed to within 2 seconds of the figure accepted today. Aristarchus [AR-uh-STAHR-kuhs] of Samos speculated that the earth and the planets moved around the sun—an idea known as the *heliocentric theory.* However, he was unable to prove his ideas, and

the best minds of the Hellenistic Age failed to develop the theory. As a result, the *geocentric*—earth-centered—theory remained as the generally accepted view of planetary motion until the time of Copernicus, about 1,800 years later (see Chapter 16).

Another outstanding Hellenistic scholar was Eratosthenes [ER-uh-TAHS-thuh-NEEZ]. According to some modern experts, Eratosthenes calculated the earth's circumference to within 200 miles (322 kilometers) of the correct figure. He also argued that all the world's oceans are connected. He used the tides of the Atlantic and the Indian oceans to demonstrate his idea. Eratosthenes also believed that a voyage could be made from the western Mediterranean Sea around Africa to India—a trip that was not attempted for 16 centuries (see Chapter 16). In addition, an astronomer named Hipparchus [hip-AHR-kuhs] learned to use latitude and longitude to find places on the earth's surface. Working in the mid-100's B.C., he cataloged nearly 900 stars and developed many of the principles of trigonometry.

MATHEMATICS Probably the most important scientific developments during the Hellenistic Age took place in mathematics. Around 300 B.C., Euclid [YOO-kluhd] gathered together much of the Greeks' mathematical knowledge—most of which dealt with geometry—in a work entitled *Elements.* Euclid's approach is still found in geometry textbooks today.

During the third century B.C., Archimedes [AHR-kuh-MEED-eez] wrote on many subjects and was perhaps the greatest scholar of the Hellenistic Age. His list of accomplishments was long and included many practical uses for his discoveries (see Biography on page 126). Archimedes developed laws for the sphere and the cylinder, for the lever and balance, and for floating bodies. He also laid the foundations of calculus. Archimedes developed the compound pulley, cranes,

(*Text continued on page* 127.)

Biography

Archimedes

Very few of the Greek scholars who lived during the Hellenistic Age rivaled the brilliant Archimedes. Born around 287 B.C., in the Greek city-state of Syracuse on the island of Sicily, Archimedes studied in Alexandria. He returned to Syracuse and began studies that led to the discovery of many of the mathematical laws of science.

Perhaps the best-known story surrounding Archimedes' life involved his discovery of the principles of floating bodies. According to tradition, Archimedes was asked by Hieron, the tyrant of Syracuse, to find out whether a crown made for him by a local goldsmith was made of pure gold. The tyrant felt that the goldsmith had kept some of the gold for himself and had mixed silver, which was less valuable, with gold to make the crown. Archimedes had to solve the problem without melting down the new crown.

Several weeks later, at the public baths, Archimedes noticed that the water rose higher and overflowed the tub according to how deeply he immersed himself. Suddenly, the answer to the puzzle came to him. He dashed home yelling, *"Eureka!"* —"I have found it!"

Archimedes discovered, by placing an object into a full tub of water, that the object loses weight in an amount equal to the weight of the water that has overflowed the tub. Archimedes reasoned that if he placed an ounce (28.35 grams) of gold in water, it would displace less water than an ounce of silver. This is because gold has less volume than silver. Archimedes placed the crown in water and found that more water was displaced by the crown than by an equal weight of gold. He knew that the crown contained some silver and that Hieron had indeed been cheated.

In 212 B.C., Archimedes was asked to help defend Syracuse from attack by a Roman fleet. He built several mechanical devices to defend the city. Among these were enormous catapults that hurled huge rocks and giant cranes that grabbed ships by large hooks and dashed them against rocks along the shore.

For several months, Archimedes' inventions prevented the Romans from overrunning the city. When Syracuse finally fell, the Roman general ordered that Archimedes be spared. But while a Roman soldier was on patrol, he came across an old man drawing figures in the sand. The old man would not go with the soldier until he had completed his drawings. Enraged by this, the soldier killed the old man. Archimedes was dead.

Although Archimedes developed many mechanical devices during his lifetime, he believed that these inventions were little more than practical demonstrations of his mathematical ideas. Yet today, more than 2,000 years after his death, many of the devices that Archimedes used to demonstrate his ideas remain in use.

One Archimedean invention that is still in use today is called Archimedes' screw. This device can be used to raise water, for example, from one field to a higher field for irrigation.

Artstreet

and a way to pump water out of ships or out of farmers' fields. He is also said to have used his machines to nearly single-handedly defend his native city of Syracuse when the city was under attack.

Archimedes was the best example of Hellenistic scientists, who not only developed ideas and concepts but also developed practical applications for science. However, science and mathematics were not the only fields in which practical uses for Hellenistic ideas developed. Hellenistic philosophers, too, sought to develop practical systems of thought that could guide everyday life.

HELLENISTIC THOUGHT During the Hellenistic Age, the center of philosophy remained in Athens. Two philosophies arose during this period that were based upon a search for happiness rather than for truth. The two philosophies were Epicureanism [EP-i-kyu-REE-uh-NIZ-uhm] and Stoicism [STOH-uh-SIZ-uhm]. Systems of proper conduct—the right way to live—were developed within each of these philosophies.

Epicurus began teaching in Athens around 300 B.C. To Epicurus, the search for happiness was a search for pleasure. He was not, however, concerned with pleasures of the senses. Rather, Epicurus believed that the development of the intellect and of a calm mind would lead to happiness. Thus, spiritual pleasure would be brought to the individual. Unfortunately, later followers of Epicurus misunderstood and distorted his teachings. They believed that only physical pleasure should be sought.

Zeno [ZEE-noh]—the founder of Stoicism —was a contemporary of Epicurus. Zeno believed that peace of mind could be reached by being free of human desires and needs. Zeno taught that people should use their intelligence to accept their lives with indifference and without emotion. Only in this way could they reach a harmony with the universal spirit that existed in all living things. Three centuries later, the influence of Stoicism was still strongly felt in the Mediterranean world.

THE IMPACT OF HELLENISTIC CIVILIZATION Hellenistic civilization helped to reshape the cultures of the Middle East and the Mediterranean. However, Greek culture did not entirely replace the older cultural patterns of this region. Beyond the Mediterranean coast and away from the Greek cities of Asia, the age-old customs and traditions of the native populations remained. These people continued to practice their own religions. And while Greek remained the language of government and of commerce, it never replaced the local languages in everyday use.

The dream of Alexander to unite Greek and non-Greek cultures into a single, worldwide civilization was never fulfilled. But his conquests changed the world dramatically and added much to the development of Western civilization. Increased trade led to an exchange of ideas between Greeks and non-Greeks that enriched many cultures.

During the Hellenistic Age, the order and balance of classical Greek art gave way to emotion and energy, as can be seen in this sculpture of 100 B.C.

Science and mathematics blossomed. Libraries were founded to collect and to preserve the knowledge acquired over the centuries by Mediterranean civilizations. Many of the scientific discoveries and principles developed by Hellenistic scholars are still in use today.

Hellenistic sculpture introduced realism into art and it stressed emotional and active subjects. However, it lacked the harmony and balance of classical Greek sculpture. Architecture became more ornate and town planning became essential as a result of the many new cities built during this period.

Changes in philosophy helped to form new systems of conduct. These ideas set the stage for the teachings of a new religion—Christianity—that arose at the end of the Hellenistic Age (see Chapter 7). Finally, Hellenistic civilization was an important factor in molding a rising new power in the Mediterranean world. That power was Rome.

QUESTIONS FOR REVIEW

1 *What was the Museum of Alexandria?*

2 *How did Aristarchus' view of the earth, sun, and planets differ from that of other astronomers of the Hellenistic world?*

3 *Why do you think Greek culture did not entirely replace the older cultural patterns of the Middle East and the Mediterranean?*

CHAPTER SUMMARY

As the Greek city-states were steadily weakened by inter-city warfare during the fourth century B.C., the northern kingdom of Macedonia grew in power. Eventually its leader, Philip II, united the Greek city-states under his rule. After Philip's death, his son Alexander continued to expand the Macedonian Empire. He conquered the lands from Greece to India, including Egypt. Alexander's conquests also spread Greek culture into these ancient lands. This marked the beginning of the Hellenistic Age, which lasted for nearly three centuries.

During the Hellenistic Age, trade increased between Asia and the Mediterranean world. However, the leaders of the empires created by Alexander's generals were constantly at war with each other or with the people they ruled. As a result, the empires of the Hellenistic world gradually became smaller and weaker until they eventually collapsed.

Although the Hellenistic Age was a time of political uncertainty and change, it was also a time of great cultural and scientific achievement. Scientists made many lasting discoveries, and they often applied their knowledge to the everyday world through useful inventions. Hellenistic philosophies—Stoicism and Epicureanism—attempted to develop guides for everyday living. But by the end of the first century B.C., the influence of Hellenistic culture diminished as the Roman Empire expanded.

CHAPTER 6 IN REVIEW

IMPORTANT WORDS, NAMES, AND TERMS

1 Explain, define, or identify each of the following:

Thebes	Issus	Library of Alexandria
Macedonia	Hellenistic Age	Aristarchus of Samos
Philip II	Seleucus	Archimedes
League of Corinth	Alexandria	Zeno

FACTS AND IDEAS

2 What was the result of the battle of Chaeronea?

3 What practice did the kings of the Hellenistic Age introduce into their rule?

4 What resulted from the establishment of Greek governments and the founding of Greek cities in Alexander's conquered lands?

5 In what ways were the monsoons important to trade during the Hellenistic Age?

6 In what ways did astronomy advance during the Hellenistic Age?

ANALYZING VISUAL MATERIAL

7 Compare the classical vase painting on page 117 with the Hellenistic sculpture on page 127. Describe the differences in these two pieces of art, completed 250 years apart.

8 Study the map on page 123 carefully. What cities were major crossroads of East-West trade in the Hellenistic world? Why?

CONCEPTS AND UNDERSTANDINGS

9 How did the Spartans attempt to unify Greece in the early fourth century B.C.?

10 Why did Alexander's army go no farther east than the Indus Valley?

11 How was trade important to the spread of Hellenistic culture?

12 Why are modern historians indebted to the work of the Museum of Alexandria?

13 In what ways did scholars of the Hellenistic Age improve knowledge of the earth?

PROJECTS AND ACTIVITIES

14 Although science flourished during the Hellenistic Age, *astrology*—the belief in the influence of the stars and planets on human behavior and events—became accepted. Make a chart of some of the astrological beliefs and practices of the Hellenistic Age, and show how they might differ from modern beliefs. Use encyclopedias and other sources, such as histories of astrology, to find your information.

15 As a result of the growing trade during the Hellenistic Age, many early banking practices were used by merchants of this time. Prepare a report to the class outlining some of these banking practices and discussing how they may have been used in the ancient world.

CHAPTER 7 THE ROMAN WORLD

1 The Conquest of Italy   2 From Republic to Empire
3 Life and Religion in the Roman World   4 The Decline and
Fall of the Empire

Over a period of six centuries, Rome grew from a small
farming village on the Italian Peninsula to a world state that
dominated a vast empire. At its height, the Roman Empire
stretched from Britain and Spain eastward to the Euphrates
River and south into Africa. The Romans brought together the
known western world through the power of their army and the
diversity of their commerce. Roman civilization helped to
preserve and to pass on much of the cultures of Greece,
Egypt, and the Middle East to the developing European
civilization of the Middle Ages. But Rome was much more
than the tie that bound these cultures together. The distinctive Roman culture, law, and government enriched later
western civilization. In addition, the influence of a new
religion—Christianity—founded in the Middle East during
Roman times can still be felt today.

Sven Samelius

The half-ruined Colosseum—scene of Roman spectacles and gladiatorial contests—stands today in the city of Rome.

1 THE CONQUEST OF ITALY

Between about 1600 B.C. and 500 B.C., civilization developed on the Italian Peninsula. Influenced by many factors, the civilization eventually became centered in the growing city-state of Rome. One of the most important developments of early Rome was the establishment of a form of government known as a republic, in which elected officials governed. Today, we can trace many elements of our government to the ideals of the Roman Republic. By about 260 B.C., Rome had conquered and unified neighboring peoples and effectively controlled the entire Italian Peninsula.

THE LAND AND THE EARLY SETTLEMENT OF ITALY The Roman civilization began to develop on the boot-shaped peninsula of Italy nearly 2,700 years ago (see map on this page). The Italian Peninsula was partly isolated from the bulk of continental Europe by the high mountains known as the Alps. Stretching southward from the Alps down the entire length of the Italian Peninsula were the Apennine Mountains. Along the east coast of Italy, the Apennines formed a barrier as they dropped sharply to the Adriatic Sea. The west coast, however, had many low hills and fertile plains, as well as many good harbors. The relatively mild climate of the peninsula enabled farmers to harvest more than one crop each year on the rich lands.

By about 1600 B.C., Indo-European-speaking peoples had slowly migrated down the western coast of the Italian Peninsula. This migration took place at roughly the same time as similar movements in the Indus Valley and in Greece (see Chapters 3 and 5). One of these migrating groups—the Latins—settled on the Latium plain, south of the Tiber River (see map on this page). The Latins traditionally herded animals. But by the early 900's B.C., they had settled

The Italian Peninsula

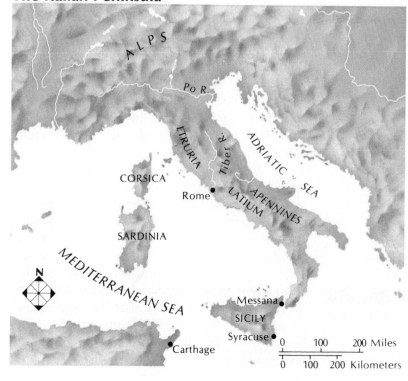

The geographic conditions of the Italian Peninsula—its rough terrain and its spine of mountains—made travel and communication difficult and challenged the Romans' engineering skills in building roads and aqueducts.

POLITICAL		SOCIAL AND ECONOMIC

B.C.

	c. 1000	Rome founded
	c. 800	Etruscans settled north of Tiber River
Romans overthrew Etruscan rulers	*c.* 500	Roman Republic began as plebeians gained rights from patricians
	494	
Laws of the Twelve Tables proclaimed	450	
Rome plundered by Gauls	387	
	312	Appian Way began
Hannibal invaded Italian Peninsula	219	
Jewish kingdom of Judea established	141	
	c. 120	Gracchi's land reforms failed
Julius Caesar murdered	44	
	27	Pax Romana began

A.D.

	c. 30	Jesus crucified
	70	Temple in Jerusalem destroyed by Romans
Romans conquered Britain	77	
	166	Plague in Rome
Diocletian divided empire	286	
	303	Last official persecution of Christians began
Roman Empire reunited	324	
	395	Christianity proclaimed state religion of empire
Eastern and Western Empires established	*c.* 400	
Western Empire fell	476	

down to cultivate the fertile Latium plain, which was nearly 60 miles (96 kilometers) long and 30 miles (48 kilometers) wide.

An important early Latin development was the settlement of a small village on the Tiber River that eventually became the city of Rome. The small farming village was built about 15 miles (24 kilometers) from the sea, near a shallow and easily crossed part of the river. The founding of Rome was traditionally placed by Roman historians around 750 B.C. However, many archaeologists today believe that the first settlements on the hills around Rome may have been established shortly after 1000 B.C. In either case, by the seventh century B.C. Rome was a growing settlement in Latium and faced a powerful threat from a people from the north—the Etruscans [i-TRUHS-kuhnz].

ROME'S ETRUSCAN HERITAGE About 800 B.C., Etruscan settlers arrived on the western shore of the Italian Peninsula. Most historians believe that the Etruscans came from the Middle East, probably from Asia Minor. They settled north of the Tiber River in an area that became known as Etruria— roughly modern Tuscany (see map on page 131). At nearly the same time, Greek city-states were establishing colonies along the southernmost coast of the peninsula and on the island of Sicily. Eventually, the Etruscans, the Greeks, and traders from Carthage in North Africa became involved in a struggle for control of trade in the western Mediterranean.

By the end of the seventh century B.C., the Etruscans had expanded southward and had taken over the settlement of Rome. To the Etruscans, Rome was part of a natural pathway for travel and for trade between lands to the north and lands to the south of the Tiber River. Moreover, Rome was far enough from the sea to be protected from invasion. Yet, the river was navigable and could be used for seagoing trade. The settlement was also protected by hills and by marshes.

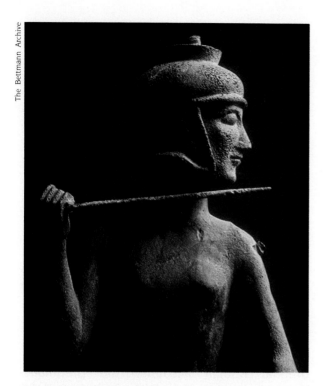

Etruscan art greatly influenced the development of Roman art. The bronze Etruscan sculpture of a warrior shown above dates from about 600 B.C.

The Etruscans slowly built Rome—once a small Latin farming village—into a growing center for trade. By 600 B.C., the Etruscans had drained a marshy area near the river and paved a central market and meeting place. This eventually became known as the Roman Forum. The Etruscans also built a bridge across the Tiber, fortifications for the growing city-state, and a sewer system. They set up irrigation systems in Latium that led to great increases in the farm production of the plain.

The Etruscans made several contributions to Roman culture. Later Roman religion was developed mainly from Etruscan beliefs. The arches and vaults that characterized Roman architecture were probably learned from the Etruscans. In addition, the Etruscans introduced a form of the Greek alphabet to the Romans, from which our present-day alphabet has slowly evolved.

Etruscan kings ruled Rome for more than a century. However, during the 500's B.C., the Etruscans were slowly weakened by battles with the Greeks and with the Carthaginians for control of the western Mediterranean. Shortly before 500 B.C., the Romans overthrew their Etruscan rulers and set about establishing a powerful city-state.

THE EARLY REPUBLIC Following the overthrow of the Etruscan monarchy, the Romans established a *republic*. The Roman Republic was a form of government in which citizens elected representatives to carry out the powers of government.

Beginning around 500 B.C., two leaders, called *consuls*, were elected each year from the *patrician*—upper—class to govern Rome. The full power of government was held by the consuls. These powers included commanding the army, proposing new legislation, and interpreting and carrying out the laws.

The consuls were prevented from becoming too powerful in several important ways. First, their terms were limited to one year. Second, by necessity the consuls had to agree with each other on all decisions. Each consul had the authority to *veto*—forbid or prohibit—the actions of the other. However, in extreme circumstances, such as war, a dictator could be chosen by the Senate and given all government powers for a maximum of six months.

The early Roman Republic also included two important governing bodies of citizens —the Senate and an assembly. The Senate primarily advised the consuls on important aspects of government, such as foreign policy, taxation, and finances. Senators also proposed new laws. Senators, who served for life, were patricians. Patricians made up less than 10 percent of the citizens of Rome.

Laws proposed by the consuls or by the Senate were passed in the early republic by an assembly. This body also elected the consuls and other government officials. The assembly consisted of both patricians and *plebeians* [pli-BEE-uhnz]. The plebeians were

The sculpture of a Roman senator shown above dates from the first century B.C. and is a classic example of Roman art.

freeborn citizens who had little property and who had to serve in the army. They included small farmers, shopkeepers, craft workers, and laborers.

The citizens of the assembly were divided according to their wealth. The assembly—known as the *Comitia Centuriata*, or Assembly of Centuries—was further divided into units of 100 citizens. These divisions—called centuries—also served as the basic divisions of the Roman army. Each century had only one vote in the business of the assembly, which the patricians usually dominated because of their wealth and power.

From almost the beginning of the Roman Republic, the division of Roman society between the influential patricians and the poorer plebeians led to social conflict. For nearly 200 years, the plebeians struggled to gain equal rights.

THE PLEBEIAN STRUGGLE Shortly after 500 B.C., the plebeian class began to demand more rights from the patricians who controlled the Roman government. At that time, plebeians were prohibited from holding the position of consul and from becoming high government officials. They could not marry patricians. Plebeians were also often treated severely and arbitrarily under Roman law. For example, many small farmers, who were often away at war, might be unable to pay their debts. As a result, their land could be taken from them, and in some cases they could be enslaved by those to whom their debts were owed.

Beginning in 494 B.C., according to traditional Roman accounts, the plebeians banded together to gain more rights. They left Rome and threatened to establish a rival city. In this way, they would deprive Rome of much of its army and labor force. A compromise between the patricians and the plebeians quickly followed, and the plebeians gained their first important demand. They gained the right to elect their own leaders—called *tribunes*. The tribunes directly protected plebeian rights and had the power to veto any actions taken by the Senate that were unjust or that hurt the interest of the plebeians. The tribunes were chosen by a newly organized plebeian assembly that was based upon geographical divisions, rather than upon wealth. This body became known as the *Concilium Plebis*, or Council of Plebeians.

Around 450 B.C., the plebeians sought more protection from unwritten laws that they felt were too vague or unfair. As a result, Roman law was brought together in a single written law code, known as the *Twelve Tables*. The code covered most aspects of Roman public and private life. The Twelve Tables defined property and family rights and duties. They also guaranteed all citizens the right to appeal severe court sentences.

The plebeians made important gains in other areas, too. Beginning sometime in the mid-fourth century B.C., plebeians were elected consuls and gained the right to hold most high public offices. At first, the plebeian council could only make recommendations for laws, which had to then be approved by the Senate. But by about 287 B.C., the council had gained the power to pass laws directly, without the consent of the Senate. However, the patrician-dominated Assembly of Centuries still elected the consuls and advised them on matters of war and peace. Thus, the legislative powers of Rome were shared between the patricians and the plebeians. Participation in the government of Rome had been extended to nearly every citizen, regardless of social class.

ROME UNIFIES ITALY At the same time that the plebeians were gaining a greater voice in the government of Rome, the city-state was gradually expanding its influence. Surrounded by enemies and potential rivals for power, the Romans worked to gain loyal allies. By the end of the 400's B.C., the Romans dominated many of the neighboring Latin tribes in central Italy. By this time, Rome had also crushed a rival Etruscan city-state. In addition, Etruria to the north and Campania to the south soon came under Roman control.

In 387 B.C., Rome was threatened with destruction by invaders from north of the Alps. Celtic-speaking people—known as Gauls—overran northern Italy and plundered Rome. However, the Gauls were interested only in treasure and not in expansion, and they suddenly retreated when their own homeland was threatened by invaders. In the decade that followed, the Romans built a new wall to protect their city. The wall was made of volcanic stone and was 12 feet (3.6 meters) thick and 24 feet (7.2 meters) high.

The Romans often treated conquered peoples as allies. Rome's allies were allowed self-government but were required to sign treaties of alliance with Rome. These mutual defense treaties required that the allies provide the Roman army with a specified number of troops in time of war. Thus, Rome was generally able to maintain good relations with the states that it conquered. In addition, this policy enabled the Roman army to grow into the largest and best fighting force in Italy.

Several other well-reasoned policies were used to expand Rome's influence. Colonies were often founded at strategic points on the Roman frontier. The soldier-farmers who settled these lands provided Rome with loyal outposts in unfriendly areas. Moreover, partial Roman citizenship was frequently extended to Rome's allies. Although the right to hold a Roman office or to vote in Roman elections was withheld, these new citizens gained many special privileges, such as making a contract protected by Roman law. This policy helped to maintain Roman domination over a neighbor, and it allowed Rome to keep control of the conquered lands without troops.

By 264 B.C., the Romans had taken over the southern part of the Italian Peninsula, including the Greek city-states of the region. As a result, Rome controlled nearly all of Italy. But another threat—the powerful city-state of Carthage—loomed in front of the growing Roman state.

QUESTIONS FOR REVIEW

1 *What was the Latium plain?*

2 *In what ways did the Etruscans contribute to Roman culture?*

3 *Why did the barriers that existed between the plebeians and the patricians of ancient Rome slowly fall away?*

2 FROM REPUBLIC TO EMPIRE

During the third century B.C., several events led the Romans into the affairs of the Mediterranean world. The result, nearly a century and a half later, was the creation of a Roman empire that covered a vast area. Internal struggles constantly plagued Rome at home. As a result of these struggles, the Roman Republic soon disintegrated. In its place, the government of the Roman Empire was formed, dominated by a single individual—the emperor.

CONFLICT WITH CARTHAGE Carthage was founded on the north coast of Africa during the ninth century B.C. by traders from the Phoenician city of Tyre (see map on page 137). During the next five centuries, Carthage became the leading commercial power in the western Mediterranean. By the mid-third century B.C., the population of prosperous Carthage was three times that of Rome. In addition, the wealthy merchants of Carthage had opened trade routes and established ports along the North African coast and in Sicily and Spain.

In 264 B.C., Carthage threatened to take over the Sicilian city of Messana—present-day Messina (see map on page 131). With control of Messana, Carthage would dominate the straits between Sicily and Italy. Rome and its allies in southern Italy and Sicily opposed the Carthaginian advances. Because of this network of Roman alliances and the threat of Carthaginian influence in Sicily, Rome entered what has become known as the First Punic War—from the Latin word for Carthaginian, *punicus*.

Rome began the war by building a fleet to match Carthage's naval strength. For nearly 25 years, Rome battled Carthage on the seas. Losses on both sides were staggering. But the Romans' great material resources and their unbending patriotism proved to be decisive advantages. And in 241 B.C., the leaders of Carthage were forced to make peace. As a result, Rome gained control of all of Sicily and, shortly after, gained the islands of Corsica and Sardinia.

Several years later, the Carthaginians moved to expand their influence in Spain. In 219 B.C., Carthage—led by Hannibal, a young and brilliant general—attacked a Spanish Roman ally. Hannibal then invaded Italy by leading 40,000 soldiers, 37 war

Hannibal met a Roman army on the plain near Zama in North Africa in 202 B.C. The great Carthaginian general had effectively used elephants against the Romans in earlier battles. After 17 years of fighting Hannibal's army, however, the Romans had developed new tactics that led to their decisive victory at Zama.

elephants, and 8,000 cavalry across the Alps. Only 26,000 survivors, exhausted by the terrible hardships of the winter march across the Alps, reached the Po River valley in northern Italy. This marked the beginning of the Second Punic War.

For nearly 15 years, Hannibal won many victories on the Italian Peninsula. But he was unable to capture the walled cities of the peninsula or to completely defeat Rome and its allies. The Romans had learned to follow a strategy of avoiding pitched battles against Hannibal in Italy. The Romans wore down Hannibal's forces with widely dispersed raids and battles, forcing him to divide his army.

Finally, the Roman general Scipio attacked Carthage itself and forced Hannibal to return to North Africa to defend his native city. In 202 B.C., Hannibal was defeated south of Carthage and Rome gained control of the entire western Mediterranean, including Spain and the north coast of Africa. Hannibal was forced to flee into the Balkans, where he committed suicide in 183 B.C. Following this victory, Rome turned to the affairs of the eastern Mediterranean.

ROME AND THE EASTERN MEDITERRA-NEAN In 200 B.C., a Roman army invaded Macedonia, whose king, Philip V, had sided with Hannibal during the Second Punic War. The Romans also felt that a pact that had been made between Macedonia and the Seleucid Empire threatened Roman interests in the eastern Mediterranean.

The mobile and well-equipped Romans were able to defeat the slower and more heavily armed Macedonians in several battles. By 197 B.C., Macedonia had been conquered. The Greek city-states, which had been dominated by Macedonia for more than a century, gained a large measure of self-government following the Roman victory. However, the Greeks remained formally under the protection of the Roman government. Fifty years later, Greece became a Roman province.

Between 190 B.C and 130 B.C., Rome continued to gain lands throughout the Hellenistic world. In 190 B.C., Rome defeated the Seleucid ruler Antiochus III and gained all the lands to the north and west of the Taurus Mountains (see map on page 138). Rome's protection was extended to Egypt in 168 B.C., after Egypt was threatened by advances made by the Seleucids.

Some of the leaders of Rome feared that Carthage would again rise to a powerful position in the Mediterranean. As a result of this fear, or perhaps as a symbol of Roman strength, Carthage was demolished and burned to the ground in 146 B.C. The captured Carthaginians were sold into slavery. Rome won control of the rich grain fields near Carthage.

By the end of the 100's B.C., Rome ruled an empire that stretched from Spain in the west to Asia Minor in the east (see map on page 138). Great wealth poured into Rome from the conquered lands. However, not every Roman had a share in the prosperity. As a result, discontent grew among the lower classes and among others who lacked political power.

DISCONTENT AND REFORM Changing social and economic conditions in Rome during the 200's and 100's B.C. challenged the power of the ruling nobility. Improved farming methods, the growth of large estates worked cheaply by slaves, and grain imports from Sicily and northern Africa made it impossible for small farmers to compete with large landowners. As a result, small farmers often lost their lands. These unemployed and landless workers flooded Rome. The government became increasingly corrupt and served only the upper class. The position of tribune, for example, had been devised to protect the rights of the plebeians. During the second century B.C., however, the office became a stepping-stone to power, personal gain, and a seat in the Senate.

In 133 B.C., Tiberius Gracchus [GRAK-uhs],

The Expansion of the Roman Empire

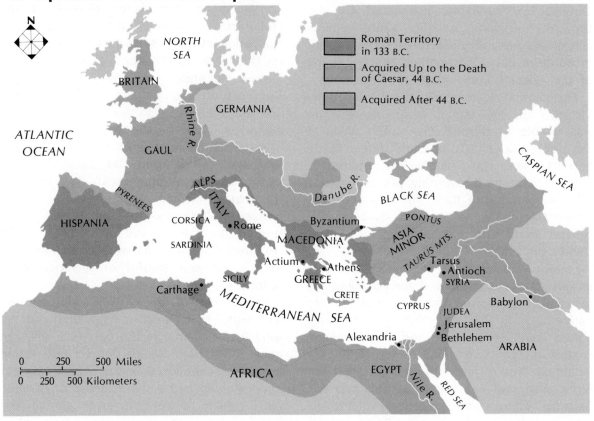

Three centuries after Rome had gained control of the Italian Peninsula in 264 B.C., Roman influence had spread throughout the Mediterranean.

a member of one of Rome's most respected noble families, was elected tribune. He recognized that reform—particularly land reform—was needed to head off growing unrest among the poor in Rome. Tiberius was able to have a law passed that limited individual ownership of public lands to no more than 300 acres (122 hectares). The remaining public land was to be divided among the poor citizens of Rome. However, his methods of gaining this measure and of keeping his power angered Tiberius' senatorial opponents. He was slain the next year.

The younger brother of Tiberius, Gaius [GAY-uhs] Gracchus, was elected tribune in 123 B.C. and restored his brother's land-reform program. Gaius also planned to establish colonies for the landless, unem-ployed people of Rome on lands that had been gained by conquest. Gaius began a program in which the government fixed grain prices and sold grain to Roman citizens below the market price. He also sought to extend full citizenship rights to Rome's Latin and Italian allies. These reform programs enraged the wealthy and powerful Romans in the Senate. They refused to enforce many of the tribune's laws. A short time later, about 3,000 of Gaius' followers were rounded up and executed. To avoid being captured, Gaius committed suicide.

CIVIL WAR The changes begun by the Gracchi did not end with their deaths. These changes were speeded up by a basic reorganization of the Roman army. Prior to 110 B.C., the Roman army required that a soldier own a certain amount of property. These citizen-soldiers, it was believed, had a greater stake in defending Rome. They could also equip themselves with the necessary arms. However, new conditions greatly changed this organization.

In the years beginning about 110 B.C., Rome had to meet a succession of outside challenges. An African king named Jugurtha threatened Rome's Mediterranean commerce. Also, Germanic-speaking barbarians threatened to invade Italy. To meet these threats, a Roman leader, Marius, recruited an army from among the landless poor of Rome. Instead of an army consisting of temporary recruits who were mainly small farmers, Marius formed a professional army whose members were personally loyal to him. These soldiers shared in the spoils of their general's victories. This new kind of Roman army, loyal only to its general, eventually became a threat to the stability of the Roman Republic.

In 88 B.C., the rise of an ambitious leader in the kingdom of Pontus in Asia Minor challenged Rome's power in the eastern Mediterranean. Sulla, a Roman consul, was supported by many wealthy and powerful citizens for the command of the Roman army sent to conquer the Pontian king. Other factions in the Roman government, however, supported Marius as commander. Thus, Marius and Sulla opposed one another for sole leadership of Rome's army in Asia.

In the confusion that followed, Sulla and his army marched on Rome to seize command of the city. For the first time the city of Rome was occupied by one of its own armies. Sulla's subsequent campaign against the rebellious Asian king was successful and he returned to Italy. Upon his arrival civil war broke out between the supporters of Marius and Sulla. Marius managed to raise an army and capture Rome. However, he died shortly after being elected consul.

By 81 B.C., Sulla had again occupied Rome and he had begun to destroy his opponents with utter cruelty. He restored power to the patrician Senate and, for a time, brought order to the Roman Republic. Two years later, Sulla gave up his dictatorial powers and retired. His changes did not last. The inability of a small, republican city-state to rule a large empire became more clear. Moreover, the new Roman armies of career soldiers enabled ambitious and unscrupulous leaders to gain tremendous power. The years of civil war had only temporarily ended.

CAESAR Between 79 B.C. and 59 B.C., Rome came increasingly under the control of military leaders. An ambitious general named Pompey led victorious campaigns in Spain and in Asia. He returned to Rome in 61 B.C. and joined forces with a wealthy noble, Crassus, and with a rising military and political leader named Julius Caesar. The coalition of Pompey, Crassus, and Caesar brought together the three most powerful men in Rome. By combining their power, the three leaders were able to dominate the Roman government.

During the years that followed, Julius Caesar sought to build his power by gaining fame as a military leader. He did this by becoming governor of the Roman province of Gaul—much of which is present-day France. In his drive for military success, Caesar extended the boundaries of Gaul to the Rhine River and to the Pyrenees Mountains. He also briefly invaded Britain (see map on page 138).

In 49 B.C., the Senate, fearful of Caesar's growing power and popularity, demanded that he surrender his troops. Caesar replied by marching on Rome. Crassus had died four years before in an ill-fated invasion of western Asia. Pompey, who had been elected consul and who now opposed Caesar, fled to Greece. Pompey's soldiers were defeated by Caesar's army the next year. Pompey fled to Egypt, where he was murdered. In 46 B.C., Julius Caesar was appointed dictator. He also assumed the offices of consul and tribune. The next year,

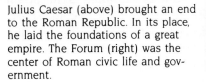

Julius Caesar (above) brought an end to the Roman Republic. In its place, he laid the foundations of a great empire. The Forum (right) was the center of Roman civic life and government.

Caesar had become the sole ruler of Rome. The Senate became a rubber stamp for his policies.

Julius Caesar used his dictatorial powers over Rome and the Senate to begin to tackle many of the republic's problems. He resettled much of the surplus Roman population, including many army veterans, in the provinces. Public building projects that would put many Romans to work were planned. Owners of large estates were required to fill at least one third of their labor needs with unemployed citizens. Also, Roman citizenship was extended to many of the conquered peoples of Italy and Spain.

Caesar did not live to see many of his plans carried out. In early 44 B.C., his dictatorship was extended for life and the power of the Senate was completely broken. On March 15, 44 B.C., Julius Caesar was stabbed to death in the Senate.

THE EARLY EMPIRE Following the death of Julius Caesar, Octavian—Caesar's adopted son and chosen heir—and a leading Roman general and consul, Mark Antony, combined their power to rule Rome for nearly 11 years. During this time many of Caesar's enemies were put to death. In 32 B.C., civil war broke out between the forces of Octavian and those of Antony. The following year at Actium, in western Greece, Octavian defeated Antony, who fled to Egypt and later committed suicide.

Octavian immediately set about consolidating his power and reorganizing the Roman government. The years of civil war between 44 B.C. and 32 B.C. had made it clear that the empire could not be ruled effectively under the old republican system. However, the fate of Julius Caesar had also made it clear that at least several powerful Roman citizens would not accept supreme power's being held by one individual. Therefore, Octavian carefully disguised his growing power by appearing to restore the republic. Many republican practices, including the election of officials, were continued. Although it appeared that the republic still existed, Octavian firmly controlled the Roman government. No laws could be passed without his approval. He selected all government officials for election. Most importantly, Octavian commanded the Roman army. Octavian ruled as emperor of Rome.

The rule of Augustus—a title meaning "great one" given Octavian by the Senate—went unchallenged. After years of devastating warfare, the Romans welcomed a strong ruler who could bring peace and order to the empire. The foundations laid by Augustus gave the Roman Empire a stable government for the next two centuries.

Augustus' reign may have signaled the end of the Roman Republic, but it was also the beginning of a period known as the *Pax Romana*—or Roman Peace. This period lasted until about A.D. 180 and was based on the strength of the Roman army. No major wars took place during this time. Increased commerce brought prosperity to every corner of the empire.

The strength of the imperial system created by Augustus was tested when, after his death in A.D. 14, several poor rulers came to power. The emperors Caligula and Nero were fearsome examples of the brutal and corrupt leaders who ruled the Roman imperial state. Beginning around A.D. 100, a succession of wise leaders brought nearly a century of relative peace and prosperity to the Roman Empire. These good times, during which Roman civilization reached its peak, ended with the death of Marcus Aurelius in A.D. 180.

QUESTIONS FOR REVIEW

1 *Who was Hannibal?*

2 *How did Gaius Gracchus plan to solve some of Rome's economic problems during the 120's B.C.?*

3 *Why do you think Octavian sought to restore the appearance of a republic in Rome?*

3 LIFE AND RELIGION IN THE ROMAN WORLD

Early in the first century A.D., the Roman Empire stood unchallenged in the Mediterranean world and in much of northern Europe. Enforced by the strength of the Roman army, the Pax Romana influenced the lives of millions.

During this time, a new religion, based upon the teachings of Jesus Christ, arose in the Middle East. Slowly, this new faith conquered the old Roman religious beliefs and became the empire's official religion.

THE PAX ROMANA At the time of Augustus' death in A.D. 14, the Roman Empire extended over a tremendous area and took in many different peoples and cultures. Furthermore, the effective government administration formed by Augustus brought stability and prosperity to the empire. The Pax Romana reigned supreme eastward to the Persian Gulf, westward to Spain, and northward to Britain (see map on page 138).

During the years of the Pax Romana, the expansion of the empire was halted and the frontiers became well-defined and well defended. Communication, trade, and travel were vastly improved by a network of roads built throughout the empire. Made of crushed stone overlain by layers of stone blocks, these roads lasted for centuries.

Trade between the empire's provinces and cities greatly expanded during the first and second centuries A.D. Markets for trade goods were created by colonies of Roman citizens that sprang up in the provinces and near the growing towns and cities of the empire. The Mediterranean Sea was cleared of pirates, and new trade routes were opened. *Duties*—the taxes paid on goods shipped between ports—were eliminated within the empire, thus encouraging greater trade. A reliable money system and improved banking practices further encouraged commerce. Exotic luxury goods—such as

Roman spectators delighted in games of all types. This mosaic from the third century A.D. shows a Roman chariot race.

spices, perfumes, and jewels from India and silk from China—were also brought into the empire during this period.

LIFE IN THE ROMAN WORLD The society of the Roman Empire during the Pax Romana differed little from that of the late days of the republic. Landowning aristocratic families and a growing class of wealthy merchants dominated Roman society and government. Agriculture remained the basis of the economy throughout the empire.

At the same time, many industries were beginning to develop in the empire's prospering cities. The rise of industry helped to increase commerce, because finished goods were traded from one end of the empire to the other. Skilled Roman citizens filled most of the craft and trade occupations. During the early years of the empire, much of the hard labor, particularly in Rome, was still done by slaves. Moreover, the living conditions of the unemployed citizens in Rome remained crowded and horribly wretched. The tenements of the poor lined the streets of the city. In A.D. 64, many of these buildings were destroyed as nearly three quarters of Rome burned to the ground in a raging fire.

Most Romans—even those of the lower classes—enjoyed a varied social life. Admission to the public baths, for example, often cost very little. There, the people enjoyed hot baths and exercise. The more elaborate Roman bathing establishments contained libraries, art galleries, and rich gardens.

Romans typically enjoyed viewing the brutal events of chariot racing and contests between gladiators. These events were held in large arenas, such as the Colosseum, that held thousands of people. The theater was also popular. Mime—in which actors portrayed roles solely through body movements—was the favorite. Cities and towns throughout the empire copied Rome's baths, arenas, and theaters.

ROLE OF RELIGION IN EARLY ROME Religion was central to Roman culture. The proper rituals and sacrifices that honored the Roman gods were important parts of the Romans' everyday life. From earliest times, Roman religion was polytheistic. The early Romans made gods of spirits as well as the forces of nature. Moreover, during the reign of Augustus, emperor worship became a practice required of all Roman citizens and subjects.

Roman beliefs were very practical and flexible. Because the Romans tolerated most religions, their gods often took on the characteristics of the gods and the religions with which the Romans came into contact. The Romans seemed to be concerned only that the new religion did not replace the existing Roman beliefs entirely and that it neither was immoral nor encouraged rebellion. As a result, Greek religion influenced the development of ideas that Romans had about their gods. For example, the Roman god Jupiter, like the Greek god Zeus, was "lord of the sky." Ares, the Greek god of war, became identified with the Roman god, Mars. Venus, the Roman goddess of love, was the counterpart to the Greeks' Aphrodite.

This assimilation of foreign beliefs did not always take place, however. In fact, religion occasionally became the basis of conflict between the Romans and the peoples they conquered. In the Middle East, the struggles over Judaism—and later, over a new religion, known as Christianity—were important examples of this conflict.

JEWS AND THE ROMAN WORLD Among the many religions that existed within the Roman Empire was Judaism. This religion, unlike the religions of ancient Greece and Rome, was *monotheistic*—that is, based upon a belief in one supreme god.

Between the sixth and second centuries B.C., Jewish Palestine in the Middle East was ruled in succession by the Persians, the Ptolemies, and the Seleucids. In 141 B.C., much of this area gained its independence from the Seleucid Empire. As a result, a Jewish state known as Judea was established and ruled by the Hasmonaean—or Maccabean—dynasty.

In 64 B.C., Judea officially came into the Roman world after being annexed by Pompey. Thirty years later, the Romans installed Herod—later called the Great—on the Judean throne. Herod reigned until his death in 4 B.C.

Shortly after Herod's death, the province of Judea came under a Roman governor—an official, nonroyal appointee of the emperor. Throughout this period, the Jews were allowed a large degree of self-rule. The Romans were reluctant to step directly into Jewish affairs. A council of Jewish leaders and scholars—known as the *Sanhedrin*—led the Jewish community in Judea. This council was headed by a chief priest.

Some Judeans, however, disliked living under Roman rule. In A.D. 66, many of the Judeans revolted. Four years later, the Roman army burned Jerusalem and destroyed the Temple. A second revolt broke out during the A.D. 130's. By A.D. 135, the revolt was crushed and the rebel survivors were sold into slavery. Others were forbidden to visit Jerusalem. Still other Jews left Judea and settled in many places throughout the Roman world.

ORIGINS OF CHRISTIANITY A new religion arose in Judea and the Middle East early in the first century A.D. It grew out of the teachings and the healing works of a man known as Jesus, although it was based in large part upon the ideas of Judaism.

Jesus' life and message have been preserved in the *New Testament Gospels* of the Bible. According to biblical accounts, Jesus was born in the Judean town of Bethlehem about the time of the death of Herod the Great (see map on page 138). At the age of 30, Jesus embarked on a mission to spread his doctrines throughout Galilee and Judea. Jesus taught about God's boundless love and about the importance of love and compassion between human beings. Jesus condemned violence and greed and told his followers that eternal life could be gained by believing in him and in the ideas that he preached.

Many Jews believed that Jesus was the *Messiah*—the savior (in Greek, *Christos*)—prophesied in earlier Jewish writings. Other Jews, however, opposed this view and denounced Jesus' teachings as *blasphemous*—false and irreligious. In addition, Roman officials in Judea came to believe that Jesus' doctrines threatened the authority of Rome throughout the region. These officials finally

143

arrested Jesus, and fearing the popularity of his ideas, sentenced him to death.

After the crucifixion of Jesus Christ, a small group of believers—Christ's apostles—set about spreading Christianity. Perhaps the greatest missionary of the new religion was Saul of Tarsus, better known by his Roman name, Paul. Born in the Hellenistic city of Tarsus in Asia Minor, Paul was Jewish, a Roman citizen, well-educated, and spoke Greek. He helped to clearly develop many of the ideas of Christianity. Paul's letters outlined the new faith and guided early Christians. These letters became part of the New Testament. Paul was a tireless traveler who carried the new religion to people in Asia Minor, Greece, Macedonia, and Rome. Paul's work greatly influenced the development of Christianity into a major religion.

EARLY CHRISTIANITY The beliefs and practices of Christianity developed gradually during the first centuries of its existence. By about the third century A.D., the Christian Scriptures—the New Testament of the Bible—had evolved into their final form. During these years, the early Christians were often *persecuted*—made to suffer for their beliefs—by the Romans.

The growth of Christianity was tolerated within the Roman Empire as long as it did not challenge Roman authority. However, the early Christians would not accept the Roman gods, nor would they worship the emperor as a god. As a result, they were often punished for their beliefs. The emperor Nero used members of Rome's small Christian community as scapegoats for the fire that devastated much of the city in A.D. 64. Many Christians were executed.

Other Roman emperors tried to ignore the early Christians. Belief in Christianity, however, was still regarded as a crime. During the reign of Trajan—A.D. 98–117—the emperor wrote to a governor of an eastern province of the empire:

> They [Christians] are not to be searched out. If they should be brought before you, and the crime [of being a Christian] is proved, they must be punished; with the restriction, however, that where the party denies himself to be a Christian, and shall make it evident that he is not, by invoking [appealing to] our Gods, let him . . . be pardoned upon his repentance. Information without the accuser's name . . . ought not to be received . . . as it is introducing a very dangerous precedent, and by no means agreeable to the equity [justice] of my government.

Early Christian art conveyed, as well as celebrated, the message of Christianity. This mosaic of Christ and the apostles Peter and Andrew is from the Church of St. Apollinaire in Ravenna, Italy.

The first widespread, organized persecutions of Christians took place during the third century A.D. The last occurred in A.D. 303 under the emperor Diocletian [DI-uh-KLEE-shuhn]. Christians, however, refused to allow their faith to be stamped out.

By the early fourth century A.D., Christianity had gained a strong foothold in the empire. The emperor Galerius legalized Christianity in the eastern part of the empire in A.D. 311. Two years later, Emperor Constantine applied Galerius' proclamation to the entire empire in the Edict of Milan. By the time of his death in A.D. 395, Theodosius I had outlawed the old Roman religious beliefs and had made Christianity the state religion.

QUESTIONS FOR REVIEW

1 *What was the Pax Romana?*

2 *In what ways did Christ's apostle Paul help to spread Christianity?*

3 *Why were early Christians persecuted by the Romans?*

4 THE DECLINE AND FALL OF THE EMPIRE

During the three centuries that followed the Pax Romana, the Roman Empire slowly declined. During this time, tremendous economic and social problems, the decay of government, and constant pressure from invaders combined to bring the Roman Empire to an end. Much of Roman culture survived, however, and has continued to influence the development of Western civilization to the present.

DECAY OF THE EMPIRE In the years after the death of the emperor Marcus Aurelius in A.D. 180, the Roman Empire slowly sank into chaos and disorder. For the next century, corrupt leaders with few qualifications except the support of the powerful Roman army became emperor. Civil war seemed unending. Economic and social disintegration added to the growing turmoil within the empire. At the same time, barbarian raids along the empire's borders forced the Romans to maintain large armies and expensive fortifications.

In A.D. 284, Diocletian became emperor and, for a time, brought order to the empire. He reorganized the government by dividing the empire into eastern and western regions (see map on page 146). The empire was also subdivided into smaller units of government called *prefectures, dioceses,* and *provinces.* It was hoped that this reorganization would improve the efficiency of the Roman government. Diocletian ruled the Eastern Empire and chose a coemperor to reign in the west. Provisions were also made for imperial successors. However, under Diocletian the emperor was now an absolute monarch and was free to ignore the empty institutions, such as the Senate, held over from the days of the Roman Republic.

Following the reign of Diocletian, the empire was united for a time under one ruler, Constantine. However, after the death of Constantine in A.D. 337, the empire was again split. By the end of the fourth century A.D., the Roman Empire was officially divided into two parts. The Eastern Empire was ruled from the city of Constantinople, and the Western Empire was controlled from Rome.

Throughout the fourth and fifth centuries A.D., the problems that had plagued the Western Empire persisted. Industry and trade declined. Money gradually became worthless. Improper fertilization techniques led to declining farm production. Moreover, the long borders of the empire were constantly threatened with attack. The cost of

The Divided Roman Empire, c. A.D. 395

By the end of the fourth century A.D. the Roman Empire had been permanently divided into a Western Empire and an Eastern Empire.

maintaining these borders became almost unbearable for the heavily taxed citizens of the empire.

THE BARBARIANS Between the third and the fifth centuries A.D., the boundaries of the Roman Empire were challenged by invaders. The Germanic tribes that lived to the east of the Rhine River and to the north of the Danube River had lived peacefully for generations on the frontiers of the empire. Increasingly, however, these peoples became a threat to the security of the empire.

Historians are uncertain of the reasons underlying the movement of the Germanic peoples into the empire after the second century A.D. One reason may have been that these seminomadic herders sought new lands for their growing populations. In addition, increased pressure from other groups further east and north may have driven the Germanic tribes into conflict with the empire. For whatever reason, these tribes challenged the authority and power of Rome by the late A.D. 300's.

In A.D. 376, one of these Germanic groups —the Visigoths—sought peaceful entry into the empire. The Huns—fierce warriors from central Asia—had pushed across the Volga River and threatened the Visigoths. However, the Romans failed to live up to a promise of land and food for the Germans. As a result, the Germans rose up under their leader, Alaric, and decisively defeated the Roman army at Adrianople in A.D. 378. By A.D. 410, the Visigoths had reached (*Text continued on page* 148).

Life at the Time

A Glimpse of the Barbarians

Much of the information that modern historians have concerning the events of ancient Rome comes from Roman sources. Perhaps the best-known historian of Roman times was Tacitus, who lived during the first century A.D. As a public official, Tacitus was able to travel widely and is believed to have held a major military post, defending the empire's border along the Rhine River. The following excerpt is taken from Tacitus' *Germania*, written in A.D. 98. In this excerpt, the ancient historian describes the Germanic tribes along the Rhine River who, he believed, might one day threaten Roman Gaul. Clearly, he often injects his Roman point of view and bias when describing the lifestyle of the Germanic tribes. Nevertheless, this is the first written description of these peoples and gives modern historians an invaluable understanding of their culture.

"On the field of battle it is a disgrace to the chief to be surpassed in valour by his companions, to the companions not to come up to the valour of their chief. As for leaving a battle alive after your chief has fallen, *that* means lifelong infamy and shame. To defend and protect him, to put down one's own acts of heroism to his credit—that is what they really mean by "allegiance." The chiefs fight for victory, the companions for their chief. . . .

"It is a well-known fact that the peoples of Germany never live in cities, and will not even have their houses set close together. They live apart, dotted here and there, where spring, plain or grove has taken their fancy. Their villages are not laid out in Roman style, with buildings adjacent or interlocked. Every man leaves an open space around his house, perhaps as a precaution against the risk of fire, perhaps because they are such inexpert builders. They do not even make any use of little stone blocks or tiles; what serves their every purpose is ugly timber, both unimpressive and unattractive. They smear over some parts of their houses with an earth that is so pure and brilliant that it looks like painting or coloured mosaics. They have also the habit of hollowing out caves underground and heaping masses of refuse on the top. In these they can escape the winter's cold and store their produce. . . .

"The universal dress is the short cloak, fastened with a brooch, or, failing that, a thorn. . . . The richest are not distinguished, like the Persians and Sarmatians, by a long flowing robe, but by a tight one that shows the shape of every limb. They also wear the pelts of wild animals, the tribes near the Rhine without regard to appearance, the more distant peoples with some refinement of taste, for there is no other finery that they can buy. . . ."

Beginning in the third century A.D., *fierce battles between Romans and barbarians became common as Roman power waned.*

The Barbarian Migrations

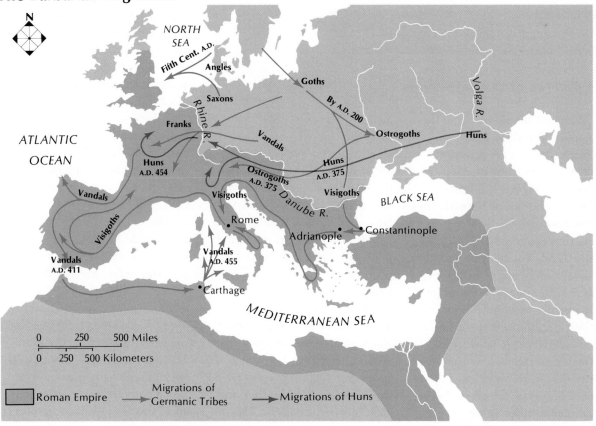

By about A.D. 400, barbarian tribes had entered the Roman Empire and had challenged the power of Rome.

Rome. The marauders shocked the empire by plundering the city. The Visigoths' victory opened a floodgate through which barbarian peoples—including the Ostrogoths, the Vandals, the Franks, the Angles, the Saxons, and others—poured into the empire (see map on this page).

By the mid-400's, the Germanic tribes had claimed large parts of the Western Empire. The eastern half of the empire, however, was stronger and more prosperous and was able to resist the outsiders. Rome was again plundered and sacked in A.D. 455, this time by the Vandals. In A.D. 476, Odoacer [OHD-uh-WAY-suhr], a Germanic general, seized control of Italy and proclaimed himself king. Other Germanic kingdoms were soon carved out of the remaining lands of the Western Empire. The once-great Roman Empire came to an end.

A.D. 476 The fall of Rome and the rise of the Germanic kingdoms in the west culminated centuries of decline. The causes for this decline were varied and complex. Many historians note that the rapid growth of the empire in its early years, and the increase in slavery that it brought, created a mob of unemployed in the cities. Despite measures taken by the Roman government, including the distribution of free grain to the poor, this problem was never satisfactorily solved.

During the later years of the empire, some historians point out, the economy became stagnant. Nearly all land in the empire had come under the control of a small group of aristocrats. Agriculture, the basis of the Roman economy, was dominated by large estates. The total area of land that was under cultivation steadily declined. Small farmers were often forced either to rent land from large landowners or to flee to the cities, there to join the ranks of the unemployed. Eventually, the half-free peasants on the large estates became tied to the land. This development foreshadowed the rise of manorialism during the Middle Ages (see Chapter 12).

Commerce also declined drastically during the later years of the empire. Moreover, prices rose beyond control. Short-sighted Roman leaders had constantly debased the money supply by using valueless metals to make coins. As a result, money had become worthless. Heavy taxation practically destroyed the middle class of Roman citizens. The payment of taxes and salaries during this time was often made in produce or in clothing. By the end of the empire, the economy in many areas had been reduced to a barter system.

Other factors also played a part in the disintegration of the empire. Among these were the transition of the Roman army from a citizen army to a group of ruthless professionals, many of whom were barbarians. The empire also suffered a decline in population that resulted from wars, epidemics, and a low birthrate. This, too, led to the decline of the Western Empire. And even as the empire was breaking apart from these enormous internal pressures, the invasions of the Germanic tribes occurred.

Thus, by the middle of the fifth century A.D., the Roman Empire had suffered blows from which it could not recover.

THE HERITAGE OF ROME Perhaps the greatest Roman contributions to later civilizations were in the fields of government and law. Many of the ideas formed during the period of the Roman Republic were the basis for the development and growth of constitutional governments in modern times. Moreover, such things as the divisions of local government and the organization and framework of the Christian Church during the Middle Ages were based upon practices of the Roman Empire.

Roman law became the foundation of many of the legal systems of the Western world. During the time of the empire, the Romans developed a system of law that could be applied to a vast world state and to a variety of foreign customs and practices. Protection of private property, assumption of innocence until guilt is proven, and equality before the law are major Roman principles found in our legal system.

Roman architects and engineers also enriched the culture of Rome. Their use of arches, arched ceilings—called vaults—domed roofs, and concrete has greatly influenced Western architecture. Developing new principles of engineering, the Romans built

Ruins of Roman engineering feats still dot Europe today. This aqueduct carried water from surrounding highlands to the Roman city on the site of present-day Segovia, in Spain. The aqueduct, built between A.D. 100 and A.D. 110, is still in use today.

149

aqueducts, which carried fresh water to the Roman cities, and bridges. Moreover, a network of roads that increased the speed of communications and trade throughout the empire was built.

Roman literature and language also influenced the development of Western culture. The Roman writers Cicero, Virgil, Horace, Ovid, and Juvenal; the Greek writer Plutarch; and the Roman historian Tacitus added to the wealth of Roman literature. Latin, the language of Rome, formed the foundation of the Romance languages—including French, Italian, Portuguese, and Spanish—as well as greatly affecting the development of English.

The end of the Roman Empire did not extinguish Roman culture. Rather, the civilization of Rome lived on and had a great impact upon the development of European civilization and, later, upon our own culture.

QUESTIONS FOR REVIEW

1 *Who was Diocletian?*

2 *In what ways did the economic problems of the Roman Empire help to bring about its end?*

3 *Why do you think modern historians describe the end of the Roman Empire as a long, slow decline rather than as an abrupt fall from greatness?*

CHAPTER SUMMARY

Rome was founded on the Italian peninsula, along the Tiber River, sometime between about 1000 B.C. and 750 B.C. By about 600 B.C., the Etruscans, who are believed to have migrated to the Italian Peninsula from Asia Minor, had taken over Rome. They turned a sleepy farming village into a bustling crossroads for trade. A century later the Romans regained control of their government. Thereafter, Rome became a powerful city-state and developed a form of government known as a republic.

During the second and first centuries B.C., the Roman Republic slowly decayed. Under Julius Caesar and Augustus Caesar the republican government was transformed into an imperial government controlled by the emperor and the army. The reign of Augustus began nearly two centuries of peace and prosperity, known as the Pax Romana.

Early in the first century A.D., a new religion began in Judea, a Roman province in the Middle East. The new faith was based upon the teachings of Jesus Christ and upon many of the ideas of Judaism and was spread by the missionary work of Paul.

By the end of the Pax Romana, the Roman Empire was in decline. Over the next 300 years, the lust for personal power, the decay of Roman government, the endless economic and social crises, and the attacks by barbarous invaders gradually brought down the Roman Empire.

CHAPTER 7 IN REVIEW

IMPORTANT WORDS, NAMES, AND TERMS

1 Explain, define, or identify each of the following:

Etruscans	Twelve Tables	Sanhedrin
republic	Hannibal	persecution
patricians	Julius Caesar	Constantine
plebeians	Pax Romana	Visigoths

FACTS AND IDEAS

2 Who were the Latins?

3 What was the office of consul?

4 Describe the policy by which Rome maintained good relations with conquered peoples during the years of the republic.

5 Who was Paul—or Saul of Tarsus?

ANALYZING VISUAL MATERIAL

6 Study the map on page 148 carefully. From which general direction did the barbarians enter the Roman Empire? What invading tribe probably set in motion the migration of the easternmost Goths?

7 What does the illustration on page 149 indicate about the level of Roman engineering nearly 2,000 years ago?

CONCEPTS AND UNDERSTANDINGS

8 How did Julius Caesar begin to solve some of Rome's pressing problems before his death?

9 In what way did the reign of Augustus Caesar mark the end of the republic?

10 Why do you think Roman religious beliefs might be described as "practical and flexible"?

11 Why do you think the Romans persecuted early Christians?

12 Why did Diocletian divide the empire into an eastern half and a western half?

13 What factors led to the decline and fall of the Roman Empire?

PROJECTS AND ACTIVITIES

14 Make a classroom display showing the influence of Roman architectural design on modern structures.

15 *Oratory*—the art of public speaking—was one of the most valued assets of Roman public officials. Organize a class debate on an issue from the days of the Gracchi, such as the merits of land reform or of free grain for the poor of Rome. Use library sources to find information that might be useful to you.

CHAPTER **8** THE CLASSICAL AGE IN INDIA AND CHINA

1 The Classical Age of Indian Civilization 2 Dynastic China Under the Han Rulers 3 Internal Strife and the Reunification of China

Beginning in A.D. 320 and lasting for more than 200 years, a classical civilization existed in India. Many facets of modern Indian culture developed during this time. A rich literary tradition was created. Great advances in science and mathematics were also achieved. The patterns of culture established during this golden age survived for centuries, even though kingdoms in India rose and fell.

China enjoyed a time of great cultural and intellectual development under the Han dynasty, which ruled from 202 B.C. to A.D. 220. One of the most important developments of this time was the beginning of trade between China and lands to the west, including the Roman Empire. Moreover, many elements and institutions of Chinese civilization that developed during the Han rule have lasted into modern times. After the fall of the Han rulers, China suffered through 400 years of invasions, division, and unrest.

Robert Freck/Odyssey

Art flourished during the time of India's Gupta Empire, as this detail from the tower of the Meenakshi Temple in Madurai, India, shows.

1 THE CLASSICAL AGE OF INDIAN CIVILIZATION

During the early part of the fourth century A.D., northern India was united in a great state known as the Gupta Empire. During this time, Indian civilization reached new peaks. Indian art, literature, science, and mathematics were enriched by many important achievements. Although the Gupta Empire eventually declined and disappeared, the culture of northern India continued to develop under a strong new ruler.

THE GUPTA EMPIRE Following the decline of the Kushan Empire in northern India during the third century A.D., much of the Indian subcontinent was divided into many small kingdoms (see Chapter 3). The prosperous trade with the Roman Empire that had begun in the first century B.C., however, continued to flourish.

Early in the fourth century A.D., a ruler named Chandragupta came to power in a small kingdom on the plains near the Ganges River. By A.D. 320, Chandragupta—no relation to Chandragupta Maurya—had established a new empire in northern India—the Gupta Empire. He then set about restoring the magnificence of the time of the Mauryas, who had ruled India six centuries earlier.

Chandragupta died in about A.D. 330, and his son and successor, Samudragupta, took the throne and ruled for nearly 50 years. Samudragupta, a remarkable leader, extended the empire across all of northern India and led an expedition southward along the eastern coast of the subcontinent. The kingdoms that were not brought directly into the empire paid tribute to the Guptas and acknowledged their power (see map on this page).

Around 375, Samudragupta's son came to power as Chandragupta II. During his reign, the Gupta Empire enjoyed a golden age of Indian culture. Modern historians owe a

The Gupta Empire

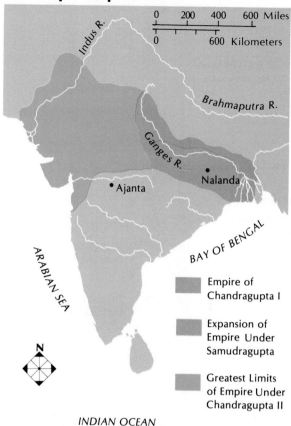

The Gupta Empire was founded in northern India by Chandragupta I and was enlarged by his son Samudragupta.

great debt to the Chinese Buddhist traveler Fa-Hsien [FAH-shi-EN], who lived and traveled in India around 400, during the time of Chandragupta II. Fa-Hsien's sharply perceptive observations of the Gupta Empire provide historians with valuable information about life in northern India during that time.

Fa-Hsien wrote that the government of the Guptas was fair and tolerant. Taxes were not excessive. Towns were large and prosperous. Fines were the most common form of punishment, and capital punishment for serious crimes was rarely inflicted. The government also tolerated many religions. People traveled freely.

During the middle of the fifth century A.D., barbarians from central Asia known as the Huns began streaming through the mountain

POLITICAL		SOCIAL AND ECONOMIC
	B.C.	
Han dynasty founded	202	
Emperor Wu Ti began 54-year reign in Han China	140	
	c. 100	Chinese traded over Silk Road
	A.D.	
Wang Mang usurped Han throne	9	
Wang Mang died	23	
	c. 50	Buddhism introduced into China
	c. 105	Process of paper-making developed in China
Han dynasty overthrown	220	
Gupta Empire established in India	320	
	c. 400	Chinese Buddhist pilgrim Fa-Hsien traveled and wrote in Gupta India
Huns invaded northern India	c. 450	Indian poet Kalidasa died
	c. 500	Indian astronomer and mathematician Aryabhata taught
Sui dynasty began	589	
Harsha took power in northern India	606	
	611	Grand Canal completed in China
T'ang dynasty founded in China	618	

passes into India. This took place at about the time that other tribes of Huns were invading the Roman Empire (see Chapter 7). By about 550, these invasions and the declining power of the Guptas led to the breakup of the empire into many small kingdoms.

DEVELOPMENTS IN RELIGION AND IN THE ARTS During the time of the Gupta Empire, the Indian civilization blossomed. Many of the cultural gains of this period were inspired by religion. Hinduism, which had declined in popularity for several centuries, became widely accepted once again. During this period, Hinduism gradually evolved into its present form. The Hindu gods Vishnu, the compassionate and loving Preserver, and Siva, the fearsome Destroyer, were exalted. The ancient epic poems of Hinduism—the *Ramayana* and the *Mahabharata*—were put into the forms that survive today.

The increasing popularity of Hinduism also resulted in the decline of Buddhism. However, Buddhism continued to survive for many years in India and eventually became a major religion in other parts of eastern and southeastern Asia.

A rich literature developed during this golden age of Indian civilization. The greatest writer of the time was Kalidasa [KAHL-i-DAHS-uh]. A sensitive observer of nature and of human emotions, Kalidasa wrote many poems and plays. One play, *Sakuntala*, is perhaps his finest work and is still performed today. In the play, Kalidasa presented a beautiful farewell to the story's heroine as she leaves her home:

Thy journey be auspicious [favorable]; may the breeze,
Gentle and soothing, fan thy cheek: may lakes,
All bright with lily-cups, delight thine eyes;
The sunbeam's heat be cooled by shady trees;
The dust beneath thy feet the pollen be Of lotuses.

Tales of the Hindu god Krishna were favorite subjects of artists during the reign of the Guptas. Krishna's popularity became so widespread that Brahma—the creator—was shown bowing to the god.

The literature of this period also included many fables and fairy tales. The story of Sinbad was eventually included in the collection of stories known as the *Arabian Nights*.

During the time of the Guptas, Indian art, which had been influenced for centuries by the Greeks, emerged with a character of its own. Sculpture was one area that revealed the uniqueness of Indian art. The famous cave paintings at the Buddhist monastery near the village of Ajanta show the high level of Indian painting. The monastery—a series of caves carved into the rock walls of a ravine—also included many beautiful sculptures and shrines.

SCIENCE AND MATHEMATICS The period of the Guptas was also a time of achievement in the fields of science and mathematics. In mathematics, Indian scholars made many advances that were not achieved in Europe for several centuries. In fact, the number symbols that we use today—called Arabic numerals—were probably developed in India. The numerals may have been brought to Europe by the Arab traders of the Middle East. Moreover, Indian mathematicians used the zero and developed the decimal system. The value of *pi*—the ratio of the circumference to the diameter of any circle—was computed to 3.1416. Indian mathematicians also added to the development of algebra. Negative quantities were known at this time. Systems of finding square and cube roots were also developed.

Along with mathematics, astronomy was highly developed by Gupta scholars. Indian astronomers understood solstices and equinoxes and they could accurately predict eclipses. The moon's diameter was also calculated. Perhaps the greatest Gupta astronomer, Aryabhata [AHR-yuh-BUHT-uh] believed that the earth was a sphere and rotated on its axis. By the seventh century A.D., many of the properties of gravitation were also understood.

During the golden age of Indian civilization, medicine was greatly advanced. Many

The Buddhist cave-temples and statues at Ajanta were carved into rock between the second century B.C. and the seventh century A.D.

different types of surgery, including a kind of plastic surgery, were performed. Different kinds of medicinal drugs were also known. The oil of the chaulmoogra tree, which was used to treat leprosy, is still used today for this disease. Fa-Hsien noted in his writings that free hospitals for the poor were also common.

Ways of making soap, glass, and cement, and of tempering steel and dyeing cloth were improved during this period. Moreover, many different kinds of fabrics, such as calico, cashmere, and chintz, originated in India at this time.

Higher learning was greatly valued in classical India. Buddhist and Hindu monasteries and temples were often centers for advanced studies. The most famous classical Indian university was the Buddhist monastery at Nalanda. Dormitories, libraries, lecture rooms, swimming pools, and observatories could all be found at Nalanda.

The classical culture in India was maintained for several centuries following the decline of the Guptas. And by the early

600's, an educated and cultured king named Harsha had again reunited much of northern India.

THE RISE OF HARSHA In 606, a 16-year-old Indian noble named Harsha came to power in a small kingdom in northern India. Determined to rule the entire subcontinent, Harsha began an organized campaign to bring the many separate kingdoms under his control. Within six years, Harsha extended his rule and controlled India from the Punjab to Bengal.

During Harsha's reign, a Chinese Buddhist pilgrim, Hsüan Tsang [shoo-AHN DZAHNG] traveled throughout India and recorded his observations, much like the Chinese traveler Fa-Hsien had done two centuries earlier. Hsüan Tsang became a close friend of the king and a member of the royal court. From Hsüan Tsang's writings, modern historians have learned much about the administration of Harsha's government. Many kings who had been defeated by Harsha were allowed to retain their thrones. However, they pledged their allegiance and paid taxes to Harsha's government.

Education was very important during the reign of Harsha. Monasteries provided free education for many. Teaching methods relied upon discussion and upon debate of such topics as medicine, philosophy, logic, and grammar. Harsha himself was educated and was an accomplished poet and playwright.

After Harsha's death in 647, his kingdom quickly broke up. Many of the smaller kingdoms that had made up Harsha's domain had been held together by the force of Harsha's personality. Without his stern hand, the kingdoms quickly became more independent. For five centuries after Harsha's death, India remained divided.

Following the breakup of Harsha's kingdom, members of a warrior class called the *Rajputs*—"sons of kings"—managed to maintain control of most of northwestern India for several centuries. The Rajputs were descendants of the central Asian barbarians who had entered India between the fifth and sixth centuries A.D. Accepted as part of the aristocratic warrior caste of India, the Rajputs have continued to form an important element in Indian society until present times.

By 1000, followers of *Islam*, a new religion that developed in lands to the west of India, had begun to invade the subcontinent (see Chapters 10 and 15). Two centuries later, these people had conquered all of northern India. As a result, the classical civilization of India underwent many further changes.

QUESTIONS FOR REVIEW

1 *Who was Fa-Hsien?*

2 *In what ways did the Gupta scholars add to the development of mathematics?*

3 *Why did Harsha's kingdom break up after his death?*

2 DYNASTIC CHINA UNDER THE HAN RULERS

After the rule of the Ch'in emperor Shih Huang-ti had ended in 210 B.C., another dynasty—the Han—was established. The Han dynasty ruled during a time of important cultural and intellectual development in China. Many of the patterns of later Chinese civilization were formed during this time. Moreover, the Han created a Chinese empire and expanded Han influence in all directions. As a result of this expansion, trade between China and western Asia began. This contact enriched many different cultures and peoples.

THE HAN DYNASTY During the late third century B.C., a Chinese empire was formed under the leadership of Shih Huang-ti (see Chapter 4). During Shih Huang-ti's brief reign China suffered greatly from the severe laws and heavy taxes imposed by the emperor. Public building projects, such as the Great Wall in northern China, also sapped the strength of the Chinese people. Following the death of Shih Huang-ti, the country erupted in rebellion. By 202 B.C., the revolts had been put down and a new dynasty—the Han—was established. Historians refer to this dynasty as the Western, or Former, Han.

Changan [CHAHNG-AHN], on a plain near the Wei River, was the site of the capital of the new dynasty (see map on page 158). Early Han rulers reorganized the country into principalities controlled by family members or by trusted generals. Moreover, an official emphasis was placed upon the philosophy of Confucianism (see Chapter 4). The influence of Confucianism on the government of China has continued throughout Chinese history.

By about 140 B.C., China had fully recovered from the turmoil of the third century B.C. Emperor Wu Ti then began to extend Han rule northward into Manchuria and into what is now Korea. The influence of the Han rulers also reached southward to the Red River, in modern-day Vietnam (see map on this page). In addition trade routes to western Asia were established. From the kingdoms of Bactria and Parthia, Chinese goods entered the Roman Empire along a route known as the Silk Road (see map on this page).

During the first century B.C., a series of poor rulers weakened the Han dynasty. In A.D. 9, Wang Mang, a member of a powerful Chinese family, seized control of the government. A popular Confucian scholar, Wang Mang had been appointed regent in A.D. 6 for an infant emperor. Three years later, Wang Mang declared himself emperor and founded a new dynasty. However, the new ruling house did not survive very long after his death.

Wang Mang began many reforms. The large estates owned by many Chinese nobles were divided among small farmers. Private slavery was ended for a time, and prices were fixed to protect people from profit-seeking merchants. Learning was also greatly encouraged. These reforms angered the wealthy and powerful elements of Chinese society, and as a result, Wang Mang was assassinated. The Han dynasty was reestablished and the imperial capital was moved eastward to Loyang.

During the early years of the reestablished dynasty, known to modern historians as the Eastern, or Later, Han dynasty, Chinese culture thrived and spread to new areas of the empire. Confucianism continued as the official government philosophy. Trade with the kingdoms of central and western Asia prospered. Weak leadership, however, eventually undermined the power of the Han rulers. And in 220, the dynasty collapsed.

THE GOVERNMENT OF IMPERIAL HAN CHINA The early Han rulers depended upon military leaders or family members to rule the provinces of China for the central government. Later, however, the emperors adopted the Confucian ideal that "only the most learned serve" and sought out scholars for government posts. Ability became

The Silk Road stretched across Asia to the Middle East. It was the major trade link between Han China and the Mediterranean world.

The Silk Road, c. Second Century A.D.

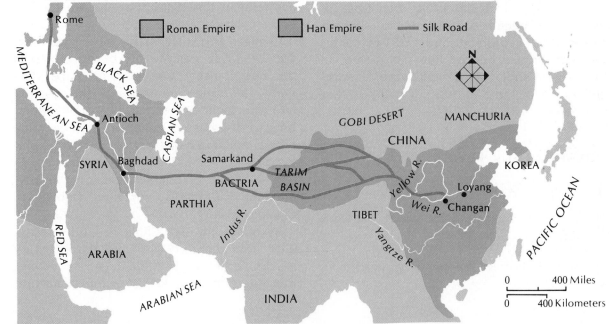

one of the most important requirements for those who sought public office. Talented individuals were recommended or recruited for service by local officials. A system of evaluating potential government workers based upon their knowledge of the Confucian *Classics* was also begun.

Education became very important in China at this time. A school for advanced studies was set up at the capital to train government officials. Education was also supported in the provinces by the Han rulers. Moreover, from the time of the earliest Han rulers, the ideas of Confucius shaped the official government philosophy. The study of the five Confucian *Classics*, which were entitled "History," "Odes," "Rites," "Changes," and "Spring and Autumn Annals," was required.

The central government of the Han was led by the emperor and a small circle of advisers. The government was further divided into several ministries, or departments. Frequently, two ministries were given the same functions or duties. In this way, the growth of power of each ministry was limited so that neither could gain more power than the other. Separate provincial governments, each headed by a governor and a military commander, ruled the outlying areas. Provincial officials were often checked by visiting government inspectors.

Local government officials were generally headquartered in walled towns. It was the local official's duty to collect taxes, to settle disputes, and to recruit individuals for military or for government service, or for the many public building projects. The imperial system formed under the Han continued without major changes into the present century.

THE SILK ROAD During the reign of Emperor Wu Ti, about 100 B.C., China's expansion reached the westernmost edge of the desolate Tarim Basin (see map on page 158). As a result, the Han came into direct contact with the fringes of the Hellenistic world, where knowledge of Greek culture had reached its farthest eastward advance. A prosperous trade was begun and eventually reached through many kingdoms from China to Rome. A Roman writer noted that during the latter part of the first century B.C., the elegant Cleopatra of Egypt owned a beautiful gown of silk. The cloth had probably been made from precious Chinese silk. By the end of the first century A.D., a Chinese army had reached the Caspian Sea. About 100 years later, according to Han historians, a Han traveler reached the shore of a "great sea" in the west. Many modern experts believe that "great sea" was a reference to the Black Sea.

The commerce between East and West crossed central Asia primarily along a route known as the Silk Road (see map on page 158). Caravans laden with goods made many stops as they wound their way through mountain passes and across arid plains. Raw silk, silk thread, silk cloth, furs, and cinnamon were among the goods sent westward by the Chinese. Traders from the West brought glass, jade, horses, ivory, pearls, diamonds, asbestos, wool, and linen to China. A sea route from India to China also existed, although little is known of its importance to trade between the two civilizations.

Historians also remain uncertain about the impact that these contacts with outsiders had upon China. Contact with the West may have influenced Han art and perhaps Chinese musical ideas as well. The increase in commerce probably sparked the development of Chinese trades and crafts. Certainly, the way was opened for the introduction of Buddhism from India, the land of its origin, to China.

CHINESE CIVILIZATION UNDER THE HAN As the Chinese came into contact with other peoples and cultures through trade and expansion, new ideas began to spread throughout the empire. In large part, Buddhism was brought to China in this way.

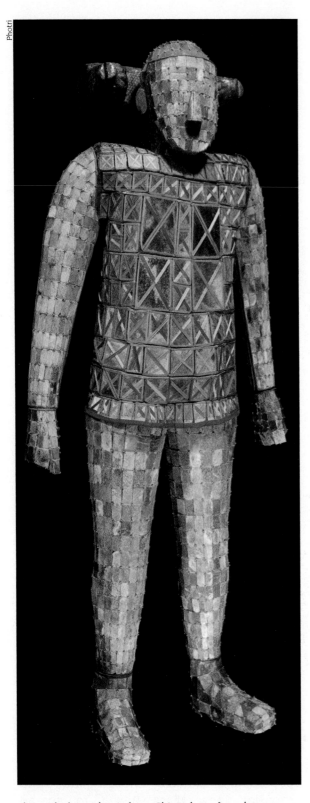

This jade funeral suit from China dates from late second-century B.C. It was made of 1,700 pieces of jade held together by gold thread.

Buddhist Kushans, the rulers of north-western India during the second and first centuries B.C., controlled lands along the trade routes between China and western Asia (see Chapter 3). As a result, Buddhism began to emerge in China during the first century A.D. Slowly, the religion grew in popularity. By A.D. 91, the first Chinese Buddhist temple had been erected. A century later, several thriving Buddhist communities existed in the Han capital of Loyang.

The Han dynasty brought a large measure of peace and prosperity to China. As a result, Chinese culture continued to develop steadily. The state philosophy of Confucianism, with its emphasis upon scholarship, stimulated learning and encouraged careful study of the *Classics*. By A.D. 100, the Chinese had begun to manufacture paper (see Myths and Realities, on page 161). They had also created a common script for writing. Many developments in literature took place as well. Poetry and new styles of prose flourished. The first history of China was written by Ssŭ-ma Ch'ien [SU-MAH chi-YEN]. Today, this relatively unbiased and well-written Chinese work is still being studied.

The period of the Han dynasty—202 B.C. to A.D. 220—established a style of Chinese government that lasted until the early 1900's. Chinese civilization had been vastly enriched during this time of intellectual and cultural development. Following the end of Han leadership, however, China slipped into nearly four centuries of uncertainty and warfare.

QUESTIONS FOR REVIEW

1 Who was the Emperor Wu Ti?

2 How did the selection of public officials change during the Han dynasty?

3 Why was education important during the Han dynasty?

Myths and Realities

Early Chinese Technology

For many years, modern Western scholars were reluctant to recognize many of the technological achievements of the ancient Chinese. Part of the reason for this view may have been the great gap in the level of technology in modern times between China and the West. It was easy for most Westerners to assume that the development of Western technology had always been fueled by the genius of Western science. Careful study in recent years, however, has led to a change from the old view that Chinese technology was historically inferior to Western technology.

Today, historians trace at least three important inventions —the magnetic compass, paper, and the earliest form of printing—to Han times. These inventions were not accidents, as many Westerners once believed. Rather, they were the result of careful observation and experimentation. In fact, many of these Chinese inventions did not reach Europe for several centuries.

By the beginning of the Han dynasty, and probably much earlier, the magnetic properties of lodestone—a type of iron ore—had been discovered. By about 100 B.C., an early form of magnetic compass was made by shaping a piece of lodestone into an object resembling a large spoon. When the spoon-shaped lodestone was placed on its base, the handle pointed south. Other directions could then be readily found. It also seems that at this time the Chinese knew that magnetic north was not true north.

Eventually, the Chinese developed a sensitive, magnetic steel needle to determine direction. This development probably occurred in the fifth century A.D., when the Chinese had developed a high degree of skill in making steel. At that time, the magnetic needle was either hung by a silk thread or floated in water to locate direction. The compass was used by Chinese soldiers and sailors and for such things as the laying out of city streets.

Around A.D. 105, the process of making paper was developed in Han China by Ts'ai Lun [TSY-LUN]. The fibers of the inner bark of the mulberry tree were pounded into flat sheets and dried to produce paper. The invention of paper also led to the development of printing. During the Han dynasty, pictures or inscriptions were carved into stone, and later into wood blocks. These objects were then inked and stamped onto paper. By 1000, an early form of movable type—separate characters made of clay—had been invented.

In later times, the Chinese developed many other important inventions that did not reach Europe for many centuries. For example, the stirrup, the crossbow, and a shoulder harness that enabled horses to pull great loads were among these inventions.

The process of making paper in ancient China began by boiling pulp from mulberry trees and then drying the mixture in sheets on a drying wall.

Photos by The Bettmann Archive

3 INTERNAL STRIFE AND THE REUNIFICATION OF CHINA

With the fall of the Han dynasty, China was plunged into four centuries of chaos and disorder. Barbarians from the fringes of China continually raided the northern part of China and eventually overthrew the Chinese rulers and gained control of vast areas. Gradually, however, the barbarians were totally assimilated into Chinese society. Also during this period, Buddhism became increasingly popular in China. For several centuries, Buddhism greatly influenced the development of Chinese culture. China was finally reunited in A.D. 589 under the Sui dynasty.

DISUNITY IN CHINA The last 30 years of the Han dynasty were filled with turmoil and destruction. Poor leadership had weakened the dynasty's power. As a result, rebellions were ignited throughout the empire. Rebel groups were formed that continually fought for control of the provinces. In 220, the last Han ruler was overthrown. Nearly 400 years passed before the Chinese were once again united under a single government.

After the fall of the Han dynasty, warfare continued as the rulers of small Chinese kingdoms struggled to win control of the entire country. At the same time, barbarians who occupied the vast arc of land stretching from Tibet to southern Manchuria began to raid northern China (see map on page 158). By the beginning of the fourth century A.D., much of northern China was under the control of barbarian tribes. Upheaval continued as one tribal chief after another seized power in northern China by force. During a period of less than 100 years, 16 kingdoms rose and fell in the north. The barbarian invasions caused many wealthy and aristocratic Chinese families to migrate southward. Some historians estimate that as many as 7 out of every 10 upper-class families in the north moved southward at this time.

During the next 200 years, the northern barbarian tribes adopted Chinese customs and language and were thus absorbed into China's culture. Intermarriage and laws passed by the barbarian rulers requiring the northern tribes to practice Chinese customs greatly speeded this process of assimilation.

South of the Yellow River, a succession of strong generals ruled from their capital near the site of the modern city of Nanking. By 589, China was united under a single ruling house—the Sui [SWI]. The centuries of disunity, rebellion, and invasion had ended.

THE GROWTH OF BUDDHISM IN CHINA
The 400 years of chaos in China that followed the fall of the Han dynasty were times of cultural development and change. During these years, the philosophy of Taoism was formed into a set of popular religious beliefs. Probably the most important development of this period, however, was the growing popularity and influence of Buddhism.

The basic ideas of Buddhism were formed in ancient India during the sixth and fifth centuries B.C. These ideas stressed escape from life through the attainment of *nirvana* (see Chapter 3). However, as early as the time of the Kushan rulers in India, Buddhism had been split into two sects. *Mahayana* Buddhism—meaning "greater vehicle"—emphasized life in the present. The believers in Mahayana Buddhism regarded Buddha as a *bodhisattva*—an individual who worked for the salvation of all beings after reaching nirvana. The goal of the bodhisattva was to help lead others to salvation. This was to be accomplished through charity and good works in this life. *Theraveda* Buddhism—called *Hinayana*, or "lesser vehicle," by its rivals—stressed the earlier, simpler teachings of Buddha. It was Mahayana Buddhism rather than Hinayana that became widespread in China and in other parts of Asia.

Chinese Classic Art
Publishing House, Peking

The Chinese mind has been, in large part, shaped by three philosophies. In this painting, a Confucian, a Buddhist, and a Taoist discuss the three ways and the wisdom and the toleration common to each.

Buddhism provided many Chinese with a guide for everyday living. It also promised a better world and salvation in an afterlife. Some historians estimate that by about 405 as many as 9 out of every 10 families in northern China followed Buddhism. The remaining families—mainly educated and upper-class—adhered to either Confucianist ideals or those of the Taoists. Later, Buddhism also reached the south.

Buddhism greatly influenced many aspects of Chinese culture. Literature, philosophy, and art all felt the impact of Buddhist ideas. In architecture, traditional Buddhist temples were gradually transformed into the Chinese *pagodas*.

THE REUNIFICATION OF CHINA UNDER THE SUI In 589, the ruler of northern China, Yang Chien, overwhelmed the kingdoms in the south and reunified the country. The conqueror established the Sui dynasty, which ruled China for the next 30 years. To bring all of China under a central government, Yang Chien reorganized the system of local governments. He appointed loyal officials to local posts. This helped to break the hold of powerful noble families on local affairs. As a result, local officials governed more effectively and remained loyal to their Sui rulers. National granaries were also built to store grain for times of famine and to better control grain prices.

Yang Chien began a canal system known as the Grand Canal that eventually brought together northern and southern China. By connecting ancient canals and existing rivers, the Grand Canal improved transportation and communication. In 611, Yang Chien's successor, Yang Ti, completed the canal system. The entire eastern region of China was finally linked together.

During his reign, Yang Ti built magnificent palaces and spent vast sums of tax money on military campaigns. Through these campaigns, Chinese rule was again extended south to the area of what is now Vietnam. Yang Ti also led three expensive and unsuccessful invasions of Korea.

Discontent with Yang Ti's policies and endless military campaigns grew. By 616, revolts had begun to break out in many parts of China. Two years later, Yang Ti was murdered and the Sui dynasty fell.

Although the Sui dynasty did not remain in power for very long, China had been reunified under its rule. Government reorganization and improved transportation and communications helped to pave the way for another great dynasty—the T'ang.

QUESTIONS FOR REVIEW

1 What group of people gained control of northern China by the beginning of the fourth century B.C.?

2 In what ways did Buddhism meet the everyday spiritual needs of the Chinese?

3 Why do you think many historians believe that the Sui dynasty laid a solid foundation for succeeding dynasties?

CHAPTER SUMMARY

The northern Indian empire known as the Gupta was founded in A.D. 320. During this golden age of Indian culture, Hinduism evolved into its present form. Hindu literature also flourished. Indian mathematicians, astronomers, surgeons, and other scientists also made great strides. By the middle of the seventh century, the Gupta Empire had disintegrated. Soon after, a strong leader named Harsha came to power in northern India. Indian civilization continued to flourish under this educated ruler. However, following Harsha's death in 647, India was divided into many smaller kingdoms, and the classical civilization of India declined.

In 202 B.C., the Han dynasty rose to power in China. Expansion by the Han rulers eventually brought China into contact with the West. Trade between China and western Asia prospered across the trade route known as the Silk Road. During the Han dynasty, Confucianism also became the official state philosophy.

The Han dynasty fell in A.D. 220 and four centuries of disorder followed. During this time, Buddhism became widely accepted throughout China. In 589, all of China was brought under a single government by the establishment of the Sui dynasty.

CHAPTER 8 IN REVIEW

IMPORTANT WORDS, NAMES, AND TERMS

1 Explain, define, or identify each of the following:

Chandragupta II	Hsüan Tsang	Ssǔ-ma Ch'ien
Fa-Hsien	Wu Ti	Nanking
Kalidasa	Wang Mang	Mahayana Buddhism
Aryabhata	Tarim Basin	Yang Ti

FACTS AND IDEAS

2 Who were the Huns?

3 What are Arabic numerals?

4 The Buddhist monastery at Nalanda was used for what purpose?

5 What were some of the goods traded between the East and the West by way of the Silk Road?

ANALYZING VISUAL MATERIAL

6 Study the map on page 153. Under which ruler did the Gupta Empire reach its greatest extent?

7 How does the painting on page 163 attempt to portray the harmony of Chinese philosophies?

CONCEPTS AND UNDERSTANDINGS

8 How did Fa-Hsien describe the government of the Gupta Empire under Chandragupta II?

9 In what ways did the Gupta scientists advance their knowledge of astronomy?

10 How did the rulers of the Han dynasty hope to improve the quality of government officials?

11 Prior to the founding of the Sui dynasty, how was the absorption of the northern barbarian tribes into Chinese society greatly speeded?

12 What was the significance of the Grand Canal that was built in China during the rule of the Sui?

PROJECTS AND ACTIVITIES

13 Prepare a chart or a bulletin-board display showing the steps by which paper was made during the Han dynasty.

14 Mathematics and science were areas of great achievement in Gupta India. Research and demonstrate for the class all or any one of the following: the importance of the zero, the significance of pi, the use of positive and negative numbers, and the calculation of solstices and equinoxes.

Using Geography Skills

The growth of efficient transportation networks during the era of the Roman Empire did much to build closer ties of communication and exchange throughout the classical Mediterranean world. Travelers and traders carried new ideas, inventions, and techniques to every corner of the far-flung empire. The Roman government, too, encouraged the spread of ideas by constructing roads, canals, harbors and docks, and lighthouses.

Geographic conditions greatly influenced the development of transportation routes—and therefore the spread of new ideas—during the classical era. In particular, the physical features—or landforms—of the empire played a major role in the development of trade and transportation networks. By studying a physical map of the Roman Empire, we can better analyze the geographic conditions that affected trade and travel in the classical world.

We can also understand more clearly the factors that promoted—or in some cases limited—the spread of classical ideas.

The physical map below shows the surface features and elevations of a portion of the Roman Empire. Study the map and the map key carefully. Then answer the following questions:

1 The city of Ledosus was an important pottery-producing center during the imperial era. According to the map, what was probably the fastest route for traders carrying pottery from Ledosus to Rome?

2 If you were a Roman merchant carrying goods overland to the city of Brundisium, what route would you take to reach your destination? Assuming the Valerian Way had not yet been built, where would you cross the mountains? Why? If you could travel an average of 18 miles (29 kilometers) a day, approximately how many days would you take to reach Brundisium?

3 Why do you think the Tiber River was so important to Roman economic life? In which general direction does the Tiber flow? Explain your answer.

4 What geographic obstacles did Roman engineers probably encounter when they built the Valerian Way?

5 What other city on the Italian Peninsula had nearly as favorable a geographic location and geographic conditions as Rome's? What geographic feature did Rome have that this city lacked?

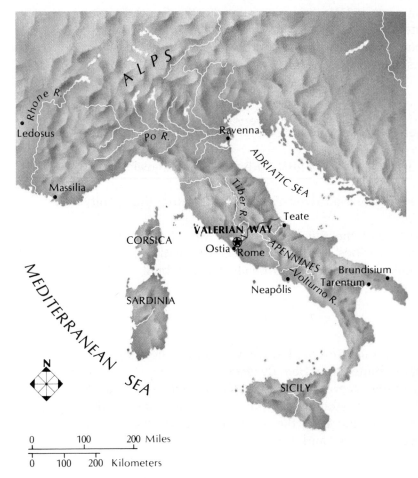

UNIT 2 IN REVIEW

CONCEPTS AND UNDERSTANDINGS

1 How did geography affect the earliest development of the Greek and Roman civilizations?

2 In what ways did the early republican government of Rome fail to represent all the people? How did the government of Rome change between 500 B.C. and 100 B.C.?

3 What were some of the important factors that led to the decline and fall of the Roman Empire?

4 What was the significance of the travels of Fa-Hsien and Hsüan Tsang?

QUESTIONS FOR DISCUSSION

1 The government of Athens is one of the first examples of a direct democracy—the participation of all citizens in the decisions of the government. Today, some people point out that it could be possible to use telecommunications to get immediate responses from all the citizens regarding proposed laws. Do you think that this form of democracy would be practical? Explain your answer.

2 Why do you think many historians argue that Roman civilization bound together the civilization of classical Greece with the developing European civilization?

3 Why do you think so many varied religious beliefs and philosophies, such as Buddhism, Taoism, and Confucianism, could exist side by side in the Chinese mind?

SUGGESTED READING

Evslin, Bernard. *Greeks Bearing Gifts: The Epics of Achilles and Ulysses.* New York: Scholastic Book Services, 1976.

Flagaur, Florence, and Mark Brokering, eds. *The First Christians: An Illustrated History of the Church.* Drury, John, tr. from Italian. Minneapolis: Winston Press, Inc., 1980.

Galbraith, Catherine A., and Rama Mehta. *India Now and Through Time.* Boston: Houghton Mifflin Co., 1980.

Hamey, L. A., and J. A. Hamey. *The Roman Engineers.* Minneapolis: Lerner Publications, 1981.

Lewis, Brenda R. *Growing Up in Ancient Rome.* North Pomfret, Vt.: David and Charles, Inc., 1980.

Nivedita, R., and Ananda K. Coomaraswamy. *Myths of the Hindus and Buddhists.* Mystic, Conn.: Lawrence Verry, Inc., 1972.

Stewart, Philippa. *Growing Up in Ancient Greece.* North Pomfret, Vt.: David and Charles, Inc., 1980.

Wilkes, John. *The Roman Army.* Minneapolis: Lerner Publications, 1977.

Wise, William. *Monster Myths of Ancient Greece.* New York: G.P. Putnam's Sons, 1981.

UNIT 3

CIVILIZATIONS IN TRANSITION

1000 B.C. to A.D. 1200

9 Early Africa and the Early Americas 10 The Byzantine and Islamic Civilizations 11 The Growth of Feudalism 12 Life in Feudal Europe

Fifteenth-century painting of a French castle

The interior of a Byzantine church, c. 650

Many important changes took place in Africa, the Americas, the Middle East, and Europe between 1000 B.C. and A.D. 1200. In Africa and the Americas, kingdoms emerged that grew powerful and achieved great cultural development. Some of these kingdoms lasted a short time, but others survived for several hundred years.

The collapse of the Western Roman Empire in A.D. 476 brought an end to Roman civilization in western Europe. The eastern half of the Roman Empire, however, survived for many centuries. At the same time, a new religion arose in the Middle East. Under this religion, the Arab peoples united and built a magnificent empire.

By the early 500's, Germanic peoples had settled in most of the lands that were once part of the Western Roman Empire. Within 300 years, a new and powerful Germanic empire had been built in these lands. A major factor in the development of the Germanic empire was the Catholic Church, which became an important social and political force in western Europe. After the Germanic empire declined, a time of disorder followed. Slowly, new political and economic systems emerged that helped restore stability in western Europe.

EPA

Mayan ruins at Chichén Itzá in Mexico

169

CHAPTER 9 EARLY AFRICA AND THE EARLY AMERICAS

1 Early African Kingdoms   2 Migration and Change in Eastern Africa   3 Early Life in the Americas   4 Early Civilizations in the Americas

Over 3,000 years ago, important changes began to take place within the vast continent of Africa. For example, rulers expanded their power, and kingdoms with great cities began to emerge. Trade was often an important factor in bringing about these changes.

In the Americas, too, many changes took place, but they began much earlier. Perhaps as long as 40,000 years ago people began a slow migration to the American continents. Over thousands of years, successive groups of people moved southward and eastward across the land. These groups settled in various regions of the Americas, and eventually developed important civilizations.

Christina Loke/Photo Researchers

The majestic, snow-capped peak of Mount Kilimanjaro in Kenya, East Africa, is the highest mountain on the African continent.

1 EARLY AFRICAN KINGDOMS

The great continent of Africa has many different geographical features and climatic conditions. These factors influenced early African peoples as powerful kingdoms began to develop about 3,000 years ago. These early African kingdoms had advanced ways of life. Governments were set up, great buildings were constructed, ways of writing were devised, and trade was begun with other parts of the world. Thus, the early kingdoms of Africa were influential in the development of human civilization.

THE GEOGRAPHY OF AFRICA Africa is an immense continent that covers about one fifth of the earth's land surface. Within this great continent are many different geographic features that have influenced the people of Africa for centuries. For example, in western and central Africa, a belt of tropical rain forests extends north and south from the equator (see map on this page). North and south of the rain forests are vast stretches of grassland known as the savanna. These lands, which cover about one fourth of Africa, tend to be dry for much of each year.

The African continent also contains huge deserts. The Kalahari [KAL-uh-HAHR-ee] and the Namib deserts are located in southern Africa. In addition, the largest desert in the world—the Sahara—is found in northern Africa. This huge expanse of sand and rock covers an area almost as large as the United States.

Many rivers flow through the vast African continent. For example, the longest river in the world—the Nile—is found in eastern Africa. This mighty waterway has been used for centuries as a transportation route between the Mediterranean Sea and the interior of Africa. In addition, annual floods have left rich deposits of topsoil many feet deep along parts of the Nile's course. Thus, the

Nile floodplains are among the world's most fertile farmlands. The other major rivers of Africa, such as the Niger, Congo, and Zambezi, are located south of the Sahara. Even though there are many rapids and waterfalls, these rivers are navigable for long stretches. Consequently, they have been used for travel through the interior of the land.

A few mountain ranges can be found in Africa, such as the Atlas Mountains in the northwest above the Sahara (see map on this page). Other mountain ranges are located in eastern and southern Africa. In addition to adapting to these different geographic features, Africans have also faced the challenge of living in different climatic conditions.

Africa's geographic features vary greatly. Deserts in the northern and southern areas give way to tropical rain forests in the central part of the continent. Much of Africa is ringed by highlands.

Africa

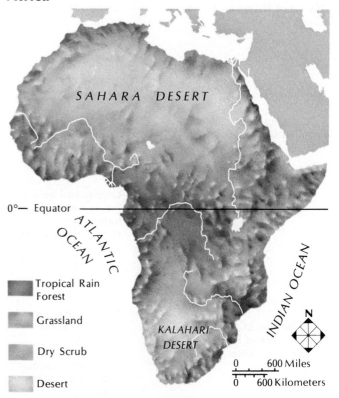

SAHARA DESERT

0°— Equator

ATLANTIC OCEAN

INDIAN OCEAN

Tropical Rain Forest

Grassland

Dry Scrub

Desert

KALAHARI DESERT

N

| 0 | | 600 Miles |
| 0 | | 600 Kilometers |

POLITICAL		SOCIAL AND ECONOMIC
	B.C.	
	c. 35,000	**Migration of first Americans across Bering Strait**
Ancestors of American Indians moved into Great Plains	*c.* 9000	**Cultivation of squash, beans, and peppers began in Americas**
	c. 1500	**Farming common in Central America**
Chavin civilization in South America	*c.* 1000	
Height of Kushite civilization (300 B.C.– A.D. 100)	*c.* 300	
Mochica culture in South America	*c.* 200	**Ironworking at Meroë in Africa**
	A.D.	
Emergence of Kingdom of Axum Ghana founded	*c.* 100	**Start of Bantu migrations**
Destruction of Meroë Height of Mayan civilization (A.D. 300–900)	*c.* 300	**Christianity reached Axum**
	c. 500	**Decline of Axum's trade**
Soninke people controlled Ghana	*c.* 700	
	c. 1000	**Copper and gold mining by Bantus in Zimbabwe** **Great Zimbabwe built**
	1324	**Pilgrimage to Mecca by Mansa Musa**
Decline of Mali Empire of Monomotapa emerged	*c.* 1400	
	c. 1500	**Portuguese traders sailed into Indian Ocean**

CLIMATE AND CULTURE People have lived in Africa for thousands of years, even though the climate in much of the continent tends to be very warm. Thus, the way of life of the African peoples has been influenced to a great extent by the different climates of the land. For example, the hot and dry desert regions are not suitable for farming. As a result the peoples of the deserts have turned to animal herding as a way of life. Bordering the African deserts is the dry savanna. Rainfall is very light in these lands, and the dry season lasts for about nine months each year. The people in these areas have become nomadic cattle herders, since little can be grown on the dry lands.

On the other hand, heavy rains in the tropical areas of Africa erode the soil and dissolve the minerals in the ground through a process called *leaching*. The process of leaching results in soil that is poor and easily exhausted. Thus, the Africans of the tropical lands have moved often as they looked for good soil in which to grow crops.

The best soils and the most favorable weather conditions are found in the highland regions of eastern, central, and southern Africa. Over the years, these lands have become heavily populated because of the good soil and climate.

As Africans have adapted to their environment, two major ways of life have emerged. One way of life is based on farming, and the other is based on cattle herding. Sometimes these life-styles have been combined, but in general, cattle herding has been found in the drier lands where there is little farming.

Just as different ways of life have developed among Africans, so too have different language groups. A language group is composed of peoples who may be scattered geographically but who share similar language patterns and cultural traits. Language groups have played an important role in African history. One of the largest language groups is the Bantu group, which consists of different languages that are related. Swahili is one of the most important Bantu lan-

The way of life of African cattle-herders has changed little since these massive Kushite pyramids were constructed about 2,000 years ago.

guages, since it is spoken by many of the peoples of eastern and central Africa. Thus, African peoples have developed many different ways of life over the years as they adapted to their environment.

THE EARLY AFRICAN SCENE Recent studies have shown that Africa was probably one of the first areas in the world where human beings lived. The earliest peoples of Africa lived by hunting and by food gathering. Later, as agriculture became important, more-complex ways of life emerged among many African peoples.

The development of agriculture in Africa helped to stimulate the rise of permanent villages. As early African village dwellers learned to work together to meet their needs, new ways of organizing people began to emerge. For example, governments were set up, and social classes and specialized occupations began to develop. Eventually, kingdoms began to appear in different areas of Africa.

One of the first and most impressive African kingdoms was that of Egypt (see Chapter 2). But there were also other kingdoms in ancient Africa. Until recently, little was known about many of these kingdoms, but continuing research has uncovered new information about these early civilizations. And as studies continue, the important contributions of the early African civilizations will become more clearly understood.

KUSH AND AXUM One of the earliest kingdoms that developed in Africa was the kingdom of Kush. Kush was located along the Nile River south of Egypt in a region of Africa called Nubia (see map on page 175).

Kushite civilization reached its highest level between the third century B.C. and the first century A.D. Trade between the Red Sea, Egypt, the Mediterranean Sea, and the interior of Africa passed through Meroë [MER-uh-WEE], the capital of Kush. This trade brought ideas from other cultures to the city. Since the lands around Meroë had

173

an abundance of iron ore and of wood to provide fuel to melt the ore, the city became one of the first ironworking centers in Africa. In addition, the Kushite civilization was very advanced in that the people built great temples and palaces and developed a system of alphabetical writing.

By the third century A.D., the kingdom of Kush grew weak. In the fourth century A.D., armies from the neighboring kingdom of Axum invaded Kush and destroyed the city of Meroë.

The kingdom of Axum emerged during the first century A.D. The capital of Axum became an important trade center, since it straddled major trade routes that went from the interior of Africa to the port city of Adulis on the Red Sea (see map on page 175).

During the fourth century, Christianity was introduced into Axum. After the conversion of Axum's King Ezana, Christianity became the official religion of the kingdom.

By the fifth century, Axum had become a culturally advanced commercial and military power. Caravans arrived frequently with goods from different areas of Africa. The Axumites built impressive fortresses and palaces with huge columns and elaborate walls.

Late in the sixth century, the Persians conquered Arabia, which was across the Red Sea from Axum (see map on page 175). As a result, Axum's trade along the Red Sea declined, since the trade routes were no longer secure.

By the seventh century, Axum was surrounded by Muslim powers (see Chapter 10). For the next few centuries Axum struggled with its rivals for land, but its power continued to decline. Axum's political power faded, but much of its culture survived and became the basis of the kingdom of Ethiopia.

GHANA The ancient kingdom of Ghana, like Kush and Axum, developed over many centuries. Ghana was located in western Africa northeast of the Senegal River and northwest of the Niger River (see map on page 175). Although the exact origins of Ghana are uncertain, experts believe that it was founded sometime between A.D. 100 and A.D. 300, when Berber nomads from North Africa invaded the area and set up a kingdom. The Berbers ruled for several centuries, but around A.D. 700, the Soninke [suhn-IN-kay] people of Ghana revolted and established their control over the land. Under the Soninke rulers, Ghana became the first great West African kingdom in the Sudan—an area south of the Sahara.

An important factor in Ghana's rise to power was the development of trade in western Africa. Many different goods passed through Ghana, but salt and gold, as well as slaves, were important items in the kingdom's trade. Salt, which was scarce in the western Sudan, was brought into Ghana from the Sahara and exchanged for gold taken from mines controlled by the Soninke rulers. This flourishing trans-Saharan trade was important because the goods that passed through Ghana were heavily taxed. These tax revenues were then used to support the government and to maintain peace and stability throughout the kingdom.

Between the eighth and the tenth centuries, Ghana's power increased, and by the eleventh century, Ghana had become a large empire. This empire encompassed lesser kingdoms that had been brought under Ghana's control by military force.

Ghana's king was considered a god by his people. As befitted a god-king, the royal palace in the Ghanaian capital of Kumbi Saleh [KUM-bee SAY-luh] was elaborately decorated with fine sculptures and paintings. Muslims who visited Ghana were deeply impressed by the magnificence and ceremony at the court of Ghana's kings. Although Ghana was not a Muslim kingdom, Muslims were welcomed. In fact, many Muslims lived in the capital, where they served as merchants, interpreters, and government officials.

Ancient Kingdoms of Africa

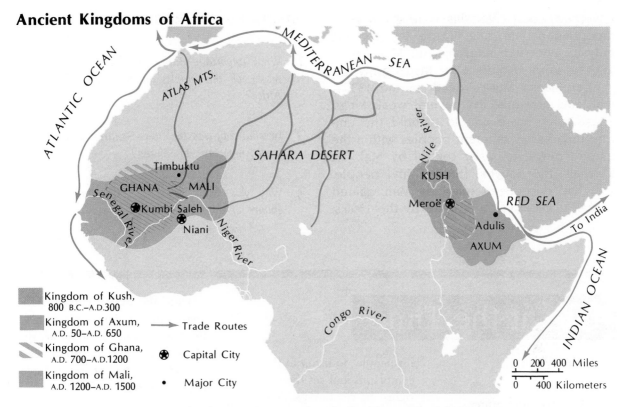

Traders faced the dangers of sea travel or the hardships of the Sahara Desert to reach the ancient kingdoms of Africa.

By the middle of the eleventh century, neighboring kingdoms were jealous of Ghana's power. A North African Muslim sect—the Almoravids [AL-muh-RAH-vuhdz]—attacked and captured Kumbi Saleh in 1076. Although Almoravid control was short-lived, the attack seriously weakened Ghana. Trade was disrupted and some of the kingdoms under Ghana's control declared their independence. During the 1200's, the empire of Ghana disintegrated. It was replaced by Mali, a new imperial power that emerged in western Africa.

MALI With the breakup of Ghana in the early 1200's the West African kingdom of Mali began to expand. Under the leadership of Sundiata [sun-di-AH-tah], Mali gained control of surrounding lands that had once been ruled by Ghana. By the mid-1200's, Mali had become the greatest imperial power in western Africa.

Sundiata expanded Mali's boundaries and set up a central government. The capital was moved to the city of Niani, which became a center of trade. The government encouraged trade, especially the profitable gold-for-salt trade. Mali's rulers adopted the earlier Ghanaian practice of taxing this trade to provide revenue for the government.

In the early 1300's, Mali's greatest emperor, Mansa Musa, came to power. This remarkable ruler extended Mali's borders through diplomacy and conquest. In addition, Mansa Musa encouraged cultural progress in Mali. For example, great *mosques* —buildings for Muslim worship—and palaces were built in several cities. The thriving city of Timbuktu attracted Muslim African scholars and became a thriving center of learning.

Mali's rulers successfully controlled a large empire of diverse peoples. This was because of the way that the empire was

175

governed. Local chieftains were given great independence to rule. These leaders had only to give their allegiance to Mali's ruler and to supply soldiers for Mali's army.

After Mansa Musa's death in the 1330's, Mali was governed by several weak kings. These rulers were unable to hold the empire together as different peoples within the empire began to resist control by Mali. As a result, the Songhai [SAWNG-hiy] people, who had once been ruled by Mali, gained control of most of the empire by the 1500's.

QUESTIONS FOR REVIEW

1 What important Bantu language is spoken by many of the peoples of eastern and central Africa?

2 In what way was the trans-Saharan gold-for-salt trade important to Ghana?

3 Why was Mali successful in ruling a large empire of diverse peoples?

Life at the Time

Imperial Ghana

By the eleventh century, Ghana was a powerful empire in the western part of Africa. People who visited Ghana at that time were often dazzled by the glittering wealth of Ghana's kings. In 1067, an Arab named Abdullah al Bekri visited the ancient African empire. Following his visit, al Bekri vividly described an audience that he had witnessed given by King Tenkaminen of Ghana. According to the visitor's account:

"The king who governs them [the people of Ghana] at present . . . is called Tenkaminen; . . . Tenkaminen is the master of a large empire and a formidable [strong] power . . . The king of Ghana can put two hundred thousand warriors in the field, more than forty thousand being armed with bow and arrow . . .

"When he gives audience to his people, to listen to their complaints and set them to rights, he sits in a pavilion [large tent] around which stand ten pages [young attendants] holding shields and gold-mounted swords: and on his right hand are the sons of the princes of his empire, splendidly clad [dressed] and with gold plaited [woven] into their hair. The governor of the city is seated on the ground in front of the king, and all around him are his viziers [advisers] in the same position. The gate of the chamber is guarded by dogs of an excellent breed, who never leave the king's seat: they wear collars of gold and silver, ornamented with the same metals. The beginning of a royal audience is announced by the beating of a kind of drum which they call *deba*, made of a long piece of hollowed wood. The people gather when they hear this sound . . ."

Thus, the king of Ghana appeared before the people to settle their disputes amid an array of attendants and wealth. Such magnificence had obviously impressed al Bekri.

Many African people used gold to make jewelry and other ornamental objects. This finely detailed gold weight is from the West African kingdom of Ghana.

The Collections of the University Museum, Philadelphia

2 MIGRATION AND CHANGE IN EASTERN AFRICA

Almost twenty centuries ago, a great migration of people began through much of Africa. This movement took place gradually and spanned hundreds of years, as people moved slowly from one location to another in the African continent. As these people moved, they adapted to new conditions and helped to bring about changes that eventually affected much of central, eastern, and southern Africa.

THE BANTU MIGRATION Among the many different language groups in early Africa were the Bantu-speaking peoples. The Bantus began a great migration through central, eastern, and southern Africa about 2,000 years ago. Small groups of Bantus left their homeland in the Benue [BAYN-way] River valley and began moving into the Congo River basin (see map on this page). Some experts believe that this migration was due to a rapid increase in the population, which caused the Bantus to look for lands on which to grow more food.

As the Bantus migrated through the African continent, they helped to spread their knowledge of ironworking and of farming to other peoples in Africa. During the migration, the Bantus sometimes encountered less advanced societies that were usually absorbed peacefully. Sometimes, however, these societies resisted the Bantus. Such groups were often defeated and forced to move to less desirable lands.

During the great migration, which spanned many centuries, the Bantu culture spread through much of Africa. Life for the Bantus usually centered around several villages ruled by a chief, who was assisted by a council of elders. The chief and the elders interpreted and defined the laws that governed conduct among the Bantu peoples. Some Bantu groups, who believed that they

The Bantu Migration

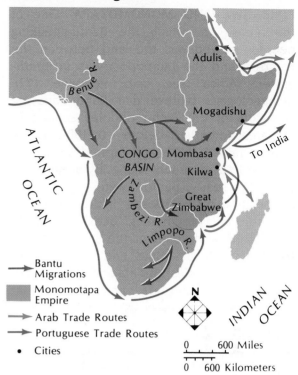

Bantu migration routes across Africa were often determined by geographic features. The East African coastal city-states settled by Bantu peoples after about A.D. 100 quickly became active trade centers.

were descendants of a common ancestor, formed loosely united kingdoms.

Some experts believe that during the fourth century, the Bantus reached the coast of eastern Africa along the Indian Ocean. As the Bantus dispersed in this area, they encountered new foods that had been brought to eastern Africa by sailors from Southeast Asia. Such foods as the banana, Asian yam, and cocoyam, or taro, grew well in the tropical regions of Africa.

The Bantu migration through central, eastern, and southern Africa was one of the greatest movements of people in history. Eventually about one third of the African continent became the home of Bantu-speaking peoples. And many of the kingdoms that developed in central and eastern Africa during the first *millennium*—thousand years—A.D. were in lands settled by the Bantus.

177

ZIMBABWE AND MONOMOTAPA One of the areas into which the Bantu-speaking peoples moved was the land between the Zambezi and the Limpopo rivers in south-eastern Africa (see map on page 177). Archaeologists believe that Bantu-speaking ancestors of the Sotho peoples settled in the area sometime before A.D. 1000. These people raised cattle and farmed, and they were skilled in metalworking. By around A.D. 1000, the early Bantus were mining the copper and gold deposits of the region. As a result of the mining activities, trade developed with some of the port cities on the Indian Ocean. Gold and copper were sent to these cities and traded for goods—such as cotton, brass, and beads—that came from as far away as India.

The outer walls of the ruins of Great Zimbabwe were built without cement and, in places, were 17 feet (5 meters) thick.

P. Raba/ZEFA

About 900 years ago another group of Bantu-speaking peoples moved into the lands between the Zambezi and Limpopo rivers. The newcomers were probably the ancestors of the Shona people. They took over the trading activities and drove out the Sotho people, who went farther south in Africa.

Archaeologists believe that sometime between the eleventh century and the thirteenth century, the Bantu-speaking peoples of the area began building great stone structures enclosed by walls. Some of the buildings within the walls were apparently used for worship while others served as the king's palace. Research has led scholars to conclude that the Bantu king was looked upon as a god who lived away from the common people. The most spectacular of these ancient structures is known as Great Zimbabwe [zim-BAHB-wee]. Some of its buildings are still standing today.

During the 1400's, one of the powerful Bantu-speaking groups, the Shonas, began building the empire of Monomotapa [mah-noh-muh-TAH-puh] between the Zambezi and Limpopo rivers. The Shonas were divided into many different *clans*—groups of families descended from a common ancestor. The ruler of one of the clans, King Mutota [moo-TOH-tuh], conquered surrounding lands and dominated trading activities through taxes on imports and exports. Following the death of Mutota's son, the empire quickly declined as rival clans fought for power. By the late 1500's, Europeans who had traded with the city-states on the coast of eastern Africa (see Chapter 19) began to assert their control over the once-powerful empire of Monomotapa.

EAST AFRICAN CITY-STATES An important factor in the development of city-states in eastern Africa was the growth of trade. Sometime between A.D. 100 and 1000, Bantu-speaking peoples migrated to the coast of eastern Africa and settled in villages along the Indian Ocean (see map on page 177). Since ancient times, such villages had exchanged goods from Africa for goods from other areas of the world.

During the centuries of settlement, the Bantus came into contact with traders, settlers, explorers, and adventurers from the Middle East and from Asia. As a result of the mixture of the cultures of these peoples with that of the Bantus, a unique civilization—Swahili [swah-HEE-lee]—emerged in eastern Africa. Although the Swahili civilization was mainly African, it was heavily influenced by the culture of the Arab Muslims (see Chapter 10) who settled along the coast of eastern Africa sometime between the seventh and ninth centuries. For example, the Swahili language spoken today is a mixture of Bantu and of Arabic.

As trade between eastern Africa, the Middle East, and Asia expanded, the eastern coastal trading villages grew into towns, and some developed into city-states. Mombasa [mahm-BAHS-uh], Mogadishu [MAHG-uh-DISH-oo], and Kilwa became prosperous trading centers where gold, iron, copper, ivory, and palm oil from the interior of Africa were exchanged for cloth from India and porcelain from China. The merchants in these cities grew wealthy from the increasing trade. In addition, the rulers prospered from the taxes that were levied on trading privileges and on imports and exports.

During the 1500's, however, Portuguese traders sailed into the Indian Ocean and gained control of the East African coast (see Chapter 16). As the Indian Ocean trade came under Portuguese domination, the city-states of eastern Africa entered a period of decline.

QUESTIONS FOR REVIEW

1 *Into what areas of Africa did the Bantu-speaking peoples move during the Bantu migration?*

2 *How did King Mutota build the empire of Monomotapa?*

3 *Why did the city-states of eastern Africa decline during the 1500's?*

The extensive ruins of Kilwa show that this city-state was one of the most active commercial centers on the east coast of Africa.

Marc and Evelyne Bernheim/Woodfin Camp

3 EARLY LIFE IN THE AMERICAS

Most archaeologists believe that the American continents were completely uninhabited until about 50,000 years ago. Then slowly, groups of people started moving to the Americas from Asia. Scholars, however, are not certain when this migration began. Over thousands of years, people filtered through North America, and into Central America and South America. These first Americans moved about as they inhabited the vast continents and adapted to the different geographic and climatic conditions that were encountered. Eventually, some of the early peoples began settling in permanent villages as farming began to emerge as a way of life among early Americans.

ORIGINS OF THE EARLIEST AMERICANS
Archaeologists are not certain when the first humans came to the Americas. Many scholars believe that migration to the American continents may have started sometime between 12,000 and 40,000 years ago. At times during that period, large areas of North America, as well as Europe and Asia, were covered with thick ice sheets. Because enormous quantities of water were locked in these vast ice sheets, the water level of the world's oceans was much lower than today. As a result, a great land bridge connecting Siberia in Asia and Alaska in North America was exposed (see map on page 183).

Experts believe that the land bridge was used by people to migrate to the Americas from Asia. Small bands of roving hunters may have crossed the land bridge as they followed the various animals that were a source of food. The migration was a slow process that lasted for thousands of years. Groups of people drifted slowly southward and eastward from Alaska through mountain passes and river valleys. Eventually, people filtered southward into the heart of North America and then into Central and South America.

As early peoples moved through the Americas, a gradual warming of the climate began throughout the world. The great ice sheets gradually melted, and the oceans began to rise. Perhaps around 10,000 years ago, the land bridge disappeared beneath the rising water. Thus, Asia and North America were separated by a narrow sea passage that today is known as the Bering Strait.

Many scholars believe that after the land bridge disappeared, the early peoples of the Americas were isolated from contact with the rest of the world. However, other experts think that people from Asia may have continued to cross the Bering Strait in crude boats after the disappearance of the land bridge. Some scholars have even suggested that as late as A.D. 1000, there may have been contact between the Americas and islands in the Pacific Ocean. As the American continents were slowly inhabited, the early peoples gradually adapted to the new environments in which they settled.

GEOGRAPHY AND CLIMATE The early peoples who trekked through the American continents for thousands of years encountered a variety of climatic and geographic conditions. One of the first geographic obstacles was the vast mountain ranges that extend from the Arctic Ocean to the tip of South America. Today, these mountains are known by various names—the Rockies in North America, the Sierra Madre in Central America, and the Andes in South America. Gradually, most of the early peoples moved into the valleys of these mountain ranges or crossed them into areas of the Americas that were more hospitable.

Some of the early peoples, however, remained in the frigid climate of the far northern regions near the Arctic Ocean. These groups lived by hunting such animals as seals, caribou, and walrus, and by fishing. Other groups who moved to areas close to

A mammoth struggles to escape from early American hunters, whose spears are tipped with flint points like the one shown in the inset.

the Pacific Ocean or near the lakes and rivers of the interior or to eastern North America also hunted and fished.

The interior region east of the Rockies was a vast expanse of forests and grasslands. Giant moose, musk-oxen, and mammoths roamed through this region while mastodons wandered through parts of eastern North America. In addition to the abundance of animals, the early peoples discovered that the interior of North America had another advantage. The great waterways of the interior such as the Missouri and the Mississippi rivers could be used to travel from one area of the continent to another.

Few of the early peoples moved into the dry areas of North America, Central America, and South America. These regions had little plant or animal life to support human populations. In addition, areas of Central and South America close to the equator had few people because the hot and humid climate of these regions made living difficult. Thus, most of the early peoples in the Americas moved to lands where the temperatures were moderate or where the climate varied from season to season. Eventually, farming began to emerge in some of these areas as many of the early peoples endeavored to meet their need for food.

FARMING IN THE AMERICAS Archaeologists believe that farming in the Americas probably began in the highlands of central Mexico. Thousands of years ago, the people of that region lived by hunting small animals and by gathering wild plants and

181

seeds. Gradually, these early peoples became increasingly reliant on plants for food. But over the centuries, the early Americans discovered that some plants grew better than others. These people also found that more plants could be grown by planting seeds rather than by depending only on wild plants. Thus, sometime between 9000 and 5000 B.C., early Americans learned to cultivate such plants as squash, avocados, beans, and peppers.

Scholars believe that many centuries later —perhaps between 5000 and 3000 B.C.—the peoples of central Mexico began raising a type of corn called maize. This maize was not like the corn grown today, for the cobs and kernels were very small. Over the centuries, an improved kind of maize with large cobs and kernels was developed.

As farming became more widely practiced, many of the early peoples in America began to settle in permanent farming villages. The lands around these villages could provide more food for people than was possible when they wandered from place to place. As a result, populations may have increased, since food supplies were more reliable.

By 1500 B.C., farming was fairly common throughout much of Central America. From these areas, farming eventually spread into North America and South America and influenced the developing cultures of those vast continents.

QUESTIONS FOR REVIEW

1 *What was the probable reason for the disappearance of the land bridge that scholars believe once connected Asia and North America?*

2 *How did early Americans use the great waterways of the interior of North America?*

3 *Why might populations among early Americans have increased after people began to settle in permanent farming villages?*

4 EARLY CIVILIZATIONS IN THE AMERICAS

The peoples who moved into the vast emptiness of the American continents centuries ago eventually were called Indians. This name was the result of an error made by the European explorer Christopher Columbus when he came to the Americas in the late 1400's. At that time, Columbus mistakenly believed that he had reached the Indies in Asia, and he called the native Americans that he met Indians. Since then, the native Americans have been known by that name.

Over the centuries, the early Indians settled in many different regions of the Americas and adapted to the various conditions they encountered. And as the Americas were inhabited, some remarkably advanced Indian civilizations developed and then declined.

EARLY CULTURES OF THE FAR NORTH
The early peoples who remained in the cold regions of the far north faced difficult living conditions. These people settled in the lands south of the Arctic Circle to the present boundary between the United States and Canada (see map on page 183). In time, the early peoples who settled in these frigid lands came to be known as Arctic Indians or Eskimos.

Although the Eskimos lived in areas where the environment was extremely harsh, these people adapted to their surroundings and made use of the few resources they found. For example, the Eskimos hunted and ate seals, walrus, caribou, and reindeer. The Eskimos also ate fish and, in some areas, gathered wild berries for food. The skins of fur-bearing animals were made into clothing by the Eskimos to protect themselves from the bitter cold. In addition, sealskins were used as the covering for the one-person canoes—called *kayaks*—that the Eskimos used to hunt and to fish. This

Early Indian Migrations

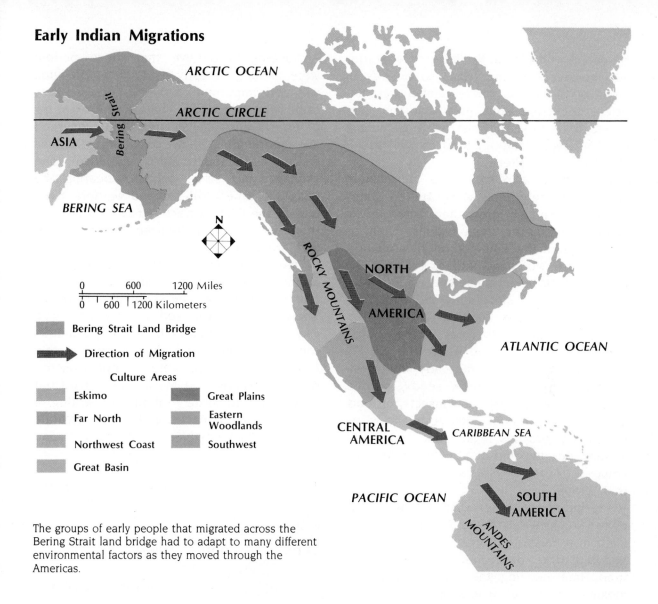

The groups of early people that migrated across the Bering Strait land bridge had to adapt to many different environmental factors as they moved through the Americas.

dependence on animals forced the Eskimos to spend much of their time moving from place to place as they followed the animals that were used for food and clothing.

The Eskimos made further use of the resources of their environment in the shelters that they built for protection from the harsh weather. In the summer, tents were made from animal skins stretched over poles. During the bitterly cold Arctic winters, shelters were made from stones, driftwood, and sometimes from logs. In some areas of northern Canada, the Eskimos used blocks of ice and snow to build unique dome-shaped shelters known as *igloos*.

Thus, the Eskimos were able to survive in the harsh conditions of the northern regions of the Americas because of their adaptation to the environment. Other Indians also faced the challenge of adaptation as they moved into different areas of the Americas.

INDIANS OF THE UNITED STATES The Indians of the United States settled in five areas—the Great Plains, the Eastern Woodlands, the Southwest, the Great Basin, and the Northwest Coast. Archaeologists think that ancestors of the Indians may have moved into the interior grasslands—the Great Plains—of the United States about 11,000 years ago. At that time, the early Plains Indians secured food by hunting and by eating wild plants. By the early centuries A.D., however, farming began to emerge in areas of the Plains where rainfall was sufficient for crops. But many Indians continued to rely on the vast herds of buffalo on the Great Plains for food as well as for clothing and shelter.

The Indians who moved to the eastern and southeastern areas of the United States hunted in the lush forests and fished in the rushing streams of these regions. Then, as farming gradually emerged in these lands, the Eastern Woodland Indians began living in villages. However, these settlements were not permanent, since the Indians often moved when soils became unproductive.

In the southwestern areas of the United States, the Indians lived where the climate was dry. Consequently, the early southwestern Indians depended on seeds, berries, reptiles, rodents, birds, and insects for food. Then, perhaps around 2,500 years ago, farming spread into this region from Mexico. As farming became important, the Indians developed irrigation systems to bring water to their crops.

The Indians who moved to the lands west of the Rockies called the Great Basin also lived in a harsh, dry environment. Scattered bands of Great Basin Indians spent most of their time roaming the area hunting and looking for edible plants and insects. On the other hand, the Indians of the Pacific Northwest encountered a more hospitable environment. These people hunted game animals in the forests and fished in the waters of the region.

Thus, the early Indians of North America were able to survive by adapting and by utilizing the resources of their surroundings. At the same time, other Indian groups were developing important civilizations in Central America.

EARLY INDIANS OF CENTRAL AMERICA
One of the oldest Indian civilizations in Central America was that of the Olmecs in what is now Mexico (see map on this page).

Archaeologists believe that these people were farming as early as 1200 B.C. Religion was very important to the Olmecs, for they built large ceremonial centers where groups of priests and officials lived and governed the surrounding farm populations. These centers contained temples, immense stone carvings, and stone columns bearing the images of chiefs, priests, and warriors. Even though the Olmecs declined around 200 B.C., their way of life influenced other cultures that arose later in Central America.

One of the most impressive of the early Indian civilizations in Central America was that of the Maya (see map on this page). These people achieved a very advanced way of life by around A.D. 300. For example, the Maya built huge religious centers that contained highly decorated temples on top of flat pyramids. The Maya also worked out a complicated system of picture writing, a system of mathematics, and a very accurate calendar. The movements of the sun and

The ancient tribes of Central America and South America lived in mountainous areas or close to the sea.

Early Indian Tribes of Central and South America

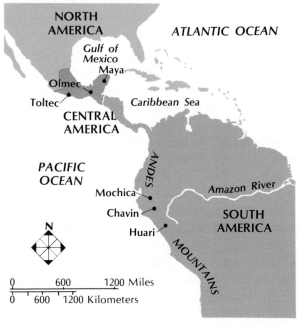

Robert Frerck/Odyssey Productions

A huge carved head (above) shows the artistic skill of the Olmec Indians, and the impressive ruins of a great temple (left) reflect the power and might of the Mayan empire of Central America.

the moon were carefully watched by Mayan astronomers, who could predict solar and lunar eclipses. Sometime after A.D. 900, the Maya began to decline for reasons that are still unknown. Some scholars have speculated that an increase in the population along with overuse of the soil brought on a food crisis, which led to revolts against the priests who were the rulers of the Maya. Thus, by the 1200's, the Maya were no longer a dominant civilization in Central America.

Another important Indian culture in Central America was that of the Toltecs, who lived west of the Maya in what is now central Mexico (see map on page 184). Like the Olmecs and the Maya, the Toltecs built pyramids and carved stone statues. The Toltecs were also the first people in Central America to do skilled work in gold and copper. By the 1200's, internal conflicts, disease, and pressure from outside peoples led to the decline of the Toltecs. Thus, Central America was affected by the rise and fall of three important civilizations

between 1200 B.C. and A.D. 1200. At the same time, other Indian cultures developed in South America.

EARLY INDIANS OF SOUTH AMERICA
One of the earliest Indian cultures that developed in South America was the Chavin [CHAY-veen] culture. This farming civilization developed in the Andes Mountains of what is now Peru sometime close to 1000 B.C. The Chavin people built ceremonial centers similar to those of the Indians of Central America. These centers had great platformlike temples decorated with stone carvings of animals and humans. Experts believe that the Chavins may have worshipped a jaguar-god, since figures of such a creature have been found in the ruins of Chavin temples and on Chavin pottery and textiles. The Chavins were also skilled in metalworking, for they made plaques, necklaces, and rings from copper and gold. The Chavin culture declined around 200 B.C. as different groups competed for land and for power in the Andes.

185

About the same time that the Chavin culture was declining, the Mochica [moo-CHEE-kuh] Indian culture was emerging along the north coast of what is now Peru. The Mochicas were farmers, and they developed irrigation systems to water their fields. Much has been learned about the Mochicas from their pottery. These vessels were often decorated with scenes from the daily life of the people. Archaeologists believe that the Mochicas were governed by a powerful ruling class of warrior-priests. These rulers controlled Mochica lands by building numerous forts that were connected by roads. The Mochica culture began to decline sometime around A.D. 600 as other Indian groups in the Andes expanded.

After A.D. 600, the Huari [WAH-ree] peoples dominated much of the coastal and highland areas of what is now Peru, probably through military force. These people constructed stone buildings and worked in metals. The Huari empire began to break apart during the 800's, and by the year 1000 Huari rule had disappeared. Thus, by the end of the first millennium A.D., many important civilizations in Central America and in South America had risen and then declined. However, the greatest Indian civilizations of the Americas—the Aztecs and the Incas—began to emerge sometime during the 1100's and 1200's (see Chapter 19).

QUESTIONS FOR REVIEW

1 What were some of the animals that the early Eskimos used for food?

2 In what ways were the Toltecs similar to the Olmecs and the Mayas?

3 Why did some of the early Indian cultures of South America decline?

CHAPTER SUMMARY

Several important kingdoms developed in different areas of Africa many centuries ago. For example, the kingdom of Kush had one of the first ironworking centers in Africa, and Axum was an important trade center. Ghana and Mali were other powerful kingdoms in early Africa. Trade was important in these ancient kingdoms, and they were known for their cultural achievements.

About 2,000 years ago, a great migration of Bantu-speaking peoples through central, southern, and eastern Africa began. Some important kingdoms and city-states developed in the lands to which the Bantus moved. For example, prosperous city-states emerged along the east coast of Africa. These city-states became wealthy through their control of trade between the interior of Africa and other parts of the world.

Thousands of years earlier, people from Asia gradually began to migrate to the Americas. These early American Indians successfully adapted to their surroundings as they settled in different areas of the Americas. Some of the Indians who moved to Central and to South America eventually developed civilizations that were very advanced.

CHAPTER 9 IN REVIEW

IMPORTANT WORDS, NAMES, AND TERMS

1 Explain, define, or identify each of the following:

Sudan
Almoravids
Sundiata
mosques

Timbuktu
millennium
Great Zimbabwe
clans

land bridge
maize
kayaks
igloos

FACTS AND IDEAS

2 What two resources found in the lands around Meroë enabled that city to become one of the first ironworking centers in Africa?

3 What culture heavily influenced the Swahili civilization?

4 According to archaeologists, in what areas did farming begin in the Americas?

5 How did the Eskimos use the skins of fur-bearing animals found in the cold regions of North America?

ANALYZING VISUAL MATERIAL

6 Study the map on page 175. What natural features added to the difficulty of traveling overland from the shores of the Mediterranean Sea to the ancient kingdoms of western Africa?

7 Look at the picture of the Olmec head on page 185. What skills do you think the Olmecs needed to create this sculpture?

CONCEPTS AND UNDERSTANDINGS

8 How has leaching affected the soil of the tropical areas of Africa?

9 How did the city-states on the coast of eastern Africa become prosperous?

10 Why did few of the early peoples of the Americas settle in areas of Central America and South America close to the equator?

11 Why did the Eskimos spend much of their time moving from place to place?

PROJECTS AND ACTIVITIES

12 The Mayan civilization was very advanced. Some students might prepare a bulletin-board display of Mayan achievements for the class. Be sure to include some of the great Mayan accomplishments in science, art, and architecture.

13 Some students might like to prepare a research report on Mansa Musa's great pilgrimage to Mecca in 1324. Information about this event might be found in encyclopedias, or in books about early Africa or the empire of Mali. The students should report their findings to the class. Then have the class discuss how this pilgrimage might have impressed those living in the lands through which Mansa Musa passed.

CHAPTER **10** THE BYZANTINE AND ISLAMIC CIVILIZATIONS

1 Origins of the Byzantine Empire   2 The Nature of the Byzantine Empire   3 The Rise of Islam   4 The Islamic Civilization

The western half of the once-powerful Roman Empire collapsed in the late 400's after repeated attacks by German invaders. But the eastern half of the empire, centered around the capital city of Constantinople, endured for many centuries. As this empire grew, a rich and splendid culture emerged that was admired by many different peoples around the world.

Less than 200 years after the fall of the Western Roman Empire, a new religion arose in the Middle East. Under this faith, different Arab peoples joined together and built a large empire. In time, this empire, which reached from India to Spain, became the basis of a great civilization.

Emperor Justinian, accompanied by church officials and soldiers, is in the center of this sixth-century mosaic in a church in Ravenna.

1 ORIGINS OF THE BYZANTINE EMPIRE

Late in the third century, the Roman Empire was divided into an eastern half and a western half. The Western Empire came to an end in the late 400's. But the Eastern Empire did not fall. It became the center of a great civilization that is known as the Byzantine Empire. Even though many enemies attacked the empire, the Byzantine civilization was a powerful influence in the world for many centuries.

ROME'S EASTERN CAPITAL During the latter part of the third century A.D., the emperor Diocletian divided the Roman Empire into a western half and an eastern half (see Chapter 7). The Western Empire included much of what is now Western Europe and North Africa. The Eastern Empire included Greece, the Middle East, and a large part of what is now Turkey. Diocletian spent much of his time in the Eastern Empire, while a trusted general was chosen as emperor for the western lands. After Diocletian's retirement, the emperor Constantine I rose to power in the early 300's and ruled both halves of the empire alone.

Constantine wanted a capital built in the Eastern Empire that would equal the magnificence of Rome. So a new capital named Constantinople was constructed on the site of an ancient Greek settlement known as Byzantium. Constantinople was located on the Bosporus, a narrow waterway separating Europe from Asia. Thus, the city was ideally situated to be a cultural and commercial center as people and goods moved between Europe and Asia.

Following Constantine's rule, the empire was again divided. The western part of the empire was ruled by an emperor in Rome. The Eastern Empire continued to be governed by an emperor in Constantinople. During this time, Europe began to experience growing unrest. Barbarian peoples began to press upon the borders in both the east and the west.

Finally, in the early 400's, barbarian invaders gained control of much of the land in the Western Empire. And in 476, the Western Empire collapsed when German invaders drove the emperor in Rome from power (see Chapter 7). The Eastern Empire, however, did not collapse. Instead, it became the center of a great civilization known as the Byzantine Empire. Under the leadership of several skillful rulers, Byzantine civilization flourished for many centuries after the collapse of the Western Empire.

THE REIGN OF JUSTINIAN One of the most outstanding Byzantine rulers was the emperor Justinian who came to power in 527. Justinian wanted to retake the western lands that had been lost to barbarian peoples before the fall of Rome. After a short campaign, Byzantine armies recaptured lands in North Africa. By 554, Justinian's soldiers had also regained land in Spain and set up Byzantine authority in

A bust of the emperor Constantine reflects the determination and strength of this Roman ruler.

POLITICAL		SOCIAL AND ECONOMIC
Roman Empire re-united under Constantine	c. 324	
	330	Constantinople dedicated by Constantine as the capital of the Roman empire
	c. 422	Petrine supremacy promoted by Pope Celestine I
Western Roman Empire collapsed	476	
Reign of the emperor Justinian began	527	
	529	Code of Justinian established
	c. 570	Muhammad born
Muslims conquered most of Arabian Peninsula	627	Persians defeated by Emperor Heraclius I
	c. 630	
	632	Death of Muhammad
Umayyad dynasty founded	661	
Muslims defeated by Charles Martel after invading France	732	
	c. 751	First paper mill in Muslim world established
Reign of the emperor Charlemagne began	771	
	c. 850	University of Constantinople founded
Reign of the emperor Basil I began	867	
	c. 950	Constantinople became the center of the Mediterranean world for the manufacture of luxury goods
	1054	Final break between eastern and western Christians
The First Crusade began	1096	
	c. 1110	Seljuk Turks defeated in war with Byzantine Empire

Italy. But the victory in Italy was very costly, since the campaign lasted for more than 15 years.

Within the empire, Justinian started a great building program that included the construction of roads, bridges, aqueducts, forts, and churches. Justinian also worked to improve the government. For example, the sale of public offices was stopped in an effort to cut down corruption. In addition, taxes were carefully collected, and government accounts were checked to end waste and the misuse of tax money.

One of Justinian's greatest contributions was in the field of law. The emperor ordered a group of legal experts to gather the laws of the empire into a *code* —an organized set of laws. The result, called the Code of Justinian, contained the main ideas of Roman legal thinking. Over the centuries, this code influenced the development of laws in many countries.

Justinian's wife Theodora was an important influence on the emperor during his reign. She often helped Justinian and took an active part in the government. Theodora also worked to improve the place of women in Byzantine society.

Despite Justinian's accomplishments, the empire was bankrupt by the time of his death in 565. Justinian's great building projects and his long military campaigns had emptied the imperial treasury. And while Byzantine armies were recapturing western lands, the eastern frontiers had been neglected. As a result, the empire was increasingly threatened by enemies from the east.

THREATS TO THE EMPIRE The rulers who followed Justinian faced many problems along the borders of the empire. Enemy peoples known as Slavs and Avars moved into the Balkans—the lands north and west of Constantinople—and weakened Byzantine control there. In the late 500's, the Lombards took much of Italy, while during the early 600's, the Persians attacked and

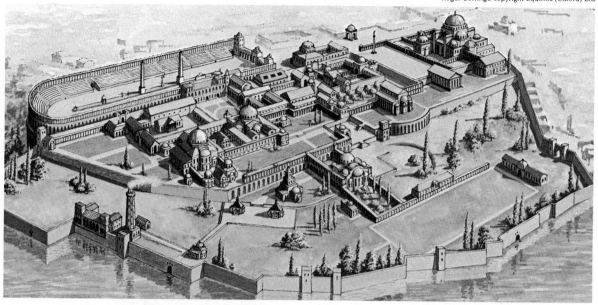

The great church of Saint Sophia at the upper right dominates this modern reconstruction of imperial Constantinople.

captured Syria, Mesopotamia, and parts of what is now Turkey.

The emperor Heraclius [HER-uh-KLIY-uhs] came to power in 610 as these threats to the empire were growing. To meet the danger, Heraclius mobilized Byzantine power and took the offensive against the Persians. After a decisive defeat in 627, the Persians were forced to return all conquered Byzantine lands. Heraclius also worked to reestablish Byzantine power in the Balkans, but the area remained a constant trouble spot.

A new threat to the empire arose in the east in the 630's. Muslim Arabs (see page 197) invaded the eastern lands, and by 642 they had captured the Byzantine lands of Syria, Palestine, and Egypt. In the 670's, the Arabs tried to capture Constantinople itself, but failed. The city was saved because of its strong defensive walls and because the Byzantine navy drove off the Arab fleet with *Greek fire* —a chemical mixture that burned furiously on contact with water. But the Arabs continued expanding into other lands. By the early 700's, they controlled North Africa and had moved into Spain.

During the mid-700's, however, the Byzantines won many victories against the Arabs and were able to check Arab expansion in several areas. For the next 200 years, the Byzantine Empire once again flourished, and its control reached from Italy in the west to Mesopotamia in the east.

Then, late in the eleventh century, the empire was threatened as the Seljuk [SEL-JOOK] Turks from central Asia defeated Byzantine forces and occupied lands east of Constantinople. By the early 1100's, however, the Seljuks had been defeated in several battles, and Byzantine forces had recaptured much of the land in the east.

QUESTIONS FOR REVIEW

1 *What emperor divided the Roman Empire into an eastern half and a western half?*

2 *How did Justinian try to reform the government of the Byzantine Empire?*

3 *Why was the Byzantine Empire bankrupt by the time of Justinian's death in 565?*

191

2 THE NATURE OF THE BYZANTINE EMPIRE

All power in the Byzantine Empire was centered in the emperor, who controlled the government and the church. The Christian church was an important influence in Byzantine life, but through the centuries differences arose between Christians in Rome and in Constantinople. In time, the two groups separated and followed different leaders.

Despite these problems, the Byzantines grew rich from the busy trade that took place throughout the empire. The government was in charge of all trade and industry and collected taxes on all trade goods. At the same time, Byzantine culture flourished and had a deep and lasting influence upon other civilizations.

THE BYZANTINE GOVERNMENT The Byzantine Empire had a form of government known as an *absolute autocracy*. This meant that the emperor had unlimited power to rule. For example, the emperor controlled all government finances, appointed and dismissed all government officers, made all laws, and directed the army and navy. To help the ruler, the government was divided into many specialized departments run by people who were part of the *civil service*. These people had to pass tests before they could hold government jobs.

The lands of the empire were divided into provinces—districts—that were ruled by generals who reported directly to the emperor. Government-held lands within each province were divided among the peasants who served in the empire's army. This system provided soldiers who were more loyal than the *mercenaries*—paid soldiers—who were often hired to fight for the empire.

The Byzantine ruler lived apart from the people in beautiful palaces amid great wealth. Since the ruler was looked upon as

above the people, every ceremony at the Byzantine court was designed to show the emperor's high place in society. For example, the Byzantine ruler wore fine clothes that were decorated with precious stones. Moreover, clothing of certain colors—

An eleventh-century painting of the Byzantine emperor Nicephorus III reflects the emperor's religious role as head of the Orthodox Church.

Bibliothèque Nationale

especially purple—could be worn only by the emperor. In addition, the emperor was always attended by many finely dressed servants. Every person who appeared before the ruler had to kneel three times as an act of submission.

The emperor was also looked upon as having been divinely chosen as God's representative on earth. Thus, the Byzantine ruler was looked upon as the supreme head of the church, even though the emperor was not an ordained member of the clergy. As the head of the church, the ruler could choose and dismiss all church officials, settle all church disputes, and decide all religious beliefs. The place of the emperor in church matters was very important because the church was a vital part of Byzantine life.

THE ROLE OF THE CHURCH During the 300's, Christianity became the official religion of the Roman Empire. But after the empire was divided into western and eastern halves, religious differences arose between Rome in the west and Constantinople in the east.

One agrument between eastern and western Christians concerned the power of the bishop of Rome—the pope. Many Christians looked upon the pope as their leader because of the idea of Petrine supremacy. According to this idea, the bishop of Rome is the successor of the apostle Peter, who was the first leader of the Christian church. Many Christians felt that the pope was the highest church authority. The eastern Christians, however, did not accept this idea. Instead, they looked to the highest ordained church leader in Constantinople—the *patriarch*—and to the emperor for religious leadership.

There were also other differences between eastern and western Christians over such matters as beliefs, religious images, and ceremonies. Then during the 800's, the Byzantine missionaries Cyril and Methodius began converting the Slavs and other peoples of eastern Europe to Christianity. These missionaries are believed to have devised the Cyrillic [suh-RIL-ik] alphabet to help the eastern peoples learn about the Christian faith. But the conversion of these peoples caused bitter differences between eastern and western Christians, since each group wanted to control the new converts.

The final break between eastern and western Christians came in 1054, after many years of argument. The eastern church became known as the Orthodox Church, and the western church was called the Roman Catholic Church.

The continuing religious differences with western Christians did not affect other aspects of life within the empire. For example, the economy grew as trade and industry brought wealth to the empire.

THE BYZANTINE ECONOMY The Byzantine Empire was located at the meeting point of Europe and Asia, where busy trade routes from all parts of the known world came together. As a result, the empire grew rich from the trade that took place in Byzantine cities.

The government benefited greatly from this trade, since taxes were charged on all imports and exports. The government also controlled the profitable silk industry, which began after silkworms were brought into the empire from China during the time of Justinian. The silk industry was an important source of money for the government, since Byzantine silk was sold all over Europe.

All trading activities in the empire were carefully watched by the government. No goods could be sent out of the empire without a government seal, and certain goods could not be exported at all. Traders from other lands had to report their arrival at Byzantine trading cities. Shops were sometimes searched, and business records were inspected, to keep traders from selling goods without paying the required taxes.

Each worker within the empire had to belong to a *guild*—a group of workers who followed the same trade or craft. The government set down rules for these groups. For example, a worker could not belong to more than one guild. The government also set the wages and hours of the guilds and told certain guilds where they could carry on their trade.

As trade grew, the Byzantine Empire became known for the high quality of its luxury goods. Brightly colored silks, fancy brocades, sparkling jewelry, and delicate ivory carvings were some of the fine products made in Byzantine workshops. On the other hand, the Byzantines imported such goods as spices, wheat, salt, furs, exotic foods, and even slaves. Thus, the empire's economy prospered through trade and industry. At the same time, Byzantine culture flourished and reached a high level of achievement.

BYZANTINE CULTURE The Byzantine Empire was the center of a civilization in which cultural achievements were highly valued. Many rich Byzantines spent their time and money in the study of literature, science, and philosophy. Byzantine rulers spent much money to support artists and scholars. Since learning was important to the Byzantines, their libraries contained many great works of Greek and Roman philosophers and writers. These writings were looked upon as important treasures to be carefully studied by Byzantine scholars.

One of the finest expressions of Byzantine culture was in the architecture of the churches. The Byzantines discovered a way to build churches with large domes that rested on 4 columns. The great church of Saint Sophia in Constantinople is the best example of such a building. Ten thousand people worked for about 5 years to build this church. Saint Sophia still stands today, even though it was built more than 1,400 years ago.

Most Byzantine churches were carefully adorned with beautiful *mosaics*—pictures made from tiny pieces of colored stone or glass set in fine plaster. Some churches were decorated with *frescoes*—pictures painted in damp plaster on the walls or ceilings of a building. Such paintings became part of the building.

The Byzantines also made beautiful *illuminated manuscripts*—religious books adorned with small paintings and decorative letters. The covers of these books were sometimes made of gold and silver. Silk and other fine cloths were used to make beautiful robes and clothing for church leaders and for the emperor.

The Byzantines created a rich culture that was used to emphasize religion and the glory of the ruler. As this great culture developed and spread, it influenced other lands. Remnants of Byzantine culture can be

The dome of Saint Sophia in Istanbul is characteristic of Byzantine architecture.

found today in parts of eastern Europe and the Middle East.

THE IMPACT OF THE BYZANTINE EMPIRE

The influence of Byzantine civilization lasted for centuries and reached far beyond the empire. For example, missionaries brought Byzantine culture to the Slavic peoples of eastern Europe. As a result, the Orthodox faith is an important part of life in many European countries today.

The Byzantine Empire also helped to keep alive the ideas of Roman law through the Code of Justinian and other Byzantine legal works. In time, these ideas were passed on to the kingdoms of western Europe. The Byzantines also preserved the writings of the early Greeks. Thus, Greek ideas were kept alive for scholars in other lands.

The influence of the Byzantine Empire extended to architecture and to art. Some of the churches that were built in western Europe followed the Byzantine style. In addition, the religious art of the Byzantines was admired and sometimes copied by the artists of other lands.

One of the most important contributions of the Byzantines related to the defense of Europe. For centuries Byzantine armies kept the Muslims from marching across Europe. Thus, the Byzantine Empire nurtured and maintained the cultural traditions that became part of the heritage of European civilizations.

QUESTIONS FOR REVIEW

1 *What was the form of government in the Byzantine Empire?*

2 *How did the Byzantine government benefit from the trade that took place in the empire?*

3 *Why did Byzantine libraries contain many great works of Greek and Roman philosophers and writers?*

3 THE RISE OF ISLAM

During the seventh century, one of the world's major religions was founded in the Middle East. The Arab peoples united under this religion and built an empire that reached through the Middle East into Asia, and across North Africa into Spain. Over the years, the leadership of the empire changed. Eventually, the unity of the empire came to an end as religious and political differences arose and led to the development of several centers of power.

MUHAMMAD Two of the world's major religions, Judaism and Christianity, began in the lands of the Middle East. Another great religion that started in the Middle East was founded by a man named Muhammad [moh-HAM-uhd]. He was born around A.D. 570 in the trading city of Mecca in what is now Saudi Arabia. As a youth, Muhammad worked as a herder. Later, he married a wealthy widow and became a successful merchant by managing her caravan business.

Muhammad often traveled with the trade caravans. During some of these trips, he met Christians and Jews and thus learned about their religious ideas, including *monotheism*—belief in one God.

Muhammad was a religious person and spent much time in meditation. One day while meditating, Muhammad had the first of many visions. In this vision, Muhammad was told by an angel to preach that there was only one God—*Allah* [AL-uh]. At that time, most Arabs believed in many gods. The images of some of these gods were kept in shrines in Mecca. There was also a shrine in Mecca called the Kaaba [KAHB-uh] that housed a sacred black stone. The ideas preached by Muhammad eventually became the religion of *Islam*, which means "submission (to Allah)." The people who joined this faith were *Muslims*—"those who surrender (to Allah)."

The painting of Muhammad instructing his followers reflects the Muslim belief that the face of the Prophet should not be shown. The small picture shows the Koran, the sacred text of Islam.

Muhammad gained few converts when he first began preaching because of opposition to his ideas. The merchants of Mecca were afraid that people would stop coming to Mecca to visit the Kaaba and the other shrines if the belief in one God became popular. Muhammad was also disliked by the wealthy people because he said that they should share their wealth with the poor.

Because of this opposition, Muhammad fled to the city of Medina, north of Mecca. This move, called the *Hegira* [hi-JIY-ruh], took place in 622. Muslims use that date as the beginning of the Muslim calendar. Muhammad gained many converts to Islam in Medina and became the religious and political leader of the city. In 630, Muhammad returned to Mecca and brought the city under his control. Muhammad also destroyed the images of the Arab gods and made the Kaaba a Muslim shrine. When Muhammad died in 632, most of Arabia had been united under Islam. Then the Arabs launched a campaign to spread the beliefs of the new religion.

ISLAMIC BELIEFS Much of Islam is based on a sacred book called the *Koran* [kuh-RAN]. Muslims believe that the revelations made to Muhammad by the angel are recorded in this book. Since the Koran has many references to the Bible, Muslims honor Abraham, Jesus, and others as prophets who came before Muhammad. The Koran also gives rules on how Muslims should live. For example, there are rules for marriage, family life, divorce, inheritance, and military activities. In addition, the Koran prohibits Muslims from eating certain foods, from gambling, and from worshiping idols.

The religious practices of Muslims center around five duties called the Five Pillars of Islam. The first duty asks Muslims to believe in one God and to believe that Muhammad was God's prophet. The second duty requires Muslims to pray five times each day. During these prayers, Muslims must face Mecca and kneel with their foreheads touching the ground. The third duty involves charity, for Muslims must share what they have with the poor. The fourth duty requires the faithful to fast during the month of Ramadan [RAM-uh-DAHN]. All Muslims, except the aged and the sick, must not eat or drink between sunrise and sunset during the month. The fifth duty asks each Muslim to make a journey to Mecca at least once in a lifetime. During this visit, each person must say certain prayers and follow prescribed ceremonies.

Muslims also believe in the idea of a holy war—*jihad* [ji-HAHD]. However, such a war can be fought only to correct a wrong or for protection. In addition, certain rules must be followed when fighting a holy war. For example, women and children are not to be harmed, and crops, sacred objects, and homes of the poor are not to be destroyed. These rules were designed to control the way wars were fought. In the years after Muhammad's death, however, a *jihad* was sometimes used by Muslims as a reason to expand into other lands.

THE EXPANSION OF ISLAM Following the death of Muhammad, Islam continued to spread rapidly under leaders who were given the title *caliph* [KAY-luhf]—"successor." During the reigns of the first four caliphs, the Arab-inhabited lands of Syria and Palestine came under Muslim rule. In addition, lands where non-Arabs lived—such as Egypt, part of North Africa, and the Persian Empire—also came under Muslim control (see map on page 198). The Arab soldiers who helped capture these lands expected to gain converts to Islam, fertile lands, and *booty*—captured goods.

As the Islamic Empire grew, the peoples of the conquered lands found that the Muslims were not harsh rulers. For example, few changes were made in the traditional ways of life in conquered lands. In addition, non-Muslims, such as Christians and Jews, were tolerated but had to pay a tax called a poll tax. This was done to encourage non-Muslims to convert to Islam.

A change in leadership took place in 661 after differences arose among groups of Muslims. At that time, a new group—the Umayyad [u-MIY-yad] dynasty—came to power. The Umayyad rulers moved the capital to Damascus in Syria. All of North Africa was captured, and the non-Arab Berber people living there were converted to Islam. In 711, the Muslims moved into Spain, and later they attacked the Germanic people in what is now France. However, the

Muslim armies were defeated and moved back into Spain. Muslim forces in the east, however, reached lands that are today part of Pakistan.

As the size of the Islamic Empire continued to grow, the Arab ruling class began to be outnumbered by non-Arabs. Resentment grew among the non-Arabs, for they were treated as second-class Muslims. For example, non-Arabs received less pay and less booty when serving in Muslim armies. At the same time, serious religious differences also arose among the Muslims.

In 750, there was a revolt against the Umayyads, and the Abbasid [AB-uh-sid] dynasty came to power. The Abbasids ruled from 750 to the 1200's, but in time, the Islamic Empire began to decline under the Abbasid leaders.

THE DECLINE OF THE EMPIRE Many changes took place in the Muslim world during the years of Abbasid rule. For example, the Abbasid caliphs became absolute rulers. Their power was based on a strong army that was mainly Persian and on a large *bureaucracy*—a group of appointed government workers. Many of these workers were also Persians and other non-Arab Muslims. Thus, Arabs no longer dominated the government of the empire.

The capital was moved to Baghdad, where the caliph lived in a beautiful palace surrounded by great wealth. The caliph was attended by many slaves, and meals were served on gold and silver plates decorated with jewels. Baghdad was also a prosperous trade center because of its location on east-west trade routes. Tax money from trade as well as from land taxes and poll taxes paid by non-Muslims helped support the government.

As the years passed, the power of the Abbasids began to decline as the caliphs neglected the affairs of the empire and spent most of their time enjoying the luxuries of court life. Discontent among the people grew as taxes were raised to pay for

Islamic Expansion

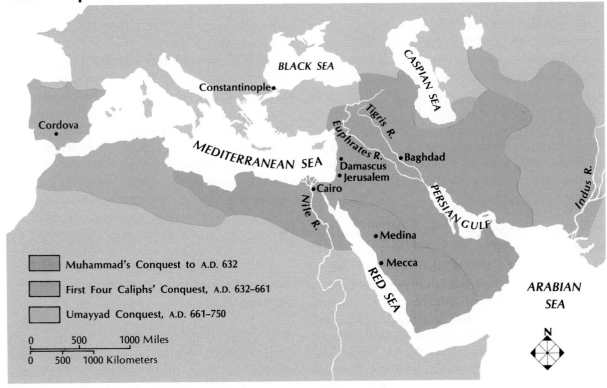

By A.D. 750, the Muslims ruled many different peoples in a vast empire that extended from the Atlantic Ocean to the Indus River.

the lavish life of the caliph and the nobles. At the same time, trade declined because the caliphs failed to protect the empire's trade routes.

The Abbasid rulers were also unable to maintain control of the outlying lands of the empire. In 756, a member of the Umayyad family took over the leadership of Spain and set up an independent dynasty at Cordova. And in the tenth century, leaders of the Fatimid [FAT-i-mid] dynasty gained control of Egypt and made Cairo the capital. Thus, by the late tenth century, there were three centers of power in the Muslim world—Cordova, Cairo, and Baghdad.

About the same time, nomadic peoples called Seljuk Turks moved out of central Asia westward into Abbasid lands. The Seljuks converted to Islam, and their power within the empire grew. As a result, the

Seljuks took Baghdad in 1055. The Abbasid caliph was allowed to remain as the religious leader, but the Seljuks took political control of Abbasid lands. By the 1100's, however, outside pressures and internal rivalries among the Seljuks had greatly weakened their power.

QUESTIONS FOR REVIEW

1 What religious belief of Christians and Jews did Muhammad learn about during his travels with trade caravans?

2 As the Islamic Empire grew, how were the peoples of the conquered lands treated by the Muslims?

3 Why did the power of the Abbasid caliphs decline?

4 THE ISLAMIC CIVILIZATION

The Islamic world prospered as trade grew within the empire and with other lands. At the same time, the government worked to improve farming. While Muslim scholars studied many different subjects, builders and artists contributed to architecture and to art. In time, the achievements of the Islamic world were passed on to other lands.

THE IMPACT OF TRADE Trade was an important factor in the Islamic economy. Muslims looked upon trade as an honorable profession because Muhammad had managed a caravan business when he was young. Most trade took place between different parts of the empire, but Muslims also traded with faraway lands. Trade with other lands grew, in part, because foreign merchants and craft workers could live in the empire and still carry on trade with their homelands.

Within the empire, trade was aided by two important factors. First, there were no import taxes on goods that passed between different parts of the empire. Second, a sound money system that could be used to finance trading activities had been set up.

To pay for trade expeditions to other parts of the world, merchants formed trade associations through which members pooled their money. Such groups allowed merchants to send out much larger expeditions than could be sent by only one or two merchants.

Goods from all over the world poured into the *bazaars*—markets—in Baghdad. Indian spices, Chinese porcelain, Asian gems, Russian honey, and African ivory were some of the goods sold in Muslim markets. Within the empire, Muslim craft workers made fine carpets, beautiful leather goods, fine silks and linens, and delicate jewelry. Paper, which was almost unknown in the Western world before the twelfth century, was another of the goods sold in Muslim bazaars. And in addition to trade, agriculture was also important to the prosperity of the empire.

AGRICULTURE IN ISLAMIC LANDS Farming was an important economic activity in Islamic lands. Since much of the land was dry, the government built irrigation systems to bring water to crops. In some places, swamps were drained to provide more land for farming. The government also encouraged crop rotation and the use of fertilizer to increase yields.

Muslim farmers grew many different crops to meet the needs of the people. In the Nile Valley, wheat and other grains were

Muslim mosques were often elaborately decorated with beautiful geometric patterns.

raised. In other parts of North Africa, cotton, flax, and sugarcane were grown, and from Spain there came a large supply of olives, fruits, and fine wines.

Farmers also worked to improve the quality of their farm animals. Sheep were raised for their fine wool, which was used to make woolen cloth. Arabian horses were well-known for their speed and endurance.

Most of the farming in the empire was done on great estates owned by rich landowners. Even though slavery was common, most slaves served as household servants. Most of the farm work was done by peasants. The solid agricultural basis of the economy produced a rich and progressive civilization. This civilization also made important discoveries in science and in medicine.

SCIENCE AND MEDICINE Islamic scholars were interested in many different fields of science. While Europe was in a time of warfare and chaos, Muslim scientists were studying light and how it behaved under different conditions. The Muslims were also interested in *alchemy* [AL-kuh-mee], an Arabic word for the art of mixing metals. The Muslims hoped to change certain common metals into precious metals, such as gold, but they failed to reach this goal. However, the study of alchemy led to the later development of chemistry.

Another field in which the Muslims were interested was astronomy. They built observatories, made charts of the sky, and discovered several stars. Muslim mathematicians studied the world of the Greeks and the Hindus. Hindu numbers were used by the Muslims and were later passed on to Europe. These numbers became the basis for the number system we use today. The Muslims also made the use of zero a common practice and invented the study of mathematics called algebra.

Muslim physicians made outstanding contributions in the field of medicine. For example, a doctor known as Rhazes [RAY-zeez]

wrote an important medical encyclopedia. The great scholar Avicenna [AV-uh-SEN-uh] wrote a book called the *Canon of Medicine* (see feature on page 201). This work, which combined Greek and Arabic medical learning, was studied in Europe for centuries.

Throughout Muslim lands, doctors had to be licensed before they could treat people. Druggists also had to pass an examination before they could sell medicines. Muslim hospitals were well equipped, and the best hospitals had separate rooms for people with different sicknesses. However, the Islamic civilization did not limit its achievements only to the fields of science and medicine. Muslims also made important contributions to architecture and to art.

ISLAMIC ARCHITECTURE AND ART Islamic architecture was used mainly in the building of mosques and palaces. The *mosques*—places of prayer—often had large interiors, great domes, and beautiful arches. The domes of the mosques were like those of Byzantine churches. The walls and the ceilings of the mosques were often covered with beautiful mosaics. Sometimes, words from the Koran were written on the inside and outside walls of these buildings. Next to each mosque was a tall tower called a minaret [MIN-uh-RET]. From this tower, people were called to prayer five times each day. The mosque and minaret in each city and town often stood apart from other buildings.

The Islamic faith did not allow the use of pictures showing people or animals. Thus, Islamic art consisted mainly of beautiful geometric and floral designs. Even carpets and robes made use of such designs.

The Muslims also built great cities that had many conveniences. Cordova in Spain, for example, had paved streets and street lighting. Some homes in Cordova even had hot and cold running water. Many Muslim cities also had libraries, schools, and colleges. Thus, as Muslim civilization reached its highest level of achievement between the eighth and the twelfth centuries, the people of the empire enjoyed an advanced way of life.

THE IMPACT OF ISLAM During the years that the Islamic Empire was growing, the Muslims encountered many different peoples and learned of their achievements. For example, the Muslims learned about paper-making and gunpowder from the Chinese. In time, knowledge of these inventions was passed on to Europeans by the Muslims.

Many fine universities were also founded by the Muslims in such cities as Baghdad, Cairo, and Cordova. Europeans came to these universities and studied Muslim writings on many different subjects. At the

Biography

A Great Scholar and Doctor

The well-known Muslim scholar and doctor Avicenna was born about 980 in a Persian town that today is part of the Soviet Union. Avicenna was taught by his father, whose house was a meeting place for well-educated people. As a youth, Avicenna often spent much of his time with these people. By the age of 10, Avicenna had memorized the Koran—the sacred Muslim book—as well as much Arabic poetry. As Avicenna grew, he studied *logic*—reasoning—and other advanced subjects with excellent teachers until he knew more than his teachers. By the age of 21, this remarkable Persian had mastered all branches of formal learning and had gained a reputation as a fine doctor.

After Avicenna's father died, he spent some time moving from place to place because of political instability within the Islamic Empire. Despite the unsettled times, Avicenna continued learning and writing for the rest of his life. Eventually, he became a doctor to the court of a Persian prince. Later, Avicenna lived in the court of another Persian noble. He became ill in 1037 and died in the same year.

One of Avicenna's greatest achievements was the *Canon of Medicine*. This work was divided into five books, and the material ranged from general comments on medicine and diseases to the making of medicines. The *Canon of Medicine* was used as a medical textbook for more than 600 years in both Europe and the Middle East.

Even today, this book is still used in some parts of Asia.

Avicenna also wrote books on philosophy and on religion. His ideas later influenced some of the great philosophers of western Europe. In the Middle Eastern world, Avicenna has been honored with the title The Leading Wise Man, while in the Western world he has been called the Prince of Physicians.

The great Muslim doctor Avicenna devoted much of his time to teaching and to discussing his ideas with others. Avicenna's interests ranged from medicine to philosophy and religion.

Historical Pictures Service

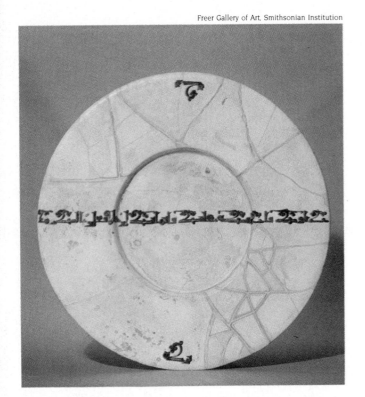

This dish dates from the tenth century. Sets of such dishes, decorated with Islamic proverbs, were widely used throughout lands ruled by the Muslims. Each dish usually had a different proverb across its surface.

same time, Muslim contributions to mathematics, science, and medicine helped Europeans gain greater understanding in these fields.

The Muslims were very interested in philosophy and carefully studied the works of Plato and Aristotle. Some Muslims, such as Avicenna, wrote commentaries on the writings of the Greeks. Many of these works were later translated into Latin and were spread through Europe. Thus, the Islamic Empire helped to preserve ancient learning, which in time was passed on to the peoples of Europe.

QUESTIONS FOR REVIEW

1 *For what reason did Islamic merchants set up trade associations?*

2 *How did the Muslims hope to change common metals into precious metals?*

3 *Why were minarets built close to mosques?*

CHAPTER SUMMARY

After the fall of the western half of the Roman Empire in the late 400's, the Byzantine Empire arose in the eastern lands once ruled by Rome. Even though the Byzantines were attacked many times by enemies and suffered from internal problems, the empire flourished for centuries. The empire was ruled by an emperor whose power was unlimited. As the empire grew rich from trade, a great culture arose that in time influenced other lands.

In the early seventh century, the religion of Islam was founded in the Middle East by an Arab named Muhammad. The Arab peoples united under this faith and built the great Islamic Empire. In time, this empire, which stretched from Asia to Spain, grew rich from trade. In addition, scholars and artists helped build the impressive Islamic culture. Later, some of the great achievements of this culture were passed on to other lands.

CHAPTER 10 IN REVIEW

IMPORTANT WORDS, NAMES, AND TERMS

1 Explain, define, or identify each of the following:

Greek fire	mosaics	caliph
civil service	monotheism	booty
mercenaries	Allah	bazaars
patriarch	Koran	minaret

FACTS AND IDEAS

2 What was the Code of Justinian?

3 By what name was the eastern church known after the final break between eastern and western Christians in 1054?

4 What duty are Muslims required to perform during the month of Ramadan?

5 How did the Islamic government try to increase farm yields in Muslim-held lands?

ANALYZING VISUAL MATERIAL

6 Look at the picture of the dome of Saint Sophia on page 194. What difficulties did Byzantine builders probably face in constructing this huge structure?

7 Study the map entitled Islamic Expansion on page 198. During which of the three periods indicated on the map was Muslim expansion greatest? During which period did Muslim expansion pose the greatest threat to the kingdoms of western Europe?

CONCEPTS AND UNDERSTANDINGS

8 How was Constantinople ideally situated to be a cultural and commercial center?

9 Why did many Christians look upon the pope in Rome as their religious leader?

10 Why is the Hegira important to Muslims?

11 Why did resentment grow among non-Arabs as the Islamic Empire expanded?

PROJECTS AND ACTIVITIES

12 The artistic achievements of the Byzantine Empire were outstanding. Find examples of Byzantine mosaics or illuminated manuscripts and prepare examples of these art forms to display in class.

13 Prepare a research report on the Five Pillars of Islam. Information might be found in encyclopedias and in books on Islam. Be sure to include the way Muslims observe Ramadan and the ceremonies and prayers that are required during a pilgrimage to Mecca. Report your findings to the class. Then ask the class to discuss how Saudi Arabia today might be affected by the annual influx of thousands of pilgrims to Mecca.

CHAPTER 11 THE GROWTH OF FEUDALISM

1 An Unsettled Time   2 European Kingdoms of the Early Middle Ages   3 The Role of the Church   4 The Growth of Feudalism

The fall of the Western Roman Empire in A.D. 476 brought important changes to western Europe. Germanic tribes moved into the former Roman lands, but there was no effective central government.

In the late 400's, a Germanic tribe known as the Franks began to unite and to expand. By the 800's, most of western Europe was part of a great Frankish empire. Following the death of Charlemagne, the most powerful Frankish ruler, the empire declined. The one stabilizing influence for the people of Europe during these years of change was the Church.

Political instability returned to western Europe when the Frankish empire declined. Conditions improved, however, as a new political system arose in the tenth century.

EPA/Scala

The great Frankish ruler Charlemagne, surrounded by splendidly dressed members of his court, was crowned emperor by Pope Leo III in A.D. 800.

1 AN UNSETTLED TIME

Many changes took place in western Europe between A.D. 476 and A.D. 1500. After the fall of the Western Roman Empire, western Europe was divided into many different kingdoms ruled by Germanic kings. Since there was no central government, lawlessness and disorder spread through western Europe. Unsettled conditions led, in turn, to a decline in intellectual and economic activity. Thus, the early years of the Middle Ages—from about A.D. 476 to about A.D. 800—have sometimes been called the Dark Ages.

THE END OF POLITICAL UNITY The long, steady decline of the Roman Empire after about A.D. 200 deeply affected European civilization. St. Cyprian, an early church leader, pessimistically described conditions as Roman power weakened in the third century:

> The world has grown old and lost its former vigour . . . the fields lack farmers, the sea sailors . . . there is no longer any . . . discipline in daily life . . . epidemics decimate [destroy] mankind . . . the Day of Judgment is at hand.

As St. Cyprian indicated, the world seemed to be collapsing. The growing weakness of the Roman government, along with continuing foreign invasions, caused many people to feel that the end of the world was near.

The power of Rome continued to weaken, and the Western Roman Empire finally came to an end in A.D. 476. Then western Europe entered a period known as the Middle Ages. This is the name given to the time between the fall of Rome and about the year 1500.

During the early Middle Ages, conditions in the area that had once been the Western Roman Empire were chaotic. This was due to the collapse of Rome's centralized power.

The Germanic peoples were fierce warriors whose lifestyles were characterized by violence, danger, and rivalry.

At the same time, there seemed to be little intellectual and cultural progress. This has led some scholars to call the early centuries of the Middle Ages the Dark Ages. However, this term is misleading, for learning and culture did advance during these years, but at a slower rate than they did at some other times in history.

After the final collapse of Rome, the lands of the Western Empire came under the control of Germanic tribes. These lands were then divided into many kingdoms ruled by the kings of the various tribes. Each of these Germanic kings looked upon their kingdoms as private property to be ruled as they pleased.

In most cases, the Germanic kings were not interested in preserving Roman institutions. One of these institutions, the Roman tax system, was allowed to disappear completely. As a result, there was no money to support a centralized government. And

POLITICAL		SOCIAL AND ECONOMIC
End of Western Roman Empire	476	
	c. 496	Clovis converted to Christianity
Frankish lands divided after death of Clovis	511	
	c. 529	Rule of Saint Benedict for monastic life
	c. 570	Gregory, bishop of Tours, wrote history of Merovingians
	596	Saint Augustine of Canterbury began conversion of England
Mayor of the palace began to dominate Frankish government	c. 629	
Muslim conquest of Spain began	711	Saint Boniface began conversion of Germanic tribes
	723	
Muslim advance stopped at Battle of Tours	732	
Pepin consecrated as king of Franks by Pope Stephen II	754	
Charlemagne crowned emperor in Rome by Pope Leo III	800	Use of *missi dominici* introduced by Charlemagne
	802	
Disintegration of Carolingian Empire began	814	
Reign of Alfred the Great in England began	870	Bulgars converted to Christianity
	871	
	c. 880	Patronage of learning by King Alfred in England
	910	Abbey of Cluny founded in France
Election of Hugh Capet as king of France	987	
Death of Edward the Confessor of England	1066	

since there was no central government to keep order, lawlessness spread through most of western Europe. Eventually, this lack of order and political unity had a deep effect on the economic life of the region.

ECONOMIC DECLINE Economic activity in western Europe changed greatly during the early Middle Ages. Travel often became very dangerous, as robbers roamed the roads of western Europe. Not surprisingly, trade declined, because merchants did not want to risk losing their goods to thieves. The outlaws had little to fear, since there was no central government to protect people from crimes. Trade was also affected as roads and bridges in the former Roman lands fell into disrepair. This happened because there was no government responsible for their upkeep.

In the seventh century, the Muslim conquests of North Africa and of Spain brought areas of the Mediterranean Sea under Islamic control (see Chapter 10). Since European ships were often attacked by the Muslims, overseas trade between Europe and the Middle East declined.

The decline in trade led to a lower demand for goods and for craftwork. At the same time, the use of money disappeared in many places because so few goods were bought and sold.

As economic activity in western Europe lessened, many city people moved to rural areas in search of food and work. Thus, the number of farming villages grew steadily during the early Middle Ages. These villages were usually isolated and self-sufficient. The people in these settlements raised their own food and made their own tools and clothing. For this reason, most villagers had little contact with people from other settlements.

The early Middle Ages were times of economic change and adjustment to new conditions. At the same time, the intellectual life of western Europe was also affected by changing conditions.

Most schools in the Middle Ages were run by the Church. Latin, theology, and classical history were among the subjects taught in these schools.

INTELLECTUAL DECLINE The time between the late 400's and the 900's was a period when education declined in western Europe. The fall of the Western Roman Empire had a serious impact on education, for the schools that had existed in Roman times disappeared. In addition, the Germanic rulers of the different kingdoms in western Europe were deeply involved in military and political problems. As a result, many of these leaders had little concern for education.

Because of the decline in education during the early Middle Ages, knowledge of ancient literature, architecture, painting, and sculpture was almost lost. Most people at that time were concerned with meeting their day-to-day living needs. These needs were more important than learning Latin, the language of the educated, or learning about ancient cultures. Such knowledge was of little practical use to people who had to struggle daily for food, clothing, and shelter.

The search for knowledge, however, did not die out completely during the early Middle Ages. The study of ancient Greek and Roman cultures was carried on in some of the few schools that were maintained in palaces and monasteries. The Church became a center for learning. Church schools provided the basis for many of the intellectual achievements that came later in the Middle Ages.

QUESTIONS FOR REVIEW

1 *For what reason have some scholars referred to the early Middle Ages as the Dark Ages?*

2 *How was European overseas trade affected by the Muslim conquests in the seventh century?*

3 *Why did the Germanic rulers of the early Middle Ages have little interest in education?*

Contributions

The Saddle, the Stirrup, and the Harness

During the Middle Ages, several devices that increased the usefulness of horses began to be used in western Europe. For example, the newly introduced saddle and stirrup improved the fighting capability of mounted combat forces, and a new kind of harness led to greater use of horses on farms.

When the Frankish ruler Charles Martel defeated the Muslims who were moving into Gaul in the early 700's, he noted the effectiveness of the Muslim cavalry. As a result, the Frankish leader began to build up a force of professional mounted soldiers.

Two important pieces of equipment used by these soldiers were the saddle and the stirrup. The saddle helped mounted soldiers stay on their horses while fighting. Formerly, riders could easily fall from their horses, since the seating was precarious. The saddle was developed in China and reached Europe sometime during the first century A.D.

The stirrup, which was also invented in Asia, began to be used in Europe during the eighth century. Before the stirrup came into use, mounted warriors could thrust their lances only with the power of their arms. The stirrup, however, allowed riders to deliver a blow to the enemy with the combined weight of the warrior and his charging horse. Thus, riders and horses were welded into a single fighting unit.

Horses were also increasingly used for farm work during the Middle Ages. This usage was made possible by an improved kind of harness that was introduced in Europe sometime around A.D. 800. The old type of harness, which had been used with oxen, was not suited for horses because it did not fit them well. When horses began pulling with the old-style harness, parts of it affected the horses' circulation and breathing. The new style of harness, however, rested on the horses' shoulders and permitted free breathing. In addition, the new harness enabled horses to throw all of their weight into pulling. As a result, a team of horses could pull loads four or five times heavier than could be pulled with the old kind of harness. Thus, technological changes during the Middle Ages improved the effectiveness of horses both in warfare and in farm work.

The improved harness developed during the Middle Ages helped horses to pull wagons and plows more efficiently.

Oxford University Press

2 EUROPEAN KINGDOMS OF THE EARLY MIDDLE AGES

In the late 400's, the Franks began to unite and to extend their power over much of western Europe. Under the leadership of strong kings who allied themselves with the Catholic Church, the Franks built a large kingdom. In the ninth and tenth centuries, however, this kingdom broke apart, as invaders attacked Frankish lands. During the early Middle Ages, England was also affected by Germanic invasions.

THE MEROVINGIANS A number of major changes took place in the political structure of western Europe during the early Middle Ages. In the late 400's, one of the tribes of Franks that lived along the east side of the Rhine River began to assert its power. Under the aggressive, sometimes ruthless leadership of King Clovis, the different Frankish tribes were united. At the same time, Clovis expanded Frankish power and brought most of Gaul—the region of present-day France and part of present-day Germany—under Frankish control. Clovis belonged to the Merovingian family, which became the ruling dynasty of the Franks for over 200 years.

Around 496, Clovis and his followers were converted to Christianity. This conversion was important, for it brought Clovis the loyalty of Christians in Gaul and the support of the pope in Rome. After Clovis's conversion, close cooperation developed between the Franks and the Catholic Church. For example, the Franks were expected to defend the Church against its enemies in return for Church support in political matters.

Clovis died in 511, and the kingdom was divided among his sons. Over the years, Clovis's sons and grandsons expanded the Frankish domain until it included all of what is now France and Belgium and much of what is now Germany. However, the practice

King Clovis fought many battles as he expanded the power of the Franks during the late fifth century.

of dividing land among the sons of the Merovingian ruler led to constant civil war. As a result, the power of the king began to decline. Eventually, the Merovingians were replaced by a new dynasty, which came to power in the seventh century.

CAROLINGIAN RULE By the late 600's, the Merovingian kings had little power, and the Frankish kingdom was divided. The real power of the king had gradually been taken over by a royal officer, who was called the mayor of the palace.

In 687, a member of a great Frankish landholding family—the Carolingians—became the mayor of the palace. As a result, the Carolingian family became a powerful influence in the affairs of the Franks. In 714, a Carolingian named Charles Martel became mayor of the palace. Charles was a strong leader who worked to subdue rebellious nobles and to unify the Franks. In addition,

Charles strengthened the eastern frontiers of the Frankish lands and defeated a Muslim force that had moved into southern Gaul from Spain in 732. This defeat ended further Muslim advances into western Europe.

In 741, Charles was succeeded by his sons Pepin and Carloman, who both held the office of mayor of the palace. Within ten years, Pepin had become king in all but name, for he directed most of the kingdom's daily affairs, while Carloman retired to a monastery. And in 751, Pepin moved to gain the Frankish crown for himself.

Pepin's claim was supported by Pope Zacharias, who agreed with Pepin that the Merovingian ruler of the Franks was a mere figurehead. With the pope's backing, Pepin became the king of the Franks and founded the Carolingian dynasty. In 754, Pepin was consecrated as king by the pope, and a strong alliance between the Carolingians and the Church was forged. This alliance drew the Church into greater political involvement in western Europe.

When Pepin died in 768, the Frankish kings ruled one of the largest kingdoms in western Europe. Pepin's two sons inherited the throne, but within a few years one son died, leaving the other son the sole ruler. This son, known as Charlemagne, became the greatest leader of the Franks.

CHARLEMAGNE Under the leadership of Charlemagne, the Carolingian dynasty extended the power of the Franks and built one of the greatest empires in the history of western Europe. For example, the Saxons, who lived between the Rhine and Elbe rivers (see map on page 211), were brought under Frankish rule and forced to accept the Christian faith. When the Lombards in Italy threatened the lands of the pope, Charlemagne moved into northern Italy and made himself king of the Lombards. Charlemagne also set up defense districts on the borders of the empire to protect the Frankish lands from invasion.

A ninth-century bronze casting portrayed Charlemagne on horseback, carrying the orb that symbolized royal power.

By A.D. 800, the Franks held an imposing empire that reached from the Danube River to the Atlantic Ocean and from Rome to the Baltic Sea. This empire was united under one leader—Charlemagne—and under one religion—the Catholic Church. On Christmas Day of A.D. 800, Charlemagne, who was visiting Rome, was crowned by the pope as the emperor of the Romans. This coronation showed that there was a desire to restore the political unity of Rome by looking upon Charlemagne as the successor of the Roman emperors.

To rule his great kingdom, Charlemagne divided the lands into districts run by local officers called counts. Royal messengers known as *missi dominici* were sent out by the emperor each year to check on these officers and to listen to complaints.

Charlemagne also worked to promote learning in the empire. For example, he urged priests to study and to improve their education. In addition, the emperor ordered that the handwriting used in Frankish lands be changed. This was done to replace the hard-to-read writing used under the Merovingian rulers. Charlemagne also had a palace school set up at his capital of Aix-la-Chapelle [AYK-SLAH-shuh-PEL]. At the same time, Irish copyists were brought to the empire to correct and to rewrite old manuscripts. As a result, many valuable writings were preserved for the future.

Charlemagne's rule brought law and order to western Europe. However, within a short time after his death in 814, the once-mighty empire of the Franks broke apart amid confusion and bloodshed.

THE DIVISION OF THE CAROLINGIAN EMPIRE Following Charlemagne's death, his son Louis inherited the Frankish kingdom. Louis divided the land among his three sons, but there was bitter rivalry over who should rule. After Louis died, his sons agreed to divide the empire into three kingdoms. Despite this agreement, however, the power of the Carolingians continued to decline in the years that followed.

As the Frankish empire grew weaker from internal feuds, the kingdom was also attacked by outside enemies. For example, during the ninth and tenth centuries, a fierce nomadic people from Asia called the Magyars terrorized the region of present-day Germany, northern Italy, and eastern Gaul.

At the same time, Muslim forces gained almost complete control of the Mediterranean Sea and drove all non-Muslim trade out of the great waterway. The Muslims also invaded southern Italy and attacked coastal towns in the Frankish lands that bordered the Mediterranean Sea.

The most feared raiders of all were the Vikings, who came from lands in Europe that today make up Norway, Sweden, and Denmark. The Vikings were excellent sailors and fierce warriors. They used specially built ships to make surprise attacks on coastal villages and towns in the Frankish lands. After an attack, the Viking raiders withdrew quickly by boat before a defending army could be gathered to attack

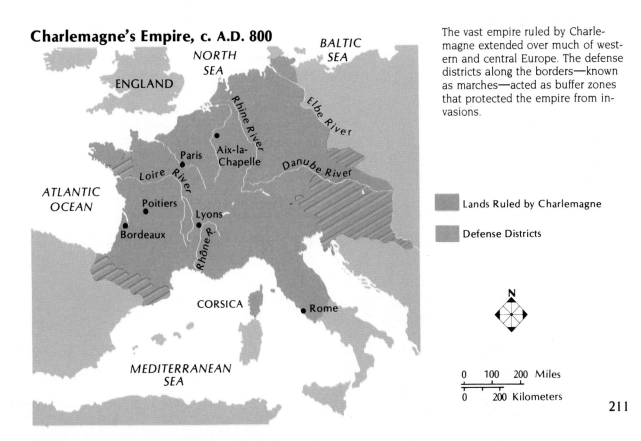

Charlemagne's Empire, c. A.D. 800

NORTH SEA
BALTIC SEA
ENGLAND
Rhine River
Elbe River
Paris
Aix-la-Chapelle
Loire River
Danube River
ATLANTIC OCEAN
Poitiers
Lyons
Bordeaux
Rhône R.
CORSICA
Rome
MEDITERRANEAN SEA

Lands Ruled by Charlemagne

Defense Districts

N

0   100   200 Miles
0   200 Kilometers

The vast empire ruled by Charlemagne extended over much of western and central Europe. The defense districts along the borders—known as marches—acted as buffer zones that protected the empire from invasions.

the Vikings. Whenever the Vikings struck, they plundered villages and towns, destroyed churches and monasteries, and spread terror among the people.

The confusion in the Frankish lands caused by outside attacks brought an end to Carolingian rule. For example, in the lands that became France, the Carolingians were replaced by a new dynasty—the Capetians [kuh-PEE-shuhnz]—who came to power in 987. In other areas, local officials often gained power as they worked to defend Frankish lands from attack. As the Frankish empire disintegrated amid new conditions, changes were also taking place in England during the early Middle Ages.

EARLY ENGLAND After the Roman legions withdrew from England early in the fifth century, the island was invaded by different Germanic groups, such as the Angles and the Saxons. These tribes fought the native Celtic peoples and enslaved many of them. By the end of the sixth century, the Anglo-Saxons had settled permanently and held

This helmet from the Sutton Hoo burial site in England probably belonged to a Saxon chieftain.

most of the island except for the western region of Wales. Under the Anglo-Saxons, England became a collection of small independent kingdoms.

In the ninth and tenth centuries, Danish Vikings invaded England and conquered much of the island. The Danes attacked the English kingdom of Wessex, which was ruled by King Alfred in the late 800's. This remarkable leader was able to organize English forces and to defeat the Danes. Under the terms of the peace agreement, the Danes were allowed to settle in England. Over the years, many Danes intermarried with the Anglo-Saxons.

There were many important accomplishments in England during King Alfred's reign. For example, the king set up a palace school and brought scholars to England to teach Latin and to translate Latin works into the Anglo-Saxon language. In addition, Alfred improved the army and founded the English navy.

In the late 900's, the Danish Vikings again attacked England. The Danes were successful, and in 1016, the Viking King Canute became the ruler of England. A few years after Canute's death in 1035, the English crown passed to an Anglo-Saxon named Edward, who belonged to the family line of King Alfred of Wessex. When Edward died in 1066, he had no heirs, so there was no one to succeed him. Thus, the stage was set for a dispute over who would be the ruler of England.

QUESTIONS FOR REVIEW

1 *To what ruling dynasty did King Clovis of the Franks belong?*

2 *How did Charles Martel's son Pepin become the king of the Franks?*

3 *Why was the coronation of Charlemagne as emperor of the Romans important?*

3 THE ROLE OF THE CHURCH

The Christian religion was an important part of life in western Europe during the Middle Ages. As the Catholic Church became better organized, different groups developed among the clergy. The clergy members who lived apart from the world in religious communities performed many important services and helped spread the Christian faith through much of Europe. During the Middle Ages, the Catholic Church greatly influenced the cultural life of western Europe.

THE ORGANIZATION OF THE CHURCH

During the Middle Ages, the only Christian religion in Europe was the Catholic Church. This faith was an important influence in western Europe between A.D. 500 and A.D. 1500.

After the fall of Rome, many of the Germanic peoples who had moved into the lands once held by Rome became Christians and became members of the Catholic Church. These people attended local churches in districts called parishes, which were served by priests. Parish priests held services and taught the people about the Catholic Church. The priests were supervised by higher Church officials—bishops—who looked after lands containing many parishes, called dioceses (DIY-uh-suh-suhz). Sometimes a number of dioceses were joined together and put under the control of a church leader called an archbishop.

The next highest Church officials were known as cardinals. During the 500's, cardinals served as advisers to the bishop of Rome—the pope. Over the years, the power of the cardinals grew, and by the 1000's, they had gained the right to elect the popes.

The pope was the head of the Church, but this role developed over many years. When the Roman government declined in the late 400's, succeeding popes had taken responsibility for running the city of Rome. This action added to the popes' prestige and power. At the same time, many Christians looked upon the popes as leaders of the Church because of the idea of Petrine supremacy (see Chapter 10). The office of the pope became known as the papacy, and all of the Church officials together were called the clergy.

As the power of the Church in western Europe grew during the Middle Ages, two groups emerged among the clergy. One group was the *secular clergy*, whose members handled the daily affairs of the Church. The second group was called the *regular clergy*. The men and women in this group lived apart from the world in monasteries and convents. During the Middle Ages, the clergy was very important to the members of the Church.

THE ROLE OF THE CLERGY The Church taught that its members must follow the

Members of the clergy often wore elaborately decorated vestments and robes when carrying out their church duties.

St. Apollinare Nuovo, Italy, *c.* 490

Abbey of Cluny, France, *c.* 1000

Palatine Chapel, Germany, *c.* 800

The churches of the Middle Ages featured different building styles. The architectural characteristics and elaborate decorations found in these structures represented an effort to glorify God.

Baptistry of St. Jean, France, *c.* 600

laws of Christ and the laws of the Church in order to gain salvation after death. The Church also believed that the people needed *grace*—spiritual help—to remain close to God in this life. According to the teachings of the Church, people received this grace through sacraments. These sacraments, as well as the Catholic Church itself, were looked upon as channels through which God's grace was given to the members of the Church.

By the 1100's, seven sacraments were being used by the Church. These sacraments were Baptism, Confirmation, Holy Eucharist (Communion), Penance, Extreme Unction, Holy Orders, and Matrimony. The sacraments were most often given to the people by an ordained member of the clergy. The clergy, therefore, was most important because its members acted as intermediaries between God and the people. Thus, Church members believed that salvation could be gained only through the direct help of the clergy. In addition, the way of life of the regular clergy was important because of its influence on the development of western European civilization during the Middle Ages.

MONASTICISM The idea of withdrawing from the world to follow a *monastic life*—a life of religious contemplation and prayer with other people—started among Christians during the third century. Men who followed such a life were known as *monks*. Women who left the everyday world to lead a contemplative life were called *nuns*.

In the early sixth century, a monk named Benedict wrote a set of rules that became the basis of monastic life during the Middle Ages. Those who followed Benedict's rules lived a life given to prayer and to manual labor. These people promised to obey the head of the monastery or the convent, to remain unmarried, and to own no worldly goods.

During the Middle Ages, a network of monasteries and convents spread through-out western Europe. Members of these religious communities were usually self-sufficient, for they grew their own food and made their own clothing. In addition, the monks often taught their farming methods to farmers who lived close to the monasteries.

Monks and nuns also performed other important services. For example, schools were set up in many monasteries, which became centers of learning. Some monks spent their lives studying and copying Roman and Greek writings. In some monasteries, monks recorded the events of the times in journals called *chronicles*. These records helped people of later times learn about life during the Middle Ages. Other monks and nuns ran hospitals for the sick and orphanages for homeless children. Some monks helped people by giving them a safe place to rest for the night while traveling.

The missionary work of the monks was one of the most important contributions made to European civilization by the regular clergy. As a result of these efforts, the Catholic faith was carried throughout western Europe during the early Middle Ages.

THE EXPANSION OF CHRISTIANITY The spread of Christianity through most of western Europe took place mainly between about A.D. 400 and A.D. 1000. Around 432, Pope Celestine chose a monk named Patrick to bring the Christian faith to the Celtic people of Ireland. As a result of Patrick's work, Christianity gained a strong foothold in Ireland. Monasteries were set up that became centers of learning and of missionary work. Irish monks later went to Scotland and northern England to bring Christianity to these lands. Patrick became known as the Apostle of Ireland and was later declared a saint by the Catholic Church.

Late in the sixth century, Pope Gregory I sent a group of missionaries led by a monk named Augustine to convert England to

Christianity. Augustine and his fellow missionaries were very successful, for thousands of people—including the ruler of the kingdom of Kent—became Christians. In 601, Augustine was made an archbishop as the Christian faith spread through England. Later, Augustine was made a saint in the Catholic Church.

In the late 600's, Irish and English monks began working to bring Christianity to the Germanic peoples. In 718, Pope Gregory II sent an English monk named Winfrid, whose name was changed to Boniface, to convert the Germanic tribes. As a result of his work, the Germanic peoples became Christians, and many religious communities were set up. In 722, Boniface was made a bishop. He became known as the Apostle of Germany. Like Patrick and Augustine, Boniface was made a saint in the Catholic Church.

Thus, Christianity spread throughout Europe during the Middle Ages. At the same time, European civilization benefited from the many cultural achievements of the Church.

THE CONTRIBUTIONS OF THE CHURCH

The cultural contributions of the Catholic Church during the Middle Ages enriched European civilization. For example, the Church helped preserve some of the early writings of the Greeks and the Romans, which were studied and copied in many monasteries. The highly decorated works —illuminated manuscripts –done by the monks were kept in monastery libraries. These writings were carefully studied by scholars in the Middle Ages. In addition, these manuscripts were preserved for use by scholars in later years.

Few Europeans knew how to read or to write during the Middle Ages. However, some people did learn these skills in schools run by the monks and the nuns. For example, boys who were preparing to join the clergy were taught by monks. In addition, other people who wanted to learn

Historical Pictures Service

The illuminated manuscripts of the Middle Ages were decorated with delicate and colorful script.

were taught in monastery schools. Thus, the monastery and convent schools of the Middle Ages helped keep learning alive during those years.

The Church was also an important political influence during the early Middle Ages. In the years after the centralized government of Rome came to an end, the Church provided unity and leadership for the people of western Europe. Thus, the Catholic Church was the one institution that gave stability to the lives of the people during the years of change.

QUESTIONS FOR REVIEW

1 *What was the only Christian religion in Europe during the Middle Ages?*

2 *How was the Christian faith brought to the Celtic people of Ireland?*

3 *Why were the schools run by the monks and the nuns important?*

4 THE GROWTH OF FEUDALISM

After the death of Charlemagne, the Carolingians grew weak, and there was no longer any effective central government. Disorder and lawlessness once again increased in western Europe. Thus, Europeans looked to the landed nobility for protection. As the power of the nobles grew, a new way of life emerged in western Europe. And by the tenth century, a new political system, based in part on Roman and Germanic customs, had arisen in western Europe.

THE ORIGINS OF POLITICAL CHANGES

Both the Romans and the Germans followed customs that later became part of a new political system that emerged in Europe during the tenth century. These customs involved the ideas of landholding and mutual protection.

During the years of Rome's decline, many nobles who owned great estates began to add to their landholdings. But, because of the size of these landholdings, their management became increasingly difficult for the nobles. As a result, the nobles began to give some of their land to others in return for certain kinds of service. Usually, the people who received land were expected to perform military service for the landowner. This custom later influenced ideas about landholding during the Middle Ages.

By the fifth century, Roman rulers had so little power that they could no longer protect their people. Thus, Roman nobles began to organize groups of citizens to serve as personal bodyguards. In return for this service, the nobles looked after the needs of their bodyguards. This idea of mutual protection was also carried over into the Middle Ages.

When the Germanic tribes moved into Roman lands, they brought their customs with them. One custom was called the *comitatus* [KAHM-uh-TAHD-uhs]. This was a relationship in which a tribal chief gave food and military goods to warriors who had been chosen as personal attendants to the chief. The *comitatus* was based on mutual protection, for the warriors promised to be loyal to the chief.

These Roman and German customs later influenced political developments in western Europe as changes became necessary. The need for such changes grew after Carolingian power started to decline.

THE NEED FOR CHANGE During the early 800's, the Carolingian dynasty was at the height of its power and ruled most of western Europe. However, as internal problems grew after Charlemagne's death, the power of the Carolingian government faded.

These freemen pledged their loyalty and service before a lord's magistrate. In return, the lord promised to extend his protection and justice to the freemen.

Giraudon/EPA

In their sturdy, high-prowed vessels, the Vikings sailed from their Scandinavian homelands to invade the lands once ruled by Charlemagne.

The end of centralized government in western Europe again led to an increase in lawlessness. Since there was no government with the power to enforce law and order, bands of robbers roamed the countryside raiding and plundering. As a result, neither people nor property was safe from attack.

In addition to the lawlessness, there were other problems. For example, fields were not plowed, so crops were not grown. There were food shortages, and the population declined in much of western Europe.

At the same time, the successors of Charlemagne were not able to defend Frankish lands from foreign invaders, such as the Vikings and the Magyars. And Muslim control of the Mediterranean Sea prevented European ships from using this great waterway. Thus, European port cities declined because of the lack of trade.

The lawlessness and economic distress in western Europe that followed the end of Carolingian power led to many changes. Frightened Europeans began to look to the landowning nobles for help during the troubled times. As conditions changed, a new way of life emerged in western Europe in the tenth century.

FEUDALISM Many people turned to the landholding nobles for protection when centralized government came to an end in western Europe after the breakup of Charlemagne's kingdom. Some people even gave their lands to the nobles in return for protection.

As conditions in Europe grew more unsettled in the mid 800's, the kings who ruled the lands once held by Charlemagne could no longer keep order. People in these lands were told by the kings to place themselves under the protection of landowning nobles. As a result, the nobles of western Europe gained new power and responsibility. For example, these nobles settled legal questions, maintained their own armies, controlled food supplies, and collected taxes in the lands that they owned.

As the landholding nobles became more powerful, a new political system arose in western Europe. This system—*feudalism*—was an elaborate set of rules that governed the relationships between the nobles and those who lived on the nobles' lands. Even though feudalism gave the people some security, it did not provide a strong central government. This was because feudal lords generally did not govern huge land areas. In addition, feudalism varied in form and practice in different parts of Europe. Despite these limitations, however, a measure of law and order returned to western Europe as feudalism became the way of life for several centuries.

QUESTIONS FOR REVIEW

1 *The customs of what two peoples were later made part of a new political system that emerged in Europe during the tenth century?*

2 *How did Muslim control of the Mediterranean Sea affect European port cities during the Middle Ages?*

3 *Why was feudalism unable to provide a strong central government in Europe during the Middle Ages?*

CHAPTER SUMMARY

The fall of the western Roman Empire led to many changes in western Europe after A.D. 500. Germanic tribes began to occupy and to rule the lands once held by Rome. While the Germanic peoples were moving into Roman lands, conditions were unsettled, since there was no strong central government to enforce law and order. At the same time, there was an economic and intellectual decline in western Europe.

The most important Germanic tribe to become powerful in western Europe in the early Middle Ages was the Franks. Under the leadership of strong rulers, the Franks built an empire that included most of western Europe. However, after the death of the great emperor Charlemagne, the Franks grew weak and their empire broke apart.

During these years of change, the Catholic Church was an important influence in western Europe. The Church helped preserve learning and made many contributions to European culture.

When the Frankish empire collapsed, conditions again became very unsettled. In time, conditions improved as a new political system, known as feudalism, emerged in western Europe.

CHAPTER 11 IN REVIEW

IMPORTANT WORDS, NAMES, AND TERMS

1 Explain, define, or identify each of the following:

Dark Ages	Vikings	clergy
Carolingian	Capetians	monastic life
mayor of the palace	dioceses	*comitatus*
missi dominici	papacy	feudalism

FACTS AND IDEAS

2 What was the language of the educated people in Europe during the Middle Ages?

3 How did Charlemagne work to promote learning in the Frankish empire?

4 What were some of the important services performed by monks and nuns during the Middle Ages?

5 What were some of the powers that the landholding nobles of the Middle Ages exercised in the lands that they owned?

ANALYZING VISUAL MATERIAL

6 According to the picture on page 205, how would you describe the life-styles and the living conditions of the Germanic peoples in the years after Rome's collapse?

7 Study the picture of the illuminated manuscript on page 216. What skills do you think were needed by the monks who made these complex manuscripts? Why do you think that these manuscripts were so elaborately decorated?

CONCEPTS AND UNDERSTANDINGS

8 Why did trade decline in Europe in the early Middle Ages?

9 For what reason were the attacks of the Vikings on Frankish lands so effective?

10 Why were the chronicles written by the monks of the Middle Ages important to the people of later times?

11 How was Europe affected by the end of centralized government after the death of Charlemagne?

PROJECTS AND ACTIVITIES

12 The ships used by the Viking raiders of northern Europe helped them to reach many different lands. Find pictures of these ships to display in class. Some students might construct models of the Viking ships.

13 One of the oldest monastic communities in the world is the monastery of Monte Cassino in Italy, founded by St. Benedict in the early 500's. Prepare a research report on this ancient religious institution. Information might be found in encyclopedias and in books on the Middle Ages. Be sure to include how the monastery was affected by World War II. Report your findings to the class.

CHAPTER **12** LIFE IN
FEUDAL EUROPE

1 Feudalism 2 Manorialism 3 Political Changes in Feudal
Europe

The decline of Carolingian power during the tenth century
led to widespread political unrest in western Europe. But
slowly, a form of government known as feudalism began to
emerge. During the next 400 years, feudalism was an important
influence in western Europe.

The feudal economy was based on farming. This system
involved an exchange of land and labor between landowning
nobles and peasant farmers. The system, however, led to
sharp differences between the upper and lower social classes
during the Middle Ages.

The unsettled times brought on by the fall of the Carolingians
led to many political changes in western Europe.
Since there was no strong central government, strong rulers
began to build their power and to unify their lands.

Castles of the Middle Ages were imposing structures, designed to withstand
repeated enemy attacks.

1 FEUDALISM

Feudalism was based on ties between nobles that centered around land use and military service. Land was the measure of wealth during the Middle Ages. As a result, most nobles spent their time trying to gain land or to protect lands that they already held.

Feudal society was divided into three classes, but movement from class to class was limited. Even though feudalism had many weaknesses, it did bring a measure of stability to western Europe.

THE FEUDAL STRUCTURE The feudal system of the Middle Ages was based on a set of obligations between a landholding noble and a person to whom the noble gave certain land rights. The noble was called the *lord*, and the person to whom the noble granted land was known as a *vassal*. The land that the vassal received from the lord was called a *fief* [FEEF].

The feudal land grant was made after the lord and the vassal had exchanged certain promises. In a ceremony called the *act of homage*, the vassal knelt and promised to be loyal to the lord. Then the vassal vowed to carry out certain duties for the lord. These duties were generally of a military nature.

Following these promises, a ceremony known as *investiture* was held. At that time, the lord gave the vassal something, such as a glove, a lance, or a piece of earth. This gift symbolized the right of the vassal to use and to govern the fief, even though the vassal did not own it. The land rights, however, were hereditary, which meant that the rights to the fief could be passed on to the vassal's oldest son.

The obligations of the lord and the vassal were looked upon as sacred duties. The most important duties of the lord were to protect the vassal and to provide justice for him in a court of law set up by the lord. In

Promises made by vassals and lords in the act of homage, shown in a scene from an illuminated manuscript, were viewed as solemn, lifelong pledges.

Historical Pictures Service

return, the vassal usually supplied the lord with soldiers for military duty for a set number of days each year. In addition, the vassal had to be part of the lord's court of followers, to give money to the lord at certain times, and to house and entertain the lord when he visited the vassal. The vassal was also expected to help pay ransom if the lord was captured by enemies. If either party failed to carry out these duties, the feudal obligations were ended. But this rarely happened.

Feudalism became the dominant political system in western Europe during the Middle Ages. Eastern Europe, however, was not affected as much by feudal influences because conditions there were much different (see Chapter 14).

The military features of feudalism showed that warfare was an important part of life in the Middle Ages. As a result, most nobles spent years in learning the skills needed for combat.

KNIGHTHOOD The nobles of the Middle Ages spent much of their time fighting. Since land was the main source of wealth, nobles often tried to enrich themselves by taking land from each other. Most of the fighting was done by *knights*—members of the nobility who had been well trained for combat.

This training usually began at the age of seven when the son of a noble became a *page* in the household of another noble. The young page was taught religion, good manners, hunting, and obedience. He also was taught the use and care of horses and of weapons.

When the page reached 15, he was made a *squire* and was ordered to serve a knight. Under the knight's training, the squire improved his skill with horses and with weapons. The squire also went into battle with the knight. While still in his teens, a squire might become a knight if he was brave on the battlefield. But most squires became knights at the age of 21. Almost all men in the nobility became knights. But a few failed to gain this rank. Unless they joined the clergy, these nobles were often criticized for failing to become knights.

The Church was involved in the ceremony of knighthood, since a knight's duty included serving God by protecting the Church. A candidate for knighthood spent the night before the ceremony in prayer and fasting, watching his weapons before the church altar. He also confessed his sins to a priest and promised to carry out the duties of knighthood faithfully. The next morning during a special church service, the young candidate was given a sword blessed by the priest and was made a knight.

Knights were expected to follow a set of rules called the *code of chivalry*. According to these rules, a knight was to be faithful to his lord, to defend the Church, and to protect women, children, and the sick. However, many knights failed to live up to these ideal goals (see *Myths and Realities*, page 224).

POLITICAL		SOCIAL AND ECONOMIC
	590	Reign of Pope Gregory the Great began
	c. 756	Papal States established
Saxony conquered by Charlemagne	785	
Muslims conquered Sicily	827	
Carolingian Empire divided under the Treaty of Verdun	843	Leonine wall built by Pope Leo IV to protect Saint Peter's from the Muslims
	847	
Paris attacked by Scandinavian raiders	885	
Reign of Henry the Fowler began	919	
Magyars defeated at Battle of Lechfeld	955	
Otto the Great crowned emperor by Pope John XII	962	
	999	First French pope—Sylvester II—elected
	c. 1040	Truce of God proclaimed to limit feudal fighting
Reign of Edward the Confessor began	1042	
	1059	College of Cardinals emerged
Norman conquest of England; William the Conqueror crowned king of England	c. 1066	
	1175	Building of Canterbury Cathedral began

223

As wars became more destructive during the Middle Ages, the Church tried to limit the fighting. Late in the tenth century, the Church refused to give the sacraments to any person who attacked holy places or innocent people. In the eleventh century, the *Truce of God* came into use. This meant that the Church set aside certain times of the year when fighting was forbidden. These limits, however, were often ignored. Thus, war continued to be the main activity of the nobles. The other social classes in western Europe, however, generally followed less warlike occupations.

FEUDAL SOCIETY There were three main social classes among the people of western Europe during the Middle Ages. The highest social class was the nobility, which was also the ruling class. The male members of this class were mainly professional warriors, whose lives centered around fight-

Myths and Realities

The Code of Chivalry

The code of chivalry that arose in western Europe during the Middle Ages influenced ideas about knights. The code was a set of rules about the way knights should behave. These rules were a model of behavior that knights could try to reach. Since the code was an ideal that knights were supposed to follow, the idea arose over the years that knights always behaved correctly. According to this idealized view of knightly conduct, knights loved the Christian faith and were ready to die defending the Church. In addition, knights protected the weak, aided the helpless, and treated all women with courtesy and respect. Knights were also faithful to their lords. In dealing with each other, knights were fair and honorable. Knights were always on the side of truth and fought injustice. And when fighting an enemy, knights were brave and ready to die rather than give up.

Even though these high ideals were the basis for knightly conduct, they were ideals that many knights never reached or even tried to reach. For example, some knights followed the code of chivalry only when dealing with members of their own class—the nobility. The people in the lowest class—the peasants—were treated any way that these knights pleased. Noblewomen were sometimes treated rudely, and most peasant women were looked down upon and treated with contempt by many knights.

Since violence was part of life during the Middle Ages, violations of the code of chivalry were hard to stop. However, those knights found guilty of being cowardly or of breaking the code were punished severely. They had their swords and spurs taken from them and broken during a public ceremony. Thus, the code of chivalry was often broken by many knights, even though it was meant to encourage knights to lead exemplary lives.

The ideals of courtesy and honor were aspects of the code of chivalry.

ing. In addition, the nobles enforced laws in the lands that they held and protected the people who lived on these lands. Since the nobles had many responsibilities, and since they formed a powerful and well-armed group, they held an honored place in society.

The second social class was the clergy. The men and women in this group spent their lives serving the Church by handling church affairs, teaching religion, and helping the poor, the sick, and the homeless. Sometimes, members of the nobility joined the clergy and became high officials in the Church. People in the lowest social class could also join the clergy. Occasionally, one of these people rose to a high church office. In general, however, members of the lowest class who entered the clergy became parish priests. Such priests were respected, but they were usually as poor as the people they served.

The lowest social class in western Europe during the Middle Ages was the peasant class. This group was also the largest social class. Peasants did all farm work, as well as any other work that a lord might want done. Most peasants were *serfs* and had few rights. For example, serfs could not leave the land that they farmed without the permission of the lord who owned the land. In addition, the status of a serf was hereditary, so the children of serfs remained in the same social class as their parents. However, for various reasons, a few peasants never became serfs. These peasants had the right to move from place to place without the permission of a lord. The men and women in this group were known as *freemen*.

Feudal society was, in many ways, harsh, cruel, and unfair. Most people in western Europe during the Middle Ages, however, accepted the feudal social structure without question. Since these Europeans were deeply religious, they believed that their place in society was based on the will of God. As a result, most people did not try to change society or to move from one

Noblewomen spent much of their time at such tasks as weaving and spinning wool.

social class to another. In addition, few people questioned the place of women in feudal society.

THE ROLE OF WOMEN Women in the Middle Ages had few rights in comparison to men. Noblewomen, however, had more privileges than did peasant women. For example, a noblewoman could be involved in a legal matter, but she could not appear in court. Instead, she was represented by her husband, father, or other male relative. When a noblewoman married, her husband was often chosen by her parents, and she was expected to obey her husband without question. A wife who did not obey could be beaten or cast off by her husband. A noblewoman had the right to inherit and to own land. However, a widow or young noblewoman with an estate could be forced to marry by her guardian.

One of the main duties of a noble's wife was to help her husband run the estate, especially when he was away. If the lands were attacked while the lord was gone, his wife was in charge of defending the estate. In addition, the noble's wife supervised the children, ran the household, and took care of the poor and sick on the estate. The noblewoman also learned music, supervised the sewing and weaving, and entertained guests who visited her husband.

Some women entered convents during the Middle Ages and rose to prominence within the Church. A nun in charge of a convent—the *abbess*—was responsible for other nuns and also gave orders to the peasants who farmed the convent's lands. Saint Clare of Italy and Saint Hildegard of Bingen were two abbesses who became well-known for their work. Sometimes, however, nobles sent their wives to convents as a way of disciplining them.

Thus, women were not treated as the equals of men during the Middle Ages. In many ways, this inequality was a direct result of the feudal system. Despite this limitation, however, the feudal system did have many good points.

AN EVALUATION OF FEUDALISM Under feudalism, western Europe was divided into thousands of local governments. Even though there was no central authority, these governments did bring some political order to western Europe after Carolingian power came to an end. In addition, feudal relationships between lords and vassals instilled ideas of personal honor and mutual obligation among the nobility. Feudalism also led to the formation of strong military forces in western Europe that were ready for battle on short notice. These armies helped stop the barbarian attacks that threatened to overrun all of western Europe at times during the Middle Ages.

The nature of the feudal system, however, caused many problems. For example, the complex feudal obligations led to divided loyalties, since a lord could owe allegiance to several lords at the same time. Feudal lords also fought each other to gain more land. Thus, western Europe was the scene of

endless small wars during the Middle Ages. These wars, however, were limited and did not lead to the great destruction of life and property caused by the wars of today.

Another problem involved high-ranking members of the clergy who held fiefs and thus were vassals of feudal lords. These clergy members had to decide whether to be loyal to the Church or to the feudal lord to whom they had promised to be faithful.

Even though feudalism had many drawbacks, it was used in western Europe for hundreds of years. In a time when violence and hardship were part of everyday life, feudalism brought a measure of order to European society.

QUESTIONS FOR REVIEW

1 *What were two important duties of a lord toward a vassal?*

2 *How did the Church try to limit fighting during the Middle Ages?*

3 *Why did most people in Europe accept the feudal social structure without question?*

2 MANORIALISM

The economic system used in western Europe during the Middle Ages was based on farming. This system began to emerge as the power of Rome declined. Over the years, important relationships developed between landholding lords and the peasants who farmed the lords' lands. Life was harsh for the peasants as they toiled long and hard at their work. While the landowning nobles did not live in great luxury, their lives were free of the backbreaking work that was done by the peasants.

The typical manor house often overlooked adjacent farm buildings and surrounding lands controlled by the feudal lord.

THE ORIGIN OF MANORIALISM The economic system used in western Europe during the Middle Ages evolved over a long period of time. It originated during the last years of the Roman Empire. As Rome's power weakened, disorder and lawlessness spread through Roman lands. Small landowners could not defend themselves from wandering outlaws and invaders. So these landowners gave up their lands to more-powerful landowners in return for protection. Thus, the small landowners became tenant farmers who paid for the use of land with the crops they raised. The tenant farmers also did certain kinds of work for the large landowners. Over the years, these customs were used by the Germanic tribes and later became part of the economic system of western Europe.

The basis of western Europe's economy during the Middle Ages was agriculture. By the year 1000, thousands of farming units—*manors*—were scattered throughout western Europe. These manors were owned by feudal lords and worked by peasants—freemen and serfs. A set of rules—the *manorial system*—governed the relationships between the peasants and the lords.

Each manor was made up of farmlands, grazing lands, woodlands, one or more peasant villages, and the *manor house*—the lord's house or castle. Some manors contained thousands of acres and several peasant villages, while others included only a few hundred acres and one peasant village.

The lords who owned the manors had complete control over them. However, most lords followed a belief called *noblesse oblige* [noh-BLES-uh-BLEEZH]. According to this idea, people of high rank and birth had a duty to treat those of a lower rank fairly. As a result, feudal lords often helped the peasants in times of need. For example, some lords gave food to the peasants during famines. Many lords also protected the peasants from attack and helped them in sickness and in old age.

Thus, manorialism became the basis of western Europe's economy during the Middle Ages. And under the manorial system a

227

unique way of life emerged during those years.

FEATURES OF MANORIALISM During the Middle Ages, most of the important needs of the people on the manor were met on the manor itself. For example, grain, vegetables, and animals were raised to provide food. In addition, clothing and footwear came from crops or animals grown on the manor. Since each manor produced most of what was needed, there was little demand for goods from towns or cities. Thus, the manorial system did little to promote the growth of urban centers.

The spiritual needs of the people on the manor were met by the village priest. The priest held services and taught the people about the Church.

Since running the manor involved many duties, the lord appointed several officers to help him. The highest official was called the *steward*. This person gave legal advice to the lord. A person known as the *bailiff* supervised the peasants' work, collected rents and fines, and kept financial records. One officer—the *reeve*—was chosen by the villagers and was usually a peasant. This person helped the bailiff oversee the farm work.

The lord's income came from the crops grown on the manor and from rents and fees paid by the villagers. Since the grinding mill, bake oven, and winepress usually belonged to the lord, peasants had to pay each time they used these facilities.

Farming on the manor was usually based on the three-field system. This meant that two fields were planted each year while one field was left idle to regain its fertility. All lands on the manor were divided into strips, and each peasant was given a total of about one acre (0.4 hectare). The grazing lands and the woodlands were shared as were the farm tools and the animals used to pull the plows. The peasants, however, could not hunt for wild game in the woodlands. Hunting was a privilege that was reserved for the lords.

One of the most important buildings on the manor was the lord's house or castle. In times of danger, the peasants went to the lord's house for protection, since it was usually fortified. The lord was anxious to protect the peasants because his wealth

Feudal peasants spent most of their time working for nobles, on whose lands the peasants lived. In the picture on the left, a bailiff supervises a group of peasants who are cutting grain by hand. In the other picture, peasants carefully shear their lord's sheep. The wool from these animals was used to make the rough garments worn by the peasants.

and power generally depended on the work of these humble people.

THE ROLE OF THE PEASANTS The labor of the peasants was an important part of manorialism. Peasant workers toiled from sunrise to sunset at many different jobs on the manor. For example, peasants usually worked for two or three days each week planting and caring for the lord's crops. The peasants also worked at such jobs as digging ditches, cutting firewood, building fences, and repairing bridges and roads. Peasant women not only toiled in the fields but also made clothing for the lord and his family. In addition, these women made the rough woolen tunics and stockings worn by the peasants.

The lord of the manor had almost total control over the peasants who lived on his land. The feudal lord, for example, decided whom a peasant could marry. A lord, however, could not remove peasants from manorial lands as long as they paid their rents and performed their services. Even though the peasants could refuse to work if a lord did not respect their rights, the life of these

people was very harsh. Many lords looked upon the peasants as stupid, dirty, and lowly. Peasants were generally regarded more as property than as human beings.

The simple huts of the peasants were typically very crude, for they usually had dirt floors and only one or two rooms. Pigs and chickens were often sheltered in the peasants' huts during bad weather.

The peasants had little variety in their food. They usually ate vegetables, brown bread, cereals, cheese, and soup. Eggs and salt pork were also eaten when they were available.

Despite the harshness of their lives, the peasants did have occasional times of enjoyment. One historian has described the peasants' lives in the following terms:

. . . life was not all gloom and discomfort, of course. The many church holidays and saints' days, and local events such as marriages, served as excuses for village celebrations. . . .

Thus, peasants' lives were generally characterized by constant work and few pleasures. At the same time, the lord of the manor did not live a life of ease.

LIVING CONDITIONS AMONG MEDIEVAL NOBLES

In the early Middle Ages, the homes of most lords were made of wood. In the twelfth century, however, powerful lords often built great stone castles to serve as manor houses or as permanent fortresses. These castles often had high walls and were surrounded by *moats*—water-filled ditches. The moat made it difficult for enemies to reach the castle.

Life in the castle was neither comfortable nor luxurious. There were no large windows, so the rooms were dark, gloomy, and damp. Huge fireplaces were used both for cooking and for heating, but they did not bring much warmth to the large rooms. The floor of the dining hall was usually covered with straw, which was often filthy. This was because the lord and his guests threw scraps of food on the floor for the dogs that roamed through the castle.

For entertainment, the lord hunted and took part in *tournaments*—contests between knights. Another popular sport was hunting with falcons. In the evenings, the lord's family and guests played such games as backgammon and chess. In addition, they listened to the songs of wandering minstrels and watched traveling jesters and clowns, who entertained the lord's household.

Manorialism was the basis of western Europe's economy for many centuries. This system, however, had few real advantages and a number of serious weaknesses.

THE PROBLEMS OF MANORIALISM

As an economic system, manorialism had few good features. One major benefit was that each manor was largely self-sufficient. This meant that people did not have to look outside the manor for food or other needed goods. Since the basic needs of the people were met in this way, there was considerable economic security for the people of western Europe under manorialism.

In general, however, manorialism was both a clumsy and inefficient economic system. For example, the peasants had to farm widely separated strips of land on the manor. As a result, the peasants often wasted much of their time just going from one strip of land to another. In addition, the size of the crops from manorial fields was often quite small. This was because neither fertilizers nor crop rotation were used.

Despite these problems, manorialism was used by Europeans for several hundred years. But by the twelfth century, changes were taking place in western Europe that, in time, brought an end to manorialism.

Armored knights tested their fighting skills against one another at the tournaments of the Middle Ages.

The British Museum

QUESTIONS FOR REVIEW

1 *For what reason did small landowners give their land to large landowners as the Roman Empire declined?*

2 *How did the lord of the manor generally regard the peasants?*

3 *Why was the manorial system clumsy and inefficient?*

3 POLITICAL CHANGES IN FEUDAL EUROPE

Many political changes took place in western Europe between the ninth and the twelfth centuries. Following the death of Charlemagne, disunity and lawlessness became commonplace. However, forceful leaders in the Germanic lands tried to bring independent nobles under control and to build a united kingdom. In England, Anglo-Saxon rule came to an end as the result of invasions and conquest. This conquest eventually led to the rise of a strong monarchy in England. French lands were also deeply divided by the end of Carolingian rule. But a new dynasty that came to power in the tenth century slowly increased the power of French kings.

DEVELOPMENTS IN GERMAN LANDS
During the ninth and tenth centuries, the Germanic lands once ruled by Charlemagne were broken into several small states called *duchies*. These duchies were very loosely united, even though each of them was independently ruled by a duke and had its own army.

In 919, Henry the Fowler became ruler of the German duchy of Saxony. By the 930's, Henry had succeeded in bringing all the German duchies under his leadership. As a result, the rulers of the other duchies recognized Henry as their overlord, even though they kept some of their independent power. Henry also fortified towns, monasteries, and convents to protect them against raids by the fierce invaders from southeastern Europe known as Magyars.

Henry was succeeded by his son, Otto the Great, in 936. This aggressive ruler subdued independent nobles and worked closely with the Church. For example, Otto gave land to bishops and to *abbots*—heads of monasteries. In return, these church officials were expected to give money to Otto and to provide soldiers for his army. At the same time, Otto made bishops and abbots his vassals by appointing them to their church offices. In time, this practice led to a power struggle between the Church and the German rulers.

In 955, the Magyars again invaded German lands. Otto gathered a large army and decisively defeated the Magyars at the Battle of Lechfeld. Otto also moved eastward into Slavic lands, which were then colonized by the Germans. In 951, Otto invaded Italy and eleven years later, he was crowned emperor by the pope. The lands that were ruled by Otto became known as the Holy Roman Empire (see map on page 232).

The defeat of the Magyars by Henry the Fowler in 933 ended a truce that had been in effect for nine years.

The Holy Roman Empire, c. A.D. 1000

NORTH SEA

Danzig

ENGLAND
London

Elbe River

HOLY

Rhine River

Aix-la-Chapelle

Krakow

Seine River

Paris

ROMAN

Prague

Danube River

Vienna

KINGDOM

OF

KINGDOM OF BURGUNDY

EMPIRE

Lyons

FRANCE

Belgrade

Genoa

Venice

Arles

0   100   200 Miles
0 100 200 Kilometers

Florence

N

Rome

PAPAL
STATES

The Holy Roman Empire reached from the North Sea to the Mediterranean Sea and included most of the central portion of western Europe.

MEDITERRANEAN SEA

Although Otto expanded German power, his heirs were not able to maintain the empire. As a result, the power of the German rulers gradually declined. The nobles regained much of their power, and a time of unrest descended on the Germanic lands. While these political changes were taking place among the Germans, political changes were also occurring in England.

POLITICAL CHANGES IN ENGLAND In 1042, a pious Anglo-Saxon noble named Edward became the king of England. Edward worked to restore order to the country after the unsettled times that followed the death of King Canute (see Chapter 11). But Edward died in 1066, without an heir. As a result, the English *witan*—council of royal advisers—chose a powerful noble named Harold to be the new king. However, Ed-

ward's powerful relative, William of Normandy, also claimed the English throne. William was the ruler of the descendants of Viking peoples who had settled in western Frankish lands after the death of Charlemagne. These lands, which became known as Normandy, are today part of France.

After careful preparation, William gathered a well-organized army, crossed the English Channel, and invaded England. In October 1066, the English and the Normans met in a furious battle at Hastings, in southeastern England. One description of this battle stated

. . . The battle commenced on both sides. They fought with ardour [courage], neither side giving ground, for [a] great part of the day. . . . This vicissitude [changing situation] of first one party conquering, and then the other, prevailed as long as the life of Harold continued; but when he fell, . . . the flight of the English ceased not until night.

The defeat of the English ended Anglo-Saxon rule in England, and William became known as William the Conqueror.

As the ruler of England, William worked to strengthen his power. For example, he took land from the English nobles and gave it to his Norman followers. Thus, the Norman nobles became vassals of King William and had to promise to be loyal to him.

William the Conqueror laid the foundation for a strong monarchy in England by his forceful rule. While England developed under William's leadership, political changes were also taking place across the English Channel in the lands that became France.

POLITICAL DEVELOPMENTS IN FRANCE For more than a century after the death of Charlemagne, the Carolingian kings struggled to stay in power in the lands that became France. These rulers were being challenged by feudal nobles who set up many small states that were independent of the Carolingian monarchs.

In 987, the last Carolingian king died, and the French nobility chose Hugh Capet [KAY-puht] as the new king. When Capet came to power, however, he actually ruled only a small royal domain—Île-de-France [EEL-duh-FRAHNS]—that included the city of Paris and some surrounding lands. The rest of the country was held by the feudal lords, who ruled their lands according to their own laws. As a result, these nobles paid little attention to the French king.

The Capetian [kuh-PEE-shuhn] kings, however, patiently worked to assert their power. Their first step was to make certain that order and obedience were enforced within their royal domain. Slowly, these capable rulers extended their power over other lands. They did this by arranging marriages between members of the Capetian family and members of landholding noble families.

The Capetians also gained land by waging small wars against unruly, but less-powerful, nobles. Thus, the Capetian kings carefully brought more towns and fiefs under royal control. As a result, the power of the French monarchy grew steadily during the 1100's. And during the next century, the power of many western European monarchs continued to expand.

NEW POLITICAL TRENDS By the late 1100's, the political organization of western Europe had begun to show signs of change. Strong monarchies led by powerful rulers slowly began to appear in parts of western Europe. These rulers worked to build unified kingdoms under centralized governments. Thus, localized feudal control slowly

Hugh Capet, crowned in 987, founded the Capetian dynasty, which ruled France for over 300 years.

gave way to a political system in which power was concentrated in the hands of individual rulers.

The strong monarchies that slowly grew in western Europe were different from one another in many ways. The German empire begun by Henry the Fowler and Otto the Great, for example, was never entirely unified. For this reason, the power of the German rulers depended, in large part, upon the goodwill and cooperation of their nobles.

The monarchies founded by William the Conqueror in England and by the Capetians in France, however, were more successful. This was because William and his heirs and the Capetians followed policies that gradually undermined the power of the nobles. The English and French kings alike forced their nobles to become vassals of the crown. Thus, the nobles owed allegiance to the crown—not to other nobles.

The rulers of France and of England generally worked to increase their royal landholdings and revenues. Their growing wealth helped the English and French kings to secure control over their feudal nobles.

In the course of many years, the rulers of France and of England built their power at the expense of the nobility. As a result, political power became increasingly centralized in both countries. This early trend toward increased political centralization marked an important development in the growth of western European civilization.

QUESTIONS FOR REVIEW

1 *For what reason did Henry the Fowler fortify German towns, monasteries, and convents?*

2 *How did Otto the Great work to bring officials of the Church under his control?*

3 *Why was the political structure of western Europe slowly changing by the 1200's?*

CHAPTER SUMMARY

During the Middle Ages, a complicated system of relationships between landowning nobles developed in western Europe. Under this system, known as feudalism, European noble lords gave land rights to other nobles called vassals. In return, these vassals promised to be loyal and obedient.

Since land was the major source of wealth in the Middle Ages, feudal lords often went to war to gain more land. These wars were fought by members of the nobility called knights.

The economic system of western Europe during the Middle Ages was called manorialism. Under this system, which was based on farming, humble peasants worked to provide the food, goods, and services needed by feudal society.

After the death of Charlemagne, strong leaders worked to unify Germanic lands. England came under the rule of William the Conqueror. The French kings, too, became more powerful after about the year 1000. The Capetian rulers, who followed the Carolingians, worked to unify France and to build it into a single powerful kingdom.

CHAPTER 12 IN REVIEW

IMPORTANT WORDS, NAMES, AND TERMS

1 Explain, define, or identify each of the following:

vassal

fief

act of homage

knights

page

code of chivalry

serfs

manorial system

noblesse oblige

tournaments

Hastings

Île-de-France

FACTS AND IDEAS

2 What were some of the duties of a vassal toward a lord?

3 How might a squire become a knight on the battlefield?

4 What was the intention of the Church in using the Truce of God?

5 What action could the peasants take if the lord failed to respect their rights?

6 How did Otto the Great make bishops and abbots his vassals?

ANALYZING VISUAL MATERIAL

7 Study the picture on page 221. Why do you think that enemy forces would find it difficult to capture such a fortress? What architectural features of this castle do you think show that the structure was built for defense?

8 Study the map on page 232. What natural features might have been used for travel within the Holy Roman Empire?

CONCEPTS AND UNDERSTANDINGS

9 Why was the Church involved in the ceremony of knighthood?

10 How did the nature of feudalism lead to endless small wars during the Middle Ages?

11 Why were feudal lords anxious to protect the peasants of the manors?

12 How did the Capetians slowly extend their power over other lands?

PROJECTS AND ACTIVITIES

13 Many different weapons were used during the endless wars of the Middle Ages. Look for pictures of weapons used during that time. Some students might construct a model of a castle under attack, showing the weapons used by the attackers and the defenders.

14 Music was important to the people of the Middle Ages for entertainment and for religious services. Find recordings of the music of the Middle Ages. Information about such recordings might be found in a record catalog. Then have the class listen to recordings of this music. Discuss how the music of the Middle Ages differs from the church music and the popular music of today.

Using Geography Skills

Political maps are extremely important in the study of history. Such maps are useful because they can provide much information about specific political events and about long-term political trends. For example, maps can show the historical expansion of political power as various peoples have extended their control over new lands throughout the world.

Many territorial changes took place in the Middle East and in Europe during the Middle Ages. These changes occurred as powerful rulers worked to expand their domains. The political map below shows Muslim expansion eastward and westward from the Arabian Peninsula, as well as Byzantine lands and Frankish lands around A.D. 750. Study the map carefully. Then answer the following questions:

1 What group of people controlled much of North Africa after 750?

2 What land was under Muslim control before 632?

3 What eastern land had come under Muslim rule by 750?

4 In whose lands was the city of Jerusalem located in 750?

5 Why do you think that control of Constantinople was important?

6 Why do you think that the Muslims did not expand their empire northward from Spain and southward into Africa?

7 What factors do you think might have limited the efforts of Byzantine rulers to expand the boundaries of their empire in 750?

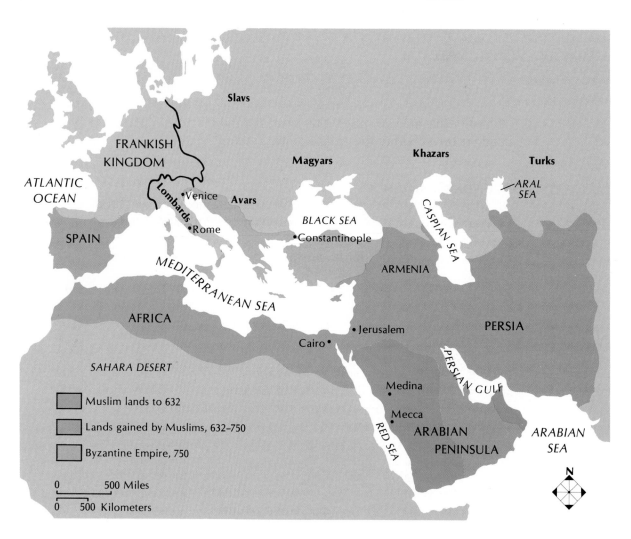

UNIT 3 IN REVIEW

CONCEPTS AND UNDERSTANDINGS

1 How have the different climates of Africa influenced the way of life of the African peoples?
2 What was the relationship between the Byzantine emperor and the Church?
3 What are the five duties around which the religious practices of Muslims are centered?
4 How did economic activity in western Europe change during the early Middle Ages?
5 What were some of the cultural contributions to European civilization made by the Church during the Middle Ages?
6 What was the role of women in feudal society?
7 How were the peasants important to the operation of the manorial system?

QUESTIONS FOR DISCUSSION

1 To what extent would you agree or disagree with the following statement: "The land bridge that connected Siberia in Asia to Alaska in North America was of great importance in the settlement of the Americas." Explain your answer.
2 What, in your opinion, are the advantages and disadvantages of an absolute autocracy?
3 After the Roman Empire fell, many schools that existed in Roman times disappeared. How do you think the disappearance of schools might affect a civilization?
4 In your opinion, could the manorial system work in today's world? Explain your answer.

SUGGESTED READING

Asimov, Isaac. *Dark Ages*. Boston: Houghton Mifflin Company, 1968.

Curtin, Philip, et al. *African History*. Boston: Little, Brown and Company, 1978.

Gann, T. *History of the Maya*. New York: Gordon Press Publishers, 1976.

Joseph, Alvin M., Jr. *The Indian Heritage of America*. New York: Alfred A. Knopf, Inc., 1968.

July, Robert W. *A History of the African People*. New York: Charles Scribner's Sons, 1980.

Lane, Peter. *The Middle Ages*. North Pomfret, Vt.: David and Charles, Inc., 1980.

Murphy, E. Jefferson. *Understanding Africa*. New York: T.Y. Crowell Company, 1978.

Stearns, Monroe. *Charlemagne*. New York: Franklin Watts, Inc., 1971.

Tames, Richard. *The World of Islam*. New York: Viking Press, Inc., 1976.

UNIT 4

THE LATE MIDDLE AGES

1100 to 1500

13 Changing Medieval Europe 14 Eastern Europe in the Late Middle Ages 15 Asia in the Middle Ages

The Bettmann Archive

EPA/Scala

Eastern Orthodox monastery in Bulgaria

Medieval Italian city

During the late Middle Ages, western Europe was changing. The feudal system declined, but the number of merchants, artisans, and craft workers increased as towns developed and prospered. In general, the nobility grew weaker as monarchs strengthened their own authority. At the same time, the political role and the spiritual influence of the Roman Catholic Church waned.

Eastern Europe remained largely agricultural in nature during this period. In many regions the feudal system became more firmly established as the nobility maintained their power over the peasants. In addition, eastern Europe was also plagued with invasions throughout the late Middle Ages. Even the once powerful Byzantine Empire succumbed to the attacks of the Ottoman Turks.

High levels of civilization developed in Asia during the late Middle Ages. Although invaders sometimes threatened the cultures of India, China, and Japan, the peoples of these lands made great strides in creating beautiful art, architecture, and literature during this period.

Japanese samurai leader of the late Middle Ages

CHAPTER 13 CHANGING MEDIEVAL EUROPE

1 The Expansion of Secular Authority   2 Competition and Conflict: Papacy and Monarchy   3 The Growth of Trade and Urban Societies   4 Intellectual and Cultural Development

In the late Middle Ages, western Europe was a region in flux. Historians often point out four major areas of change. Political institutions were changing—the feudal system was slowly being replaced by national monarchies. In addition, the supreme authority of the Roman Catholic Church was questioned by both religious and civil leaders. Furthermore, towns and cities were growing in wealth and power, and trade increased. Western Europeans exchanged ideas with people from distant lands. More-complex methods of commerce replaced simple barter, and a system of banking aided trade. At the same time, people developed a renewed interest in education. Universities were founded throughout Europe. This increase in education caused further changes in medieval society.

Studio Jon, Fishguard

The enormous size of this bishop's palace shows the important place of the Roman Catholic Church and its clergy in medieval society.

1 THE EXPANSION OF SECULAR AUTHORITY

European civilization changed in many important ways during the period from A.D. 1100 to A.D. 1500. Medieval institutions reached their height in the thirteenth century and then started to decline. The feudal system and the Roman Catholic Church began to weaken. In western Europe, powerful monarchs were increasing their authority over the nobility. This increase in secular authority was especially conspicuous in England, France, and Spain.

THE RISE OF THE ENGLISH MONARCHY As you read in Chapter 12, William, Duke of Normandy, conquered England in 1066. In the years that followed, he built the foundations of a strong monarchy in England. After becoming king, William—called William the Conqueror—increased his power by redistributing land to his nobles according to the customs of Norman feudalism. In return, the nobles owed him military service, feudal dues, and loyalty. However, to keep the major nobles weak, William granted each of them land scattered in different parts of the country. As a result, it was nearly impossible for any one noble to gather a large army—threatening William's authority—without William's being aware of it.

William also authorized the *Domesday Book*—a survey of all landholdings in the country according to their size, their owners, and their value. This survey helped William to collect feudal dues more easily. Most of the English rulers in the next century were able to maintain the tradition of strong feudal government.

THE BEGINNING OF COMMON LAW In 1154, Henry II—of the Plantagenet family—became king of England. Henry was determined to continue the work started by William the Conqueror. Henry's plans decreased the power of the nobles and, at the same time, increased his own authority. Henry strengthened royal authority in several ways. One important way was that Henry made the king's law the law of the land. Royal law was more just and more efficiently administered than was the crude feudal law. Over time, this law became known as *common law*.

When a crime was committed, the visiting judge and a jury of 12 men—women were excluded—decided guilt or innocence. Decisions were based on the king's law. These trials were the beginning of what is now known as the jury system.

During the corrupt reign of King John, the major English nobles joined together in 1215 and forced John to sign the *Magna Carta*—the Great Charter. This medieval document reaffirmed the rights of the English nobles and limited the power of the

King John's signing of the Magna Carta in 1215 marked the first time that a written agreement limited the power of the English monarch.

POLITICAL		SOCIAL AND ECONOMIC
William, Duke of Normandy, invaded England	1066	
	1095	Pope Urban II called for First Crusade
Henry Plantagenet became king of England	1154	
	1163	Building of Cathedral of Notre Dame was begun
	c. 1200	High Middle Ages
King John of England signed Magna Carta	1215	
Philip the Fair became king of France	1285	
	1291	Crusades ended when Turks captured Acre
Model Parliament in England	1295	
	1309	Pope Clement V moved papacy to Avignon
Hundred Years' War began	1337	
	1347	Black Death struck Europe
	1381	Wat Tyler's Rebellion
	1385	Chaucer began writing the Canterbury Tales
	1417	Great Schism ended; Martin V became pope
Treaty of Troyes	1420	
Joan of Arc led French troops at Battle of Orléans	1429	
	c. 1450	Gutenberg invented movable type
Wars of the Roses began in England	1455	
Ferdinand and Isabella unified Spain	1492	
	c. 1500	Paper money issued

monarch. Some of the provisions of the Magna Carta were

> 12. Scutage [tax in place of military service] or aid [payment to the lord] shall be levied in our kingdom only by the common counsel of our kingdom, . . .
> 20. A freeman shall be amerced [fined] for a small offence only according to the degree of the offence; . . .
> 39. No freeman shall be captured or imprisoned or disseised [dispossessed] or outlawed or exiled or in any way destroyed . . . except by the lawful judgment of his peers or by the law of the land.
> 40. To no one will we sell, to no one will we deny or delay right or justice.

The provisions applied only to the nobles. However, the Magna Carta is often cited by historians as the beginning of democratic government in England.

ENGLAND'S MONARCHY IS STRENGTHENED Four years after the signing of the Magna Carta, John died and was succeeded by his son Henry III. During Henry's reign the Great Council—a group of nobles who advised the king—grew in power. This council came to be called Parliament sometime in the 1240's.

The central role of the English monarch was again strengthened under Edward I, who ruled from 1272 to 1307. Edward completed the reforms begun by Henry II. One of Edward's greatest accomplishments was making Parliament—now composed of the nobles and the townspeople, or burgesses—a primary tax-granting body.

Earlier English rulers had sometimes consulted the Great Council. But Edward began a tradition when he invited the nobles to meet with the rich burgesses—called *commons* because they had no titles of nobility. Edward called the meeting because he needed money to pay for his wars with Wales and Scotland. The Parliament that Edward called in 1295 was the most representative of any such meeting up to that time. It became known as the Model Parliament. Soon, it became customary for the nobles and the burgesses to meet as separate bodies. In later years, the two groups developed into the two houses of Parliament—the House of Lords and the House of Commons.

The money that Parliament voted to give to Edward I increased his power. But later monarchs found that before Parliament granted them money, it demanded a voice in how the money would be spent and demanded that certain laws be passed. Thus, the English Parliament, which began as a tax-granting body, developed a great deal of power.

THE GROWTH OF A STRONG CENTRAL GOVERNMENT

Three crises faced England in the fourteenth and fifteenth centuries. The plague, or Black Death, ravaged Europe, killing an estimated one third of the people in England in the fourteenth century. At the same time, the Hundred Years' War had begun (see page 244). When the war ended in 1453, the English had lost all their landholdings in France except the port of Calais [ka-LAY].

The third crisis arose in 1455 when a civil war broke out between two branches of the English royal family—the house of York and the house of Lancaster. This civil war, called the Wars of the Roses because each of the royal houses used a rose as its symbol, lasted for 30 years. The Wars of the Roses finally ended in 1485 when Henry Tudor, a descendant of the Lancastrian house, defeated the Yorkist King Richard III in the Battle of Bosworth Field. Henry Tudor married Elizabeth of York and thus united the two royal houses. Under the Tudors, another dynasty of strong monarchs ruled England.

By the late fifteenth century England was, for the most part, a unified country with a strong monarch aided by a national Parliament. A common language, a national law, and the decline of the feudal system helped to unify the country. Furthermore, the English crown—having lost almost all its land on the European continent—could concentrate on strengthening England.

FRANCE BECOMES A STRONG KINGDOM

The growth of the French monarchy began with the election of Hugh Capet as king in 987. The Capetian kings ruled France from 987 to 1328. During this time, they worked to increase their power. King Philip II, known as Philip Augustus, ruled from 1180 to 1223. He is often called the first great king of the Capetian dynasty. Philip added the province of Picardy to his kingdom. Philip also conquered most of the English lands in France. By the time of Philip's death in 1223, he was stronger than any of the nobles of his kingdom.

Philip IV, called Philip the Fair, came to the throne in 1285. He also worked to strengthen the French monarchy. Through marriage, he added the area of Champagne to his kingdom. Philip quarreled with Pope Boniface VIII because the king had taxed the French clergy against the pope's orders. Later, in 1305, Philip succeeded in having a

One of the earliest known illustrations of the English Parliament shows King Edward I presiding. Edward I called the Model Parliament in 1295.

French archbishop elected pope. The new pope, Clement V, moved from Rome to Avignon [A-veen-YOHN], France (see page 250). From Avignon, the pope carried out the French king's orders.

Philip was also responsible for calling the first *Estates-General*, a body representing each of the three groups, or estates, of French society—the clergy, the nobility, and the common townspeople. Philip called the Estates-General to try to win the support of the kingdom in his struggle with the pope.

The French Estates-General, however, did not become a powerful governing body as did the English Parliament. Traditionally, the Estates-General in Paris was not required to approve legislation concerning taxation. The French nobles were more interested in remaining independent of the crown than in gaining control of the government. The

nobles were unwilling to cooperate with the townspeople in checking royal authority.

THE HUNDRED YEARS' WAR The last Capetian king, Charles IV, died in 1328, leaving no male heir. According to an old French custom, women were not permitted to succeed to the throne. A cousin of Charles IV succeeded him as King Philip VI. However, King Edward III of England, a nephew of Charles IV, also claimed the French throne. In 1337, Edward invaded France to make good his claim.

Edward's invasion of France began the Hundred Years' War—a series of conflicts between England and France that lasted from 1337 to 1453. England won most of the early battles. England's success was due, in large part, to its use of foot soldiers armed with the longbow.

France During the Hundred Years' War

- English Landholdings in France, 1337
- English Landholdings in France, 1360
- English Landholdings in France, 1453

0 100 Miles

0 100 Kilometers

The main cause of the Hundred Years' War was the claim of the English kings to the throne of France. As a result of the war, England lost all its land on the European continent except Calais. France, however, had begun to develop a strong, centralized monarchy.

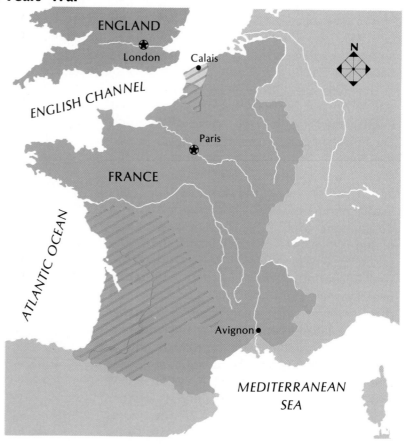

The use of the longbow was a key factor in many of the English victories over the French during the Hundred Years' War.

With the longbow, a skilled archer could fire 10 to 12 arrows a minute, reach 300 yards (274 meters), and penetrate heavy armor. The use of the longbow showed that common foot soldiers armed with the right weapons could defeat heavily armed knights. In addition, the English coordinated the efforts of the longbow archers and the mounted cavalry.

The French, on the other hand, clung to the feudal traditions of warfare. There was little planning for battle on the part of the French. The French nobles saw warfare as a knightly endeavor and looked down on the commoners that made up the infantry. The lack of cooperation between the knights and the foot soldiers contributed greatly to the French losses. By 1360, Edward III had won control of southwestern and west central France.

The next period of the Hundred Years' War was characterized by many small battles, ending with the French regaining most of their land. Then in 1415, King Henry V of England landed in France with 30,000 troops. Henry met the French army at Agincourt [AJ-uhn-KOHRT] and won a major victory. English power in France reached its height between 1415 and 1420. France, weakened by the fighting, concluded a truce—the Treaty of Troyes—in 1420. Under the terms of the Treaty of Troyes, Charles, the rightful heir to the French throne—called the *dauphin*—was excluded from the throne in favor of Henry V of England.

JOAN OF ARC In 1429, a peasant girl, Joan of Arc, claimed she had had visions and had heard voices of saints telling her to rid France of the English. Joan went to see the dauphin to ask for an army. At first Charles and his advisers did not believe Joan. But because of her persistence, Joan received the troops she needed. Joan of Arc's bravery inspired the French troops. She led them to victory at Orleans. Other victories followed. In 1431, Joan was captured. She was put on trial, convicted of heresy, and burned at the stake. But the French victories continued. By 1453, the city of Calais was the only English possession in Europe. France became a unified kingdom under the rule of Charles VII (see map on page 244).

The end of the Hundred Years' War had important results. The French victory ended England's attempts to conquer France. In addition, the feudal system—with its emphasis on loyalty to the lord—declined. Perhaps most important, a sense of *patriotism*—loyalty to one's country—began to develop in France and in England. Consequently, the power of the nobles declined and stronger monarchies developed.

THE EMERGENCE OF SPAIN AND PORTUGAL As you read in Chapter 10, followers of Islam, called *Moors*, conquered most of the Iberian Peninsula—present-day Spain and Portugal—in the eighth century. There they developed a high level of culture. But the Christians, who still lived in the northern parts of Spain, fought to drive the

Moors out. The period in Spanish history from 722 to 1492, when the last Moorish kingdom was defeated, is called *la Reconquista*—the Reconquest.

During the Reconquest several Christian kingdoms—Navarre, León, Castile, and Aragon—were set up. Portugal became an independent kingdom in 1139 when King Alfonso I defeated the Moors. However, the two most important and powerful of these kingdoms were Castile and Aragon.

In 1469, Isabella, heir to the throne of Castile, married Ferdinand, heir to the throne of Aragon. By 1479, Ferdinand and Isabella were jointly ruling their kingdoms. They succeeded in defeating the Moors and capturing Granada, the last Moorish kingdom in Spain, in 1492. The reconquest of the Iberian Peninsula was complete.

The joining of Castile and Aragon was one of the major developments in Spain in the late Middle Ages. Another major development was the rise of secular, royal authority. The Spanish monarchs granted many freedoms to the growing towns and cities. The monarchs joined with the towns and cities to weaken the power of the nobility. The townspeople thus owed loyalty only to the crown.

DEVELOPMENTS IN GERMANY AND ITALY

Strong monarchies did not develop in either Germany or Italy in the late Middle Ages, as they did in England, France, and Spain. In the tenth century, Henry the Fowler and then Otto the Great—who became the Holy Roman emperor in 962—started to unify Germany and strengthen the crown. However, later rulers failed to increase their power. One of the chief reasons for their failure was that imperial succession was not hereditary. The German nobles retained the right to elect the Holy Roman emperor. Thus, a noble family seldom ruled long enough to develop the power and the loyalty necessary to proceed to unify the country. To keep their own power, the nobles usually elected relatively weak emperors.

In addition, the emperors lost power north of the Alps because of their continual attempts to hold northern Italy. The idea of uniting Germany and Italy under one ruler was started in 962, when Otto the Great was crowned Holy Roman emperor by the pope. This idea was perpetuated by later rulers. These later rulers made numerous attempts to consolidate their power in Italy. In the process, however, the emperors failed to unify the German duchies and towns.

A strong central government did not emerge in Italy in the late Middle Ages partly because of the interference of the Holy Roman emperors. Small countries—such as the Kingdom of Sicily and the city-states of Venice, Florence, and Milan—developed on the Italian Peninsula. Furthermore, the existence of a temporal domain of the popes—the Papal States—contributed to the lack of unity in Italy.

Although strong monarchs did not emerge in Germany and Italy at this time, the rise

The unification of Spain was completed in 1492, when the Moors were driven from Granada.

The Unification of Spain, 1492

FRANCE

KINGDOM OF NAVARRE

KINGDOM OF ARAGON

KINGDOM OF PORTUGAL

KINGDOM OF CASTILE

MEDITERRANEAN SEA

GRANADA

N

0   100 Miles

0   100 Kilometers

Kingdom of Spain

Last Moorish Kingdom Conquered by Spain

of other secular authorities—Holy Roman emperors, dukes, and counts—weakened the power of the Roman Catholic Church. The expansion of secular authority within the Holy Roman Empire was a major development of the late Middle Ages.

QUESTIONS FOR REVIEW

1 *Who set up the beginning of the English jury system?*

2 *What were three important results of the Hundred Years' War?*

3 *Why did a strong monarchy fail to develop in Germany in the late Middle Ages?*

2 COMPETITION AND CONFLICT: PAPACY AND MONARCHY

The growth of monarchies during the Middle Ages inevitably led to conflicts with the leaders of the Church. Popes and monarchs competed for power, control of land, and revenues. Changing attitudes and internal problems plagued the Church and influenced the outcome of the struggle between the secular and spiritual leaders of western Europe. By the end of the Middle Ages the once all-powerful Church no longer was the dominant force it had been just a few centuries earlier.

THE ROLE OF THE CHURCH It would be difficult to understate the importance of the Roman Catholic Church during the Middle Ages. After the fall of the Roman Empire in western Europe, the Church was a stabilizing factor. The Church kept learning alive. It helped preserve literature, sculpture, and architecture. Furthermore, the Church offered a spiritual goal—salvation—to all Christians. The Church was central in

the lives of the people of the Middle Ages—a time often referred to as the Age of Faith.

The Roman Catholic Church was at the height of its power by the beginning of the thirteenth century. The time when the Church reached this height is sometimes referred to as the High Middle Ages. After 1200, however, the power of the Church began to decline. The next three centuries brought political, intellectual, and religious changes—changes that eroded the once-powerful position of the Church.

THE CHURCH AND THE CRUSADES The Crusades were military campaigns by Christians to capture the *Holy Land*—the land where Jesus lived and died—from the Muslims. The Holy Land was captured by the Seljuk [SEL-JOOK] Turks, who were Muslims, in 1071. The Seljuk Turks interfered with the Christian pilgrimages to the Holy Land. In 1095, Pope Urban II called upon the Christians of Europe to join a Crusade to free the Holy Land from the *infidels*—the non-believing Muslims.

Many people became crusaders because of deep religious convictions. People were told that those who were killed in a Crusade would achieve immediate salvation. Other people saw the Crusades as an opportunity. Some merchants viewed the Crusades as an opportunity to expand their trade. Knights saw a chance for adventure, and many nobles hoped to expand their power and gain new land.

Four major Crusades were carried out between 1096 and 1204 (see map on page 248). After 1204, there were several less-important Crusades. The First Crusade, started in 1096, resulted in the crusaders' capturing Jerusalem and parts of Asia Minor. The crusaders founded four states on the eastern Mediterranean—the County of Edessa, the Principality of Antioch, the County of Tripoli, and the Kingdom of Jerusalem. However, by 1147, the Turks had conquered the County of Edessa, and this

The Routes of the Four Major Crusades

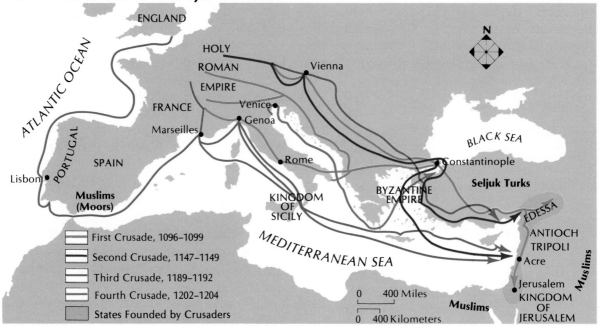

Crusaders traveled by land and by sea to the eastern shore of the Mediterranean Sea in attempts to recapture the Holy Land.

Turkish victory caused the western Europeans to organize the Second Crusade. Overall, the Second Crusade was a triumph for the Muslims.

After the Muslims recaptured Jerusalem in 1187, the Third Crusade was organized. Richard the Lion-Hearted, king of England, defeated the Turkish leader, Saladin, in several battles and captured the city of Acre. Although Richard could not capture Jerusalem, he arranged a truce with Saladin. Under this truce, Christians were allowed to enter Jerusalem freely.

The Fourth Crusade against the Turks turned into an expedition for political and economic gain. The crusaders had arranged for the Venetians to take them by ship to the Holy Land. However, when the crusaders reached Venice, they found that they could not pay the cost. The Venetians then agreed to transport the crusaders if they would help the Venetian army attack the Byzantine Empire. The crusaders, allied with the Venetians, captured the town of Zara and then went on to attack Constantinople. The successful crusaders removed the Byzantine emperor and set up the Latin Empire, which lasted until 1261. The crusaders, however, never reached the Holy Land.

Other Crusades were organized in the 1200's, but these met with little success. In 1291, the Turks captured Acre, the last Christian stronghold in the Holy Land, and the Crusades ended.

RESULTS OF THE CRUSADES A significant outcome of the Crusades was an increase in trade. The Crusades did not cause Europeans to discover the "luxuries of the East," as is commonly believed. But it can be said that the Crusades stimulated and increased trade with the East.

Trade between Europe and the East had never ended. The Crusades occurred at about the same time that western Europe was beginning to expand its trade with the East. Traders—one of the most famous is Marco Polo—traveled to the East and organized thriving international businesses. Rice, sugar, spices, lemons, melons, apricots, and other typically Eastern foods became common in the West. New types of cloth—cottons and satins—and new colors were also brought to the West.

During the Crusades, an emerging group of town dwellers benefited most from the increased trade. Merchants and business people lent money to the crusaders and sold them supplies. Many peasants and serfs bought their freedom from masters who needed money for the Crusades. Many of these newly freed people moved to the growing towns. The Crusades thus helped speed up the decline of the feudal system.

At first, the Crusades strengthened the Roman Catholic Church. The enthusiasm of the early crusaders added to the Church's sense of a spiritual mission. But as the Crusades continued unsuccessfully, the crusaders became discouraged and their fervor decreased. The type of people joining the Crusades changed. Many of the later crusaders lacked religious motivations. For example, judges often gave criminals the choice of going to jail or joining a Crusade. In time, the failure of the Crusades to free the Holy Land from the Turks and the pope's support of these wars undermined the spiritual authority of the Church.

THE POPE AND THE HOLY ROMAN EMPEROR CLASH During the late Middle Ages, the Church suffered in ways other than the unsuccessful Crusades. Several corrupt practices troubled the Church. One of these was *lay investiture*—the practice through which a monarch or a lord would invest a person with, or appoint a person to, a Church office. A second corrupt practice was *simony*—the selling of Church offices. A third abuse was marriages among the clergy. And a fourth problem was the interference of monarchs and the nobility in the election of the pope.

The practice of lay investiture caused serious confrontations between the popes and the Holy Roman emperors. The Holy Roman emperors believed that it was their right to appoint the bishops within the Empire. However, in 1075 Pope Gregory VII issued a decree that ordered an end to lay investiture. The Holy Roman emperor, Henry IV, felt threatened by the pope's decree for two reasons. The Church owned almost one third of the German land. In addition, important members of the clergy served Henry as administrators and political advisers. Naturally, Henry resented the pope's decree.

Henry refused to accept the pope's ruling. He continued to appoint people to Church offices. Pope Gregory threatened Henry with *excommunication*—a decree that would keep Henry from receiving the sacraments of the Church and would free his subjects from their feudal duties. Henry responded by calling a council of German bishops. The council voted that Pope Gregory VII should be deposed. Henry informed the pope of the bishops' decision in a letter that concluded: "I, Henry, king by the grace of God, together with all our bishops, say unto thee: 'Come down, come down, to be damned throughout all eternity'!" Gregory excommunicated Henry. The pope also declared that Henry's subjects should no longer recognize him as king, saying, "I absolve all Christians from the oath they have taken to him [Henry], and forbid anyone to recognize him as king."

The papal denunciation of Henry provided a convenient excuse for the German princes, dukes, and other nobles to rebel. They planned a meeting, with the pope presiding, to elect a new emperor. Given the situation, Henry admitted defeat. Henry decided to try to regain the pope's favor.

Henry met the pope to ask his forgiveness at Canossa, a castle high in the mountains of northern Italy. Pope Gregory described Henry at the gates of the castle as follows: "[Henry] stood in wretchedness, barefooted and clad in woolen, for three days before the gate of the castle, and implored with profuse weeping . . . until he had moved all who saw or heard it to . . . pity." Gregory removed the excommunication and Henry's imperial authority was safe.

But Henry and Gregory continued to argue. The conflict over lay investiture was not settled until after Gregory and Henry died. In 1122, a compromise, the *Concordat of Worms*—a formal agreement signed at the city of Worms, Germany—provided that the Church would decide who was to be appointed to a Church office. But the worldly feudal obligations of the bishops—and their loyalty—were retained by the emperor.

The controversy over lay investiture and other abuses caused members of the Church to call for reforms. The leaders of reform movements were frequently monks in the many new monasteries that were founded during the tenth and eleventh centuries. One of the most famous movements was established at Cluny, France, in A.D. 910. The Cluniac monks were against lay investiture, simony, marriage of the clergy, and lay interference in papal elections. Later, other groups, such as the Franciscans and the Dominicans, also founded monasteries throughout Europe and worked for reform.

THE TROUBLED PAPACY As you read earlier in this chapter, Philip IV of France secured the election of a French pope, Clement V, in 1305. The new pope moved from Rome to Avignon, France. The time the papacy remained in Avignon (1309–1377) is often called the Babylonian Captivity. The popes at Avignon were strongly influenced by the French rulers. During the Avignon papacy, the popes and the Church lost power and prestige, especially in countries other than France.

Pope Gregory XI, another French pope, returned the papacy to Rome in 1377. When he died in 1378, the cardinals, threatened by a Roman mob, elected an Italian pope—Urban VI. The cardinals later declared the election of Urban VI invalid because of the threats of the mob and elected another pope. There were now two popes—one at Rome and one at Avignon. This split in the Church, called the Great Schism, lasted for about 40 years. The Great Schism divided the peoples and the rulers of Europe in their allegiance to the Church. It soon became clear that there should not be two popes. Questions arose over Church appointments and Church revenues. In 1409, a Church council met at Pisa in northern Italy to heal the schism. The council called for both popes to resign and then elected a new pope. However, since neither of the popes were willing to obey the council, there were now three popes. Finally in 1417, another Church council deposed all three popes. The council then elected a new pope—Martin V.

The troubles of the papacy during the Babylonian Captivity and the Great Schism greatly weakened the prestige and the au-

Clement V was the pope who moved the seat of the papacy from Rome to Avignon, France.

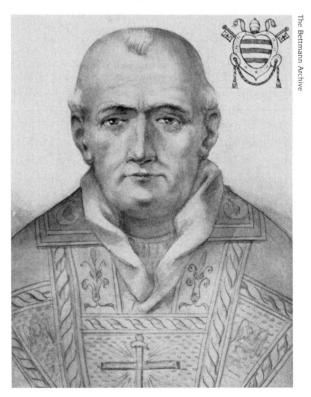

thority of the Church. Catholics throughout Europe were shocked and seriously worried about the salvation of their souls because they did not know which pope to believe. Scholars questioned the legitimacy of the pope as God's representative on earth. These papal troubles, combined with other criticisms, resulted in a weakened Church that never regained its supreme role in most people's lives.

CRITICS CALL FOR CHURCH REFORMS

Not surprisingly, the changing conditions of the late Middle Ages influenced the way that many people viewed their Church. Rather than spiritual and moral leadership, the Church seemed to reflect incompetence and intrigue. One of those who spoke for changes in the Church was John Wycliffe.

Wycliffe was an English priest at Oxford University. After the Great Schism in 1378, Wycliffe began teaching that the Bible, not the pope, is the highest religious authority. He spoke out against pilgrimages, the worldliness of the clergy, and some of the sacraments. He also taught that the Church has no right to interfere in government and that all clergy are subject to secular laws.

At first, Wycliffe was supported by the nobles. But he lost this support after his followers—called Lollards because of the way they mumbled their prayers—were accused of stirring up a revolt among the peasants. Many Lollards were beheaded or burned at the stake as heretics. Wycliffe's ideas became unpopular in England, but they spread to other places in Europe.

Ideas similar to Wycliffe's were taught around 1400 by John Huss, a professor at the University of Prague in Bohemia (now in Czechoslovakia). Huss's ideas had gained a great deal of local support. His followers, called Hussites, became an important religious movement. To check this movement, the Church summoned Huss to appear before a Church council. Because Huss refused to recant his teachings, he was accused of heresy and burned at the stake.

Historical Pictures Service

John Wycliffe, who lived from 1320 to 1384, was an English theologian who challenged many of the religious beliefs of his time.

By the mid-fifteenth century, most of the calls for reform of the Church had been suppressed. But the teachings of Wycliffe, Huss, and other reformers laid the foundation for greater changes that would come about in the sixteenth century during the Reformation (see Chapter 17).

QUESTIONS FOR REVIEW

1 *What were the Crusades?*

2 *What four corrupt practices troubled the Roman Catholic Church during the late Middle Ages?*

3 *Why did the pope and the Holy Roman emperor come into conflict?*

3 THE GROWTH OF TRADE AND URBAN SOCIETIES

Another characteristic of the Middle Ages was the increased growth and development of towns and cities. Trade increased during this period, and the beginnings of modern banking developed. As serfdom began to disappear, the number of free workers increased. In many instances, these workers moved to the towns, where they formed associations to protect their trades. The social and economic changes that occurred during the late Middle Ages helped to bring an end to the feudal system.

THE RISE OF TOWNS AND CITIES Towns and cities, which had never totally disappeared from western Europe, began to grow as early as the eleventh century. Towns developed in western Europe at different times and for different reasons. However,

some generalizations concerning the growth of towns in the Middle Ages can be made.

Towns often developed from peasant villages. Many of the towns grew because their location was favorable to trade. Often, people came to the towns because the walls of the towns offered protection from invaders.

After a period of time, many towns were granted charters by kings and princes. The town's charter usually granted specific privileges—such as the right to move freely—to the town's residents. The right to move freely was one of the most important privileges because it meant that the townspeople were to be treated as free people, not as serfs. They were no longer bound to the old feudal customs of vassalage and loyalty. This provision of town charters helped to destroy the feudal system.

In some instances, a town charter was granted by a powerful lord, especially if the lord needed money. The townspeople would willingly pay for the privileges granted in a

After medieval merchants and townspeople bought their freedom from a feudal lord, they received a town charter. The charter guaranteed certain rights to the townspeople and freed them from most feudal obligations.

charter. However, monarchs were usually more sympathetic to the townspeople and granted town charters more readily. Thus, monarchs helped assure the loyalty of the townspeople and, at the same time, decreased the power of the nobles. Furthermore, the granting of charters by the monarchs supplemented the royal revenues that came from taxing the growing trade of the towns.

The artisans and the merchants who lived in the towns were forerunners of the modern middle class. They were neither nobles nor peasants. Their importance was political and social, as well as economic. They wanted stable governments to protect property and trade. Thus, they usually favored the rising monarchs over the nobility. The monarchs, in an effort to decrease the power of the nobles, often employed educated town dwellers in government positions.

The growth of towns contributed to the decline of serfdom. Towns offered serfs the opportunity to become free people. A common saying at the time was "Town air makes men free." Furthermore, those serfs that continued to farm the land outside the towns sold their surplus crops to the townspeople. As the population of the towns grew and as trade increased, some medieval townspeople organized themselves into business associations.

MERCHANT AND CRAFT GUILDS Merchants and craft workers in the medieval towns worked to protect their businesses by organizing into associations called *guilds*. The guilds set up rules regulating business. The guilds organized the economy of the late Middle Ages.

The merchant guilds wanted all the trading within the towns to be done by their own members. Merchant guilds strictly regulated trade with other towns. Competition did not exist within the guilds. They fixed prices and punished members who cheated customers.

A guild master carefully inspected all the work done by the journeymen and the apprentices.

The craft guilds each represented a particular trade. The purpose of the craft guilds was to promote the economic well-being of its members. The craft guilds guaranteed full employment at high pay by restricting membership. A craft guild in a town held a monopoly of its product. The guild regulated work procedures and hours, forbade advertising, and set wages. It also standardized the quality and the price of a product.

The price that could be charged for a product was called the just price. The just price included only the cost of the materials and the labor used in making the product. The just price did not include any profit.

Craft guilds were made up of apprentices, journeymen, and masters. A young apprentice worked without pay for a period of time, usually seven years. The apprentice received food, clothing, shelter, and training in the craft from the employer, a master. After the apprentice had become skilled at the craft, the apprentice became a journeyman and earned wages. Finally, after several

(*Text continued on page 255.*)

Life at the Time

A Paris Homemaker in the Fourteenth Century

Men have often written books telling women how to behave. This was certainly true in the Middle Ages. Women in the Middle Ages—at all levels of society—were subject to their fathers, brothers, or husbands. In many regions, a woman could not inherit land, make a legal will, or testify in court.

The following excerpts are taken from a book written by a man identified as the House-holder of Paris. The instructions given in the book are representative of how a woman was expected to conduct herself. The author, well over 60 years old, was wealthy and well educated, as well as very particular. He wrote his book between 1392 and 1394 to instruct his young wife. The book covers numerous topics, including religious and moral duties, household management, cooking, and clothing.

"Know . . . that if you wish to follow my advice you will have great care and regard for what you and I can afford to do, according to our estate. Have a care that you be honestly clad, without new devices and without too much or too little frippery [nonessentials]. And before you leave your chamber and house, take care first that the collar of your shift, and of your [petticoats], do not hang out one over the other, as happens with certain drunken, foolish or witless women, who have no care for their honour . . . When you go to town or to church go suitably accompanied by honourable women according to your estate, and flee suspicious company, never allowing any ill-famed woman to be seen in your presence. And as you go bear your head upright and your eyelids low and without fluttering, and look straight in front of you about four rods [66 feet or 20.1 meters] ahead, without looking round at any man or woman to the right or to the left, nor looking up, nor glancing from place to place, nor stopping to speak to anyone on the road. . . .

"[C]herish the person of your husband carefully, and, I pray you, keep him in clean linen, for 'tis your business. [When on a journey, a husband] is upheld by the hope that he has of his wife's care of him on his return, and of the ease, the joys and the pleasures which she will do to him, or cause to be done to him in her presence; to have his shoes removed before a good fire, his feet washed and to have fresh shoes and stockings, to be given good food and drink, to be well served and well looked after, . . .

"[R]emember the rustic proverb, which saith that there be three things which drive the goodman from home, to wit, a dripping roof, a smoking chimney and a scolding woman."

The wife of the Householder of Paris, an "ideal" woman of the late Middle Ages, cooked supper with the aid of his book.

years of additional work, a journeyman could become a master. However, a journeyman could become a master only with the approval of the guild. Normally, the guild limited the number of masters within the guild. In addition, to become a master, a journeyman had to produce a very fine piece of work—a masterpiece. With enough money, the new master could then open a shop.

THE ROLE OF WOMEN Women's roles in the late Middle Ages varied from place to place and depended upon the social class to which the women belonged. Women of all social classes were considered to be subservient to their husbands. However, once widowed, women were usually free to choose for themselves whether to remarry or not.

In the guilds, women held a monopoly of certain crafts, such as spinning, ale making, and producing certain foods. In some guilds, women were excluded, except for the members' wives and daughters. In other guilds, women did the same work as men.

Similarly, the life of a merchant's wife was very busy. A merchant's wife was responsible for managing the household and, in the merchant's absence, the business as well. The merchant's wife supervised the sewing, weaving, candle making, and marketing and directed the household servants. She might also keep the accounts of the merchant's business.

Some women in the late Middle Ages were professors and doctors. And at least one woman, Christine de Pisan, earned her living as an author. Many of her books and poems were concerned with women's education and their treatment by their husbands. Even though they often did the same work as men, women were considered legally and socially inferior.

MEDIEVAL FAIRS Medieval fairs were important events that helped stimulate trade. Merchants probably started the idea of a trade fair by selling goods at religious festivals. The fairs became meeting places for merchants from Italy and northern Europe.

Fairs were special events, held only seasonally or annually. Fairs were important because they were places where people exchanged goods and ideas. People from all over Europe traded information about new methods of farming, transportation, and industry. Fairs were also important because they helped develop an economy based on money rather than on barter.

The people at the fairs came from many different countries and frequently had different types of money. Money changers were needed to figure out how much one currency was worth in terms of another. Some money changers became moneylenders. They were able to lend out money because merchants often left large amounts of money with the money changers for safekeeping. Thus, many moneylenders developed into bankers.

Early banking and moneylending activities were often done in the moneylender's home.

THE BEGINNINGS OF BANKING Banking as we know it today developed in the Middle Ages. The word *bank* comes from the Italian word *banca*, meaning the money changer's bench or table. The first bankers—moneylenders and goldsmiths—stored gold or other valuables for the merchants. The merchants received receipts, or letters of credit, for their deposits, and the goldsmiths promised to return the deposit on demand—whenever the receipts were presented. These receipts began to be used as payments for goods. In other words, the receipts were used as money. Similar banking practices developed throughout western Europe.

In time, the goldsmiths realized that not all the merchants came to withdraw their deposits at the same time. Thus, the goldsmiths could also lend money. The development of an economy based on money and banking was important. It allowed merchants to travel without carrying large amounts of cash with them. Arrangements were made among banks of different towns to issue money to the merchants in exchange for letters of credit. Banks began issuing paper money around the year 1500.

The Jews were among the first moneylenders and bankers in Europe. Often, Jews became moneylenders for three reasons. Jews were not bound by Church teachings forbidding *usury*—the charging of interest on loans. In addition, religious intolerance barred Jews from the guilds. Finally, Jews were often forbidden to own land. Thus, moneylending was one of the few jobs open to them. The Jews' risk in lending money was often very great. This was because many people used religious prejudice as an excuse for not repaying their loans to Jewish bankers. Futhermore, Jews were often humiliated for carrying on business. Many Jews also had to wear a Star of David or a horned cap. Later, Christians in the trading cities in northern Italy became the leading bankers. Officially, these Christian bankers did not charge interest on their loans.

However, they often charged service fees and late charges if the money was not paid back on time.

THE ITALIAN TRADING CITIES By the 1200's the cities of northern Italy had, for the most part, become independent city-states. These cities—Venice, Florence, Milan, Genoa, and others—became centers of trade. The location of these cities—between western Europe and the Byzantine Empire—was a major reason for their importance. They were commercial cities controlled by merchants and bankers. These cities became very wealthy through their trading activities.

For example, in the thirteenth century, the merchants of Venice owned a fleet of about 3,000 ships. Florence developed into an important city of industry. Florentine bankers became some of the most powerful in the world. Milan and Genoa also became important cities of trade and industry. In time, other European cities also became important trading centers.

THE HANSEATIC LEAGUE The Hanseatic League was a trade association of cities in northern Germany. These cities formed the Hanseatic League to protect their trading interests. Cities such as Lübeck, Danzig, Cologne, and Hamburg were among the important cities of the league in the late thirteenth century. Later, other cities joined.

The Hanseatic League was important because of its influence on trade in northern Europe. It controlled the fur trade with Russia and the fishing trade with Norway and Sweden. The league also carried on a thriving trade with England and Flanders. The league remained a powerful trading organization well into the late fifteenth century.

TOWN LIFE IN THE LATE MIDDLE AGES The typical city of the late Middle Ages was relatively small by modern standards. Medieval cities were usually walled towns built in a series of ever-widening circles. Whenever the citizens decided to expand the town, the old walls were torn down and new walls were built. The plan of Paris shows this type of development.

Though relatively small in population, medieval cities tended to be overcrowded. Streets, especially in the older towns and cities, were usually dark and narrow. People tended to construct buildings five or six stories high because the city walls limited expansion.

THE BLACK DEATH An epidemic of bubonic plague struck Europe in late 1347. The plague was a disease caused by a type of bacterium that was spread by certain fleas. These fleas were carried by rats. After a person was infected, the disease produced dark patches over the entire body and turned the tongue black. Thus, the disease was called the Black Death. People infected with the disease died within three days.

The Black Death was brought to Europe by merchant ships from Asia. It spread rapidly through most of the cities and towns of Europe. By 1348 the plague had reached England and Germany; by 1349 it had spread to Scandinavia and Poland; by 1351 it had ravaged Russia. Only gradually did the disease disappear.

Exactly how many people died during the Black Death is not known. But we do know that entire villages were wiped out. Most historians generally conclude that one third to one half of Europe's population died.

As a result of Europe's loss of population, the number of workers declined sharply. Some of the poor who had survived the Black Death realized that they could get higher pay. Often, the serfs demanded and received freedom and wages for their work. When the nobility refused to grant the peasants' requests and imposed new taxes, the peasants rebelled.

Wat Tyler's Rebellion was a revolt of the English peasants in 1381. The peasants demanded an end to serfdom and to oppressive labor laws. About the same time, a more widespread revolt of the peasants occurred in France—the uprising of the Jacquerie. These revolts were violently put down by the nobility.

By the late 1400's, the general economic problems in western Europe were easing. Wages and prices rose. Aided by improving conditions, the rising monarchs of western Europe increased their power and further decreased the nobles' power. Feudalism was ending in western Europe and new forces of learning and culture were developing, starting in the cities of northern Italy.

The triumph of the bubonic plague is illustrated by this fresco of the late Middle Ages.

EPA

QUESTIONS FOR REVIEW

1 *Why were town charters important?*

2 *What was the purpose of the guilds?*

3 *How did medieval fairs contribute to the growth of trade?*

4 INTELLECTUAL AND CULTURAL DEVELOPMENT

The social and economic changes that occurred during the late Middle Ages reflected the changing attitudes and ideas of the people. None of the changes were immediate. Instead, they were part of a gradual development that took place in much of western Europe from the eleventh century through the fifteenth century. It was during this period that new methods arose in science, education, literature, and architecture. The feudal system in western Europe was giving way to a new way of life and thought.

MEDIEVAL UNIVERSITIES The late Middle Ages witnessed a revival of education. During the 1100's the rise of the town dwellers, monastic reforms, the growth of trade, and new contacts with other cultures stimulated the educational interests of the western Europeans. In addition, the Church and secular leaders needed lawyers and people trained in civil matters. To meet this demand, scholars and students formed organizations similar to guilds.

Students who joined these organizations came mostly from the ranks of the nobility and the town dwellers. The early universities of the Middle Ages were not planned; some developed from Church schools. Often, the professors and the students realized that it would be to their advantage to form a guild. Their guild organization was called a university. Later, outstanding universities were founded at Bologna, Paris, Oxford, and Cambridge and elsewhere throughout Europe. In time, the universities were granted charters by monarchs and popes, which gave the universities legal status. An individual with a university degree could teach, practice law, or practice medicine.

LITERATURE IN THE LATE MIDDLE AGES As the educational activity of the late Middle Ages increased, the general level of culture rose. The ability to read and write became more common. The *vernacular*—the everyday language of the people—began to replace Latin as the dominant literary language in western Europe. The use of the vernacular made literature more accessible to the common people. In addition, improved methods of manufacturing paper developed during this time. In the fifteenth century, the use of paper replaced the use of the more expensive parchment. As a result, books became more common. The literature of the late Middle Ages was often instructive in nature, delivering a moral or pointing out some injustice. The favorable educational and literary climate of the late Middle Ages produced several influential authors, most of whom wrote in the vernacular.

Dante Alighieri [DAHN-tay AL-uhg-YER-ee] lived in northern Italy in the late 1200's and early 1300's. He is famous for his epic poem the *Divine Comedy*. The poem traces Dante's imaginary journey through hell, purgatory, and paradise. At the end of the poem, Dante's lesson becomes clear: Love for God complements human love in the search for happiness. Many scholars consider the *Divine Comedy* a summary of medieval thought as well as a magnificent poem of scholarly learning. Dante's works influenced many later writers, including Geoffrey Chaucer and John Milton.

Geoffrey Chaucer was the greatest English poet of the late Middle Ages. His major work—the *Canterbury Tales*—is a group of stories reflecting life-styles of the time. The stories are told by a group of pilgrims on their way to the shrine of Thomas à Becket in Canterbury. Chaucer wrote in Middle English—the form of English used from about 1100 to about 1485.

ARCHITECTURE IN THE LATE MIDDLE AGES The architecture of the late Middle Ages is best illustrated by the striking cathedrals built during that time. The earlier

The Cathedral of Notre Dame was begun in 1163 and was completed 150 years later. Located on the Seine River in Paris, the cathedral is considered one of the finest examples of Gothic architecture, utilizing flying buttresses to support the outside walls.

style of medieval architecture is called *Romanesque*, meaning *like the Roman*.

The cathedrals of the Romanesque style are characterized by thick walls and curved stone roofs called *barrel vaults*. The walls of the cathedrals had to be strong to support the weight of the heavy roofs. Because windows weaken walls, Romanesque cathedrals had few windows. This style is also characterized by rounded arches over doors and windows.

In the late twelfth century, a new style of architecture developed—*Gothic*. Architects in the late twelfth century discovered ways of building that enabled them to construct impressive cathedrals with thinner walls and larger windows. Gothic cathedrals used *flying buttresses*—wooden or stone structures built against the walls, thus giving support to the

roofs and the walls. The superior construction methods of the Gothic cathedrals allowed for large windows. Huge stained-glass windows, often illustrating religious and Biblical scenes, let in light. Gothic cathedrals also exhibited more sculpture and stone carving than did Romanesque cathedrals. The Gothic style of architecture spread from northern France throughout western Europe.

PROGRESS IN SCIENCE In general, progress in science and medicine in the late Middle Ages was slow. People were often superstitious. Medieval medicine was crude, and little was known about anatomy. Most scholars of the Middle Ages were interested in the study of religion and philosophy, not in the facts of science. This was most likely because a majority of the people were concerned with life after death rather than with their earthly life.

However, one leader in the development of scientific progress in the thirteenth century was Roger Bacon. Bacon, an English philosopher, is often called the founder of experimental science. Bacon believed that experimentation is the best way to gain knowledge. He also studied *optics*—the branch of physics that deals with light. Bacon accurately described the anatomy of the eye.

Progress was made in other areas as well. *Alchemy*—a medieval study in which people tried to turn base metals into gold—led to the development of modern chemistry. *Astrology*—the study of the planets and the stars and their effect on human life—contributed to the development of modern astronomy. A few scholars studied physics at the universities at Oxford and at Paris. During the late Middle Ages, the foundations were laid for scientific discoveries in the sixteenth and seventeenth centuries.

QUESTIONS FOR REVIEW

1 *What factors contributed to increasing the educational interests of western Europeans in the late Middle Ages?*

2 *What two medieval studies contributed to the development of modern science?*

3 *Why were religion and philosophy, rather than science, studied in the late Middle Ages?*

CHAPTER SUMMARY

The late Middle Ages was a time of change. The feudal system was giving way to the development of strong monarchies in England, France, and Spain. However, the rulers in Germany and Italy were not able to unite their respective countries.

The Roman Catholic Church was very important to the people of the late Middle Ages. In 1095, Pope Urban II called upon the people of Europe to fight a Crusade against the Muslims who had captured the Holy Land. The Crusades did not succeed in freeing the Holy Land. But the Crusades helped stimulate trade and aided the development of towns and cities. However, problems began to trouble the Church. Corrupt practices, the Avignon papacy, the Great Schism, and the unsuccessful Crusades contributed to a decline in the authority of the Church.

Towns and cities grew at this time and the townspeople flourished in the urban environment. Many of these people organized themselves into guilds. The members of the guilds trained people in the various trades and crafts, and banking aided the growth of trade and commerce.

Universities were organized in the Middle Ages, and the increased use of the vernacular contributed to the growth of literature. Advances were also made in architecture and science.

CHAPTER 13 IN REVIEW

IMPORTANT WORDS, NAMES, AND TERMS

1 Explain, define, or identify each of the following:

Domesday Book	*la Reconquista*	guilds
Magna Carta	Crusades	Christine de Pisan
Hundred Years' War	Holy Land	usury
Joan of Arc	lay investiture	Black Death

FACTS AND IDEAS

2 What were the Wars of the Roses?

3 What was the Estates-General?

4 What were some of the teachings of John Wycliffe?

5 What was the Hanseatic League?

6 How did the Black Death affect feudalism?

ANALYZING VISUAL MATERIAL

7 Examine the picture on page 243. What groups are represented at that meeting of Parliament?

8 Study the map on page 248. According to the map, what European countries participated in the Crusades? Which Crusade failed to reach the Holy Land?

CONCEPTS AND UNDERSTANDINGS

9 Why did Holy Roman Emperor Henry IV and Pope Gregory VII clash?

10 How did medieval guilds organize the economy of the late Middle Ages?

11 How did medieval fairs stimulate trade?

12 How did universities begin to develop in the late Middle Ages?

PROJECTS AND ACTIVITIES

13 Prepare a bulletin-board display illustrating the differences between the Romanesque style and the Gothic style of architecture. On the bulletin board, label the innovations that helped develop the Gothic style.

14 Guilds were an important part of the economic system of the late Middle Ages. Prepare a research paper outlining the life of a member of a guild. Information may be found in books about life in the Middle Ages. Be sure to show how the guild supported, as well as restricted, the various activities of the guild member.

EASTERN EUROPE
CHAPTER **14** IN THE LATE MIDDLE AGES

1 Life in Eastern Europe 2 The Emergence of Czarist
Russia 3 Byzantine Influence in Eastern Europe
4 The Ottoman Empire

Eastern Europe in the late Middle Ages was noticeably
different from western Europe during the same period of time.
Eastern Europe, for the most part, did not develop lasting
countries ruled by strong monarchs. Furthermore, many
eastern European countries were subject to outside invasions
and frequent internal conflicts. The kingdoms of Hungary,
Bohemia, and Poland rose to positions of prominence for a
period of time and then declined. For nearly 250 years, from
about 1240 to about 1480, Russia was controlled by Mongol
invaders from Asia. In addition, the Byzantine Empire—which
had preserved the Greco-Roman heritage for nearly 1,000
years after the fall of Rome in the West—fell to Turkish
invaders. In place of the Byzantine Empire rose a new
power—the Ottoman Empire. The Ottomans became the
dominant force in the eastern Mediterranean region.

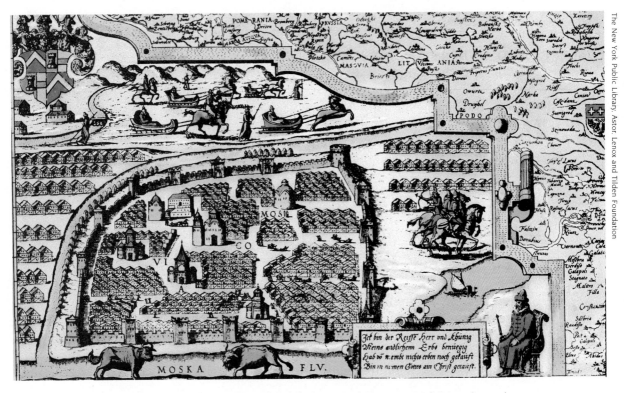

A medieval map shows Moscow and the surrounding countryside near the end
of the reign of Ivan the Great.

1 LIFE IN EASTERN EUROPE

Conditions in eastern Europe in the Middle Ages differed significantly from those in western Europe. Because many different groups of migrating peoples settled in eastern Europe, various cultures and languages developed there. As a result of this diversity, rulers in eastern Europe were not able to develop strong central governments, and the nobility often retained more power than did their counterparts in the west. Feudalism therefore lasted in eastern Europe for several hundred more years than did feudalism in the west.

THE GEOGRAPHY OF EASTERN EUROPE

The northern section of eastern Europe is part of a vast plain that stretches from the central highlands of Siberia westward to the Alps of central Europe. The mountains of eastern Europe—the Sudeten [soo-DAYT-uhn] and the Carpathian [kahr-PAY-thee-uhn] mountains—are low in elevation and contain many passes. Farther to the south are the Hungarian plain and the Rumanian plain. The southernmost region is made up of mountains and valleys.

The geography of eastern Europe has aided the movement of various peoples and the transportation of goods for trade. Transportation within the region was made easier by a series of rivers—most of which flow north and south—that created a system of natural waterways. However, in the southern area of eastern Europe—the Balkan Peninsula—numerous mountains tended to separate people into small and partially isolated groups.

PEOPLES OF EASTERN EUROPE

In general, the peoples of eastern Europe can be divided into two basic groups. The larger of these groups—classified as Slavs because they speak Slavic languages—originally came from the marshy areas of Poland and Russia. Later, as certain Germanic tribes moved southward into the Roman Empire, Slavic tribes occupied their lands, and within a relatively short time the Slavs had populated most of eastern Europe. The Slavs were organized into tribes, and for the most part, were farmers, herders, and hunters.

The Slavs can be further divided according to their geographic distribution—eastern Slavs, western Slavs, and southern Slavs. The eastern Slavs settled in the European part of what is now the Soviet Union; the western Slavs lived in the area that is now Czechoslovakia and Poland; the southern Slavs populated the Balkan Peninsula. The Slavs became divided into these three broad groups partly because of natural geographic divisions and partly because invading tribes often settled among the Slavs, separating them into different groups.

The non-Slavic peoples of eastern Europe were the Greeks, the Albanians, the Lithuanians, the Latvians, the Rumanians, and the Hungarians. Some of these peoples lived in areas of eastern Europe before the Slavs, while others settled in the area after the various Slavic groups had arrived.

MIGRATIONS FROM THE EAST As noted earlier, the geography of eastern Europe did not prevent attacks of the area by invaders. In the seventh century, the Hungarian plain was overrun by a group of Asian invaders—the Avars. Also in the seventh century, another group of Asians—the Bulgars—attacked the southern part of eastern Europe. The Bulgars set up a weak empire and, over the centuries, became Slavic in their language and culture.

New invaders from Asia attacked eastern Europe during the late 800's. These new invaders—the Magyars [MAG-yahrz]—conquered the Slavs living in the region of the Danube River. In the early 900's Magyar armies also attacked towns in southern Germany and northern Italy. However, in 955 Otto the Great of Germany defeated the

Eastern Europe

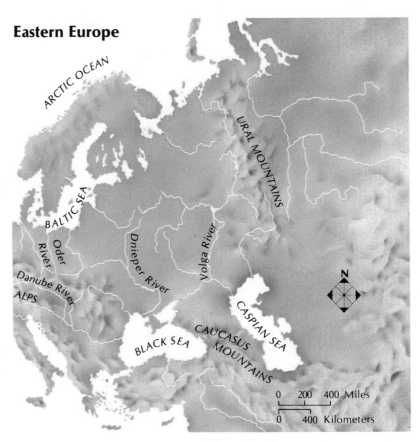

Eastern Europe is often divided into the following four geographic areas: the Great European Plain in the north, the central mountains and highlands, the plains of the Danube River, and the southern mountain regions.

Magyars at the Battle of Lechfeld. The Magyars then settled peacefully in the area of what is now Hungary.

These early invasions of eastern Europe helped shape the history of the region in several ways. The invasions kept the region in a state of conflict and thus prevented large-scale political and economic development. The constant warfare also contributed to the power of the nobles and tended to strengthen the feudal system in eastern Europe.

MIGRATIONS FROM THE WEST At about the same time that Asian invaders were attacking eastern Europe, Germanic invaders came from the west. These invasions are referred to by the German phrase *Drang nach Osten*—the drive to the east.

In the ninth century, the Germanic Bavarians moved eastward and settled on the Hungarian plain. Other Germanic groups

settled as far east as the Oder River. Germanic invasions east of the Oder River —carried out by Christian monks known as the Teutonic Knights—occurred in the eleventh century. In response to a request from the ruler of Poland, the Teutonic Order set out to convert the pagan Prussians to Christianity. When the Prussians refused Christianity, they were killed; German immigrants colonized the area and founded the German province of East Prussia. Other Germanic groups settled in the Slavic regions of Silesia and Bohemia.

In contrast to the relatively primitive invaders from the east, the Germanic invaders brought with them a relatively high level of culture. The Germanic settlers that came after the invaders were often merchants, artisans, and missionaries. For the most part, the Germanic peoples were not absorbed by the Slavic groups of eastern Europe. Instead, the Germanic groups set up their own communities, retained their own culture, and influenced the Slavic culture of the area. The settlement of these Germanic groups promoted the development of towns and increased the trade and the commerce of the region. The towns of Krakow and Riga became members of the Hanseatic League in the later part of the Middle Ages.

RELIGIOUS DIFFERENCES Another major reason why eastern Europe developed differently from western Europe in the late Middle Ages was the lack of religious unity in the east. In the west, the vast majority of the people were Roman Catholic. In eastern Europe, many groups of people—Poles, Lithuanians, Czechs, Slovaks, Hungarians, and Croats among them—were also followers of Roman Catholicism. But several other large groups—Russians, Serbians, Bulgarians, Greeks, and Rumanians—were members of the Eastern Orthodox Church.

While both Christian churches adhered to basically the same teachings, there were essential differences between the churches. In the west, the leader of the Roman Catholic Church—the pope—claimed supremacy over kings and emperors. In addition, religious unity was maintained in the west because all Church services were performed in Latin. Furthermore, the monasteries of the west played a major role in the development of universities and the intellectual growth of western Europe.

In contrast, the churches of the Eastern Orthodox faith were state or regional churches. The heads of these churches usually yielded to the demands of the king or the emperor. As a result, eastern churches usually taught the view that the people should be obedient to their ruler. In the Eastern Orthodox Church, services were performed in the different languages of the various groups of people. The monasteries of eastern Europe developed magnificent religious liturgies but did little to advance learning. For the most part, monasteries in

POLITICAL		SOCIAL AND ECONOMIC
	c. 850	Rus settled in western Russia
	c. 860	Cyrillic alphabet developed
Magyars invaded eastern Europe	c. 870	
Battle of Lechfeld	955	
	c. 988	Orthodox Christianity established in Russia
	c. 1040	Prince Yaroslav furthered Kievan cultural growth
Latin Empire established at Constantinople	1204	
Mongols destroyed Kiev	1240	
	1274	Byzantium committed to reunion with Roman Catholic Church
	c. 1300	Novgorod developed as commercial center
Ottoman state most powerful of Islamic principalities	c. 1380	
Constantinople fell	1453	
Moscow renounced Mongol rule	1480	
	c. 1500	Istanbul became center of east-west trade
Ivan the Terrible crowned	1547	
	1549	*Zemskii sobor* in Russia
Battle of Lepanto	1571	
Ottomans defeated at Battle of Vienna	1682	

265

Under the feudal system in Russia, the czar's agents were sent to collect taxes from the serfs. The feudal system, which lasted into the nineteenth century in some parts of Europe, kept most of the serfs living in impoverished conditions.

eastern Europe did not make great contributions to the growth and development of universities or to intellectual thought.

FEUDALISM IN EASTERN EUROPE In the early Middle Ages, feudalism in eastern and western Europe was generally structured in the same way. However, feudalism in eastern Europe differed in several ways from feudalism found in western Europe. The duties and obligations between lord and vassal, for example, were not set forth by the terms of a formal feudal contract. Nor were the relations between lord and vassal controlled by custom or by religious restrictions. Instead, the individual noble landowners merely imposed feudal duties upon their vassals much as they saw fit. The landowners were able to do this because of their position as soldiers and warriors.

In the twelfth and thirteenth centuries, when feudalism in western Europe was beginning to decline, the life of the average eastern European peasant was becoming even more restricted. In contrast to the west, eastern European landlords increased their power and nearly enslaved the peasants.

The relatively short growing season found in most of eastern Europe also contributed to the continued existence of feudalism. In the short growing season of the area, wheat and barley could not ripen. Rye, however, which yielded less grain per acre, ripened in the eastern European growing season. This meant that the rye farmers could not support the larger populations that the wheat and barley farmers of western Europe supported. Thus, few urban centers developed and the feudal system was strengthened.

Another reason why feudalism persisted in eastern Europe was the need for military service from the landowning nobles. The feudal rulers often rewarded the nobles with additional grants of land for military service. Thus, the feudal system was maintained.

Furthermore, feudalism continued in eastern Europe because strong central governments failed to develop. In the west, aggressive monarchs weakened the power of the nobility and helped bring about the decline of feudal society. In the east, the nobility increased their power, checked the development of central governments, and thus perpetuated feudal society.

EASTERN EUROPE IN THE LATE MIDDLE AGES The social and political history of eastern Europe is long and varied. Only with a great deal of caution can some generalizations be made. During the major portion of the Middle Ages (A.D. 800–A.D. 1400) most of the tribes living in eastern Europe settled down and organized themselves into tribal kingdoms. In some instances, these kingdoms were powerful and relatively stable. For example, in the tenth century, six Slavic tribes founded the kingdom of Poland by accepting the rule of a single monarch.

However, the kingdoms that developed throughout most of eastern Europe were generally smaller and weaker than their counterparts in western Europe. One reason for this situation was that many of the monarchs of eastern Europe were elected by the nobles, who were eager to preserve their own power. The refusal of the nobles to elect strong rulers greatly hindered the development of kingdoms in eastern Europe.

Nevertheless, some eastern European states—Bulgaria in the twelfth century and Poland in the fifteenth century, for example—obtained for a time a position of prominence in European affairs. But the periods of greatness were brief and generally occurred only when the nobles rallied around a strong leader during a period of crisis.

ECONOMIC DEVELOPMENT IN EASTERN EUROPE Varying degrees of trade existed in eastern Europe in the early Middle Ages. However, trade grew more important in eastern Europe in the late Middle Ages. Trading routes connected eastern Europe to the west. Tar, furs, hides, and timber from the area of the Baltic Sea were traded for wool from England or for luxuries brought from China by Italian merchants. Goods from Asia also reached eastern Europe via the Black Sea. In the late Middle Ages, the kingdoms of Bohemia, Hungary, and Poland carried on an active trade with Asia and with western Europe.

In general, however, there was less overall economic development in eastern Europe than in western Europe during the late Middle Ages. Eastern Europe depended more on farming than did the west. However, a few urban centers—for example, Prague and Krakow—developed into trading cities. Towns, sometimes built by powerful lords, remained small, and little industry developed.

QUESTIONS FOR REVIEW

1 *What two basic groups can the people of eastern Europe be divided into?*

2 *In what way did the various migrating peoples of eastern Europe tend to separate the Slavic peoples?*

3 *Why did the feudal system remain in eastern Europe for a longer period of time than in western Europe?*

2 THE EMERGENCE OF CZARIST RUSSIA

The development of the Russian state began in the Middle Ages. Tribes of eastern Slavs settled in the region and became a basically agricultural people. The leaders of these tribes set up small rival principalities that vied for political supremacy. During the tenth century, Kiev became the dominant principality in the region. The Kievan princes expanded their power and ruled dictatorially. This tradition was affirmed by the teachings of the Orthodox Church and reinforced by the cruel and harsh rule of the Mongols in the thirteenth and fourteenth centuries. Later rulers continued this tradition and expanded their power over the Russian people.

EARLY SETTLEMENT By the eighth century, tribes of eastern Slavs had occupied most of the area that makes up the European part of what is now the Soviet Union. Originally an agricultural people, the eastern Slavs built towns along the Russian rivers. These rivers, which flow either north or south, provided a system of natural water transportation. From these towns the settlers carried on a thriving trade with the Scandinavians to the north and the Byzantine Empire to the south.

During the ninth century, the eastern Slavs became associated with the name *Russians*. Historians debate the origin of the name. Some historians believe that the name is derived from a Scandinavian tribe, the Rus. These historians believe that in the mid-800's the Rus came to the region at the invitation of quarreling Slavic tribes to rule the area and ultimately founded the Kievan state. However, other historians believe that the Rus were a Slavic tribe that eventually dominated the other Slavic peoples in the area. The exact origin of the name *Russian* may never be discovered. However, it is certain that a group of people known as the Rus founded Kiev in the later part of the ninth century.

THE RISE OF KIEV In the early centuries, the eastern part of Europe called Russia was made up of several small states, or principalities, each trying to dominate the others. By the early 900's, Kiev was becoming the dominant principality in Russia.

The first known ruler of Kiev, Prince Oleg, came to power in about 882. Oleg worked to increase his land and brought several of the surrounding Slavic tribes under his rule. In the tenth century, Oleg's successors expanded the power of Kiev. By about 988, most of the Russian people had adopted Orthodox Christianity from Constantinople. Russia was thus linked culturally to Byzantium and not to Rome.

However, Kiev often had difficulty maintaining its dominant position. A major reason for this difficulty was the series of civil wars that resulted over succession to power

Prince Yaroslav, known as the Wise, advanced the cultural development of Kiev and strengthened the role of the Christian religion in Russia.

after a ruler died. The concept of *hereditary succession*—the idea of the oldest child inheriting the throne—did not become established in Russia until centuries later. As a result, civil wars often broke out among the various sons and brothers who were striving for power. These civil wars tended to severely weaken Kiev.

The leader who brought Kiev to the high point of its power was Prince Yaroslav [yuh-ruh-SLUHF], who ruled from 1019 to 1054. Despite his political accomplishments, however, Yaroslav's greatest contributions to Kiev were cultural.

Yaroslav built churches and monasteries and strengthened the role of the Eastern Orthodox Church in Russia. In addition, he was responsible for the first Russian legal code, *The Russian Justice*. Furthermore, Yaroslav added to Russian culture by patronizing artists and architects and establishing schools and libraries in Kiev.

Unfortunately, before his death Yaroslav divided Kiev into five principalities, giving one to each of his sons. Yaroslav thus hoped to avoid a civil war. Instead, this seriously weakened the country. For almost two centuries, the dominant position of Kiev faded as civil wars and outside invaders devastated the country.

RUSSIAN SOCIETY IN THE MIDDLE AGES

The social and cultural aspects of Russian life varied somewhat from one principality to another during the Middle Ages. However, some overall characteristics of Russian life remained relatively constant.

In general, Russian society was divided into four groups. The royal families of the princes made up the ruling class. Over the years this group became rather large; some princes had nothing to rule and served a more powerful relative. The *boyars*, or nobility, made up the next group. The power and authority of the boyars varied; some actually ruled a principality when the heir to the throne was a child.

Traders and artisans made up the next group in Russian society. However, this group was always small in number. A few principalities—for example, Novgorod and Moscow—became trading centers, but for the most part, the economy of Russia was based on farming. Thus, the fourth group— the peasants—made up the bulk of the Russian population. In general, the conditions of the peasants worsened during the late Middle Ages until, by the sixteenth century, most peasants had been forced into serfdom.

In general, most of the common people living in the Russian principalities during the Middle Ages lived lives of hardship. The people were constantly subject to raids from outside invaders; they scraped a poor existence from the land. For the most part, the common people had no rights and little freedom.

Orthodox Christianity, adopted by the vast majority of Russians, played a central role in the life and culture of the people. Much of the Russian literature and art of the late Middle Ages was Church inspired. Furthermore, the Church aided the development of the dictatorial rule of the Russian princes. This was because the Russian *patriarch*—the head of the Russian Orthodox Church—taught submission to the wishes of the secular rulers. Thus, secular authority in

The boyars often had a great deal of influence over the rulers of early Russia, but their power had diminished by the late 1500's.

Russia developed unchallenged by the Church. The Orthodox Church, by teaching submission to secular rulers, continued to maintain its position in Russian society after the fall of Kiev to the Mongols—a warlike people from Asia—in 1240.

THE MONGOLS CONTROL RUSSIA Originally, the Mongols were a group of nomadic tribes living in the area that is now Mongolia. For many centuries, the Mongols had fought among themselves. However, in 1206 a strong leader—Genghis Khan—became head of all the Mongol tribes (see Chapter 15).

In the early part of the thirteenth century, the Mongols began a campaign of westward expansion. The Mongol armies defeated the Volga Bulgars and the various Russian principalities. A Church leader described the Mongol invasion of Kiev as follows:

. . . they went against Russia and enacted a great massacre in the Russian land, they destroyed towns and fortresses and killed people, they besieged Kiev which had been the capital of Russia, and after a long siege they took it and killed the inhabitants of the city; for this reason, when we passed through that land, we found lying in the field countless heads and bones of dead people; for this city had been extremely large and very populous, whereas now it has been reduced to nothing: barely two hundred houses stand there, and those people are held in the harshest slavery.

By 1240, the Mongols had overrun most of the other Russian principalities.

The Mongols later went on to defeat the combined armies of Poland and the Holy Roman Empire at the Battle of Legnica. By late 1241, the Mongol army had reached as far west as the Adriatic Sea.

The Mongols attacked southeastern Russia in 1223 and then went on to devastate eastern Europe as far west as the Adriatic Sea.

Mongols in Europe

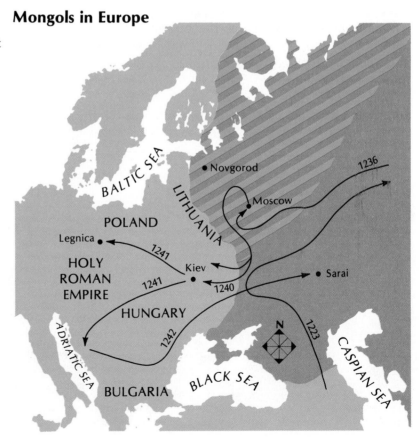

Lands of the Golden Horde

Russian Principalities Indirectly Ruled by the Golden Horde

Routes of Mongol Invaders

0 200 400 Miles

0 400 Kilometers

No European army was able to stop the Mongols. However, in 1241, the Mongol leader died, and the Mongol armies returned to their homeland to choose a new ruler. Although the Mongols retreated east to the region near the Caspian Sea, all of Russia remained under their control.

The Mongols established a capital at the city of Sarai, and the Golden Horde, as the Mongol Empire was called, ruled Russia from there. Mongol domination of Russia meant that the ruler of the leading Russian principality—called the grand prince—recognized Mongol overlordship and that the Mongol leader invested the Russian grand prince with his office. It also meant that the Russians paid tribute—in money and in military aid—to the Mongols.

THE IMPACT OF MONGOL RULE Mongol rule of Russia lasted for almost 250 years—from 1240 to about 1480. In general, it had destructive effects on the development of Russian society.

The first of these negative effects was the devastation and massacre of the Russian population. The cruel and harsh rule of the Mongols may have set up a pattern for later Russian rulers. Mongol control isolated Russia from the Byzantine Empire and from western Europe. Russia was thus cut off from the political, social, and religious developments that occurred in Europe during the fourteenth and fifteenth centuries. In addition, the financial tribute imposed by the Mongols kept the Russian economy impoverished.

NOVGOROD After the conquest of Kiev by the Mongols in 1240, Novgorod emerged as the leading Russian principality. Novgorod—located in the northern part of Russia—was not invaded by the Mongols, but Prince Alexander Nevski submitted to Mongol rule because he felt that resistance against them was hopeless.

Nevski became a favorite of the Mongol leader and was invested as grand prince of Russia from 1252 until his death in 1263. Nevski's cooperation with the Mongols was significant because he saved Novgorod from Mongol destruction and preserved Russian culture and the Russian Orthodox Church.

Novgorod's power and importance grew from its position as a commercial center. Novgorod traded the goods of the northern Russian forests with traders from England, Flanders, and Germany. Merchants from Novgorod also traded with members of the Hanseatic League. Novgorod remained an important Russian principality for nearly two centuries until it fell to a new power, the grand duchy of Moscow.

THE RISE OF MOSCOW The town of Moscow was founded in the mid-twelfth century, and very little is known about its early history. By the late thirteenth century, Moscow had become a grand duchy, with Daniel —Alexander Nevski's son—as ruler.

Daniel and several of his successors expanded the land under Moscow's control,

A primary goal of the Russian princes was the territorial expansion of Moscow.

The Growth of Moscow

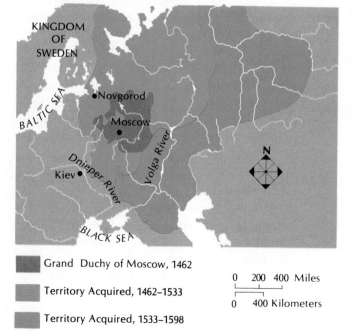

KINGDOM OF SWEDEN

BALTIC SEA

•Novgorod

Moscow •

Dnieper River

Kiev •

Volga River

BLACK SEA

N

■ Grand Duchy of Moscow, 1462

■ Territory Acquired, 1462–1533

■ Territory Acquired, 1533–1598

0 200 400 Miles

0 400 Kilometers

and at the same time kept a relatively peaceful relationship with the Golden Horde. Moscow also grew in power because its leaders collected the tribute due the Golden Horde from the other Russian principalities. Although Moscow's economy was based mainly on agriculture, a thriving commercial trade aided Moscow's rise as a powerful and wealthy principality.

After much interfamily intrigue, Ivan Kalita—meaning *John the Moneybag*—became grand prince of Moscow in the mid-1300's. Ivan used his wealth to purchase additional land and to ransom Russian prisoners from the Mongols to settle on Muscovite lands.

The history of Moscow in the last half of the fourteenth century is characterized by a series of relatively weak rulers, interfamily warfare, and attacks by the Mongols and by the Lithuanians. In 1389 Basil I became grand prince. Basil concluded a peace treaty with the Lithuanians and enlarged Muscovite territory by capturing the lands of the Volga Bulgars. Moscow was becoming increasingly independent of the Mongols.

The death of Basil I in 1425 brought about a civil war concerning succession to the throne, which lasted for almost 25 years. In 1448, Basil II—the son of Basil I—prevailed over his rivals and became grand prince. During Basil II's reign the land of the Golden Horde began to break up into several smaller states. By 1452, Moscow was almost completely free from Mongol rule. At about the same time, the Russian bishops declared the Russian Orthodox Church independent of the Byzantine Church.

MOSCOW THROWS OFF MONGOL RULE
Many historians consider the reign of Ivan III, who ruled from 1462 to 1505, to be the beginning of a new age in Russian history. Ivan III, called the Great, forcibly asserted his rule over two rival Russian principalities—Novgorod and Tver. Ivan brought most Russian land under his control, including the lands once occupied by the principality of Kiev.

One of the most significant events of Ivan the Great's reign was his renunciation in 1480 of allegiance to the Golden Horde. The Mongols attacked the Russians in an effort to reassert their authority, but their efforts failed. Ivan thus established Russia as an independent kingdom.

During his reign, Ivan authorized a widespread building program in Moscow and developed a new legal code for the country. In addition, Ivan increased Russian contacts with western Europe; Ivan himself married Sophia, the niece of the last Byzantine emperor.

After Ivan III's reign, the idea of Moscow as the Third Rome developed. The idea stemmed from a letter written by a Russian Orthodox priest to Ivan's son and successor, Basil III. The priest noted that Rome fell because of heresy; that Constantinople—the Second Rome—fell to the Muslim Ottomans; but that Moscow, now the center of the Russian Orthodox faith, would stand permanently as the Third Rome, for there would be no fourth. Although the priest was referring to Moscow as a religious center, some Russian leaders interpreted this concept as meaning that Moscow was the political heir to the old Roman and Byzantine empires.

THE REIGN OF IVAN THE TERRIBLE
Ivan IV became heir to the Russian throne at age three, upon the death of his father, Basil III. During Ivan's childhood, Russia was ruled by boyars. As a child, Ivan was often cruelly treated by the boyars.

In 1547, Ivan IV was officially crowned as the first czar. Although Ivan has become known to history as Ivan the Terrible, the first part of his reign was characterized by relatively wise rule. For example, in 1549, Ivan called a type of parliament known as the *zemskii sobor* [ZEM-skee SAW-bor]. The *zemskii sobor* approved Ivan's reforms. Ivan worked to bring about the reform of local governments by allowing the people to elect certain officials. Ivan also worked to reorganize the military by making certain regiments permanent. In addition, Ivan improved the legal code.

In the first years of Ivan's reign, Russia was subject to raids from various Mongol groups in search of slaves and riches. Ivan's army beat back the Mongols, and he expanded Russian control over former Mongol lands in the south and east. Ivan also waged war against the Poles and the Lithuanians and seized lands in the northwest.

Ivan sent ambassadors in 1547 to western Europe and invited various specialists—doctors, teachers, artists, and technicians—to Russia. The Russians and the English soon developed a brisk commercial trade.

Biography

Ivan the Terrible

During his 37-year reign as czar, Ivan IV of Russia acquired the title "The Terrible." The first part of Ivan's reign was characterized by relatively wise rule and attempts at governmental reform; the second part was filled with bloodshed, destruction, and terror. Ivan's irresponsible behavior is perhaps best illustrated by the infamous accidental murder of his son and heir—Czarevich Ivan.

The accidental murder of the Czarevich was a consequence of Ivan's temper. The 27-year-old Czarevich was living in the Kremlin with his wife. One evening Ivan entered the Czarevich's apartment and was greeted by his daughter-in-law wearing a dress that Ivan considered inappropriate. Ivan began to scold her. The Czarevich, who was present at the time, resented his father's scolding of his wife, and defended her. Soon, father and son were verbally abusing each other. Ivan, outraged at what he considered his son's lack of respect, suddenly struck the Czarevich in the temple with the iron-tipped staff that he always carried with him. The Czarevich fell to the floor, mortally wounded; five days later he died.

As an absolute ruler, Ivan the Terrible had unlimited power in Russia.

The Bettmann Archive

For weeks after the tragedy, Ivan mourned his son's death and pleaded with God for forgiveness. He tore out his hair and his beard. He wandered through the halls of the Kremlin, calling upon his dead son to return to life. No one could console Ivan.

Even in his grief, Ivan realized not only that he had committed a horrible deed but that he had plunged all of Russia into a situation that might prove disastrous. For with the Czarevich dead, the heir to the Russian throne was Ivan's younger son, Theodore, a feebleminded weakling.

As it turned out, Ivan's fears for the future of Russia were justified. The long-range effect of the tragedy caused the boyars to engage in a struggle for the throne that lasted an entire generation and became known as the Time of Troubles. By killing the Czarevich, Ivan wiped out his direct line of heirs—Theodore died childless, and Dmitri, Ivan's only other living son, was mysteriously murdered after Ivan's death in 1584.

THE LATTER PART OF IVAN'S REIGN

After 1553, Ivan the Terrible underwent a series of changes. Several events most likely contributed to Ivan's dramatic change, including his grave illness and the death of his first wife, Anastasia. Ivan became increasingly distrustful of the boyars and his rule became completely *autocratic*—with unlimited authority. Ivan deposed his closest advisers and never consulted the *zemskii sobor*.

In 1565, Ivan set up the *oprichnina* [aw-preech-NEEN-yah]—a division of the Muscovite state ruled directly by the czar. The people appointed to serve Ivan were similar to a secret police force. Their purpose was to destroy Ivan's enemies.

A reign of terror followed. Hundreds of boyars, their families, and their friends were killed. Entire towns that Ivan felt were not loyal to him were leveled. The lands of the victims were confiscated by Ivan. This terror lasted until the early 1570's. Ivan the Terrible appeared to have lost his emotional balance and often suffered from outbreaks of wild rage. In 1581, during a violent fit, Ivan struck and mortally wounded his son and heir with a pointed staff. Ivan's condition continued to deteriorate until his own death in 1584.

During the reign of Ivan the Terrible, feudalism became entrenched as the basis of the Russian economy. Ivan—and later czars—passed laws that bound the peasants to the land as serfs. Thus by the end of the Middle Ages, feudalism, which was disappearing from western Europe, became firmly established in Russia and lasted there into the nineteenth century.

QUESTIONS FOR REVIEW

1 *Who was the first known ruler of Kiev?*

2 *How did Yaroslav weaken the unity of Kiev?*

3 *Why is the reign of Ivan the Great significant?*

3 BYZANTINE INFLUENCE IN EASTERN EUROPE

During the early Middle Ages, the Byzantine Empire had developed into a major civilization that contributed many outstanding cultural achievements to Western heritage. By the eighth century, the Byzantine Empire stood as a bulwark against the expansion of Islam into Europe. In the centuries that followed, the Byzantine Empire had a tremendous influence upon the development of religion, politics, and the social climate of Europe. Until its final collapse in the late Middle Ages, the impact of the Byzantine Empire was perhaps greatest in the area we know as eastern Europe. From its capital at Constantinople, the Byzantine Empire's rich cultural heritage served as a civilizing influence on the various peoples throughout the area.

CONSTANTINOPLE: CENTER OF TRADE
Constantinople—the capital of the Byzantine Empire—remained the most important trading center in the eastern Mediterranean area throughout the Middle Ages. Located at the crossroads between Europe and Asia, Constantinople was the city through which passed many of the goods being transported between the Orient and Europe, as well as goods from Russia and Scandinavia. In addition, Byzantine trade was supported by the use of a stable money economy based on gold currency.

Constantinople was a thriving city that was not only a center for trade but also the site of the Byzantine government. It was also the religious and intellectual center of the empire. As a meeting place for travelers and traders, the Byzantine Empire became the source from which other areas drew their ideas about religion and politics.

ORTHODOX CHRISTIAN BELIEFS SPREAD
Perhaps one of the most significant contributions of the Byzantine Empire to eastern

Europe during the Middle Ages was Orthodox Christianity. Most of the Slavic groups in the Balkan Peninsula and in Russia were deeply influenced by the Orthodox Church. Missionaries from Constantinople brought the faith—and civilization—to the pagan Slavs. Monasteries based on those found in the Byzantine Empire spread throughout eastern Europe. The monastic life—with its emphasis on solitude, hard work, and poverty—extended throughout Serbia, Bulgaria, Rumania, and Russia.

Because many eastern European peoples adopted the Orthodox Christianity of Byzantium—rather than the Roman Catholicism of western Europe—most eastern European cultures adopted other aspects of the Byzantine culture. Much of the art, architecture, and literature and many political ideas of eastern Europe are rooted in the Byzantine traditions. Many historians note that the autocratic rule of the Russian czars is patterned to a large extent upon the idea of the supremacy of the Byzantine emperors. Even the term *czar*, meaning *Caesar*, came to Russia from the Byzantines. In addition, the alphabet used in many Slavic languages was derived from the Greek letters used in the Byzantine Empire.

The alphabet developed by two Byzantines—SS. Cyril and Methodius—strongly influenced the language and the literature of eastern Europe.

OTHER CONTRIBUTIONS OF BYZANTIUM

Another significant contribution of Byzantium to eastern Europe was its system of law. During the later medieval period, Byzantine law, based on the Emperor Justinian's code of Roman law, spread throughout eastern Europe. In most cases, Byzantine laws replaced the existing traditional laws that were usually based on local or tribal customs. Frequently the traditional laws proved to be inadequate in the face of changing ways of life. The adoption of Byzantine law helped eastern European rulers deal with the increasingly complex social and economic conditions that were developing in the late Middle Ages. Byzantine law—which stressed the supremacy of the state over individuals—also was favored because it aided rulers in their efforts to increase their own power. In addition, the spread of Byzantine law through most of eastern Europe was accepted because it accompanied the spread of Orthodox Christianity.

The literature of eastern Europe was also influenced by the Byzantine culture. The earliest literature showing Byzantine influence is religious in nature. The Bible, *Lives of the Saints*, and other religious works were translated from Greek into Slavic languages, using the Cyrillic alphabet. Later, nonreligious literature and poetry—strongly influenced by the Byzantine culture—developed in eastern Europe.

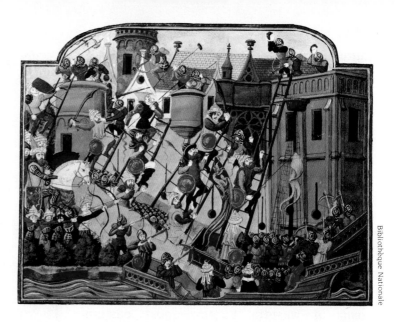

Ottoman forces stormed the walls of Constantinople during their siege of the city in 1453. The city was battered by cannon fire for six weeks before being overrun. The capture of Constantinople marked the end of the Byzantine Empire.

The art and architecture of eastern Europe in the late Middle Ages also exhibits the Byzantine influence that came with the adoption of the Orthodox Christian faith. Many of the churches, the mosaics, and the frescoes found in eastern Europe reflect Byzantine styles. This was especially true in Serbia and in Russia.

THE LATIN EMPIRE AT CONSTANTINOPLE

Despite its high level of culture and its wealth and strength, the Byzantine Empire was not invincible. As you read in Chapter 13, the soldiers of the Fourth Crusade, allied with the Venetian rivals of the Byzantines, attacked Constantinople in 1204. The city was taken by the crusaders and pillaged ruthlessly. Churches, palaces, and monasteries were robbed and destroyed by the Christian soldiers. Much of the art and treasure accumulated at Constantinople over nine centuries was stolen, lost, or destroyed by fire.

After the destruction of the Byzantine Empire by the crusaders, Baldwin, Count of Flanders—a leader of the Fourth Crusade—set up a new empire, called the Latin Empire. Other Crusade leaders established small principalities in the former Byzantine lands. At the same time, the Venetians seized several Byzantine port cities as well as many islands in the Aegean Sea.

Having fled from Constantinople, Byzantine leaders set up three separate principalities—the most important at Nicaea—from what remained of the Byzantine Empire. In 1261, Michael VIII—the Nicaean leader—allied himself with the Bulgarians and the Genoese and succeeded in recapturing Constantinople from the Latins. Michael VIII reestablished the Byzantine Empire. But in the years that followed, the empire set up by Michael VIII was plagued by civil wars, religious conflicts, and threats from foreign invaders.

THE COLLAPSE OF THE EMPIRE

The years between 1261 and 1453 witnessed the slow decline and the final collapse of the Byzantine Empire. Continual disputes among rivals for the throne severely weakened the government of the empire. Income from taxes and customs duties decreased, and the power of the military and naval forces crumbled.

The Byzantine Empire was also weakened by continual religious disputes. Over the years, attempts had been made to reunite the Eastern Orthodox Church and the Roman Catholic Church. At the Council of Lyons in 1274, Michael VIII committed the Byzantines to reunion with Rome. His motive was to gain political allies in western Europe. But the vast majority of the clergy and the people of Byzantium were too loyal to the Orthodox Church to make concessions to Rome merely for political gain. Michael VIII's unsuccessful attempts at the reunification of the two churches only caused further disagreements within the empire.

In addition, the Byzantine Empire was threatened by foreign rivals. The Venetians and the Genoese controlled several port cities and worked to weaken Byzantine trade. At the same time, the Slavic countries in the Balkan Peninsula drained the empire's military strength with continued attacks.

However, the most serious threat to the Byzantine Empire came from the east. The Ottoman Turks, former subjects of the Seljuk Turks, became independent and expanded the territory under their control. The Ottoman Turks conquered most of Asia Minor, bypassed Constantinople, and attacked the Balkan Peninsula. By 1400, all that remained of the Byzantine Empire was Constantinople itself and the immediate area to the north of the city. Surrender was simply a matter of time.

The end of the Byzantine Empire came in 1453. Emperor Constantine XI and about 9,000 soldiers defended the city against a Muslim army of about 160,000. After a Muslim siege of about seven weeks, the city fell. Thus ended the Byzantine Empire. It had survived nearly 1,000 years longer than the Roman Empire in the West. It was replaced by the powerful forces of Islam—the Ottoman Empire.

QUESTIONS FOR REVIEW

1 *What were three significant contributions of the Byzantine Empire to eastern Europe?*

2 *How did Michael VIII reestablish the Byzantine Empire?*

3 *Why did the Byzantine Empire decline after 1261?*

4 THE OTTOMAN EMPIRE

The Ottoman Turks, descendants of nomadic peoples, built a large and powerful empire in eastern Europe and Asia Minor. The Ottoman rulers expanded the land under their control until they ruled most of the area once held by the Byzantines. In 1453, the Ottomans conquered Constantinople and thus finally ended the Byzantine Empire. The Ottomans reached the height of their power in the late sixteenth century but then entered into a period of decline.

THE ORIGINS OF THE OTTOMAN EMPIRE
The Ottoman Turks were the descendants of a nomadic people who had once roamed the Eurasian plains. These groups of nomads eventually settled in the Middle East. Another Turkish group—the Seljuk Turks—at first became the ruling tribe in the area, and the Ottomans remained subservient to the Seljuks. By the tenth century, most of these Turkish groups had adopted the Islamic faith. Later, in the 1200's, the Ottomans threw off Seljuk rule and set up a small independent state in western Asia Minor.

The Ottoman state was at first one of many small Islamic principalities in Asia Minor that were founded in former Byzantine lands. In the middle of the fourteenth century, the Ottomans slowly began to increase their power over surrounding states. By about 1380, the Ottoman state was the most powerful of the Islamic principalities.

THE OTTOMANS ENTER EUROPE After the Ottomans established their power in Asia Minor, they bypassed the fortress city of Constantinople and tried to gain a foothold in the Balkan Peninsula. A major reason why the Ottomans sought to expand their land was their desire to convert all nonbelievers to Islam. The Ottomans embarked on a holy war and conquered the city of Gallipoli, on the Balkan Peninsula. From there, the Ottomans slowly expanded the area under their control, until by 1400 the Ottomans controlled much of the Balkan Peninsula. Many Christian countries in the Balkans became vassal states—paying tribute and sometimes providing troops to the Ottomans.

The Ottomans established their authority in the Balkans without much difficulty. With the decline of Byzantine power in the Balkans, many small, relatively weak principalities and kingdoms were founded. These weak states were no match for the military strength of the Ottomans, which was based upon highly trained soldiers known as Janissaries [JAN-uh-SER-eez].

The Janissaries were professional soldiers who served under the direct command of the Ottoman rulers. The term *janissary* means *new troops* in Turkish. The Janissaries were slaves, captured Christians, and selected Turkish soldiers. The slaves and captured Christians were forcibly converted to Islam. In addition, the Janissaries received special military training. By the fifteenth century, they formed the first standing army in Europe.

Another reason why the Ottomans encountered mild resistance in the Balkans was that the Ottomans employed a type of feudal system. Under this system, a conquered prince was allowed to rule as a vassal of the Ottoman sultan. The vassal ruler was responsible for maintaining peace in the region and for paying tribute to the sultan. In return, the Ottomans allowed conquered peoples to keep their land, religion, and customs as long as they remained loyal to the sultan.

However, this system contained one significant weakness. The vassal rulers—who maintained some measure of power—were able to assert their independence whenever the central authority of the Ottoman ruler was weakened. This weakness became evident in the early 1400's.

THE INTERREGNUM During the last part of the fourteenth century, the Mongols—led by the famous Tamerlane—were expanding westward in central Asia. In 1402 Tamerlane attacked Ottoman lands in eastern Asia Minor. The Ottoman sultan was captured in the ensuing battle, and Tamerlane was victorious.

A great number of the troops that made up the Janissaries were former Christians, who had often been taken from their homes and forcibly converted to Islam.

Expansion of the Ottoman Empire

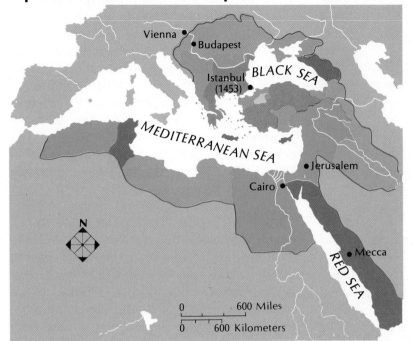

Lands Acquired by the Ottoman Turks

	1300
	1300–1359
	1359–1451
	1451–1481
	1512–1520
	1520–1566
	1566–1683

——— Boundary of the Ottoman Empire at its greatest extent, 1683–1699

Between 1300 and 1683, the Ottoman Empire expanded its boundaries until it included much of the land formerly held by the Byzantine Empire. The Ottoman Empire reached its greatest limit between 1683 and 1699.

With the Ottoman state severely weakened by this defeat, the vassal rulers in the Balkans and in Asia Minor quickly set up independent states. In those lands that remained under Ottoman rule, civil war and dynastic rivalries became common. After a period of confusion and continued warfare—known as the Interregnum—the Ottomans, under the leadership of a strong ruler, regained a position of dominance in the Middle East and again extended their control over the Balkans. By about 1450, the Ottoman Empire had reasserted itself as the most powerful force in the Middle East and in the Balkan Peninsula.

THE OTTOMAN EMPIRE In 1451, Muhammad II became ruler of the Ottoman Empire. Muhammad, who reigned from 1451 until 1481, started a new era of Ottoman expansion. Early in 1451, Muhammad began to plan the final assault on Constantinople. Muhammad laid siege to the city in April 1453. After Ottoman forces broke through the city wall, they pillaged the city for three days. Muhammad entered the city and declared, "Hereafter my capital is Istanbul." Thus the city of Constantinople, former capital of the Byzantine Empire, became Istanbul, capital of the Ottoman Empire.

Muhammad II then worked to expand Ottoman influence. He strengthened Ottoman control over areas of the Balkans and of Asia Minor. He also expanded Ottoman influence to areas around the Black Sea.

Muhammad II's successors continued to expand the land under Ottoman rule. By 1520, the Ottomans had conquered Syria and Egypt. At about the same time, the Ottomans gained control of Arabia, including the Islamic holy cities of Mecca and Medina. The Ottoman Empire was the most powerful country of the Muslim world.

THE OTTOMAN EMPIRE BECOMES A WORLD POWER During the sixteenth century the Ottoman Empire emerged as a world power and was often involved in international politics. For example, in the 1520's the French allied themselves with the Ottomans against the Holy Roman Emperor Charles V. Later, the Ottomans attempted to

The Battle of Lepanto, in which the Ottoman Turks were defeated, was the last great sea battle fought between Christian and Turkish forces.

make Hungary a vassal state by their efforts to influence the selection of the Hungarian king.

In the mid-sixteenth century, Czar Ivan the Terrible of Russia unsuccessfully challenged Ottoman power in the Black Sea region. In addition, the Ottomans fought against several Asian states and interfered in the affairs of Venice and of Poland. The Ottoman Empire also maintained close diplomatic relations with the countries of northern Europe. In 1571, an alliance of Venice, Spain, and the Papal States sent a fleet to the eastern Mediterranean Sea to recapture the island of Cyprus and other formerly Christian lands from the Ottomans. The Ottomans were soundly defeated at the Battle of Lepanto. However, they quickly recovered from this loss and reestablished themselves as a major naval power.

During the late 1500's through the mid-1600's, the Ottomans continued to engage in many wars with European and Asian countries. In 1682, the Ottomans—hoping to secure all of Hungary—declared war on the Hapsburgs of the Holy Roman Empire. In June 1683, the Ottomans attacked Vienna, Austria, where they were beaten back by combined Austrian and Polish forces. The defeat at Vienna marked the beginning of the nearly 250-year decline of the Ottoman Empire.

TRADE AND THE OTTOMAN EMPIRE A major reason why the Ottoman Empire rose to a position of power in the world was its location. Like the Byzantine Empire in earlier centuries, the Ottoman Empire was a highway for east-west trade. Merchants from the Italian trading cities met caravans from the Far East and Persia at the port cities of Asia Minor and, after 1453, at Istanbul. In addition, traders from the north of Europe and Russia brought their goods to these same busy trading centers. Later, Ottoman merchants established trading routes in Europe. The trading activities within the empire brought great amounts of wealth to the Ottoman Empire.

The Ottomans were able to use trading privileges within the empire as a political weapon. For example, when the city of Marseilles, which had extensive trading rights within the empire, supported an enemy of the Ottomans, the Ottomans abolished the commercial privileges of Marseilles. The Ottoman Empire remained a center for European commercialism through the sixteenth century.

IMPACT OF THE OTTOMAN EMPIRE IN EUROPE In general, the Ottoman Empire had negative effects upon eastern Europe. One negative effect was that the Ottoman domination of the Balkan Peninsula prevented the development of strong, independent countries in the region. A second effect was that the military strength of the Ottoman Empire, especially in the 1500's and 1600's, often posed a serious threat to the peoples of Europe.

However, the Ottoman Empire had some positive effects. The Ottoman Empire helped trade by providing growing markets for European goods. The cities of the empire developed into important trading centers. During times of peace, the empire provided protection for merchants and maintained roads that aided trade.

Although the importance and influence of the Ottoman Empire began to decrease, it still remained a factor in European affairs into the 1900's. The Ottoman Empire had reached the height of its political and economic power by the late sixteenth century. But by 1600, the Ottoman Empire began losing its importance as a major commercial center. With the discovery of America, Europe's attention turned westward toward the New World. As trade shifted from the Mediterranean Sea, Ottoman economic and political power declined. In later years, the empire was called "the sick man of Europe."

QUESTIONS FOR REVIEW

1 *Who were the Janissaries?*

2 *How did Muhammad II expand the power of the Ottoman Empire?*

3 *Why was trade important to the Ottoman Empire?*

CHAPTER SUMMARY

Eastern Europe did not, for the most part, develop strong monarchies. The nomadic peoples that settled in eastern Europe lacked a common culture, heritage, and language. Furthermore, the nobility in these countries often prevented a strong leader from centralizing power.

The Russian principality of Kiev grew in power during the tenth and eleventh centuries. However, in 1240, a warlike tribe from Asia—the Mongols—subdued Russia. After nearly 250 years of Mongol rule, another Russian principality—Moscow—threw off Mongol rule and began to dominate Russia.

The Byzantine Empire influenced eastern European religious beliefs, law, art, architecture, and literature in the late Middle Ages. In 1204, the Byzantine Empire was conquered by the forces of Venice and the soldiers of the Fourth Crusade. Although the Byzantine Empire was reestablished by Michael VIII in 1261, it never regained the dominant position it once held in southeastern Europe and Asia Minor, and it finally fell to the Ottoman Turks in 1453.

The Ottoman Turks grew in power by conquering neighboring lands, and by the mid-fourteenth century they were expanding into the Balkan Peninsula. In 1453, the Ottoman Sultan Muhammad II conquered Constantinople, renamed it Istanbul, and made it his capital city.

CHAPTER 14 IN REVIEW

IMPORTANT WORDS, NAMES, AND TERMS

1 Explain, define, or identify each of the following:

Slavs	Mongols	Nicaea
Magyars	czar	Gallipoli
Rus	*zemskii sobor*	Muhammad II
Kiev	Latin Empire	Battle of Lepanto

FACTS AND IDEAS

2 About when did the Magyars invade eastern Europe?

3 What was the *Drang nach Osten*?

4 What was the Golden Horde?

5 What were five Byzantine contributions to eastern Europe?

6 About when did the Ottoman Turks become independent of the Seljuks?

ANALYZING VISUAL MATERIAL

7 Examine the map on page 264. What geographic characteristics shown on the map may have influenced the early settlement of this region? How do you think these geographic characteristics may have influenced the culture and the languages of the people who settled in this area?

8 Study the map on page 270. According to the map, what cities and countries did the Mongols attack? What Russian city escaped destruction by the Mongols?

CONCEPTS AND UNDERSTANDINGS

9 How has the geography of eastern Europe influenced the history of the region?

10 Why did feudalism persist in eastern Europe for a longer period of time than did feudalism in western Europe?

11 How did Mongol rule of Russia influence that nation's history?

12 How did Ivan the Terrible control the government of Russia after 1565?

13 How did the Janissaries increase the power of the Ottoman rulers?

PROJECTS AND ACTIVITIES

14 Many buildings in the Kremlin, the seat of the Russian government, were built in the late Middle Ages. Search newspapers and magazines to find pictures of the Kremlin that illustrate the architecture of these buildings. Using these pictures, prepare a bulletin-board display in your classroom.

15 The Byzantine Empire influenced the countries of eastern Europe in many ways. Use library sources to prepare a brief paper outlining the areas of Byzantine culture that influenced eastern Europe. Present your paper to the class.

CHAPTER 15 ASIA IN THE MIDDLE AGES

1 India and the Muslim Conquest   2 China During the Middle Ages   3 The Rise of Early Japan

Asia in the Middle Ages saw the rise of high levels of culture in India, China, and Japan. At various times, however, these civilizations were threatened by invasions of peoples from other parts of Asia. The foreign culture of the invaders was never fully assimilated into the culture of India. However, the Mongols adopted many aspects of the superior Chinese culture into their own life-style. The Japanese, on the other hand, borrowed heavily from the culture of mainland Asia to develop their own distinctive culture. One reason the Japanese people were able to perfect their own culture was that the islands of Japan were not occupied by outside forces until the twentieth century.

Eastfoto

The exquisite art of China is exemplified by the more than 50,000 Dazu stone carvings found in the Szechwan province.

1 INDIA AND THE MUSLIM CONQUEST

The Muslim conquest of India, which began as early as the eighth century, has had far-reaching effects that have lasted to the present day. Although periods of the Muslim rule of India were characterized by religious conflict, massacre, and warfare, high levels of cultural achievement were attained during these centuries. For example, some of the finest architectural achievements of Indian society date from the years of the Muslim conquest.

FIRST MUSLIM CONTACTS The earliest Indian contact with the Muslims occurred in 711, when a Muslim Arab leader invaded northwestern India and captured the region of Sind. The Muslim rule of Sind had almost no lasting political effects upon India. However, the period of the eighth century through the tenth century was a time of active cultural exchange between the Muslim Arabs and the Hindu Indians. Knowledge and ideas in the fields of astronomy, mathematics, and medicine were carried from India to the Arab world. Eventually, many of these ideas made their way to Europe.

In the tenth and eleventh centuries new invaders—Turkish Muslims from the area of Afghanistan—attacked northern India. Filled with Islamic religious fervor, these Muslims conquered India as far as the Indus River. At first, the Muslims were determined to convert the Hindus to Islam.

To the Muslims, Hinduism—with its many deities, elaborate rituals, and fondness for images—was the exact opposite of all that Islam held sacred. The Muslim invaders destroyed Hindu temples. Thousands of Hindus, offered the choice of conversion or death, clung to their own religion and were then put to death by the Muslims.

In addition, the social beliefs of the Muslims contrasted with those of the Hin-

India in the Middle Ages

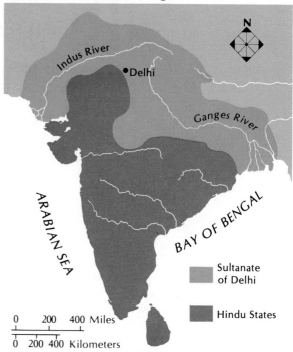

During the greater part of the Middle Ages, the Delhi Sultanate controlled most of northern India, and Hindu states controlled southern India.

dus. Islamic beliefs could not be reconciled with the caste system that formed the basis of Hindu society. Despite the religious and cultural differences between the groups, over a period of time ways were found for both groups to live side by side in relative peace. One of the chief ways was the *jizya*—a tax—imposed upon the Hindus. If the Hindus paid the tax, their way of life was not disturbed.

The Turkish Muslims finally gained firm control over northern India in the twelfth century. Social and economic conditions slowly became more settled. Then, in 1206, the sultan was murdered and his general founded what became an autocratic state—the Delhi sultanate.

THE DELHI SULTANATE The Delhi sultanate became a strong Muslim kingdom covering most of northern India. The sultanate lasted until the early fifteenth century, and during the height of its power (1206–1388), it gave northern India political unity. The Delhi sultans extended Muslim authority and religious beliefs southward into the Deccan region. By the early fourteenth century, the Delhi sultanate had reached southernmost India. However, the Delhi sultanate was not able to unify the southern region, and it soon lost control of this region.

The Delhi sultanate was characterized by rulers who were often cruel but who were also scholars and patrons of the arts. For example, Sultan Mohammed Tughlak [mu-HAM-muhd tag-LAK], who ruled from 1325 to 1351, allegedly came to the throne by killing his father. During his reign he often disposed of his opponents by having them flayed alive. Despite his cruelties, he is also remembered as a scholar, a writer, and a philosopher.

In contrast, Firuz Shah Tughlak [fee-ROOZ SHAH tag-LAK], who ruled from 1351 to 1388, was the most enlightened Muslim ruler up to that time. He devoted himself to the welfare of his subjects, established agencies to take care of Muslim widows and orphans, and abolished torture as a punishment for crimes.

TAMERLANE The death of Firuz Shah Tughlak in 1388 threw the Delhi sultanate into a civil war that greatly weakened the country and left it unprotected from invaders. Timur the Lame, called Tamerlane—a Mongol Turk descended from Genghis Khan—who had already conquered central Asia, invaded the Delhi sultanate in 1398. Tamerlane and 90,000 warriors plundered Delhi and massacred the city's inhabitants. The Delhi sultanate lay in ruins and the political unity of northern India was destroyed. Tamerlane then deserted Delhi and went on to attack other parts of Asia.

Succeeding Delhi sultans were weak and ineffectual rulers. As a result, a number of petty sultanates were established in northern India.

POLITICAL		SOCIAL AND ECONOMIC
	c. 550	Buddhism brought to Japan
T'ang dynasty founded in China	618	
	c. 625	Block printing emerged in China
	c. 650	Taika reforms in Japan
Earliest Indian contact with Muslims	711	
Fujiwara established rule of Japan	794	
	c. 880	Kana system of writing developed in Japan
Sung dynasty established in China	960	
	c. 1170	Chu Hsi's philosophies promoted science
Delhi sultanate set up	1206	
Genghis Khan attacked Peking	1215	
Kublai Khan conquered all of China and established Yüan dynasty	1269	Marco Polo set out for China
	1279	
	c. 1300	Chinese culture spread to other parts of Asia
Ming dynasty founded in China	1368	
Tamerlane invaded Delhi sultanate	1398	
	c. 1400	Tea ceremony and No drama developed in Japan
	c. 1500	Sikhism founded

The Taj Mahal, seen here from a distant archway, is one of the finest examples of Indo-Islamic architecture. The close-up at the right shows the delicate detail of this style of architecture.

THE EFFECTS OF MUSLIM RULE One of the most significant results of the Muslim rule of India was the introduction of the Islamic faith. The spread of Islam led to religious conflicts in the years that followed. Many Hindus became Muslims to escape death, while others became Muslims to avoid paying high taxes. Other Hindus adopted the Islamic faith to escape their low-caste status; some administrators accepted Islam as a way to gain power in the service of Muslim rulers. However, most Hindus—especially those of the upper castes—clung to their faith. The religious conflicts that arose in the tenth and eleventh centuries have caused serious problems well into the twentieth century.

Not surprisingly, the impact of the Muslim conquest resulted in lasting changes in the Hindu culture. The Muslim practice of *purdah*—the strict seclusion of women—was introduced among the Hindus, and it was adopted by some groups in parts of India. In addition, many aspects of the Muslim style of dress and Muslim ceremony were adopted by some of the Hindu people.

A new language—Urdu—was developed by the Muslim ruling class. Urdu, a combination of Turkish, Persian, and Arabic words, used the language construction of the Hindi tongue. Today, Urdu is one of the dominant languages in India and in Pakistan.

ARCHITECTURE AND RELIGION In the field of architecture, elements of the Hindu and Muslim styles were combined during the twelfth and thirteenth centuries to form a new style, called Indo-Islamic. The Hindu influences can be seen in the decorative ornaments and lacework patterns on the buildings. The Muslim contributions included the pointed arches and the domes characteristic of Islamic architecture.

The introduction of Islam into predominantly Hindu India resulted in the creation of a new religion—Sikhism [SEEK-IZ-uhm]. Developed around the year 1500, Sikhism tried to unite Hinduism and Islam by combining beliefs from both faiths. Today, about 10 million people in India are followers of Sikhism.

A COMMON CULTURE A culture common to the Hindus and the Muslims developed in many parts of India because of centuries of interaction and because many of the Muslims in India were converts from Hinduism. The Hindus and the Muslims in India also shared ways of living and artistic tastes. This was especially true in northern India, where Muslims and Hindus lived together peacefully as one people. They often spoke the same language—Hindi—and they developed a common life-style and faced similar economic problems.

A common culture developed in India despite religious differences and the caste system, both of which tended to keep people apart. Generally, it was the men of the society who participated in the common culture. In most areas, many women of the upper social groups were restricted by the purdah and isolated from women of other faiths and of other castes.

Despite the many common cultural traits that developed among the Hindus and the Muslims in India during the time of the Muslim conquest, basic differences remained. A major problem was religion. While some Muslim rulers tolerated religious differences, other Muslim rulers ruthlessly persecuted members of the Hindu faith. Many of the problems arising from religious differences have lasted to the present day.

QUESTIONS FOR REVIEW

1 *What was the jizya?*

2 *How did Tamerlane's invasion affect the Delhi sultanate?*

3 *Why did a common culture develop among the Hindus and the Muslims in many parts of India?*

2 CHINA DURING THE MIDDLE AGES

The history of China during the Middle Ages—from the beginning of the T'ang era to the time of the Ming—is a story of the rise and fall of ruling dynasties. For the most part, each Chinese dynasty built upon the political and social accomplishments of earlier ruling families. Though dynasties rose and fell, a sense of Chinese cultural unity was maintained over the centuries, even through the years of foreign domination. New heights of artistic, literary, and architectural achievement were reached, especially during the T'ang and Sung eras. Later dynasties maintained these cultural achievements.

THE T'ANG DYNASTY As you read in Chapter 8, the last Sui emperor was murdered in 618. China was then plagued with rival groups struggling to gain power. By 623, the T'ang [TAHNG] rulers had established firm control over most of China. The T'ang era (618–907) was a golden age in Chinese history. At a time when European civilization was at a relatively low level, China was becoming the most civilized society in the world.

The first great emperor of the T'ang dynasty—T'ai Tsung [TIY DZUNG]—reigned from 627 to 650. A great warrior, T'ai Tsung extended the borders of the Chinese Empire. At its height, the Chinese Empire under the T'ang extended from Korea through central Asia to the borders of India and Persia.

In addition to his military achievements, T'ai Tsung was responsible for improvements in the administration of the Chinese Empire. He governed the empire through educated officials recruited under the civil service system that had been started in the Han period. Laws concerning land reform were also passed.

During the T'ang era, economic prosperity

These pottery figurines, unearthed from a tomb near the city of Sian, represent noblewomen of the T'ang dynasty.

was a great demand for religious and educational materials. However, reproducing materials by hand took enormous amounts of time. The demand for new materials could be met only if a new, faster means of making copies was found. By the seventh century, block printing—printing from an image carved into a wooden block—emerged in China. From this beginning, the Chinese developed movable type.

THE FALL OF THE T'ANG DYNASTY Divisive forces were at work during the later part of the T'ang era. The nobles lived in splendor, but the living conditions of peasants worsened. Because of the increasingly poor economic conditions, many peasants were forced to give up their land and become tenant farmers of the lesser nobles. The poor conditions led to revolts among the people that seriously weakened the government. In 907, the Chinese emperor was assassinated and the T'ang dynasty ended.

A period of anarchy followed the fall of the T'ang dynasty. Between 907 and 960 five short-lived dynasties attempted to assert control over northern China; independent petty kingdoms arose in the south. War and bloodshed were commonplace throughout China. During this time, economic conditions deteriorated and barter replaced the money economy of earlier times. However, in 960 a powerful family succeeded in reuniting China and founded the Sung dynasty.

THE SUNG DYNASTY The Sung dynasty was established in 960, and by 979 the Sung had completely subdued the rebellious petty kingdoms in the south. Thus, China was again united. The founder of the Sung dynasty, Chao K'uang-yin [JOW-KWAHNG-YIN], reorganized the administration of the Chinese government. The government now directly controlled taxes, and its income increased greatly.

Throughout the period of the Sung dynasty, China was faced with the threat of

stemmed from an expansion of the trade with Tibet and India. Caravans from central Asia brought Chinese goods—such as silk, porcelain, and pottery—to markets as distant as Jerusalem and Cairo. Many new foods—almonds, dates, beets, and pepper—were made available to the Chinese during the T'ang era as a result of trading.

CULTURAL ACHIEVEMENTS OF THE T'ANG Culture and learning flowered under the T'ang dynasty. Scholarly achievements included the writing of two encyclopedias designed to assist students preparing for the civil service tests. Teams of scholars were employed by the T'ang government to write detailed histories of preceding eras.

Literature also flourished at this time. Two famous poets of the T'ang era were Li Po and Tu Fu. Much of their poetry reflects universal themes that are easily understood by twentieth-century people.

Printing was developed in China during the T'ang period. During the T'ang era, there attack by fierce nomadic tribes from the north. The Khitan Tatars—a tribe from northeastern Asia—were a major threat until a peace treaty was negotiated in 1005. The Sung maintained peace by paying the Khitan 100,000 ounces of silver and 200,000 bolts of silk annually.

The Sung dynasty witnessed attempts at far-reaching reform guided by a leading Chinese official and economist, Wang An-shih [WAHNG AHN-SHIR]. Wang rose to power through the civil service system and eventually gained the confidence of the emperor. Wang favored educational reforms that stressed practical knowledge rather than memorization. His economic reforms included the government's controlling trade and production to increase government income, setting the prices of certain goods, and providing agricultural loans to farmers. Wang's reforms provided pensions for the aged and aid for the unemployed. However, corruption, the opposition of the wealthy class, and the impracticality of some of Wang's projects combined to prevent their complete adoption or permanent operation.

In 1100, Emperor Hui Tsung [HWAY DZUNG], who was chiefly interested in art, came to the throne. He knew little about government and was not able to rule effectively. At this time, new invaders from Manchuria attacked the Sung. The ineffective Sung government was not able to withstand the attack and lost all of northern China to the Manchurian invaders. In 1141, a peace treaty, which required the Sung to pay tribute in silver and in silk, was concluded between the warring parties. For the next century, China was divided into two empires. The Sung continued to rule in the south, and the Chin—the dynastic name of the Manchurian invaders—ruled in the north.

ACHIEVEMENTS OF THE SUNG ERA The cultural achievements of the earlier T'ang dynasty were built upon during Sung times. Literature became more common as the use of printing spread. Sung art reached new heights of beauty. Sung art—generally more secular in nature than the art of the T'ang era—stressed the beauty of landscapes and of nature. Sung craft workers created fine, delicate porcelain bowls and vases.

The philosopher Chu Hsi [JOO-SHEE] believed that people should study through the "investigation of things." The adoption of Chu Hsi's idea during the Sung era resulted in advances in the applied sciences. Numerous works concerning botany, zoology, and chemistry were published. The Chinese development of algebra was the most advanced in the world. Progress was also made in agriculture. Improved farming techniques doubled the rice harvest, and tea and cotton became important crops.

THE MONGOLS CONQUER CHINA While the Sung dynasty was reaching new levels of cultural development, the Mongols—fierce warriors from central Asia—were consolidating their power north of the Great Wall. A nomadic people, the Mongols were ignorant of farming techniques and they lacked a written language.

Under the leadership of Genghis Khan, the Mongols attacked the Chin capital of

Genghis Khan (center) became the leader of the Mongols in 1206 and united the various Mongol tribes.

China: The T'ang Dynasty to the Ming Dynasty

T'ang Dynasty A.D. 750

Yuan Dynasty A.D. 1290

Ming Dynasty A.D. 1600

✗✗✗ The Great Wall of China

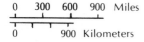
0   300   600   900   Miles

0   900   Kilometers

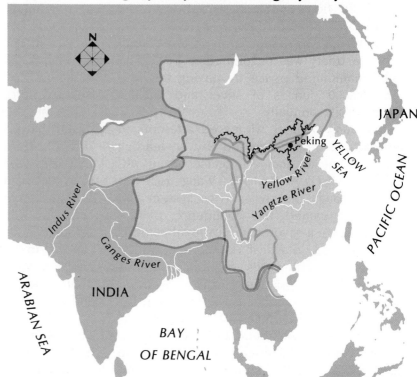

The boundaries of the Chinese Empire varied greatly over the centuries as the dynasties that ruled China attempted to extend their control throughout eastern Asia.

Peking in 1215. The Mongol army, entirely made up of cavalry, devastated the capital city and massacred the population. After the fall of Peking, Genghis Khan's army campaigned to the west, conquering much of Asia and parts of Russia and threatening western Europe. Later, the assault on the Chin Empire was renewed, and the Mongols subdued the Chin completely.

The Mongols then proceeded to conquer the Sung dynasty in the south. The Sung Empire resisted the Mongol attacks for almost 50 years. By 1279 the last Sung ruler was defeated and all of China was in Mongol hands. Kublai Khan—a descendant of Genghis Khan—founded the Yüan [yoo-AHN] dynasty. For the first time in history, all of China was ruled by foreign conquerors.

Mongol China was ruled separately from the rest of the Mongol Empire in Asia. After the Mongols came to power, Chinese society was divided into five groups. The Mongols made up a small but privileged minority. The second group was a special-status group made up of non-Chinese people who often held high-level government jobs. The next group was the northern Chinese; this group sometimes served the Mongol government in various low-level positions. The fourth group was the southern Chinese, the former subjects of the Sung. This group made up the majority in Chinese society. At the lowest level of Chinese society were the slaves.

Through the years, however, the Yüan dynasty became more Chinese than Mongol in nature. Kublai Khan and his successors recognized the superiority of the Chinese culture. Although the Mongols adopted the ways of Chinese culture, they remained a ruling class, separate from the rest of Chinese society.

Most of our knowledge about Kublai Khan and China at this time is based upon the book by Marco Polo, *The Travels of Marco Polo* (see Contribution on page 291). As a youth,

(*Text continued on page* 292.)

Contributions

The Writings of Marco Polo

The Travels of Marco Polo has been called one of the greatest books of all time. It begins

Royal Princes, Emperors and Kings, Dukes and Marquises, Counts, Knights, and Burgesses! and People of all degrees who desire to get knowledge of the various races of mankind and of the diversities of the sundry regions of the World, take this Book and cause it to be read to you.

Dictated to a fellow inmate while he was in prison in Genoa, the advice given by Polo has proved to be as fitting and appropriate throughout the past seven centuries as it was in 1298, when the book was compiled.

Polo's book is more than simply a travelogue of his 24-year journey across Asia. It records the customs of several Asian peoples, including the Persians, the Tartars, and the Mongols. It also notes their forms of government, the life-styles of their societies, and their religious practices. It also includes detailed descriptions of the plants and animals that Polo found on his journey. Polo recorded his observations with accuracy and clarity, without making harsh judgments on the people he encountered or on their strange customs.

Marco Polo's book has influenced people for centuries. Prince Henry the Navigator, Christopher Columbus, and the other explorers of the fifteenth and sixteenth centuries had read or were familiar with Polo's book. It was one of the only books that could have given these early explorers firsthand information about the lands of China, India, and Persia. Later, in the beginning of the twentieth century, scientists, using Polo's book as a guide, discovered the ancient Silk Road and found the towns through which Polo traveled on his journey across Asia. These scientists found that Marco Polo's system of measuring distances by days' journeys proved to be extremely accurate. Some geographers have called Polo's work the forerunner of scientific geography. However, perhaps the greatest contribution of Marco Polo's book is that it is a source of enjoyable historical reading.

This detail of Marco Polo's two uncles and their trading companions traveling by camel caravan was taken from an atlas dating from the late 1300's.

Marco Polo went with his father and his uncle, two Venetian merchants, to China on a trading expedition that lasted 17 years. Marco Polo described the palace in the capital city of Peking as follows:

> The Hall of the Palace is so large that it could easily dine 6000 people; and it is quite a marvel to see how many rooms there are besides. The building is altogether so vast, so rich, and so beautiful, that no man on earth could design anything superior to it. The outside of the roof also is all coloured with vermilion [bright red] and yellow and green and blue and other hues, which are fixed with a varnish so fine and exquisite that they shine like crystal . . .

CHINA UNDER KUBLAI KHAN Kublai Khan and his successors had rebuilt and beautified Peking and other cities in the empire. As a result of the Mongol rule of most of Asia, roads were improved and travel was made safe. Trade between East and West increased greatly.

The Mongol rulers also encouraged education and expanded the existing schools. Public welfare for the aged, the blind, and the orphaned was also established under the Yüan rulers. In general, religious tolerance was practiced by the Yüan.

Despite the attempts of the Yüan at wise rule, the economic conditions of China during the later part of the Yüan dynasty deteriorated. Inflation, high taxes, unsuccessful wars, and excessive spending weakened the Chinese economy. Furthermore, the overall level of the culture of China did not improve greatly under the Yüan.

Although Chinese culture under the Yüan dynasty generally reflected earlier historical periods, it remained an important factor throughout Asia. Chinese culture influenced many areas of Asia during the later part of the Middle Ages. For example, Chinese medical books were translated into Persian; examples of Persian painting of the thir-

teenth and fourteenth centuries reflect the influence of Chinese art. In addition, the Japanese borrowed much of the basis of their own culture from the Chinese.

THE MING DYNASTY The Ming dynasty restored a Chinese ruling house to China. The Mongol rulers had grown weak over the centuries, and Mongol unity in Asia had disintegrated. The weak leadership of the later Mongol rulers resulted in numerous rebellions, especially among the peasants in southern and central China. By the mid-1300's, China was in a state of political, social, and economic chaos. From this disorder emerged a strong military leader, Chu Yüan-chang [JOO yoo-AN JAHNG], who expelled the Mongols from Peking and founded the Ming dynasty in 1368. Chu Yüan-chang's role in Chinese history is important because he restored to China a Chinese dynasty and reunified the country.

The Ming government reflected anti-foreign reaction by returning to the traditions established during the T'ang and Sung times. Confucianism once again became the guiding philosophy of China. After defeating the Mongols, Chu Yüan-chang reorganized the government according to Confucianism and reestablished the civil service system.

The Ming period until about 1500 was characterized by peace and prosperity. Gold and silver coins circulated throughout the empire. Trade with surrounding countries increased. New land was brought under cultivation through the use of irrigation canals and water reservoirs. Despite the prosperous times, the Ming period was generally lacking in new cultural achievements. Most of the art, the architecture, the literature, and the philosophy of the Ming period imitated or interpreted the styles of the earlier T'ang and Sung eras.

The first century of the Ming period was characterized by an increase in trading expeditions with the rest of the world. However, after 1500, the expeditions were stopped by the emperor's orders. The Chinese began to consider themselves culturally superior to outsiders. Foreigners were considered barbarians. Cut off from foreign trade and non-Chinese cultures, China became increasingly isolated.

Later Ming emperors were, for the most part, ineffective rulers. The isolationist policies of the later Ming severely limited trade. As the government's income declined, taxes were increased, and living conditions grew worse. Uprisings occurred throughout the country. At the same time, new invaders from the north—the Manchus—began attacking China. In 1644, the last Ming ruler hanged himself; the Ch'ing dynasty of the Manchus became the rulers of China (see Chapter 25).

QUESTIONS FOR REVIEW

1 *Who was T'ai Tsung?*

2 *How did Wang An-shih attempt to reform Chinese society?*

3 *Why is Chu Yüan-chang's role in Chinese history important?*

3 THE RISE OF EARLY JAPAN

The early history of Japan is clouded in legend. However, the early people of Japan were strongly influenced by Chinese culture from the mainland of Asia. Later, the Japanese modified and adapted Chinese ideas to form their own unique culture. During the Middle Ages, a type of feudalism developed and became the basis of the Japanese social and economic systems. At this time, the Japanese emperor held little or no authority; instead, powerful warriors ruled Japan.

Japan

The mountainous terrain of Japan has influenced Japan's development throughout history.

THE GEOGRAPHY OF JAPAN Over 3,000 islands make up the Japanese *archipelago* [AHR-kuh-PEL-uh-goh]—chain of islands. However, only 4 islands are relatively large. Historically, the vast majority of the Japanese people have lived on the 4 main islands—Hokkaido, Honshu, Shikoku, and Kyushu.

Japan is a land of limited resources. Mountains and hills make up nearly 90 percent of Japan's land; only one seventh of the land is suitable for farming. Much of the food required to support a population of nearly 120 million must be imported. Because of its limited resources, Japan must also import large amounts of minerals and raw materials. Japan has no long rivers, but hundreds of short rivers and streams flow down from the mountains. The rivers and streams have aided transportation and are used to irrigate crops.

The geography of Japan has influenced its history in two important ways. Because Japan is an island country, it was shielded from the numerous hostile invasions that plagued the peoples on the Asian mainland. Japan was able to develop a unique culture by borrowing aspects of Chinese culture because its geography separated it from the Asian mainland.

EARLY JAPANESE LEGENDS Much of the early history of Japan is colored by legends. According to one Japanese legend, the god Izanagi married his sister Izanami. The marriage of these two gods produced several children, including the sun goddess, the moon god, and the storm god. According to the legend, the marriage also produced the islands of Japan, thus giving the islands a sacred quality.

Later, a grandson of the sun goddess descended to earth on the island of Kyushu. He then proceeded northward and started to unify Japan. The unification of Japan was completed in 660 B.C. by Jimmu, another descendant of the sun goddess. Jimmu became the first emperor of Japan and he is considered to be an ancestor of all later emperors. Thus, from the beginning of oral Japanese history, the emperor was believed to be divine.

Many variations of the Japanese legends exist. This fact may suggest that Japan was originally settled by more than one cultural group. Over the centuries, the different legends of the various groups were orally passed on to succeeding generations, and eventually the stories began to overlap.

EARLY PEOPLE OF JAPAN The first people may have lived in Japan as early as 200,000 B.C. Most likely, these people came to the islands from the Asian continent. The primitive culture of these early inhabitants did not have a lasting effect on Japan.

Three later civilizations, however, contributed to the traditional culture of early Japan. The Jomon [JOH-mahn] people, who flourished from about 3000 B.C. to 250 B.C., developed elaborate religious ceremonies. They also made crude pottery and began to raise farm animals. Later, the Jomon gave way to the Yayoi [yah-yoh-ee] people.

The Yayoi people lived in Japan between 250 B.C. and A.D. 250—about the time that the Han dynasty ruled in China. Basically an agricultural people, the Yayoi learned from the Chinese how to grow rice. The Yayoi also used metal tools and weapons, learning how to use bronze and iron from the Chinese and the Koreans. The last of these civilizations, known as the Tomb Culture, existed from about A.D. 250 until A.D. 645. As the name implies, these migrants from mainland Asia were noted for the massive tombs they built for their rulers. These early civilizations developed a basic social structure that influenced Japanese society for many centuries.

EARLY JAPANESE SOCIETY Historians have concluded that the early Japanese people were organized into numerous clans, each controlled by a chief. The Japanese emperor gave many of the clan chiefs official hereditary ranks, similar to the titles of nobility in Europe during the Middle Ages. Some of these ranks were given to the emperor's relatives, but other ranks were given to powerful chiefs that the emperor did not wish to fight. The chiefs who held high ranks were expected to be loyal to the emperor, but the chiefs were more often interested in expanding the wealth and power of their own families. The clan system of social organization in early Japan aided the rise of powerful families at the expense of the emperor's authority.

Many of the clans had their own hereditary guilds of craft workers, artisans, and farmers. The guilds of farmers made up the largest group. The people in the guilds were considered free persons, but they could not leave the service of their clan. At the lowest level of society were the slaves.

THE SHINTO RELIGION The native Japanese religion—Shinto—differs from the Chinese philosophies in that it has no known founder, no books of teachings, and few organized religious ceremonies. Central to the Shinto religion is the idea of *kami*. *Kami* is sometimes translated as "gods," but the concept of kami can be applied to anything that inspires awe or wonder. Thus, many kami are found in the beauty of nature.

Shinto has no regular days of worship and few sacred holidays. Individuals go to Shinto shrines to say private prayers for the things they want. Today, the Shinto faith is held by about 60 million people.

CHINESE INFLUENCE IN JAPAN Elements of Chinese culture made their way into Japan as early as the Han dynasty (202 B.C.–A.D. 220). Chinese and Korean craft workers, artisans, painters, and silkworm breeders brought their skills to Japan and enriched the Japanese culture. The Chinese calendar was adopted by the Japanese. Most important, Chinese scholars brought the written Chinese language to Japan. By the fifth century A.D., tutors from mainland Asia were teaching Japanese students to write Chinese characters. Early Japanese literature was strongly influenced by Chinese literary works.

During the sixth century, Buddhism was brought to Japan by Chinese missionaries. At first, the Japanese were hesitant to adopt the new faith. Slowly, however, Buddhism was accepted by many government leaders. In time, both Buddhism and Shinto became the two most influential faiths in Japan.

In the mid-600's, the Japanese rulers reorganized the government, using the T'ang bureaucracy of China as the model. Government reform measures, called the Taika reforms, were instituted. The emperor was recognized as having complete political, as well as religious, authority over the people. The emperor was believed to be divine, and rebellion against the throne was considered a religious crime. Thus, throughout Japanese history, the emperor retained the throne even when military dictators ruled the country.

Under the Taika reforms, the Japanese instituted a system of civil service tests as the means to gain government positions. However, only people of high rank were

Japanese art was influenced by Buddhism. These statues of Buddha (below) and Vajrapani, a fierce guardian deity of Buddhism, are located at Nara.

allowed to take the tests. Unlike those in China, the important positions in the Japanese government eventually became hereditary posts, and thus the power of the upper social ranks was increased.

Early in the eighth century the Japanese capital was moved to the city of Nara. This period in Japanese history—called the Nara period—was characterized by a strengthening of the government. During the Nara period, a money economy based on copper coins spread throughout Japan. The acceptance of a money economy, rather than barter, strengthened the Japanese government. Also during this period, Buddhism gained importance in Japan. Nara became an important Buddhist center and attracted scholars and artists from the mainland. Thus, the Japanese art and literature of the Nara period exhibits strong Chinese influence.

THE FUJIWARA PERIOD In 784 the capital was moved from Nara, and by 794 it was established at the site of present-day Kyoto. At this time, a powerful noble family—the Fujiwaras—began to dominate the government. From 794 to 1160, the Japanese emperor reigned but did not rule; the real power of governing was in the hands of the noble Fujiwara family.

An important development of the Fujiwara period occurred in the late ninth century. The Japanese began to simplify the Chinese character system of writing by developing a phonetic system based upon 48 symbols or letters. The development of this system, called the *kana* system, led to the growth of a native Japanese literature, including poetry and novels. Writing based upon the kana system became widely used by the ordinary Japanese people, and it aided in the development of Japan's unique culture. However, Chinese remained the official language of the emperor's court.

During the Fujiwara period, the number of tax-free estates increased significantly. On these estates there developed a system that was similar to the feudal system that had developed in medieval western Europe. Although the Japanese had borrowed many aspects of Chinese culture, the feudal system in Japan developed without influence from the mainland.

The Japanese term for the rights or income from the tax-free estates was *shiki*. The shiki was unequally divided among those who owned, managed, protected, and worked the estate. Receiving the greatest share of the shiki was the patron, a person similar to the lord in western European feudalism. The patron received the largest share because of high social rank. Second in rank, and also receiving a large share of the shiki, was the proprietor who managed the estate. The next group was the warriors who protected the estate and its tax-free status. The next-to-lowest group was the farmers, who eventually became tied to the estate and could not leave. The lowest group—the laborers—also became tied to the land. Of course, the lowest groups received the smallest share, if any, of the shiki.

The Fujiwara family had weakened the bureaucratic system of government that had become established during the Nara period. The Fujiwara had gained almost complete control of the government by making heredity and family connections the most important factors in obtaining government positions. In time the hereditary system of the Fujiwara family grew increasingly inefficient. Eventually, the warrior class filled the void left by the continuing powerlessness of the Fujiwara family.

THE SHOGUN AND THE SAMURAI In 1192 the leader of the most powerful military family, Minamoto Yoritomo [mi-nah-moh-toh yoh-ri-toh-moh], forced the emperor to appoint him as *shogun*, or great general. From the city of Kamakura, Yoritomo ruled Japan as military dictator. Yoritomo did not overthrow the emperor but was the power behind the throne. Yoritomo did not destroy the existing Japanese system of government. Instead, he set up a military organization called the *bakufu* [bah-ku-fu]. The bakufu kept law and order and collected taxes.

At the same time, the feudal system that had developed during the Fujiwara period became firmly established. The warrior nobles, now called *samurai*, became protectors, and thus rulers, of the large estates. The unarmed peasants had no alternative but to accept the protection of the samurai. Each of the samurai had an army of sword-wielding protectors, who were loyal only to him and who were awarded a share of the shiki. The samurai practiced a strict code of chivalry and honor—called Bushido since the sixteenth century. It stressed qualities such as courage, bravery, loyalty, and kindness.

In 1199, governing power passed from Yoritomo's family to the Hojo family. They continued the military-style governing methods of Yoritomo. During the Hojo period, laws were codified. The Hojo period also witnessed an increase in trade with China and the introduction of tea and porcelain from the mainland.

THE MONGOL INVASIONS The Mongol rulers of China, having heard of the fabled wealth of Japan, planned to invade and conquer the islands. Kublai Khan sent an unsuccessful expedition to Japan in 1274. After this setback, Kublai Khan gathered an army of over 150,000 warriors, who set sail for Japan in 1281.

Meanwhile, the Japanese had been preparing to withstand the Mongol attack. In August 1281, while the Mongol army was fighting on the coast, a great storm blew up and scattered the invading forces. The typhoon—known as the *kamikaze*, or divine wind—destroyed the Mongol forces. The *kamikaze* was interpreted as an example of divine intervention protecting the islands. To the Japanese, the *kamikaze* symbolized how divine forces helped make their country superior to other countries.

The enormous cost of defending Japan from the Mongols and then maintaining those defenses for several more years, drained the Japanese treasury. This drain severely weakened the power of the Hojo family. In the thirteenth century, quarrels over succession to the throne broke out between supporters of the emperor and supporters of the shogun. An army general, Ashikaga Takauji [ah-shi-kah-gah tah-kah-u-ji], destroyed the power of the Hojo family. Takauji then founded the Ashikaga shogunate, which ruled Japan for nearly 250 years.

THE ASHIKAGA PERIOD In general, during the Ashikaga period—1333 to 1598—Japanese society remained organized according to the system of feudalism. The samurai

Ashikaga Takauji established a new shogunate, which lasted for over 250 years in Japan. Many of the late Ashikaga shoguns were able and resourceful rulers.

protected the estates of the nobility. The shogun remained the military dictator of the government; the emperor held no governing power.

A unique culture flowered during the time of the Ashikaga shogunate. The tea ceremony—a formal ritual designed for silent meditation—was developed during the Ashikaga era. The architecture of the period was simple yet elegant. It was designed to blend with natural settings. The artists of the Ashikaga period often painted inspiring landscapes that reflected the ideals of Zen Buddhism. The No drama—a carefully controlled dance in which the actors wear decorative masks—developed at this time.

During the Ashikaga era, Japan's economy grew as vigorous trade within the islands developed. Japan also traded with China at this time. However, Japan did not carry on significant commercial activities with the rest of the world until 1542, when the Portuguese gained minor trading rights.

QUESTIONS FOR REVIEW

1 *What are kami?*

2 *How did the kana system develop?*

3 *Why was Japan influenced by China during the Nara period?*

CHAPTER SUMMARY

Although the first Muslim conquerors of India, in the eighth century, were chiefly interested in trade, later Muslim conquerers were determined to convert the people to Islam. In 1206, the Muslims founded the Delhi sultanate—a strong kingdom that unified northern India. Later, however, a weakened Delhi sultanate was devastated by Tamerlane in 1398. Although aspects of the Muslim and Hindu cultures blended, basic differences have caused problems in India to the present day.

In China the T'ang dynasty, which ruled from 618 until 907, was characterized by government reforms and economic prosperity. Printing was developed and literature flourished. After the fall of the T'ang, a period of confusion ensued until, in 960, the Sung dynasty came to power. During the Sung era, the philosopher Wang An-shih instituted many reforms. By 1279, all of China had fallen under the control of the Mongols. Kublai Khan—a Mongol leader—founded the Yüan dynasty. Over the centuries, Mongol rule grew weaker, until it was replaced by the Ming dynasty in 1368.

Because of its position as an island country, Japan was able to develop a unique culture. Early Japan was influenced by Chinese art, architecture, and literature. During the Fujiwara period, a system of feudalism developed in Japan. By the twelfth century, the Japanese emperors had lost their power to the shoguns, who ruled Japan as a military dictatorship.

CHAPTER 15 IN REVIEW

IMPORTANT WORDS, NAMES, AND TERMS

1 Explain, define, or identify each of the following:

jizya	T'ang dynasty	archipelago
Urdu	Chu Hsi	Shinto
Indo-Islamic style	Kublai Khan	shiki
Sikhism	Marco Polo	tea ceremony

FACTS AND IDEAS

2 When did the Muslims gain permanent control of northern India?

3 Who was Tamerlane?

4 What were three significant cultural achievements of the T'ang era in China?

5 When did the Mongols gain complete control of China?

6 What was the *kamikaze*?

ANALYZING VISUAL MATERIAL

7 Examine the picture on page 288. What tokens of social and cultural status on the figurines may indicate that the women represented were of noble birth?

8 Study the map of Japan on page 293. How would you describe the geography of Japan? In what ways might the geography of Japan have influenced its cultural development? What role might the geography of Japan have played in the development of its agriculture? Cite examples to support your answers.

CONCEPTS AND UNDERSTANDINGS

9 What were some of the major cultural effects of Muslim rule upon India?

10 Why did religious differences remain a major problem among the Hindus and the Muslims in India?

11 How did T'ai Tsung of the T'ang dynasty improve the government of the Chinese Empire?

12 How did Mongol rule affect China?

13 What were some of the cultural achievements of the Ashikaga period in Japan?

PROJECTS AND ACTIVITIES

14 Look through books and magazines to find examples of Japanese art and literature. Prepare a bulletin-board display with your findings. Label those examples that may illustrate the influence of Chinese culture.

15 Choose one of the emperors of the T'ang, the Sung, or the Yüan dynasty. Using library materials, prepare a biography of that ruler. Include the contributions that the emperor made to China. Present your paper to the class.

Using Geography Skills

The term *climate* refers to the average weather conditions of a region over a long period of time. The climate of a particular region may affect its development in several ways. For example, climate affects the growing season of a region. In addition, climate may be one factor that influences the growth of towns and cities.

A *climatic map* shows the various types of climates that exist in a particular region. By looking at a climatic map, it is possible to make some generalizations concerning the lifestyle that the people of that region have developed.

The climatic map below shows the various types of climate found in Europe. It also shows the major medieval European cities. Study the map carefully. Then answer the following questions:

1 Compare the number of medieval cities in western Europe with the number found in eastern Europe. Basing your opinion on the information on the map, why, do you think, did more medieval cities develop in western Europe than in eastern Europe?

2 What other geographic characteristic shown on the map may have been a determining factor in the location of many medieval cities? Why?

3 In what way may the growing season of a particular region be related to the development of towns and cities? How might the growing season affect the levels of urban population? Explain.

4 In what ways did geographic factors aid the development of medieval cities in western Europe more than in eastern Europe? Explain.

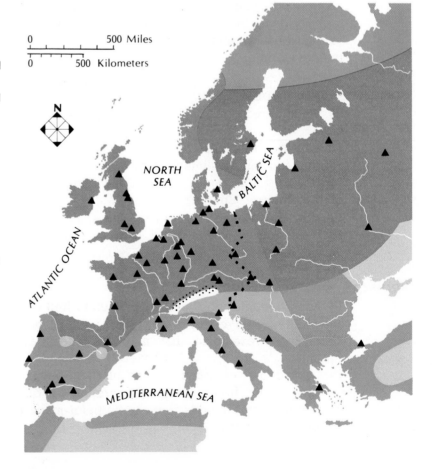

Climate

Steppe—very hot summer, very cold winter, little rainfall

Mediterranean—dry summer; moist, mild winter[1]

Humid Subtropical—long, humid summer; short, mild winter[1]

Maritime—mild temperatures all year, dependable rainfall[1]

Warm Summer Continental—warm summer, cold winter, dependable rainfall[1]

Cool Summer Continental—warm but short summer, cold winter, dependable rainfall[2]

Subarctic—short summer; long, cold winter

Highlands—temperature and rainfall vary over short distances at different altitudes

[1]These regions tend to have a long growing season with a relatively high agricultural yield.

[2]These regions tend to have a short growing season with a relatively low agricultural yield.

▲ Major Medieval European City

- - - - Approximate division between eastern and western Europe

UNIT 4 IN REVIEW

CONCEPTS AND UNDERSTANDINGS

1 How did the development of the English Parliament differ from the development of the French Estates-General?
2 In what ways did the Crusades bring about changes in western Europe during the late Middle Ages?
3 How did the repeated invasions of eastern Europe affect the development of the region?
4 In what ways did Ivan the Great and Ivan the Terrible contribute to the development of czarist Russia?
5 How did the Muslim rule of India affect the culture of that country?
6 How did Chu Hsi influence Chinese thought during the Sung era?
7 How did the increase of tax-free estates in Japan during the Fujiwara period affect the Japanese social structure?

QUESTIONS FOR DISCUSSION

1 In what ways do you think the merchant and craft guilds contributed to the decline of feudalism in western Europe?
2 To what extent do you think the influence of the Byzantine Empire in eastern Europe hindered the development of strong monarchies in that region?
3 Do you think that the creation of Sikhism in India was a realistic alternative to the faiths of Hinduism and Islam? Why or why not? Explain your answer.
4 Japan was not successfully occupied until the twentieth century. To what extent do you think this fact may have influenced Japan's history and culture? Explain your answer.

SUGGESTED READING

Asimov, Isaac. *Constantinople: The Forgotten Empire*. Houghton Mifflin Company, 1970.
Duke, Dulcie. *Lincoln: The Growth of a Medieval City*. Cambridge University Press, 1974.
Leonard, Jonathan N. *Early Japan*. Time-Life Books, 1968.
Mango, Cyril. *Byzantium: The Empire of New Rome*. Charles Scribner's Sons, 1980.
Morgan, Gwyneth. *Life in a Medieval Village*. Lerner Publications Company, 1981.
Rugoff, Milton. *Marco Polo's Adventures in China*. Harper & Row Publishers, Inc., 1974.
Schulberg, Lucille. *Historic India*. Time-Life Books, 1968.
Wallace, Robert. *Rise of Russia*. Time-Life Books, 1967.
Watson, Percy. *Building the Medieval Cathedrals*. Lerner Publications Company, 1978.

A NEW EUROPEAN ORDER

(c. 1300 to c. 1750)

Raymond V. Schoder, S.J.

Renaissance cathedral in Florence, Italy   Cavalry skirmish during the Thirty Years' War

During the late Middle Ages, many forces were combining to change the way that Europeans viewed themselves and their world. Slowly, the medieval emphasis on spiritual matters was replaced by a growing awareness of the individual's role and importance in the world. This shift of emphasis helped begin a time of intellectual, scientific, and cultural renewal that was to change almost every part of European society.

At the same time, strong monarchies were replacing feudalism throughout Europe. Kings and queens also began challenging the role of the Roman Catholic Church as the strongest political power in Europe. Then, in the 1500's, the power of the Church was further weakened as some Europeans, who felt that the Church had become too worldly and corrupt, called for change. Rather quickly, new religious groups were started throughout Europe. As the power of the Church declined, the monarchs claimed increasing political and religious authority. In addition, the monarchs backed voyages of exploration that led to European dominance in many parts of the world.

By the eighteenth century, medieval ideas and institutions had been completely altered by the many changes that had taken place in Europe. The modern era had begun.

Port of Lisbon, Portugal, in the sixteenth century

CHAPTER 16 THE EUROPEAN RENAISSANCE

1 The Nature of the Renaissance   2 The Italian Renaissance
3 The Spread of the Renaissance   4 The Age of Exploration

By the late Middle Ages, Europe was in a state of cultural and intellectual change. People were faced with new problems and challenges. When traditional teachings did not provide all the answers to the problems, people slowly turned away from the medieval way of life. But changes did not take place in all parts of Europe at the same time. The reshaping of the European way of life began in the Italian city-states and then spread to other parts of Europe.

It was a time when the limits of learning were extended. Because of this, important advances were made in many cultural and intellectual fields. These achievements laid the foundations for many present-day institutions. In time, a new and vital period of history—the early modern age—began.

A noted humanist of the Renaissance, Cardinal Bessarion, in a painting by the Italian artist Carpaccio

1 THE NATURE OF THE RENAISSANCE

Historians often refer to the period of European history between about 1300 and about 1600 as the Renaissance [REN-uh-SAHNS]. During these years, European civilization began to show a number of characteristics that we generally classify as modern. But it would be misleading to think that the Renaissance was a sharp break with the Middle Ages. Instead, the Renaissance owed much to classical and medieval traditions.

THE IMPORTANCE OF THE RENAISSANCE

Many historians agree that the Middle Ages reached its peak during the early 1300's. At the same time, however, new ways of life began to emerge in parts of western Europe. During the next 300 years, European life and thought were gradually reshaped. Interest in earthly life and in human achievement was renewed.

The slow change from a spiritual to an earthly focus during these years was based, in part, upon a revival of classical Greek and Roman ideals. Because of this, the years between about 1300 and about 1600 have become known as the *Renaissance*—rebirth—of European culture.

There was much that was new and fresh in the culture of Renaissance Europe. But it is important to remember that Renaissance culture was built partly upon medieval foundations. For example, religion continued to be an important aspect of everyday life during the Renaissance. And even though the political influence of the Roman Catholic Church declined after 1300, the Church continued to play a powerful role in European society.

The Renaissance helped to shape present-day European thought and culture. Many of today's social and political ideas were shaped during the Renaissance. But the beginnings of these ideas can often be traced back even further—to the late Middle Ages.

MEDIEVAL ORIGINS OF THE RENAISSANCE

For nearly a thousand years, the civilization of medieval Europe grew and adapted to changing conditions. Important institutions, such as feudalism, the Church, and the manorial system, formed a framework within which the society of the Middle Ages flourished.

By the late Middle Ages, however, many of the institutions that had shaped medieval life had become outdated. The rise of powerful central governments did much to undermine feudalism. Moreover, the spread of trade and commerce and the development of towns and cities helped to change medieval social and economic life.

By the early 1300's, the Church, too, was no longer as powerful as it had once been. In part, this was due to the conflict between the Church and local rulers who were jealous of the Church's power. By the late Middle Ages, this conflict had sapped the strength of the Church. And throughout the 1300's, problems within the Church lessened its prestige. These problems will be discussed further in Chapter 17.

The growth of a strong middle class led to new ideas about life, which further weakened Church influence. Middle-class goals, such as wealth, success, and a better life on earth, became increasingly widespread in medieval society. Thus, by the late Middle Ages, a growing number of Europeans were no longer concerned only with their spiritual well-being.

Traditional views of society and of the role of the individual also changed greatly during the late Middle Ages. As more people began to seek a better way of life, the role of the individual became more important. A new emphasis upon personal worth, achievement, and individualism began to be felt.

Thus, many of the cultural and social patterns that gave birth to the European

POLITICAL		SOCIAL AND ECONOMIC
	1420 –	Prince Henry of Portugal founded navigators' school
	1441 –	Portuguese began African slave trade
Lorenzo de' Medici, future ruler of Florence, born	– 1449	
	1452 –	Leonardo da Vinci born
Conclusion of Hundred Years' War	– 1453	
Wars of the Roses began	– 1455	
	1456 –	Johannes Gutenberg developed movable-type printing press
	1473 –	Copernicus, European astronomer, born
Spain united under Ferdinand and Isabella	– 1479	
	1488 –	Bartholomeu Dias discovered Cape of Good Hope
Spanish defeated Moors in Granada	– 1492 –	Columbus voyaged to Americas
Treaty of Tordesillas signed	– 1494	
	1497 –	John Cabot searched for northwest passage
	1498 –	Michelangelo finished "Pietà" sculpture
Vasco da Gama founded Portuguese colony at Cochin, India	– 1502	
Portuguese founded trading post at Goa	– 1510	
	1516 –	Thomas More's Utopia published
Portuguese expelled from China	– 1523	
	1534 –	Jacques Cartier explored St. Lawrence River

Renaissance came about during the late Middle Ages. Many of these patterns emerged first in the small but wealthy and aggressive city-states of northern Italy.

ITALY IN THE FOURTEENTH CENTURY
Medieval Italy, unlike France and England, was never unified under a single, centralized government. Instead, Italy in the 1300's was divided into a number of independent city-states and kingdoms. Among these were the wealthy city-states of northern Italy.

By 1300, the northern city-states, such as Florence, Milan, and Venice, had grown powerful through trade and commerce. Venice, for example, had become a leading sea power. Venetian traders called at ports throughout Europe, the Byzantine Empire, and the Muslim world. Other Italian city-states, such as Florence, became banking and manufacturing centers.

During the 1300's, many northern Italians grew enormously wealthy through trade and commerce. And because wealth often brought political power, rich merchants and bankers were frequently government leaders as well. By the 1300's, then, political power was no longer held only by the nobility. Instead, it was increasingly held by those who had shown themselves able to achieve economic success.

Trade and commerce speeded the growth of worldly values and ideas. Many people depended upon economic success for their livelihoods. To those people, the deeply spiritual outlook of the Middle Ages had little attraction.

Moreover, trade with other parts of the world brought Italians of the northern city-states into contact with new ideas and new ways of doing things. And the emphasis upon personal achievement and competition demanded by life-styles based on trade and commerce encouraged feelings of individualism in the people of the city-states.

Thus, life in the Italian city-states in the 1300's had many characteristics that, today,

In addition to its importance as a manufacturing and banking center, the northern Italian city-state of Florence led the way in artistic expression during the Renaissance.

we view as modern. In their intellectual outlooks, too, a growing number of northern Italians moved away from accepted medieval points of view.

THE BEGINNING OF THE ITALIAN RENAISSANCE By the late Middle Ages, changing living conditions had brought about new patterns of thought in parts of Europe. Scholasticism, the major philosophy of the Middle Ages, slowly began to lose its broad appeal.

In northern Italy, the movement away from Scholasticism took the form of a new interest in classical Greek and Roman thought. This movement has become known as the *humanist revival* because it stressed human—rather than spiritual—values. For this reason, the humanist revival marked a clear break with the religious focus of the Middle Ages.

Earlier Greek and Roman authors were chiefly interested in the quality of human life on earth and in the present. These ideas were strongly favored by many fourteenth-century Italians. Also, classical writings seemed to justify and to explain many of the changes that faced Renaissance Italians.

Classical thinkers, for example, valued individual development and achievement. Moreover, they generally held that effective communication and a willingness to accept change were needed in an orderly, prosperous society. These and other classical values were ideally suited to the city lifestyles of northern Italy in the 1300's. For this reason, Italian authors and teachers worked to use classical ideas to meet their society's changing needs.

The humanist revival had a major impact upon life in fourteenth-century northern

Italy. In time, humanist ideas greatly changed ways of thinking about society. Ultimately, these changes gave rise to what is now known as the Italian Renaissance.

QUESTIONS FOR REVIEW

1 *What approximate period of time did the Renaissance span?*

2 *How did the northern Italian city-states grow powerful by 1300?*

3 *Why did the growing interest in classical Greek and Roman thought during the late Middle Ages become known as the humanist revival?*

2 THE ITALIAN RENAISSANCE

It is difficult to assign exact dates to the Renaissance. It had its beginnings in northern Italy sometime during the mid-1300's, and it lasted in that area for over 200 years. During that time, remarkable accomplishments were made in literature, art, and science.

Much of the Renaissance had its beginnings in the late Middle Ages. But it was during the Renaissance that the greatest achievements were made. For many historians, the Renaissance looms not only as a time of great achievement but also as an age of change. It was a time when Europe moved from the Middle Ages toward what we now view as modern times.

ITALIAN RENAISSANCE LITERATURE The literature that emerged in Italy during the Renaissance is often described as humanistic. The noted authors of the time shared a passion for the study of ancient Greek and Roman literature and a belief in what is today called humanism.

During the Renaissance, Italian authors produced a wide variety of prose and poetry, both in the *vernacular*—the language of their society—and in Greek and Latin. Even though these authors shared ideas and points of view with earlier medieval scholars, they brought to their writing a greater emphasis on the importance of the individual and the ideas of change and progress. Some of the noted authors of the time were Francesco Petrarca (1304–1374), Giovanni Boccaccio (1313–1375), and Lorenzo Valla (1406–1457).

Francesco Petrarca, or Petrarch, was an Italian poet of the early fourteenth century. Early in life, Petrarch developed an interest in classical Roman literature. His poems reflected his humanist ideas. They expressed Petrarch's feeling that people should concern themselves more with earthly questions and less with spiritual questions. Petrarch's view showed the continuing change from the medieval spiritual concerns to a concern for the present-day world.

Petrarch and his friend Giovanni Boccaccio, the author of *The Decameron*, were important writers of the humanist school. Writing in Italian rather than Latin made them popular with many people and influenced other authors who followed them. One such writer was Baldassare Castiglione (1478–1529), whose book, *The Courtier*, popularized the idea of the well-rounded, multitalented individual, "the Renaissance man."

Through the influence of the humanist authors, people developed new interests. One of these interests was the study of history. A leading figure in the 1400's was Lorenzo Valla, who used his knowledge of classical Latin to challenge documents and doctrines of the Christian Church. Valla's work influenced later humanists, who began to question the practices and the authority of the Church.

RENAISSANCE ART IN ITALY As great as were the writings of Italian authors, perhaps even greater were the remarkable works of art produced in Italy. The city of Florence led the way in artistic progress. The new and energetic environment of the Italian city-states led to the development of a new style of art.

During much of the Middle Ages, painting was generally meant to fulfill a practical purpose—the decoration of churches and public buildings. Medieval paintings were always religious, and little if any attention was paid to secular, or everyday, matters. These paintings were created to show the people's devotion to God. But with the growth of humanism and of the concern for the more practical life of individuals, painting began to change. Painting became more lifelike and the subject matter of the paintings became more worldly. Even though religious themes were still portrayed, other subjects were also painted.

The first steps away from the medieval style of painting were taken by the Florentine painter Giotto di Bondone (1266?–1337). He brought realism to art by painting animated and far more lifelike figures than was done before.

Another influential painter was Masaccio (1401–1428). In his brief career (it was rumored that he was poisoned), he introduced *perspective*—a technique that brought a three-dimensional look to painting. In his paintings Masaccio also tried to give his subjects a more human quality than had medieval artists.

With these changes, people began to see painting as an art, not just as decoration. People began to appreciate paintings for their beauty. And wealthy merchants and princes had their portraits painted by the leading artists of the time.

LEONARDO AND MICHELANGELO A number of outstanding painters followed Giotto and Masaccio. But perhaps the greatest of them all was Leonardo da Vinci (1452–1519).

Masaccio's painting *The Tribute Money* is an excellent example of how Renaissance artists used realism and perspective in their works.

Scala/EPA

In addition to painting such masterpieces as the portrait of Ginevra de'Benci (below), Leonardo da Vinci sketched machines, like the ones at the right, that were similar to modern weapons.

Born in the small mountain town of Vinci in 1452, Leonardo da Vinci grew to become the outstanding genius of the Italian Renaissance. Skilled in painting, he was also acclaimed for his abilities as a sculptor, architect, mathematician, philosopher, scientist, and engineer. More than any one individual, Leonardo da Vinci represented the talented, well-rounded Renaissance ideal.

As a youth, Leonardo was sent to study painting in Florence. By the time he was 25, he had become recognized as one of the outstanding painters of his time. During his illustrious career, he produced a number of masterpieces. Critics today generally agree that two of his most memorable works are *The Last Supper* and the *Mona Lisa*. Through his paintings, Leonardo da Vinci pioneered many art techniques that are widely used by painters today.

No discussion of Renaissance art can be complete without a consideration of Michelangelo Buonarroti. Born in 1475, Michelangelo lived for 89 years. His first love was sculpture, but he also painted. Considered to be his masterpiece are the frescoes on the ceiling of the Sistine Chapel in Rome. Today, Michelangelo is thought to have been the greatest sculptor of the Renaissance, and some people think he was the greatest sculptor of all time. His major works of sculpture include the *Pietà* and his *David*. Upon his death in 1564, Michelangelo was buried with honors by the citizens of Florence.

OTHER CONTRIBUTIONS Overall, the Italian Renaissance was a time of great intel-

Michelangelo's powerful statue of Moses shows how Renaissance sculptors were influenced by the works of the classical Greeks and Romans.

lectual change. Renaissance scholars and scientists developed new ideas that led to advances in many areas of learning.

One idea, for example, that interested Italian humanists concerned the relationship between government and the people. The noted political philosopher Niccolò Machiavelli [MAK-ee-uh-VEL-ee] tried to define this relationship in his writings, particularly in his book *The Prince*. Machiavelli (1469–1527) believed in the idea of a strong state. He wrote that a ruler should use whatever means needed to remain in power and to build a powerful state. Even though many of Machiavelli's ideas appear to be immoral or, at best, unethical, his ideas influenced later political philosophers and, not surprisingly, some rulers.

Medicine was another field of intellectual development in Italy during the Renaissance. Italian universities made great strides in the study of medicine. In time, discoveries made in these schools helped Andreas Vesalius (1514–1564) to write the first accurate book on human anatomy.

Renaissance scientists also made important discoveries in the field of astronomy. The Italian-educated Polish scientist, Nicolaus Copernicus [koh-PUR-ni-kuhs], for example, discovered that the sun was the center of our solar system. Before this discovery, the earth was thought to be the center of the solar system. Copernicus (1473–1543) also described how the earth and the other planets moved around the sun. Copernicus' discovery became known as the *heliocentric*—sun-centered—theory. Later, an Italian, Galileo Galilei (1564–1642), greatly improved the telescope. With the aid of the telescope, Galileo confirmed the heliocentric theory. Challenged by the Church, Galileo stopped his teaching of the theory but never changed his belief in its accuracy.

The work of Italian teachers and scientists helped to bring about the transition from medieval times to the modern world. Even more important was the fact that Italian scholars and scientists of the Renaissance no longer believed without question the accepted teachings of the past. Careful observation and an open-minded, scientific approach became the methods of science. In this way, the intellectual contributions of the Italian Renaissance gave rise to a new age, an age of modern thought.

QUESTIONS FOR REVIEW

1 *What form of writing helped make Petrarch and Boccaccio popular with many people?*

2 *In what ways did the Florentine painter Giotto di Bondone bring realism to art?*

3 *Why was Copernicus' theory known as the sun-centered theory?*

Life at the Time

The Renaissance Ideal

Throughout the Renaissance, great emphasis was placed upon the complete development of the individual. The ideal individual during the Renaissance was expected to be well educated and socially graceful. Women, however, enjoyed far less social freedom and opportunity than did men. In addition, Renaissance standards of social behavior generally applied only to members of the wealthy classes.

The ideal Renaissance standards of behavior were summarized and described in an influential book, *The Courtier*, written by Baldassare Castiglione in 1528. Castiglione's important book gives today's reader a clear picture of Renaissance life-styles and manners. The excerpt below, taken from *The Courtier*, provides an insight into Renaissance social ideals and thus helps us to better understand the nature of Renaissance culture.

". . . I would have the Courtier . . . endowed by nature not only with talent and beauty of person and feature, but with a certain grace and (as we say) air that shall make him at first sight pleasing and agreeable to all who see him . . .

"[In battle,] let the man we are seeking, be very bold, stern, and always among the first, where the enemy are to be seen; and in every other place, gentle, modest, reserved, above all things avoiding ostentation [unnecessary display] and that impudent self-praise by which men ever excite hatred and disgust in all who hear them. . . .

"I would have him more than passably accomplished in . . . those studies that are called the humanities, and conversant not only with the Latin language but with the Greek . . .

"[He should] be also a musician and . . . play upon divers [various] instruments. . . .

"[O]ur Courtier ought . . . to know how to draw and to have acquaintance with the . . . art of painting. . . .

"I believe that many faculties of the mind are as necessary to woman as to man . . . [such as] to be naturally graceful in all her doings, to be mannerly, clever, prudent, not arrogant, not envious, not slanderous, not vain, not quarrelsome, not silly . . .

"[I]n the matter of bodily exercises it does not befit women to handle weapons, to ride, to play tennis, to wrestle, and to do many other things that befit men. . . .

"[I]n dancing I would not see her use too active and violent movements . . . when she starts to dance or make music of any kind, she ought to bring herself to it . . . with a touch of shyness. . . ."

Harrach Collection/Photo Meyer KG

The Renaissance emphasis on complete personal development included musical study by the women, as well as by the men, of the wealthy classes.

3 THE SPREAD OF THE RENAISSANCE

By the late 1400's, the humanistic values and the ideas of Renaissance Italy had begun to filter northward, greatly influencing culture and society in other parts of Europe. Important changes in the social, political, and economic life-styles of northern Europeans began to take place at this time. As a result, from the late 1400's to the 1600's, great strides were made in the art, the literature, and the science of northern Europe.

THE SPREAD OF RENAISSANCE THOUGHT

By the mid-1400's, northern Europe had begun to recover from the turmoil and destruction of the Hundred Years' War (see Chapter 13). With the return of peace, travel along roads and rivers became safer. Increased safety made it more profitable for merchants to carry on trade between towns. Rather rapidly, towns and cities grew throughout northern Europe.

The revival of trade and of town life after the mid-1400's helped to spread Renaissance ideas northward. Increased trade made closer communication among people of different areas possible. As merchants moved northward from town to town, they helped to spread the knowledge of the new ideas and techniques of the Italian Renaissance. In this way, the humanist ideas of Renaissance Italy slowly spread throughout northern Europe.

The spread of Renaissance ideas into northern Europe was also aided by the invention of the printing press by Johannes Gutenberg in 1456. The new movable-type press made it possible to print large numbers of books cheaply and rapidly. As books became available, the literacy rate increased in many places.

By the end of the fifteenth century, printing presses were being set up all over Europe. Textbooks, religious works, and other important books were becoming more common. By 1500, about 6 million books had been printed in Europe. The development of the printing press helped to spread the humanist ideas and points of view of Renaissance Italy throughout much of Europe.

NORTHERN HUMANISM During the late 1400's, humanist views about achievement, individualism, and the importance of life on earth attracted a growing number of northern Europeans. Many people found that humanist ideals related closely to their personal goals and values. Among middle-class Europeans, for example, support for humanist ideals became more widespread. Moreover, a growing number of authors, artists, and government and Church leaders accepted the ideas of the Italian humanists. Rather quickly, the ideals of humanism mixed with the traditional values of northern Europe. Together, they formed a new culture—the culture of the Northern Renaissance.

In some cases, the humanism of the Northern Renaissance was strongly shaped by northern European religious ideas. For this reason, northern humanism was generally more spiritual in tone than was the humanism of Renaissance Italy. Nevertheless, northern humanists—like their Italian counterparts—believed in individual development, personal achievement, and earthly progress.

Perhaps the most important humanist thinker of the Northern Renaissance was Desiderius Erasmus [i-RAZ-muhs]. Erasmus (1466?–1536) used satire in such works as *Praise of Folly* to state his views. Erasmus wanted to rid the world of injustice and corruption. His humorous but critical writings set the standard for much of the intellectual progress made during the Northern Renaissance.

Throughout the 1400's, humanist ideas changed northern values and ways of living.

Humanism also played a part in the development of new styles of art and literature in northern Europe.

NORTHERN ART By the late 1400's, northern art clearly showed the influence of humanism. Northern artists learned to combine their traditions with the style and techniques of the Italian artists. These artists no longer dealt solely with religious subjects, but instead they worked to portray the real world as they saw it.

Artists of the Northern Renaissance learned to show their subjects in realistic, everyday settings. Typical of this trend was the painter, Pieter Brueghel [BROO-guhl]. Brueghel (1520?–1569) vividly captured the way of life of northern peasants.

Equally outstanding was Hans Holbein the Younger. Holbein was the most famous northern portrait painter of the 1500's. Because Holbein tried to capture exact likenesses of his subjects, his paintings have a realistic, almost photographic, look. As the court painter to King Henry VIII of England,

Holbein had a lasting influence on English artists.

Thus, when northern artists broke away from the medieval tradition, a new style of northern art grew. The artistic style that emerged during the fifteenth and sixteenth centuries emphasized realism, accuracy, and the present. In much the same way, the humanist authors of the Northern Renais-

Pieter Brueghel's *Peasant Wedding* (below) and Hans Holbein's *The Ambassadors* (right) show the contrast in lifestyle and dress between the upper and the lower classes during the northern European Renaissance.

sance created new and important forms of literature.

THE LITERATURE OF THE NORTHERN RENAISSANCE

During the fifteenth and sixteenth centuries, humanist ideas spread throughout northern Europe. These ideas led to the development of new forms of literature. Northern authors no longer confined themselves to religious and spiritual subjects. Instead, they began to write about social and political ideas, about human behavior, and about earthly matters.

The literature of the Northern Renaissance emphasized subjects of immediate interest. Northern humanists, such as Erasmus and the English philosopher Sir Thomas More, discussed various ways to improve society. These northern authors felt that institutions, like people themselves, had to adapt to changing conditions in order to survive and improve. For example, More's classic work, *Utopia*, stated his belief that society should be built upon ideas of justice, equality, and opportunity for all.

Humanist authors of the Northern Renaissance used many different approaches and wrote on a variety of subjects. The French writer François Rabelais [RAB-uh-LAY], for one, used an earthy, humorous style to portray human feelings. And the Spanish author and soldier Miguel de Cervantes [suhr-VAN-teez] first used the literary form that later became the novel.

Among the most creative northern authors was the English dramatist, William Shakespeare. A great number of Shakespeare's plays are still enjoyed by people today. Among these works are *Hamlet*, *Romeo and Juliet*, *The Taming of the Shrew*, and *Othello*. A master of drama, Shakespeare portrayed human relationships with great clarity and insight.

Humanist authors of the Northern Renaissance aimed to entertain, as well as to educate, their readers. Literature, like other works of art, was meant to be appreciated for its beauty as well as for its meaning.

SCIENTIFIC ADVANCES

During the Northern Renaissance, advances in art and literature were matched by important developments in science. Northern European scientists began to question the accepted teachings of the past. Through careful experiments and observations, northern Europeans proved that some of the views held by traditional authorities were wrong or outdated. The work of Northern Renaissance scientists led to many new and important scientific discoveries.

Medicine was one field in which northern scientists made important breakthroughs. Careful experimentation and observation led northern scientists to discover helpful new drugs. Among these drugs were sulfur compounds and copper sulfate, which were used to treat wounds. Moreover, improved surgical techniques and a better understanding of human anatomy were developed by northern doctors, led by the French physician Ambroise Paré. And the work of the English doctor William Harvey led to new understandings of the human circulatory system. These and many other findings brought about major improvements in medicine.

During the Northern Renaissance, major advances were made in the field of astronomy. For example, a German, Johannes Kepler, did much to clarify the heliocentric theory. Kepler's studies helped to explain the movement of the planets.

Progress was also made in mathematics. During the 1500's, northern Europeans first used plus, minus, and equal signs, as well as the symbols for square roots and decimal points. Because of this, more detailed calculations were made possible. In this way, mathematics became a more useful tool of science.

In general, the Northern Renaissance was a time when a growing number of people challenged once-accepted explanations and ideas. People worked to find their own answers. They were more inclined to test long-held ideas and beliefs and to search for new information. Thus, early researchers opened the door to modern science.

RESULTS OF THE NORTHERN RENAISSANCE During the late 1400's, changing cultural conditions in northern Europe led to new points of view and to new ways of living. Much progress was made in many areas of society as northern Europeans, influenced by humanist ideas, worked to build a better life on earth. Religion still played an important part in daily life. But a growing number of northern Europeans were no longer concerned only with their spiritual well-being. The influence of humanism led to changes in many traditional ideas and institutions. And as a result, new ways of living slowly emerged in northern Europe.

The development of new artistic points of view was one of the most important aspects of the Northern Renaissance. Humanist artists and authors worked to show life in a realistic and vivid way. Their new ideas and skills helped northern artists and authors to produce masterpieces that are still full of meaning and impact today.

The characteristic Northern Renaissance desire to question and to test led to many important scientific discoveries. Northern scientists began to follow new approaches to learning. Experimentation and careful observation became standard methods of science. New information was discovered that helped Europeans to better understand themselves and the world around them.

QUESTIONS FOR REVIEW

1 *What invention made it possible to print large numbers of books cheaply and rapidly?*

2 *How did artists of the Northern Renaissance depict people in their paintings?*

3 *Why do you think so many important scientific discoveries were made during the Northern Renaissance?*

4 THE AGE OF EXPLORATION

The European Renaissance was a time of exploration and discovery as well as of cultural growth and change. European desires to explore new lands were caused, in part, by new economic needs. In addition, improved shipbuilding and navigational techniques enabled Europeans to make longer sea voyages than ever before.

Portugal and Spain were among the first European countries to engage in large-scale overseas exploration. Their successes brought other European powers into the race for land and wealth. By the early 1500's, Europeans had discovered new overseas routes to the fabled Far East. They had also begun to open the vast new world of the Americas.

REASONS FOR EXPLORATION European trade with the Middle East and the Orient expanded throughout the Middle Ages and the Renaissance. Before 1500, however, this trade was virtually monopolized by the city-states of northern Italy—particularly Venice. Goods from India and China were brought to the Middle East by Arab traders, who sold them to Italian merchants. The Italians, in turn, carried these goods to the markets of northern and western Europe. But since the spices and other products had to be handled by Arab traders on the route to Europe, prices for Eastern goods were very high.

Not surprisingly, merchants and traders from other parts of Europe resented the Italian monopoly and wanted to share in the profitable trade. Thus, European rulers and merchants alike worked to encourage the discovery of new trade routes to the East. With these new trade routes, they could buy goods directly from India and China. The Arab and Italian traders could therefore be eliminated from the East-West trade, and Eastern goods could be bought at lower prices.

In addition to searching for new trade routes, Europeans wanted to find markets for their products and to find new sources of gold and silver. By the 1400's money coined from gold and silver had begun to replace barter as the method of paying for goods in much of Europe. As a result, greater amounts of gold and silver were needed so that countries could expand their trade.

However, exploration was not a result of economic factors alone. Religion also played an important role. In the 1400's, some European leaders viewed overseas exploration as a chance to spread Christianity. In Spain and Portugal, the crusading spirit was very strong at this time. This spirit, coupled with their strong religious views, encouraged the Spanish and the Portuguese to spread Christianity to foreign lands.

TECHNOLOGICAL ADVANCES The creative spirit of the European Renaissance was also a factor in the Age of Exploration. By the fifteenth century, technological advances had helped to make overseas exploration possible.

One of these developments was the magnetic compass, which enabled sailors to keep their ships on course without the aid of the sun or stars. Another was the astrolabe, an instrument used to determine latitude. By using these instruments, a ship's course and approximate position could be determined.

New developments occurred in shipbuilding as well. The ships of medieval Europe were very difficult to maneuver and were not suitable for long voyages in the open seas. By the mid-1400's, the Spanish and the Portuguese had built two new kinds of oceangoing ships—the caravel and the carrack. In these new vessels, the single sail of medieval ships was replaced by five or six smaller, more easily handled sails. Both types of ships had rudders that greatly improved maneuverability. Crude by modern standards, these new vessels never-

The perfection of navigational devices like this astrolabe made it possible for European explorers to embark on long overseas voyages.

theless were able to make long overseas voyages. Thus, by the end of the 1400's, the desire for exploration, as well as the technical achievements to make it possible, had started a new era of discovery in Europe.

PORTUGUESE EXPLORATIONS The first European country to engage in extensive overseas exploration and discovery in the fifteenth century was Portugal. This was due, in large part, to the efforts of one Portuguese leader—Prince Henry the Navigator. Around 1420, Prince Henry founded a school near Sagres, on the southwestern coast of Portugal. There he gathered navigators, mariners, scientists, and mapmakers who could provide sailors with the latest information and techniques in explorations.

Henry's major goals were to send expeditions down the African coast to find new sources of gold and silver and to discover a sea route to India. Under Prince Henry's leadership, the Portuguese had built a thriving trade with coastal Africa by the 1450's.

After Henry's death in 1460, Portuguese explorers continued to search for an overseas route to India (see map on page 318). And in 1488, Bartholomeu Dias reached the southernmost point of Africa—the Cape of Good Hope. The Portuguese now knew that the Far East lay just across the Indian Ocean.

However, it was not until 1498 that the Portuguese finally reached the Far East. In that year, a Portuguese fleet led by Vasco da Gama arrived in India. The Arab traders in India tried to stop da Gama from taking on a cargo of spices because they felt that trade with India was their monopoly. Nevertheless, da Gama loaded one of his four ships and returned to Portugal with a cargo that paid a handsome profit, despite the loss of many men and three vessels.

Within a few years the Portuguese were able to establish a fairly large empire in the East. The Portuguese were not particularly interested in founding colonies. Rather, their empire existed almost exclusively for trade. Although the Portuguese sent priests to convert native peoples to Catholicism, they made few attempts at large-scale conquest or colonization.

EUROPEANS REACH AMERICA At the same time that the Portuguese were exploring eastward, other Europeans believed that Asia could be reached by sailing west. One Italian navigator, Christopher Columbus, wanted to make such a voyage. In 1486, he asked King Ferdinand and Queen Isabella of Spain to pay for an expedition that would sail westward to Asia. At first, Columbus' request was refused. In 1492, however, the Spanish rulers finally agreed to finance the voyage. Columbus set sail westward for Asia with three small ships from Palos, Spain, in August 1492.

On October 12, 1492, Columbus set foot on an island that he assumed was near the coast of Japan. In reality, he had landed on a Caribbean island—now known as San Salvador—about 500 miles off the coast of

In the fifteenth and sixteenth centuries, courageous European explorers, backed by powerful monarchs, voyaged throughout the world.

European Voyages of Exploration

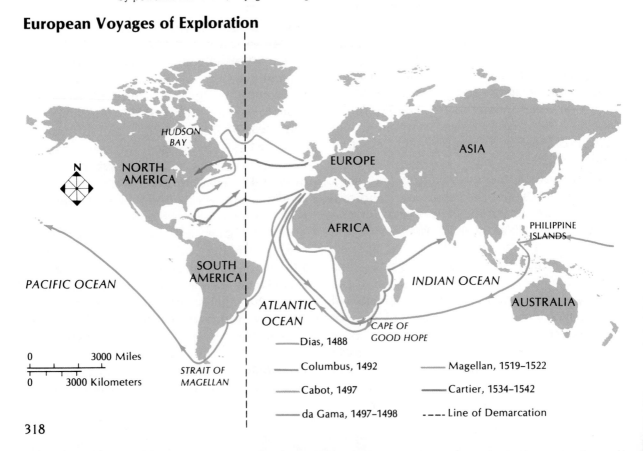

Florida. Until his death in 1506, however, Columbus remained convinced that he had reached Asia, and during three later voyages he continued to search for mainland Asia.

Although the results of Columbus' voyages excited Europe, Columbus was probably not the first European to reach America. Scandinavian sagas told stories of earlier Viking explorations of North America. Recent discoveries now seem to indicate that the sagas were true. For example, in the 1960's, archaeologists discovered what they believe to be the remains of Viking settlements in Newfoundland. Because of these findings, historians now are almost certain that the Vikings settled parts of North America about 500 years before Columbus.

SPANISH EXPLORATIONS Following Columbus' voyages, the Spaniards quickly began settling in the Americas (see map on page 318). The Spanish plan for an empire placed great emphasis on conquest, colonization, and missionary work. Consequently, most Spanish expeditions contained soldiers, settlers, and priests. Thus, the Spanish sought to build an empire that was based upon permanent settlement, in contrast to the Portuguese, who worked to establish an empire based on trade.

The Spanish and the Portuguese wanted to guarantee their right to control their growing empires without going to war. Therefore, the rulers of both countries asked the Pope to help them divide the world into two spheres of influence. In 1494, Spain and Portugal signed the Treaty of Tordesillas, which set up a line of demarcation running from pole to pole (see map on page 318). All of the New World except for Brazil—which was claimed for Portugal by Pedro Cabral—was granted to Spain. The Portuguese were granted control of Africa and Asia.

Following the Treaty of Tordesillas, many Spanish explorers began to suspect that Columbus had discovered a new land,

rather than merely islands off the coast of Asia. Their suspicion was confirmed when Amerigo Vespucci, exploring the coast of South America in 1499, determined that the land was, in fact, a new continent.

Then, in 1513, Vasco Núñez de Balboa, another Spanish explorer, crossed the narrow Isthmus of Panama and discovered a magnificent calm sea—the Pacific Ocean. It was thus proven that another body of water lay between the Americas and the Far East. The search for a way around America began.

MAGELLAN CIRCLES THE WORLD Ferdinand Magellan, a Portuguese navigator living in Spain, believed that a passage through the Americas linking the Atlantic and Pacific oceans existed. Magellan realized that a sea passage through the Americas would offer a new route to Asia. He therefore asked the Spanish king, Charles V, to sponsor a voyage to search for a "southwest passage" to the Indies. Magellan's idea was accepted enthusiastically, and he began his historic journey in September 1519. Magellan's five ships crossed the Atlantic and reached the southern tip of South America. After suffering extreme hardships, the small fleet discovered a route to the Pacific, the Strait of Magellan.

Throughout the journey, Magellan had trouble with mutinous sailors and with poor supplies, but his problems became worse in the vast Pacific. The tiny fleet's supplies quickly ran out, and the men were reduced to eating rats and sawdust. When the ships finally reached Guam, new provisions and water were taken on board.

In the Philippines, Magellan was killed in a battle with natives. The remnants of his crew, in a single ship commanded by Juan Sebastián del Cano, finally reached Spain in September 1522. Thus, it was proved that it was possible to reach the fabled East by sailing west.

THE NORTHWEST PASSAGE Other European countries quickly joined the race to find a new route to India and China. Portugal controlled the route around Africa, and Spain dominated the areas around the Caribbean. Therefore, the explorations sponsored by other European countries focused on finding a "northwest passage" through North America.

In 1497, England dispatched the Venetian seaman John Cabot, who explored Newfoundland and Nova Scotia and returned to England believing that he had found mainland China. In 1509, Cabot's son, Sebastian, explored as far north as Hudson Bay. Despite continued disappointments, English explorers continued their search for a northwest passage until the beginning of the 1600's.

The French also wanted to find a northwest passage. In 1523, Giovanni da Verazzano, an Italian sailing for France, explored the entire coast of North America. He finally concluded that the Chesapeake Bay was the entrance to the northwest passage. Later, the French sent Jacques Cartier, who explored the St. Lawrence River in 1534.

Cartier soon realized that he had found a river and not the fabled northwest passage, but he continued his explorations into the interior of North America and claimed the land for France.

Both the French and the English failed to find a northwest passage to India. The explorers did, however, claim lands for their countries during their voyages. These claims, in turn, became the basis for vast French and English colonial empires in North America.

QUESTIONS FOR REVIEW

1 *Who controlled trade with the Far East before the Age of Exploration?*

2 *How did new inventions make exploration possible?*

3 *Why were the French and the English efforts to find a northwest passage important to those countries?*

CHAPTER SUMMARY

By the end of the Middle Ages, many Europeans were developing an increased interest in classical Greek and Roman thought. Humanism, a new movement that emphasized earthly matters rather than spiritual well-being, replaced Scholasticism as the dominant school of thought. As a result of humanist ideas, European religious values slowly changed. Changing spiritual points of view in Europe led, in turn, to changing social, economic, and political values.

This time of great cultural change, known as the Renaissance, lasted from the 1300's to the 1600's. During these years, increasing trade and contact between towns and cities, as well as the invention of the printing press, helped to spread the ideas of the Renaissance.

The Renaissance was also a time of discovery and exploration. The Spanish and the Portuguese took an early lead in the search for new trade routes, for markets for their products, and for gold and silver. Other countries soon competed with Spain and Portugal. As a result, the foundations for worldwide empires were laid.

CHAPTER 16 IN REVIEW

IMPORTANT WORDS, NAMES, AND TERMS

1 Explain, define, or identify each of the following:

Renaissance	vernacular	Utopia
individualism	The Prince	astrolabe
humanist	heliocentric	Henry the Navigator
revival	Gutenberg	Ferdinand Magellan

FACTS AND IDEAS

2 When did the Middle Ages reach its peak?

3 What values did middle-class Europeans tend to share?

4 What brought Italians of the northern city-states into contact with new ideas and techniques?

5 How did the movable-type printing press affect Renaissance ideas?

6 What influential humanist thinker set the standard for Northern Renaissance writers?

ANALYZING VISUAL MATERIAL

7 According to the map on page 318, who was the first European explorer to enter the Indian Ocean?

8 Study the paintings on page 314. What differences do you see between the lives of the upper classes and those of the lower classes as depicted by the artists?

CONCEPTS AND UNDERSTANDINGS

9 How did political development in medieval Italy differ from the political development of France and of England?

10 In what way did the humanist revival break with the concerns and values of the Middle Ages?

11 In what ways did Leonardo da Vinci represent the talented, well-rounded Renaissance ideal?

12 How did the revival of trade and of town life help to spread Renaissance ideas northward?

13 How did the Spanish idea of empire differ from the Portuguese idea?

PROJECTS AND ACTIVITIES

14 Renaissance artists introduced the concepts of realism and perspective into painting. Find an example of a painting in this chapter that you think shows these two characteristics. Then look through the beginning chapters of the text to find a painting that doesn't show realism or perspective. Compare and contrast the two artworks.

15 Prepare a bulletin-board display of outstanding Renaissance painting and sculpture. Look in newspapers and magazines for these pictures. Identify the artist, when and where the work was completed, and where the work is presently located.

CHAPTER 17 THE REFORMATION AND ITS IMPACT

1 Causes of Religious Discontent in Europe 2 Martin Luther and the German Reformation 3 Reformation and Counter Reformation 4 Effects of the Reformation

The leadership of the Roman Catholic Church in Europe weakened during the 1300's and the 1400's. Corruption within the Church was a major cause of this change. Moreover, a growing number of Europeans believed that Church leaders were more concerned with worldly aims than with religious ideals. Because of this, some people began to call for reforms that were intended to rebuild the moral and spiritual strength of the Roman Catholic Church.

During the sixteenth century, the call for Church reform led to the rise of new religions that were Christian—but not Roman Catholic—in character. The Roman Catholic Church, in turn, worked to rebuild its influence and to halt the spread of new religions. By the end of the 1500's, however, the thousand-year era of religious unity in Europe was ended. Thus, the sixteenth century marked a new period of spiritual and political conflict throughout western Europe.

An early painting shows French Protestants gathered for services in Lyons, France, in 1564.

1 CAUSES OF RELIGIOUS DISCONTENT IN EUROPE

Throughout the 1300's and the 1400's, the influence of humanism caused a growing number of Christians to question the aims of the Roman Catholic Church and its leaders. Many Europeans felt that their religious leaders had become too concerned with everyday political and economic matters. The apparent desire of some Church leaders to gain worldly power and wealth seemed, to many, to contradict Church claims of spiritual purity. Thus, some people began to question Church teachings and practices.

DECLINE OF THE MEDIEVAL CHURCH

The Roman Catholic Church in the Middle Ages was the single most powerful institution in western Europe. Church leaders influenced spiritual and cultural conditions alike. But as changes in European society took place during the late Middle Ages, the Roman Catholic Church was faced with new problems.

The Church did not willingly adapt to the changing times that it faced. One result of the Church's resistance to change was the rise of religious discontent in Christian Europe during the late Middle Ages. A growing number of Christians in these years began to lose faith in the ability of the Church to meet their religious needs. This trend led to a slow decline of Church power and prestige. A major cause of Church decline during the late Middle Ages was the growing political and economic rivalry between European rulers and Church leaders.

POLITICAL AND ECONOMIC RIVALRIES

During the late Middle Ages, Church leaders became deeply involved in European political affairs. The growing political power of Europe's secular rulers caused much alarm within the Church. For this reason, Roman Catholic leaders increasingly came into conflict with the rulers of European countries.

One source of rivalry between the papacy and individual rulers was economic in nature. Traditionally, Christians had given money and goods in the form of a *tithe* to support the Church. As a result, large amounts of wealth were drained from the countries of western Europe to flow into the Church's treasury. Many rulers, however, disliked this practice. Money given to the Church could not be collected as taxes by the rulers. Thus, secular rulers could not use this wealth to build their countries.

Another source of rivalry between Church and state had to do with the amount of land owned by the Church. It has been estimated that at the beginning of the 1500's the Church owned between one fifth and one third of all the land in western Europe. According to Church law, these lands were free from secular taxes. The tax-free status of Church lands meant that rulers could not share in the revenues that these lands produced.

A growing number of rulers began to resist the power of the Roman Catholic Church during the late 1200's. In 1296, for example, King Philip IV of France taxed the

The collection of tithes was disliked by many feudal rulers, who felt that they could better use the money to strengthen their domains.

POLITICAL		SOCIAL AND ECONOMIC
	1415 ~	John Huss burned as a heretic
	1417 ~	Great Schism ended
Ottomans conquered Constantinople	~1453	
	1456 ~	Johannes Gutenberg printed the Bible
Hapsburgs acquired the Netherlands	~1477	
	1478 ~	Spanish Inquisition established
Mohammed II, founder of Ottoman Empire, died	~1481	
	1484 ~	Huldreich Zwingli born
Tudor dynasty began in England	~1485	
Henry VIII became king of England	~1509	
	1517 ~	Martin Luther wrote the Ninety-five Theses
Charles V became Holy Roman emperor	~1519	
Thirty Years' War began	~1520	
	1521 ~	Diet of Worms excommunicated Martin Luther
Spanish and German troops sacked Rome	~1527	
Henry VIII broke with Roman Catholic Church	~1534 ~	Ignatius Loyola founded Society of Jesus
Sir Thomas More executed in England	~1535	
	1536 ~	John Calvin wrote *Institutes of the Christian Religion*
	1545 ~	Council of Trent met

French clergy. Before this time, the Church had been free from paying government taxes. But Philip, despite the pope's angry objections, was determined to use the French Church as a new source of income.

Philip's move to tax the French clergy helped him to build a stronger royal treasury. But more than this, Philip proved his desire to uphold royal authority over his French subjects—including the clergy. Thus, the king's actions clearly signaled the growing willingness of secular rulers to compete with the Church for political leadership.

DIVISIONS IN THE CHURCH Philip IV's challenge to papal power did not end with his move to tax the French clergy. In 1305, Philip arranged the election of a French cardinal as pope. The king was also instrumental in moving papal headquarters from Rome to Avignon, in southeastern France (see Chapter 13).

The shift of Roman Catholic headquarters from Rome to Avignon led many people to believe that the popes had allied themselves with the French crown. Whether or not this was true, it was clear that strong rulers, such as Philip of France, could successfully challenge the papacy.

After the return of the papal residence to Rome in 1377, another situation that weakened papal prestige began to develop. Within a year, two different popes were elected by two rival groups of cardinals. Each pope had his own headquarters—one in Rome and the other in Avignon. And each rival claimed to be the only true head of the Roman Catholic Church.

This confusing situation, known as the *Great Schism*, lasted for nearly 40 years. Finally, in 1417, Church leaders declared the rival popes deposed. A new pope was elected, and the Church was once again united under a single leader. However, the prestige of the Church had been greatly weakened by the Great Schism.

Confusion and discontent grew among Christians as a result of the Great Schism.

These feelings led, in turn, to increasingly widespread calls for Church reform in the years after 1417. During these same years, growing public awareness of corruption and irresponsibility within the clergy itself also resulted in demands for Church reform.

THE CHANGING CLERGY The widespread custom of *primogeniture* that was generally followed in the Middle Ages held that only the eldest son in the family could inherit family land and wealth. Therefore, younger sons had to find other ways to make a living.

In many cases, noble families had their younger sons enter the Church as officials, such as bishops and cardinals. Often, this was done for political and economic reasons, rather than for religious causes. Since only a limited number of high-ranking Church positions existed, appointments often went to those willing to make large donations to the Church. As a result, *simony*—the buying and selling of Church offices—was common. The practice of simony brought a great deal of wealth into the Church. Unfortunately, this practice sometimes gave power to Church officials who were more interested in personal gain than in religious life. It also led, in some cases, to bribery and to other corruption within the Church.

Large incomes accompanied many Church offices. For this reason, ambitious office seekers often paid for more than one Church position. But Church officials who had several positions in different areas could not be available in all places at the same time. Thus, some Christians suffered from poor religious leadership. As a result, the Church could not always meet the spiritual needs of its members.

Among the lower clergy, there were many sincerely devout people who worked to serve the Church and the community. But the common people, faced with a growing number of ambitious Church officials, began to lose faith in their religious leaders. Thus,

the prestige of the Church was further weakened.

The general loss of prestige suffered by the Church during the late Middle Ages led some Christians to call for Church reform. But Church leaders often saw the demand for change as a threat to their own power. Because of this threat, they were slow to improve Church organization and practice.

EARLY ATTEMPTS AT REFORM Criticism aimed at the Church and its leaders became increasingly widespread during the fourteenth and fifteenth centuries. Among the more influential Church critics of these years were two priests—John Wycliffe (1320?–1384) and John Huss (1374?–1415).

As you learned in Chapter 13, John Wycliffe was a teacher at Oxford University, in England. Disillusioned with some of the Church's actions, he called for a series of reforms. Wycliffe and his followers were particularly outspoken in their opposition to the worldly aspects of the Church and its clergy.

Wycliffe's calls for religious leaders to give up their material possessions and political ambitions were not well received within the Church. But perhaps his most controversial teaching was that Christians should read and interpret the Bible for themselves. This concept struck at one of the basic tenets of the Church, for it attacked the position and the importance of the clergy.

The Church condemned Wycliffe's ideas as heretical. But his teachings quickly spread throughout Europe and influenced many Christians. One Catholic clergyman, John Huss of the German state of Bohemia, became an especially outspoken follower of Wycliffe.

Huss, like Wycliffe, believed that the Church had become too concerned with worldly matters. He also believed that Church leaders and members of the clergy should devote their lives to serving the spiritual needs of Church members. Huss went further than Wycliffe, however, and attacked the papacy itself. He felt that the papacy had given up its position as the earthly representative of Christ. John Huss was accused of heresy and was burned at the stake in 1415.

The death of John Huss did not quiet the demand for Church reform. For the next 100 years, people continued to call for change and reform. But during these years, the Church generally resisted the demands of the growing reform movement.

QUESTIONS FOR REVIEW

1 *What three causes contributed to the decline of Church prestige during the late Middle Ages?*

2 *In what way did the tax-free status of Church lands cause friction between the Church and some national rulers?*

3 *Why did some of Wycliffe's teachings strike at the basic beliefs of the Church?*

2 MARTIN LUTHER AND THE GERMAN REFORMATION

The early 1500's marked the birth of a sweeping religious reform movement in Germany and throughout western Europe. At the center of this movement was Martin Luther, an uncompromising religious leader and reformer. When Church leaders rejected Luther's demands for reform, he broke with the Roman Catholic faith and founded a new Christian church. Thus began a new era of European history, during which religious change and conflict led to major social and political developments.

LUTHER'S EARLY LIFE Martin Luther was born in the German duchy of Saxony on November 10, 1483. Luther's father, a well-to-do peasant, wanted his son to become a

This famous portrait of Martin Luther was painted by his friend Lucas Cranach.

lawyer. And in 1501, young Luther entered the University of Erfurt to study law.

At the university, Luther was known for his outstanding speaking skills. Because he took life very seriously and freely stated his strong opinions, Luther was called "the philosopher" by his classmates.

Luther received his master's degree in 1505. He appeared to have every chance to build a successful legal career. But during his years of study, Luther became increasingly interested in the question of heavenly salvation. Luther's religious feelings were so powerful that he abandoned his plan to become a lawyer. Instead, he decided to enter the clergy. Much to his father's disappointment, Martin Luther was ordained a priest in 1507.

Within a short time, Luther became a professor of theology at the University of Wittenberg. As he searched the Scriptures for answers to his religious questions, Luther became more troubled and confused. In spite of engaging in long periods of prayer and fasting, he experienced no release from his troubles. Later, he wrote, "I felt myself in the presence of God to be a sinner with a most unquiet conscience." Clearly, Luther felt much guilt for his sins, even though he tried to live a pure life.

By 1517, Luther had become deeply concerned with the nature of God's judgment of the human soul. He concluded that Church teachings regarding this major Christian idea were wrong. Moreover, Luther believed that other Church doctrines and practices were also wrong or misleading. Thus, he began to call for reform and for an end to Church practices that he felt abused the Christian ideal.

LUTHER THE REFORMER In 1517, Luther became involved in an issue that quickly brought him to the front of the growing reform movement. This issue revolved around the sale of *indulgences*. An indulgence was a papal pardon that, when combined with true repentance, freed a sinner from some of his or her guilt. An indulgence could be gained by doing good works on behalf of the Church.

Church leaders, in need of money to rebuild Saint Peter's Basilica in Rome, offered indulgences in return for donations to this cause. But when some Church agents tried to sell indulgences, they failed to explain that indulgences were valid only when accompanied by true repentance.

Luther was outraged by this means of raising money. In reply, he wrote the Ninety-five Theses in 1517. This work described the abuses involved in the Church's sale of indulgences. It stirred an immediate and fiery response among dissatisfied Germans—clergy and lay people alike.

Luther opposed the whole idea of indulgences. He felt that donations were of little spiritual value. Instead, Luther agreed with St. Paul's statement that "the just shall live by faith." Luther interpreted this biblical passage as meaning that forgiveness for sins was gained by belief and trust in God.

Dominican priest Johann Tetzel's zeal in collecting money while granting indulgences led to Martin Luther's posting of his Ninety-five Theses.

This idea of *justification by faith* became one of Luther's major teachings.

Luther also taught that Christians should be their own priests. That is, only by reading and interpreting the Bible for themselves could people build a direct relationship with God. And only in this way could Christians win forgiveness for their sins. This doctrine became known as the *priesthood of all believers*.

By about 1520, Luther had become a symbol of the call for Church reform. His ideas had attracted a growing number of followers. Thus, Luther had become a danger not only to Church leaders but to government leaders as well.

LUTHER AND THE EMPIRE A growing number of German nobles had begun to support Luther by the early 1520's. These nobles viewed Luther's attack on the Church as a chance to rid their states of papal control. For this reason, Luther received protection and encouragement from some powerful German nobles. Other nobles supported Luther because they sincerely agreed with his religious views.

Luther, however, as well as the German leaders who supported him, owed allegiance to the Holy Roman emperor, Charles V. And Charles was determined to stop Luther's religious protest. The emperor was a faithful Catholic. Moreover, he wanted to maintain religious unity in order to stabilize the Holy Roman Empire. Thus, Charles called a *diet*—a meeting of nobles and religious leaders—to be held in the city of Worms in 1521. Martin Luther was ordered to go before the diet to defend his views. But Luther refused to deny any of his teachings. He told the assembly "I cannot and I will not recant [withdraw] anything, for to go against conscience is neither right nor safe."

The diet's response to Luther's stand was stated in the E*dict of Worms.* The edict declared Luther a heretic and an outlaw and forced him to flee. Outlawed and in hiding, Luther worked to clarify his religious views. Moreover, he translated the New Testament from Greek into German. In addition to its religious impact, Luther's translation of the New Testament helped to establish the modern German language.

THE SPREAD OF RELIGIOUS WARFARE

As the number of *Protestants*—those who protested against the Roman Catholic Church's teachings—grew, fighting between Protestant and Catholic armies increased. Years of bitter violence and of widespread civil war—called the era of religious wars—engulfed Germany from the 1520's to the 1550's. For more than 30 years, the German states were plagued by religious turmoil. Both Protestants and Catholics were determined to have their own religion established in their areas. But as the conflict dragged on, both sides realized that neither would destroy the other.

In 1555, an agreement was reached between the Catholics and the Protestants of

Martin Luther's defense of his views at the Diet of Worms in 1521 won him many supporters but led to his expulsion from the Church.

the Holy Roman Empire. This agreement, called the Peace of Augsburg, gave German nobles the power to decide whether their subjects would follow Catholic or Lutheran teachings. All other religious teachings were forbidden in the Empire. As a result, for the first time Luther's followers officially gained equal standing with Roman Catholics.

The Peace of Augsburg was a compromise. Neither side—Catholic or Lutheran—was completely satisfied with its terms. Yet the agreement saved the German states from further civil war and brought about a general peace for the next 50 years.

QUESTIONS FOR REVIEW

1 What Church abuse did Martin Luther attack in his Ninety-five Theses?

2 How did Luther interpret St. Paul's statement that "the just shall live by faith"?

3 Why did Luther refuse to deny his teachings at the Diet of Worms?

Contributions

Modern Printing Techniques

The speed with which Protestant doctrines spread throughout sixteenth-century Europe was largely a result of major improvements made in European printing techniques. Among the most important of these improvements were the development of the printing press and the use of movable metal type.

Johannes Gutenberg (1400–?1468), a goldsmith from the German city of Mainz, is credited with the invention of the *type mold*, a machine used to cast permanent *type*—the individual metal characters used in combination with a printing press to produce sheets of printed pages. Gutenberg also pioneered the development of mass-printing techniques that utilized the printing press and movable type to create quantities of printed material.

As you have learned, the Chinese were probably the first people to invent and use a printing press. But their method of block printing, using type generally carved from wood, was a slow process that produced very expensive books. Moreover, because the Chinese system of writing included thousands of characters, the use of movable type was impractical.

Movable metal type could be used in Europe, however, because written European languages were based upon a much smaller alphabet. And because books printed on movable-type presses were less expensive than those copied by hand, more people could afford to own them.

By 1500, 20 million books—including classical and philosophical works, scientific studies, and lighter works dealing with conduct and manners—had been printed on presses. The first *newssheets*—the ancestors of today's newspapers—were published even before 1500. And by the end of the sixteenth century, roughly 200 million machine-printed books were in circulation.

The use of the printing press, of movable type, and of mass-printing techniques helped to spread the ideas of the Reformation. Martin Luther's Ninety-five Theses, for example, was printed and widely distributed soon after it was written in 1517. Thus, the development of modern printing techniques helped Europeans to become better informed of the revolutionary religious ideas that arose during the Reformation. Moreover, the Protestant emphasis upon individual biblical study, and the greater availability of printed materials brought about by developments in printing, encouraged literacy and education throughout sixteenth-century Europe.

Johannes Gutenberg's development of a hand-operated printing press (above) and movable metal type had a dramatic impact upon much of Europe. The Gutenberg Bible (below) was probably printed in 1455. It is estimated that by 1500, more than 8 million books had been printed by printers using Gutenberg's ideas.

3 REFORMATION AND COUNTER REFORMATION

The rise of the Lutheran Church after 1517 marked the end of the old religious order in western Europe. New religious teachings and new Protestant churches spread quickly during the 1520's and the 1530's. At the same time, the Roman Catholic Church took bold steps to restore religious unity throughout Europe. Thus, the years of the mid-1500's were times of religious conflict that, in turn, brought about major political changes in Europe.

HULDREICH ZWINGLI A growing number of Europeans in the 1520's began to follow Martin Luther's movement away from the Roman Catholic Church and its teachings. During this important period of European history—known as the *Reformation*—several religious leaders helped to shape the Protestant movement. One of the most notable of these reformers was Huldreich Zwingli [ZWING-lee] of Zurich, a city in northern Switzerland.

Zwingli (1484–1531), a Roman Catholic priest, was strongly influenced by the humanist ideas of Desiderius Erasmus (see Chapter 16). Zwingli felt that the Church and its clergy must set an example of spiritual purity for all Christians to follow. And he argued that the Church could fulfill its religious role only by returning to the simple faith of the earliest Christians. Zwingli also believed that many Church ceremonies served only to separate the clergy from the people. For this reason, he favored a form of worship that was largely free from traditional ceremony.

In the late 1520's, the Protestants of Zurich, under Zwingli's leadership, became involved in a bitter struggle with Catholic forces from the surrounding countryside. During a battle between the two sides in late 1531, Zwingli was killed.

Soon after Zwingli's death, peace was restored between Protestant Zurich and its Catholic neighbors. The Peace of Kappel, signed in November 1531, guaranteed to both Catholics and Protestants the right to freely practice their religious beliefs. Thus, a Protestant church based upon Zwingli's religious ideas became firmly established in parts of Switzerland during the early 1530's.

JOHN CALVIN John Calvin (1509–1564) was another major figure in the Protestant movement of the mid-1500's. Calvin, born into a middle-class French family, studied at the famous University of Paris. During his studies, Calvin learned about the teachings of Martin Luther. By about 1533, Calvin had become an active and outspoken Protestant.

In 1534, a wave of religious persecution caused Calvin and many other French reformers to flee from Catholic France. Calvin soon settled in the lovely Swiss city of Geneva, a center of Protestant belief. In 1536, Calvin outlined his religious ideas in *Institutes of the Christian Religion*, a book that did much to shape the Protestant movement.

At the center of the Calvinist doctrine was the idea of *predestination*. Calvin felt that Christians were born already judged by God. "All are not created on equal terms,"

An old engraving shows John Calvin, who ruled Geneva, Switzerland, until his death in 1564.

he wrote, "but some are preordained [predestined] to eternal life, others to eternal damnation."

Christians who were predestined to receive salvation were known as the *Elect*. Members of the Elect could not be identified with certainty because God's will was often unknown. But according to Calvinist ideas, the Elect were successful during their earthly lives. Thus, wealth and personal success were viewed as outward signs of goodness.

Calvin, like Luther and Zwingli, believed that each Christian should study and interpret the Bible independently. Thus, every Christian would act as his or her own priest. In Calvin's view, this doctrine of universal priesthood meant that all Christians should have a voice in the operation of their church.

Calvin's reforming ideals and his strong personality soon brought him to power in Geneva. By about 1541, the city had become a *theocracy*—a community governed by religious leaders—under Calvin's control. Within a few years, Geneva—which Calvin called the City of God—was a Protestant stronghold in Europe. And Calvin, who governed the city until his death in 1564, became both a religious and a political leader in the Protestant movement.

CALVIN'S GENEVA John Calvin believed that church reform should be coupled with social reform. This reasoning prompted Calvin to establish his theocratic government in Geneva. Calvin's aim was to build an ideal society based upon religious faith and social justice.

The theocratic government that Calvin built in Geneva was, in some ways, stern and rigid. Geneva's citizens had to obey the religious and civil rules that Calvin decreed in *The Lawes of Geneva*. Among the laws that made up this code were rules stating that

> . . . every one . . . is bound to come to heare the word of GOD, principally upon the Sundaies, and the dayes of prayer, and other dayes when they may have time and leisure. . . .

> . . . none shall play, or run idlely in the streets, during the time of the Sermons on Sundayes, nor dayes of prayer, nor to open their shops during the Sermon time . . .

> . . . none . . . walke by night in the Towne after nine of the clocke, without Candle light and also a lawfull cause, except those which bee appointed for the Watch [town guard], upon paine to be put in Prison three dayes . . .

> . . . no manner of person, of what estate, condition, or quality soever they be, men or women, shall wear above 2 rings upon their fingers . . .

Some of Calvin's laws seem strict by today's standards. But it is important to remember that many towns and cities of the 1500's had similar laws. Moreover, Calvin and other Protestant leaders in Geneva were working to build a godly city. Their aim was to shape a society that reflected the high moral standards of their religious ideals.

Calvin's ideas about predestination and the Elect had important social and economic effects in Geneva. Because wealth and success were viewed as outward signs of God's blessing, Calvinists were encouraged to follow thrifty, hardworking lifestyles. This teaching appealed to many Genevans of the middle class, who felt that Calvinism gave a moral justification for their material goals.

The Protestant beliefs of Calvin, Zwingli, and Luther had taken firm root in parts of western Europe by the mid-1500's. From these areas, the ideas of the Protestant reformers spread quickly to other European countries.

SPREAD OF PROTESTANT BELIEFS Many Europeans adopted Protestant religions between 1520 and the end of the sixteenth century. Luther's teachings gained wide acceptance in much of Germany and Scandinavia. Calvinism rapidly spread to France and to parts of England, Scotland, and the Netherlands. There were also many Calvinists in areas of Germany and central Europe. And in 1534, King Henry VIII of England broke political ties with the papacy and established the Protestant Church of England.

The Roman Catholic Church was strongly affected by the successes of the new Protestant churches. By the late 1500's, the Roman Catholic Church was no longer the all-powerful institution it had once been. As more Protestant churches were established, the age of religious unity in Europe was ended. But the Catholic Church was not idle during this period of Protestant growth. Instead, Catholic leaders worked to reform the Church and to check the spread of Protestant doctrines.

THE COUNCIL OF TRENT   The rapid spread of Protestant ideas in northern and western Europe proved to be a major threat to the Roman Catholic Church. Leaders of the Church, in turn, worked to reform Church practices and to stop the growth of Protestant faiths. Thus, in 1545, Pope Paul III began to organize a religious movement that became known as the Counter Reformation. The pope called a Church *council*—a meeting of Church leaders—to be held in the Italian city of Trent. The Council of Trent met to explain Roman Catholic teachings and to rid the Church of corruption.

To more clearly distinguish Catholic teachings from those of the new Protestant faiths, the Council of Trent redefined many Catholic beliefs. The Council also acted to rid the clergy of corruption. Many of the practices involving simony and the selling of indulgences were eliminated. In addition, bishops were given stricter rules for their supervision of Church members. And in order to build a better-trained clergy, the Council called for seminaries and schools to be founded throughout western Europe. Moreover, in the hope of spreading the Roman Catholic faith into lands outside of Christian Europe, missionary work was promoted by the Council. The overall effect of the Council of Trent, which met between 1545 and 1563, was to restore vitality and strength to the Roman Catholic Church.

THE CATHOLIC REFORMATION   To counteract the Protestant movement, Catholic leaders took important steps to strengthen and reform the Church. In 1542, for example, the Church renewed the Inquisition—a special Church court—to stop the spread of

The Inquisition was established in 1231. It reached its peak in Spain in the late 1400's and then fell into disuse until its revival in 1542.

Protestant teachings. The function of the Inquisition was to find and punish Protestants and others who the court determined were guilty of holding non-Catholic beliefs. Furthermore, the Inquisition was intended to uphold orthodoxy within the Catholic Church itself. In countries in which the Inquisition was active, Protestants were in danger of losing their property, being tortured, or even being executed. Wherever the Inquisition was in force, Protestant ideas made few inroads.

Even before the Council of Trent was called, new religious *orders*—groups of priests or nuns—were founded with the aim of reforming the Church. One of the most important of these new orders—the Society of Jesus—was founded in 1534 by Ignatius Loyola. Members of the order, called Jesuits, entered into educational missionary work. They won back to the Roman Catholic faith many people who had earlier become Protestants.

The Ursulines, an order of Catholic nuns, was founded by Angela Merici in 1535. This teaching order worked to provide for the education of girls and young women in the doctrines and beliefs of the Catholic Church.

The Roman Catholic Church lost many of its members to Protestant churches during the 1500's and the 1600's. But at the same time, the Catholic Church gained new members through the work of its dedicated missionaries. And because of the changes made during the Catholic Reformation, the Church strengthened and reformed itself.

QUESTIONS FOR REVIEW

1 What was the importance of the Peace of Kappel?

2 In what general way did Calvin's teachings appeal to middle-class Genevans?

3 Why did the Council of Trent meet?

4 EFFECTS OF THE REFORMATION

Western Europe in the late 1500's was no longer unified under a single, universal church. The breakdown of religious ties that began during the 1520's led to widespread disorder and conflict. But these years were also times of important social and economic development. In many cases, European life-styles and viewpoints changed dramatically. At the same time, the Reformation led to political reorganization in many parts of western Europe.

CHANGING SOCIAL CONDITIONS The coming of the Reformation led to important changes in European life-styles and living conditions. One of the most important social changes that grew out of the Reformation was in the field of education.

Many of the new Protestant faiths stressed individual study and interpretation of the Bible. Moreover, religious leaders— both Catholic and Protestant—quickly saw the need to train church members in the teachings and ideals of their respective churches.

The growing emphasis upon Bible study and religious training helped to speed the rise of literacy and of education in general in western Europe. Catholic and Protestant faiths alike began to build church schools in which reading, writing, religion, and other subjects were taught. Thus, the Reformation brought about important educational opportunities in many parts of western Europe.

Religious persecution and warfare in sixteenth-century western Europe divided and disrupted society. The German states, especially, suffered a general breakdown of peace and order during the Reformation. Thus, religious conflict led to major social problems and to widespread lawlessness and terror during the sixteenth century.

Europe's economic growth led to an increase in the demand for goods (left)
and to the production of coins (right) for use as money.

THE ECONOMIC IMPACT OF THE RE-FORMATION The Reformation had an important influence upon economic development in western Europe. New social and religious conditions led to new points of view toward trade and commerce. And new political realities in many parts of western Europe brought about changing economic needs and aims.

The Reformation led to the spread of new attitudes toward economic activity in Europe. Some Protestant faiths—Calvinism, for example—taught that personal success was an outward sign of God's favor. This outlook, in turn, tended to encourage economic growth in parts of western Europe.

Trade and commerce were also stimulated by the Reformation and the loss of Church influence. Church teachings had, in many cases, placed limits on certain business practices, such as the charging of interest on loans. The Church had also set limits on the prices of many goods and services. With the decline of Church power, however, these limits were removed. As a

result, bankers, tradespeople, and commercial leaders were able to operate more profitably.

As you have learned, Protestant government leaders often confiscated Church lands and property. In this way, royal treasuries were built, and rulers won greater economic power.

Some rulers actually benefited from the turmoil of the 1500's. But, in general, social upheaval during the Reformation led to economic breakdown. Farms and towns alike were destroyed by widespread religious wars. Farm output and trade were often greatly cut as a result of continued fighting. Moreover, the wars of religion led to a huge loss of life and to economic ruin in many parts of Europe.

POLITICAL ADJUSTMENTS The far-reaching social and economic effects of the Reformation led to important political changes as well. Europe became divided, with some exceptions, into the Protestant north and the Roman Catholic south. The papacy was no longer a great power in international politics. In Protestant countries, papal influence had largely come to an end by the late 1500's.

Even in Roman Catholic countries, the Church gave up much of its power to the central governments. This was because Church leaders often needed the help of powerful Catholic rulers to fight the spread of Protestant teachings. In return for helping the Church, Catholic rulers sometimes demanded a stronger voice in the religious affairs of their countries. As a result, the political power of the Church declined throughout western Europe after the mid-1500's.

The Reformation led to the development of new political ties in western Europe during the middle and late 1500's. The rulers of Europe no longer followed a common religious ideal. As a result, they tended to form new political alliances based upon shared religious loyalties as well as upon political and economic aims. Religious differences between countries increasingly led to political differences and to open conflict. Thus, the Reformation, which began as a spiritual movement, also helped to shape political, social, and economic conditions in Europe.

QUESTIONS FOR REVIEW

1 *What impact did the Reformation have upon education and literacy in western Europe?*

2 *In what way did some Protestant doctrines, such as Calvinism, affect economic activities in parts of western Europe?*

3 *Why did the political influence of the papacy decline in both Protestant and Roman Catholic countries in Europe?*

CHAPTER SUMMARY

At the beginning of the 1500's, the Roman Catholic Church was still a unifying force throughout western Europe. But corruption within the Church helped to weaken its power and influence. As demands for Church reform strengthened during the early 1500's, a new religious movement—known today as the Protestant Reformation—spread throughout Europe.

The doctrines of early Reformation leaders—such as Luther, Zwingli, and Calvin—appealed to many European Christians. In general, these early Protestant leaders shared a desire to purify the Christian faith. They called for an end of elaborate religious ceremony and for a return to the spiritual simplicity and material poverty of the early Church. Many also spoke out against the clergy, which they believed stood between God and the individual Christian.

Roman Catholic leaders sought to overcome the Protestant movement by reforming the Church from within. But they were unable to rebuild religious unity in western Europe. As a result, religious conflict spread throughout Europe. By the late 1500's, the Protestant movement was firmly established and had done much to shape European life-styles, as well as spiritual beliefs.

CHAPTER 17 IN REVIEW

IMPORTANT WORDS, NAMES, AND TERMS

1 Explain, define, or identify each of the following:

tithe	John Huss	predestination
Great Schism	indulgence	theocracy
primogeniture	Ninety-five Theses	Inquisition
simony	Protestant	Jesuits

FACTS AND IDEAS

2 What effect did the Great Schism have upon Church prestige during the 1300's?

3 Why did many secular rulers resent the tax-free status of Church lands in the early 1500's?

4 Who is generally thought to be the leader of the sixteenth-century Reformation?

5 What agreement, signed in 1555, gave German rulers the power to determine the religion of their people?

6 What belief prompted John Calvin to establish a theocracy in the Swiss city of Geneva?

ANALYZING VISUAL MATERIAL

7 After studying the painting of the French Protestants on page 322, how would you describe the nature of their church and their manner of worship?

8 On pages 329 and 334 are pictures of fifteenth-century printing and manufacturing. In what ways were these early industries different from industries today? What reasons can you give to explain these differences?

CONCEPTS AND UNDERSTANDINGS

9 How did the practice of simony lead to corruption within the Church during the late Middle Ages?

10 Why did Martin Luther oppose the sale of indulgences?

11 What was the concept of predestination?

12 Why did many Reformation leaders encourage literacy and education?

PROJECTS AND ACTIVITIES

13 Prepare a chart of the various Protestant churches in the United States. Include the Protestant religions influenced by Luther, Zwingli, and Calvin; the Reformed Churches; and the American form of the Church of England.

14 Write a biography of one of the Protestant or Roman Catholic reformers who was active during the time of the Reformation. Research material for your report may be found in encyclopedia articles, journals, and book-length studies. Present your report to the class.

CHAPTER 18 THE RISE OF NATION–STATES

1 The French Monarchy   2 The English Monarchy   3 The Holy Roman Empire and Prussia   4 The Growth of Russia

During the late Middle Ages, powerful monarchies began to replace feudalism as the dominant political system in many parts of Europe. This process, which took hundreds of years to complete, was often interrupted. To set up strong central governments, rulers had to limit the powers of the feudal lords. Not surprisingly, these nobles often opposed the loss of their personal power. And only very able rulers were able to successfully challenge these nobles. Moreover, rulers were faced with religious conflicts that prevented the growth of stable governments.

Due, in large part, to the unique conditions that were present in different parts of Europe, central governments did not develop at the same time or in the same way. By the early 1700's, however, strong governments whose rulers had varying amounts of power had been set up in France, England, Prussia, and Russia. The era of the modern nation-states had begun.

Leo de Wys Inc.

A bedroom in the palace of Versailles reflects the wealth of the French monarchy under Louis XIV.

1 THE FRENCH MONARCHY

During the Middle Ages, political power in France was centered in the hands of the nobility. Slowly, however, French kings were able to challenge the authority of the nobles and to begin building a strong central government. Not surprisingly, the nobles were against the growth of a strong monarchy because it meant a decline in their own powers. Even though the growth of royal power was disrupted by conflict and weak rulers, by the early 1700's, the French monarchy had become one of the strongest in Europe.

THE RISE OF THE MONARCHY As you read in Chapter 13, a series of able kings had begun to build a strong monarchy in France during the late Middle Ages. Even though feudal lords remained powerful during that time, the French kings steadily increased their domains. This was possible, in part, because of the support of the emerging merchant, or middle, class. These wealthy merchants realized that feudalism could not guarantee the law and order that were essential to the growth of trade. Therefore, the merchants supported the kings in their efforts to diminish the powers of the nobility. In return for this support, the French kings appointed members of the middle class to government offices. Unlike the nobles, the merchants were loyal to the king rather than to their own interests or to feudal lords.

During the Hundred Years' War (1337–1453), the growth of royal power in France was interrupted as fighting spread throughout the country. As the war continued, however, an increasing number of French people looked to the king as a symbol of unity and as a focal point of national pride. Then, in 1439, the Estates-General gave the king the right to levy a tax on land to be used to raise a standing national army. The new tax made it possible for the king to maintain an army that was loyal to the monarch rather than to a specific noble as in feudal times. The right to tax greatly increased the power of the king. In the future, a king faced with a financial crisis could simply raise taxes without convening the Estates-General. The Estates-General had never been a very strong legislative body. By granting the king the right to tax, however, the Estates-General virtually guaranteed that it would never become a powerful force in French politics.

The French kings also were able to control the French Church. The Great Schism had seriously weakened papal power in France. Then, in 1516, Pope Leo X agreed to the Concordat of Bologna, which gave French kings the right to nominate bishops and abbots. This control over top French Church officials made the French king the true leader of the French Church.

THE GROWTH OF ROYAL POWER In 1461, Louis XI became the king of France and continued to strengthen the monarchy at the expense of the nobility. Since the tax on land had become permanent, Louis XI could ignore the Estates-General. Louis further increased royal power by restricting the powers of the *parlements*—courts of justice—which were headed by nobles.

At the same time, Louis strengthened the royal alliance with the middle classes by encouraging businesses, guaranteeing peace and order, and appointing lawyers and administrators to government posts. In return, the middle class supported the king.

With this support, Louis was able to challenge French feudal lords, who at times were more powerful than the king. Through political agreements, war, and inheritance Louis took over many of the lands that had been controlled by the nobles. By the time Louis died in 1483, almost all of France as we know it today was under royal control.

ROYAL DECLINE IN FRANCE After Louis XI's death, the political ambitions of his successors and the religious upheaval of the Reformation brought on a period of decline in royal authority. In 1494, the new king of France—Charles VIII—invaded Italy in an attempt to increase his power and prestige. This invasion began a series of unsuccessful wars that drained the French economy. The resulting shortage of money limited the continued development of a strong centralized monarchy in France. Without enough money, Charles could not maintain a strong army.

In addition to the political and financial problems caused by the Italian wars, the French kings were faced with a religious conflict. As you read in Chapter 17, the Reformation was spreading throughout western Europe in the 1500's. By 1560, there were many French Protestants, called Huguenots. Even though the Huguenots were persecuted by the Catholic kings of France, the Protestants continued to gain converts. Then, in 1562, a series of civil wars broke out between the Catholics and the Huguenots.

In reality, the civil wars were political as well as religious. A series of weak kings made it possible for the nobles to regain some of their powers. These nobles, in turn, backed two powerful French families—the Guises (Catholics) and the Bourbons (Protestants)—who were fighting to take over the French crown.

The political and religious war continued until the 1590's. By that time, the Huguenot Henry de Bourbon—Henry IV—had seized the French throne.

THE RESTORATION OF THE MONARCHY
When Henry IV became king of France in 1589, the country faced political and religious problems. Rather quickly, Henry IV began to reconstruct a strong French government. The new king ensured Catholic support by becoming a Catholic. Then in 1598, he issued the Edict of Nantes. The edict gave French Huguenots many of the religious, civic, and legal rights enjoyed by Catholics. In addition, the Huguenots were

POLITICAL		SOCIAL AND ECONOMIC
Charles V elected Holy Roman emperor	~1519~	Reformation in Switzerland began
	1534~	Anglican Church established
Ivan IV crowned czar of Russia	~1547	
Ivan IV died	~1584~	Time of Troubles began in Russia
Invincible Armada defeated	~1588	
	1598~	Edict of Nantes proclaimed
Mikhail Romanov elected czar of Russia	~1613	
	1616~	William Shakespeare died
Thirty Years' War began	~1618	
Civil war began in England	~1642~	Puritans closed all theaters in London
Peace of Westphalia ended Thirty Years' War	~1648	
	1665~	London's great plague began
Glorious Revolution in England	~1688	
Great Northern War began	~1700	
	1712~	St. Petersburg became capital of Russia
Frederick the Great assumed power	~1740	Freedom of worship granted in Prussia
Catherine the Great became ruler of Russia	~1762	
	1773~	Pugachev's rebellion in Russia
Catherine the Great died	~1795~	French adopted metric system

339

Massacres of both Catholics and Huguenots were common during the religious wars that wracked France in the 1500's.

allowed to fortify certain towns to ensure that they could defend themselves in case of further religious warfare. Even though some restrictions on religious freedom remained, the Edict of Nantes did much to establish peace between French Catholics and Huguenots and thus to end civil war in France.

Henry also acted to solve France's financial problems. The large debt was paid off by reducing government corruption and inefficiency. In addition, government programs to encourage industry, to build roads and bridges, and to make marshes into productive farmland helped to strengthen the French economy.

The restoration of order as well as the new economic policies made Henry IV popular with the middle classes and helped renew the royal alliance with that part of society. Backed by this support, Henry IV began to subdue the nobles. The most prominent nobles were bribed with gold or titles, and other nobles were forced to obey

the king's rule. As a result, by the time of Henry's death in 1610, the monarchy had once again become the most powerful political force in France.

THE GROWTH OF ABSOLUTISM UNDER RICHELIEU

Henry IV's son and successor, Louis XIII, proved incapable of ruling France. During the early years of Louis' reign, the nobles again tried to regain their lost powers. In 1624, however, Louis XIII appointed the able Armand Jean du Plessis —Cardinal Richelieu [RISH-uhl-OO]—as his chief minister. Although a high Church official, Richelieu was devoted to strengthening the French monarchy, and he worked to make the crown the sole political authority in France. In addition, Richelieu acted to establish France as a major European power.

To consolidate royal power inside France, Richelieu worked to destroy the political power of the Huguenots. He believed that the Huguenots' right to hold fortified towns was a threat to the monarchy and used the royal army to attack many of these towns. Faced with the superior royal forces, the Huguenots surrendered. In 1629, under the Peace of Alais, the Huguenots were forced to give up their right to fortified towns, but they were allowed to keep their religious and civil freedoms. In this way, Richelieu hoped to avoid a recurrence of the bloody religious wars of the 1500's.

Richelieu acted to further reduce the powers of the nobles. He ordered the destruction of fortified castles that had provided refuge for rebellious nobles in the past. He also expanded the system of royal *intendants*—commissioners of justice and finance. This system had been started by Henry IV to reduce the power of the nobles in rural France. Intendants, who were almost always from the middle class, were sent into the provinces by the central government and were given wide-ranging financial, judicial, and police powers.

By the time Richelieu died in 1642, royal power in France was firmly established.

Neither the Huguenots nor the nobles threatened the crown, and peace was restored throughout France. Moreover, Richelieu's expansion of the intendant system extended royal authority into every corner of France.

THE REIGN OF LOUIS XIV Shortly after Richelieu's death in 1642, Louis XIII died and was succeeded by his four-year-old son, Louis XIV. During the early years of Louis XIV's reign, his chief minister—Cardinal Mazarin [MAZ-uh-RAN]—controlled the government. When Mazarin died in 1661, however, Louis XIV took over personal control of the government. Continuing the policies of centralization begun by his predecessors, Louis XIV made the French monarchy the *absolute*—unlimited—power in France. Because Louis believed that he was the center of France just like the sun was the center of the solar system, he became known as the *Sun King*.

Louis XIV's *absolutism*—government by a ruler who has unlimited power—was based upon the theory of the divine right of kings. According to this theory, rulers received their power from God and were responsible only to God. Therefore, absolute monarchs ruled without consulting legislative assemblies or the people.

During his reign, Louis XIV further reduced the powers of the nobles and increased the royal alliance with the middle class. Fearing the potential power of the nobles, Louis XIV refused to appoint nobles to high government offices. Instead, the Sun King chose middle-class ministers who were loyal only to the king. Moreover, Louis XIV improved the intendant system by increasing the powers of the royal intendants over local affairs and thus further decreasing the powers of the nobles.

As a symbol of his power, Louis XIV built the beautiful Palace of Versailles. The king's ministers and the leading nobles had to live at Versailles. These nobles, deprived of governmental offices and provincial power, became increasingly dependent upon the king for their livelihood. Not surprisingly, the king only rewarded, with money or land, those nobles who were unquestionably loyal to the government.

To make France the leading power in Europe, Louis XIV began a series of wars. Other European powers, fearing a strong France, banded together to oppose Louis XIV's territorial ambitions. As a result, between 1667 and 1713, France was defeated in four separate and costly wars.

These unsuccessful wars proved disastrous for the French economy, for they drained the royal treasury and led to higher taxes on the peasants. The economy was further weakened in 1685 when Louis XIV revoked the Edict of Nantes. The Huguenots, who were among the wealthiest and most hardworking citizens of France, fled the country, leaving a significant void in French society.

By the time that Louis XIV died in 1715, the absolutism of the French king was firmly established. Louis' expensive life-style and

The French monarchy reached its height of absolutism and power under Louis XIV—the Sun King.

his unsuccessful wars, however, left the government with financial problems that were to plague his successors.

QUESTIONS FOR REVIEW

1 *When did the Estates-General give French kings the right to tax?*

2 *How did the Edict of Nantes end civil war in France?*

3 *Why was the theory of divine right important to Louis XIV?*

2 THE ENGLISH MONARCHY

In England, as in France, a strong nationalist monarchy slowly replaced feudalism after the Hundred Years' War. There were, however, important differences between political developments in the two countries. While the Estates-General of France never became an important factor in the French government, the English Parliament developed into an active legislative body that effectively limited royal power.

THE ENGLISH MONARCHY REESTABLISHED As you read in Chapter 13, the War of the Roses had ravaged England for more than 30 years after the end of the Hundred Years' War in 1453. By 1485, however, the founder of the Tudor dynasty— Henry VII—had claimed the throne. As in France, the middle class wanted the peace and order of a stable government. Accordingly, the growing middle class was ready to support a strong king who would curb the powers that the nobles had seized during the years of civil unrest. Henry VII, in turn, openly encouraged the growth of business.

By this time, Parliament—including the House of Lords and the House of Commons —had become a strong legislative body.

Henry's rule was highly effective, in part, because he recognized Parliament's power and worked closely with its leaders to strengthen the central government at the expense of the nobles.

Henry set up a special court to hear cases involving only the powerful nobles who often overawed the judges and juries of regular courts. The court of *Star Chamber* had no jury and was allowed to use torture to get information. Because the court reported directly to Henry VII, the judges were not afraid to try even the most powerful nobles.

Another characteristic of Henry VII's rule was the spread of royal power into the kingdom's town and village governments. The king gave greater authority to *justices of the peace*—local judicial and administrative officials—chosen from the middle class. Since the justices of the peace were responsible to the king, they helped increase the authority of the central government.

GOVERNMENT CONTROL OF THE CHURCH When Henry VIII, the son of Henry VII, became king of England in 1509, he continued the efforts to increase royal power. Perhaps Henry VIII's most important contribution to the rise of the English monarchy was his expansion of royal power to include control of the Church.

Since Henry VIII was only the second ruler of the Tudor dynasty, he was desperate for a male heir to ensure the continuation of Tudor rule. Henry VIII's marriage to Catherine of Aragon, however, only produced a daughter—Mary. Therefore, Henry VIII asked the Pope to annul the marriage so that the king could remarry. When the Pope refused to grant the annulment in 1529, Henry VIII asked Parliament to pass the laws necessary to set up an independent English church. Then, in 1534, Parliament passed the Act of Supremacy that made the king, not the Pope, the head of the Church of England—the Anglican Church.

With his marriage annulled by the new

Hans Holbein the Younger, court painter for the Tudors, did this portrait of Henry VIII.

Anglican Church, Henry went on to marry five more times and to have two more children—Elizabeth and Edward. Edward's birth assured the continuation of the Tudor dynasty.

During Henry VIII's rule, the Anglican Church was not accepted by everyone in England. Catholics believed that the Anglican Church was heretical, and they wanted to reestablish Catholicism in England. At the same time, Protestants, influenced by the Reformation, wanted more religious reforms. The resulting religious dissension dominated English domestic affairs for decades to come.

THE REIGN OF ELIZABETH I Many historians believe that the most successful Tudor monarch was Henry VIII's daughter—Elizabeth I. When Elizabeth became queen in 1558, there was religious turmoil throughout England. Elizabeth's predecessor and half sister, Queen Mary, was a devout Catholic who restored the Catholic Church to its former power. She persecuted Angli-

cans and other Protestants. In contrast, Elizabeth reestablished the Anglican Church and changed its ceremonies and doctrines in order to make a church service that was accepted by most English people. Even though many restrictions were placed on English Catholics, Queen Elizabeth avoided religious wars like those that disrupted the French monarchy.

During most of Queen Elizabeth's rule, England was able to stay out of foreign wars, despite a growing rivalry between England and Spain. King Philip II of Spain hoped to unite England and Spain under his rule and to restore Catholicism in England. Philip's ambitions were finally ended when, in 1588, a powerful Spanish invasion force—the Armada—was defeated off the English coast (see Myths and Realities on page 346). As a result Spain was no longer a threat to English independence.

Under Queen Elizabeth's strong leadership, a prosperous England emerged as new industries were started and more money was made available for investment in trade and exploration. England's prosperity, in turn, increased the wealth and the power of the middle class. Supported by the new prosperity, many members of the upper middle class devoted more time to governmental affairs and began to demand greater authority for Parliament. The end of Elizabeth's rule was marked by increased friction between the crown and Parliament. After Elizabeth's death in 1603, royal relations with Parliament deteriorated even further due, in large part, to the personalities of her successors.

CROWN VERSUS PARLIAMENT Because Queen Elizabeth died without a direct heir, her cousin, King James VI of Scotland, became King James I of England in 1603. King James—founder of the Stuart dynasty—thus became the first king to rule both Scotland and England.

Like Louis XIV of France, King James was a champion of the theory of divine right.

Not surprisingly, James's belief in this theory led to bitter conflict with Parliament.

The struggle for power between Parliament and the king continued during the reign of Charles I, James's son, who ruled from 1625 to 1649. Almost as soon as he became king, Charles dissolved Parliament and attempted to rule as an absolute monarch. In 1628, Charles, in need of money, was forced to summon Parliament to ask for new taxes. In return, Parliament insisted that the king accept the *Petition of Right*. The petition clearly defined English liberties and placed important limits on royal powers. For example, Charles's policy of imprisoning people who refused to "loan" him money was forbidden, as was his practice of forcing his subjects to house royal troops. After the taxes were granted, however, Charles again dissolved Parliament and ignored the Petition of Right. By carefully managing the royal finances, Charles was able to rule without Parliament.

THE ENGLISH CIVIL WAR In 1640, the financial needs of a war forced Charles to call Parliament again to ask for new taxes. Political tensions continued to rise until, in 1642, a war broke out between the supporters of Parliament and the supporters of the king.

The king's supporters, known as Cavaliers, were opposed by Parliament's soldiers—Roundheads—who were led by a landowner named Oliver Cromwell. For the most part, the Cavaliers were nobles and wealthy landowners, while the Roundheads were farmers, skilled craft workers, and middle-class landowners and townspeople. Moreover, some Cavaliers were Catholics who hoped to restore Catholicism in England. In contrast, a powerful group within the Roundhead army was made up of *Puritans*—Protestants who wanted to organize the English Church along Calvinist lines. Thus, the English Civil War was a religious, as well as a political, war.

In 1648, Cromwell and his well-trained army defeated the Cavaliers and captured King Charles. A short time later, Parliament tried the king as an enemy of the people and executed him on January 30, 1649.

CROMWELL AND THE COMMONWEALTH
Soon after the execution of Charles I, the House of Commons set up the *Commonwealth*—a republican form of government. Both the monarchy and the House of Lords were abolished. A council of state was founded as the new executive power. The army, however, was the real power in England, and Oliver Cromwell, the army's leader, ruled as a military dictator. Despite rebellions led by monarchists who recognized Charles I's son—Charles II—as king, Cromwell was able to remain in power because of his strong army.

Since Cromwell was a devout Puritan, he acted quickly to guarantee the rights of that religious group under the Commonwealth. Although most Protestants were given freedom of religion, the Anglicans and Catholics—supporters of monarchy—were severely restricted.

In 1653, Cromwell dissolved Parliament and founded a new form of English government called the Protectorate. At this time, Cromwell and his leading military officers composed the only written constitution England has ever had. It was called the *Instrument of Government*. Cromwell was made Lord Protector, and he was assisted by a council of state and a newly elected Parliament. The Instrument, however, did not define Parliament's role in the new government, and a struggle for power between Parliament and Cromwell began. This struggle—similar to the conflict between Parliament and the Stuart kings—lasted until Cromwell's death in 1658.

THE RESTORATION OF THE MONARCHY
Shortly after Cromwell's death, the Protectorate collapsed because Cromwell's son and heir could not control the army. After a period of unrest, the upper middle class and the nobility joined forces, hoping to put

an end to disorder. The Parliament of 1640 was recalled, and Charles II was invited to return as king if he agreed to certain restrictions on his power. For example, Parliament forced Charles to agree to govern with Parliament. At the same time, the English army was disbanded so that the king could never control the government through military might. After Charles agreed, he was made king in 1660.

Although Charles favored Catholicism, he agreed to the restoration of the Anglican Church as the official church in England. Moreover, only Anglicans could hold posts in local government or conduct religious services for more than five people.

As Parliament became more powerful, two political factions—forerunners of modern political parties—developed. The Whig faction represented England's business interests and called for greater Parliamentary control of royal power. The second faction—the Tories—were supported by the land-owning upper middle class and the clergy and favored the expansion of royal power.

Charles II wanted to add to his own powers, but he did not want to return to exile. Therefore, he grudgingly worked with Parliament. When Charles's brother, James II, became king in 1685, however, relations between the crown and Parliament quickly became more strained.

James II was a Catholic who wanted to restore Catholicism in England. James chose Catholics as advisers and reopened Catholic churches in London. The idea of a Catholic restoration alarmed Parliament. Whigs and Tories temporarily forgot their differences and acted quickly to replace James with a Protestant ruler. Parliament secretly asked James's Protestant daughter, Mary, and her husband, William of Orange, leader of the Dutch Republic, to come to England.

THE GLORIOUS REVOLUTION In November 1688, William and Mary landed in England with a small army. James II, fearing for his life, fled to France, and in 1689, Parliament offered the crown to William and Mary. In return, the new monarchs accepted the Declaration of Rights, which became a part of the Bill of Rights later that year. This document, one of the most important in English history, guaranteed individual liberties such as the freedom from excessive bail and the right to a jury trial. Moreover, the Bill of Rights limited the royal power to suspend Parliament or to keep a standing army during peacetime. The Bill of Rights, along with the Magna Charta and the Petition of Right, helped to prevent the rise of an absolute monarchy in England. Thus, without bloodshed or chaos, William and Mary ascended the throne in what has become known as the Glorious Revolution.

Oliver Cromwell dissolved Parliament and set up the Protectorate in 1653.

QUESTIONS FOR REVIEW

1 What did Henry VIII accomplish in 1534 with the Act of Supremacy?

2 In what way did the prosperity of England during Queen Elizabeth's reign encourage the development of Parliament?

3 Why was the English Bill of Rights important to the development of representative government?

Myths and Realities

The Invincible Armada

The story of the Spanish Armada is covered in most history books. As most students learn, in 1588 King Philip II of Spain sent a mighty invasion fleet—the Invincible Armada—to conquer England and to restore Catholicism in that Protestant country. On July 29, the Armada, which consisted of 130 ships and 30,000 sailors and soldiers, sailed into the English Channel. There, the Spanish ships began ten days of battle with the English fleet that numbered 197 ships with about 18,000 sailors. By August 8, the small, highly maneuverable English ships had defeated the lumbering Spanish galleons, and the remnants of the Armada had escaped from the English fleet.

Based on this type of account, it was commonly believed that the English navy had destroyed most of the Armada. In fact, however, the English sank only two Spanish ships during the battle. In addition, the Spanish lost five ships that ran aground in France and Holland. They abandoned two more that were badly damaged during battle. The remaining Spanish ships were scattered, ending the immediate threat of invasion. Nevertheless, the Spanish fleet was still a powerful naval force. The English victory could well have proved to be only a temporary delay in King Philip's plans for conquest.

In the final analysis, the destruction of the Spanish Armada was due more to weather conditions on the long trip home than to the battle. Fortunately for the English, high winds and strong currents forced the Spanish galleons and the armed merchant ships to sail northward into the stormy North Sea after their defeat. From there, the ships of the Armada tried to return to Spain by sailing through the unfamiliar seas around Scotland and Ireland. In those waters, treacherous weather forced many of the Spanish vessels to run aground along the rugged coasts. Other ships, badly damaged in the battle with the English, sank at sea.

Although exact numbers are not available, historians estimate that the Spanish lost approximately 54 ships as the Armada sailed back to Spain. This loss represented nearly one half of the once-mighty Armada, and many of those ships that managed to reach port were unseaworthy.

The loss of life among the sailors was equally staggering. Of the 30,000 who set sail with the Armada, approximately 1,500 died in battle, while 18,500 died on the trip back to Spain.

Thus, the terrible weather conditions that the Armada encountered after its running battle with the English proved to be the decisive factor in the Spanish defeat. King Philip never again attempted to invade England.

The lumbering Spanish galleons of the Armada were also designed as troop transports to aid in Philip II's planned invasion of England.

3 THE HOLY ROMAN EMPIRE AND PRUSSIA

Much of what went on in Europe following the Reformation concerned the Holy Roman Empire, or more specifically the house of Hapsburg. Conditions in central Europe during the sixteenth and seventeenth centuries were quite different from those in England and France. These conditions in Germany led not toward unity but toward disunity. Instead of the decline of the nobility and the rise of royal power, just the opposite occurred. Finally in the 1700's the nucleus of a unified Germany emerged.

THE HOLY ROMAN EMPIRE During the seventeenth century the Holy Roman Empire occupied an area of central Europe that is roughly present-day East and West Germany. It also contained land that today is part of Austria, Czechoslovakia, Yugoslavia, and Poland.

As you read in Chapter 13, the Holy Roman Empire, whose origin goes back to Charlemagne, arose in 962 when a strong German king, Otto the Great, was crowned emperor. Its location in the center of Europe made the empire an important factor in European politics.

In reality the empire was a collection of competing feudal domains, principalities, and kingdoms. And the various emperors had little actual control over this collection of states. These states, or domains, often were divided by language, customs, cultures, and conflicting goals. After 1520 and the rise of Protestantism, the empire also was divided by religious differences.

Several factors limited the powers of the Holy Roman emperors and prevented them from bringing the empire together as a unified nation. One factor was that the emperors could not inherit the throne. Instead they were elected by the *Imperial Electors*—rulers—of the empire's major states. Real power in the empire was shared by these electors. To safeguard their power, these electors resisted efforts by the emperors to unify the empire under a single strong government.

Another factor affecting the power of the emperors was their limited power to tax their subjects. German princes jealously held on to their feudal rights to tax their subjects and to raise local armies. Unable to finance their own armies, the emperors had to rely upon powerful nobles for support.

THE IMPERIAL HAPSBURGS Although a member of the Hapsburg family was elected Holy Roman emperor as early as 1273, no dynasty was established. Later, however, after the mid-1400's, the powerful Hapsburgs gained control of the imperial throne.

Since the eleventh century the house of Hapsburg had increased its landholdings and its political power through marriage and inheritance. As Holy Roman emperors, the Hapsburgs continued to add land to their holdings. By the 1500's, the Hapsburg family controlled Spain, the Netherlands, Burgundy, Austria, and land in Italy and in Hungary.

In 1519, the head of the house of Hapsburg, who was also the king of Spain, became Charles V, Holy Roman emperor. The only rival to the Hapsburgs as the dominant power in Europe was France. Hapsburg landholdings stretched from the Netherlands in the north to Spain in the south, virtually encircling France. Warfare between France and the Hapsburgs had erupted in 1494. Throughout the reign of Charles V this warfare continued.

DECLINE OF HAPSBURG POWER Under different conditions, Charles V might have unified the empire. However, the problems faced by Charles, and by his successors, made this impossible. For years, Charles V fought with France and the Ottoman Empire to protect Hapsburg lands in western and eastern Europe. Meanwhile, jealous German princes resisted efforts to establish order within the empire. As a Catholic, Charles also faced opposition from many Protestant princes who feared that he might try to reestablish Catholicism throughout Germany.

Finally in 1556, Charles, tired and in poor health, surrendered his throne. To his son Philip he gave Spain and its possessions, plus Burgundy, the Netherlands, and Hapsburg lands in Italy. To his brother Ferdinand he gave the Hapsburg landholdings in central and eastern Europe. He also had Ferdinand elected Holy Roman emperor. Charles then retired to a monastery, where he died in 1558.

Now split into two branches—Spanish and Austrian—the Hapsburg rulers continued to face problems. In Spain, Philip squandered the wealth pouring in from the Americas on costly wars. In the east, Ferdinand and his heirs faced the continuing threat from the Ottoman Turks and the growing religious differences within the empire. By 1618, these religious differences became so great that Europe's last great religious war erupted.

THE THIRTY YEARS' WAR As you read in Chapter 17, the earlier religious wars that had wracked the Holy Roman Empire ended in 1555 with the Religious Peace of Augsburg. Under its terms each German prince could choose either Catholicism or Lutheranism. Each prince's subjects then were forced to accept their prince's choice or to leave. The uneasy religious truce lasted until 1618 when the Thirty Years' War broke out. This war began with a revolt in Bohemia in 1618.

Bohemia was strongly Protestant. When a Catholic Hapsburg, Ferdinand II, became king of Bohemia and Holy Roman emperor, his pro-Catholic actions led to a revolt. Ferdinand's imperial forces crushed the Bohemian revolt in 1620. Punishments, executions, and seizures of Bohemian estates followed. These actions alarmed other Protestants in Europe who feared Ferdinand's growing power.

Following Bohemia's defeat, Christian IV, the Lutheran king of Denmark, invaded Germany in 1625 to defend Protestantism as well as Denmark's landholdings in Germany. Faced with this new threat, Ferdinand allowed a Bohemian noble named Wallenstein to raise an army that was to be paid from whatever loot they were able to seize. By 1629 Christian's forces were defeated. Ferdinand's subsequent actions against Protestants provoked Gustavus Adolphus, king of Sweden, who invaded Germany the following year. Several Swedish victories followed, but in 1632 Gustavus Adolphus was killed in battle. Protestant forces continued the war, and France, a Catholic country interested in destroying the Hapsburgs' power, entered the war on the Protestant side. As the war dragged on, the imperial forces slowly weakened. In 1648 a peace treaty ended the war.

THE EFFECTS OF THE WAR The Thirty Years' War and the resulting peace treaty had several direct effects on Germany. On the positive side, the Peace of Westphalia brought a degree of religious tolerance. Calvinism, as well as Lutheranism and Catholicism, was recognized.

However, for Germany some of the other effects were less welcome. Some areas were hard hit by war. It is estimated that Germany's population decreased by 30 to 50 percent. Certainly the economic decline of Germany that had begun before the war continued.

The Peace of Westphalia also began the idea that all states, regardless of size or power, were equal diplomatically. In essence, each German prince's domain became a sovereign state. This idea, coupled with the diminished prestige of the emperor, postponed the growth of a unified nation under one strong government. But from the destruction of the Thirty Years' War a new, powerful German state began to emerge.

THE RISE OF PRUSSIA By the end of the Thirty Years' War, Germany was made up of

Europe in 1648

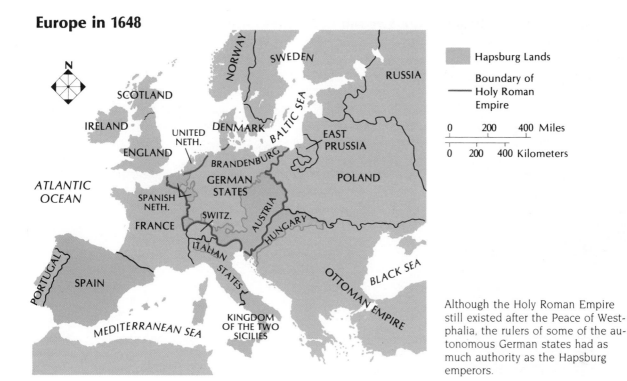

Although the Holy Roman Empire still existed after the Peace of Westphalia, the rulers of some of the autonomous German states had as much authority as the Hapsburg emperors.

more than 360 individual states. One of these states was Brandenburg.

Since 1415, the Hohenzollern family had ruled Brandenburg. Through marriage and inheritance the family increased its landholdings until, by 1618, they controlled land stretching across Germany.

Although the Hohenzollerns' lands suffered heavily during the Thirty Years' War, the peace treaty added to their holdings. In the next 100 years these lands became the powerful kingdom of Brandenburg-Prussia, and finally the kingdom of Prussia.

The Hohenzollern leader who laid the foundation for Prussian power was Frederick William of Brandenburg, who was known as the Great Elector. When he came to power in 1640, during the Thirty Years' War, he inherited a domain that was largely occupied by enemy troops. At the end of the war in 1648, Frederick William moved quickly to rebuild Brandenburg and to establish his control. With a small, well-trained army, he reduced the power of the nobility within his domain. A well-organized central

government was established. Many of the government officials were drawn from the middle class rather than from the nobility. In this way Frederick William removed the nobility from positions of power and replaced them with a trained civil service loyal to their ruler. At the same time the army was equipped with the most modern weapons. Although small in size, the army was extremely effective in maintaining Brandenburg's security and in controlling the nobility.

The Great Elector died in 1688. He was succeeded by his son, Frederick I, and then by his grandson, Frederick William I. Both of these rulers recognized the need to carry on the policies of the Great Elector.

To provide the revenue needed to maintain a strong army, economic growth was encouraged. Local industries were aided and protected by the government. New farming methods were also introduced. In addition, swamps were drained and forests cut down to provide land for new farms. At the same time, foreign workers and farmers

The Bettmann Archive

The Growth of Brandenburg-Prussia, 1415–1795

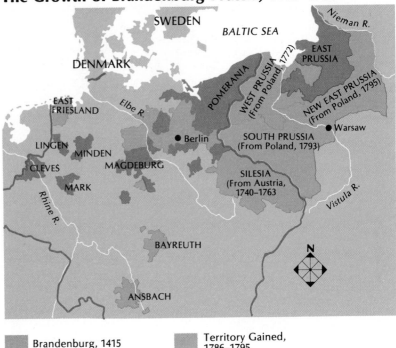

Under the able leadership of Frederick the Great, the Prussian army became the best fighting force in Europe and added new territories to the Hohenzollern domains.

Brandenburg, 1415	Territory Gained, 1786–1795
Territory Gained, 1415–1740	Boundary of Holy Roman Empire, 1786
Territory Gained, 1740–1786	

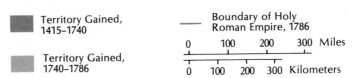

were encouraged to migrate to Brandenburg-Prussia, where their talents were welcomed.

A growing military tradition was a characteristic of the Hohenzollern rule. Under Frederick William I, the army was doubled in size through a draft. A lifetime professional officer corps was established. Its members were drawn from the landowning nobility. Thus when Frederick William I died in 1740, the kingdom of Brandenburg-Prussia was secure and beginning to prosper. The next ruler was Frederick II, who came to be known as Frederick the Great.

FREDERICK THE GREAT Frederick the Great was cultured and artistic. As a youth he showed a strong interest in art, music, and literature. Although he retained these interests as an adult, he also was an outstanding military leader who used the Prussian army to gain new land. Under Frederick's rule Silesia was taken from Austria in the 1740's. In 1772 Frederick joined forces with Russia and Austria in the first partition of Poland. This collaboration netted Frederick the area of West Prussia, thus linking Brandenburg and East Prussia (see map on this page). Later, in 1793 and in 1795, Prussia gained additional land from Poland.

During his reign, Frederick the Great personally supervised his government. As an enlightened ruler, he promoted religious tolerance, moved to reform the legal code, encouraged industries, and worked to improve agriculture. Frederick died in 1786. He left an efficient government loyal to the king. In addition, the Prussian army was the best in Europe. Thus, by the beginning of the nineteenth century, Prussia was a European power and it was the dominant state in a fragmented Germany.

QUESTIONS FOR REVIEW

1 What factors limited the powers of the Holy Roman emperors?

2 How did the Hapsburgs manage to acquire vast landholdings?

3 Why was Brandenburg-Prussia able to become the dominant state in Germany?

4 THE GROWTH OF RUSSIA

The history of Russia in the two centuries following the death of Ivan the Terrible in 1584 is a story of expansion, westernization, and alienation. During these two centuries, Russia expanded eastward to the Pacific Ocean, southward to the Black Sea, and westward to within 200 miles (323 kilometers) of Berlin.

In its process of expansion, Russia also began to adopt some western ways. However, it remained a backward country in comparison to Great Britain and France. The growth of the powers of the czar was similar in some respects to the rise of powerful monarchs in western Europe, but it was accompanied by the spread of serfdom among the Russian peasants. As a result, the *alienation*—the separation—of the Russian people from their rulers increased.

THE EARLY ROMANOVS The death of Ivan IV in 1584, brought a period of confusion and civil war to Russia. This period, known as the Time of Troubles, was characterized by weak rulers, peasant revolts, nobles striving for power, and foreign invasion. Both Poland and Sweden seized the opportunity to intervene in Russian affairs. Sweden invaded an area near the Baltic Sea, and for several years, Polish forces occupied Moscow.

Finally, the Russians rallied and forced Polish forces out of Moscow. In 1613, representatives from 30 of Russia's towns met in Moscow to choose a czar. Their choice was a 16-year-old noble named Mikhail Romanov. This choice established the Romanov dynasty that was to rule Russia until 1917.

Mikhail ruled for 32 years, from 1613 to 1645. During that time, some degree of law and order was restored. But to win the support of the nobility, Mikhail had to grant them favors. Most importantly for the future, the czar expanded serfdom. Many formerly free peasants were ordered bound to land owned by the nobility.

Upon Mikhail's death in 1645, his son, Alexis, became czar. During his reign Alexis I continued his father's policies. The result of the efforts of Mikhail and Alexis was the growth of an absolutism in Russia that was as great or greater than the absolutism enjoyed by most kings in western Europe. It was an absolutism that gave the czar complete control over all Russians and the Orthodox Church.

PETER THE GREAT Czar Alexis I married twice. Two sons, Fëdor and Ivan, were born to the first marriage. The czar's second marriage produced one of Russia's greatest rulers, Peter, who was born in 1672.

After Alexis I died in 1676, his son Fëdor III served as czar until his death in 1682. At that time Ivan and his half brother Peter became joint rulers. Sophia, who was the daughter of Alexis I from his first marriage, became regent, ruling Russia for her mentally defective brother Ivan and for her half brother Peter, who was only ten. This situation changed when Peter seized power in 1689 and sent Sophia to a convent. In theory, if not in fact, Peter shared power with Ivan until Ivan's death in 1696. Then,

Peter I became the sole ruler of Russia until his death in 1725.

Peter was, in many ways, a strange ruler. Barely literate, he was crude, ill-mannered, cruel, and given to excesses. He was also strong, vigorous, hardworking, and truthful. Physically he was inspiring, standing six feet eight inches tall. He had very little formal education and his main interests were in technical areas, such as carpentry and ship-building. Despite his limitations, he was to become known as Peter the Great, one of Russia's outstanding rulers.

THE WESTERNIZATION OF RUSSIA In the first few years of his reign Peter devoted most of his attention to his army and to a war with Turkey. Hoping to form a league of Christian countries to oppose Turkey, Peter—disguised as Corporal Peter Mikhailov—traveled to western Europe with other Russian officials. Peter's exposure to the culture of the West led to his desire to modernize and to westernize Russia.

When Peter returned to Russia in 1698, he was determined to change Russian society. To a large extent, many of Peter's efforts affected only the nobility. For example, Peter's ruling that beards had to be shaved and long gowns shortened applied only to nobles; priests and peasants were excepted. Two practices—the seclusion of noble-women and the wearing of veils in public—also were stopped. While Peter's attempts to westernize Russian customs had little impact on most of his subjects, many of Peter's other changes had a greater and a longer-lasting impact.

The changes that took place in Russia's economy were the result of Peter's desire to strengthen Russia. Determined to build up Russia's army and navy, Peter saw the need for a strong economy to support the military. Peter encouraged the growth of factories and manufacturing. Russia's iron industry was built up, and skilled workers from western Europe were invited to come to Russia to produce goods.

At the same time taxes were raised. Most of these taxes fell upon the peasants. Many free peasants fell into debt and ultimately into serfdom. The expansion of serfdom was seen by Peter as a way to place peasants in a class to serve the state. Serfdom was further expanded when more land was granted to nobles loyal to the czar. The peasants on these lands became serfs subject to the control of the landowner. With no legal rights, a Russian serf could be sold, traded, or used as a worker on the land or in factories.

The reorganization of Russia's government along Western lines was also undertaken. The country was divided into provinces and the government organized into departments. Each department was run by an official loyal to the czar. Peter's absolutism was further enhanced through his nearly total control of the Orthodox Church.

PETER'S FOREIGN POLICY Throughout the reign of Peter the Great, Russia's foreign policy had one basic goal. This goal was to seize warm-water ports—ports that were open year-round—which would give Russia

As part of a program to westernize Russia, Peter the Great decreed that the nobles could not wear traditional Russian dress or have long beards.

access to the West. Russia's few ports were closed by ice for months each year.

Peter's quest for warm-water ports to the east was limited by the harsh climate and by distance. To the west, on the Baltic Sea, Poland and Sweden stood in the way. To the south, on the Black Sea, the Ottoman Empire blocked Russia's expansion. Assuming Sweden's 18-year-old king Charles XII to be his easiest opponent, Peter—allied with Denmark and Poland—prepared to attack Sweden.

The Great Northern War lasted from 1700 to 1721. It began when Charles XII seized the initiative and invaded Denmark. After defeating Denmark, Charles turned to Russia. In 1700, at Narva, the Swedish army routed a Russian army five times its size. Sweden then invaded and defeated Poland. While Charles was involved in Poland, Peter reorganized the Russian army and invaded Sweden's territory—Ingria and Karelia—along the Baltic Sea. The construction of a new capital of Russia, named St. Petersburg, was begun on the conquered territory. Charles retaliated and marched on Moscow. The Russian forces fell back, burning everything in Charles's path. A harsh winter and a lack of supplies forced the Swedish forces to turn south to regroup. On July 8, 1709, the Swedish army was decisively defeated and Charles fled to Turkey for safety. Although the fighting continued for many years, Sweden's power declined. Shortly after Charles's death in battle, the war was ended. The Treaty of Nystadt (1721) gave Estonia, Livonia, Ingria, and Karelia to Russia. This new territory gave Russia its access to the Baltic Sea.

Peter the Great died in 1725, four years after the end of the Great Northern War. Even though Russia remained a backward country when compared to countries in the West, some progress had been made. Russia had emerged as a European power, and its large army was a force that demanded respect. In the years that followed, the army was used to expand Russia's boundaries.

Russian Expansion, 1721–1795

| From Sweden, 1721–1743 | From Turkey, 1774–1792 |
| From Turkey, 1730–1769 | From Poland, 1772–1795 |

In a quest for warm-water ports, Russia conquered territory on the Baltic and Black seas.

THE YEARS AFTER PETER The policies of Peter the Great had been designed to create a strong and independent Russia. However, a series of weak rulers followed Peter's death and many of Peter's policies were discontinued. From 1725 to 1762, Russia suffered under the rule of six ineffectual monarchs. It was a period of confusion and rebellions, during which the nobility regained much of their power.

The Russian nobility deeply resented a system established by Peter the Great that required a lifetime of government service for all male nobles. Under Peter's order, at the age of 16 all male Russian nobles entered either the military or the government. Each noble was required to begin at the lowest rank and was promoted according to merit. Following Peter's death the nobility worked to end their service and to weaken the czar's powers. Rebellions by the nobles broke out and service requirements were gradually lowered until 1762, when they were abolished.

Unrest among the peasants was also common after 1725. The head tax, introduced by Peter in 1718, fell most heavily upon the lower class. As living conditions grew worse, peasant uprisings increased, but they were unsuccessful. Reprisals against the peasants were harsh. Slowly the gap between the peasants and the nobility widened.

CATHERINE THE GREAT The succession of weak rulers that followed the death of Peter ended in 1762. At that time, Catherine II, Empress of Russia, came to power.

A German by birth, Catherine had married the Romanov heir to the throne. Attractive, courageous, and intelligent, Catherine quickly adapted to her new country and its language and customs. She was well liked by most of the Russian people.

Catherine's husband became Czar Peter III in 1762. Raised in Germany, Peter was afflicted with a weak mind, a lack of judgment, and a contempt for Russia that angered the people. Within six months he was deposed by Catherine and killed. Catherine quickly gained control of the government.

As empress, Catherine II was a strong and hardworking ruler. Well educated, she corresponded with intellectuals in western Europe. Although she shared many of their views regarding reform, she was a practical ruler who did little to improve conditions for the Russian lower class. As a result, peasant uprisings were common throughout her reign.

The most serious uprising was Pugachev's Rebellion in 1773. Claiming to be the dead Peter III, Pugachev raised an army of peasants. Promising to free the serfs and to hang the landlords, Pugachev had some initial success. However, in 1775, Pugachev was captured, put in a cage, and taken to Moscow, where he was executed. In reprisal for the revolt more peasants were forced into serfdom and the power of the nobles

The Bettmann Archive

Catherine the Great's minister, Potemkin, hid the real poverty of Russia by allowing the empress to see only well-dressed and happy peasants.

over the peasants was increased. The gap between the people and their rulers continued to grow.

CATHERINE'S FOREIGN POLICY The primary goal of Russia's foreign policy under Catherine the Great was expansion. She is quoted as having said, "If I could live to be two hundred years all of Europe would be brought under Russian rule." During Catherine's rule, about 213,000 square miles (551 671 square kilometers)—an area about the size of France—was added to the Russian Empire. This territory came largely from Turkey and Poland.

In the south, Catherine's goal was to gain access to the Black Sea. From 1768 to 1792, Catherine waged war against Turkey and succeeded in gaining the Crimean Peninsula, Bessarabia, and other land along the Black Sea. Catherine's plan to partition Turkey was blocked by other European powers, who began to fear Russia's growth.

However, this fear of Russia's growth was not a factor in Catherine's early reign. Both Prussia and Austria joined with Russia in first partitioning and finally in removing Poland from the map of Europe.

In the 1770's Poland was a weak and disunited country. Lacking natural barriers for defense, Poland was a country in need of a powerful and stable government. However, nobles, jealous of their power, resisted all efforts to unify their country. Realizing Poland's weak condition, Russia, Prussia, and Austria joined together to partition Poland in 1772. As a result Poland lost about one third of its land and about one half of its population.

A second partition of Poland occurred in 1793. Poland had begun to develop a central government, and it was growing in strength. Fearful of this development, Catherine ordered Russian forces into Poland. The Polish defenders were defeated and Russia and Prussia helped themselves to more of Poland. The following year the Poles rebelled. Moving quickly, Russia, Prussia, and their old ally Austria ended the rebellion and seized the last Polish lands.

Thus, in 1795, Poland disappeared from the map of Europe.

The following year, November 17, 1796, Catherine died. She had done little during her reign to benefit the Russian people. But she had made Russia a European power, and she had expanded Russia's borders. As she said, "I came to Russia a poor girl. Russia has dowered me richly, but I paid her back with Azov, the Crimea, and Poland."

QUESTIONS FOR REVIEW

1 *What was the Time of Troubles?*

2 *How was serfdom extended in Russia under the Romanovs?*

3 *Why did Peter the Great and Catherine want to gain access to the Baltic Sea and the Black Sea?*

CHAPTER SUMMARY

In France, after the Hundred Years' War, a series of able kings successfully suppressed the feudal powers of the nobles and founded a strong monarchy. This process was often interrupted by religious wars or by weak rulers. However, by 1700, the French monarchy had reached its height of absolute power under Louis XIV—the Sun King.

In England, a strong government, which was very different from the one in France, arose. The English Parliament severely limited the rulers' attempts to set up an absolute monarchy. After a bloody civil war and a time of republican government, the rights of citizens and Parliament were guaranteed, and a monarchy with limited powers was founded.

Unlike the rulers of England and France, the Holy Roman emperors were never able to build a strong government in central Europe. Instead, the Hohenzollerns of Prussia set up a powerful monarchy, which developed a highly efficient military class that supported the central government.

In Russia, powerful rulers with absolute powers followed policies that made their empire the largest in Europe. In so doing, however, most of the Russian people became serfs and were totally alienated from the elite ruling class.

CHAPTER 18 IN REVIEW

IMPORTANT WORDS, NAMES, AND TERMS

1 Explain, define, or identify each of the following:

parlements	justices of the peace	Frederick the Great
Huguenots	Glorious Revolution	Mikhail Romanov
intendants	Imperial Electors	Great Northern War
absolutism	Hohenzollern	Pugachev

FACTS AND IDEAS

2 What was the theory of divine right?

3 What was the purpose of the court of Star Chamber?

4 What were the effects of the Thirty Years' War in Germany?

5 What did Peter the Great hope to accomplish in his visit to the West?

6 What territories did Catherine the Great add to the Russian Empire?

ANALYZING VISUAL MATERIAL

7 Study the map of Europe in 1648 on page 349. What modern-day nations, or parts of nations, were ruled by the Hapsburgs at that time?

8 Study the picture on page 352. How do you know that these nobles are not willingly obeying the czar's decrees?

CONCEPTS AND UNDERSTANDINGS

9 How were the powers of the French Estates-General and the English Parliament different?

10 How did Cardinal Richelieu expand royal power in France?

11 Why did the English and the French middle classes support their kings in their efforts to decrease the authority of the nobles?

12 Why were the Hapsburgs unable to found a unified nation in central Europe?

13 How did Peter the Great's policies force more peasants into serfdom?

PROJECTS AND ACTIVITIES

14 Make an outline map of present-day Europe and label all the countries. Then, outline the boundaries of the Holy Roman Empire in 1648 according to the map on page 349. At the bottom of your map list the present-day countries or parts of countries that were a part of the Holy Roman Empire in 1648.

15 You have learned about the growth of powerful monarchies in France, Russia, Prussia, and England. Monarchies were also established in other countries of Europe. Prepare a research report on the rise of a monarchy in one of the other European countries or German kingdoms that were part of the Holy Roman Empire.

CHAPTER 19 IMPACT OF EUROPEAN EXPANSIONISM

1 European Mercantile Ventures in the Far East
2 Sub-Saharan Africa and the Europeans   3 Indian Empires
in the Americas

The European voyages of discovery of the fifteenth and early sixteenth centuries were rapidly followed by large-scale trading expeditions throughout the world. In the Far East, the Portuguese took the early lead in establishing trade. As the potential for vast profits became apparent, however, other European countries successfully competed for a share of the wealth. In sub-Saharan Africa, where many African societies had built powerful empires and kingdoms, the Europeans set up outposts to trade for gold and slaves. Meanwhile, the Spanish were conquering the advanced civilizations of the Americas and setting up a colonial society. As a result of all these ventures, large European trading and colonial empires were set up during the sixteenth century. This drive for new lands and trade enriched the lives of many Europeans. Unfortunately, it had devastating effects on the social, the cultural, and the political development of many non-European peoples.

Historical Pictures Service

Small and highly maneuverable Dutch ships helped make Amsterdam the center of a worldwide trading empire in the 1600's.

1 EUROPEAN MERCANTILE VENTURES IN THE FAR EAST

During the sixteenth century, the Portuguese set up a far-flung trading empire in the Far East. Throughout most of the 1500's, the Portuguese retained a virtual monopoly of European trade with Asia. But by 1600, the English and the Dutch—encouraged by the decline of Portugal's power—had begun to compete for a share of this lucrative trade.

Rather quickly, the Dutch and the English became commercial rivals. For most of the seventeenth century the Dutch controlled much of the trade with the Far East. But by 1700, the formidable English East India Company had surpassed the Dutch in many Asian markets.

THE PORTUGUESE EMPIRE After Vasco da Gama returned from his voyage to India in 1501, the Portuguese acted quickly to set up a trading empire in the Far East. At that time, the Arabs regarded the trade in spices as their monopoly and opposed Portuguese attempts to enter the field. The small Arab ships, however, were no match for the strong Portuguese navy, and most of the Arab traders were soon forced out of India and eastern Asia by the Portuguese.

In founding their trading empire, the Portuguese had two major objectives. First, they hoped to monopolize the spice trade. Second, they wanted to convert local peoples to Christianity. To accomplish these goals, the Portuguese relied upon their superior naval power, fortified trading posts, and missionaries. The Portuguese, however, made few attempts to found large colonies.

Having defeated the Arab traders, the Portuguese first established permanent forts in India. There, Portuguese merchants bought cargoes of pepper, cloves, nutmeg, and mace from local merchants who had brought the products from the Moluccas (see map on this page). Rather quickly, the Portuguese then moved to increase their revenues by eliminating the local merchants' share of the profits. In 1511, under the leadership of Alfonso de Albuquerque, the Portuguese moved eastward and set up a series of strategic outposts. From these outposts, they established direct trade with the Moluccas. By the middle of the six-

Adventurous Europeans set up trading outposts in India on the way to their ultimate goal of establishing direct trade with the fabled Spice Islands of the East Indies.

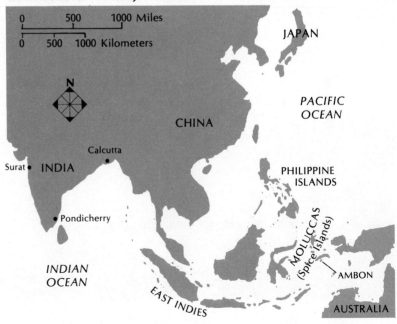

Southeastern Asia, c. 1600

358

teenth century, Portugal controlled the spice trade and had founded trading bases in Japan and China as well.

DECLINE OF PORTUGUESE POWER From its peak in the mid-sixteenth century, Portugal's power and dominance in the Far East slowly declined in the years that followed. In part, this decline was the result of a growing resentment against greedy and corrupt Portuguese traders and officials.

Portugal's small population provided too few trained and competent people who were willing to work and live in the East. As the quality of Portuguese officials in the Far East declined, resentment among local rulers grew. As a result, these rulers welcomed traders from other European nations, who were anxious to participate in the highly profitable trade with such countries as India, China, and Japan.

Portugal's problems were further complicated by events in Europe. In 1580, the Spanish king, Philip II, claimed the throne of Portugal, and after a short period of Portuguese resistance, the two countries were united under Spanish rule. England and the Netherlands, which at the time were enemies of Spain, became enemies of Portugal. As a result, Portugal lost many valuable markets in northern Europe. As Portugal's trade declined both in Europe and in Asia, so did its economy. By the end of the sixteenth century, Portugal had lost much of its wealth and power.

DUTCH AND ENGLISH FAR EAST COMPANIES By the early 1500's, the Dutch had built a large commercial fleet that conducted a profitable European trade. After 1516, when Spain and Holland were united under King Charles I of Spain, Dutch trade continued to grow. Dutch merchants carried northern European goods to Spanish and Portuguese ports. At these ports, they purchased spices and other products, which they sold throughout northern Europe.

In the mid-1500's, however, the Dutch

POLITICAL		SOCIAL AND ECONOMIC
Incas began large-scale conquest	~1438	
Sunni Ali became ruler of Songhai	~1464	
Montezuma II became ruler of Aztecs	~1502	
	1512~	First African slaves reached Cuba
Cortes conquered Aztecs	~1521~	Silk manufacturing began in France
Mogul Empire began	~1526	
Pizarro conquered Incas	~1533	
	1543~	Portuguese brought guns to Japan
Spain and Portugal united	~1580	
Moroccans invaded Songhai Empire	~1591	
	1600~	Dutch East India Company founded
	1602~	English East India Company founded
English founded trading post at Surat, India	~1612	
English massacred at Ambon	~1623	
	1632~	Taj Mahal begun
	1660~	Boers settled in South Africa
Bahadur Shah I of India died	~1712	
	1727~	Quakers demanded abolition of slavery
British won Battle of Plassey	~1757	

The revenues from the Dutch trading empire helped raise the standard of living for members of the growing Dutch middle class.

revolted against Spanish rule and fought for their independence. Almost all Dutch trade with Spain immediately stopped. When the Spanish took over Portugal in 1580, the Spanish king closed Portuguese ports to Dutch traders. The Dutch, deprived of Spanish and Portuguese markets, turned to Asia and began to challenge the Portuguese for a share of the profitable spice trade. In 1596, the first Dutch merchants, under Cornelis de Houtman, arrived in what is today known as Indonesia. Then in 1602, the Dutch government granted the Dutch East India Company the exclusive right to the Indies trade.

The Dutch were well equipped to compete with the Portuguese. Their ships were smaller, better armed, and more maneuverable than Portuguese ships. In addition, many Dutch sailors had served on Portuguese ships and knew their trading routes in the Far East. Using the wealth they had gained through earlier trading ventures, the Dutch were able to finance long and costly expeditions. They soon became the leading competitors for control of European trade in the Far East.

At about the same time, the English sought a share of the Far East trade. With the defeat of the Spanish Armada in 1588, the English established themselves as a strong naval power. Three years later, the English began sending expeditions to Asia. England's success in these ventures led Queen Elizabeth to grant the English East India Company a monopoly of England's growing trade with the Indies.

Both the English East India Company and the Dutch East India Company were granted almost unlimited power in the Far East. Both companies were free to establish their own fleets, armies, and legal systems.

Unlike the Portuguese, the Dutch and the English were only concerned with profits. No attempts were made to convert people to Christianity or to interfere in local politics. These attitudes often gained the Dutch and the English the support of local rulers who resented the corruption and the religious zeal of the Portuguese.

DUTCH SUPREMACY In Europe during the late 1500's and the early 1600's, the Dutch and the English were allied against the

Portuguese and the Spanish. In the Far East, however, the intense competition for the profitable spice trade soon developed into open warfare between the Dutch and English trading companies. Minor fighting first broke out in the Moluccas in the early 1600's. Skirmishes between the forces of the two companies continued until finally, in 1623, the Dutch massacred the entire staff of the English trading station on the island of Ambon. At the time, England was in the midst of a domestic struggle between Parliament and the king. As a result, the English East India Company was given very little support by the English government and thus was unable to offer much resistance to the Dutch. Within a short time, England was forced to withdraw from the spice trade.

Under the leadership of Jan Pieterszoon Coen, the Dutch continued their efforts to increase trade with Japan, China, and India at the expense of the Portuguese. By 1641, the Portuguese were replaced by the Dutch as the dominant European trading power in Asia. However, this dominance did not last. Once its domestic problems had been solved, England once again turned its attention to the Far East.

EUROPEAN SETTLEMENT OF INDIA The rivalry among European nations on the subcontinent of India increased during the seventeenth and eighteenth centuries. En-

gland's interest in India began with a trading outpost that was established in Surat in 1612. For years, powerful Mogul rulers like Akbar (see biography on page 363) had wanted to decrease Portuguese influence in India. Therefore, the Indian leaders welcomed the English as competitors to the Portuguese.

In the years that followed, the Dutch and the French also established trading posts. The Europeans set up *factories* in many Indian locations. These so-called factories consisted of residences, offices, and warehouses where goods were stored. Throughout the 1600's the English, the French, the Portuguese, and the Dutch competed for control of trade in India. As long as the Europeans were fearful of angering the strong Mogul rulers, they avoided open warfare in their struggle for supremacy.

However, after the death of the last powerful Mogul emperor, Bahadur Shah I, in 1712, the situation changed. The power and stability of the Mogul government declined as Indian leaders fought among themselves for power. As disorder spread throughout India, the Europeans began to fear that their investments might not be safe. The Europeans—primarily the French and the British—began to fortify their factories. Inside these factories, the Europeans maintained their own legal systems and armies, levied their own taxes, and circulated their own money.

The European settlements in India became almost independent states in the eighteenth century. In this illustration of Bombay, European architectural styles, as well as European dress, are apparent.

The cost of maintaining and supplying these fortified factories soon began to be a drain upon the financial resources of the trading companies. To lower the cost, the companies began to occupy the land near the forts in an effort to make the forts self-supporting. In these areas, European laws and institutions were established. The factories, and the areas that surrounded them, soon became small, almost independent states within India.

ENGLISH SUPREMACY IN INDIA As the Mogul power in India continued to decline, the British and the French emerged as the most powerful European rivals. Under Joseph Dupleix, the French had been the first to begin territorial settlements. Dupleix, who was the governor-general of the French possessions in India, was convinced that order in India could be restored only under European control. Quite naturally, he wanted the French to exercise that control.

Dupleix hoped to achieve his objective by gaining the support of local Indian leaders and by training *sepoys*—Indian troops —to aid the French in driving the British out of India. In retaliation, the British quickly adopted the French policy of using Indian troops to do much of the fighting.

One Indian leader, Siraj-ud-daula [suh-RAHJ-uh-DOW-luh], from the rich province of Bengal took advantage of the Anglo-French rivalry. Siraj-ud-daula wanted to end the Europeans' interference in India. Seeing that the British were preoccupied with the French, he attacked the British at Calcutta in 1756. Most of the British fled, but what was left of the British garrison was placed in a tiny cell—later called the Black Hole of Calcutta—where many suffocated.

The story of the Black Hole of Calcutta led Robert Clive, the leader of the British forces, to mount an attack against Siraj-ud-daula and his French advisers. In 1757, at the battle of Plassey, the French-led Indian troops were defeated. Four years later, in 1761, the British captured the last leading French base at Pondicherry, and the French never again threatened British power in India. Finally, in 1858, India became a colony of Great Britain.

IMPACT OF EUROPEAN TRADE In general, European trade with Asia from 1500 to about 1770 had little impact on the lives of most Asians. Where local governments were relatively strong, the Asians effectively kept European influence to a minimum. This was especially true in Japan and China, where powerful governments severely limited European trade.

One reason for the limited impact was that the Europeans had few products that were of any interest to the people in China and Japan. Although Christianity itself might be considered an export of the Portuguese, it had little lasting effect after the Portuguese ceased to dominate trade. In the years that followed, the British and Dutch traders made almost no attempts to spread Christian beliefs.

In the Philippines, India, and what is today known as Indonesia, the presence of Europeans had considerably more impact upon local ways of life than it did elsewhere in Asia. In all three areas, by the late eighteenth century, Europeans had become colonial masters rather than traders. As colonial rulers, they imposed European ideas of government and culture upon the local peoples. At the same time, the local peoples were usually relegated to the lowest position in the colonial social structure.

QUESTIONS FOR REVIEW

1 *What were the two major objectives of the Portuguese in the Far East?*

2 *In what ways were the Dutch well prepared to compete with the Portuguese?*

3 *Why did the Europeans in India acquire territory around their factories?*

Biography

Akbar the Great

Jalal-ud-Din Muhammad, today known as Akbar the Great, became emperor of Mogul India in 1556 when he was about 14 years old. At first, the young ruler was dominated by powerful advisers. By the age of 25, however, Akbar had eliminated those advisers who had tried to manipulate him, and he had begun programs to unify India un-

Historical Pictures Service

der his personal rule. By the time he was 33, Akbar had made major conquests throughout northern India and had set up a powerful empire with an efficient administration and competent officials.

Accounts written at the time show that Akbar was an immensely strong and imposing figure with wide-ranging interests that included sports and music. Moreover, Akbar embodied the ideal of royal dignity. As one observer reported, "his expression is tranquil, serene and open, full also of dignity, and when he is angry [,] awful majesty." Even though he was illiterate, Akbar openly encouraged learning throughout India. During Akbar's rule, the imperial court became a center of culture and learning where people of all religious and cultural backgrounds were welcomed.

In addition to setting up a mighty empire, Akbar did more to unify the Indian people than any other Mogul emperor. In Akbar's time, there were many religious groups in India. These groups often opposed the rule of the Muslim Moguls who discriminated against non-Muslims. Akbar, however, followed policies of religious toleration that helped unify these groups be-

hind Mogul rule. By marrying a Hindu princess, for example, Akbar gained the support and the loyalty of that large religious group. Akbar further unified the Indian people by abolishing the taxes that had been levied on all non-Muslims and giving all religious groups the same rights that Muslims had. Even though Akbar's attempts to begin a religion that would completely unify the people of India failed, his policies of fairness for all religious groups did much to stabilize India. As a result, the Mogul empire under Akbar was not divided by religious conflicts like those that disrupted life in many European countries during the 1500's and the 1600's.

Akbar also encouraged the development of the arts. In painting and in architecture, for example, Akbar's reign saw the rise of a delicate new style. This style blended Islamic and Hindu traditions and reflected the religious tolerance and the unity of India under Mogul rule.

At the time of Akbar's death in 1605, the Mogul Empire was well established. Akbar's policies had brought about greater unity than ever before. India was a stable country with an efficient government and a rich culture. Only long after Akbar's death were Europeans able to take advantage of India's weak rulers and bring colonial rule to India.

Akbar personally led his vast army, which included Hindu as well as Muslim soldiers, on campaigns of conquest throughout India.

2 SUB—SAHARAN AFRICA AND THE EUROPEANS

During the fifteenth and sixteenth centuries, many African kingdoms and empires arose in the lands south of the Sahara. At first, these societies, with economies based upon agriculture and trade, grew without any significant contact with the Europeans. The Age of Exploration, however, brought European traders from many countries to Africa in search of gold and of markets for their products. Then, with the founding of colonies in the Americas, a transatlantic slave trade began. For three centuries, massive numbers of Africans were enslaved and brutalized by the Europeans. This cruel trade severely affected the future of African social, economic, and cultural development.

BACKGROUND Immediately to the south of the Sahara is the *savanna*—a wide belt of flat, semiarid, almost treeless lands. For centuries, trans-Saharan trade routes linked North Africa with the savanna. One of the most important of these trade routes led from western North Africa to a gold-rich region in the western savanna, known as Wangara (see map on page 365). Following this route, Arab caravans from North Africa brought salt from the Sahara into the savanna. There, they traded with Africans for the gold of Wangara.

African societies of the savanna that lived along this vital trade route profited from this gold-for-salt trade. In general, these societies grew rich because they taxed the many caravans that passed through their lands. As you read in Chapter 9, by 1400 the western savanna had been the site of two great African empires—Ghana and Mali.

To the east of these trade routes, the fertile shores of Lake Chad attracted various nomadic groups. Probably around 700, these groups settled permanently in the area, began farming, and established a thriving trade with North Africa and Egypt.

South of the western savanna is a region of tropical forests that extends to the Gulf of Guinea. Here too, societies were flourishing by 1400. Unlike those of the savanna, the societies of this area were largely dependent upon subsistence farming. These societies did, however, carry on limited trade with the empires of the savanna.

Through the trade network between the western savanna and North Africa, the societies of the western savanna learned about the Islamic religion. As a result, many people accepted the Islamic faith during the period from the twelfth century through the fifteenth century.

SONGHAI Historians are not certain about the early history of Songhai [SAWNG-hiy]. They do know that sometime in the seventh century the Songhai people had settled in the town of Gao, near the Niger River. Also, recent archaeological discoveries have shown that as early as the eleventh century, the people of Songhai had accepted Islam and established extensive trade with other Muslim areas.

Songhai was conquered by the powerful empire of Mali in 1325. Although it paid tribute to the emperor of Mali throughout the fourteenth century, Songhai kept a great deal of its independence. Then, when weak rulers and internal unrest grew in Mali, Songhai was able to challenge Mali's position as the leading power of the western savanna.

Under the powerful ruler Sunni Ali (ruled 1464–1492), Songhai conquered much of the former empire of Mali and took over control of the traditional gold-for-salt trade. In his military campaigns, Ali was often ruthless, and anyone suspected of aiding enemies of Songhai was killed. The victims often included educated Muslims, and their executions made Ali's rule unpopular among the many devout Muslims in Songhai territories.

After Ali's death in 1492, one of his generals led a revolt against Ali's son and

Kingdoms and Empires of Western Africa, c. 1000–1896

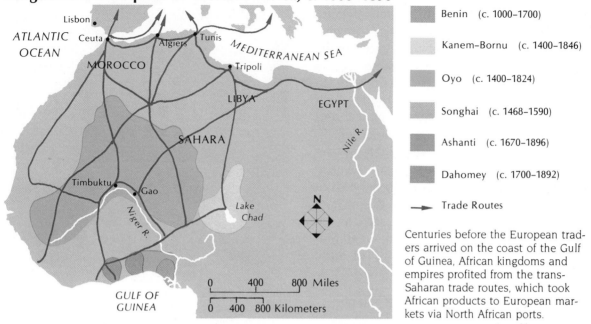

Benin (c. 1000–1700)

Kanem–Bornu (c. 1400–1846)

Oyo (c. 1400–1824)

Songhai (c. 1468–1590)

Ashanti (c. 1670–1896)

Dahomey (c. 1700–1892)

→ Trade Routes

Centuries before the European traders arrived on the coast of the Gulf of Guinea, African kingdoms and empires profited from the trans-Saharan trade routes, which took African products to European markets via North African ports.

successor, Sunni Baru. The general, later known as Askia Muhammad, seized the throne and continued to expand Songhai power. It was during Askia's rule that the Songhai Empire reached its peak as a political and commercial power (see map on this page).

In contrast to Sunni Ali, Askia tried to spread Islam and Islamic law and institutions throughout the empire. The fabled city of Timbuktu, which had fallen into decline under Ali, once again became a center of Islamic learning and culture.

Another of Askia's contributions was the development of a highly efficient system of government. Under Sunni Ali the Songhai Empire had been divided into provinces, each with a governor and a bureaucracy that were directly responsible to the emperor. Askia expanded this organization and improved it by setting up permanent government offices that were supervised by ministers responsible to the emperor. This administrative structure made it possible for Songhai to control an empire larger than any other empire in the history of the western savanna.

THE MOROCCAN INVASION In 1528, Askia Muhammad was overthrown by his sons. For eight years opposing groups struggled for power. This internal unrest weakened the empire. Order was finally restored, but Songhai never again was as powerful as it had been during the reign of Askia Muhammad. Then, in 1591, Moroccans from the north, armed with guns from Europe, invaded the Songhai Empire. The Songhai armies were no match for the well-armed Moroccan forces, and the invaders quickly captured Timbuktu and Gao.

The Moroccans' goal was the control of the gold-for-salt trade, but their goal was never achieved. Even though the Moroccans won nominal control over part of the Songhai Empire, Songhai forces launched guerrilla activities that successfully disrupted trade. Moreover, many of the groups who had been conquered by Songhai now revolted against Moroccan authority. As a result, the formerly stable area of the western savanna became a vast battleground.

Another factor that hampered the Moroccans' attempt to control trade was the presence of Europeans on the shores of the

Gulf of Guinea. These European traders had arrived in the mid-1400's in search of gold. By the late 1500's, Europeans were drawing off some of the trade that had traditionally passed through the western savanna. As a result, the Moroccans were never able to reap the vast profits that they had anticipated. Faced with continual revolts and unimpressive revenues, the Moroccans finally withdrew in 1621. Nevertheless, the power and authority of the Songhai Empire had been destroyed. As Es-Sadi, an African historian of the 1600's explained, the Moroccan invasion severely affected life in the western savanna region. The thirty-year Moroccan occupation, as described by Es-Sadi, was a time when

> security gave place to danger, wealth to poverty, distress and calamities, and violence succeeded tranquility. Everywhere men destroyed each other; in every place and in every direction there was plundering, and war spared neither property nor persons.

The regions of the western savanna that had not been under Songhai control escaped the destruction and war caused by the Moroccan invasion. On the shores of Lake Chad was the kingdom of Kanem-Bornu (see map on page 365). This kingdom had originally been two separate kingdoms —Kanem and Bornu. By the end of the 1500's, however, the two were united under the powerful ruler Idris Alooma. During his rule, Kanem-Bornu increased its power and extended its territory. Much of the kingdom's wealth came from its control of the vital trade routes from Lake Chad to Libya and Egypt. Kanem-Bornu remained strong until it was overrun by invaders in 1846.

THE FOREST KINGDOMS In the forests north of the Gulf of Guinea, other advanced societies also flourished. Unlike the empires of the western savanna, which left complete chronicles written in Arabic, these societies produced few written records. Therefore, their history is based largely upon archae-

The bronze sculptures of Benin showed advanced levels of artistic expression, as in this work entitled *The Oba of Benin and His Court.*

ological discoveries and the writings of early European explorers.

Today, historians believe that as early as the thirteenth century, the societies of this forest region were beginning to found small empires and kingdoms. The largest of these kingdoms were Benin, Oyo, Ashanti, and Dahomey (see map on page 365). Each established trade with the empires of the western savanna and, after 1500, with the Europeans who had founded outposts on the coast of the Gulf of Guinea.

The kingdoms of the forest region achieved high levels of social and political organization. The Ashanti, for example, developed a form of constitutional government in which a council of local rulers advised the king on legal and political decisions. Benin was well-known for its exquisite bronze statues and relief sculptures. In Oyo there was a system of checks and balances that prevented the king from becoming too powerful. Any king who was considered to be a poor ruler could be deposed by a council of nobles. Dahomey had a highly centralized government. The kingdom was divided into six provinces, and a large corps of royal officials ensured that the king's wishes were met.

THE SLAVE TRADE Undoubtedly, one of the most tragic and disruptive factors in African history was the growth of the slave trade. It began with the arrival of Europeans in the fifteenth century.

As early as the mid-1400's, Portuguese traders had brought the first African slaves back to Lisbon. Even though almost every other Portuguese ship brought back a few slaves, the slave trade was not very extensive during the fifteenth century. Europe's growing population provided a large pool of inexpensive workers, and there was little demand for slaves. In fact, Europe was never a major market in the slave trade.

However, the slave trade became an important aspect of Afro-European commerce during the 1500's. This was due, in large part, to the European colonization of the Americas. Spain, with its plantations and mines in the West Indies, needed a supply of cheap labor. The native Indian populations in the West Indies had been virtually wiped out by the Spanish in the many wars of conquest. The remaining Indians that were enslaved often died from overwork or disease. Therefore, the Spanish colonies experienced labor shortages, which they solved by importing African slaves.

The first slaves probably reached Cuba in 1512, and by the end of the century, slavery was an integral part of Spanish colonial society. At first, the Africans were only used in Spanish colonies. In later years, however, English, French, and Portuguese colonies also became markets for slaves from Africa. Many European nations competed to capture a part of this lucrative trade. By the seventeenth century, Dutch, French, English, German, and Portuguese ships carried their captive human cargoes across the Atlantic.

Types of slavery have existed in many parts of the world for centuries. However, before the transatlantic slave trade began in the 1500's, those enslaved were almost always war captives, debtors, and criminals. These people often became household slaves. In general, these slaves were looked upon as members of the master's family. In addition, slaves could own property and were protected by law from cruelty. The European slave trade was completely different in that slaves were viewed as products that would bring huge profits rather than as human beings.

In the early years of the slave trade, African chieftains delivered prisoners of war or criminals to the Europeans. But as demand grew, Arab and African traders began to raid villages, seizing captives for shipment to the Americas.

IMPACT OF THE SLAVE TRADE The exact effects of the European presence in Africa from the fifteenth century through the early nineteenth century can only be approximated. Historians do, however, agree that the slave trade of that period severely

As the demand for African slaves rose, an increasing number of African men, women, and children were kidnapped from their homes and sold to the Europeans.

Aldus Archives

367

disrupted the progress of African societies. This was particularly true in the coastal area of West Africa, where most of the slave trade was centered.

An exact figure for the number of Africans sold into slavery is not available. However, it is estimated that at least 20 million West Africans were sent into slavery during the more than 300 years of the trade. This number appears even more staggering when it is considered that only young, able-bodied Africans were enslaved. These were the most productive members of African societies. Deprived of this segment of the population, African civilizations could not progress in a normal manner.

The constant slave raids prevented the growth of stability throughout West Africa. Often whole societies were forced to seek out new lands when raiders destroyed their villages. Since the people never knew when these raiders would strike, they lived in a constant state of fear and uncertainty.

Most slaves were taken from West Africa, because it was closer to their final destination—the Americas. After about 1750, however, East Africa figured prominently in the slave trade. The expansion of the slave trade into this area was due, in large part, to the founding of European plantation systems in Mozambique and the islands of the Indian Ocean. Because the slave trade in East Africa lasted for a briefer period, that area was not as severely affected. In all areas where the slave trade existed, however, it brought unbelievable suffering and hardship to its victims.

QUESTIONS FOR REVIEW

1 What contributions did Askia Muhammad make to the Songhai Empire?

2 In what way did the Moroccan invasion affect life in the western savanna?

3 Why was there an increased demand for slaves during the 1500's?

3 INDIAN EMPIRES IN THE AMERICAS

During the late 1400's and the early 1500's, Indian civilizations established powerful empires in Central and South America. Rumors of the great wealth of these empires excited the Spanish adventurers who were exploring and colonizing the islands of the Caribbean at that time. In the early 1500's, these adventurers launched expeditions to search for the riches of these Indian empires. Quite rapidly, the Spanish were able to conquer these civilizations and to found a large Spanish empire in the Americas. Unfortunately, these conquests destroyed the great civilizations of Central and South America.

RISE OF THE AZTECS As you read in Chapter 9, the power of the Toltecs, in what is now known as Mexico, declined around the year 1200. For about 200 years afterward, several groups struggled to dominate the region.

During this period, many nomadic peoples migrated to the region from the north. These nomads moved throughout the area and eventually gave up their wandering life-styles to become farmers.

One of these groups was the Aztecs, who founded a city—Tenochtitlán [tay-NAWCH-tee-TLAHN]—on a swampy island in Lake Texcoco around 1325 (see map on page 369). Here the Aztecs built reed huts, began farming, and erected a temple to their chief god, Huitzilopochtli [WE-tsee-loh-POHCH-tlee].

At first, many Aztecs served as mercenaries for the more powerful societies of the region. In 1427, however, the Aztecs made an alliance with two of these societies. The combined armies of the three allies then began a period of conquest that lasted throughout the 1400's. Gradually, as their population grew and their warriors became more skilled, the Aztecs emerged as the most powerful of the three allies. By 1500, the Aztecs were the leaders of a new empire.

In governing their empire, the Aztecs did not try to spread their culture or to build a sense of loyalty to Aztec rule among conquered societies. Instead, the Aztecs allowed local leaders to retain complete control of their domestic affairs if they agreed to worship Huitzilopochtli and to pay tribute to the Aztecs. As a result, these conquered societies remained loyal to their own leaders, and they paid tribute only because they feared Aztec military reprisals if they refused.

AZTEC SOCIETY When the Aztecs were one of the many nomadic groups migrating through Mexico, they were probably democratic, with all warriors taking part in group decisions. As Aztec power grew, however, their society became divided into social classes. At the very top of Aztec society was the emperor. He was considered a god by his people and was always elected from the eligible males in the royal family by a group of electors representing the nobility. Below the emperor were the nobles, then the warriors, the artisans, the farmers, and the slaves in that order. Throughout Aztec history, this class system remained flexible. A person could move up the social ladder as a result of bravery in battle or service to the government.

By 1500, Aztec engineers had made Tenochtitlán into one of the most beautiful cities in the world. The capital had massive pyramid-temples, many parks, and magnificent palaces for the nobility as well as simple adobe homes for the many artisans and farmers. Aqueducts brought fresh water to public fountains, and there was an extensive sanitation system that made Tenochtitlán far cleaner than any European city of its time.

Historians are unsure of the exact population of Tenochtitlán at the height of Aztec power, but they believe that it was around 400,000. To support such a large population, the Aztecs had developed a unique method of farming known as *chinampa* [chuh-NAHM-puh] agriculture. The farmers constructed false islands of matted reeds on Lake Texcoco. Onto these islands, the Aztecs placed fertile soil. The resulting fields yielded very good harvests and ensured an adequate food supply for the capital.

To instill the ideals of good citizenship in the people, the Aztecs required that all male children attend school. Students studied Aztec history, religion, arts and crafts, and warfare. In addition, there were special schools for the nobility where some children were trained to be priests or priestesses. Except for priests, all males over the age of 15 had to serve in the Aztec armies.

Religion was an important part of the Aztec society. Some historians believe that the early Aztecs worshiped peaceful nature gods who accepted sacrifices of agricultural

By the time that the Europeans were exploring the world, the Aztecs and the Incas had already established advanced civilizations and large empires.

The Aztec and Inca Empires

products and animals. By the time the Aztecs were founding an empire, however, they worshiped more-warlike gods who, they believed, demanded human sacrifices.

In the arts, the Aztecs were very advanced. Unfortunately, most Aztec artworks were destroyed when their empire was conquered by the Spaniards. The remaining examples, however, show that they were outstanding goldsmiths and jewelers. Moreover, Aztec artisans produced exquisite statues to adorn their temple-pyramids and palaces.

THE SPANISH INVASION While the Aztecs were building their empire, the Spaniards were founding colonies throughout the West Indies. Rumors of the Aztec wealth prompted Hernando Cortes, the mayor of the Spanish settlement of Santiago, Cuba, to lead an expedition to Mexico in 1519. Cortes and around 600 *conquistadors*—Spanish soldiers of fortune—landed on the eastern coast of Mexico.

When the Aztec emperor, Montezuma II, learned of the Spanish force, he thought that Cortes was the fair-skinned Aztec god Quetzalcoatl [ket-SAHL-KWAHT-uhl]. According to Aztec legends, Quetzalcoatl had been banished from Mexico in ancient times, but he had promised to return and fight the other Aztec gods for control of Mexico.

Montezuma, fearing a war between the gods, sent rich gifts to the Spaniards as well as requests that they leave Mexico. The gifts, however, merely excited the greed of the Spanish, and Cortes, burning his ships to prevent mutiny, began to move inland. At first, the non-Aztec Indian societies fought against the conquistadors. Soon, however, these societies, believing that the Spaniards could help destroy the hated Aztecs, became allied with the conquistadors.

SPANISH VICTORY The Spaniards and their Indian allies reached Tenochtitlán on November 8, 1519. Montezuma, still fearing that Cortes was Quetzalcoatl, welcomed

By 1521, Cortes had defeated the Aztecs and received homage from the Aztec emperor.

them to the city and prepared magnificent palaces for them.

The conquistadors were dazzled by the wealth that they saw in Tenochtitlán. As one of Cortes's soldiers later wrote,

> . . . we were amazed . . . on account of the great towers and cues and buildings rising from the water, and all built of masonry. And some of our soldiers even asked whether the things we saw were not a dream . . . seeing things as we did that had never been heard of or seen before, not even dreamed about.

Cortes, realizing that a few hundred Spaniards would have no chance if Montezuma ordered the Aztec armies to attack, soon took Montezuma as a hostage. Cortes had correctly assumed that the Aztecs would not risk harming their sacred emperor. Therefore, the conquistadors were relatively safe from attack as long as Montezuma was their prisoner.

When Cortes learned that more Spanish soldiers had landed on the eastern coast of Mexico, he left Tenochtitlán to convince them to join his forces. During Cortes's absence the Spaniards, under Pedro de Alvarado, killed many Aztec warriors during a religious feast. The Aztecs, who no longer respected Montezuma's authority because of the emperor's refusal to act against the conquistadors, besieged the Spanish palace. Even after Cortes returned with reinforcements, it was evident that the Spaniards were no match for the Indians. Accordingly, Cortes led the conquistadors out of the city. As they fled, the Spanish were ambushed and three fourths of Cortes's soldiers were killed.

The remaining Spaniards regrouped and attacked Tenochtitlán. The Aztecs fought valiantly for more than four months. The conquistadors, however, had an advantage over the Aztecs because the Spaniards were armed with guns and steel swords and were aided by thousands of Indian allies. By August 1521, the conquistadors had conquered and almost completely destroyed what Cortes called "the most beautiful city in the world." The era of Spanish rule in Mexico had begun.

THE INCA EMPIRE At about the same time that the Aztecs of Mexico were building an empire, the Incas of South America were also increasing their power. Originally, the word *inca* meant "leader," but the term now has two meanings. The word means the entire Indian civilization, and it is the title of the emperor.

Although the exact origins of the Incas are unknown, historians believe that around 1200 they were living in the Urubamba Valley in the Andean highlands. There they founded a town—Cuzco—and began farming. Gradually, the Incas developed an efficient army that enabled them to conquer and rule the other societies of the Urubamba Valley.

In 1438, the Incas began an era of large-scale military conquest. By 1530, the Incas ruled an empire that extended from what is now known as Colombia as far south as what is now known as central Chile. The vast empire covered about 350,000 square miles (910 000 square kilometers).

Unlike the Aztecs, the Incas spread their culture, customs, language, and government throughout their empire. Conquered societies had the same rights and duties as the Incas, and local leaders were often made into Inca nobles. By the early 1500's, the many societies of the Inca Empire were united by a common language and a single set of laws. Moreover, all the subjects of the empire worshiped the Inca in Cuzco, whose authority and absolute power were never questioned.

To ensure total obedience to the Inca in Cuzco, the Incas built a highly efficient government that was based upon the basic unit of the Inca society—the *ayllu*, or clan. The empire was divided into groups. And each group was made up of 10 to 50 ayllus. A government supervisor oversaw each group and reported any violations of the laws to higher officials. These officials, in turn, reported to still higher authorities, who were directly responsible to the Inca in Cuzco.

INCA SOCIETY Like the Aztecs, the Incas were divided into social classes. At the very top of this class system was the Inca in Cuzco, who was considered to be a god and a direct descendant of the sun. Below the Inca were nobles who served as high government officials, priests, or military officers. Still lower on the social ladder were the classes of skilled artisans and farmers.

Social position was determined by birth, and people could rarely move up the social ladder. Moreover, schools were only open to male children from the nobility.

The vast majority of people were farmers. Inca farmers used an extensive irrigation system and terrace agriculture on steep mountainsides to increase harvests. In addition to working their own fields, farmers had to till community lands that were reserved for the Inca in Cuzco and the priests.

According to Inca beliefs, all individuals and land belonged to the Inca in Cuzco. The lives of all the people were regulated by laws that dictated such things

The magnificent Inca city of Machu Picchu was built in such a remote area of the Andes that archaeologists did not discover its remains until 1911.

as marriage age, family relationships and responsibilities, personal conduct, and obligations to the Inca. In return, the Inca believed that it was his sacred duty to look after his people. When a poor harvest caused food shortages in certain areas, food was shipped to those regions. People too old to work were cared for, and the sick received medical care that often included surgical procedures.

Unlike the Aztec religion, the Inca religion did not demand tremendous numbers of human sacrifices, although the practice was certainly carried on in a limited way. The Inca rituals were elaborate and were most often related to the harvesting of crops and the curing of disease.

The Incas were advanced architects and engineers. Well built roads and suspension bridges connected all areas of the empire with Cuzco. Moreover, the Inca cities contained great palaces and public buildings, whose massive stone walls were so well built that many are still standing. These buildings were often covered with gold or silver that had been obtained through advanced mining and smelting techniques. Artists also used these metals to make delicate jewelry, figurines, plates, and vases.

THE SPANISH CONQUEST Shortly after Cortes's successful conquest of the Aztecs, a group of about 180 Spanish adventurers set sail from Panama in search of the wealth of the Incas. These conquistadors, led by Francisco Pizarro and backed by a promise of aid from the Spanish king, landed in what is now known as Ecuador in 1530.

Fortunately for the conquistadors, they entered South America when the Inca Empire was extremely unstable. In 1525, the emperor Huayna Capac [WY-nah KAH-pahk] had died after deciding to divide the empire between two of his sons. Each son claimed that he was the only legitimate and divine Inca, and a civil war soon broke out. The war was still raging when the conquistadors, with their guns and horses, landed. Although the rival Incas knew that the conquistadors had entered Peru, neither brother thought that the small Spanish force was a threat to Inca power. Consequently, the Spaniards encountered little resistance as they made their way toward the center of the Inca Empire.

In 1532, Pizarro's force entered the undefended Inca city of Cajamarca, high in the Andes. At that time, the Inca Atahualpa [AHT-uh-WAHL-puh], who had defeated his brother, was camped with thousands of warriors outside the city.

Soon after entering Cajamarca, Pizarro sent emissaries to invite Atahualpa to visit the Spanish in the city. Surprisingly, the Inca agreed and entered the city with thousands of unarmed attendants. At that point, Pizarro, copying Cortes's policy in Mexico, fired upon the Incas and took Atahualpa captive.

In captivity, Atahualpa continued to issue orders, and he was treated very well. Meanwhile, Inca nobles were reluctant to attack the Spanish for fear that such a move would bring harm to the sacred emperor.

Atahualpa soon realized how much the Spaniards wanted gold. He then offered to fill a huge room with gold and to fill another room twice with silver in return for his release. Pizarro hastily accepted the offer. Nevertheless, when the ransom was complete, Pizarro had Atahualpa executed on the grounds that the Inca had plotted against the Spaniards. Without an emperor to guide them, the Incas were unable to organize any effective resistance.

The conquistadors, with reinforcements that had arrived from Panama, proceeded to Cuzco. There, they installed a puppet ruler and accumulated all the gold they could find. Despite some limited opposition from the Incas, the Spaniards were able to keep control of Peru for the next three hundred years.

SPANISH ADMINISTRATION With the conquest of the Incas, Spanish control of the wealthiest and most powerful civilizations in the Americas was complete. To govern the vast empire, the Spanish king divided it into two viceroyalties. In the north was New Spain, composed of California, Mexico, and Central America. Farther south was the viceroyalty of Peru, which included all of Spanish South America. A viceroy—royal governor—appointed by the Spanish king governed each area. Both viceroyalties, in turn, were divided into smaller governmental units that were administered by colonial officials.

Eager for riches and land, Spaniards flocked to America. The king of Spain, who was considered the owner of all Spanish lands, granted these adventurers large estates, where they farmed or began mining for silver and gold. In addition, through a policy known as *encomienda* [en-KOH-mee-EN-duh], the Indians who lived on these vast estates were entrusted to the new owners' care. Theoretically, the Indians were not slaves. In reality, however, the Indians

were bound to the land and were slaves in all but name. Gradually, as disease and overwork killed off most of the Indian population, slaves from West Africa were imported to ensure an adequate labor supply.

Despite the low status of Indians and Africans in Spanish America, Spaniards often married Indian or African women. Their children, although considered socially inferior to Spaniards, were able to improve their status through personal effort and education.

A major goal of the Spanish was the spread of Christianity throughout their empire. Accordingly, many of the early settlers were missionaries, who usually were successful in their attempts to convert the Indians to Christianity. Frequently, these missionaries spoke out against the mistreatment of the Indians.

In the Americas, as in Africa and Asia, a number of European countries quickly began to compete for a share of the land. During the 1600's, the French, the English, the Dutch, and the Portuguese all founded permanent settlements in other parts of the Americas.

THE IMPACT OF EUROPEAN EXPANSION The early European conquest and settlement of the Americas had profound effects upon traditional American societies. The Europeans destroyed advanced civilizations and replaced them with European-dominated societies. Traditional Indian life eventually remained only in remote villages. Throughout the Americas, wherever the Europeans expanded, the Indian societies were destroyed, and the Indians were forced to the bottom of the social system. Some Indian societies refused to submit to the Europeans and sought new lands, where they continued their traditional ways of life.

The most devastating effect of the Europeans was the decimation of Indian populations through sickness and mistreatment. The Europeans brought new diseases such as smallpox, measles, and the common cold. Since the Indians had no natural immunities against these diseases, epidemics that were often deadly for the Indians spread throughout the Americas. Moreover, the many Indians forced to work in mines or on plantations often died from overwork and mistreatment.

Historians do not know what the population of the Americas was before the Europeans arrived, but it has been estimated that in Mexico there were between 11 million and 20 million people in 1500. By 1650, only 1.5 million Indians remained—a decrease of 85 percent. Historians believe that elsewhere in America the toll was equally severe.

In Spain, the colonization of the Americas also had profound effects. The large supplies of gold and silver made the Spanish Empire very wealthy. However, most of the wealth was concentrated in the hands of the king and the upper classes. Frequently, the Spanish king and the nobility used the money to make their lives more luxurious or to wage wars. Few attempts were made to found commercial enterprises, to develop prosperous farms, or to set up industry inside Spain. As a result, Spain never developed a strong economy. When the flow of gold and silver later decreased, Spain did not have an economic base that was sufficient to maintain its prosperity. Thus, even though Spain retained control of Latin America, Spanish power began to decline in the 1600's.

QUESTIONS FOR REVIEW

1 *What was chinampa agriculture?*

2 *In what ways did the Aztecs show that they were great architects and engineers?*

3 *Why did the Aztecs and the Incas fail to drive the conquistadors out of their lands as soon as the Spaniards arrived?*

CHAPTER SUMMARY

In the Far East during the sixteenth century, the Portuguese founded a successful empire based on trade. Because of the vast profits of trade in the Far East, other European countries soon competed for a share of the wealth. First the Dutch, and then the English, succeeded the Portuguese as the leading European power in the Far East.

Meanwhile, in the savanna and forest regions of West Africa, many kingdoms and empires were flourishing. Soon after European traders began setting up outposts on the shores of the Gulf of Guinea in the fifteenth century, an inhumane transatlantic slave trade began. This cruel trade, which lasted for more than three centuries, totally disrupted the orderly development of African societies.

By 1500, Indian civilizations of Mexico and Peru had built large and powerful empires. However, the Spanish conquistadors, lured by stories of great wealth, were able to conquer these civilizations in a relatively short time. The Spanish conquerors established a new society, in which the formerly powerful Indians, decimated by disease and mistreatment, were relegated to the bottom of the social system.

CHAPTER 19 IN REVIEW

IMPORTANT WORDS, NAMES, AND TERMS

1 Explain, define, or identify each of the following:

Ambon massacre	Songhai	Montezuma II
factories	Kanem-Bornu	conquistadors
sepoys	Huitzilopochtli	ayllu
savanna	Hernando Cortes	viceroy

FACTS AND IDEAS

2 What factors contributed to the decline of Portugal's power in the Far East?

3 What was the Black Hole of Calcutta?

4 What four major African kingdoms arose in the forest regions near the Gulf of Guinea?

5 Why did the conquistadors invade Mexico and Peru?

6 What was the policy of encomienda?

ANALYZING VISUAL MATERIAL

7 Study the map on page 369. Why do you think that the Spanish invaded the Aztec Empire several years before the conquistadors attacked the Inca Empire?

8 Study the picture of Cortes on page 370. How does the style of this painting differ from European paintings of about the same time period?

CONCEPTS AND UNDERSTANDINGS

9 How did Askia Muhammad's rule differ from Sunni Ali's?

10 How did the slave trade affect the development of African cultures?

11 How did the traditional concept of slavery differ from the European concept of slavery that developed during the centuries of the transatlantic slave trade?

12 How did the ways that the Incas and the Aztecs ruled their empires differ?

13 How did the European invasions affect the future development of native American cultures?

PROJECTS AND ACTIVITIES

14 The local societies of Africa developed advanced levels of artistic expression through sculpture. Using the text, find illustrations of African, as well as of European, sculpture of the sixteenth or the seventeenth century. Compare and contrast these artworks.

15 There were many kingdoms and empires in Africa when the European traders first arrived. Prepare a research paper that includes a description of the social organization, the government, and the trade of one of these kingdoms or empires.

Using Geography Skills

In order to locate a place on the globe, we use lines of longitude and latitude. Lines of longitude—meridians—are drawn from the North Pole to the South Pole. These lines measure the distance east or west of the prime meridian. Lines of latitude—parallels—are drawn from east to west and run parallel to the equator. Latitude measures the distance north or south of the equator.

Lines of latitude and longitude are divided into degrees (°). Each degree, in turn, is divided into 60 minutes ('). If we know both the latitude and the longitude of a given point, we can easily locate it on a map or a globe.

Illustration A shows the lines of latitude and longitude on the globe. Illustration B is a map showing some of the important trading outposts of the Far East trade as well as lines of latitude and longitude. Study these maps and answer the following questions:

A

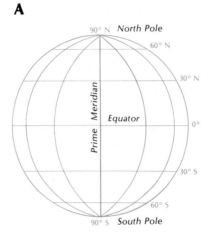

1 What settlement is located at approximately 7°N and 80°E?
2 What settlement is located at approximately 3°S and 129°E?
3 What are the approximate coordinates for Manila?
4 Why would the coordinates 52° 41° be useless in pinpointing a location?
5 What direction would a ship travel to go from 22°N 89°E to 2°N 100°E?
6 Before sailors could calculate latitude and longitude, what route do you think they took to get from 12°N 80°E to 2°N 103°E?
7 How did the use of latitude and longitude alter the route taken in question 6?

B

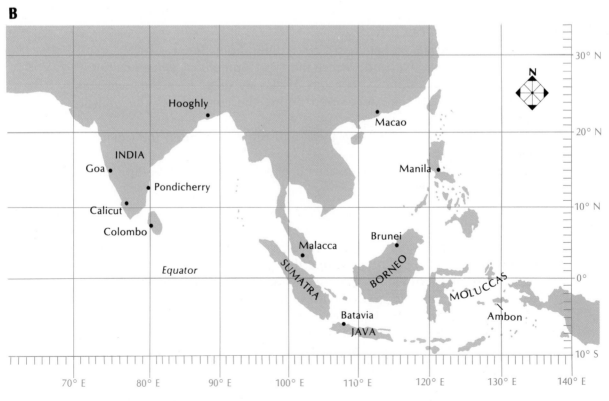

UNIT 5 IN REVIEW

CONCEPTS AND UNDERSTANDINGS

1 Who were three of the major Italian writers who helped break with the ideals of the Middle Ages and allied themselves with the humanistic movement?
2 Why is the period between about 1300 and about 1600 known as the Renaissance?
3 Why did the authority of the Roman Catholic Church decline in the 1300's and the 1400's?
4 How did the Reformation contribute to the rise of strong monarchies in western Europe?
5 How did monarchs in Prussia use their military forces to help establish their absolute powers?
6 How were the native civilizations of the Far East, Africa, and the Americas affected by contacts with the Europeans between 1500 and about 1700?

QUESTIONS FOR DISCUSSION

1 In what ways do you think that the many cultural, scientific, artistic, religious, and political changes of the Renaissance period affected the daily lives of the common people of Europe?
2 Why do you think that Parliament in England developed into a strong legislative body, while the Estates-General of France remained weak?
3 As the Spanish colonized the Americas, many people protested the enslavement of the Indians. When African slaves were introduced, however, their enslavement was generally accepted. Why do you think Indian slavery was condemned while African slavery was condoned?

SUGGESTED READING

Fehlauer, Adolph. *Life and Faith of Martin Luther.* Milwaukee: Northwestern Publishing House, 1981.

Lane, Peter. *Elizabethan England.* North Pomfret, Vt.: David and Charles, 1981.

O'Dell, Scott. *The Feathered Serpent.* Boston: Houghton Mifflin, 1981.

Ofosu-Appiah, L. H. *People in Bondage: African Slavery in the Modern Era.* Minneapolis: Lerner Publications Co., 1971.

Powell. *Renaissance Italy.* New York: Franklin Watts Inc., 1980.

Rosenthal, R. *The Splendor That Was Africa.* Dobbs Ferry, N.Y.: Oceana Publications Inc., 1967.

Stern, Steve J. *Peru's Indian Peoples and the Challenge of Spanish Conquest: Huamanga to 1640.* Madison, Wis.: University of Wisconsin Press, 1982.

Wallace, Robert. *Rise of Russia.* Morristown, N.J.: Silver Burdett Co., 1967.

UNIT **6**

REVOLUTION AND REFORM IN EUROPE

1650 to 1870

20 A Changing European Society **21** The Era of Revolution **22** Industrialization and Rebellion **23** Imperialism and Nationalism

The Granger Collection

The Mansell Collection

Galileo studying the movements of the planets   An early ironworks in Coalbrookdale, England, 1805

By the seventeenth century, Europe had begun to undergo economic, social, and political changes that would—within 300 years—shatter the old European order. The economic life of Europe was transformed during these years by increased world trade and by the astonishing developments brought about by industrialization. During this time, the discovery that humans could identify and explain the laws of nature, thereby increasing their knowledge of the universe, resulted in an age of "enlightened" thinking. As a result, the ideas of human rights and of liberty became more widely accepted.

At the end of the 1700's, many Europeans still lived under the authority of monarchies that had been evolving since the Middle Ages. One event, the French Revolution, helped to spark movements that eventually brought down the old political order throughout Europe. During the early decades of the 1800's, nationalism became an important factor in many of these movements as the nations of modern Europe were formed. Thus, European life-styles in 1870 barely resembled those of 1650.

Henri Félix Philippoteaux's painting of the "Battle of Waterloo, 1815"

CHAPTER **20** A CHANGING EUROPEAN SOCIETY

1 The Commercial Revolution   **2** The Impact of Science on European Society   **3** The Age of Reason

The three centuries between 1500 and 1800 were times of tremendous change in Europe. The Age of Exploration had changed the European view of the world. During this time, increased world trade brought many of the countries of the world closer together. Economic changes during these years formed the basis of the modern western European economy and transformed European society. The rise of modern science changed the way in which Europeans viewed themselves and the world around them. The individual began to play a more important role in society. In addition, the impact of scientific thinking led to the development of new ideas in religion, government, and the arts.

In this painting, members of the French Academy of Sciences surround Louis XIV and the founder of the academy, Jean Baptiste Colbert.

1 THE COMMERCIAL REVOLUTION

By the early 1500's, the economy of western Europe was experiencing the beginning of the *Commercial Revolution*. Over the next two centuries, economic changes and increased overseas exploration and trade shaped new economic policies in many western European nations. This combination of events, it should be understood, did not take place in eastern Europe. Trade and commerce were generally of less importance to the economies of eastern European countries for several centuries to come.

The Commercial Revolution in western Europe brought about the use of new business methods and the creation of new financial institutions. Moreover, during this period an expanding middle class gained enough wealth and influence to challenge the old order of western European society.

THE CHANGING EUROPEAN ECONOMY

As early as the eleventh century, the economy of western Europe began to undergo changes brought about chiefly by the rise of towns and the growth of trade. One of these changes involved the replacement of the old barter system—which had been the basis of western Europe's local, manorial economy—with the use of money to purchase goods. With the spread of an economy based upon money, new banking and credit practices were soon developed.

As late as the eighteenth century, farming continued to be the primary basis of the western European economy. Peasant farmers and their families made up more than 80 percent of the population. Nevertheless, a small and prosperous middle class—later called the bourgeoisie [BURZH-WAH-ZEE]—arose. The merchants and craft workers who made up the bourgeoisie became increasingly powerful because of their growing wealth. Moreover, the bourgeoisie generally supported strong monarchs, whose efforts to build centralized governments often led to greater political order and social stability. Eventually, many of the kings of Europe's rising nations came to depend heavily upon the support of the bourgeoisie. As a result, the governments of Europe often formed policies to protect the bourgeoisie and to encourage trade.

During the 1500's and the 1600's, commerce grew rapidly as the countries of western Europe increased their national strength and wealth. The Age of Exploration provided opportunities to expand into new lands and to establish colonies. Eventually, far-flung empires were created. The effect on trade and commerce that resulted from this expansion is known as the Commercial Revolution. It helped to shape the modern European economy.

THE GROWTH OF MERCANTILISM

During the sixteenth and seventeenth centuries, an economic policy known as *mercantilism* emerged in Europe. Mercantilism arose alongside absolutism, as European kings tried to gain more power by increasing the strength and the wealth of their lands. Mercantilists believed that a kingdom could only become truly powerful by being self-sufficient. This could be accomplished by the accumulation of *bullion*—precious metals, such as gold and silver. The economic decline of bullion-rich Spain during the 1500's, however, showed that mercantile success depended upon more than gold and silver bullion. Other factors, such as commercial and agricultural growth, were equally important if a country was to build lasting prosperity.

Perhaps the most important goal of mercantilism was to gain a favorable *balance of trade*. This meant that a country had to export more goods than it imported. Thus money paid for goods would flow into a country, rather than out of it. However, the manufacture of goods for export demanded raw materials, many of which were scarce in

	1600~	**English East India Company** established
First permanent colony in North America founded	~1607	
	1609~	**Amsterdam Bourse** founded
	1628~	**Harvey demonstrated** circulation of blood
English Civil War began	~1642	
First English Navigation Acts passed	~1660	
English Bill of Rights enacted	~1689	
	1690~	**Locke published** *Two Treatises of Government*
Parliament established Bank of England	~1694	
	1709~	**First piano built**
Louis XIV of France died	~1715	
	1718~	**First bank notes in Britain** issued
Peter I declared Emperor of Russia	~1721	
	1727~	**Newton died**
	1735~	**Linnaeus systematically classified plants**
Frederick the Great gained Prussian throne	~1740	
	1742~	**Handel's** *Messiah* **first** performed
	1752~	**Franklin experimented with electricity**
George III crowned in Britain	~1760	
	1776~	**Adam Smith published** *The Wealth of Nations*

the mercantile countries of Europe. Often, raw materials had to be imported. Mercantile nations tried to avoid importation of raw materials by founding overseas colonies. These colonies were expected to provide the home country with a steady supply of cheap raw materials. The colonies also would become markets for manufactured goods produced in the home country. Mercantilist policies therefore discouraged certain colonial industries in order to avoid competition with the home country.

The Navigation Acts passed by the English Parliament after 1660 provided a model for the practice of mercantilism. These laws resulted in closer economic ties between England and its colonies. Principally, the Navigation Acts involved the English government directly in the regulation of commerce. These laws were designed to provide English manufacturers with a steady supply of raw materials and with colonial markets for their goods.

The increase in commerce during the sixteenth and seventeenth centuries led to important changes in European business practices. Merchants as well as governments sought new ways to finance and to protect their overseas interests.

NEW BUSINESS METHODS During the late Middle Ages, merchants formed trade associations to protect and to regulate the trade of individual members (see Chapter 13). These associations often enjoyed a monopoly of trade. In England, for example, one group monopolized the exportation of woolen cloth, while another group controlled the trade of raw wool.

The tremendous cost of overseas ventures made it increasingly difficult for individuals to finance their businesses. As a result, the idea of the *joint-stock company* developed. Joint-stock companies were groups of merchants and investors who pooled their resources in the hope of making profits from overseas trade. To gain the money needed for long voyages and overseas trade, mer-

Atlantic Trade, c. 1700

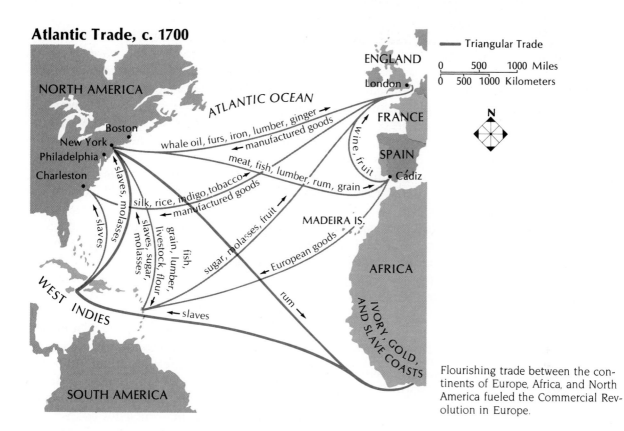

Flourishing trade between the continents of Europe, Africa, and North America fueled the Commercial Revolution in Europe.

chants and investors combined their capital by purchasing *stock*—shares in a company. It was not necessary for shareholders to become directly involved in the operation of the company. Any profits gained by the company were distributed among the shareholders. Losses were shared by all of the company's stockholders. Thus, no one individual took the entire risk for a trading venture. The modern corporation traces its origins to the structure of the joint-stock company.

Joint-stock companies were formed by seagoing merchants and traders in a number of European countries. Probably the most successful and best known joint-stock companies were the East India companies that were chartered by the English, the Dutch, and the French in turn.

Beginning in the early 1600's, other business practices developed. The formation of joint-stock companies led to the trading of shares of company stock. A stock exchange was set up in Amsterdam in 1609 for that purpose. The *Bourse*, as it was known, provided an organized setting for buying and selling stocks.

THE IMPACT OF OVERSEAS TRADE The Commercial Revolution brought many changes to Europe. One important change was the rise in prices that resulted from the influx of Spanish gold and silver from the New World. Between about 1550 and 1650, this flood of precious metal touched off a period of *inflation*—rapidly rising prices. Prices in some parts of Europe increased by as much as 400 percent during this 100-year period. Rising prices were brought about, in part, by greater demands for goods and by increases in the European money supply.

In general, the rise in prices during the 1500's and the 1600's benefited the merchant class. Workers' wages changed little during the period and, as prices increased, workers could afford fewer goods.

The impact of increased trade was felt all over Europe as new products changed the habits and the tastes of European consumers. Coffee, cocoa, tobacco, tea, sugar, potatoes, and corn were among the new products that entered the European market.

The mines and the sugar plantations of the New World colonies required vast amounts of cheap labor. A tragic outgrowth of the increased labor demands brought about by overseas trade and exploration was slavery. Beginning in the early 1500's, Spanish and Portuguese slave traders raided the west coast of Africa for slave laborers. On ships bound for the Spanish West Indies and for Portuguese Brazil, slaves were crammed into tight, suffocating quarters. Many died en route. Those who

Slavery was one of the most cruel outgrowths of European economic development. This French engraving from the late 1700's illustrated the crowded shipboard conditions that captive Africans had to endure during passage to the West Indies.

The Granger Collection

reached the Americas were often brutally treated. Traders from other nations soon joined the profitable slave trade. Some modern scholars estimate that between the early 1500's and the mid-1800's, over 20 million people were shipped as slaves from Africa to all parts of the Americas.

THE RISE OF AN INFLUENTIAL MIDDLE CLASS The prosperity brought about by the Commercial Revolution was not shared by all western Europeans. In 1700, most of western Europe's population was still made up of peasants who farmed the land. Many peasants still lived at a subsistence level and produced only enough for their own needs and, if they were lucky, for their taxes. The merchants who profited from the expanding European economy formed a small but increasingly important middle-class group. Between the sixteenth and the eighteenth centuries, money—rather than land—became the new measure of wealth in Europe. As a result, wealthy European merchants gradually gained power and influence, especially in the governments of northern and western Europe.

The shift of political power from the landed nobility to middle-class merchants and tradespeople was one of the most important developments of this period. In England, there was little evidence of social prejudice against business people. English nobles, free to enter the business world, became successful farm owners, a trend that continued until well into the nineteenth century. The wealthy English middle class also met little resistance to their entry into the English aristocracy.

In France, however, different social and political traditions existed. Commerce was less developed in France than in England during the 1600's. For this reason, the bourgeoisie lacked an influential position in society. Many wealthy members of the French middle class sought to enter the nobility rather than to build the power of the middle class. As a result, the French middle class did not often seek or gain much political power.

THE IMPACT OF MERCANTILISM As we have seen, mercantilism greatly expanded European trade. Colonies sprang up on many continents. Mercantilism also aided in the formation of a small, but influential bourgeoisie, or middle class. As the bourgeoisie emerged, the nobility continued to decline. Finally, under mercantilist policy, new business methods came into use and new financial institutions were formed.

However, many merchants believed that one aspect of mercantilism stood in the way of further development. That aspect was government regulation, which continually hindered free competition. Governments created trade monopolies, fixed prices, and placed other restrictions upon commerce.

By the late 1700's, the influence of mercantilism began to decline. New factors, especially the rapid growth of industry, began to shape economic development in western Europe. The Industrial Revolution that transformed the world during the next century was already well underway in England (see Chapter 22).

During the mid-1700's, the idea of a marketplace free from government control developed. Adam Smith, a Scottish scholar, wrote a book in 1776 entitled *The Wealth of Nations*. In this book, Smith stated that every person in society was motivated by self-interest, not by the interest of others. He said:

> It is not from the benevolence [kindness] of the butcher, the brewer, or the baker, that we expect our dinner, but from their regard to their own interest. . . . Every individual is continually exerting himself to find out the most advantageous employment for whatever capital he can command. It is his own advantage, indeed, and not that of society, which he has in view.

Smith went on to point out that government interference in a nation's economy should not exist. His idea, called *laissez-faire* [LE-SAY-FAIR]—or hands-off—economics, was that business and commerce should be allowed to develop free from government regulation. Eventually, economic growth stimulated by free competition among traders and manufacturers became the basis for the system of *modern capitalism* that developed during the 1800's.

QUESTIONS FOR REVIEW

1 What was the bourgeoisie?

2 How did a favorable balance of trade result in greater wealth for a mercantilist nation?

3 Why were many European merchants unhappy with mercantilist policies?

2 THE IMPACT OF SCIENCE ON EUROPEAN SOCIETY

The methods and goals of scientific study changed a great deal in Europe during the seventeenth and eighteenth centuries. Scientific inquiry became more systematic. Many great scientific advances were made as a result. Also, many professional societies devoted to the study of science and to the spread of scientific information were founded during this time. Scholars began to realize that it was indeed possible for humans to discover and to understand the scientific laws of the physical world. The knowledge that the principles governing the universe could be understood through science led, in turn, to important changes in the intellectual life of Europe.

BACON AND THE INDUCTIVE APPROACH TO SCIENCE Prior to the 1600's, science in Europe was greatly influenced by religious thought. When their observations seemed to contradict religious beliefs, few European scientists were willing to challenge church authority. However, it became increasingly hard for the Church to ignore the discoveries of science. For example, the heliocentric theory of Copernicus and the work of Galileo were, at first, condemned by church leaders (see Chapter 16). By about 1650, however, most scientists accepted the Copernican theory that the earth and the planets revolved around the sun. And a century later, Copernicus's book, *Concerning the Revolutions of the Heavenly Bodies*, was removed from a list of books prohibited by the Roman Catholic Church. By the seventeenth century, science was no longer an extension of religious thought.

During the early 1600's, it became clear that an organized and systematic way of thinking was needed for science. Among the first Europeans to put forward such a system was the English scientist Sir Francis Bacon (1561–1626). Although he was trained as a lawyer, Bacon's interests were wide-ranging and he had a great impact upon the development of science.

Bacon believed that the search for knowledge was often slowed by false beliefs and prejudices that were held by all people. Bacon observed that people saw only the facts that they wanted to see or that supported their opinions. Moreover, Bacon realized that people were prejudiced in certain ways as a result of their environment and the way in which they were brought up and educated. Bacon also felt that people tended to accept popular ideas easily. They also held to traditional beliefs and understandings, even if those ideas could not be reasonably defended.

Bacon's views led him to form a systematic approach to science. This approach has become known as the *inductive method*. Basically, Bacon's inductive method stressed the careful observation and recording of events or experiments. From these observations and records, a scientist could draw preliminary conclusions, which could then be tested. The goal of this careful work was to uncover a general scientific law. Bacon's ideas helped to open the way for further developments in science.

Spontaneous and unconstrained gatherings of scholars, writers, and others who were interested in and challenged by the exchange of new ideas were commonplace in European cafés during the Enlightenment.

RENÉ DESCARTES Another individual who helped chart the course for science during the 1600's was René Descartes [day-KAHRT] (1596–1650). Descartes was mainly a mathematician who is well-known today for his contributions to the development of geometry. He formed the ideas for analytic geometry, which combines the principles of algebra and geometry. The coordinate system of plotting points on a graph was developed by Descartes. However, Descartes was also a philosopher and a scientist. The origin of modern philosophy can be traced back to the ideas and the methods of this seventeenth-century genius. Furthermore, Descartes introduced the mathematical approach to scientific study. This is known today as the *deductive method*.

Descartes, like the Greek philosopher Aristotle, firmly believed that knowledge could be gained only through logical reasoning. A simple truth or a general principle first had to be stated. Then, by using reason and logic, a person could deduce more-complex truths from the original principle.

The methods of René Descartes and Sir Francis Bacon seem to be very different. Bacon relied upon observed facts and upon carefully directed experiments to increase scientific knowledge. Descartes, on the other hand, believed in the intuition and the ability of each thinker. By the end of the 1600's, however, these methods had been combined, and together they helped to propel Western science forward. The superstitions of the Middle Ages were left far behind.

THE ORDERED UNIVERSE Into the vigorous seventeenth-century atmosphere of scientific study and questioning, one of the greatest scientists of the period, Sir Isaac Newton (1642–1727), was born. By the age of 24, this mathematical genius had made several monumental scientific discoveries. In 1669, Newton was made a professor of mathematics at Cambridge University in England. He spent the next 34 years teaching, studying, and publishing his work. From 1703 until his death in 1727, Newton served as the president of the prestigious Royal Society, which had been founded by English scientists to share their knowledge and their discoveries. Few scientists have ever achieved the worldwide renown of Newton, who was readily accepted into the innermost circles of European nobility.

In 1666, Newton formulated the law of gravitation. This was the basis for his theory that the planets attract each other and remain in orbit by the force of gravity. During the same year, Newton developed the principles of calculus, which were also reached independently by the German mathematician and philosopher Gottfried Leibniz (1646–1716).

Calculus was a major scientific development because it could be used to explain the physical laws of the universe in mathematical terms. As a result, calculus could be put to many practical uses. For example, calculus could be used by engineers to determine stresses in construction as well as by astronomers to measure the movement of stars. Calculus also helped to explain the properties of matter and the behavior of gases. Calculus proved invaluable to Newton's development of the law of gravitation.

Newton was also a pioneer in the science of optics. In 1666, he demonstrated his theory that light was made up of the entire spectrum of colors. This discovery, and the many others that Newton made, greatly changed the studies of physics, engineering, astronomy, religion, and philosophy.

Newton's discoveries helped to convince Western scientists that the universe was a well-ordered system. He had shown that natural laws govern the universe and that these laws could be understood. Thereafter, science came to be looked upon as a way to study the natural laws that control the physical world. Moreover, Newton admired Descartes and formulated many ideas by using Descartes's deductive method. But

Sir Isaac Newton discovered the compound nature of sunlight, and his experiments revealed that white light is made up of many colors.

Newton also relied upon careful scientific experimentation in his work. Thus, Newton helped to bring together the inductive and deductive methods of gathering knowledge. After Newton's death in 1727, the eighteenth-century poet Alexander Pope (1688–1744) wrote, "Nature and Nature's laws lay hid in night: /God said, Let Newton be! and all was light."

ACHIEVEMENTS IN SCIENCE Unencumbered by past superstitions and fired by the ideas of Newton, science flourished during the late 1600's and throughout the 1700's. Another important scientist in England during this time was Robert Boyle (1627–1691). Boyle founded the modern science of chemistry and was typical of the bright, wealthy nobles who studied science during this time.

Boyle rejected the mysterious and mystical notions of chemistry that had existed during the Middle Ages. Instead, he relied upon experimentation. Boyle pointed out that the basic chemical elements were not the traditional medieval elements earth, fire, water, and air. Rather, elements were basic substances that could be combined by chemical action to create compounds. This idea is basic to chemistry today. Boyle also formulated a law about the relationship between the volume and the pressure of gas that later contributed to the development of the steam engine.

The emergence of modern science during the 1700's was marked by many other achievements. For example, oxygen and its role in chemical action was discovered. The study of electricity had its beginnings in the experiments of an American, Benjamin Franklin (1706–1790), and an Italian, Alessandro Volta (1745–1827). Volta created the first steady flow of electricity from a crude battery. The modern unit of electrical measurement, the *volt*, was named for this Italian scientist.

The view that the earth's surface was static and unchanging was also challenged during this time by James Hutton (1726–1797). In general, Hutton believed that the earth's surface was constantly *eroded*—worn down—by the forces of water and wind. Perhaps the best example of this action is the erosion of mountains. Hutton also pointed out that new layers were constantly added to other areas of the earth's surface, such as ocean or valley floors, through the same forces. These changes occurred over vast stretches of time. Thus, Hutton's ideas revealed the tremendous age of the earth.

ADVANCES IN MEDICINE Many changes also took place in medicine between 1500 and 1700. One of the first physicians to bring scientific methods to the practice of medicine was Philippus Paracelsus [PAR-uh-

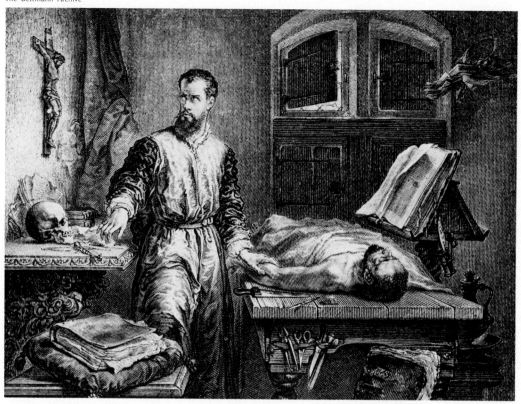

Human anatomy was first described accurately in 1543 by Andreas Vesalius in his work *Concerning the Fabric of the Human Body.*

SEL-suhs] (1493–1541). Paracelsus was among the first to realize the importance of certain types of chemicals in the treatment of disease. He developed and used many different medicines in his work. Among these was zinc oxide ointment, which is still used today to treat some types of skin disease. Paracelsus also openly challenged the medical authorities and texts of his day and strongly supported experimentation.

Andreas Vesalius (1514–1564) made great strides in the understanding of the human anatomy. Vesalius's findings were used by Ambroise Paré (1507–1590) to develop many new surgical techniques. While serving in the army, Paré discovered new ways to treat wounds and to stop severe bleeding.

In a book written in 1628, entitled *Anatomical Exercise on the Motion of the Heart and Blood,* the English scientist William Harvey described the function of the human circulatory system. Harvey traced the continuous flow of blood from the heart through the arteries and veins. As a result of Harvey's discoveries and those of other physicians during this period, modern medicine, based upon scientific techniques, emerged.

QUESTIONS FOR REVIEW

1 What is the inductive method of gathering knowledge?

2 In what ways did Descartes's deductive method differ from the inductive approach?

3 Why might the work of Sir Isaac Newton be described as bringing order to the universe?

3 THE AGE OF REASON

The scientific and philosophical gains of the sixteenth and seventeenth centuries brought about profound changes in many aspects of western European life. Gradually, these changes led to the widespread rejection of traditional authority. Instead, Europeans began to emphasize the value of reason as a basis for social and political development.

During the 1700's, the forces of change gave birth to an era of intense questioning and widespread criticism of traditional European society. Concern for the freedom and well-being of all members of society became an important ideal. New ideas about government and about religion also emerged during these years.

THE AGE OF REASON The reliance upon reasoned, logical thought that began to take hold in Europe during the late 1600's reached a peak in the next century. This period, which lasted from about 1650 to about 1790, became known as the *Age of Reason*, or the *Enlightenment*. Many traditional ideas about government, religion, art, music, and philosophy were challenged. Reason was looked upon as the way to solve the social and political problems faced by western Europeans.

Among the most outspoken critics of society during the Age of Reason were the *philosophes* [FEE-luh-ZAWFS]. Well educated and worldly, these sharp-witted writers and

This eighteenth-century engraving shows several philosophes at the dinner table of Voltaire (with upraised arm), enjoying a friendly exchange of ideas. Seated directly across from the host is Diderot.

philosophers hoped to change many of the inequalities, foolish customs, and unjust laws of their time. Often, the philosophes were forced to defy the censorship laws of their own nations to publish their attacks.

The best known of the skeptical, often caustic, French philosophes was a writer who took the name of Voltaire (1694–1778). During his long life, Voltaire continually criticized the French monarchy and nobility. Some of his most widely read books also pointed out the hypocrisy and the intolerance of the Protestant and Roman Catholic churches.

The function of government was carefully studied by another philosophe, Baron de Montesquieu (1689–1755), in his popular work *The Spirit of Laws*, written in 1748. Montesquieu analyzed many of the governments of the world. He particularly respected the English parliamentary system of government because of its separation of legislative, executive, and judicial powers. This idea of separation of powers influenced others and it became an important part of the American Constitution, written almost 40 years later.

Many of the new ideas of eighteenth-century Europe were brought together into an encyclopedia by Denis Diderot [dee-DROH] (1713–1784). The most widely read writers of the time, including Voltaire and Montesquieu, contributed articles that praised reason and science and that denounced intolerance and superstition. Many of the articles also indirectly criticized the French monarchy. The *Encyclopédie*, as it was called, helped to spread the ideas of the Age of Reason throughout Europe.

The philosophes of the eighteenth century were greatly concerned with the quality of human life. They believed in the worth of each person. They felt that governments were responsible for such things as public health, better prisons, and better care for the sick and the insane. Many of the philosophes began to apply scientific methods to solving social problems. In the process, many of the social sciences were born, including psychology, criminology, economics, and political science. Religion was also challenged. As a result, new views of the nature of God took hold in Europe.

CHANGING RELIGIOUS VIEWS The new ideas of the Age of Reason questioned traditional religion. Many educated Europeans at this time felt that logic and science left little room for religious belief. During the 1600's and the 1700's, many European thinkers attempted to solve this dilemma.

Descartes was among the first to offer a solution to the growing spiritual crisis. He believed that all humans were made of two substances—mind and matter. Matter was governed by reason and by the laws of nature. On the other hand, faith and belief were part of the mind and were impossible for science to understand. This idea became known as *dualism*. Many dualists believed that by dividing the world into two realms, the gap between science and religion could be narrowed.

Another seventeenth-century thinker, Baruch Spinoza (1632–1677), accepted many of Descartes's ideas. However, Spinoza went further by declaring that everything in the universe—the human mind as well as nature—was part of God. Spinoza's ideas became known as *pantheism*, which means "all God." Pantheism greatly influenced later religious developments during the Age of Reason.

By the eighteenth century, science and religion had finally been combined into a new philosophy known as *deism*. Perhaps the best-known eighteenth-century deist was Voltaire.

Basically, the deists believed that God created the universe. But from the time of creation, the laws of nature and of logic governed the universe. It was as if God was a master watchmaker who had made a watch, wound it, and left it alone to run on its own. Deists believed in life after death and in the need for all people to atone for their sins. Deists also felt that reason must be used to solve social problems. Many deists held that regardless of the name given to Him, the same God was worshiped the world over.

CHANGING POLITICAL VIEWS The ideas of the Age of Reason also affected the way in which people viewed their relationship with government. One writer, Thomas Hobbes (1588–1679), provided a justification for European absolutism. Hobbes believed that strong centralized government was necessary to prevent people from living in what he called a state of nature. He felt that in a state of nature, people lived uncontrolled by laws or by respect for the rights of others and that they were basically barbaric, selfish, and cruel. According to Hobbes, strong government by an absolute monarch was the best way to maintain order in society.

An English philosopher, John Locke (1632–1704), did not agree with Hobbes's pessimistic view of human nature, nor with his concept of absolute monarchy. In 1690, Locke published a work entitled *Two Treatises of Government.* In these two essays, Locke described his optimistic view of people and of the ideal government. Locke did not believe in the divine right of kings. Instead, he believed that government should be based upon the principle of consent of the governed. Locke wrote that the citizens of a nation entered into a type of contract or agreement with their government. The government was to rule wisely and to protect the basic, natural rights of all people. These included each citizen's right to life, liberty, and property. In return, the government could expect the obedience of the people. However, Locke stated that if the government abused or took away the basic rights of its citizens, the citizens would then have the right to overthrow the government.

A French political thinker named Jean Jacques Rousseau [ru-SOH] expanded some of Locke's ideas. Rousseau (1712–1778) observed that people are by nature good, not evil, as Hobbes and other writers had proposed. Rousseau championed the simple, primitive life and believed that people had been corrupted by the development of civilization.

In his famous book, *The Social Contract,* Rousseau argued that people would obey the laws of a government only if they made the laws for themselves. Rousseau argued that in a just society, each individual must act out of concern for the good of all, not out of self-interest. Rousseau thought that people were thus bound by what he termed the general will. The general will was, in effect, the welfare of the entire nation. People in such a society, Rousseau held, would not act as individuals. Rousseau's writings helped to encourage widespread discontent with the monarchy in France during the latter half of the 1700's.

THE ARTS The 1600's and the 1700's were also times of great artistic development. This period is generally known as the *baroque* era. The baroque style of art and architecture had emerged in many parts of Europe by about 1600. Baroque art was grand and emotional. Baroque architecture was extravagant and highly decorative. The French palace at Versailles, begun by Louis XIV in the 1660's and finished 40 years later, was a fine example of baroque art.

Peter Paul Rubens (1577–1640) was one of the greatest baroque artists. Rubens's paintings were rich and exciting. The works of the Italian baroque sculptor Giovanni Bernini (1598–1680) achieved the illusion of rapid movement. Bernini's colonnade and plaza at St. Peter's Basilica in Rome provided a grand setting for the center of the Roman Catholic religion. By the early 1700's, another, even more ornate, style of art, called *rococo,* developed within the baroque form.

During the 1700's, many artists and architects reacted against the elaborate styles of

The main altar of St. Peter's Basilica in Rome lies beneath a beautiful bronze *baldacchino*—canopy—designed by the baroque artist Giovanni Bernini.

baroque and rococo art. They returned to the classical forms of Greek and Roman art. This type of art became known as *neoclassical*. It was probably best represented by the paintings of the French artist Jacques Louis David (1748–1825).

The seventeenth and eighteenth centuries were years of rich literary achievement. One of the most important writers in France during the 1600's was Molière [mohl-YER]. His satires poked fun at the life-styles and the formal manners of the rich. In England during the first half of the eighteenth century, Alexander Pope embodied the ideas of the Enlightenment. His precise and descriptive style was modeled after the Roman satirists. Pope praised the reasoned thinking of the age.

Popular books of eighteenth-century England included Jonathan Swift's *Gulliver's Travels*, Daniel Defoe's *Robinson Crusoe*, and Henry Fielding's *Tom Jones*.

MUSIC Music, like art, architecture, and literature, flourished during the baroque period. Many important changes in music also took place during this time. A new musical form known as the opera was developed by Claudio Monteverdi (1567–1643). Many other composers in this period broke with past traditions and concentrated upon the use of instruments rather than voices in their compositions. Keyboard instruments became more versatile and gained in popularity. Although baroque music was written during an age when many people doubted their faith, the finest works of the period were inspired by deep religious convictions.

One of the great composers of the baroque period was Johann Sebastian Bach (1685–1750). Bach, a German-born Protestant, composed many kinds of *polyphonic* music—that is, a kind of music that blends several melodies into a harmony. Bach is probably best known for his organ works and for bringing European church music to a brilliant peak in the first half of the eighteenth century. His religious compositions include *The Passion According to St. Matthew* and *Mass in B Minor*. Bach's other works include *The Well-Tempered Clavier*, which explores all the possible keys in which keyboard music can be played.

Another important musical figure of the baroque was George Frederick Handel

(Text continued on page 395.)

Contributions

The Piano

Developments in music during the eighteenth century included the building of the first piano in 1709 by an Italian, Bartolommeo Cristofori. Cristofori called his instrument "gravicembalo col piano e forte," which means "harpsichord with soft and loud." Eventually, the term was shortened to *piano-forte*, and still later to *piano*.

The strings of Cristofori's first piano were struck by small hammers when the keys were pressed. The piano could thus produce soft and loud tones and "shade" music.

The forerunners of the piano can be traced to many types of stringed instruments, including the zither of ancient Asia and Africa and the dulcimer of medieval Europe. The strings of these instruments were either plucked or struck by hand to create sound.

Between about 1200 and 1400, the clavichord was developed in Europe. The clavichord was a stringed instrument with a keyboard. The keys, when pressed, lightly struck the strings, creating a fragile and delicate sound. By the 1500's, the clavichord had become the favorite practice instrument of many organists.

Also gaining in popularity during the 1500's was the harpsichord. The harpsichord's strings were plucked when the keys were pressed, producing a clear tone. The harpsichord was larger than the clavichord and produced a greater volume of sound. Many harpsichords were built with two keyboards to increase the volume. Many beautiful works were composed for the clavichord and the harpsichord by several great composers, including Johann Sebastian Bach.

Shortly after the first pianos were built, problems began to arise in their basic construction. For example, the piano needed heavier strings than other keyboard instruments in order to withstand the hammering the strings received when struck. This made stronger and sturdier frames necessary, which, in turn, began to change the look of the piano. In the 1790's, the pianos built in England by John Broadwood were vastly improved versions of earlier instruments. The sounds produced by Broadwood's pianos were richer and had greater volume than the first efforts of Cristofori.

During the early 1800's, the popularity of the piano grew rapidly. By the 1830's, the clavichord and the harpsichord were often ignored by keyboard musicians in favor of the piano. Over the next 150 years, many improvements were made in the piano, and today it remains one of the most popular of musical instruments.

The first pianoforte was developed in 1709. The model shown below, built by Bartolommeo Cristofori around 1720, resembled an Italian harpsichord in styling.

The Bettmann Archive

One of the great composers of the baroque period was George Frederick Handel, who has become known for his dramatic vocal works. Handel presented his orchestral composition *Water Music* to King George I of Great Britain around 1717.

(1685–1759). Born in Germany, Handel became a citizen of England. Handel was famous for his monumental work, *Messiah*. When it was first performed in Dublin, Ireland, in 1742, one reviewer wrote that the *Messiah* was "performed so well that it . . . was allowed by the greatest Judges to be the finest Composition of Musick that ever was Heard."

During the late 1700's, a new period in music, known today as the *classical* period, emerged. The center of classical music was the Austrian city of Vienna. The modern symphony was developed during the classical period by Franz Joseph Hadyn (1732–1809), who wrote more than 100 symphonies.

Hadyn sponsored a young musical genius named Wolfgang Amadeus Mozart (1756–1791). Mozart further developed the symphonic form. In addition, he wrote many other works, including several operas, such as *The Magic Flute* and *The Marriage of Figaro*. Mozart also composed several masterful pieces of chamber music. Chamber music was written to be performed by a small group of musicians in private homes or in small concert halls.

THE IMPACT OF THE AGE OF REASON

The Age of Reason began to wane during the late 1700's. The reliance upon reason that characterized the Enlightenment era broke the hold of medieval superstition. Although many of the solutions proposed by the thinkers of the Age of Reason may seem overly simplistic today, many important questions were raised.

The Age of Reason was a time of growing concern for the welfare of all people. The philosophes effectively attacked many of the evils of society and advocated many reforms. The need for personal freedom and the importance of freedom of thought and expression were popularized by the writers of the period. These ideas greatly influenced the reforms and the development of many governments.

An important outcome of the Age of Reason—especially in France—was the impact of the political writers. By the end of the period, political discontent in France had reached a feverish pitch, as many people turned to violence to solve their problems (see Chapter 21). The writers of the Age of Reason did not advocate violence. Rather, they supported reforms and laws based upon reason and logic. The philosophes did, however, help to express the widespread discontent over the inequalities and injustices of the times.

QUESTIONS FOR REVIEW

1 *Who were the philosophes?*

2 *In what way did the ideas of Thomas Hobbes justify absolutism?*

3 *According to Rousseau, why would people not act as individuals in a just society?*

CHAPTER SUMMARY

During the 1500's and the 1600's, the economy of Europe changed rapidly, even though it continued to be based upon farming. A new economic policy known as mercantilism developed in many of the countries of western Europe. This policy, in turn, brought many changes to business. The economic changes resulted in the rise of a powerful bourgeoisie. Tragically, these changes also led to an increase in slavery.

The 1600's and the 1700's were times when science reached lofty heights. New systems of thought developed—inductive and deductive—that helped to organize scientific study. Scientific discoveries had a tremendous impact upon the ways in which people viewed themselves and the universe.

The Age of Reason, roughly the years between 1650 and 1790 was a time of great intellectual, social, and political achievement in western Europe. The writers of the age who became known as the philosophes, openly criticized the old order of European society and put forward many reforms. Political thinkers, such as Locke and Rousseau, advocated new forms of government based upon the importance of the individual. Moreover, this period was a time of great accomplishments in the arts. Many forms of modern music, including the opera and the symphony, were developed at this time.

CHAPTER 20 IN REVIEW

IMPORTANT WORDS, NAMES, AND TERMS

1 Explain, define, or identify each of the following:

bourgeoisie   laissez-faire   The Spirit of Laws
mercantilism   Sir Francis Bacon   deism
balance of trade   René Descartes   John Locke
inflation   philosophes   polyphonic music

FACTS AND IDEAS

2 What were the English Navigation Acts of the late 1600's?

3 What were the major advantages of investing in the joint-stock companies that developed during the 1600's?

4 Who benefited most from the inflation in Europe that occurred during the sixteenth and seventeenth centuries?

5 What was the significance of Diderot's *Encyclopédie*?

ANALYZING VISUAL MATERIAL

6 Study the map on page 383 carefully. Describe the type of trade and the resulting relationships between the colonies of North America, the West Indies, and England and between North America, the West Indies, and Africa.

7 What might the illustrations on page 386 and 390 indicate about the nature of the development and the spread of ideas during the Age of Enlightenment?

CONCEPTS AND UNDERSTANDINGS

8 How did the European bourgeoisie become increasingly powerful during the sixteenth and seventeenth centuries?

9 How did the inductive method of reasoning differ from the deductive method?

10 How did the deists view the universe?

PROJECTS AND ACTIVITIES

11 The piano developed during the 1700's and the early 1800's. Find examples of recordings of the early piano and of the modern piano. A music catalog will help you to locate these recordings. Play the recordings for the class. Listen carefully and compare the way the early instrument sounds to the way it sounds today.

12 Much of science during the Middle Ages was based upon the work of the alchemists. Prepare a report for the class outlining the beliefs of alchemy and compare these ideas with the changes in science that occurred in the 1600's and the 1700's. Information about alchemy may be found in the library.

CHAPTER **21** THE ERA OF REVOLUTION

1 The Impact of the American Revolution   2 The Growing Need for Reform in France   3 The French Revolution   4 The Napoleonic Era   5 Independence Movements in Latin America

The late 1700's and the early 1800's were times of political and social revolution in many parts of the world. For the first time, the concepts of liberty and equality were put into practice by the new governments created by many of these upheavals. Perhaps the most far-reaching of the revolutionary movements of this period was the French Revolution. Absolutism and feudalism were swept away in France. It took years of violence and bloodshed to bring these changes about. In North America, different circumstances led to American independence from Great Britain. In both France and the United States, however, the Enlightenment influenced the creation of new governments. A few years later, the struggle for independence swept through Latin America, and the era of European domination in the Western Hemisphere was finally ended.

In June 1789, angry French delegates of the Third Estate met and vowed to limit the king's powers. Jacques Louis David painted the event.

1 THE IMPACT OF THE AMERICAN REVOLUTION

The prosperous British colonies in North America enjoyed a large measure of independence throughout most of their history. After the early 1760's, however, the British tightened their rule in North America, stirring colonial resentment and rebellion. In 1775, fighting broke out. The American colonists declared their independence in 1776 and for the next five years, with aid from France, fought for their freedom from Great Britain. As a result of the Americans' victory, the first modern democratic republic was formed. The American experience also helped to inspire discontent and a spirit of revolution in France.

THE AMERICAN COLONIES Beginning with the founding of Jamestown in 1607, and continuing for more than 150 years, the British colonies in America grew steadily more prosperous and self-sufficient. During this time, a spirit of political freedom was nurtured in America. Many liberties were enjoyed by Americans that were not often shared by Europeans. Among these were religious toleration and freedom of the press. And even though social classes existed in colonial America, economic opportunity tended to make class divisions less rigid than in Europe.

Between 1607 and 1763, few direct controls were placed upon the colonies by Great Britain. There were many reasons for this. First, the king and the Parliament had engaged in a long struggle for control of the British government (see Chapter 18). As a result, the American colonies had often been ignored. Second, since the late 1600's, four European wars had preoccupied British leaders. Third, the British government had failed to develop an effective policy for ruling its colonies. Finally, the vast distance that separated America from Great Britain slowed communication and travel, making close supervision impractical.

The right to vote had long been extended to landowning male colonists in America. But unlike Great Britain, the colonies had an abundance of land, which enabled most colonial men to own land and to vote. As a result, direct participation in government was a cherished right in the American colonies. At the same time, *home rule*—the right of a colony to rule itself—developed. By the mid-1700's, colonial assemblies formed a part of every colonial government. These assemblies were elected by eligible voters and often exercised considerable power in local affairs.

To a large extent, the establishment of the American colonies was a result of British mercantilism as well as of the desire for

In 1619, the first colonial representative assembly in America was held at the Virginia settlement of Jamestown.

Historical Pictures Service

399

POLITICAL		SOCIAL AND ECONOMIC
First colonial assembly in America met	~1619	
	1760~	Mechanization of British industry began
Seven Years' War ended	~1763	
Townshend Acts passed	~1767	
	1770~	German composer Ludwig van Beethoven born
Americans declared independence	~1776	
	1779~	First children's clinic established in London
Paris mob stormed Bastille	~1789~	Declaration of the Rights of Man and of the Citizen written
Reign of Terror began	~1793~	
	1795~	Metric system adopted in France
Napoleon invaded Egypt	~1798	
	1800~	Population of Paris reached 550,000
Napoleon crowned emperor of France	~1804	
	1807~	Slave trade abolished in British Empire
Napoleon defeated in Russia	~1812	
Mexico declared independence	~1813	
	1830~	Regular passenger train service began in England
Texas gained independence from Mexico	~1836	
	1846~	Potato famine in Ireland
Louis Napoleon proclaimed emperor of France	~1852	
French occupied Mexico	~1863~	Slavery abolished in United States
Díaz became dictator of Mexico	~1876	

religious and political freedom. Many colonies became sources of raw materials and markets for British goods. As a result, several laws were passed in Great Britain to restrict colonial trade. However, these laws were ineffective and were often ignored in the colonies. By 1763, a need for new tax revenues forced the British to put an end to the illegal trade. They sought more effective control over the colonies.

GROWING TENSION IN THE COLONIES
During the mid-1700's, France and Great Britain competed for worldwide commercial leadership. In 1754, in a dispute that stemmed from clashes over the control of Canada, fighting broke out in North America between the two powers. This war became known in America as the French and Indian War. Two years later, political competition in Europe and the ongoing war in North America combined to engulf much of Europe in a worldwide conflict. This war, known in Europe as the Seven Years' War, had a major impact upon the colonial ambitions of Great Britain and of France. Complete British victory in these two wars led to the signing of a treaty in 1763 that gave Britain a vast colonial empire. The British won control of most of France's North American possessions, all but one French Caribbean island, French outposts in India, and France's West African slave-trading operations.

The tremendous cost of these wars nearly doubled the British national debt and placed a heavy burden upon British taxpayers. As a result, British leaders resolved that the colonies would share in the cost of governing and of protecting the colonies. The attitude of the British leaders led to the passage of new colonial tax laws in 1764. British troops and ships also remained in the colonies to enforce the laws and to stop colonial smuggling, which had cost the British government much needed revenue for many years. The smugglers were to be tried without juries in British courts. The

Many Americans resented British tax policies toward the colonies during the 1760's and the early 1770's. The cartoon shown above, drawn in the 1770's, illustrated the strong reaction of some colonists against such hated British taxes as the duty on tea.

American colonists strongly resented these measures. The next year, threats of open revolt in the colonies became stronger after Parliament passed the Stamp Act. This new law placed a tax on all printed materials and documents in the colonies. Colonial reaction was immediate. Angry mobs demonstrated against the Stamp Act and harassed tax collectors. A boycott of British goods by the colonists damaged British trade. Within a year, the British were forced to repeal the act.

In 1767, new British laws imposed duties on goods imported into the colonies. The passage of these laws, known as the Townshend Acts, also provoked strong reaction in the colonies. Tense feelings continued to simmer between the British and the Americans. In 1770, the tension boiled over in the Boston Massacre, during which five Boston demonstrators were killed by British soldiers. Three years later, further demonstrations over taxes led the British to close Boston Harbor to shipping. The British were determined to control the colonies tightly. Strong new laws were enacted. These laws became known in the colonies as the Intolerable Acts and proved to be the final step along the path toward independence in America. Since they were unable to settle their differences peacefully, war broke out between the American colonists and the British in April 1775.

THE AMERICAN REVOLUTION By the summer of 1776, many Americans were calling for complete independence from Great Britain. On July 4, 1776, the *Declaration of Independence* was approved by representatives of the 13 American colonies. Many parts of this document, written in large part by Thomas Jefferson, were based upon the ideas of the English philosopher John Locke and the writers of the French Enlightenment. The Declaration stated that if the government abused or destroyed the basic rights of its citizens, the citizens had the right to change the government. The Declaration has been an inspiration throughout the world to people opposed to arbitrary and unrepresentative government.

The turning point in the American Revolution came in 1777, with an American victory at Saratoga, New York. Thereafter, the French monarchy, which had secretly sent aid to America for two years, signed a formal treaty to help the Americans. The French sent soldiers and a fleet large enough to challenge British superiority on the high seas. Although this aid was crucial to the Americans, it placed a great burden on the French treasury.

In 1781, the combined French and American forces trapped and captured the largest British army in America at Yorktown, Virginia. The British defeat led to peace negotiations that were completed in 1783 with the Treaty of Paris.

For the next four years, the American states struggled as a weak and ineffective union. Jealously guarding their powers, the states were reluctant to support a strong central government. However, many Americans recognized the need for firmer and more effective central control. As a result, a plan of government—the Constitution of the United States—was hammered out by American leaders during the summer of 1787. The Bill of Rights was later added to the Constitution to protect the basic freedoms of all Americans. The Constitution echoed many of the ideas of the Age of Reason, particularly those of the French philosophe Montesquieu. A new nation based upon many of the democratic ideas that developed during the Enlightenment had emerged.

THE IMPACT OF AMERICA'S INDEPENDENCE Historians have found it difficult to measure the effect of the American Revolution upon the old order of European society, and particularly upon French society. By 1776, a new nation had already been developing in the North American wilderness for more than 150 years. Americans had enjoyed a large degree of freedom and of self-government. Although the Declaration of Independence and the Constitution of the United States reflected the ideas of the European philosophes, the direct causes of the war lay elsewhere. Economic and political disputes with Great Britain had, in large part, led to the conflict. It was the Enlightenment, however, that gave the Americans new democratic ideas with which to shape a new government.

Eight thousand British troops were forced to surrender to American and French armies in October 1781 at Yorktown, Virginia. The victory assured the independence of the American colonies from Great Britain.

French involvement in America between 1776 and 1783 proved to be costly. The strain placed upon the finances of the French government was great. In general, the French had supported the American cause in order to oppose British political and commercial power. The French had fought the British in Europe and in the Caribbean as well as in North America. Clearly, French leaders had not acted to establish a free and democratic nation in North America. By necessity, their desire to defeat Britain had led to their support of the American Revolution and its aims. A few years later, however, a similar republican movement in France challenged, and eventually destroyed, the French monarchy.

The American Revolution affected France in another way. The writings of the philosophes, such as Voltaire, Montesquieu, and Rousseau, were no longer mere words. These ideas had been put into action by the Americans. The growing popularity of such ideas as liberty, freedom, and consent of the governed soon threatened traditional French society. In early 1789, Thomas Jefferson, the American minister to France, wrote:

> Though celebrated writers of this [France] and other countries had already sketched good principles on the subject of government, yet the American War seems first to have awakened the thinking part of this nation in general from the sleep of despotism in which they were sunk.

QUESTIONS FOR REVIEW

1 What was home rule?

2 In what ways did British leaders hope to strengthen their control over the American colonies before 1775?

3 Why did the French government support the American War for Independence?

2 THE GROWING NEED FOR REFORM IN FRANCE

France was faced with many problems in the mid-1700's. The economy sagged under the weight of a growing debt. Taxes could not keep pace with government spending. Internal trade stagnated. In addition, French society remained tied to feudal traditions of privilege and rank. Less than 3 percent of France's population controlled most of the country's wealth and held all of its important government and church offices. Many French writers and political thinkers offered solutions for these injustices. But the centuries-old problems of France could not easily be solved.

THE FRENCH ECONOMY By the early 1700's mercantilism had nearly strangled France's economy. Government interference and regulation existed at every turn. Strong, self-interested guilds had shut off competition in many areas of the economy. Moreover, the government controlled both domestic and foreign trade. A web of toll charges and local taxes within France added to its economic problems by limiting the flow of trade goods throughout the country. Grain, for example, was generally required to be sold in the region in which it was grown. Generally, it could not be traded or transported to other parts of France. Grain brought into Paris for sale was also taxed.

Despite these burdens on France's economy, foreign trade prospered during the eighteenth century. Both the volume and the value of French trade increased. For some French people—particularly merchants and traders—the growth of foreign trade brought wealth and opportunity. This prosperity was not shared by all, however. More than 80 percent of the French people remained poor peasant farmers.

France's economy also suffered under the weight of the huge royal debt. This debt was a result of many factors, including the many wars that France had fought in Europe and America during the 1700's and the extravagance of the French court. Also, an unequal system of taxation prevented a balancing of the royal budget without a reduction in government spending. The tax burden was carried by the lower classes. The nobility and the clergy were largely exempt from taxation. Moreover, chaotic and corrupt tax collection practices increased the problem. Some historians estimate that more than one half of the taxes collected failed to reach the royal treasury. By the mid-1700's, the economy of France was badly in need of change and reform.

SOCIETY IN FRANCE Eighteenth-century French society is known as the *Old Regime*. The social order that existed under the Old Regime was based largely upon a framework of feudal privilege and obligation. In some respects, this social order resembled a pyramid. The king was at the pinnacle of the social pyramid, while the great mass of people—the peasant farmers—were at the bottom.

French society was divided into 3 *estates*—social classes. The first 2 classes included the clergy and the nobility and made up roughly 2 percent of France's population of about 26 million. A third social class consisted of peasant farmers, craft workers, serfs, and the bourgeoisie, which included merchants and professional workers. Because of various exemptions, the first 2 classes paid little if any tax. The *Third Estate* supported the entire system with its labor and its taxes.

The *First Estate* was made up of the Roman Catholic clergy. The Roman Catholic Church was a large landholder in the mid-1700's, controlling about 10 percent of the land of France. Generally, the upper ranks of the clergy—cardinals, bishops, and abbots—came from the nobility and greatly benefited from the Church's privileged position. Parish priests, however, came from the lower classes and generally lived in poverty. The parish priests ministered directly to the needs of the French people. The entire clergy made up less than 1 percent of France's total population.

During the era of the Old Regime, many of the French nobles pampered themselves and took great pride in being expensively and fashionably attired.

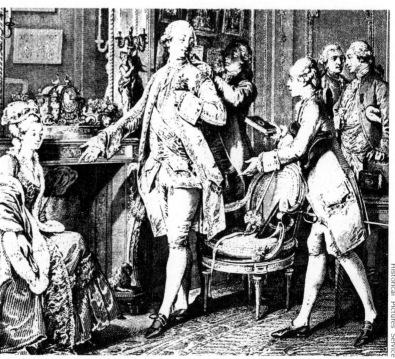

The *Second Estate*—the nobility—numbered about 400,000. Like the clergy, the nobility was divided into many different ranks, ranging from the most powerful nobles in the king's court to those nobles who barely survived on small, poorly kept farms. Together, the nobility owned about 20 percent of the land. They collected taxes and rents from the peasants who farmed the land. The nobles also held the most important and powerful government posts, and they controlled the courts of law. By the late 1780's, many of the nobles were attempting to strengthen their privileged position in society, only to be faced with fierce opposition from the Third Estate.

THE THIRD ESTATE Two main groups made up the Third Estate in France. These groups were the peasants and the bourgeoisie, or middle class. By the mid-1700's, less than 10 percent of France's population lived in cities or towns. Most of the French tilled the land. The peasantry was poor and remained so generation after generation. The peasants carried the burden of the government's taxes. The nobility received feudal dues from peasant farmers. The clergy received a *tithe*, about one tenth of a peasant's yearly income. Some historians estimate that in some years many peasants paid as much as one half of their income in taxes and other obligations. Primitive agricultural methods also prevented increased farm production and added to the problems of the peasantry.

As a result of its growing wealth, the bourgeoisie gained an increasingly powerful voice in French society during the eighteenth century. For the most part, members of the bourgeoisie accepted their position in society. However, many also dreamed of gaining the privileges of nobility. Often, wealthy members of the middle class could buy a government office or a large estate. In this way, they could gain social status and privilege, such as exemption from the taxes required of members of the Third Estate.

By the end of the 1780's, rigid social divisions and the economic problems faced by the French people had reached a critical point. The government was no longer able to finance its own operation. Huge debts crippled the French economy. Payment of the interest alone on these debts was equal to one half of the government's income by 1789. Tax reform was also badly needed. Added to these problems were crop failures in 1788 and 1789. Famine resulted in many parts of France. Reform was long overdue. No one knew, however, that reform would soon turn to revolution.

QUESTIONS FOR REVIEW

1 *What was the Old Regime?*

2 *In what way were the First and Second Estates similar?*

3 *Why was tax reform needed in France by the late 1780's?*

3 THE FRENCH REVOLUTION

By 1788, the Old Regime in France had begun to crumble. The king, the clergy, and the nobility proved to be incapable of meeting the country's growing need for drastic reform. As a result, revolution raged across France in 1789.

Initially, the leaders of the French Revolution were drawn largely from the bourgeoisie. However, war, fear, and mob violence soon led the revolution into radicalism. Radical leaders sought to destroy every remnant of the Old Regime. By 1794, these extremists had exhausted the country with their violent campaign and the radical stage of the revolution had come to an end.

The Estates-General met in May 1789, and conflict immediately arose over the Third Estate's demand to change the assembly's voting procedure.

THE BEGINNING OF REFORM France was nearly bankrupt in 1788. In August, King Louis XVI called for a meeting of the *Estates-General* for the next year to deal with France's many problems. The Estates-General had originated in the late Middle Ages and was made up of representatives of each of France's three social classes (see Chapter 13). However, the Estates-General had not met since 1614, largely because of the strength of the French kings. Unlike the British Parliament, the Estates-General did not develop as a legislative body and it had no authority over taxation.

France was divided into several districts, each of which sent many delegates to the Estates-General. The king also called for each of the districts to draw up a list of grievances and suggestions—called a *cahier*—to present to the meeting of the Estates-General. The cahiers proposed such democratic improvements as a legislative assembly, tax reform, trial by jury, freedom of the press, and equal taxation.

As a concession to the discontented middle class, Louis XVI doubled the membership of the Third Estate in the Estates-General. Thus, a slight majority of the 1200 members of the Estates-General were representatives of the Third Estate. Moreover, most of the delegates from the Third Estate were drawn from the bourgeoisie. More than half of these representatives were lawyers. Less than one tenth of the Third Estate's delegates were peasants.

The Estates-General met in May 1789. From the beginning, one issue that needed to be resolved was the way in which voting would take place within the body. Traditionally, each estate met separately and had one vote. However, the Third Estate realized that the nobility and the clergy would combine their votes to control the outcome of any proposals or changes made to the Estates-General. As a result, members of the Third Estate demanded a different voting procedure. Under this plan, the estates would meet together as one body and each delegate would have one vote. Thus, the Third Estate, which made up a majority of the Estates-General, could control the body.

For several weeks, the debate on voting continued. Finally, the Third Estate, supported by many of the lower clergy and by liberal nobles, defiantly declared themselves to be an independent representative body. The Third Estate's delegates called themselves the National Assembly. The Assembly claimed the legislative power to make laws. In answer to the Third Estate's open challenge to traditional authority, the king weakly agreed that the combined estates should meet as one body. Reform had begun to turn to revolution.

THE END OF THE OLD REGIME During the summer of 1789, several events led to the end of the French feudal system. The economic situation of the French peasants and of the lower classes in the cities had become desperate. By July, the price of bread had reached its highest point in 75 years. Unemployment was widespread and taxes were high. The National Assembly, which had been formed over the objections of the king, had made many of the Parisians bolder and more defiant. Discontent was further fueled by the radical leaders and pamphleteers of Paris. Rumors that the king's troops were gathering outside Paris added to these growing tensions. Many Parisians sought to arm themselves. On July 14, a violent mob looking for weapons stormed the *Bastille*, a fortress prison and a symbol of royal despotism. Many of the prison's defenders were killed, and the seven prisoners there were freed.

Mob violence continued in many parts of France throughout the summer. Nobles' estates were plundered and destroyed. Many of the hated feudal rolls that recorded the peasants' debts to the nobles were also destroyed. Fearing the spread of more violence, several nobles stood in the National Assembly in early August 1789 and gave up their feudal claims of privilege. Soon after, the National Assembly passed the "August Decrees," which abolished French feudalism. Serfdom, church tithes, feudal dues, and aristocratic titles were outlawed.

Three weeks later, the National Assembly approved the *Declaration of the Rights of Man and of the Citizen*. This document became the basis upon which the new French government was founded. Many of the ideas of the

Hope for peaceful reform in France dimmed on July 14, 1789, when a Paris mob stormed the hated prison fortress known as the Bastille.

The Granger Collection

philosophes and of American and British documents were reflected in the Declaration. Among these ideas was the principle that all people had basic rights guaranteed by the government. These rights included "liberty, property, security, and resistance to oppression." In addition, all people were equal before the law and were to be taxed fairly and in equal proportion.

REFORM AND A NEW CONSTITUTION
During the fall of 1789, shortages of food supplies, especially in Paris, became critical. This led to the October 5 march of thousands of poor Parisian women on the royal palace at Versailles to demand bread from the king. The crowd shouted that they would "bring back the baker and the baker's wife," referring to Louis XVI and his wife, Marie Antoinette. As a result of this demonstration, the king and queen were forced to move to Paris. They were accompanied by the National Assembly, which moved its meetings to Paris. Once the delegates were there, however, the fiery Parisian crowds often influenced the Assembly and the building of a new French government.

By the summer of 1790, many changes had been brought about by the National Assembly. Church lands were confiscated and the Church became subject to government control. Church officials were to be elected and were to be paid by the government. The pope's authority was no longer recognized in France. More than half of France's priests and nearly all of its bishops rejected these changes. The reforms also angered many peasants, who refused to support the civil church, which was dominated by the upper middle class. The conflict over religion dampened the enthusiasm of many toward the revolution.

By 1791, the National Assembly had completed the task of creating a new French government. Not surprisingly, the constitution written by the largely bourgeois Assembly generally reflected the needs and the concerns of the French middle class. Most of the powers of government were to be held by a new lawmaking body, called the Legislative Assembly. The tax requirement for voting and for holding higher office severely limited participation in the new government. Some historians estimate that of the 26 million people in France at the time, no more than 70,000 paid enough tax either to serve in or to elect the Legislative Assembly. The constitution also kept the monarchy, but greatly limited its powers.

Unable to accept many of these changes, Louis XVI and his wife tried to flee the country in June 1791. They were discovered and returned to Paris. In September, the king reluctantly accepted the constitution and the new French government took office.

THE RADICAL TURN OF THE REVOLUTION
By the spring of 1792, the revolutionary government of France faced several challenges. A large number of émigrés—emigrants—including many important nobles and moderate reformers, began to work against the French Revolution. Also, war with Austria, Prussia, and many smaller German states appeared imminent. The rulers of these kingdoms feared that the revolutionary ideas of France would spread to their countries, and they opposed the revolution. These kingdoms jointly declared that it was in the interest of all European nations to resist French ideas. Added to these problems were the growing divisions among the revolutionary leaders themselves.

In April 1792, France declared war on Austria and Prussia. However, the French army soon suffered several defeats at the hands of the well-trained Austrian and Prussian armies. By the end of the summer, the invading armies of Austria and Prussia were only 200 miles (320 kilometers) from Paris.

At the same time that these events took place, radical leaders in Paris called for the end of the French monarchy. Fearing the violent Paris mob that backed the radicals,

On August 10, 1792, a Paris mob forced the king and his family to flee the royal palace. The members of the Legislative Assembly, fearing for their own lives, suspended the monarchy and established a provisional government to rule France until new elections could be held for a convention to change the constitution.

the Legislative Assembly voted to suspend the monarchy. A new assembly, called the National Convention, was elected to change the constitution and create a democratic republic in France. In September 1792, the French Republic was proclaimed. Nearly all adult males became eligible to vote and the monarchy was abolished. The revolution had entered a more radical stage.

The poor Parisians' hatred of the Old Regime and widespread fear of the invading armies reached a peak in the late summer of 1792. During the first days of September, frenzied mobs murdered nearly 1,300 people who were suspected of supporting the monarchy and of opposing the revolution. These black days became known as the September Massacre. During the fall of 1792, many of the members of the National Convention called for the king to be tried on charges of treason. King Louis had long worked to undermine the revolution, carrying on secret correspondence with the leaders of Austria, Sweden, and Spain. Louis XVI was tried and found guilty of the charges against him. He was executed on January 21, 1793.

THE JACOBINS The newly elected National Convention met in mid-September 1792. The assembly was overwhelmingly middle class. The most radical revolutionaries in the Convention were known as the *Jacobins*. They were led by Georges Jacques Danton (1759–1794), by Jean Paul Marat (1743–1793), and later by Maximilien Robespierre (1758–1794). These radicals were strongly supported by the lower classes and by the unruly mobs of Paris. However, the Jacobins had little support in the outlying provinces, where a more moderate group, the *Girondins*, was strong.

During the summer of 1793, the Jacobins gained control of the French government. Robespierre and several Jacobins had become members of the powerful Committee of Public Safety, which was eventually given extraordinary powers by the Convention. It was from this position that Jacobin leaders conducted the Reign of Terror, which lasted from September 1793 to July 1794. Political opponents, émigrés and their relatives, and those suspected of hoarding food or of speculating for profit were exiled from

(*Text continued on page* 411.)

409

Life at the Time

The Reign of Terror

The Reign of Terror gripped Paris between September 1793 and July 1794. It is difficult to imagine the daily fear in which people lived during that time. Many who had once supported the revolution were turned away as a result. The following excerpt was written by a Parisian lawyer who had been away from the city for ten months. He had once written a glowing account of the fall of the Bastille. But when he returned, the Terror was well under way. He was stunned by what he found.

"So there I was packed into a stage-coach surrounded by sinis-

The Reign of Terror spread fear across France as thousands were arrested, tried, and sentenced quickly and without compassion.

ter faces, for at that moment, none but revolutionaries and government agents dared to move about. My mind was filled with the darkest presentiments [premonitions] and every stage on my way to Paris seemed to bring me nearer to the scaffold. As I thought of my wife and my children, I reproached [blamed] myself for having left them so rashly and for not having embraced them yet once more before we parted.

". . . [O]ne of my companions cried: 'Here we are at the barrier. We've arrived.' These words shook me out of my lethargy but they made me shudder. I put my head out of the window. It was dark, though it was scarcely eight o'clock.

"What a change! Formerly—even when I left the city not so long ago—eight o'clock was the hour when Paris was most brilliantly illuminated . . . It was the hour when the cafés were lit up and when the gleam of candles shone from every storey; when luxurious equipages [carriages] passed one another swiftly in the streets on their way to theatres, concerts and balls in every quarter of the capital. Now, instead of this bustling life, these animated crowds, this impressive brilliance, a sepulchral [funerallike] silence filled all the streets of Paris. All the shops were already shut, and everyone hastened to barricade himself in his own home. . . .

"[The next day] I walked boldly on my way when suddenly I was struck by a curious medley of colours which I had not been expecting. All the doors and all the windows carried a flagstaff on which floated the Tricolour [the revolutionary flag]. A few patriots, more republican in spirit than their neighbours, or wishing to be thought so, had hoisted this banner and from that time onwards, as it was dangerous to be less patriotic than anyone else, everyone had decorated his windows with tricolour streamers and large, coloured inscriptions on which one read the words: 'Unity, indivisibility, liberty, equality, fraternity or death.' Another notice posted up everywhere bore the inscription: 'Charity, justice and humanity are part of our daily duty.' . . . This high-light of hypocrisy reminded me of a phrase . . . 'There is nowhere so much talk of liberty as in a state where it has ceased to exist.' "

Historical Pictures Service

France or were killed. Some historians estimate that nearly 2,700 people were executed in Paris alone. Perhaps 20,000 or more were killed throughout the rest of France. Tens of thousands were arrested and jailed.

During the Reign of Terror, the Jacobins mobilized the entire nation against the foreign armies on French soil. The enemy now included Spain, England, and Holland, as well as Austria and Prussia. This alliance became known as the First Coalition. Several victories by the French army followed. By June 1794, the French had effectively defeated the First Coalition.

With final victory over the First Coalition certain, the revolution began to slow. The French people seemed exhausted from the war and numbed by the continuous fear of the "terror." Finally, in July 1794, the Reign of Terror came to an end. Robespierre and his closest followers were denounced and removed from power. On July 28, they were executed.

THE END OF THE REVOLUTION After Robespierre's death, another government, called the Directory, was formed in France. The Directory was led by a committee of five and lasted from 1795 to 1799. During these years, however, France faced many problems. Constant war, a weakened economy, and rebellion threatened to bring down the new government. By 1799, the Directory's most powerful general, Napoleon Bonaparte, had gained control of the French government. It was Napoleon who spread the ideas of the French Revolution across Europe.

The results of the French Revolution were many. The revolution completely remade France. The titles and the privileges of the aristocracy were swept away. Feudalism ended in France and was replaced with individual freedom. The bourgeoisie became a powerful influence in society, in government, and in business.

Although the middle class continued to rule France under the Directory, the peasants had gained some advantages. Confiscated church property and the lands of the émigrés were sold. Independent farmers soon became an important stabilizing force in France as a result. The arbitrary justice of the Old Regime and the radical excesses of the Reign of Terror were replaced with a legal system based upon equality before the law. Taxation became more equal and more just. The attacks upon the Church also caused France to become more secular.

The influence of the French Revolution was eventually felt throughout Europe. Ideas about government, politics, and economics and the way in which European society was organized were all affected. New feelings of nationalism replaced traditional loyalties to long-standing monarchies. The modern Western world had begun to emerge.

QUESTIONS FOR REVIEW

1 What groups made up the Third Estate?

2 How did the National Assembly help to secularize French Society?

3 Why do you think the Legislative Assembly might be termed a "bourgeois assembly"?

4 THE NAPOLEONIC ERA

By the end of the 1790's, the French people had tired of the chaos of the revolution and the incompetence of French leaders. In 1799, a popular young general named Napoleon Bonaparte seized the French government. The French people willingly turned to the strong leader.

During his early rule, Napoleon brought about many needed reforms in France. However, his thirst for conquest launched France and Europe into more than a decade of war. By 1810, Napoleon dominated nearly all of Europe. Only five years later, his empire lay in ruins.

THE RISE OF NAPOLEON On the Mediterranean island of Corsica; a newly acquired French possession, Napoleon Bonaparte was born in 1769. Beginning at the age of 10, young Napoleon attended a military academy in France. He joined the revolutionary army of France and rose rapidly in rank. The young soldier excelled at military tactics and eventually received an appointment as a brigadier general at the age of 24.

In 1796, the Directory called upon Napoleon to command one of France's three armies that were to be sent against Austria and the German states. Napoleon was to lead a French army into Italy. Inheriting an army that was ill fed and ill equipped, Napoleon soon gained his soldiers' confidence by brilliant leadership.

During April and May 1796, Napoleon's army quickly defeated the Austrian and the Sardinian armies and moved into Italy. Soon after, Napoleon took the rich city of Milan. He created a republic of these conquered lands, spreading French ideas of liberty and equality.

Following his victories in Italy, Napoleon was approached by the Directory to lead an invasion of Great Britain. Napoleon rejected this plan and instead proposed to strike at British trade routes with India. In 1798, Napoleon invaded and easily conquered Egypt. However, British sea power stranded the French army in the strange land. The long hot months and the stiff opposition that the French encountered from the Ottoman rulers of the Middle East soon wilted the French soldiers' desire for the campaign. Cornered and disgusted with the weak and corrupt leadership of the Directory, Napoleon returned to France in 1799.

Although the Egyptian campaign is generally regarded by historians as a military failure, the scientists and scholars who ac-companied the expedition greatly increased European knowledge of Egypt. The most important discovery was the Rosetta Stone, which unlocked the secrets of the Egyptian hieroglyphs (see Chapter 2).

During Napoleon's absence in Egypt, France lost most of the young general's gains in Italy and along the eastern frontier of France. In November 1799, Napoleon seized an opportunity to take control of the government. A new French government, the Consulate, was formed with Napoleon as First Consul. From this powerful position, Napoleon ruled France.

NAPOLEONIC REFORMS Two years after becoming First Consul, Napoleon defeated the armies of the Second Coalition—Great Britain, Austria, and Russia—which had threatened to invade France. In 1802, a truce was achieved between France and Great Britain. As a result, Napoleon was free to concentrate on domestic problems.

One of Napoleon's first efforts was directed toward making peace with the Roman Catholic Church. Since the days of the French Revolution, the French government and the Church had been at odds. The secularization of France had never been popular with the majority of the French people. Therefore, Napoleon brought the state and the Church closer together with the *Concordat of* 1801. This document reestablished the Church in France. All church buildings were returned. However, land confiscated from the Church during the revolution was not restored. In addition, the state was to continue the practices of paying the salaries of the clergy and of nominating the bishops to their office. The pope regained the right to install church officials. Other religious groups were also given freedom of worship.

One of Napoleon's most important accomplishments during this time was the codification of French law. The new legal system, known as the *Code Napoleon*, was finished in 1804. The code combined old French common law, Roman law, and a myriad of royal decrees. The code also declared the equality of people before the law. However, women remained in an inferior legal position. Those who committed political crimes would be dealt with harshly. The code eventually influenced the development of law in Germany, Italy, and Holland, throughout Latin America, and in the American state of Louisiana.

Napoleon made other lasting changes. He established public education in France under the supervision of a government body. He also centralized the government of France to bring the country more firmly under his control. Finally, Napoleon made tax collection more efficient, built roads, and established the Bank of France to deal with government finances. By 1804, Napoleon had achieved the height of his popularity. In that year, he crowned himself emperor of France. The First French Republic was at an end.

EMPIRE In 1805, Napoleon was opposed by a new European alliance called the Third Coalition, which consisted of Great Britain, Russia, Austria, and Sweden. During that year, Napoleon's plan of invading Great Britain was crushed at the Battle of Trafalgar, off the coast of southern Spain. The British admiral, Lord Nelson, defeated the French and Spanish navies decisively. France was never again able to challenge British naval power.

Napoleon then turned eastward with his experienced and well-equipped Grand Army. Perhaps his greatest military victory was achieved in 1805 at Austerlitz against the combined armies of Austria and Russia (see map on page 414). Napoleon then dissolved the remnants of the Holy Roman Empire and formed a republic—the Confederation of the Rhine—of the many German states.

Napoleon also gained important victories over Prussia. As a result, Prussia's gains in the partitioning of Poland a decade earlier were reorganized into the Grand Duchy of Warsaw—a French ally. The nation of Poland, however, would not reappear in Europe until 1919. By the end of 1809, Napoleon ruled over an empire that reached across nearly all of Europe (see map on page 414).

THE ROAD TO DEFEAT Since invasion of Great Britain was impossible without control of the seas, Napoleon began an economic blockade of Britain. He hoped to destroy British trade with the European continent. But the blockade was never completely

On December 2, 1804, Napoleon received the crown of the French Empire from Pope Pius VII and crowned himself emperor.

The Empire of Napoleon

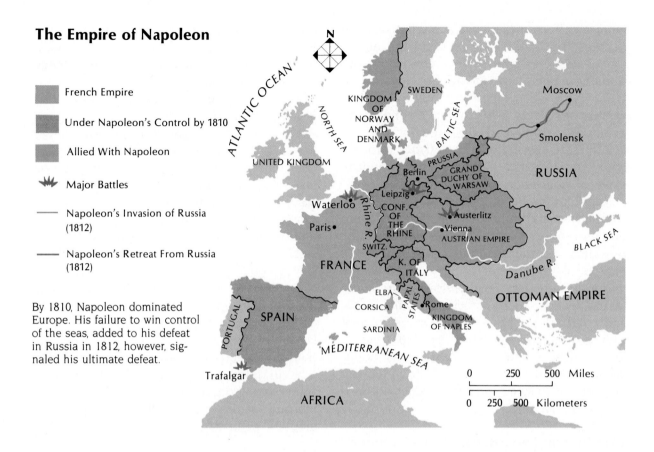

Legend:
- French Empire
- Under Napoleon's Control by 1810
- Allied With Napoleon
- Major Battles
- Napoleon's Invasion of Russia (1812)
- Napoleon's Retreat From Russia (1812)

By 1810, Napoleon dominated Europe. His failure to win control of the seas, added to his defeat in Russia in 1812, however, signaled his ultimate defeat.

successful because it could never be strictly enforced. Moreover, nationalistic feelings had grown to the point of rebellion in Portugal and in Spain. Spanish and Portuguese rebels, encouraged and aided by the British, fought a four-year war against French domination.

In 1812, Napoleon set out on a campaign that would prove to be an utter disaster. He massed more than one-half million soldiers along the Baltic Sea in eastern Prussia for an invasion of Russia. During the invasion, the Russians avoided a direct battle with Napoleon's army whenever possible. Also, as the Russians withdrew deeper into their country, they burned the fields to prevent the French from living off the land. As a result, French supplies dwindled.

Napoleon entered Moscow in October. The city had been abandoned by the Russians and was burning. A month later, short on supplies and with winter setting in, Napoleon withdrew. He was constantly ha-

rassed during the withdrawal by Russian soldiers and by the bitter Russian winter. Napoleon reached the Baltic Sea with only a fraction of his original force.

In 1813, the Third Coalition defeated Napoleon in the Battle of the Nations, near the German city of Leipzig (see map on this page). The next year, Napoleon's empire fell apart. The allied armies of the Third Coalition invaded France and entered Paris. In April 1814, Napoleon abdicated.

Napoleon was exiled to the tiny Mediterranean island of Elba. A new French government was formed and was led by Louis XVIII, brother of Louis XVI. But the government was faced with many internal problems that could not easily be solved. From exile, Napoleon saw another chance to return to power. In March 1815, he landed in France. As he marched to Paris, Napoleon again gained the confidence of many of the French people. For 100 days, Napoleon controlled the French government. Allied troops gathered at the eastern border of France to face another challenge from Napoleon. In June, Napoleon was defeated for the last time in the Battle of Waterloo. He was exiled to the South Atlantic island of St. Helena, where he died in 1821.

QUESTIONS FOR REVIEW

1 What was the Concordat of 1801?

2 In what way did Napoleon influence the development of law in France?

3 Why do you think Napoleon's invasion of Russia was a failure?

5 INDEPENDENCE MOVEMENTS IN LATIN AMERICA

Revolution spread to Latin America during the late eighteenth and early nineteenth centuries. Inspired in part by American independence and the French Revolution, nearly all of Latin America gained independence from Spain and Portugal in a 14-year period, beginning in 1810. Independence did not greatly change the many problems of Latin America, however. Wealthy and powerful individuals, aided by the strength of their armies, remained in control of many of the newly created nations.

LATIN AMERICA IN THE EIGHTEENTH CENTURY By about 1700, Spain and Portugal had lost the military and naval superiority that they had once enjoyed. Although Spain had received fabulous wealth from its American colonies, the Spanish economy remained backward in comparison to the rapidly developing economies of northern Europe. However, the highly regulated Latin American economy began to change under the leadership of the Bourbons, the ruling dynasty that came to the Spanish throne in 1701. Trading companies, modeled on European examples, were formed. Beginning around 1765, the Spanish colonies in America were opened to unlimited trade with Spain.

By the end of the 1700's, Latin America was remarkably prosperous. Sadly, its prosperity was based upon the labor of native Indians and of African slaves. Although mining and industry remained important in the colonies, agriculture had become the basis of the Latin American economy. The Spanish crown and the Roman Catholic Church still dominated life in Latin America.

During the 1700's, many Latin Americans, particularly educated creoles, began to call for independence. The writers of the Enlightenment, including Voltaire and Rousseau, were widely read among educated Latin Americans. Also, the American and French revolutions provided examples for a growing group of discontented creoles. Underlying creole discontentment were the grievances of poor mestizos, Indians, and black slaves.

In 1791, the first successful revolution in Latin America took place on the Caribbean island of Hispaniola. The western third of this tropical island was the French colony of Saint Domingue [SAND-uh-MANG]. This colony accounted for about one half of France's colonial trade. More than 400,000 slaves worked the plantations of this rich colony. But only a few thousand French ruled Saint Domingue and formed the upper class.

During the French Revolution, slavery was outlawed by the French government in all its colonies. Almost at once, violence broke out in Saint Domingue. One of the slave leaders was Toussaint L'Ouverture [TOO-san-LOO-vuhr-tur]. Ten years later, the army of Toussaint controlled most of Hispaniola, and for a time, the former slave was dictator of the island. In 1802, Napoleon sent an army to the island to reestablish French rule. The next year, Toussaint was captured and imprisoned. However, the French were finally defeated in 1804. A new nation, Haiti, was proclaimed. By 1810, other Latin American colonies began to react to Napoleon's control of Spain and the Spanish colonies through his brother, Joseph, who sat on the Spanish throne.

MEXICO'S INDEPENDENCE In 1810, a ten-year struggle for liberation began in the Spanish viceroyalty of New Spain—Mexico. Father Miguel Hidalgo, a Roman Catholic priest, organized an army of Indian peasants and mestizos. Little support came from the creoles, who sought more control of the colonial governments for themselves. After a year of battling Spanish troops and the creoles, Hidalgo was captured and shot. One of his followers, Father José Morelos, continued fighting, and by 1813, he controlled most of southern Mexico. Two years later, Morelos was also captured and executed.

During the next five years, support for independence became widespread among the Mexican creoles. They helped Mexico gain independence in 1821. At this time, the region of Central America was separated from Mexico (see map on page 417). By 1838, civil wars had divided Central America into the countries of Guatemala, Honduras, Nicaragua, El Salvador, and Costa Rica.

Mexico became a republic, at least in theory, in 1824 with the adoption of the first Mexican constitution. Although this document appeared similar to the American and French constitutions, it ignored several issues. Most importantly, the power of the president was not limited. Also, individual rights were neither guaranteed nor protected. As a result, personal power struggles and dictatorships have characterized Mexican government.

PROBLEMS IN MEXICO From its beginnings, the Mexican government was controlled by strong leaders who had gained the support of the army. These leaders were called *caudillos* [kow-THEE-ohs]. Among the most powerful of the caudillos was Santa Anna, who commanded the Mexican army during the Texan war for independence.

Continual conflict and power struggles among the leaders weakened Mexico between 1821 and the 1860's. During this time, Mexico lost much of its territory. In 1836, the territory of Texas became independent. It was annexed by the United States in 1845. The annexation led to war with the Americans the next year. As a result of this war, Mexico lost nearly one half of its land to the United States in 1848.

In the 1850's, Benito Juárez [WAHR-uhs], a liberal reform leader, came to power in Mexico. Juárez helped to write a new constitution in which the powerful relationship between the Church and the government was ended. Other reform measures ended Church landownership in the hope that the land could be divided among small farmers. However, these and other changes challenged the foundation of Mexican society, which was based upon the wealth of a few and the domination of the Church.

Civil war soon broke out between the liberals, who wanted change, and the conservatives, who supported the Church and the old structure of society. In 1860, the liberals were successful in controlling the government, and Juárez became president. However, the reforms of the liberals were never as extensive as they had once hoped.

During the early 1860's, many Europeans saw an opportunity to intervene in the chaotic atmosphere of Mexico. In 1863, the French, perhaps hoping to establish a colonial empire in America, occupied Mexico and crowned Archduke Maximilian of Austria as the Mexican emperor. His reign was plagued by continual uprisings. He was finally removed from his throne and executed in 1867. Juárez again became president and governed until his death in 1872.

Between 1876 and 1910, Mexico was ruled by a dictator, Porfirio Díaz [pawr-FEE-ryoh DEE-ahs]. Díaz brought a large measure of security and order to Mexico. During his rule, foreign capital from Europe and the United States helped to industrialize Mexico. Oil, mining, railroads, utilities, and manufacturing were all developed by foreigners during this time. However, the regime of Díaz did not attempt to solve the problems of Mexico's many landless poor. Revolutionary leaders plunged Mexico into a civil war—the *Mexican Revolution*—between 1910 and 1920.

THE LIBERATION OF SOUTH AMERICA

Two leaders—Simón Bolívar and José de San Martín—stand out in the wars for independence in Spanish South America. These brilliant generals helped to defeat the Spanish armies between 1810 and 1824. The three Spanish viceroyalties of New Granada, Peru, and La Plata were liberated (see map on page 417). These lands were eventually divided into many of the nations that exist in South America today.

Simón Bolívar was born to a wealthy creole family of the city of Caracas, in what is now Venezuela. Ambitious and educated in the ideas of the French Enlightenment, Bolívar participated in the first revolt of Caracas in 1810. For the next 14 years, Bolívar fought to free New Granada and Peru from Spain. By 1821, he had led Venezuela to independence. Next, he marched to Bogotá, in what is now Colombia, and then on to Quito, in the country now known as Ecuador. In 1822, Bolívar entered Peru and met the liberator of the southern lands of South America, José de San Martín.

Between 1812 and 1822, San Martín fought for the independence of the area that became the nations of Argentina, Chile, Paraguay, Peru, and Uruguay. San Martín shunned honors and recognition. Idealistic and highly educated, he sought only independence from Spanish rule, not personal glory.

Latin America After Independence

Countries Independent by 1828

Nearly all of Latin America was free from foreign control by 1828. It would be several years, however, before many Latin American countries would achieve stable governments.

417

In 1822, the armies of Bolívar and San Martín converged on Peru. There, the two great generals met. No records of this meeting exist. According to some sources, however, it is believed that at the meeting Bolívar and San Martín could not agree on a way to combine their talents and their armies. Afterward, San Martín quietly withdrew. Finally, in 1824, the last Spanish armies were driven from South America. In the same year, the Portuguese colony of Brazil also gained its independence.

All that remained of the once-great colonial empires of Spain and Portugal in the New World were a few Spanish holdings in the Caribbean Sea. For many Latin Americans, however, life changed little after independence. A tiny but wealthy minority and strong leaders backed by the strength of the armies still controlled the governments and the societies of these new nations. Political instability continued into the twentieth century throughout Latin America, while the desperate plight of the poor and the landless remained largely unchanged.

QUESTIONS FOR REVIEW

1 Who was Toussaint L'Ouverture?

2 In what ways did the first Mexican constitution fall short of forming a stable republic in Mexico?

3 Why did life change little for many Latin Americans after independence?

CHAPTER SUMMARY

The end of the 1700's and the first years of the 1800's were times of unrest and revolution throughout the European world. By the 1790's, the traditional feudal society of France had been completely overturned by the French Revolution, a development that would greatly influence Europe in the 1800's. The privileges of the royal court and of the powerful clergy and nobility were abolished. In their place, a shaky republican government ruled under the control of the French bourgeoisie. In 1799, Napoleon Bonaparte overthrew the republic and thus began a reign that continued for more than 15 years. During this time, Europe was rarely at peace, as the ambitious Napoleon built a European empire and then watched as it collapsed around him.

Freedom from foreign rule was gained by many British colonies in North America in the American War for Independence, which ended in the early 1780's. An American government was formed that reflected many of the important ideals of the European Enlightenment, including consent of the governed, personal liberty, and equality before the law.

Between 1790 and 1824, independence was also achieved by nearly every European colony in Latin America. Spanish, Portuguese, and French rule was ended throughout the region in all but a few small states and Caribbean islands.

CHAPTER 21 IN REVIEW

IMPORTANT WORDS, NAMES, AND TERMS

1 Explain, define, or identify each of the following:

Seven Years' War   Third Estate   émigrés
Stamp Act   tithe   Reign of
Declaration of   Louis XVI   Terror
    Independence   Declaration of the Rights   Code Napoleon
Old Regime   of Man and of the Citizen   caudillos

FACTS AND IDEAS

2 What impact did the French and Indian War have upon British policies toward the American colonies?

3 What was the direct result, in France, of French aid to the Americans during the American War for Independence?

4 What specific issue in the Estates-General led to the split between the Third Estate and King Louis XVI in 1789?

5 About when did the Jacobins take control of the French Revolution?

6 Who were Simón Bolívar and José de San Martín?

ANALYZING VISUAL MATERIAL

7 Study the political cartoon on page 401. What specific elements in the drawing portray the feelings of the American colonists toward British tax policies?

8 What was the significance of Napoleon's act in the painting on page 413? What impact do you think the act had upon French public opinion at the time?

CONCEPTS AND UNDERSTANDINGS

9 Why was the Battle of Saratoga considered the turning point of the American Revolution?

10 Why did France support the American struggle for independence?

11 In what ways did the French revolutionaries seek to make France more secular?

12 Why do you think many of the nations of Europe opposed Napoleon time after time?

13 In what ways did the caudillos stand in the way of stable government in Latin America during the nineteenth century?

PROJECTS AND ACTIVITIES

14 Organize and conduct a classroom debate on the influence of the ideas of the Enlightenment upon the American and French revolutions. Two important issues might be the economic and the social makeup of each country prior to revolution. Check library sources for more information on these revolutions.

15 Prepare a chart of the major differences in the legal systems of France, Great Britain, and the United States. Information about these various legal systems may be found in the library.

CHAPTER 22 INDUSTRIALIZATION AND REBELLION

1 The British Industrial Revolution   2 Industrialization and Its Impact   3 Changing Political Ideals in Europe   4 Reaction and Revolution in Europe

A revolution in industry, in agriculture, in transportation, and in communications transformed Europe and America during the nineteenth century. This revolution had its roots in developments that began in late eighteenth-century Great Britain. The Industrial Revolution, as it became known, brought power-driven machinery to industry. As a result, great progress and many improvements were made in society.

The Industrial Revolution also had a dark side. The human toll taken by exploitation, poverty, and unemployment during industrialization was great. Many people suffered as the first industrial society was formed. However, reforms were instituted and influential new ideas about how to reorganize society were soon put forward.

The years between 1815 and 1850 were characterized by important political developments. After the final defeat of Napoleon, the leaders of Europe reacted strongly, hoping to restore the Europe of 25 years before. Soon, however, the spread of republican ideas and of nationalism again challenged the old order in Europe.

One of the first useful steam engines—the Newcomen engine—was built in England in the early 1700's to pump water from flooded mines.

Walker Art Gallery

1 THE BRITISH INDUSTRIAL REVOLUTION

Far-reaching changes took place in Great Britain during the late 1700's and the early 1800's. Beginning around 1760, Great Britain began to undergo what many historians have commonly termed the Industrial Revolution. However, these changes were not as rapid as the term *revolution* might imply. Nevertheless, the changes were profound.

Industrialization is a process that involves a changeover from products made by hand to the mass production of goods by power-driven machinery. This process has helped create a world that is vastly different today from the world of 1700.

BRITAIN PRIOR TO INDUSTRIALIZATION
Before 1700, the English economy was almost entirely based upon agriculture. This was true even though the economy had become more commercial through increased trade and overseas colonization. Some historians estimate that at that time 75 percent of England's population was still supported by farming. Most of the people lived in small villages and tiny hamlets. London, the largest English city, had a population of about 500,000 in 1695, which was roughly one tenth of England's total population. Only a few towns had as many as 10,000 inhabitants.

Much of England's agriculture, particularly in the south and the west, was organized in the medieval common-field system. The lands surrounding a village were generally divided into three main fields from which each farmer received strips to cultivate. Every year a different field was left fallow in order to restore the soil. A separate common field and forest were also left uncultivated and were used by all the villagers to graze livestock and to hunt and fish.

During the early 1700's, many British goods, especially textiles, were manufactured by the domestic system. A merchant purchased raw materials and sold them to individual workers. Often, entire families worked in their homes to produce a finished product. In the cotton and woolen industries, for example, the work done in the home might have included spinning the raw cotton or wool into yarn and weaving the yarn into cloth. The weavers were free to work at their own pace. The merchant bought back the finished product and sold or traded it.

Although widespread, the domestic system of production was slow and often resulted in expensive products. In addition, merchants found it increasingly difficult to supply a growing market for manufactured goods. Slowly, the domestic system began to change, especially after 1750, as industrialization transformed the economic life of Great Britain.

IMPORTANT REASONS FOR BRITISH INDUSTRIALIZATION Great Britain was the first nation to undergo industrialization. Industrialization is a process by which the mass production of goods by power-driven machinery gradually replaces the production of goods by hand. Many important factors contributed to the British Industrial Revolution. Among these was the fact that Britain itself was an island. The British were isolated and protected from the destructive European wars of the eighteenth century. Moreover, during that time Britain became a leading maritime power. As a result of its geography and its naval strength, Britain became a center for international trade.

Although Britain was still primarily an agricultural nation during the early 1700's, the British had been developing a commercial economy for more than a century. The establishment of colonies provided British merchants and manufacturers with raw materials and with expanded markets for goods. The economic growth that resulted created a prosperous middle class. They demanded, and could afford, more manufactured goods. Some historians estimate that the average

POLITICAL		SOCIAL AND ECONOMIC
Seven Years' War ended	~1763	
	1769~	Spinning frame patented / Watt's steam engine built
United States Constitution written	~1787~	Power loom developed
French Revolution began	~1789	
	1793~	Cotton gin invented in America by Eli Whitney
Napoleon seized power in France	~1799	
	1807~	First practical steamship built by Robert Fulton
Congress of Vienna met	~1814~	George Stephenson successfully built a steam locomotive
Greek rebellion against Turks began	~1821	
	1825~	First public railroad opened in England / New Harmony, Indiana, founded
Reform Bill passed in Britain	~1832	
	1837~	Electric telegraph developed by Samuel Morse
British Parliament outlawed child and woman labor in mines	~1842	
Ten Hours Act established standard workday for women and children	~1848~	*Communist Manifesto* published
Louis Napoleon declared himself Napoleon III	~1852	

income in Great Britain during the mid-1700's was about 50 percent higher than in France and even higher than in other, poorer European countries. Britain's wealth meant that money was available to put into growing industries. A class of *entrepreneurs* [AHN-truh-pruh-NUHRZ]—people with new ideas on the organization and management of businesses, and with money to invest—also emerged.

Another important reason for the growth of industrialization was the development of a new technology. British inventors developed new machines and new techniques for the manufacture of goods. Natural resources that were important for manufacturing were also discovered during the Industrial Revolution. These resources, which included iron ore, water, and coal, were abundant in Great Britain.

A booming British population provided the needed labor for the advent of industrialization. Between 1750 and 1801, Great Britain's population increased by about 50 percent. During the next 50 years, the population nearly doubled. Agricultural production also increased as a result of changes in land distribution and of the development of new crops and new methods of farming.

AGRICULTURAL CHANGES Perhaps the most far-reaching of the agricultural changes in Britain during the eighteenth and nineteenth centuries was the land-enclosure movement. Land enclosure consisted of closing off open fields and commonly held lands by fences for private ownership. During the 1700's, more than 2,000,000 additional acres (809 400 hectares) were brought under cultivation in Britain, largely the result of enclosure.

Enclosure was the way in which small farmers—freeholders—or large landowners could consolidate the land that they owned. Consolidation resulted in more-efficient farm production because consolidated farms could practice more scientific agricultural techniques. However, tenant farmers and other villagers lost their rights to commonly held lands. As a result, many became farm laborers or were forced to seek work in the towns. Enclosure also led to the concentration of land in the hands of a few. By the 1870's less than 7,000 landowners held about 80 percent of the land in Great Britain.

The changes in farming during this time also included new methods of farming and the introduction of new crops. Jethro Tull (1674–1741) developed a seed drill that planted seeds in neat rows. Tull also believed that the soil around a plant should be broken up to allow better moisture absorption. As a result, he developed a hoe that could be pulled like a plow. Charles Townshend (1674–1738) introduced turnips for fodder and new methods of crop rotation and soil conservation. These and other agricultural improvements provided food for Britain's rapidly growing population.

THE REVOLUTION IN TEXTILE MANUFAC-TURING Great Britain's cotton industry had its start in the early 1700's. A small, domestic cotton industry grew up, in part, because powerful woolen manufacturers had succeeded in prohibiting cotton imports from India. Cotton goods made in Britain soon became extremely popular. In order to keep up with the demand for cotton goods, a series of laborsaving and timesaving machines were invented. The machines revolutionized the production of cotton fabric.

The first step toward the mechanization of textile production came with the invention of the flying shuttle in 1733. This device enabled weavers to double the amount of cotton cloth they wove each day. A shortage of cotton yarn quickly developed, however, because the production of yarn by spinners was still done entirely by hand.

In the 1760's, James Hargreaves invented the spinning jenny, a machine that increased the output of spinners and enabled them to keep pace with the greater production of the weavers. At first, the spinning jenny permitted a single worker to spin 8 threads onto separate spindles at the same time. As the machine was improved, as many as 80 threads could be spun by hand.

In 1769, Sir Richard Arkwright patented the spinning frame. Arkwright's water-powered machine was capable of spinning large quantities of cotton yarn with a minimum of human labor. The spinning mule, a combination water frame and spinning jenny, was

Power looms were faster than hand looms and required fewer operators. Hand weaving, which was widespread throughout Great Britain in the 1700's, declined rapidly during the early 1800's as power looms came into use and as industrialization spread.

Historical Pictures Service

developed in the 1770's. The coarse cotton and flax yarn produced by the spinning jenny soon gave way to the finer and stronger cotton thread spun by the "mule." In 1787, a power loom was first developed by Edmund Cartwright. During the 1820's, machine-powered weaving replaced hand weaving throughout England. Other improvements in the production of textiles were made in the printing and dyeing of cloth.

The quality and quantity of cotton textiles greatly increased because of industrialization. The price of cloth also continued to drop. The demand for raw cotton grew tremendously during this period. The southern United States became one of the largest suppliers of raw cotton to Britain during the first half of the 1800's. Eli Whitney's invention of the cotton gin in 1793 enabled cotton growers to clean their crop mechanically at a much faster rate than was possible by hand. Thus, American cotton growers could keep up with British demand for their product.

FACTORIES AND POWER–DRIVEN MACHINERY After the initial stages of the Industrial Revolution, several developments took place that speeded British industrial expansion. These were the development of power-driven machinery, of the factory system of production, and of new natural resources.

British textile manufacturing was first adapted to water-powered machinery in the 1770's, with the use of the spinning frame and the spinning mule. However, these machines soon grew to be too large, expensive, and complicated for a domestic worker to maintain. As a result, the machinery necessary for each step in the production of cotton textiles was soon housed in one place, rather than in a cottage or similar working area. The buildings in which all stages of the manufacturing process were carried out at the same time became known as *factories*.

Another factor that helped to speed British industrialization during the late 1700's was the development of the steam engine. As early as 1769, the Scottish inventor James Watt produced a steam engine that provided efficient machine power. Steam-powered factories, unlike those powered by water, could be located virtually anywhere. Thus, manufacturers could build factories near towns that supplied both markets for their goods and workers to operate their machines.

A tremendous expansion in Britain's industry followed the development of steam power. At the same time, towns where factories were located soon grew into large manufacturing centers.

IRON AND COAL Iron production was a sizable British industry by the 1760's. To continue expanding their industry, however, British iron manufacturers were forced to develop new fuel sources for their foundries. Supplies of charcoal that British ironmasters used to smelt iron began to run out. Thus, iron manufacturers began to experiment with coal—an abundant resource in Great Britain—as a source of fuel.

In the early 1700's, *coke*—a purified form of coal that burned cleanly and efficiently—was developed. Ironworkers soon perfected a process that used coke to smelt a highly refined type of iron. This process enabled British manufacturers to make great quantities of high-grade iron by using a cheap and readily available source of energy.

By the early 1800's, Great Britain was the world's leading producer and exporter of iron goods. At the same time, increased demands for coke led to the birth of a booming coal industry in Britain. The growth of its iron and coal industries became cornerstones of Britain's industrialization after the late 1700's. Other European countries, witnessing Great Britain's rapid industrial growth and the power and wealth that accompanied it, worked to follow the British example.

THE SPREAD OF INDUSTRIALIZATION Industrial growth on the European continent came most quickly to the tiny nation of Belgium. This probably resulted from Belgium's early adoption of British technology. Belgian coal producers, using British ideas, were soon able to outstrip the coal production of France. Belgian manufacturing also grew rapidly. During the mid-1800's, Belgium also boasted a large railroad network.

Industrialization moved at a much slower pace in France and in Germany. During the first half of the nineteenth century, French textile manufacturing and iron production began to modernize slowly. In the German states, however, political disunity greatly hindered German industrialization.

In 1834, many of the trade barriers, such as high tariffs, that had been erected among the German states were removed. German industry began to grow rapidly because of relaxed trade regulations and an abundance of raw materials. By 1900, Germany ranked among the leaders of the industrial world.

The United States, like Great Britain, began to industrialize in the late 1700's. During the early 1800's, many heavy industries were established in the northeastern United States, and the area soon became the nation's most industrialized region. By the late 1800's, the United States had also become a major industrial nation.

Initially, American industry was aided by British inventions and methods. Soon, however, American industrialists became less dependent on British ideas, as American inventors developed new machines. In fact, American inventiveness helped to overcome such limiting factors to industrialization as chronic shortages of both skilled and unskilled labor. Among the important American contributions to the Industrial Revolution was Eli Whitney's development of identical, machine-made interchangeable parts. Whitney's invention meant that the different parts of a product could be mass-produced and then assembled. To demon-

During the nineteenth century, industrialization spread throughout Europe. Industry in Germany, such as the ironworks pictured above, grew more rapidly than industry in any other European country.

strate his ideas, Whitney first used a rifle as a model.

The Industrial Revolution, however, was not a worldwide phenomenon during the nineteenth century. Many of the nations of eastern Europe, Asia, Africa, and South America became industrialized much more gradually than did western Europe and North America. Agriculture remained the economic basis of these regions well into the twentieth century. Even today, many countries throughout the world are still working to develop an industrial economy.

QUESTIONS FOR REVIEW

1 *What was the domestic system of production?*

2 *In what ways did the enclosure movement improve the agricultural productivity of eighteenth-century Britain?*

3 *Why was Belgium's industrial growth the most rapid on the European continent?*

2 INDUSTRIALIZATION AND ITS IMPACT

Industrialization led to major advances in transportation and in communication. Mechanization enabled more goods to be carried faster, farther, and more cheaply than ever before. At the same time, the development of the telegraph and the telephone sped communication among people throughout the world.

The Industrial Revolution, however, also created immense social problems. The rapid growth of cities led to unhealthy living and working conditions in many areas of industrialized Britain. Demands for cheap labor often resulted in the exploitation of women and children. Beginning in the 1830's, attempts were made to solve many of these problems.

TRANSPORTATION AND COMMUNICATION

Major advances in Britain's road system had been made even before industrialization began. Nevertheless, the transport of goods remained a slow process. As the Industrial Revolution gained momentum during the early 1800's, faster and cheaper ways to bring goods and raw materials to market were needed.

Canals were developed as a cheap form of transportation during the late 1700's and the early 1800's. New waterways that helped to lower the cost of shipping goods and raw materials were built throughout Britain by 1830. In the United States canal systems were also built to speed the transportation of goods. During the 1830's, American canal mileage tripled.

The development of steam-powered vehicles revolutionized travel and transportation. In the early 1800's, a wheeled steam engine was first used to haul coal. By the 1820's, George Stephenson, a British inventor, developed a powerful and efficient locomotive. During the next 40 years, rail systems were built throughout the United States and western Europe as well as Great Britain.

An American, Robert Fulton, built the first practical steamboat in 1807. By the 1860's, steamships had begun to replace sailing vessels for carrying goods such as mail. However, the less expensive sailing ships continued to carry most of the goods transported overseas until the early 1890's.

Other inventions revolutionized communication. The American inventor Samuel Morse developed the first telegraph. In 1866, the first intercontinental telegraph cable connected Europe with the United States. Alexander Graham Bell demonstrated the first telephone in 1876. By the end of the century, a wireless telegraph developed by the Italian inventor Marconi had transmitted a message across the Atlantic Ocean. A system of communication soon linked people throughout the world.

NEW LIFE–STYLES AND A GROWING POPULATION
The Industrial Revolution brought about many social as well as eco-

The Industrial Revolution stimulated many inventions, including Alexander Graham Bell's telephone.

nomic changes. During the early 1800's, the factory system became the primary way of manufacturing goods in Great Britain. New life-styles developed as workers had to meet the needs of the factory workday. The pace of life quickened accordingly. However, it should be understood that the Industrial Revolution did not change life in Britain overnight. Factory mechanization and hand labor existed together for many years.

Another phenomenon that accompanied industrialization and the changes in agriculture was a tremendous growth in European and American population. Between 1800 and 1900, the population of Great Britain, for example, increased by more than 250 percent. The annual growth rate in Britain reached a peak of 16 percent between 1811 and 1821.

Other industrialized countries experienced similar growth. Europe's overall population doubled during the 1800's. During the same period, Germany's population also

Poverty and crowded slums—especially in London—were two of the results of industrialization in England.

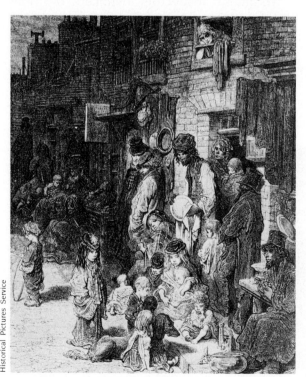

grew by 100 percent. In the United States, the population increase between 1800 and 1900 was a staggering 1,400 percent. However, this growth rate was partly due to increased immigration. In France, where industrialization was more gradual, the population increased by only about 50 percent during the same period.

Experts are unsure of the reasons for this population explosion. Early historians believed that medical advances and a declining death rate resulted in this growth. Today, many scholars add other factors to this list, including the disappearance of terrible epidemics and a rising birthrate that was due in large part to changing ideas about the appropriate age for marriage and to a growing desire for larger families in industrialized societies. Increased agricultural production during the 1800's fed the growing population.

Cities also grew rapidly during the nineteenth century. As industrialization spread, new jobs and economic opportunities drew people to the growing urban centers. By 1850, one half of the British population lived in cities. The United States and many industrialized nations in Europe also experienced rapid urban growth.

THE EFFECTS OF INDUSTRIALIZATION
The rapid rise of urban industrial centers in Great Britain during the first half of the nineteenth century helped to create a new society. However, British society, which was unprepared for this growth, was beset by immense problems. Many cities could not keep pace with the demand for housing. As a result, old buildings became dangerously overcrowded. New construction was often flimsy and hastily built. Public sanitation barely existed in many parts of the booming factory towns. In 1844, an observer wrote,

Every great city has one or more slums, where the working class is crowded together. . . . The streets are generally unpaved, rough, dirty, filled with vegetable and animal refuse, without sewers or gutters, . . .

Working conditions in the industrial towns were often deplorable. Dingy, unsafe, and poorly lit factories and long, monotonous workdays—sometimes as long as 16 hours—for low wages were all too common. In 1854, Charles Dickens bitingly described life in an industrial town in his novel *Hard Times*:

It [the town] contained several large streets all very like one another, and many small streets still more like one another, inhabited by people equally like one another, who all went in and out at the same hours, with the same sound upon the same pavements, to do the same work, and to whom every day was the same as yesterday and to-morrow, and every year the counterpart of the last and the next.

Many historians today believe that views of the Industrial Revolution as a time of declining living standards and wretched factory conditions are somewhat exaggerated. They point out that workers who moved from farms to factories often benefited economically. Moreover, large, up-to-date factories were generally better places to work than small workshops. However, most scholars agree that miserable conditions in many factory centers did indeed exist.

The most tragic and well-documented consequence of rapid industrial growth was the exploitation of children in factories and in mines. Many industrialists sought to lower their costs by employing children, who were expected to work for relatively low wages. Cruel and ruthless factory owners sometimes employed children as young as four or five years old. The first laws regulating the employment of children were not passed until the 1830's, when reform of many of the worst outrages of industrialization began in Great Britain.

REFORM The conditions that faced workers in many parts of industrialized Britain gradually gained the attention of the entire country. Such notable leaders as Lord Palmerston and Sir Robert Peel pushed reform measures through Parliament to deal with some of industrialized society's worst problems.

The first effective reform of British industry was the Factory Act of 1833. This law was aimed at child employment. Employment of children under the age of 9 was prohibited by the act. A 9-hour workday was established for children between the ages of 9 and 13. A 12-hour workday was set for workers between the ages of 13 and 18. Government inspectors enforced the new law. In 1842, an act of Parliament outlawed woman labor and child labor in British mines. In 1847, the Ten Hours Act established a standard workday for women and children.

(*Text continued on page* 430.)

A great need for cheap labor in early industrial England led to the exploitation of children in mines and in factories. This practice was not confined to Great Britain, however, and child labor was used throughout the industrializing world.

The Bettmann Archive

Biography

Charles Dickens

One of the best known social critics of the mid-1800's was the English writer Charles Dickens. Dickens was a lifelong observer of the social problems that plagued industrialized Britain. Dickens was sympathetic to the poor and the helpless, and he bitterly attacked the greed and the cruelty that he saw around him.

Dickens's writing career began in 1833, when he contributed stories to various magazines and newspapers. In 1836, Dickens became famous for *The Pickwick Papers*, a novel serialized in a monthly magazine. In 1837, *Oliver Twist*, a story about a penniless orphan in which Dickens criticized the mistreatment of England's poor, began to appear as a monthly serial. Many other works followed, including *David Copperfield*, *A Tale of Two Cities*, *Great Expectations*, *Hard Times*, and *Bleak House*. One of Dickens's most beloved books was *A Christmas Carol*, written in only a few weeks in 1843. It tells the story of a selfish old man who finally learns the true meaning of the Christmas spirit.

Dickens's vivid descriptions of contemporary English life were realistic and often bleak, particularly in his later writing. In *Hard Times*, published in 1854, he described an industrial town:

"It had a black [badly polluted] canal in it, and a river that ran purple with ill-smelling dye, and vast piles of buildings full of windows where there was a rattling and a trembling all day long, and where the piston of the steam-engine worked monotonously up and down, like the head of an elephant in a state of melancholy madness."

Dickens's social opinions often found a journalistic outlet. In 1849, he wrote a series of newspaper stories about a farm for pauper children. Conditions on the farm, Dickens claimed, had led to an outbreak of cholera that killed many of the children:

"The dietary of the children is so unwholesome and insufficient that they climb secretly over palings [picket fences], and pick out scraps of sustenance from the tubs of hog-wash. Their clothing by day, and their covering by night, are shamefully defective. Their rooms are cold, damp, dirty, and rotten. In a word, the age of miracles is past, and of all conceivable places in which pestilence [disease] might—or rather *must*—be expected to break out, and to make direful ravages, Mr. Drouet's model farm stands foremost."

During his lifetime, Dickens achieved worldwide fame and popularity, touring America in 1867–68. His masterful plots, vivid imagery, and observations of life continue to entertain readers today. Dickens's importance as a novelist, however, is matched by his significance as a social observer and a critic of life in industrialized Britain.

Charles Dickens (right) was often critical of the social problems that were caused by Britain's industrialization. Below is a scene from Dickens's novel Oliver Twist.

The first law regarding public education was passed in the 1830's, but by the late 1860's, only about one half of Britain's school-age children attended school. It was not until the 1870's that Parliament empowered local governments to set up elementary schools and to thus provide education for all children.

During the early 1800's, the first British unions were formed to fight for higher wages and for better factory conditions. By the 1820's, labor unions had become legalized in Britain. Early British unions, however, were limited in their power because union actions, such as strikes, were prohibited. Unions were finally permitted the right to strike in Great Britain in the 1870's.

Representation in Parliament was also changed during this time by the passage of the Reform Bill of 1832. The impact of this law was widely felt. New and rising industrial centers, such as Manchester and Birmingham, gained a greater voice in the House of Commons. The right to vote was extended to many well-to-do members of the middle class and was no longer limited only to aristocratic landowners. As a result, control of Parliament by the landed aristocracy was ended.

Women also gradually won equal political rights. Laws were changed to allow women to buy, sell, and inherit property, although British women did not win the right to vote until 1918.

QUESTIONS FOR REVIEW

1 *What developments sped travel during the Industrial Revolution?*

2 *How did many industrialists seek to lower their costs during the early 1800's?*

3 *Why was the Reform Bill of 1832 a democratic measure?*

3 CHANGING POLITICAL IDEALS IN EUROPE

During the mid-1800's, people worked to solve the social problems that had been created by early industrialization. Two related schools of thought—socialism and Marxism—developed during this time. Reformers of both schools were sympathetic to the plight of the poor and exploited workers and were outraged by the often miserable working and living conditions of industrial workers. As a result, many social reformers worked to transform industrialized society.

HOPE FOR A NEW SOCIETY During the early 1800's, a number of reformers believed that it was necessary to rebuild the unplanned, often unjust capitalist society of the early Industrial Revolution. These reformers became known as *socialists*. Basically, socialists felt that government action was needed to solve many of the problems of an industrialized society. Many of their ideas came from the thinkers of the Enlightenment. Like the philosophes, the early socialists believed in the basic goodness of people. Many socialists dreamed of creating an ideal society, called a *utopia*.

Among the first of the utopian socialists was Comte Henri de Saint-Simon (1760–1825), who expressed the idea that an industrial society must be planned in order to alleviate many of its worst problems. He also attacked the inequalities of industrialized society. Saint-Simon's writings influenced later socialists, who advanced the novel idea that private property should be abolished to eliminate social exploitation.

François Fourier (1772–1837) imagined a new society divided into model communities. Individuals would work at the tasks for which they were best suited. Although the products of Fourier's model communities would be shared by all, they would not be equally divided. Workers with special skills or responsibilities might receive larger shares, according to Fourier's plan.

Robert Owen's effort to build a utopian socialist community at New Harmony, Indiana, only succeeded for a short time.

The most practical socialist of this period was the British reformer Robert Owen (1771–1858). Owen believed that the environment in which people lived was crucial in molding their lives and their characters. As part owner and manager of a large textile mill in New Lanark, Scotland, Owen was able to put his ideas into practice. He provided workers in New Lanark with high wages and with safe and healthy working conditions. He strictly controlled child labor and established schools for the children of the community. Owen's mill was tremendously profitable, in large part because worker productivity reflected the mill's exceptional working environment. In 1825, Owen helped found a model American community at New Harmony, Indiana. This experiment, however, soon failed.

Although later socialists continued to disagree about the ways in which their ideas should be put into action, they generally believed in the same goals. Socialists argued that the capitalist zeal for profits often caused certain social evils. In addition, socialists held that the government should own many of the means of production, such as factories and mines, and the means of distributing goods, such as railroads and shipping. Many socialists believed that these actions would rid society of the inequalities of capitalism. Finally, these changes should be brought about gradually and peacefully. During the 1840's, however, an offshoot of socialism that preached violent revolution developed.

THE COMMUNIST MANIFESTO An obscure pamphlet, entitled the *Communist Manifesto*, was published in early 1848 by two German intellectuals, Karl Marx (1818–1883) and Friedrich Engels (1820–1895). This short essay put forward several startling and radical ideas. Although the essay appeared as revolutions were sweeping across Europe, its ideas had little impact on these movements. However, the *Manifesto* has dominated socialist thinking since the late nineteenth century.

Marx was born into a well-to-do German family. Educated in philosophy but unable to teach because of his criticism of religion, Marx turned to journalism. In Paris during the 1840's, Marx met his lifelong friend and partner, Engels. Engels and Marx were influenced by socialist thought after witnessing

The radical thinkers Karl Marx (top) and Friedrich Engels (bottom) called for a reorganization of society in their *Communist Manifesto.*

the miserable conditions faced by Europe's working classes. Constantly involved in radical circles, Marx and Engels were driven into exile, and fled first to Brussels, Belgium, and later to London.

Borrowing ideas from the German philosopher Georg Hegel (1770–1831) and from socialist thinkers, Marx developed a compelling and influential doctrine. Marx held that history was a process of continual conflict among social classes. However, according to Marx, this class struggle had not

always existed. Most prehistoric societies, Marx believed, had been classless. But as civilization emerged, classes of exploiters and exploited were formed. This conflict first appeared with the unequal ownership of land. Later, according to Marx, the development of *capitalism*—the private ownership of land, factories, and other means of production—led to great inequalities between classes. A class of owners—the bourgeoisie—had developed under capitalism. Marx believed that the bourgeoisie exploited the wage-earning working class—called the *proletariat.* In the *Manifesto*, Marx and Engels stated that the conflict between the bourgeoisie and the proletariat would inevitably lead to revolution. The revolution would not be gradual or peaceful. From the ashes of this revolution, a new society would arise.

In 1867, Marx published the first volume of his monumental work, *Das Kapital.* This book further laid out his theory of social and economic development. Two more volumes of *Das Kapital*, edited by Engels, were published after Marx's death.

THE IDEAS OF MARX Marx labeled his own brand of socialism *scientific socialism*, to distinguish it from the utopian socialism of other thinkers. Marx believed that his philosophy was based upon scientific analysis. He claimed to have discovered the true character of history, which led inevitably to the overthrow of capitalism. Marx's basic belief was that economics shaped history. Moreover, he declared, the struggle between classes had existed in each historical age. In ancient Greece, the class struggle had pitted slave against master. In Rome, plebeians had struggled against patricians. Medieval Europe was characterized by the conflict of serf against lord. The dramatic and far-reaching changes of the Commercial and Industrial revolutions had created two new antagonists, the proletariat and the bourgeoisie.

Marx also pointed to many factors of the

capitalist economic system that led to class conflict. Marx held that under capitalism, workers did not receive the full value of the goods that they produced. Put simply, if workers could live at a bare subsistence level with 6 hours of labor but were required to work 12 hours, the factory owners would be in control of 6 hours of "surplus value." This surplus value provided added profits and capital for the capitalist—the bourgeoisie. However, the workers received barely enough to survive. As a result, Marx believed, the rich became richer and the poor became poorer.

Marx believed that crises would result from the inability of the poor workers to buy the products that they manufactured. This situation would lead to an overproduction of goods. Unemployment would then result because of cutbacks in production by the manufacturers. This never-ending cycle would become steadily more severe, until the economic system collapsed into revolution. Marx went on to state that the outcome of this revolution would be a takeover of the means of production by the proletariat. A "classless society" would be established, private property would be abolished, and social conflict would end.

EVALUATING MARX From the time of Marx's first published writings, his ideas were widely criticized. Even before Marxism gained a wide audience in the late 1800's, historians and economists had begun to attack the weaknesses and oversimplifications in Marx's works. For example, the Marxist idea that economics was the sole force behind historical events and the molder of human character seemed to be a great oversimplification. Marx's interpretation of history failed to account for such personal elements as religion, idealism, and patriotism. Indeed, fervent *nationalism*—feelings of intense patriotism toward one's own country—was a constant and powerful force in world history even before Marx published his ideas.

Marx's concept of surplus value has also come under attack by many modern scholars. They argue that labor unions and progressive labor laws have allowed workers to strike, to bargain for higher wages, and to win higher living standards. As a result, workers in many industrialized countries have steadily earned a growing portion of the value of the goods they produce.

Another factor unforeseen by Marx, according to modern scholars, was the rise of a large and influential middle class. In many western countries, this class has served as a buffer between the extremes of the owning classes and the working classes.

Another Marxist idea that has been greatly altered by events in the past century is the "withering away" of government. In essence, Marx believed that after a communist revolution, government would no longer be needed, since the exploitation of workers would cease. In contrast to this Marxist belief, governments in countries in which *communism*—an economic system based upon Marxist doctrine—has been established have grown tremendously. Many communist nations of the twentieth century have created centralized governments supported by immense bureaucracies.

Marx's ideas have formed an important body of thought since the late nineteenth century. Today, the governments of many nations, such as the Soviet Union and the People's Republic of China, have been established upon the principles of Karl Marx.

QUESTIONS FOR REVIEW

1 Who was Robert Owen?

2 How did the Communist Manifesto explain the workings of history?

3 Why have scholars criticized Marx's theory of surplus value?

4 REACTION AND REVOLUTION IN EUROPE

At the same time that industrialization was transforming the economic and social life of western Europe, two new forces—liberalism and nationalism—brought many more changes to Europe. With the defeat of Napoleon in 1815, the aristocratic rulers of Europe sought to restore the political, social, and economic conditions they had enjoyed before 1789. But they failed to realize the power of the new forces that had arisen in Europe since the French Revolution. By the 1820's, liberalism and nationalism had weakened aristocratic power in many countries. For the next 30 years, revolutions spread across Europe. Although many of these movements failed, they signaled the birth of modern European social and political thought.

THE CONGRESS OF VIENNA European leaders met in the Austrian city of Vienna in September 1814. Their purpose was to bring order to Europe after years of wars, revolution, and unrest. With the defeat of Napoleon and of the republican ideas that had grown during the French Revolution, the European nobility sought to reestablish the traditions of an earlier era.

The most-influential aristocratic diplomat at Vienna was Prince von Metternich of Austria. Others who worked to restore the old order included Viscount Castlereagh of Great Britain, Czar Alexander I of Russia, and Prince von Hardenberg of Prussia. Later, the French foreign minister, Talleyrand, became an important member of this group.

To reestablish monarchial rule and the pre-Napoleonic order of Europe, delegates at the Congress of Vienna agreed to follow certain principles. These principles included creating a balance of power among European nations that was aimed at weakening France. Also, the leaders at Vienna wanted to restore the former rulers of kingdoms that had been dissolved by Napoleon. Finally, the delegates were determined to redraw the map of Europe in an effort to strengthen conservative countries that would, in turn, work to preserve Europe's traditional order. At the same time, the delegates wanted to weaken countries that might threaten the old order, as France had done under Napoleon.

One of the most important elements in the reorganization of Europe was the establishment of a balance of power. The leaders at Vienna felt that it was necessary to prevent one nation from becoming powerful enough to dominate Europe. They also feared that the growth of liberal ideas in one nation could spread to other nations, thus threatening the old order. As a result, a system of alliances that was intended to strengthen the old order in Europe was created at Vienna. This system, largely the work of Metternich, resulted in the Quadruple Alliance, which united Great Britain, Austria, Russia, and Prussia by treaty. By 1818, France had joined the alliance as well.

The leaders at Vienna also restored many of the monarchies that had been overthrown during the Napoleonic era. The Bourbons were returned to the French throne, and Louis XVIII was crowned king. However, France was confined to its 1790 frontiers. Other countries, including Spain, Holland, and Switzerland, regained their independence (see map on page 436). What had been the Holy Roman Empire remained divided, and a confederation of German states was created that was dominated by Austria.

Stability and order in Europe, however, were short-lived. Within a few years, revolutions again challenged the power of the European aristocracy.

REBELLION SPREADS ACROSS EUROPE The leaders of the Congress of Vienna failed to realize that two powerful forces had emerged in post-Napoleonic Europe. These

Europe in 1815

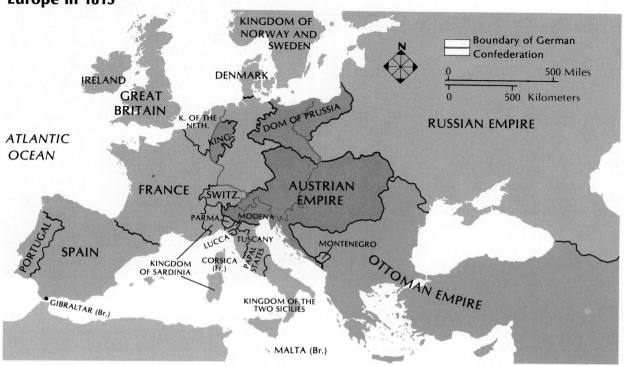

At the Congress of Vienna in 1815, the most influential leaders of Europe redrew the boundaries of many European countries in the hope of returning to the balance of power of pre-Napoleonic times.

forces were liberalism and nationalism. European leaders had hoped to maintain the power of the landed aristocracy through the agreements reached at Vienna. To accomplish this, Metternich and the other diplomats had redrawn the map of Europe with little regard for the nationalistic feelings that were growing throughout Europe. The demands of German, Italian, and Belgian patriots and of patriots in other countries were ignored in order to satisfy the old aristocracy.

The growth of nationalism in Europe was accompanied by the spread of liberalism. Liberals, who were mainly middle class, sought more of a voice in the affairs of government. They resented the ways in which many of the rulers of Europe suppressed individual freedoms after 1815.

The forces of nationalism and liberalism soon challenged European stability. In 1820, riots and demonstrations forced the Spanish king, Ferdinand VII, to restore Spain's liberal constitution of 1812, which the monarch had chosen to ignore. With the aid of a French army, the rebellion was brutally crushed. However, Spain's rulers continually battled attempts by liberals to control the government well into the twentieth century.

In 1821, a liberal revolution occurred in Italy. However, an Austrian army occupied the Italian peninsula the next year and restored the absolute rulers of the region to their thrones. By 1826, a liberal rebellion in Portugal had also failed.

Nationalism was a greater force in the revolutions of Greece and of Belgium. In 1821, the Greeks rebelled against their Turkish rulers. Eight years later, with aid from Russia, Great Britain, and France, the Greeks won their independence from the crumbling Ottoman Empire.

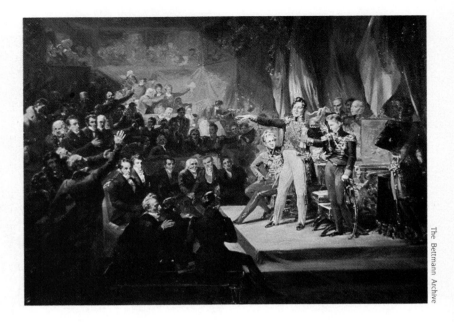

Louis Philippe became king of France in July 1830. But he did not turn out to be the liberal that many of his supporters had hoped for. By 1848, many French citizens had become unhappy with the "Bourgeois Monarchy," and revolts spread across France. As a result, Louis Philippe was forced to flee to England.

The Belgians had long resented becoming part of Holland in 1815. Language and religious differences led to clashes between the Belgians and the Dutch. In 1830, the Belgians finally succeeded in establishing their own nation. In eastern Europe, on the other hand, an unsuccessful revolt took place in 1830, when Polish nationalists failed to gain their independence from Russia.

REVOLUTIONS IN FRANCE In July 1830, the increasingly harsh regime of Charles X, the Bourbon king of France, provoked the French people into open rebellion. Unable to push his programs through the national legislature, King Charles had dissolved the body. In addition, he had censored the press and had severely limited voting rights. Outraged by these unconstitutional measures, the people of Paris revolted. The king was forced to abdicate, and a new government was set up. But France remained a monarchy, and Louis Philippe, an aristocrat who enjoyed widespread popularity among the French middle class, became king.

The new French king did not claim to rule by divine right, as his predecessors had.

Instead, Louis Philippe supported a somewhat liberal French constitution. For the next 18 years, the pro-business and pro-middle class monarch reigned. France enjoyed a measure of prosperity, and the nation's economy gradually became industrialized.

Yet the "Bourgeois Monarchy," as people referred to the reign of Louis Philippe, had many weaknesses. The right to vote was still limited primarily to the wealthy middle class. Moreover, the middle class gave little support to the call for increased political rights for the rest of the population. Louis Philippe also continued to censor the press. The fact that industrialization benefited only the bourgeoisie—and not the working class—was another injustice that Louis Philippe did nothing to correct. As a result, many of the social problems that had plagued Great Britain during the early stages of industrialization began to be felt in France.

Early in 1848, the discontent that had been brewing in France throughout Louis Philippe's reign exploded in revolution. Barricades appeared on the streets of Paris, as they had 18 years before. The rebellion gained momentum as the citizens clashed with government troops. Finally, Louis Philippe was forced to flee the country. The French monarchy was once again abolished by the republican forces. The vote was extended to every citizen, and the Second French Republic was proclaimed.

The new republican government of France, however, could not cope with France's growing number of unemployed. Weak and poorly planned reforms were often useless and angered the French workers. A bloody revolt of Parisian workers took place during the summer of 1848, but it was eventually put down by the government. Fear of continued violence frightened voters throughout the more-conservative French countryside. Many of the French hoped to recapture the magic of the Napoleonic legend. As a result, they chose Napoleon's nephew and heir, Louis Napoleon, as president of the Second Republic.

Louis Napoleon believed that he alone should rule France. In 1851, he seized control of the French government by force. The following year, he declared himself Napoleon III, emperor of a new French empire. The attempt at republican government in France again had failed.

POLITICAL CHANGE IN GREAT BRITAIN

The stability of the British political system contrasted sharply with the upheaval on the European continent between 1820 and 1850. As you have read, the British Reform Bill of 1832 marked a significant change in the political structure of Parliament. More political power was extended to the upper middle class and to the voters of the industrial centers of Britain. A major step in the peaceful evolution of a truly democratic government had been taken.

Other reforms were also made in Britain during this period. Badly needed factory reform laws were passed. Slavery was abolished throughout British-held lands in 1833. The election of local town officials was also approved by Parliament. This helped break the hold of aristocrats on local affairs.

During the 1830's, a potentially explosive movement, known as Chartism, grew up in Britain. The Chartists were made up of England's working class. The name "Chartist" came from the People's Charter, a document that members of the movement drafted to forward their demands for sweeping political changes. The Chartists demanded the extension of voting rights to all citizens. In addition, they called for the adoption of the secret ballot to eliminate coercion and unfair influence at polling places. Chartists also argued that members of Parliament should receive salaries. This, they believed, would enable poorer citizens to hold office. These demands were eventually passed into law. In large part, British democracy became based upon these principles.

Another important development in Britain during the mid-1800's was the repeal of the Corn Laws. The powerful landed interests in

In 1848, Europe was rocked by revolutions. In February and again in June of that year, revolts in Paris led to bloody fighting in the streets.

The Bettmann Archive

Britain had long succeeded in keeping high tariffs on all imported grains. But the tremendous growth of Britain's population created a need for more and cheaper foodstuffs. This need forced the repeal of the high tariffs, which in turn lowered the price of food and eased the country's growing food shortages. The repeal of the Corn Laws also led, in part, to the adoption of free-trade policies in many other areas of the British economy.

MID–NINETEENTH CENTURY REVOLUTIONS IN PERSPECTIVE Many of the revolutions that took place in Europe between 1820 and 1850 were unsuccessful. However, these upheavals helped to show the growing importance of the middle classes and helped to spread democratic ideals throughout Europe. Perhaps the greatest liberal gains were made in the commercial and industrial centers of western Europe—Great Britain, Belgium, and France—where influential middle classes had developed. It seems that where business and industry had made little progress, liberal revolutionary movements stalled or were defeated. In these areas, nationalism, more than liberalism, caused discontent among the people.

For the first time, many Europeans came to think seriously of themselves as members of national groups—German, Italian, Belgian, Greek, Polish, or any one of a number of others. Many of these national groups also supported liberal reforms, but national unity was their primary goal. By the end of the nineteenth century, successful struggles for national independence had taken place in many parts of Europe.

QUESTIONS FOR REVIEW

1 *Who was Prince von Metternich?*

2 *In what ways did the reign of Louis Philippe fail to satisfy the people of France?*

3 *Why was liberalism probably more influential in western Europe than in eastern Europe during the mid-1800's?*

CHAPTER SUMMARY

The Industrial Revolution began in Great Britain during the late 1700's. Industrialization was based upon the mass production of goods by power-driven machinery. This occurred first in British textile manufacturing and quickly spread to other areas of British industry. During the 1800's, industrialization spread to the countries of northern and western Europe, and to North America as well.

The benefits of the Industrial Revolution were great. However, severe social problems also appeared. As a result, new ideas about society, such as socialism and Marxism, emerged.

The first half of the nineteenth century was also a time of political change in Europe. The Congress of Vienna sought to reestablish the old order of Europe in 1815. In reaction to this effort, open rebellion fueled by two new powerful forces—nationalism and liberalism—took place in many countries.

CHAPTER 22 IN REVIEW

IMPORTANT WORDS, NAMES, AND TERMS

1 Explain, define, or identify each of the following:

domestic system	George Stephenson	proletariat
entrepreneurs	Factory Act	nationalism
spinning mule	utopia	Congress of Vienna
James Watt	*Communist Manifesto*	Chartism

FACTS AND IDEAS

2 What factors helped Great Britain industrialize?

3 How did the land-enclosure movement change the traditional ideas of land ownership in Great Britain during the 1700's?

4 Which machines revolutionized textile manufacturing before 1800?

5 What was the philosophy of Robert Owen?

6 What principles guided the reorganization of Europe in 1815?

ANALYZING VISUAL MATERIAL

7 How were the developments pictured on pages 420, 423, and 426 characteristic of the changes brought about by the Industrial Revolution?

8 Study the illustration of Robert Owen's utopian socialist community on page 431 and compare the organization of this community with the organization of your neighborhood or community.

CONCEPTS AND UNDERSTANDINGS

9 How did industrialization change the nature of the workday?

10 Why was improved transportation important to early industrial societies?

11 In what ways do some modern historians disagree with the traditional view that the Industrial Revolution lowered the standard of living of Britain's working class?

12 Why do you think reforms aimed at child labor did not come about until the 1830's?

13 Why did the ideas of Karl Marx come under attack almost as soon as they were published?

PROJECTS AND ACTIVITIES

14 Make a chart or a bulletin-board display showing some of the important inventions and their inventors between 1800 and 1900.

15 The first 50 years of the nineteenth century were rich in literature. Choose a few examples of writing from this period to present to the class. You may wish to describe to the class the types of subjects that concerned nineteenth-century writers. Authors might include Charles Dickens, Victor Hugo, Lord Byron, Johann von Goethe, Herman Melville, Edgar Allan Poe, Percy Bysshe Shelley, and Sir Walter Scott. Information on these and other writers of the time may be found in biographies, anthologies, and encyclopedia articles.

23 IMPERIALISM AND NATIONALISM

1 Imperial Powers of Western Europe **2** The Unification of Italy **3** Germany Unites **4** Changes in Eastern Europe

Political developments during the mid-nineteenth century helped to shape many of the nations of modern Europe. Italy and Germany became unified states in these years. At the same time, national feelings began to grow among the many diverse peoples that made up the Austrian Empire. Not all nationalistic movements in eastern Europe, however, were successful. As a result, the seeds of European conflict were sown in this period of nation building. Among the major causes of tension in Europe was the gradual disintegration of the Ottoman Empire. The breakup of the Ottoman Empire led in turn to increased European intervention in the Balkan Peninsula. Thus, the old order in Europe continued to decline during the mid-1800's in the face of new social and political realities.

National Gallery, London

J.M.W. Turner's work *Rain, Steam, and Speed—The Great Western Railway,* painted in 1844, symbolized the changes brought about by industry.

1 IMPERIAL POWERS OF WESTERN EUROPE

After the revolutionary upheavals of 1848, the states of continental Europe enjoyed a period of stability and prosperity. France flourished under the Second Empire, formed by Napoleon III. Prussia's political and economic influence over other German states continued to grow. However, the Austrian Empire, which had remained largely unchanged under the conservative policies of Prince von Metternich, experienced increasing difficulties. By 1848, the various peoples that made up the empire had begun to challenge the monarchy and to demand independence.

In the mid-nineteenth century, Great Britain was the most industrialized nation in the world. Overseas, the British controlled an expanding colonial empire. At home, they consolidated their democratic form of government. The right to vote was extended to more people, and education became more widespread. Thus, the British continued to combine economic growth with social and political reforms during the mid-1800's.

THE GROWING STRENGTH OF THE GERMANIES In the years after the Congress of Vienna, Germany remained disunited. However, two German states—Austria and Prussia—had joined the ranks of the European powers during the eighteenth century. After 1815, Prussia played an increasingly important role in German affairs. The rise of Prussia caused German nationalists to hope that the German people might one day be united.

During the first 50 years of the nineteenth century, the economies of Prussia and the other German states remained primarily agricultural. About two thirds of the German people were still engaged in farming at mid-century. During the 1830's and the 1840's, however, German industry gradually began to modernize. The Zollverein—a customs union of German states, established in 1834 to create freer trade between members—had helped to unite the economies of the various northern German states.

Another important development in the German states prior to 1850 was the rapid building of a unified railway system. Between about 1835 and 1850, private and state-funded railway construction boomed. By 1848, 1,500 miles (2 400 kilometers) of railroad track had been laid in Prussia. By the next year, over 3,000 miles (4 800 kilometers) of track existed in the German states. The expansion of railroads, like the growth of economic unity largely brought about by the Zollverein, helped to bring the German people closer together.

German liberals and nationalists joined in the revolutionary spirit that swept Europe in 1848, and they eventually brought about some liberal reforms. In 1850, the king granted the Prussian people a more liberal constitution, which established a legislative body with an upper and a lower house. German unification, however, remained a distant goal.

THE AUSTRIAN EMPIRE After 1815, the Austrian Empire and the policies of Prince von Metternich led Europe in a return to aristocratic, monarchical rule. Metternich reached the peak of his power in 1819, when he helped the leaders of several German states to put down student protests. In Austria, Metternich successfully stifled the forces of liberalism until 1848 by using strict censorship and the court police.

Unlike Great Britain, Austria was still overwhelmingly agricultural in 1840. Society was dominated by the nobility. The peasantry—the vast majority of the population—continued to pay various feudal dues and tithes. Few peasants were free of these obligations and few owned land.

The Austrian Empire was also a land of many ethnic minorities. The peoples that made up the empire in the early 1800's

SOCIAL AND ECONOMIC

POLITICAL		SOCIAL AND ECONOMIC
	1834 –	Creation of Zollverein established economic unity in northern Germany
Queen Victoria came to British throne	– 1837	
The French overthrew "Bourgeois Monarchy" of Louis Philippe	– 1848	
	1849 –	German railway system expanded to 3,000 miles
	1851 –	Great Exhibition opened in London
Cavour became Sardinian prime minister	– 1852	
Crimean War began	– 1854 –	Alfred, Lord Tennyson, wrote "The Charge of the Light Brigade"
	1856 –	Bessemer process for making steel developed
Garibaldi and the Thousand invaded Sicily	– 1860	
	1861 –	Russian serfs freed by Czar Alexander II
	1866 –	Swedish inventor Alfred Nobel developed dynamite
Dual monarchy of Austria-Hungary formed	– 1867	
	1870 –	British education expanded after passage of Education Act
German Reich created French Third Republic formed	– 1871	
	1876 –	Alexander Graham Bell invented telephone
Congress of Berlin met to redraw map of Balkans	– 1878	

included Germans, Magyars, Slovenes, Croatians, Serbians, Italians, Poles, and Czechs. During the 1840's, many of these groups began to demand greater independence and self-government.

In 1848, the forces of liberal reform and of national unity that had been brewing in the Austrian Empire led to open rebellion. Encouraged by the revolution that had broken out in Paris in March, liberals and nationalists alike rebelled. Metternich, who could not depend upon the loyalty of the Austrian army, fled the country. The emperor, feeble-minded Ferdinand I, gave in to demands for a convention to draw up a liberal constitution.

In that part of the empire known as Hungary, nationalists called for the adoption of a separate constitution. Lajos Kossuth, a Hungarian patriot, led a new government in a determined effort to establish Hungarian independence. A similar revolt by Czech nationalists took place in Bohemia. However, it was put down a short time later by the Austrian army.

In the midst of these rebellions, the weak emperor was replaced by his nephew Francis Joseph. Following the imperial victory over the Czech nationalists, the Austrian government crushed the Hungarians' dreams of independence with the help of Russian troops sent by Nicholas I. Kossuth and his rebel followers were defeated and brutally hunted down by the imperial army. Nonetheless, although the Austrian Empire remained intact, it had been seriously weakened by the Hungarian uprising.

THE SECOND FRENCH EMPIRE In France, the Revolution of 1848 had overthrown the "Bourgeois Monarchy" of Louis Philippe. In its place, Napoleon III, taking firm control of France, created the Second French Empire. Under the new emperor, domestic enterprise and foreign investment were actively encouraged, and France enjoyed two decades of growth and prosperity.

During his reign, Napoleon III also set out to restore Paris to its former position as Europe's cultural center. Many parts of Paris were torn down, replanned, and rebuilt. Streets were widened into beautiful boulevards. Museums were improved, and a new railway system, new churches, and a new opera house were added to the city as well.

The rebuilding of Paris provided steady jobs and good wages for many Parisians. As a result, there was little worker unrest in Paris during this period. Interestingly, the construction of wider streets eventually made it more difficult for Parisian rioters to build barricades, as they had done in the revolutions of the past.

Napoleon III also worked to restore French prestige in foreign affairs, which had steadily declined since 1815. In 1854, France joined Great Britain and the Ottoman Empire in a war against Russia. The Russian czar, Nicholas I, hoped to make territorial gains at the expense of the weak and crumbling Ottoman Empire. He did not bargain, however, on facing two western European powers in war.

The Crimean War, as the conflict became known, was fought in the Crimea, a peninsula jutting into the Black Sea. Incompetent generals and widespread disease were characteristics of this ill-planned war. During the conflict, the wretched conditions in British field hospitals were exposed by the legendary Florence Nightingale. She established clean and well-run facilities for soldiers wounded in the war and helped to save many lives.

Czar Nicholas I died in 1856, and the Russians, finally realizing the futility of continuing the fighting, sued for peace. Napoleon III gained an important diplomatic victory by hosting the peace conference in Paris. This was the height of French foreign achievement during the Second Empire. In the last years of his rule, Napoleon III became further entangled in world affairs and unsuccessfully attempted to extend his empire to include Mexico (see Chapter 21). As opposition to his government grew during the 1860's, Napoleon III was forced to make many liberal concessions. Finally, in 1871, he was overthrown, his empire collapsed, and the Third French Republic was established.

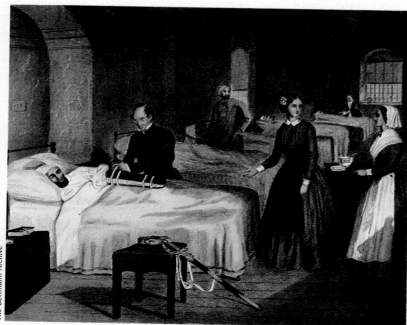

Florence Nightingale established the modern practice of nursing. During the Crimean War, she developed sanitary medical facilities for the first time in British military hospitals, thereby saving many lives. As a result of her work in the Crimea, Florence Nightingale became a world figure and a sought-after expert on medical care.

The Crystal Palace, a 19-acre (8-hectare) glass-and-iron structure, was dedicated at the Great Exhibition, which opened in London in 1851. New inventions of the Industrial Age from many parts of the world were exhibited.

The Bettmann Archive

GREAT BRITAIN AT MID–CENTURY By the 1850's, the Victorian Age in Britain—named after Queen Victoria, who reigned from 1837 to 1901—was well under way. Manufacturing, trade, and agriculture all prospered during the mid-1800's. The Great Exhibition of 1851, held in London in a new glass-and-iron structure called the Crystal Palace, was a showcase of British technology. Large overseas investments also tied the British economy to the economies of other nations.

At home, stable leadership between 1855 and 1880 was provided, in large part, by three prime ministers—Lord Palmerston, William Gladstone, and Benjamin Disraeli. During these years, the British political system became increasingly democratic. The Reform Bill of 1867, which enabled city workers to vote for the first time, increased the voting rolls by 88 percent. Many agricultural workers, however, were still unable to vote. In addition, the Ballot Act of 1872 established the secret ballot in Britain. This enlargement of the electorate made education more necessary than ever before. In western Europe, educated citizens have long been considered to be the foundation of a sound democracy. Under Gladstone's "Glorious Ministry"—1868–1874—public ed-

ucation was supported by the government. The Education Act of 1870 gave local governments control over the education of children between the ages of 5 and 13 and allowed the levying of taxes for this purpose.

During the mid-nineteenth century, the industrialized British economy was unmatched anywhere in the world. In a very real sense, Great Britain was the "workshop of the world," producing cheap, durable textiles, machinery, coal, and other goods that were traded around the world. British sea power was also at its height at this time. A stable government and progress in technology were characteristic of the Victorian Age, during which Britain continued to flourish until the end of the century.

QUESTIONS FOR REVIEW

1 *What was the Crimean War?*

2 *In what ways did Metternich stifle liberalism in Austria?*

3 *Why do you think the Austrian Empire was vulnerable to nationalistic demands in 1848?*

2 THE UNIFICATION OF ITALY

Between 1848 and 1870, the people of the Italian Peninsula united to build a new nation—Italy. The peninsula had long been dominated by such foreign powers as the Austrian Empire and the French Bourbon monarchy. But during the mid-1800's, a small group of Italian nationalists, supported by the Kingdom of Sardinia, managed to unite the Italian people and to end foreign intervention. After 1870, Italy continued to grow in importance and gained an influential voice in European affairs.

STIRRINGS OF ITALIAN NATIONALISM

Austria's Prince von Metternich once referred to Italy as being little more than a "geographical expression." It was an apt description prior to Italy's unification in 1861. Sardinia, Venetia, Lombardy, Tuscany, the Papal States, and the Two Sicilies were among the numerous separate kingdoms and duchies that made up the Italian Peninsula (see map on page 446). Austrian influence on the peninsula had been reaffirmed by the Congress of Vienna. At that time, members of Austria's ruling house of Hapsburg had taken control of many small Italian states. The rich Italian regions of Lombardy and Venetia had also been brought into the Austrian Empire. However, the republican ideas that had filtered into Italy from Napoleonic France helped to bring about the Risorgimento—the "reawakening" of Italian nationalism after 1815.

Initially, the idea of a unified Italy appealed to only a small, educated portion of the Italian population. Intellectuals and university students agitated for revolution. Although the Italians were bound together by a common religion and a common cultural tradition, most Italians remained outside the nationalistic movement.

In 1848, as demands of liberals and nationalists echoed across Europe, Italy also became embroiled in rebellions. But these rebellions led to short-lived democratic gains that were overturned by Austria. In many areas, particularly in the south, revolutions were harshly suppressed.

During the early 1850's, King Victor Emmanuel II, who had recently taken the Sardinian throne, appointed the liberal nationalist Camillo di Cavour [kuh-VUR] prime minister. Cavour began to establish Sardinia as the cornerstone on which the new nation of Italy would be built.

THE UNIFICATION OF NORTHERN ITALY

Count Camillo di Cavour was educated in the liberal spirit of nineteenth-century Europe. Above all else, however, Cavour was a nationalist. He founded a newspaper, Il Risorgimento, to aid the cause of Italian nationalism. When he became prime minister of Sardinia in 1852, Cavour encouraged railroad construction, business development, and commercial treaties in an effort to promote Italian unity. But he realized that these changes alone were not enough to create an Italian nation.

In 1855, Cavour surprised the European world by allying Sardinia with Great Britain and France in their war against Russia. Although few understood this move at the time, it enabled Cavour to bring the issue of Italian unification before the world at the Paris peace conference the following year.

At the conference, Cavour gained sympathy for the Italian cause by attacking the Austrians for their harsh rule on the Italian Peninsula. One impressed listener was Napoleon III of France. Two years later, the French emperor made a secret pact with Sardinia that promised French aid in the event of a Sardinian war against Austria. But France would fight Austria only if the Austrians began a war with Sardinia. In return for their help, the French would receive the province of Savoy and the Mediterranean city of Nice (see map on page 446).

In 1859, Cavour managed to provoke a war with Austria. The war was short and the

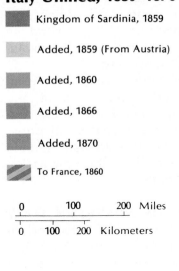

Italy Unified, 1859–1870

- ■ Kingdom of Sardinia, 1859
- ▫ Added, 1859 (From Austria)
- ▤ Added, 1860
- ▦ Added, 1866
- ▨ Added, 1870
- ▧ To France, 1860

```
0        100        200   Miles
|         |          |
0    100     200   Kilometers
```

Between 1859 and 1870, the modern nation of Italy was formed from the many small and independent states and kingdoms that occupied the Italian Peninsula.

gains were small, but the victorious Sardinians and their French allies were able to force the Austrians out of Lombardy. The war also sparked revolutions in the smaller states of northern and central Italy against their Austrian-backed rulers.

At this point, Napoleon III suddenly made peace with Austria. Several reasons may have caused the French emperor to abandon the Sardinian cause. A Prussian army stood on the banks of the Rhine, probably waiting to attack in the event of a French invasion of Austria. In addition, Napoleon III may have begun to realize that a strong and united Italy would pose a threat to France along its southern border. It is also possible that the French emperor, who cherished the support of French Roman Catholics, may have feared that the pope would lose power and lands in a united Italy.

Although he was furious over the French defection, Cavour could do little but accept the peace terms offered by Austria. Sardinia was not strong enough to carry on the war alone. During the next year, successful revolutions throughout the smaller states of northern Italy brought on other events. Voters in Tuscany, Romagna, Parma, and Modena chose to join Sardinia in a united northern Italy (see map on this page). Cavour next turned to the problem of bringing the south into a unified Italy.

THE SOUTH AND THE COMPLETION OF UNIFICATION The liberator of southern Italy was the patriot Giuseppe Garibaldi. Garibaldi was a veteran of the revolution of 1848 and of the war of 1859. A daring leader, Garibaldi turned to the conquest of the Kingdom of the Two Sicilies in 1860. The kingdom included the island of Sicily and the Kingdom of Naples.

Garibaldi raised a small army of idealistic, middle-class Italians that became known as the Thousand. Clad in red shirts, this ill-equipped band landed on Sicily in May 1860. Garibaldi had correctly guessed that the Sicilians were on the verge of revolution themselves. In less than two months, Garibaldi's army, aided by discontented Sicilians, overran the island. But Garibaldi did not stop there. He next landed his forces on the Italian mainland and triumphantly entered the city of Naples, forcing the Bourbon king to flee.

Garibaldi's victories were the finishing touches to the creation of the Kingdom of Italy. Napoleon III, who had a garrison of soldiers protecting Rome, allowed the annexation of the south and of several of the papal states by the new Italian government (see map on page 446). Only Venetia and Rome were not part of the new kingdom that was proclaimed in March 1861. Tragically, Count Cavour died two months after the Kingdom of Italy was created.

The leaders who followed Cavour lacked his diplomatic skill. Nevertheless, they wisely followed Cavour's policies and were able to complete the unification of Italy. In 1866, Italy became an ally of Prussia in the Austro-Prussian War. Prussia's victory over Austria enabled the Italians to annex the state of Venetia. However, Rome and the remaining papal states refused to join the Italian union because the pope was reluctant to give up his temporal powers. Prussia again provided Italy's leaders with the opportunity to complete the unification. In 1870, the defeat of Napoleon III during the Franco-Prussian War forced the French to withdraw their garrison from Rome. As a result, the Italian government was able to annex Rome with little opposition.

Although the unification of Italy was completed in 1870, an important task lay ahead. Only a tiny portion of the Italian population had supported the fight for unification. For the most part, the people of Italy had to be instilled with the idea of being "Italian." That is, they had to begin thinking of themselves as citizens of a nation, rather than citizens of a single city or state.

Giuseppe Garibaldi led his red-shirted army, called the Thousand, in successful invasions of Sicily and southern Italy. His victories led to the annexation of these areas by the kingdom of Italy.

Moro Romo

THE ITALIAN NATION At the time of unification, Italy was primarily a nation of farmers. Italians engaged in agriculture outnumbered those in other occupations by a margin of 3 to 1. Moreover, of the 22 million inhabitants of Italy excluding Rome and Venetia, only 20 percent could read or write. In the south, illiteracy approached 100 percent.

Italian manufacturing also lagged far behind manufacturing in other European countries. The regions of Lombardy and Venetia in northern Italy led the world in silk production, but 80 percent of the raw silk they produced was exported to other countries for the manufacture of silk goods. In 1861, Italy did not have a good transportation system, and its lack of natural resources made rapid industrialization difficult. For these reasons, between 1861 and 1870, the Italian nation teetered on the brink of bankruptcy.

Despite these problems, the new Italian nation survived. An increase in trade after 1870 helped to strengthen the economy. Through careful planning, the government's treasury ministers managed to fight off financial disaster and to reestablish Italian credit. The resulting economic growth led to internal improvements. By 1870, rail mileage in Italy had greatly increased. In addition, the introduction of mechanical looms into the Italian textile industry began to transform Italy into the center of European silk manufacturing. As a result of these and other developments, Italy began to gain an important place in the European world.

QUESTIONS FOR REVIEW

1 *What does the term* Risorgimento *refer to?*

2 *How did Cavour use the Crimean War to further the cause of Italian nationalism?*

3 *Why did Napoleon III suddenly make peace with Austria in 1859?*

3 GERMANY UNITES

A unified Germany was created between 1860 and 1871. The kingdom of Prussia served as the basis upon which the new nation was built. The diplomacy of the Prussian prime minister, Otto von Bismarck, and Prussian success in three European wars established a single, central government for Germany. It replaced the petty kingdoms and duchies that had existed for centuries. After unification, Germany became one of the dominant powers in Europe and by 1900 ranked among the leading industrialized nations of the world.

GROWING GERMAN NATIONALISM Germany, like Italy, became a nation after 1860. Prior to that time, there had been 39 independent German states, each with its own government and its own military force. However, as early as 1834, the northern German states had reached a form of economic unity under the customs union known as the Zollverein.

In many of the German states, the liberal revolutions of 1848 and 1849 had not achieved a lasting success. Reactionary rule had been reestablished, and the influence of Austria had once again been felt throughout the region. German nationalism, however, continued to grow, especially in the German kingdom of Prussia. By the middle of the nineteenth century, Prussia had achieved a dominant position in the Zollverein and had become the most economically advanced and most powerful of the German states. Many Germans believed that if they were to be united, Prussia would have to be the foundation of their new state.

When he took the Prussian throne in 1861, King William I sought to build up the strength of the Prussian army by modernizing and enlarging it. However, Prussian liberals opposed William's plans in the parliament. They feared that a strong standing army would curtail freedom in Prussia. They also feared that the taxes needed to maintain a large force would ruin the Prussian economy. The impasse between the Prussian monarch and the liberal opposition leaders in the parliament lasted nearly two years. William was considering resigning the throne when, in a last effort to resolve the issue, he brought Otto von Bismarck into the Prussian government as prime minister.

THE RISE OF BISMARCK Otto von Bismarck was born into an aristocratic Prussian family in 1815. The values of the Prussian aristocracy—the Junker—remained an important part of Bismarck's conservative outlook throughout his life. As the Prussian prime minister, Bismarck was the first great practitioner of *realpolitik* [ray-AHL-POH-li-TEEK] —the use of negotiation and of compromise

Otto von Bismarck—a Prussian aristocrat, politician, and nationalist—was primarily responsible for forging the modern nation of Germany.

Historical Pictures Service

in politics. Bismarck was never a believer in democratic rule. He declared that "the great questions of the time are not to be solved by speeches and majority resolutions . . . but by blood and iron." True to his Prussian heritage, Bismarck was loyal to the Prussian king and determined in his desire to unite the German people around Prussia. He was equally determined to end the influence of Austria in German affairs.

Bismarck found his first opportunity to help bring the German people together under Prussia's leadership in the issue of the status of Schleswig and Holstein. These two tiny northern states, each with a large German population, were governed by the king of Denmark (see map on page 450). German nationalists had long favored independence for these states. Bismarck's first step was to negotiate an alliance with the Austrians, who continually sought to extend their influence in the German states in any way they could. His next step was to provoke a war with Denmark. Bismarck's efforts were successful. In 1864, a short war between Denmark and the combined forces of Prussia and Austria resulted in the cession of Schleswig to Prussia and of Holstein to the Austrian Empire. Within two years, Austria's claim to Holstein provided Bismarck with an excuse for a war against Austria.

UNITY IN NORTHERN GERMANY Following the war with Denmark, Bismarck continued his efforts to unite Germany and to defeat Austria. Bismarck managed to secure Italy's support in the event of a war with Austria. In return for its support, Italy would receive Venetia. Bismarck then convinced Napoleon III that France should remain neutral in any war between Prussia and Austria. Undoubtedly, Napoleon III saw that much could be gained if France's two rivals weakened each other in a major conflict.

The Austro-Prussian War began in the summer of 1866. Bismarck's policies had finally provoked Austria into declaring war on Prussia. It took only seven weeks for the powerful Prussian army to defeat the combined forces of Austria and the independent southern German states allied with Austria.

After the war, Bismarck's lenient peace proposal surprised many Europeans. His plan called for the cession of Venetia to Italy and for a small indemnity to be paid by Austria to Prussia. Austria also had to accept the formation of the North German Confederation under Prussian leadership.

Through its domination of the North German Confederation, Prussia gained control of two thirds of the German people and the majority of the German states. The confederation was established and a constitution was completed in 1867. This constitution remained in effect, with few changes, until 1918. It created a two-house legislature— with members of the lower house being elected by all males of voting age. The government, however, was still tightly controlled by the Prussian king and his cabinet.

The Austro-Prussian War did not completely unify the German people. The southern German states of Bavaria, Württemberg, Baden, and Hesse-Darmstadt still remained independent. Bismarck needed yet another war, this time with France, to complete the unification of Germany.

THE FRANCO–PRUSSIAN WAR At the end of the 1860's, two important obstacles stood in the way of final German unification. The first of these obstacles was a religious one. The Germans of the south were Roman Catholic, while the Prussian-dominated north was generally Protestant. The second obstacle was political, since the liberal ideas that had spread across Europe after the French Revolution were stronger in the southern states than in the conservative north. Offsetting these religious and political differences was a fear of French aggression that was widespread in the south. It was this fear that Bismarck hoped to use in his plans for unifying Germany.

Between 1865 and 1871, the divided Germanic kingdoms of central Europe were brought together into one nation—Germany—under Prussian leadership.

Prussia, 1865

Land annexed by Prussia, 1866

Lands uniting with Prussia to form North German Confederation, 1867

German states uniting with Prussia to form German Empire, 1871

Lands annexed following Franco-Prussian War, 1871

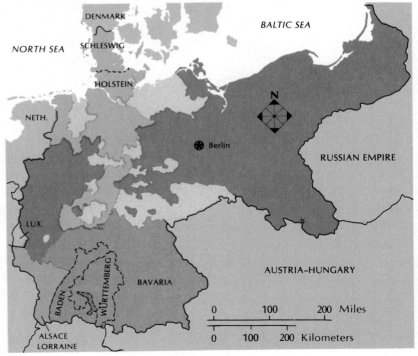

The Unification of Germany, 1865–1871

450

In late summer 1870, the battle at Vionville, France, between the French and German armies, resulted in nearly 30,000 casualties. France's eventual defeat in the Franco-Prussian War removed the last obstacle to German unification by bringing southern Germany under Prussian control.

In July 1870, Bismarck successfully provoked France into declaring war on Prussia. The final provocation that led to war was a dubious Prussian claim to the Spanish throne. The spark that ignited the war was a telegram from William I to his chief minister, Bismarck. Earlier, the French had asked that a member of the Hohenzollern family that ruled Prussia must never sit upon the Spanish throne. Bismarck cleverly condensed the telegram from William, exaggerating the French demand to make it appear insulting to the Prussians. Bismarck's version of the telegram was also greatly insulting to the French.

Bismarck released the edited telegram to the German newspapers. Within a week, public outrage in France had led to a French declaration of war on Prussia. The French hoped for a short war that would restore France's prestige abroad and strengthen the rule of Napoleon III at home. However, the Prussians scored many early victories and captured the French emperor in September 1870.

The capture of Napoleon III plunged France into near chaos. The Prussian army marched on Paris and besieged the city. In January 1871, the starving Parisians surrendered. The same month a new German *Reich* [RIYK]—Empire—was formed. In May, a peace treaty was concluded, and Germany gained Alsace and part of Lorraine—two French territories west of the Rhine River. The southern states recognized the strength of a united Germany and joined the new German empire. The unification of Germany was finally complete.

Following unification, Germany became one of the most powerful nations in Europe. Industrialization, the establishment of colonies abroad, and a strong military were important factors in Germany's rise to predominance on the European continent.

QUESTIONS FOR REVIEW

1 *What was realpolitik?*

2 *How did Bismarck provoke war with France in 1870?*

3 *Why did confusion reign in Paris in September 1870?*

451

Myths and Realities

The Charge of the Light Brigade

The Crimean War—which lasted from 1853 to 1856—produced one of the world's most famous poems about war. The British poet Tennyson immortalized part of the battle of Balaklava, which took place in October 1854, in his stirring and highly romanticized work, "The Charge of the Light Brigade." During the charge, British cavalry, numbering 673 of Europe's finest riders, charged down a valley through a cross fire from Russian guns and artillery. Over 70 percent of the Light Brigade were killed, wounded, or taken prisoner; only 195 of the Light Brigade returned. Although the romantic charge was a minor battle in a poorly led war, it has long been remembered.

I

Half a league, half a league,
  Half a league onward,
All in the valley of Death
  Rode the six hundred.
"Forward, the Light Brigade!
Charge for the guns!" he said:
Into the valley of Death
  Rode the six hundred.

II

"Forward, the Light Brigade!"
Was there a man dismay'd?
Not tho' the soldier knew
  Some one had blunder'd:
Their's not to make reply,
Their's not to reason why,
Their's but to do and die:
Into the valley of Death
  Rode the six hundred. . . .

VI

When can their glory fade?
O the wild charge they made!
  All the world wonder'd.
Honour the charge they made!
Honour the Light Brigade,
  Noble six hundred!

A common myth has grown up around the British cavalry charge at Balaklava, which blames the attack on a totally incompetent commander in chief and upon a feud that existed between the commanding officers of the British cavalry forces. A review of the circumstances surrounding the incident, however, places the blame elsewhere.

The intended point of attack that day lay on one side of the valley, where there was a group of British guns that had been captured by the Russians. This was away from the Russian battery at the far end of the valley. However, the order was vague, probably because the commander in chief of the British Army, Lord Raglan, did not realize that the Light Brigade could not see the entire valley as he could. The order was delivered to the cavalry leader, Lord Lucan, by an overly excited aide, who could not clear up the vagueness. Apparently, the aide also pointed to the Russian battery at the far end of the valley as the guns to be attacked. But in the heat of battle, an order was to be obeyed, not questioned, and

Into the valley of Death
Rode the six hundred.

The bloody charge of the Light Brigade was immortalized by the British poet Tennyson.

Historical Pictures Service

4 CHANGES IN EASTERN EUROPE

By the middle of the nineteenth century, the countries of eastern Europe were feeling the effects of the changes that were taking place in western Europe. Russia, stagnant under the heavy-handed rule of Czar Nicholas I until 1855, underwent many economic and social reforms during the rule of his successor, Alexander II. The Austrian government was modified when its policies failed to satisfy the many ethnic minorities living under its control. Unrest ultimately led to the creation of the dual monarchy of Austria-Hungary. As the nineteenth century drew to a close, the Balkan Peninsula became a hotbed of nationalistic discontent and a pawn in the struggle among the imperial powers of Europe.

AUTOCRACY IN RUSSIA In 1825, Nicholas I became czar of Russia. A conservative and reactionary leader, Nicholas ruled with an iron hand. An autocrat in thought and in action, Nicholas I sought to stamp out personal freedom and individual thought in Russia. His main instrument was the dreaded secret police force that he created to fight revolution, subversion, and liberalism. By order of the czar, only one church —the Russian Orthodox Church—was recognized. All other religions were persecuted. Strict censorship was imposed throughout the empire, and a separate department was formed to watch the censors. However, several minor reforms, such as the stabilization of the Russian currency and the allowance of a small degree of local government, were permitted at this time. Russian law was also codified by Nicholas I. Nevertheless, the 30 years of Nicholas's reign were marked by his fear of revolution and by the successful measures he took to stifle change in Russia.

After the death of Nicholas I in 1855, his son, Alexander II, succeeded to the throne.

Alexander's rule was very different from that of his father. At the time, Russia faced enormous problems. The empire was mired in the Crimean War against France, Great Britain, and Sardinia. The Russian economy was stagnant, having undergone none of the changes that had taken place in the economies of western European countries. Similarly, its social system—in which serfs still made up almost half of the population— was in sharp contrast to the progressive social systems of western Europe. Reflecting upon Russia's defeat in the Crimean War, the new ruler recognized at once the need for reform.

THE REFORMS OF ALEXANDER II Alexander II was determined to bring about both social and economic reform for the Russian people. In 1861, after long preparation, Alexander II signed the Emancipation Edict, which abolished serfdom in Russia. The immediate result of this momentous social reform was freedom for almost 22 million serfs. The government also began economic reform, encouraging landlords to sell land to peasants. The land, however, was not sold directly to the peasants. Instead, village communes—called *mirs*— were helped by the government to buy the land, which was then distributed to commune members. The mirs actually held the titles to the land. The communes probably resulted from the widespread belief among the Russian aristocracy that centuries of serfdom had not prepared the peasants for freedom.

Although the Emancipation Edict and the sale of land were both progressive steps, many scholars have argued that the reforms did not go far enough. They point out that the standard of living among the peasantry did not greatly improve after emancipation. Moreover, the peasants often did not receive enough land to farm. Also, a few wealthy peasants—known as *kulaks*—were able to gain control of much of the land by buying it themselves.

Alexander's reign also brought other reforms to Russia. A system of local governments was set up and town councils were established. The court system was reorganized and modeled after the systems of western Europe. Finally, all Russian males—not just the poor—became eligible for the military draft. Although these reforms were all beneficial, unrest and discontent—especially among the educated—remained widespread in Russia during the last decades of the nineteenth century.

UNREST IN THE BALKANS By the 1860's, eastern Europe and the Balkan Peninsula were being torn apart by severe nationalistic struggles and the ambitions of the great European powers. In 1866, the Prussian victory over Austria severely weakened the Hapsburg empire. As a result, the Hungarian-speaking Magyars, who had long worked for independence within the Austrian Empire, increased their agitation for greater political freedom. In 1867, Austria's leaders gave in to many of the Magyar demands, creating the dual monarchy of Austria-Hungary. In domestic affairs, the Empire of Austria and the Kingdom of Hungary functioned as two independent states. However, a parliament drawing its membership equally from each country was established for such matters as foreign policy and mutual defense. In addition, the monarch, Francis Joseph, reigned as emperor in Austria and as king in Hungary.

Although the dual monarchy brought some stability to eastern Europe, unrest was growing in the Balkans. During the 1870's, the many different ethnic groups that lived in eastern Europe rose in revolt against the decaying Ottoman Empire. In 1875 and 1876, the peoples of Herzegovina, Macedonia,

Long-overdue social reform came to Russia in the early 1860's, when Czar Alexander II's Emancipation Edict freed nearly 22,000,000 serfs throughout the empire.

The Bettmann Archive

Balkan Countries in 1878

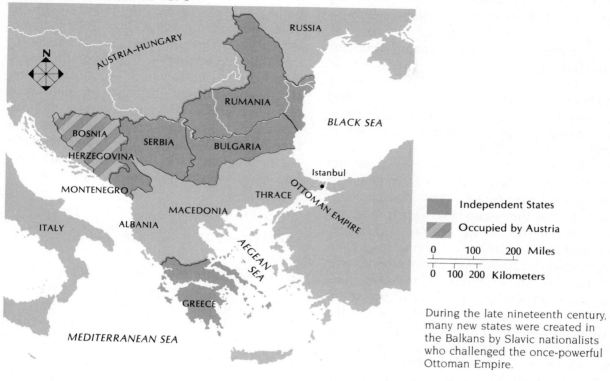

During the late nineteenth century, many new states were created in the Balkans by Slavic nationalists who challenged the once-powerful Ottoman Empire.

Bosnia, Serbia, and Montenegro rebelled against their Turkish rulers. These rebellions were encouraged by the Austrians and the Russians, who eagerly sought to expand their influence in the region at the expense of the Ottomans.

The uprisings on the Balkan Peninsula were put down by the Turkish government, but not before Russia had become involved. Great Britain, France, and Germany urged a peace conference to settle the problems of the region. But Russian ambition in the Balkans—and the Russian desire for year-round ice-free ports—soon led to a Russian invasion of the Ottoman Empire in 1877.

In 1878, Russian forces reached the Turkish capital of Istanbul. The victorious Russians forced the Turkish government to sign the Treaty of San Stefano. This treaty made Rumania, Serbia, and Montenegro independent countries. Also, the territory of Bulgaria was increased at Turkey's expense. Russia received land in the Caucasus. Fearing the influence of Russia in the Balkans, however, the major powers of western Europe asked for a conference to revise the treaty. Russian leaders feared a general European war and reluctantly agreed to the revisions made at the Congress of Berlin.

The treaty that resulted from the Congress of Berlin divided Bulgaria into three separate parts, all under the control of the rulers of the Ottoman Empire. Rumania, Serbia, and Montenegro remained independent, and each was given more land. The most important provision of the treaty, however, placed Bosnia and Herzegovina under the control of Austria-Hungary. As a result, nationalists' dreams in these Balkan lands remained unfulfilled and became a source of growing tensions in the region at the turn of the century.

DECLINE OF THE OTTOMAN EMPIRE For more than three centuries the slowly decaying Ottoman Empire was governed by a succession of weak and incompetent rulers. These weak rulers kept the Ottoman Empire isolated. As a result, the empire experienced almost none of the commercial and industrial growth common in western Europe. The once-powerful Ottoman Empire slowly but steadily declined throughout the eighteenth and nineteenth centuries. Ottoman contact with Europeans was limited largely to the battlefield.

During the mid-1800's, a strong central government replaced the old, fragmented Ottoman rule in Turkey. New Turkish leaders realized the need for widespread reforms within the aging empire. Education, law, and the military all underwent government reorganization after the Crimean War.

However, these attempts to strengthen the Ottoman Empire proved to be short-lived. The Turks were unable to meet the increasing demands for independence by their European subjects. Rebellions broke out throughout the Balkan Peninsula, and these upheavals gave Russia, which coveted Ottoman lands, repeated opportunities to challenge the decaying empire. Other European powers also began to interfere in the affairs of the Balkans. By the Treaty of Berlin in 1878, Turkish holdings in Europe were reduced to Macedonia, Albania, and Thrace (see map on page 455). In the years that followed, Ottoman rule in Europe was reduced even further until by 1915 only the city of Istanbul and the land surrounding it remained under Ottoman control. Thus, by the early 1900's, the once-mighty Ottoman Empire was no longer a major force in world affairs. By that time, the empire had truly become "the sick man of Europe."

QUESTIONS FOR REVIEW

1 *What were the major reforms in Russia brought about by Czar Alexander II?*

2 *In what ways did the Emancipation Edict change landownership in Russia during the last half of the nineteenth century?*

3 *Why do you think the major European powers became involved in the affairs of the declining Ottoman Empire?*

CHAPTER SUMMARY

During the mid-nineteenth century, France and Great Britain flourished, while the multiethnic Austrian Empire was continually in turmoil. Also during this time, the nations of Italy and Germany were also formed. By 1870, Italian nationalists, led by Cavour and Garibaldi, had gradually freed all parts of the Italian Peninsula from foreign rule, thus creating a new nation—Italy. In the German states, the diplomacy of Otto von Bismarck pieced together the Second German Reich on the solid foundation of Prussian leadership.

The steady decay of the once-great Ottoman Empire and the national movements that arose in the Ottomans' European domain eventually brought the major powers of Europe into the affairs of the region. By 1878, Turkish control had been greatly reduced in the Balkans. However, Balkan nationalists continued their struggle for independence.

CHAPTER 23 IN REVIEW

IMPORTANT WORDS, NAMES, AND TERMS

1 Explain, define, or identify each of the following:

Napoleon III	Sardinia	realpolitik
Prussia	Camillo di Cavour	*Reich*
Reform Bill of 1867	Giuseppe Garibaldi	Alexander II
Risorgimento	Otto von Bismarck	Treaty of Berlin

FACTS AND IDEAS

2 What was the importance of the Zollverein?

3 What were the goals of French foreign policy under Napoleon III?

4 How did Prussia provide important opportunities for Italian nationalists to complete the unification of Italy?

5 In what major ways did the people of northern and southern Germany differ before unification?

6 What were the Russian mirs?

ANALYZING VISUAL MATERIAL

7 Carefully compare the illustrations on pages 427 and 444. What two faces of industrialization are shown? Why do you think that industrialization might have been viewed by some people in the nineteenth century as "bringing progress at a price"?

8 Based upon the maps on pages 446 and 450, what basic political obstacle do you think had to be overcome by both Bismarck and Cavour before the nations of Germany and Italy could be successfully established?

CONCEPTS AND UNDERSTANDINGS

9 Why was there little worker unrest in Paris during the first decade of the Second Empire?

10 Why did the pope oppose the cause of Italian unification during the 1860's?

11 What factors enabled Bismarck to unite northern and southern Germany by 1871?

12 How did the decay of the Ottoman Empire draw other European countries into the affairs of the Balkans?

PROJECTS AND ACTIVITIES

13 Draw a map of eastern Europe for classroom display. Label the territories of the various ethnic groups that lived in the region at the end of the nineteenth century.

14 List the policies of Cavour and of Bismarck that resulted in the unification of Italy and of Germany. Prepare a report to the class in which you agree or disagree with these policies. An important element of your report might be to evaluate what policies may or may not be justified in unifying a people or a region.

Using Geography Skills

The Industrial Revolution began in Great Britain during the middle and late decades of the eighteenth century. In the early nineteenth century, industrialization spread to Belgium, France, and Germany. Among the more important elements needed for industrial growth in these countries were an abundance of raw materials and of sources of power, the improvement of transportation systems, and the growth of population. Germany, in particular, possessed these elements of rapid industrial expansion.

The resource and population map below shows some of the raw materials important for early German industrialization. The map also shows the regions of densest population and the industrial centers of mid-nineteenth-century Germany. This type of map can help us to better understand the relationships between the location of natural resources and of population and the development of industry. Study the map and the map key carefully. Then answer the following questions:

1 What mineral resources were important for the development of German industry in the mid-1800's?

2 Why do you think the cities of Essen, Dortmund, and Düsseldorf had become centers for German industrialization by the mid-1800's? Do you think the same factors could have been responsible for the growth of Berlin and Hanover? Explain your answer.

3 Control over the region of Alsace-Lorraine was for many years sought by both France and Germany. Explain why you think this area was coveted for military and economic purposes by both the French and the Germans.

4 Factors other than raw materials were also important to the growth of German economic life. What do you think may have led to the growth of the cities of Hamburg and Bremen? Explain your answer.

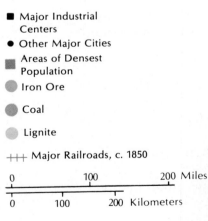

■ Major Industrial Centers
● Other Major Cities
▮ Areas of Densest Population
● Iron Ore
● Coal
● Lignite
+++ Major Railroads, c. 1850

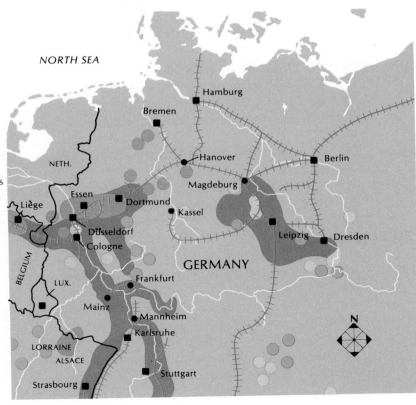

UNIT 6 IN REVIEW

CONCEPTS AND UNDERSTANDINGS

1 What effect did mercantilism have on the economic growth of western Europe during the sixteenth and seventeenth centuries?

2 What important developments in political thought took place during the Age of Reason?

3 How did Napoleon help to spread the ideas of the French Revolution?

4 In what ways did early socialists hope to remedy the worst social abuses of early industrialized Europe?

5 Who were the leaders of German and Italian unification? In what ways were the circumstances leading to the unification of Germany and those leading to the unification of Italy similar or different? Explain your answer.

QUESTIONS FOR DISCUSSION

1 To what extent would you agree or disagree with the following statement? "It was necessary for the changes of the Commercial Revolution to take place *before* the Industrial Revolution could begin." Explain your answer.

2 Why do you think many modern historians regard the French Revolution as a pivotal event in the creation of modern Europe?

3 What do you think led to the rise of nationalism as an important factor in European political affairs during the nineteenth century?

SUGGESTED READING

Baker, Nina B. *Garibaldi*. New York: Vanguard Press, Inc., 1944.

Brownlee, Walter. *The Navy That Beat Napoleon*. Minneapolis: Lerner Publications Company, 1981.

Cairns, T. *The Old Regime and the Revolution*. New York: Cambridge University Press, 1976.

————. *Power for the People*. New York: Cambridge University Press, 1978.

Clarke, Penny. *Growing Up During the Industrial Revolution*. North Pomfret, Vt.: David and Charles, Inc., 1980.

Dickens, Charles. *A Tale of Two Cities*, illus. by Charles Shaw and adapted by Patti Krapesh. Milwaukee: Raintree Publishers, Inc., 1980.

————. *Oliver Twist*. New York: Dodd, Mead and Co., 1979.

Dupuy, Trevor N. *Battle of Austerlitz: Napoleon's Greatest Victory*. New York: Macmillan, Inc., 1968.

Rosenblum, Morris. *Heroes of Mexico*, foreword by J. Montoya. New York: Fleet Press Corp., 1969.

Vialis, Christine. *The Industrial Revolution Begins*. Minneapolis: Lerner Publications Company, 1981.

UNIT 7

IMPERIALISM AND WORLD WAR I
1871 to 1920

24 The Supremacy of Imperial Europe **25** The Growth of Imperialism **26** Progress in the Industrial Age **27** Prelude to War **28** The Great War

Mary Evans Library

Historical Pictures Service

A European mission at Lake Chad

Iron and steel industry in Germany, 1895

Between 1870 and 1914, the major European powers built a delicate balance of power based upon military alliances. Europe continued to be troubled by localized wars and diplomatic clashes. But the era seemed generally peaceful, as the European powers founded colonies and established spheres of influence in Africa, Asia, and the Pacific.

The newly formed German Empire became one of Europe's strongest military powers, while a new government in France survived despite several internal problems. The era witnessed many scientific discoveries and technological innovations. In literature, philosophy, and art, new schools of thought became popular. Germany, France, and Great Britain passed many social reform bills that improved the lives of people in the lower and middle classes.

In 1914, the "Great War" began. After four years of fighting, a peace that most people hoped would be lasting was established. But the war completely changed European society. In Russia, the czarist government fell in 1917. It was replaced by a communist government. Elsewhere in Europe, empires were replaced by postwar republics, and many new countries were formed.

Armistice Day, 1918, Gifford Beal, Indiana University Art Museum; William Lowe Bryan Memorial

Armistice Day celebration, November 11, 1918

24 THE SUPREMACY OF IMPERIAL EUROPE

1 The German Empire Under Bismarck   2 The Third Republic of France   3 Great Britain in the Late Victorian Era

Many historians note that a new era of European history began around 1870. The forces of nationalism had successfully unified Germany and Italy, and nationalistic drives continued to be key factors in European politics. The period between 1870 and the turn of the century witnessed the rise of imperialism as a major force on the international scene as European powers extended their control over vast colonial empires. In addition, domestic reforms enacted by the European powers improved the living conditions of the average worker. The supremacy of imperial Europe in the late nineteenth century was characterized by developments in the German Empire, in France, and in Great Britain.

Historical Pictures Service

William I, king of Prussia, was proclaimed emperor of Germany at Versailles in January 1871.

1 THE GERMAN EMPIRE UNDER BISMARCK

After founding the German Empire in 1871, Otto von Bismarck, the German chancellor, worked to strengthen the nation. Bismarck suppressed groups that he felt threatened German unity. Later, Bismarck embarked upon an aggressive policy of overseas expansion. By the end of the century, Germany was the dominant power on the European continent as well as a leading colonial power.

THE GERMAN EMPIRE Created at Versailles in 1871, the German Empire developed into an absolutist state under the aristocratic Hohenzollern family, and ruling dynasty, of Prussia. The German imperial government, headed by the emperor, included a two-house legislature. However, the legislature had little real power. The actual head of government—the chancellor—held almost unlimited power because he was appointed by the emperor and was responsible to the emperor alone. The chancellor could ignore any action of the legislature. Unlike the British House of Commons, which could force the prime minister's resignation, the German legislature had no such power. True parliamentary democracy did not develop at this time in Germany.

Prussia was the dominant state within the German Empire. The empire was set up so that the Prussian king was also the German emperor, or *kaiser*, meaning "caesar." The kaiser controlled all the Prussian votes in the legislature. Thus he could block any legislative action. The kaiser also had great power in military and foreign affairs.

Otto von Bismarck, who had successfully engineered German unification, was appointed as the first chancellor. Now that he had politically unified Germany, Bismarck, a fervent nationalist, set out to unify the empire's social and economic systems. Dur-

In this political cartoon of 1879, Chancellor Otto von Bismarck was portrayed as a wild-animal tamer facing the muzzled members of the German Reichstag, or parliament.

ing the 1870's and 1880's Bismarck worked to achieve his goals.

BISMARCK'S POLICIES Bismarck's policies exemplified two forces that prevailed within the German Empire. *Nationalism*—a strong belief that one's own nation and culture are superior to others—dominated Bismarck's domestic policies. Later, *imperialism*—a policy of expanding the nation's power over other lands and people—was a key force of Bismarck's foreign policy.

To unify the German Empire's economy, Bismarck introduced an imperial currency in 1871, and in 1873, an imperial bank. Under Bismarck's guidance, the empire's banking system was completely reorganized, thus strengthening the empire. To coordinate the many German railroads, an imperial railway office was set up. In addition, imperial codes of law were passed, thus giving the German Empire a single system of laws.

POLITICAL		SOCIAL AND ECONOMIC
Gladstone elected British prime minister	~1868	
Third Republic of France founded	~1870	
German Empire founded	~1871~	Paris Commune set up
Disraeli elected British prime minister	~1874	
Victoria declared empress of India	~1876	
Great Britain and France controlled Egypt	~1879	
France declared Tunisia a protectorate	~1881~	Land Act gave rights to Irish peasants
	1883~	Social-reform laws passed in Germany
Southwest Africa became German colony	~1884	
	1886~	Boulanger threatened French Republic
William II ascended German throne	~1888	
William dismissed Bismarck as chancellor	~1890	
	1894~	Alfred Dreyfus arrested
Boer War began in South Africa	~1899	
	1901~	Queen Victoria died
	1906~	Dreyfus declared innocent

Bismarck also secured the passage of a *tariff*—a tax on imported goods—in 1879. This tariff was designed to protect the growing industries from foreign competition. This law also added revenue to the imperial treasury, thus strengthening the empire. Later, Bismarck passed other tariff laws that protected German farmers from foreign competition.

THE KULTURKAMPF A few years after the founding of the German Empire, Bismarck began to try to subordinate the Roman Catholic Church. Although his exact motives were never clear, Bismarck believed the Church to be an enemy of the empire. The struggle between the empire and the Church has become known as the *Kulturkampf*—battle of cultures—because some journalists in the 1870's called it a struggle between two ways of life.

Although the struggle was more political than religious in nature, it renewed the old suspicions between German Protestants and German Catholics. Protestants were concerned by the attempts of Pope Pius IX to reassert papal authority. Catholics were suspicious of Protestant Prussia's political and military successes. Furthermore, the Kulturkampf brought to mind the medieval struggle between the Holy Roman emperor Henry IV and Pope Gregory VII (see Chapter 13).

Perhaps because Bismarck so greatly desired a thoroughly unified empire, he viewed an independent Church as a threat to German unity. Therefore, Bismarck set out to weaken the power of the Church. Between 1871 and 1875 several laws designed to achieve this goal were passed. After 1872, numerous religious orders, such as the Jesuits, were suppressed or completely banished from German lands. The May Laws of 1873 gave the government the right to approve appointments to Church offices. These laws also required priests to study theology at state universities, required civil marriages, and stopped state-collected money from being given to the Church.

In response to these laws, Pope Pius IX declared them null and void and called for loyal Catholics to refuse to obey them. This, in turn, further angered Bismarck. The May Laws were strictly enforced. Many priests were imprisoned and much Church property was taken over by the government.

Despite the harshness of the repression, Bismarck was not successful in weakening the Church's power within Germany. The Kulturkampf had, however, increased the strength of Bismarck's opponents within Germany. Thus, Bismarck was forced to make peace with the Church. The chancellor's task was made easier after the death of Pope Pius IX in 1878. The new pope, Leo XIII, was more conciliatory in nature, and between 1878 and 1887 most of the anti-Catholic laws were repealed.

BISMARCK AND THE SOCIALISTS The Socialists in Germany, who traced their roots back to 1848, aroused Bismarck's suspicions for three reasons. The Socialists were internationalists, pacifists, and anti-militarists. Bismarck saw the Socialists as a threat to the German Empire's unity and power. The chancellor termed the Socialists "the red menace."

As industrialization increased in Germany, Socialist strength among the workers grew, particularly in the late 1870's. Bismarck, supported by conservative landowners and big industrialists, moved to suppress the Socialists. Bismarck's excuse for this suppression came in 1878, when two attempts were made on the kaiser's life. Although the Socialists were in no way connected to the assassination attempts, Bismarck immediately called for strong measures against the Socialists. These laws restricted the Socialists' rights to free speech and public assembly. Socialist publications were outlawed.

In the face of these severe measures, however, the Socialists' support increased rather than decreased. Bismarck then decided to weaken the Socialists' support by adopting some of their goals for improving the lot of the German workers. Bismarck declared,

> Give the workingman the right to work as long as he is healthy, assure him care when he is sick, and maintenance when he is old . . . then the socialists will sing their siren songs in vain, and the workingmen will cease to throng to their banner . . .

Mary Evans Picture Library

The assassination attempts on Kaiser William I in 1878 gave Chancellor Bismarck an excuse for suppressing the Socialists, a group that Bismarck believed threatened German unity and power.

Bismarck sponsored a series of social-reform bills that was so farsighted that it placed Germany far ahead of other nations in this field. In 1883 a health-insurance law was passed that provided financial and medical aid to workers laid off because of sickness. The following year an accident-insurance law was adopted. Under this law, disabled workers received financial benefits and widows of workers killed on their jobs received pensions. In 1889, old-age insurance was introduced.

Bismarck's social reforms greatly improved the well-being of the German worker. But despite Bismarck's efforts, support for the Socialists continued to grow.

GERMAN IMPERIALISM Throughout the 1870's, Bismarck concentrated on strengthening the German Empire's position as the dominant power on the continent of Europe. His primary goal was to isolate France and to prevent a French war of revenge against Germany. At the same time, Bismarck developed strong diplomatic ties with Russia and Austria. He also cultivated friendly relations—but not a formal alliance—with Great Britain.

German merchants and industrialists, however, favored the acquisition of colonies. These groups reasoned that Germany's rapid industrialization and steady population growth made it necessary to obtain colonies as new sources of food and new markets for goods. Other Germans believed that obtaining colonies would enhance the empire's prestige as a world power.

By 1882, Bismarck had changed his anti-colonial stand and adopted a policy of imperialism. In 1883, German merchants claimed land that was to become the colony of German Southwest Africa in 1884. Around this same time, Bismarck sent an explorer, Gustav Nachtigal, to the west coast of Africa. Nachtigal, discovering that the British were about to take over the area, declared the region to be under German protection. This claim became the foundation for the German colonies of Togoland and Cameroons.

The German Empire also asserted its sovereignty over large areas of eastern Africa. In 1884, explorers obtained treaties from local chiefs giving Germany control over vast African lands. In 1885, Bismarck claimed the region as German East Africa.

German imperialism also spread to parts of Asia. Germany acquired numerous Pacific islands and ports on the Chinese mainland. By the turn of the century, Germany's colonial empire was the third largest in the world. Only the empires of Great Britain and France were larger.

KAISER WILLIAM II William II, grandson of William I, ascended the German imperial throne in 1888. William II was determined to personally control the German government. The new kaiser resented Bismarck's power and for two years tension between the two leaders mounted. In 1890, William dismissed Bismarck.

The chancellors who succeeded Bismarck did not possess his abilities and never achieved his dominant position in the government. They were never given the unlimited power that Bismarck had held. William II autocratically ruled Germany until the end of World War I. William followed policies of intense nationalism and military aggressiveness. He greatly expanded the German navy, thus threatening Britain's dominant position as a naval power.

William II was strongly opposed to the democratic movement that developed in Germany in the 1890's. But, despite the opposition of the emperor and his conservative supporters, support for the democratic movement increased. However, the various groups that favored democracy and opposed Hohenzollern autocracy lacked unity. For example, 14 political parties were represented in the German legislature. As long as these parties failed to work together for common purposes, the emperor and his

2 THE THIRD REPUBLIC OF FRANCE

The Third Republic of France was born in the midst of the Franco-Prussian War. From very unstable beginnings, it developed into a democratic system of government that lasted until 1940. The Third Republic initiated reforms to improve the working conditions and the educational system of France. Despite much progress, the Third Republic was shaken by several scandals. In the later part of the nineteenth century, France maintained a vigorous policy of imperialism.

THE BIRTH OF THE THIRD REPUBLIC The events of the Franco-Prussian War had proven disastrous to France since its beginning in July 1870. After the French emperor Louis Napoleon was defeated and captured at Sedan by the Prussian army, the government of the Second Empire collapsed. The French government known as the Third Republic was proclaimed on September 4, 1870, during the Franco-Prussian War.

Even in the absence of an organized government, the French army stationed near Paris continued to fight the Prussians. Paris was besieged for four months. It was at this time that the king of Prussia was proclaimed the German emperor at Versailles, the former palace of the French kings. On January 27, 1871—ten days after the founding of the German Empire—France accepted Bismarck's terms for an armistice. The terms included the surrender of Paris and a 21-day truce. During this truce the French people were to elect a national assembly with the authority to make peace with the German Empire.

The elections were held on February 8, 1871. The results indicated that the French nation, as a whole, wanted peace. Adolphe Thiers [tee-ER] was selected as chief executive of the French Republic. The first task of

DROPPING THE PILOT.

This cartoon appeared in 1890, following the dismissal of Bismarck as chancellor of Germany. Bismarck, the pilot, is shown departing from the ship of state.

supporters could ignore their demands for a truly democratic system of government. Thus, Germany remained an absolutist state until 1918.

QUESTIONS FOR REVIEW

1 *What was the Kulturkampf?*

2 *How did Bismarck strengthen the German Empire?*

3 *Why did some groups within Germany favor the acquisition of colonies?*

467

this provisional government was to make peace. Thiers met with Bismarck and worked out the terms of peace. The exceedingly harsh terms of the Treaty of Frankfurt included the cession of the French provinces of Alsace and Lorraine to the German Empire. It also required France to pay Germany a huge *indemnity*—payment for loss and damage—of nearly one billion dollars. In addition, a large area of French land was to be occupied by the German army until the indemnity was paid.

The outcome of the Franco-Prussian War was a severe blow to the national pride of France. No longer was France the leading military power on the continent. The French government set up in Versailles was unable to provide adequate leadership and French society was divided into various political groups. Each group supported a different course of action.

THE PARIS COMMUNE A short time after the Treaty of Frankfurt, the Paris national guards seized power and set up a *commune*—a city council—to govern the city. The vast majority of the people of Paris were outraged by the terms of the peace. The Parisians looked to the Paris Commune as the true government of France and saw the Versailles government as traitorous. Furthermore, wide differences of opinion developed between those who favored a Socialist form of government and those who favored a more conservative form of government. Civil war broke out in Paris. Government forces from Versailles laid siege to the forces of the Paris Commune. Bitter fighting resulted in the loss of thousands of lives; much of Paris was destroyed.

The government forces succeeded in defeating the rebellious Parisians in May 1871. After the collapse of the Paris Commune, nearly 38,000 people were arrested, and many of these people were sentenced to long prison terms. Paris remained under *martial law*—military rule—until 1876.

THE THIRD REPUBLIC LASTS From its chaotic beginnings, the government of the Third Republic attempted to establish its authority and to unify the country. However, throughout the early 1870's there was disagreement between the republicans, who favored a democratic French government, and the monarchists, who called for a restoration of the French monarchy. By 1875 a number of laws, which formed the basis of the Third Republic's constitutional system, were passed by the National Assembly.

After the Paris Commune rebelled against the French government located at Versailles, the French army bombarded Paris. On May 21, 1871, French troops entered the city. The bitter fighting between the forces of the commune and the army raged for a week. During the fighting, thousands of lives were lost.

Under these laws, all adult males were given the right to vote.

In subsequent elections, representatives favoring democracy gained a majority in the National Assembly and the threats from the monarchists declined. By 1879, the Third Republic was firmly established as the French government. Various social and economic reforms were passed during the latter part of the nineteenth century that served to strengthen the Third Republic. It continued as the French government until 1940.

SOCIAL AND ECONOMIC CHANGES

As business and industry grew with the establishment of a stable French government, the need for reform became evident. Several reform acts improved the living and working conditions of the people. For example, factory acts were passed by the government to reduce the number of hours of work and to prohibit dangerous conditions in factories. Other laws provided workers' compensation benefits in cases of accidents at work.

Other reforms were also enacted after 1875. The educational system—from elementary schools through universities—was reformed so that France had a system of free, universal education. Other laws made school attendance compulsory for all children between the ages of 6 and 13. As they did in Germany, these various social and educational reforms contributed to the growth of nationalistic feelings in France during the late 1800's.

Banking also developed in these years. Although local banks continued to exist, large national banks—the *Banque de France*, for example—set up branch banks throughout the country. These banks attracted large deposits and were able to provide capital for investment. Also during this time a high proportion of French savings was invested overseas. By the turn of the century, France ranked second after Great Britain as the leading creditor nation, loaning vast sums of money to its ally, Russia.

In general, the period from about 1860 to about 1882 was characterized by slow but steady economic growth in France. After 1882, a financial crisis developed that was part of a worldwide economic depression. The depressed state of the French economy lasted until about 1897. A period of economic growth began at that time and lasted until World War I.

POLITICAL SCANDALS

Despite the development of a stable government and the success of the various reform efforts, in the mid-1880's France was shaken by a series of scandals. The most serious of these scandals threatened the very existence of the Third Republic.

The Boulanger affair was the first serious scandal to shake France. In 1886, General Georges Boulanger, the minister of war,

Supporters of Georges Boulanger, the French minister of war, took to the streets after he was dismissed from his post by the French government.

Historical Pictures Service

became a celebrity in France because of his strong stand against the Germans. Boulanger appealed to those people who wanted a restoration of the French monarchy and those who dreamed of a war of revenge against Germany. Some of Boulanger's followers talked of overthrowing the republic and replacing it with a dictatorship headed by Boulanger. Boulanger did not make his exact plans known. However, after the French government took action against him, he escaped to Belgium and later committed suicide.

Another scandal, centering around the bankruptcy of the Panama Canal Company, involved several young government officials. After completion of the Suez Canal in 1869, Ferdinand de Lesseps formed a company to build a canal in Panama connecting the Atlantic and Pacific oceans. From its beginning in 1882, the project ran into serious difficulties, including outbreaks of yellow fever and problems of construction. Perhaps the most serious problem, however, was the mismanagement and graft that plagued the company. This corruption caused the Panama Canal Company to go bankrupt in 1888 and destroyed the careers of several politicians. The bankruptcy also caused many discredited bankers to flee the country or to commit suicide. These scandals weakened the stability of the Third Republic and, later, a more serious scandal threatened the French government's existence.

THE DREYFUS CASE The Dreyfus [DRIY-fuhs] case divided France and ultimately challenged the French ideals of democracy. The crisis began when Captain Alfred Dreyfus, the first Jewish officer on the general staff of the French army, was arrested on October 15, 1894, on suspicion of spying for Germany. Throughout the trial, Dreyfus maintained his innocence. But, disliked by many of his fellow officers as a Jew, Dreyfus was found guilty by a military court. Dreyfus was sentenced to life imprisonment on Devil's Island.

Captain Alfred Dreyfus was unjustly convicted of betraying French secrets to the Germans. The outrage over his case shook the Third Republic.

The case became an issue of national significance. It raised the issue of whether *anti-Semitism*—discrimination against Jews—and injustice would be tolerated in France. It also sharpened the differences between those who favored the Third Republic and those who wanted a restoration of the monarchy. In general, the monarchists, the Church, and the army were anti-Dreyfus. Socialists and intellectuals supported Dreyfus. However, opinion turned against those who were anti-Dreyfus because it was rumored that they were planning to overthrow the Third Republic.

However, the Dreyfus case was not closed. In 1896 a fellow staff officer found documents that convinced him of Dreyfus's innocence. Army superiors, however, refused to reconsider the case. In the meantime, a spendthrift officer, Major Esterhazy—later found to be the actual criminal—was brought to trial but acquitted. During this time, the noted author Émile Zola wrote an open letter to the French president, calling for justice in the Dreyfus case. Zola attacked the military court martial and accused the judges of deliberately acquitting the guilty party—Esterhazy. Zola was convicted of libel and fled to England to avoid imprisonment.

In 1899, Dreyfus received a second trial. Anti-Semitism in the military ran high, and although Esterhazy admitted his own guilt, Dreyfus was again convicted and sentenced to ten years in prison. Fortunately, the French president was sympathetic to Dreyfus and pardoned him. Later, in 1906 the highest civil court in France found Dreyfus completely innocent. Thus, the power of the civil authority triumphed over military authority and the democracy of the Third Republic emerged victorious over its enemies.

FRENCH IMPERIALISM Throughout the nineteenth century, France's primary concern remained European affairs. Even so, imperialism was an important factor in French foreign policy. France built a worldwide empire during this period. For example, as early as 1830 the French army had occupied Algeria. By 1870, French settlers in Algeria had established successful businesses and large farming estates. Algeria was later made part of the French nation.

In 1881, Tunisia became a French protectorate. France was able to obtain political and economic control of Tunisia for two major reasons. The Tunisian government owed large financial debts to France. In addition charges that wild Tunisian tribes were attacking French interests in Algeria gave France the necessary excuses for intervention.

The French were active in Egypt, where France sponsored the building of the Suez Canal. After a financial crisis developed in Egypt, France and England took control of Egypt's finances. However, when riots broke out in 1882, the French fleet withdrew from Egypt and England occupied the country. England then set up its own Egyptian protectorate. By 1904, France had accepted

During the late 1800's, the French built a vast empire in northern and western Africa.

English control of Egypt. French imperialism spread to other parts of Africa. By 1884, the efforts of a young naval officer, Pierre de Brazza, enabled France to claim large sections of central Africa. In 1896 the island of Madagascar, off the east African coast, became part of the French Empire (see Chapter 25.)

French influence spread to East Asia as well. Starting in 1787 by securing trading rights, the French increased their hold over Indochina throughout the nineteenth century. In 1885, the Chinese government was forced to recognize French supremacy in the area. By the turn of the century, France had created an empire in Indochina twice its own size.

French imperialism in the later part of the nineteenth century was significant because it primarily served to revive French nationalism and prestige. This was especially true after France's humiliating loss to the German Empire in 1871. France did not need colonies as foreign markets because France's industrial output barely met the demands of the home market. Even though private enterprise flourished in France's colonies, the costs of administering, maintaining, and protecting the colonies offset any great economic gain to the French government.

QUESTIONS FOR REVIEW

1 *When was the Third Republic of France proclaimed?*

2 *How did Parisians react to the terms of the Treaty of Frankfurt?*

3 *Why was French imperialism in the latter part of the nineteenth century significant?*

National Portrait Gallery, London

Victoria, the queen who gave her name to an era, reigned for 63 years, from 1837 until 1901.

3 GREAT BRITAIN IN THE LATE VICTORIAN ERA

By 1870, Great Britain was already an imperial power. Throughout the late Victorian era—the latter part of the nineteenth century—Britain seldom became directly involved in continental affairs. However, Britain maintained an aggressive imperialist foreign policy. In addition, numerous domestic reforms were carried out in Britain during this time. The forces of nationalism and imperialism worked to maintain the dominant position of Great Britain in world affairs.

GREAT BRITAIN IN 1870 Without question, Great Britain in 1870 was the most powerful nation in the world. Its colonial empire was the largest and richest the world had ever known. Britain's army was superior to all others and its navy dominated the seas.

By 1870, Great Britain had also become the greatest industrial power in the world. British manufactured goods were shipped to markets around the globe. As a result, British prosperity grew and its economic power wielded influence in the affairs of other nations.

Britain in 1870 was also one of the most democratic nations in the world. After 1870, democracy continued to grow in Great Britain. The period of British history from 1870 to the turn of the century was a time of remarkable domestic reform as well as a time of British superiority in world affairs. The policies followed by Britain at this time were largely the work of two outstanding leaders—William Gladstone and Benjamin Disraeli.

GLADSTONE AND DISRAELI William E. Gladstone, a Liberal, and his political rival, Benjamin Disraeli, a Conservative, alternated with each other as prime minister from 1868 to 1880. Gladstone continued to be a dominant force in British politics after Disraeli's death in 1881.

William Gladstone was elected to the House of Commons as a Conservative in 1832, but he later became a member of the

The prime ministries of William Gladstone (left) and Benjamin Disraeli (right) were characterized by numerous social reforms.

Liberal party. Benjamin Disraeli first gained prominence by writing *Vivian Grey* and other novels. Disraeli first favored the Liberals' political philosophy, but he was elected to the House of Commons as a Conservative in 1837.

GLADSTONE'S REFORMS Gladstone's first term as prime minister, from 1868 until 1874, was characterized by numerous reforms affecting many aspects of British society. Reforms were made in the field of education, setting up local school boards and providing that school attendance could be made compulsory for all children between ages of 5 and 13.

The reform of the British government's administration was also accomplished during Gladstone's "Glorious Ministry." In the past, governmental and military positions had traditionally been dependent upon patronage and favoritism. To correct this abuse, a law passed in 1870 made employment in the British civil service dependent upon competitive examinations.

Gladstone's government also worked to correct certain weaknesses in the army that had become apparent during the Crimean War. The administration of the War Office was reorganized, giving the Commander in Chief greater power. The terms of enlistment in the army were improved—from a mandatory 12 years to 6 years on active service and 6 years in the reserve. In addition, flogging as a military punishment in peacetime was abolished. Perhaps most importantly, in 1871 the practice of buying commissions was eliminated. Before this time, an officer's rank could be sold to the highest bidder. Thus, high rank was often an indication of personal wealth rather than of military talent.

Another badly needed reform instituted during Gladstone's tenure as prime minister was the secret ballot. The Ballot Act of 1872 was important to the development of democracy in Great Britain. This was especially true after urban workers were given the right to vote.

The rich, who once exclusively held the right to vote, had few superiors who could intimidate them. But open balloting left the

Protest marches, such as this one by matchmakers, called attention to the harsh, and often dangerous, conditions under which many workers labored. Legislation, sponsored by Prime Ministers Gladstone and Disraeli, did much to improve working conditions in Great Britain.

workers exposed to pressure from employers and landlords. The secret ballot corrected this abuse and aided the growth of democracy.

PROGRESSIVE TORYISM Democracy continued to grow in Great Britain after Benjamin Disraeli became prime minister in 1874. Although a Conservative, or Tory, Disraeli advocated what he thought of as progressive Toryism. Disraeli attempted to promote an alliance between the working class and the conservative landowning class. Disraeli believed that the landowning aristocrats were the best suited to govern in the name of the common people. However, Disraeli did not especially favor the interests of the middle class.

Many significant reform laws, which laid the groundwork for the welfare state of the twentieth century, were passed during Disraeli's second term as prime minister. Several laws improved the conditions of the workers. Peaceful picketing of employers was legalized and the foundations of collective bargaining were laid. In addition, a maximum ten-hour workday was established for workers.

Many other social reforms were achieved during Disraeli's ministry. Legislation con-

cerning slum clearance and the building of new housing was passed. Public health laws setting standards for the sale of safe food and drugs, as well as laws concerning public sanitation, were enacted. Disraeli's administration did much to further the reform movement and to promote the advancement of democracy.

GLADSTONE RETURNS TO POWER Upon returning to power after the election of 1880, Gladstone sponsored several pieces of reform legislation. One of the most important of these measures was the third Reform Bill. This measure extended voting rights to farm workers. Thus, by 1884, Great Britain had extended voting rights to most adult men. Women, however, did not receive the right to vote in national elections until 1918.

Other reform measures during Gladstone's second ministry included the Employers' Liability Act. Prior to this law, when workers accepted employment, they also accepted the hazards of the job. Thus, workers could not sue their employers in case of accidents or for the carelessness of co-workers. However, the Employers' Liability Act provided for compensation for five types of accidents.

(*Text continued on page* 476.)

Life at the Time

Social Class in Victorian England

The society of Victorian England was based upon a rigid social-class system. The social-class system was, for the most part, accepted as part of life. Ministers preached to their congregations,

"God, in His infinite wisdom, had appointed a place for every man, woman, and child on this earth and it was their bounden duty to remain contentedly in their niches."

All people, even the young, were well aware of the social-class system of which they were a part. A young man living around the turn of the century described his perceptions as follows:

"Well there was the wealthy class, the Chorley New Road people and the people that lived up Seymour Road, which was a residential area. . . . The local mill-owner . . . lived in a big house there. There were some other mill-owners, Mallinsons, who had mills and bleach works, and these were the aristocrats . . . in those days. . . . [They owned] big houses and stables at the back—these were the aristocrats, the really top class.

"Then there were the distinct professional classes—the doctors and the solicitors and the schoolmasters, who we thought were a class on their own. . . .

There were certain residential areas, and Seymour Road in those days was one of them, where the professional classes lived. . . .

"We thought ourselves as the respectable working class; we were a little bit above the labouring class who lived in the poorer districts of the town. . . . Mostly artisans and craftsmen; cotton spinners would be included. . . . Father was in the foundry—he was a craftsman, a moulder. In the foundry there were different skilled crafts: moulders, pattern makers, fitters and one or two others, who had served their time at a particular trade. These were a class on their own, and would consider themselves somewhat distinct from the labouring classes, the people who used to do the fetching and carrying, and the assistants. . . .

". . . There were respectable labourers who would mix in various church activities, who took part in the religious life of the church. You would mix with them. You wouldn't look down on them in any shape or form. The only people you'd look down on was the people who used to drink and neglect their family life. . . . We were called the respectable working class. And we were taught to make the best use of every halfpenny or penny that came into the house. My mother had that ingrained in her and we had it ingrained into us."

Poor housing conditions, such as those in working-class tenements, were common in the industrial centers of Victorian England.

Gladstone resigned in 1885, but he returned to the office of prime minister in 1886 and again in 1892. Large parts of Gladstone's third and fourth ministries were spent attempting to solve the Irish Problem and conducting foreign affairs.

THE IRISH PROBLEM Historically, there has been conflict between Ireland and England since the Middle Ages, when English monarchs attempted to conquer Ireland. Even after Ireland had been subdued, the Irish people often rose in rebellion against their English conquerors. The conflict between the Irish and the English grew worse during the Reformation. The Irish remained largely Catholic, while the English were predominantly Protestant. Oppressive laws had been passed by the English Parliament restricting the political, religious, and economic freedom of Irish Catholics. The English also dispossessed—deprived—the Irish Catholics of much of their land.

The continuing troubles between the Irish people and the British government became known as the Irish Problem in the nineteenth century. During the early part of the nineteenth century some progress was made at restoring a few basic rights to the Irish people. For example, in 1829, the Catholic Emancipation Act, which permitted Catholics to be elected to Parliament, was passed. This law allowed the Catholic majority in Ireland to send its own representatives to Parliament. Later, in 1869, under Gladstone's leadership, the Irish Anglican church was disestablished. The Irish Church was thus separated from the State and tax money was no longer used to support a church to which 75 percent of the Irish population did not belong.

In 1881, Gladstone's government passed a land act that greatly expanded the earlier Land Act of 1870. The 1870 act provided only for the reimbursement of tenant farmers for improvement to the land. The 1881 act, however, aided the Irish peasants by providing what became known as "the three F's"—fair rent, fixed tenure, and free sale. Fair rent and fixed tenure meant that the county courts could, upon request by either tenant or landlord, fix rents. Once rents were fixed, eviction was forbidden. Thus the peasants were more secure on their land. Free sale meant that the peasants could sell their tenancy rights to another person. As a result of the Land Act of 1881, many Irish peasants now had a chance to earn a decent living.

IRISH HOME RULE While the Irish land problem was being resolved, the issue of Irish home rule arose. The Irish Nationalist party demanded that Ireland have its own parliament, rather than sending representatives to the British Parliament. The leader of the Irish Nationalist party was Charles Stewart Parnell, who entered the House of Commons in 1874.

In Parliament, Parnell and the 85 members of the Irish Nationalist party tried to obstruct the regular business of Parliament. By obstructing business the Irish members were determined to show that Britain would not be allowed to govern itself until Parliament allowed Ireland to govern itself. Faced with this situation, Gladstone concluded that Ireland must have home rule. In 1886 and again in 1893, Gladstone introduced home-rule bills in Parliament. The Liberal party divided over the issue and both times the bills were defeated. The matter was settled in 1914, when a third home-rule bill was passed by Parliament. However, the provisions of the 1914 bill were not enacted because of the outbreak of World War I. In 1921, Ireland received home rule when it became a British dominion.

BRITISH FOREIGN POLICY Through most of the late Victorian era Great Britain's foreign policy followed the practice of imperialism. There were imperialists among the Liberals and the Conservatives in Parliament. In general, however, the Conservatives more strongly favored British overseas expansion. During the late Victorian era, Britain obtained additional colonies throughout the world. By the turn of the century, the British Empire had reached its greatest extent.

Although British colonization had started as early as the late fifteenth century, vast lands—especially in Asia and Africa—were added to the British Empire in the last half of the nineteenth century. The British rule of India was consolidated during the eighteenth and nineteenth centuries. As Britain's industry expanded, India became a valuable market for manufactured goods. The importance of India to the British Empire was illustrated when Prime Minister Disraeli—a strong supporter of imperialism—proclaimed Queen Victoria Empress of India in 1876. Other areas in Asia—Burma, Malaya, and Hong Kong, for example—grew increasingly important to the British Empire during the last half of the nineteenth century.

The British were also active in Africa during the late Victorian era. In 1875, Prime Minister Disraeli purchased a large share of the Suez Canal, which had been built by the French between 1854 and 1869. Disraeli thus obtained control of the management of the canal. Control of the canal was important because of its location on the route to India.

Economic problems in Egypt prompted France and England to intervene in Egypt's domestic affairs. In response to foreign intervention, riots broke out in Egypt and, after the French withdrew in 1882, the British completely took over the administration of the country. Lord Cromer was sent to Egypt to reorganize the country's finances and government. Cromer actually ruled Egypt from 1883 until 1907.

The British also expanded their control in areas of southern Africa. Britain had acquired the Dutch colony at the Cape of Good Hope in 1806 during the Napoleonic Wars. Almost immediately, there were problems between the original Dutch settlers,

The fierce resistance put up by the Boers against the powerful British army was a major reason why the Boer War lasted for three years.

called Boers, and the new English settlers. Relations between the Boers and the British continued to worsen and in 1899 fighting broke out. The Boer War lasted until 1902, when the Boers surrendered. Later, in 1909, the British government permitted the English and the Dutch states to form a self-governing dominion, similar to the governments of Canada and Australia.

OTHER BRITISH ACQUISITIONS Great Britain's imperialist foreign policy also led to colonial gains in other parts of the world. Disraeli annexed the islands of Cyprus and Fiji during the 1870's. In 1879, the British fought a war with the Zulu—a Bantu tribe in southern Africa—and annexed their land. In 1885 Cecil Rhodes, the British empire builder, persuaded the British government to declare a protectorate over Bechuanaland [BECH-uh-WAHN-uh-LAND]—a region north of the former Dutch colony of Transvaal. This resulted in extending British influence farther north into Africa. Rhodes was determined to build a railroad from the Cape of Good Hope in the south to Cairo in the north, and British control of Bechuanaland was essential to Rhodes's plans.

Later, Rhodes was able to acquire mining and settlement rights farther north. Rhodes flooded the area with settlers, and despite uprisings from the natives, settlement continued. In 1890, Salisbury—the capital city—was founded and the colony was named Rhodesia. By about 1914, the colony had a European population of 25,000.

In 1884, Britain gained control over the land that became known as British Somaliland. The control of this land was important to the British because it guarded the southern approach to the Suez Canal.

Britain conquered the area south of Egypt, which became known as the Anglo-Egyptian Sudan, in 1898. By the turn of the century, Britain also had colonies on the west coast of Africa—Gambia, Sierra Leone, the Gold Coast, and Nigeria (see Chapter 25).

QUESTIONS FOR REVIEW

1 Who were William Gladstone and Benjamin Disraeli?

2 How did the Land Act of 1881 improve conditions for Irish peasants?

3 Why was control of the Suez Canal important to Great Britain?

CHAPTER SUMMARY

After the Franco-Prussian War of 1870–1871, Chancellor Otto von Bismarck worked to strengthen the newly united German Empire. Through the Kulturkampf, Bismarck tried, unsuccessfully, to weaken the power of the Catholic Church. He passed reform laws as a means to weaken the Socialists' support among the workers. After 1883, Bismarck adopted an imperialistic foreign policy. By the turn of the century, Germany ranked among the world powers.

The Third Republic of France was proclaimed during the Franco-Prussian War. After the Treaty of Frankfurt ended this war, the Paris Commune waged an unsuccessful civil war against the Third Republic. The Third Republic became a stable government after 1879. However, political scandals —the Boulanger affair and the Dreyfus case—plagued France at this time. Like the British, the French acquired a vast colonial empire during this period.

Prime Ministers William Gladstone and Benjamin Disraeli were influential and powerful leaders of the British government during the last part of the nineteenth century. Under their leadership, numerous social-reform laws protecting workers were passed and most of the adult male population was given the right to vote. During these years Great Britain's colonial empire grew to be the largest in the world.

CHAPTER 24 IN REVIEW

IMPORTANT WORDS, NAMES, AND TERMS

1 Explain, define, or identify the following:

Hohenzollern	Adolphe Thiers	William Gladstone
kaiser	indemnity	Benjamin Disraeli
Kulturkampf	Treaty of Frankfurt	secret ballot
William II	Georges Boulanger	home rule

FACTS AND IDEAS

2 What were the May Laws of Germany designed to accomplish?

3 Why was Bismarck dismissed from his position as chancellor of the German Empire?

4 When did France accept Bismarck's terms for an armistice ending the Franco-Prussian War?

5 What was the Paris Commune?

6 What was the Irish Problem?

7 When was Queen Victoria of England crowned as the Empress of India?

ANALYZING VISUAL MATERIAL

8 Study the cartoon on page 467. Who is watching Chancellor Bismarck depart from the ship of state? Why is Chancellor Bismarck referred to as the pilot?

9 Examine the picture on page 471. How are the native people indicating their submission to the French? Why do you think this symbolic act was considered important?

CONCEPTS AND UNDERSTANDINGS

10 How did Bismarck strengthen the unity of the German Empire?

11 Why did Bismarck adopt many of the programs favored by the German Socialists?

12 Why did the Dreyfus case become important to the stability of the Third Republic of France?

13 Why did Gladstone believe that the Irish should have home rule?

14 How did Great Britain's imperialist policies affect its position in the world?

PROJECTS AND ACTIVITIES

15 Use library sources to prepare a chart comparing the social-reform laws of Great Britain, France, and Germany. Note the years that the different types of social reforms were made law and the various groups within each nation that these reforms affected. Discuss your findings with the class.

16 Prepare a research report on the foreign policies of Prime Minister Gladstone, Prime Minister Disraeli, or Chancellor Bismarck.

CHAPTER **25** THE GROWTH OF IMPERIALISM

1 China and the West   2 The Rise of Modern Japan
3 British Rule of India   4 The Partition of Africa

Between about 1870 and 1914 Europeans spread their rule, their civilization, and their culture throughout the world. Imperialist powers competed for trading rights in China and divided China into areas of influence. Fearful of Western domination, the Japanese rapidly industrialized and quickly became a first-rate power. The British presence in India caused the growth of nationalist feelings among the Indian people in the late 1800's. A notable example of Western imperialism is the case of Africa, where vast colonial empires were set up in less than 50 years. The forces of imperialism had reached their height around the globe by 1914.

Foreign influence was strongly felt at the Chinese port of Canton in the mid-nineteenth century because of Western trade.

1 CHINA AND THE WEST

The Ch'ing dynasty, which ruled China for over 250 years, surpassed all previous Chinese dynasties in political and economic development. However, China's attempts to maintain its isolation proved unsuccessful as the Western powers repeatedly extracted additional trading rights and interfered in China's internal affairs. By the early 1900's, China had succumbed to foreign intervention and was in a severely weakened state.

THE CH'ING DYNASTY The Ch'ing dynasty came to power in China in 1644. Peasant uprisings had severely weakened the Ming dynasty, and after the peasants took over the capital of Peking, the last Ming emperor hanged himself. Manchu invaders defeated the rebels and founded the Ch'ing dynasty. China was again ruled by a foreign dynasty.

The Manchu consolidated their power within China, and by 1796, the outlying areas of Burma, Tibet, Indochina, and the eastern part of Turkestan had become tributary states of the Chinese Empire. Manchu authority was based mainly on ancient Chinese traditions.

The Chinese believed that their society was the center of the world and that its culture was superior to all others. Thus, the Chinese believed that all the world voluntarily looked to China for learning and culture. China was to teach civilization to the barbarians, as all foreigners were called. The attitude of the Chinese toward foreigners was a key factor in China's inability to respond effectively to growing Western influences. The Chinese view of international relations—cultural imperialism based on Confucian ideology—hindered China's relations with other countries.

TRADE RELATIONS WITH THE WEST The first Europeans to make their impact felt in China were the Portuguese. The Portuguese, motivated by the desire for profit and the desire to convert the people to Christianity, arrived at the Chinese port of Canton in the early 1500's. When the Portuguese conducted themselves in an arrogant and unruly manner, the Chinese attempted to expel them. This experience made the Chinese reluctant to trade with or to have any significant contact with Western countries.

However, after 1550, relations with Europeans improved. Portuguese merchants were tolerated on condition of good behavior, but the Chinese would not recognize the official Portuguese ambassador. The Portuguese merchants were restricted to the peninsula of Macao, and the settlement was placed under strict Chinese supervision. The Portuguese had to pay rent, customs duties, and anchorage fees. The Portuguese traders were permitted to send only two ships per year to the port of Canton. To emphasize Chinese control over the Westerners, a wall was built across the peninsula, thus separating it from the mainland. Despite the severe restrictions, Portuguese trade flourished, and soon other Western countries sought trading privileges in China.

The Portuguese traders were followed by Dutch traders in the early 1600's. The Chinese subjected the Dutch to the same restrictions they had imposed upon the Portuguese. Later, the same policy was imposed upon the British.

Great Britain's China trade began in 1699, when the Manchu granted commercial privileges to the British at Canton. This event also marked the start of the Canton system, so-called after 1757, when the Manchu restricted all foreign trade to the port of Canton. The Canton system expressed the attitude of the Chinese toward foreign relations.

The Canton system imposed severe restrictions upon all Western traders. Trade was undertaken only in Canton, and the foreign merchants were confined to their own restricted areas. At the head of the Canton system was an imperial official

POLITICAL	Date	SOCIAL AND ECONOMIC
Britain defeated France at the Battle of Plassey	~1757~	Canton system restricted all foreign trade in China
First Anglo-Chinese War began	~1839	
	1840~	Dr. Livingstone began missionary work in Africa
Taiping Rebellion broke out in China	~1850	
Commodore Perry reached Japan	~1853	
Sepoy Rebellion broke out in India	~1857	
Meiji Restoration in Japan	~1868	
	1869~	Suez Canal opened
	1885~	First meeting of Indian National Congress
Sino-Japanese War began	~1894	
Ethiopia defeated Italian army	~1895	
Open Door policy implemented	~1900~	Boxer Rebellion put down
Boer War ended	~1902	
Russo-Japanese War began	~1904	
	1906~	Muslim League formed in India
	1908~	Tz'u-hsi, dowager empress, died
Japan annexed Korea	~1910	
Manchu dynasty overthrown	~1911	

known as the *hoppo*. The hoppo's chief responsibility was to collect the tax on foreign trade. To do this, the hoppo employed a group of Chinese merchants, known as the *cohong* merchants. These merchants saw that each foreign ship paid its tax and that the ship's crew conducted itself properly. Profits from the foreign trade went directly to the Chinese government.

ANGLO–CHINESE RELATIONS In an attempt to ease trade restrictions and gain further trading privileges, the British sent an official delegation to Peking in 1793. But this mission failed and conditions grew worse at Canton. The Chinese emperor responded to the British king as follows:

> As your Ambassador can see for himself, we possess all things. I set no value on objects strange or ingenious, and have no use for your country's manufactures. . . . It behoves you, O King, to respect my sentiments and to display even greater devotion and loyalty in the future, so that, by perpetual submission to our Throne, you may secure peace and prosperity for your country hereafter.

During the last half of the eighteenth century, trade in opium with China had grown increasingly important to some European countries, especially Great Britain. In 1800 the Chinese government renewed its prohibition against the importation of opium. Although illegal, the opium trade continued to flourish as smuggling became widespread. The owners of private trading vessels made huge profits from the opium traffic, and the ineffective laws of the Chinese government were ignored. At the same time, the government of the Manchu Empire grew weaker.

Tensions mounted between the Chinese and the British over legal trading rights, the refusal of the Chinese to recognize the British as equals, and the opium trade. In 1839, after the Chinese destroyed 20,000 chests of opium found on British ships, war broke out. The immediate cause of the First Anglo-Chinese War was the opium trade, and it is thus often called the Opium War. However, the basic causes of the war were rooted in the larger conflicts between Eastern and Western cultures.

The military power of the British easily defeated the weak Chinese army. In 1842 the Chinese agreed to the Treaty of Nanking. Under the terms of this treaty, China ceded the island of Hong Kong to Britain, opened five additional ports to foreign trade, and agreed to pay for war damages.

This treaty was the first of the so-called unequal treaties forced upon China. Under these treaties, China granted favorable trading privileges to Western nations. In addition, the West demanded extraterritoriality from the Chinese. This meant that Westerners, in their disputes with the Chinese, were to be tried in Western, not Chinese, courts of law. The unequal terms of these treaties threatened the sovereignty of the Chinese Empire. Another war with Great Britain, which broke out in 1856, further weakened China.

INTERNAL PROBLEMS Throughout the last half of the nineteenth century, the Manchu government suffered from serious internal difficulties. As a result of the increasing ineffectiveness of the Manchu rulers, numerous rebellions broke out in China. The most serious revolt, known as the Taiping Rebellion, lasted from 1850 until 1864 and almost overthrew the Manchu dynasty. The revolt was suppressed only with the aid of several Western adventurers.

The reassertion of Manchu authority was chiefly the result of powerful local Chinese leaders and officials, with the support of Tz'u-hsi [TSOO-SHEE], the dowager empress. From 1861 until her death in 1908, she was the power behind the throne. Her leadership helped to put down revolts and brought back some prestige to the Chinese Empire. However, as a strict traditionalist, she believed that China should adhere to its ancient ways and she encouraged antiforeign and anti-Christian feelings.

THE SINO–JAPANESE WAR The weak and ineffective Manchu government could do little to stop the continuing interference of the Western powers. But one of the most severe blows to Chinese prestige came from

Superior British forces easily won the Opium War. The armed British steamer *Nemesis* is shown destroying Chinese war junks.

Japan. After several years of increasing tension between the two countries, war erupted in 1894.

As a result of the brief Sino-Japanese War, China was forced to recognize the independence of Korea, cede Formosa to Japan, and pay an indemnity of 150 million dollars. In addition, Japan was granted additional trading rights in China. The weakness exhibited by China's defeat caused the Western powers to renew their interference in China.

THE OPEN DOOR POLICY

By the turn of the century, China was in danger of complete disintegration. Russia dominated Manchuria and Mongolia, the Shantung Peninsula was under German control, French influence was felt in southern China, and the British controlled Hong Kong, Weihaiwei, and the Yangtze Valley.

In 1899, John Hay, the American secretary of state, asked the major powers not to interfere with the trading rights of other countries or their spheres of influence—regions where a nation has special trade or military privileges. One reason why the United States favored such a policy was that it had no sphere of influence in China. In 1900, the Open Door policy, which gave the major powers equal trading rights in China, was implemented. The United States indicated that its goal, in addition to equal trading rights, was to preserve China's territorial unity. This announcement came just as the other powers were planning to intervene in China in response to the Boxer Rebellion.

THE BOXER REBELLION

The Boxer Rebellion was a violent reaction against foreign influence in China. A secret society known as the Righteous and Harmonious Fists—called the Boxers by Westerners—demanded the removal of all foreign and all Christian influence in China. The first attacks on Christians occurred in the fall of 1898. Within a short time, the Boxers had killed many people and destroyed much property. Finally, in August 1900, an international army reached Peking and took over the Chinese government. The foreign powers insisted that the Boxers be severely punished and that China pay an indemnity of about 333 million dollars. In addition, the

Foreign Powers in China, c. 1898

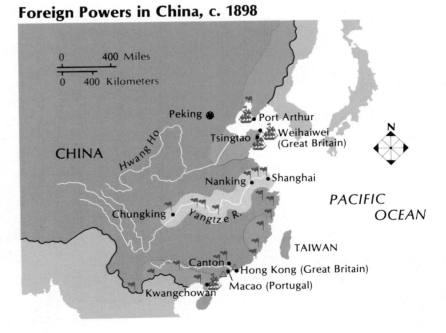

Treaty Port (Controlled by a Foreign Power)

Naval Base

△ Colony

Russia

Germany

Great Britain

Japan

France

During the Boxer Rebellion, Chinese troops stormed the buildings of Western governments in an attempt to rid China of all foreign influence.

foreign powers were allowed to station troops permanently in Peking. China was in a severely weakened state but had not been divided among the foreign powers.

After the Manchu dynasty was restored to power in Peking, the dowager empress, Tz'u-hsi, made serious attempts at reform. However, these efforts came too late. In 1911, the Manchu dynasty was overthrown.

QUESTIONS FOR REVIEW

1 What was the Chinese view of international relations?

2 How did the Canton system attempt to restrict Western trading rights?

3 Why did the United States favor the Open Door policy in China?

2 THE RISE OF MODERN JAPAN

In the middle of the nineteenth century, Japan was still a feudal state, isolated from the West, existing much as it had been for centuries. However, in the latter part of the nineteenth century, Japan underwent dynamic changes with far-reaching results. By the early 1900's, Japan had become an industrialized, autocratic nation competing with European countries for power.

TOKUGAWA JAPAN After establishing its authority in 1603, the Tokugawa shogunate consolidated its power (see Chapter 15). It strengthened its ruling position by distributing land—taken from disloyal feudal lords—among loyal supporters. Throughout the Tokugawa shogunate, the samurai warriors served as administrators of the feudal bureaucracy. The Japanese emperor remained a mere figurehead with no real power.

During the early part of the seventeenth century, Japan carried on limited but friendly relations with the Spanish, the Portuguese, the Dutch, and the English. The Westerners brought trading goods to Japan, and the Dutch and the English set up factories there in the early 1600's. The Westerners also brought Christianity with them. The Tokugawa shoguns grew suspicious of Christianity as rival feudal lords, having been converted to the Western faith, began rebelling against the Tokugawa government.

Determined to maintain its power, the Tokugawa shogunate decided that Christianity and Western influence must be eliminated from Japan. The English left in 1623 and the Spanish were expelled in 1624. An unsuccessful revolt, thought to have been encouraged by Christians, caused the Portuguese to be expelled by the shogun in 1638. In 1639, the only remaining Western traders—the Dutch—were subjected to severe trading restrictions. Japan remained almost totally closed to Western contact until the 1800's.

WESTERNERS OPEN JAPAN From about 1770 to 1840, several attempts by Russian, British, and American merchants to obtain trading privileges in Japan proved fruitless. However, in about 1840 the Japanese, warned by events in China, began to alter their strong antiforeign position.

In 1853, the American commodore Matthew Perry led a large fleet to Japan and delivered a friendly letter from President Millard Fillmore. The letter asked for better treatment of shipwrecked American sailors, the establishment of American whaling stations in Japan, and American access to Japanese trade. Perry informed the Japanese that he expected a formal reply to the letter and would return to Japan for it. Upon Perry's return in February 1854, he was informed that the shogun was willing to sign a treaty. Two Japanese ports were then opened to American trading ships.

In 1853, Commodore Matthew Perry started commercial relations between America and Japan.

The Bettmann Archive

THE END OF THE SHOGUNATE AND THE MEIJI RESTORATION The period from about 1854 to 1868 saw the shogunate's decline and, ultimately, its end. Domestic difficulties had weakened the shogun's authority. By the late 1860's, a group of feudal lords who advocated restoring power to the emperor had gained control. In 1868, supreme authority was returned to the emperor. At this time the capital city of Edo was renamed Tokyo, meaning "eastern capital."

The emperor reigned from 1868 to 1912. His reign has become known as the *Meiji* [MAY-jee]—enlightened government—and thus the return of power to the emperor is often called the Meiji Restoration. The period from 1868 to the turn of the century was a time of unprecedented change in Japan.

During this time Japan was transformed from a feudal country to a Western-style autocratic state. By 1871, the feudal system had officially been abolished and many of the samurai had been pensioned. In 1876, national *conscription*—compulsory military service—went into effect. Japan began to develop a modern, Western-style army based on the French and German armies.

Also at this time the Japanese government formulated a constitution, which went into effect in 1889. The constitution was based upon the German system developed by Bismarck. The position of premier of the Japanese government was similar to that of the German chancellor. The cabinet included nine ministers, each heading a government department and responsible only to the emperor. Since only the army and the navy could appoint the cabinet ministers, however, real governmental authority was in the hands of the military. Although the Japanese constitution adopted some Western ideas, the position and power of the emperor remained sacred.

THE WESTERNIZATION OF JAPAN Many other changes that came about during the latter part of the nineteenth century made Japan more Western in nature. Much of the Meiji emperor's reign was dedicated to making Japan equal to the Western powers and preventing Western imperialism from destroying Japan. The Japanese continued to borrow many Western ideas and institutions.

The Japanese government sponsored a program of industrialization. In 1871, the Japanese began building a system of railroads. The Japanese government also entered the fields of mining, shipbuilding, cement and brick production, and glass and textile manufacturing. The government employed Western experts and used modern equipment. After these government-controlled industries became successful, they were often sold to private owners. The government's active role in industrial development was a chief reason for the rapid westernization of Japan after the Meiji Restoration.

In 1873, the Japanese adopted the Gregorian calendar used in Western countries. The Japanese constructed a telegraph system, lighthouses, dockyards, and other modern facilities. Western experts were also brought in to teach the Japanese about engineering, farming, and medicine. Together, these various innovations worked to strengthen the Japanese government and society. By the early 1890's, Japan was well on its way to a dominant position in eastern Asian affairs.

JAPANESE EXPANSIONISM After 1894, the Japanese imperial government embarked upon a foreign policy of expansionism. Through this policy, Japan planned to gain prestige and power and increase its foreign trade. Japanese expansionism was first exhibited in the Sino-Japanese War. Tensions between China and Japan had been building for several years, especially over China's rule of Korea. War broke out in July 1894 and Japan had soundly defeated China by March 1895. As a result of the war, Japan received the island of Formosa, an indemnity of 150 million dollars, and more trading rights.

Also under the terms of the peace treaty, Japan received the Liaotung [lee-OW-DUNG] Peninsula in Manchuria from China. However, three Western powers—Russia, France, and Germany—demanded that Japan return the Liaotung Peninsula to China and hinted that they might use force if Japan refused. To avoid further confrontation, Japan returned the peninsula to China.

Later, Russia leased the ports of Dairen and Port Arthur in Manchuria from China. Japan grew suspicious of Russia's designs on

Japanese Expansion, 1875–1914

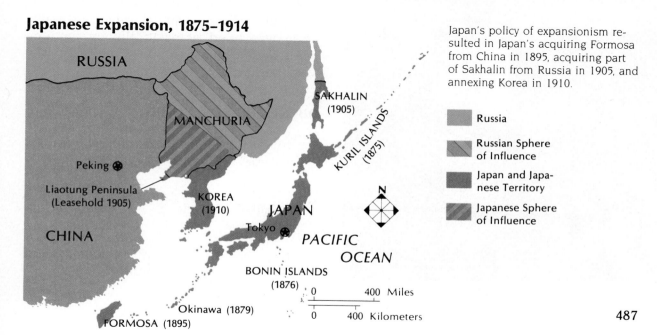

Japan's policy of expansionism resulted in Japan's acquiring Formosa from China in 1895, acquiring part of Sakhalin from Russia in 1905, and annexing Korea in 1910.

487

Manchuria and Korea and attempted to negotiate a division of the area into spheres of influence. Thinking that the Japanese could easily be defeated, the Russians refused to negotiate. In February 1904, the Japanese broke off diplomatic relations with Russia. The Japanese attacked the Russian fleet at Port Arthur, thus beginning the Russo-Japanese War. A series of Japanese victories followed.

By the spring of 1905, however, the Japanese were running short of troops and of money. The Japanese then requested that American president Theodore Roosevelt negotiate a peace treaty. By the Treaty of Portsmouth, Japan received from Russia the southern half of Sakhalin Island, the leases to the ports in Manchuria, and railway rights in southern Manchuria. Japan's interests in Korea were also recognized by this treaty, paving the way for Japanese annexation of Korea in 1910. The Russo-Japanese War marked the first time that a Western power had been defeated by an Asian nation. Perhaps the most significant result of the

Russo-Japanese War was that Japan became recognized as a first-class power.

JAPAN IN THE EARLY 1900'S Japan continued to further its industrial program in the early 1900's. The vast majority of Japan's industries were controlled by private enterprises. These industries often received government aid to encourage their growth. By 1914, Japan equaled many European nations as an industrial power and surpassed any other Asian, South American, or African country.

Despite rapid industrial growth, Japanese living standards remained low. In general, working conditions also were poor. Some workers tried to organize to improve conditions. The government passed laws that forbade strikes and other unionlike activities, but it took some steps to improve working conditions.

Japan was the first Asian nation to achieve a high degree of literacy. However, education was primarily a tool of the Japanese government, designed to produce loyal subjects of the emperor. In addition, the army instilled in its members obedience to the emperor and to the government.

By the first decade of the twentieth century, Japan had been transformed from a backward feudal state into a first-rate power. Japan appeared to be a liberal constitutional monarchy. However, in reality Japan was ruled autocratically by the emperor and a small group of ministers who were backed by the military.

Theodore Roosevelt (center) mediated the peace treaty that ended the Russo-Japanese War in 1905.

FPG

QUESTIONS FOR REVIEW

1 *What did Commodore Matthew Perry accomplish in Japan?*

2 *How did the Japanese constitution of 1889 strengthen the role of the military in the government?*

3 *Why was the outcome of the Russo-Japanese War significant to the Japanese?*

3 BRITISH RULE OF INDIA

By the early nineteenth century, Great Britain effectively controlled all of India. However, throughout the latter part of the nineteenth century, the forces of nationalism grew in India. At the same time, tensions between the Muslims and the Hindus increased. Although both of these groups called for a larger role in Indian affairs, the forces of nationalism did not unite them politically.

THE CONSOLIDATION OF BRITISH RULE After the disintegration of the Mogul Empire in the mid-1700's, France and Great Britain competed for supremacy in India. However, the French were soundly defeated by the British in 1757 at the Battle of Plassey, during the Seven Years' War. This battle marked a new period in Indian history—the period of British rule.

After the Battle of Plassey, the British East India Company—a private trading concern—virtually ruled India. Under the company's rule, the Indian subcontinent was divided into those areas that were subject to direct British rule and those areas that were ruled by local Indian princes. In return for allowing the princes to keep their thrones, the company obtained the right to administer the foreign policy of those areas.

BRITISH REFORMS IN INDIA Great Britain introduced many reforms into India during the first half of the nineteenth century. Under the administration of Lord William Bentinck, governor general from 1828 to 1835, slavery and the killing of girl babies were abolished. *Suttee*—the practice in which widows burned themselves on their husband's funeral pyre—was made illegal. In addition, Bentinck broke up *thuggee*—an organized secret system of religious murder. The thugs, disguised as pilgrims or merchants, strangled their victims as sacrifices

to the goddess Kali. Under Bentinck's administration, the secret organization was crushed.

The British also reorganized the educational system in India, introducing secondary schools and universities. English became the language used in the schools. The British employed Indians in the civil service, but usually in low-level positions. The vast majority of the Indian people were treated as second-class citizens. Indian people were not given the opportunity to take a significant part in governing their own country.

THE SEPOY REBELLION Despite the British reforms, the forces of nationalism that were beginning to develop in India reflected widespread discontent in many regions of the country. The discontent erupted into open rebellion in May 1857. The uprising centered on the mutiny of Indian troops, called sepoys. The sepoys complained that the new rifle cartridges they had been issued were smeared with the fat

By 1858, the subcontinent of India was ruled—either directly or indirectly—by Great Britain.

British Rule in India

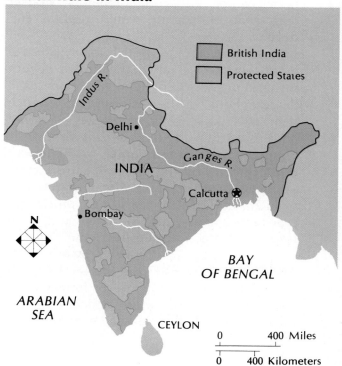

This nineteenth-century drawing shows various stages of the growth of tea plants and of the production of tea. The tea industry had become an important part of the Indian economy by about 1860. British management controlled the tea industry and Indian peasants performed manual labor.

of cows and pigs. This angered the Hindus, to whom the cow is sacred, and shocked the Muslims, to whom the pig is unclean.

In all likelihood the rebellion would have occurred without the cartridge incident, because discontent with British rule was deep-seated and growing. The British had been introducing Western ideas, building railroads, and constructing telegraph lines throughout the country, but the life of the average Indian remained miserable. The presence of British missionaries aroused fears that Christianity would replace Hinduism.

Fortunately for the British, many areas of India remained loyal to the British government during the rebellion. After months of fierce fighting, the rebellion was crushed in June 1858. As a result of the Sepoy Rebellion, the rule of the British East India Company was ended; India was afterward ruled directly by the crown. Queen Victoria appointed Lord Canning as the first viceroy of India. In addition, the queen proclaimed a general amnesty for the rebels and promised complete religious freedom.

THE IMPACT OF BRITISH IDEAS ON INDIA

The years after 1858 were formative in Indian history because the impact of British ideas changed the Indian economy and brought about changes in Indian culture. The British brought to India their basic ideas about a free-enterprise economy. By consolidating Indian markets, the British encouraged large-scale trade and stable prices for Indian goods. Indian agricultural products, such as tea, coffee, cotton, and indigo, became the chief items of foreign trade. The British built irrigation works, thus bringing new land under cultivation. In addition, communications were improved between India and other parts of the world as telegraph lines were laid and as the Suez Canal was opened. Improved communications contributed to the growth of industry and to foreign trade.

Industrialization had begun in India in the mid-1850's. Throughout the latter half of the nineteenth century the number of factories producing cotton, leather, paper, and woolen goods increased in the Indian cities. India's mineral resources, such as coal, were also developed at this time. However, the British-controlled industries in India usually produced only raw materials. Thus, in the long run, the British control of India's industries prevented the development of a manufacturing economy in India.

The effects of British rule also aided the improvement of health conditions and the prevention of famine. Advances in farming methods and agricultural planning helped ease the severity of the frequent famines that had caused the starvation of millions of Indian people.

As a result of the reduction in the number of famines the population of India increased dramatically—10 percent between 1881 and 1891. The population increase caused living conditions for the poor and the unskilled workers in the cities to deteriorate. Also, as the farm population increased, farmers began to divide their land among their children. Over a period of time, the farms became too small to support a family, and many Indian people went to the cities to find work. However, there were not enough factory jobs available.

British rule also changed India's culture. A middle class, educated with Western ideas, developed. The people who made up the middle class were educated in the English language, in English history, and in democratic ideas. These people, with their common educational background, began to develop a sense of national unity. Yet, despite the stirrings of nationalism, there was an increasing separateness between the two largest religious groups in India—the Hindus and the Muslims.

THE ISSUE OF RELIGION The growing nationalistic feelings of the Indian people became entangled with religious issues. New movements developed among the Muslims and the Hindus, and these groups grew farther apart. The division that began in the late nineteenth century between these two religious groups laid the foundation for the partition of India in 1947.

Muslim leaders encouraged their followers to accept Western education and social reforms. They successfully restored to the Muslims the sense of confidence and assertiveness that had been lost after the fall of the Mogul Empire. In time, this assertiveness became increasingly directed against the Hindus, not the British. The Muslims feared political and economic domination by the numerically superior Hindus. In 1906, the Muslims formed an organization known as the Muslim League. The Muslim League was a key factor in preventing Indian unity.

In addition, a number of movements that were influenced by Western ideas developed among the Hindus in the late 1800's. These movements stressed pride in the accomplishments of the Hindu past and its sacred traditions. Most of the Hindu movements centered on a return to strict Hindu beliefs, but some movements became militant and vigorously opposed everything foreign. In 1885, the Indian National Congress met for the first time. Its membership was primarily Hindu and was drawn from the middle class. By 1890 the Indian National Congress was the primary voice of the Hindu majority in India.

INDIAN NATIONALISM Indian nationalism grew in the decades prior to World War I. In the 1890's, the Indian National Congress had called upon the British to introduce various reforms. Later, the Indian National Congress became more revolutionary in nature. Some members advocated the use of violence as a means of achieving the congress's goals. The growing spirit of Indian nationalism was demonstrated in 1906, when the congress demanded self-rule.

Around the same time, hostility toward the British began to increase. The Indians began to express their feelings that the British were cruel, arrogant, and racist. Many British fostered these feelings by their attitude of racial superiority. Outbreaks of violence became common. The issue of race also caused an increase in the tension between the Muslims and the Hindus in India.

Although in the past the Muslims and the Hindus had been able to live in relative peace, the nationalistic pride of each group accentuated their religious and cultural differences. Despite the growing nationalistic feelings of both the Muslims and the Hindus, only a minority of the population called for a complete independence from Great Britain in the early 1900's. Although nationalism was, without question, the most powerful force in India in the early twentieth century, it failed to become unified. Instead, a Muslim nationalism and a Hindu nationalism developed. Each of these forces became pitted against the other. Nationalistic feelings, however, continued to grow through the 1920's and the 1930's.

QUESTIONS FOR REVIEW

1 What was the role of the British East India Company in India in the late seventeenth century?

2 How did the Sepoy Rebellion change the government in India?

3 Why did nationalistic forces fail to unify India?

4 THE PARTITION OF AFRICA

The partition of Africa began about 1870. By 1914 the forces of imperialism had divided the African continent, and the European powers ruled nearly 150 million African people. As the European powers scrambled for African colonies, however, little thought was given to the culture or the life-style of the African people.

BEGINNINGS OF AFRICAN COLONIZATION

During the first half of the nineteenth century, Africa was, for the most part, unknown by Europeans. About 10 percent of Africa was controlled by western European nations. The most significant of the European holdings were Algeria, ruled by the French, and Cape Colony, held by the British. Dutch settlers had set up two small republics—the Orange Free State and the Transvaal. Other European holdings were restricted to coastal ports.

European contacts with Africa south of the Sahara had begun in the fifteenth century as Portuguese explorers searched for an all-water route to India. However, these explorers failed to move into the African interior. Only in the late eighteenth century did Europeans begin to explore Africa beyond the coastal areas. British explorers searched for the sources of the Nile and Niger rivers. French and German explorers found ancient cities and mapped geographical landmarks. The penetration of European explorers into the interior often met with fierce resistance from the African people.

The famous missionary Dr. David Livingstone spent over 20 years in central Africa, performing humanitarian work among the Africans and carefully recording his observations about the land. After Dr. Livingstone's death in 1893, his friend and associate Henry M. Stanley continued the exploration. The reports about Africa and the African people that reached Western nations stimulated the interest of other European explorers and missionaries. The reports also heightened the growing imperialism of the European nations.

REASONS FOR ACQUIRING COLONIES A primary reason for obtaining colonies was economic gain. Colonies provided markets for the manufactured goods of the imperialistic powers. In addition, colonies provided an important source of raw materials—such as cotton, silk, rubber, and copper—for the growing industries of European nations. Worldwide trade on a large scale had become economically feasible only in the late nineteenth century. This was because the construction of railroads and better highways, the completion of the Suez Canal, and the building of faster and larger ships greatly aided trade. In addition, the telegraph made communication possible with even the most-distant lands.

Another reason for the scramble for colonies was the increasing population of some European countries. For example, leaders in Germany and Italy thought of the acquisition of colonies as a way of obtaining places to settle their surplus population. Still another reason for desiring colonies was nationalism. Strong nationalistic drives existed in all the imperialistic nations. The acquisition of colonies added to a nation's international prestige. Germany and Italy, having just achieved national unification, were especially eager to exhibit their new national strength.

The imperialistic drives of the late 1800's included a military factor as well. Colonies were viewed as important because they could serve as military and naval bases to protect a nation's trade routes. Colonies were sometimes thought of as huge troop reservoirs from which native armies could be recruited.

Lastly, humanitarian and religious motives played an important role in the drive for colonies. Many political leaders sincerely believed that the rule of their governments could bring law and order to those areas suffering from tribal warfare. These political leaders sought to bring the best aspects of Western civilization to the people under their rule. Similarly, many religious leaders sincerely believed that it was their task to bring Christianity to native peoples.

INTERNATIONAL CONFERENCES ON AFRICA Upon hearing explorers' reports on the Congo, King Leopold II of Belgium called the first major European conference on Africa. It was Leopold's ambition to acquire a large empire in Africa. The conference, held in Brussels in 1876, was allegedly called for humanitarian purposes. But clearly the purpose of the conference was to gain recognition by the European powers of Leopold's claim to the Congo. Leopold was successful. By 1882, he had personally acquired over 900,000 square miles (2 331 000 square kilometers) of territory in central Africa.

Later, as the rivalry over Africa increased, the threat of war between the European

European rule in Africa in 1870 was mainly restricted to coastal areas. By 1914, however, the European powers had divided nearly the entire continent into vast colonial empires.

European Rule in Africa, 1870 and 1914

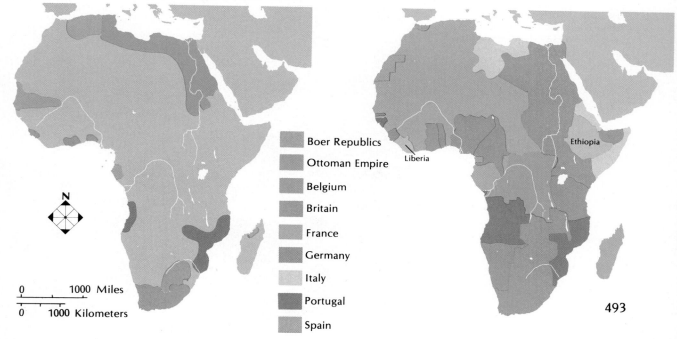

Boer Republics
Ottoman Empire
Belgium
Britain
France
Germany
Italy
Portugal
Spain

Liberia
Ethiopia

N

0   1000 Miles
0   1000 Kilometers

493

powers grew. It became apparent that careful diplomacy was necessary if war were to be averted. Therefore, in 1884, Otto von Bismarck of Germany called a conference in Berlin. At this conference the representatives condemned the illegal slave trade and prohibited the sale of liquor and guns in some areas. The most important work of the conference, however, concerned developing rules for easing international tensions in Africa. It was agreed that Leopold II of Belgium would administer the Congo and that trade in the area was to be free. In addition, no nation was to assert its claims in Africa without telling the other powers of its intentions. No land could be claimed unless it was occupied by the European power, and all disputes were to be settled by arbitration. However, these rules were frequently broken and several times war was barely avoided.

BRITISH ACTIVITY IN AFRICA Between 1870 and 1914 Great Britain established the richest and second-largest empire in Africa. British colonial activity first occurred in southern Africa, when, in 1806, the British conquered Cape Colony during the Napoleonic Wars. Almost immediately, tensions arose between the original Dutch settlers, called Boers, and the new British immigrants. In 1835 the Boers began a six-year journey, known as the Great Trek, to the interior of Africa to escape British rule. The Boers established two republics—the Orange Free State and the Transvaal.

However, the independence of the Boer states was short-lived. With the discoveries of gold and diamonds in the Boer republics from the 1860's through the 1880's, thousands of miners, most of them British, moved into the area. In 1877, the British governor of Cape Colony annexed the mine fields. Relations between the two groups worsened, and in 1899 war broke out. After three years of bloody fighting, the Boers surrendered. As a result of the Boer War, the Boer states became British colonies. In 1909 the Dutch states joined the English states to form the Union of South Africa.

Throughout the 1880's Great Britain extended its control over central and eastern Africa. In 1885 Cecil Rhodes persuaded Britain to declare a protectorate over Bechuanaland. Rhodes then brought European settlers even farther north. The area grew into a major white settlement and in 1895 became the colony of Rhodesia.

Also, in 1890, Great Britain reached an agreement with Germany over claims in

To escape British rule, 12,000 to 14,000 Boers embarked upon the Great Trek in 1835 and moved farther into southern Africa.

In this cartoon of the late 1890's, the British entrepreneur Cecil Rhodes is shown planning to extend British interests from Cape Town to Cairo.

East Africa. A treaty was reached whereby Britain's protectorate over Zanzibar and its claims to what is now Kenya and Uganda were recognized by Germany. In return, Britain recognized Germany's claims in what became known as Tanganyika. During the 1880's, Great Britain had extended its control over Egypt (see Chapter 24). Because of its position in Egypt, Britain became involved in a series of battles trying to hold the area to the south of Egypt—the Sudan. Between 1883 and 1895 thousands of British soldiers died fighting the Muslim nomads of the region. Finally, in 1898, the British conquered the Sudan.

Great Britain also acquired colonies on the west coast of Africa. These colonies grew out of trading posts that had been established in the seventeenth and eighteenth centuries. The tiny colony of Gambia, completely surrounded by French-held lands, was made a British colony in 1843. The colonies of Sierra Leone and the Gold Coast had once been bases for the slave trade. Sierra Leone was taken from the Portuguese and made a colony as early as 1808. However, British settlements and trading posts in the Gold Coast were attacked by the powerful Ashanti warriors throughout the 1800's. Finally, in 1896 British troops defeated the Ashanti.

The largest British colony in western Africa—Nigeria—became a British protectorate in 1900. Before that date, the region surrounding the Niger River was controlled and developed by a private trading concern—the Royal Niger Company. In 1900, the Royal Niger Company sold its holdings to the British government.

THE FRENCH EMPIRE IN AFRICA The first important French colonial acquisition in Africa occurred early in the nineteenth century. In 1830, under the pretext that the Algerian ruler had publicly insulted the French consul, a French army was sent to occupy the country. After 17 years of bitter fighting, the French finally subdued the fierce Algerian nomads.

The French again became active in Africa in the 1880's. In 1881 Tunisia became a French protectorate. The explorations of Pierre de Brazza allowed France to claim huge sections of the Congo region. De Brazza also urged France to claim lands around the Niger River. In 1889 the Ivory Coast became a French protectorate. After a series of brutal wars, the French annexed the African kingdom of Dahomey.

The French developed a colonial policy that called for a vast French African empire stretching across Africa from the Atlantic Ocean to the Nile River or even to the Red Sea. However, the aims of France's policy conflicted with the goals of Great Britain, and the two nations were near war more than once. For example, at the city of Fashoda [fuh-SHOHD-uh] in the Sudan an international crisis, known as the Fashoda Incident, developed. In 1898, the British had begun conquering the Sudan, and upon reaching Fashoda, they found the city occupied by the French. The French commander refused to leave the city unless ordered to do so by his government. International tensions mounted until the British and French governments peacefully resolved the crises.

As a result of the Fashoda Incident, the French did not achieve their goal of reaching the Nile River, but by 1900 they controlled the largest empire in Africa. France's empire stretched from the Atlantic Ocean eastward to the Sudan and from the Mediterranean Sea southward to the Congo River. France annexed the island of Madagascar in 1896 and in 1912 made Morocco a French protectorate.

GERMAN COLONIES IN AFRICA Germany was a late entrant into the race for African colonies. Even so, by 1900 Germany had acquired the third-largest empire in Africa. In 1883, German merchants acquired land in southwestern Africa. Bismarck then declared a protectorate over the region, which became German Southwest Africa in 1884.

During the 1880's Germany acquired control over vast lands on the west coast of Africa. The German explorer Gustav Nachtigal discovered that the British were about to claim this land and quickly declared the region to be under German protection. Nachtigal then assured German rule by negotiating treaties with the local chiefs. These lands became the colonies of Togoland and Cameroons.

On the east coast of Africa, Germany acquired its most important colonial territory. In the early 1880's, Carl Peters organized a trading company—the German East Africa Company. He set out for East Africa and obtained from local chiefs treaties that gave him control of vast stretches of land. In 1887, Peters was granted an imperial charter for his trading company, and later Chancellor Bismarck claimed the region as the protectorate of German East Africa.

OTHER EUROPEAN COLONIES Italy's imperialistic ambitions first centered on Tunisia, in North Africa. However, after France made Tunisia a protectorate in 1881, Italy turned to eastern Africa. In 1882, Italy seized part of the Red Sea coast, which became the colony of Eritrea [ER-uh-TREE-uh]. In 1889, Italy seized Somaliland, on the eastern coast of Africa.

Italy then planned to attack Ethiopia—the oldest kingdom in Africa. Ethiopia, aided by the French, soundly defeated the Italian army in 1895. As a result, Italy was forced to recognize the complete independence of Ethiopia. Italy then turned its attention to Tripoli—what is now Libya. In 1911 Italy declared war on the Ottoman Empire—the nominal rulers of Tripoli—and forced the Ottomans to cede the area in 1912. Thus, by 1914, Africa was almost completely divided into colonies ruled by European powers. Only two countries—Liberia and Ethiopia—remained independent.

THE IMPACT OF IMPERIALISM ON AFRICA Several aspects of European imperialism had an impact on Africa. Perhaps the most significant effect was the loss of native sovereignty by almost all the African people. In most areas of the continent, the African people were subjected to the will of their European conquerers. The Europeans often exercised complete control over the African people.

In addition, the territories into which Africa was partitioned by the Europeans were established without regard for tribal lands or local customs or languages. European partition lines often divided the lands formerly ruled by a single African tribe. Cruel and oppressive colonial administration of the African colonies often resulted in armed rebellions by the African peoples. These uprisings were put down by the colonial powers.

Imperialistic control of Africa was, in most cases, based upon exploitation of the
(*Text continued on page* 498.)

Contributions

The Art of Africa

For many years, Africa was often described as a primitive or backward area of the world. The people were described as if all Africans belonged to a single culture. Many old history books discussed African history as beginning with the coming of the Europeans, and many people believed that all of Africa was jungle teeming with lions and elephants. For the most part, African art was viewed as crude and unsophisticated.

Recently, however, many people have become aware of Africa's many contributions to the fine arts over the centuries. Noted one art museum director, "African art has taken its rightful place among the great art traditions of the world."

In the early twentieth century, some European artists "discovered" that African art is rich and varied. For example, one expert noted that "it was the symbolic, conceptual quality of African art that began to fascinate Picasso . . ."

Art critics have realized that there is no one style of African art. Instead, African art expresses the culture of a native group or of a particular region. African art is not static but is constantly changing with the times.

The visual arts of Africa—sculpture, textiles, painting, and architecture—have perhaps contributed the most to humanity's cultural heritage. For example, the earliest surviving African art consists of paintings and engravings found in rock shelters of the Sahara region. These early examples of African art date back to about 4,000 B.C. The traditions of African painting have been developed and refined over the centuries.

In the second half of the twentieth century, African art has been changing more rapidly than ever before. As modern society changes, the use of traditional art forms has decreased. Newer styles of art are replacing older art forms. Since the colonial period, many African artists have been educated at Western universities. Thus, in addition to receiving traditional artistic training, these artists have been exposed to Western techniques. These artists are then able to draw upon numerous artistic styles and traditions.

As one art critic notes,

". . . African art . . . is at the beginning of a new development. . . . African artists are zealously aspiring to combine the highest achievements and the best traditions of African and universal culture."

Today, the intermingling of African and Western styles is producing a striking richness in the arts of Africa.

African art has become accepted as the creative record of imaginative cultures and has influenced many Western artists.

Alpha

colony for the benefit of the controlling power. Large territories were seized from local rulers without compensation. From many colonies, valuable raw materials were transported back to factories in Europe. In some cases, forced native labor was used by colonial authorities. In most cases, missionaries failed to respect the worth and the dignity of the local people and their customs.

The social and political dominance of the Europeans over the Africans brought an influx of Western ideas. Christianity, Western economic and social ideas, and Western education have had an impact upon African thought. However, European political domination of the Africans directly affected only a small percentage of the African people. The vast majority of the African people lived much as their ancestors had lived. However, because of European influence, the forces of African nationalism began to grow during World War I and the years that followed.

QUESTIONS FOR REVIEW

1 *What parts of Africa were controlled by western Europeans during the first half of the nineteenth century?*

2 *How did King Leopold II of Belgium acquire the Congo?*

3 *Why did an international crisis develop at the city of Fashoda?*

CHAPTER SUMMARY

The Chinese under the Manchu dynasty viewed themselves as culturally superior to foreigners and tried to isolate themselves. These attempts, however, were not successful. The First Anglo-Chinese War, the Sino-Japanese War, and the Boxer Rebellion severely weakened China. Between 1840 and 1900 the imperialist powers gained broad trading rights in China and interfered in China's internal affairs.

Japan, however, rapidly became industrialized and westernized in the late 1800's. The Sino-Japanese War and the Russo-Japanese War greatly added to Japan's prestige. By the first decade of the twentieth century, Japan was recognized as a first-rate power by Western nations.

The British rule of India introduced many Western ideas into the Indian culture. After the Sepoy Rebellion of 1857, British rule brought reforms. In the late 1880's, many nationalist movements began in India. However, the major religious groups—the Hindus and the Muslims—failed to unify their political goals and impeded the growth of Indian unity.

Beginning about 1870, the Western powers started to partition Africa. France, Great Britain, Germany, Belgium, Italy, Portugal, and Spain each won shares of Africa. Imperialist control of Africa was often exercised without regard for the customs and traditions of the African people.

CHAPTER 25 IN REVIEW

IMPORTANT WORDS, NAMES, AND TERMS

1 Explain, define, or identify each of the following:

Canton system   conscription   Indian National Congress
extraterritoriality   Liaotung Peninsula   Leopold II
Tz'u-hsi   suttee   Boers
Meiji Restoration   Muslim League   Carl Peters

FACTS AND IDEAS

2 What was the Chinese view of international relations?

3 When did Great Britain's China trade begin?

4 What was the Open Door policy?

5 What steps did Japan take toward westernization in the late nineteenth century?

6 What role did the issue of religion play in the development of Indian nationalism?

7 What were four major reasons why European nations wanted to acquire colonies?

ANALYZING VISUAL MATERIAL

8 Examine the map on page 484. Which foreign power controlled the island of Taiwan? Along what river was Great Britain's sphere of influence? What city was the location of a Russian naval base? How do you think the spheres of influence resulted in China's loss of sovereignty?

9 Study the maps on page 493. Which nation lost all its holdings in northern Africa by 1914? Which nation controlled small areas of northern and western Africa in 1870? Which nation controlled most of western Africa in 1914? Why do you think the European powers acquired vast empires in Africa?

CONCEPTS AND UNDERSTANDINGS

10 How did the Chinese attempt to limit contacts with foreigners by the use of the Canton system?

11 How did the Sino-Japanese War and the Russo-Japanese War change Japan's position in world affairs?

12 How did the British rule of India affect the development of Indian culture?

13 Why was the Fashoda Incident important to French colonial aims?

PROJECTS AND ACTIVITIES

14 Using pictures from magazines and newspapers, prepare a bulletin-board display showing Western influence in Japan.

15 Select an African nation that was once under European rule. Using library materials, prepare a research report showing how that African nation came under European control and how the period of colonial rule has affected its development since it gained independence.

CHAPTER 26 PROGRESS IN THE INDUSTRIAL AGE

1 A New Scientific Revolution   2 Science and Society
3 Changes in the Arts   4 Growing Social Awareness

The Industrial Age—roughly the last half of the nineteenth century in many countries—transformed much of western Europe and America. Not only did changes occur in industry and commerce in these countries, but cultural life was transformed as well. Perhaps the most important developments took place in science. Scientific discoveries challenged familiar views of the nature of the universe and beliefs about the origins and the development of living things. Science also provided many practical achievements and greatly improved medical care throughout the industrialized world.

New forms of expression in literature, art, and music flourished during the late nineteenth century, and the limits of the classical period of the previous century were abandoned. This was also a time when women's rights became a major issue, as women in many Western countries fought for greater equality.

Sunday Afternoon on the Island of La Grand Jatte, painted by Georges Seurat, was one of the many achievements of nineteenth-century art.

1 A NEW SCIENTIFIC REVOLUTION

Science, more than any other factor in the past three centuries, has changed everyday life. Science has also influenced the ways in which people look at themselves, at their past, and at their future. Although the framework of modern science was built during the 1600's and the 1700's, it was not until the 1800's that the study of science became truly systematic. However, it was the earlier discoveries that refined scientific thought, methods, and instruments and that gave scientists of the 1800's powerful tools with which to carry on their work.

THE THEORY OF EVOLUTION One of the most far-reaching developments of the nineteenth century was the publication of Charles Darwin's book *On the Origin of Species* in 1859. In this book, Darwin put forward a controversial theory on the development of life. He held that all living things had *evolved*—gradually changed—from earlier forms of life. The British naturalist reached this startling conclusion after more than 20 years of careful thought and interpretation of data he had collected.

Simply stated, Darwin's theory held that all forms of life produced many more offspring than could survive to adulthood. According to Darwin, this resulted in a constant battle to stay alive, which he called the "struggle for existence." Darwin also believed that organisms vary within each species. Because each organism varied, it might carry a special trait that could enable it to adapt more easily to a certain environment and to survive where organisms that lacked the trait would die out. This idea became known as "survival of the fittest."

The final part of Darwin's theory dealt with a concept called "natural selection." Basically, this meant that an organism that possessed a trait helpful to survival would pass that trait on to the next generation.

The trait was then passed on to each succeeding generation, according to Darwin. In this way, Darwin believed, all forms of life gradually changed over time.

Darwin's theory of evolution was not entirely new. Another British naturalist, Alfred Russel Wallace, working independently, came to many of the same conclusions as Darwin. Furthermore, nearly a half century before, a French scientist, Jean Baptiste Lamarck, published his views on how living things changed. In fact, the idea that living things change over vast periods of time—*evolution*—can be traced back to the writings of the Greek philosopher Aristotle. Although many scientists before Darwin had worked on the idea of evolution, it had never been stated with such convincing simplicity.

Many scientists accepted Darwin's theory. However, they continued to experiment and to add their own ideas to those of the British naturalist. For example, in the 1860's Gregor Mendel, an Austrian monk, experimented with garden peas. He found that certain laws governed the changes that took place in species from one generation to the next. Mendel's work formed the basis of the science of heredity.

DISCOVERIES IN THE PHYSICAL SCIENCES During the 1800's the developments in the biological sciences were accompanied by many achievements in the physical sciences. Physicists formulated general laws of science that were developed from important inventions such as the steam engine. These generalizations formed the basis of the study of *thermodynamics*—the relationship between heat and energy—and had many practical applications in industry. For example, these laws could be used to design a better steam engine. They were later applied to the gasoline engine, as well as to other forms of energy, such as electrical and nuclear energy. The laws of thermodynamics also eventually led to the unsettling idea that the sun might not shine forever.

Great strides were also made in the field

POLITICAL		SOCIAL AND ECONOMIC
	1796	Smallpox vaccine developed by Edward Jenner
Napoleon defeated at Battle of Waterloo	1815	
Nicholas I became czar of Russia	1824	
	1827	Beethoven died
Louis Philippe became king of France	1830	
	1831	Faraday invented the electric dynamo
British Reform Act passed	1832	
Chartist movement began in Britain	1836	
	1843	Wordsworth became poet laureate of England
Louis Napoleon became president of France	1848	
	1859	Darwin's On the Origin of Species published
British women householders gained the vote	1867	
Franco-Prussian War ended	1871	Darwin's The Descent of Man published
Britain acquired Suez Canal from Egypt	1875	
	1885	Pasteur gave first inoculation against rabies
	1898	Marie and Pierre Curie isolated radium
Russo-Japanese War ended	1905	Einstein put forward Special Theory of Relativity
	1914	Panama Canal opened
British women gained the right to vote	1918	

of electricity. In 1831, Michael Faraday (1791–1867) invented the electric dynamo, a machine that converted mechanical energy into electricity. This led to the development of the electric motor, of the transmission of electric current over power lines, of the telephone, and of the electric light-bulb.

Other scientists put forward the idea that electricity moves in waves in much the same way as light. Heinrich Hertz (1857–1894) was able not only to demonstrate this property of electricity but also to measure the velocity of the electromagnetic waves. Eventually, Hertz's discoveries led to the invention of the wireless telegraph, the radio, and, later, television.

PROGRESS IN MEDICINE The nineteenth century was also a time when the quality of life in the modern world was remarkably improved by advances in medical science. In 1796, a smallpox vaccine was developed by an English doctor, Edward Jenner (1749–1823). The vaccine grew out of the idea that inoculation with a mild form of a disease could increase people's *immunity*—resistance—to the disease. They would then be protected from a more serious attack. Vaccines also dramatically slowed the spread of cholera, typhoid, and the plague.

In the 1860's, the French chemist Louis Pasteur (1822–1895) made a discovery that led to the germ theory of disease. Pasteur found that many diseases were caused by *microorganisms*—bacteria—that exist in the air. Pasteur's first development based upon this idea was to slow down fermentation in wine by killing bacteria through a heating process. This concept was quickly applied to the processing of milk and became known as pasteurization. During the 1870's, Pasteur's studies led to the development of animal vaccines made from disease bacteria. In 1880, Pasteur tackled the study of rabies. By 1885, he had inoculated a small boy who had been bitten by a rabid dog.

Several improvements were also made in surgery and in the treatment of wounds

In 1796, Edward Jenner developed the first vaccine for smallpox. In that year, the English physician successfully inoculated a small boy with cowpox, a mild disease, increasing the boy's immunity to a more serious attack of smallpox.

during the nineteenth century. Anesthetics to deaden pain and to produce unconsciousness during surgery were first used in the 1840's. Although this development removed some of the fear of surgery, patients continued to die from serious infections that resulted from operations. Beginning in the 1860's, a surgeon named Joseph Lister (1827–1912) used many of Pasteur's ideas to demonstrate the importance of antiseptic and sterile procedures in treating wounds and in performing operations. Prior to Lister's work, few surgeons bothered to sterilize their instruments or even to wash their operating coats. This was because they did not understand the causes of infection. Lister tested his ideas by sterilizing the instruments that he used, as well as the area on which he operated. He also began to disinfect open wounds. Antiseptics and sterile instruments helped to reduce the spread of serious infectious diseases in hospitals.

By the end of the nineteenth century, new ideas about the causes of diseases, new methods of diagnosis, and new instruments had dramatically improved medical care in many countries. For example, the German physicist Wilhelm Conrad Roentgen discovered mysterious invisible rays, which he called X rays. He found that X rays penetrated many objects. Other scientists soon found that X rays could be used for medical diagnosis, primarily because X rays are not stopped by flesh as they are by bone. Therefore, a shadowlike picture of a person's bone structure can be taken by using X rays. During the first years of the twentieth century, medical science continued to find new ways to treat disease and to find out more about the human body.

QUESTIONS FOR REVIEW

1 *What was the importance of Faraday's electric dynamo?*

2 *How did Darwin believe all living organisms evolved?*

3 *Why can X rays be used for the purpose of medical diagnosis?*

2 SCIENCE AND SOCIETY

During the nineteenth century, the impact of science also led many European thinkers to begin to view society as if it were a living organism, constantly changing and progressing. The assumptions of the eighteenth century that centered around a belief in the goodness and reasonableness of people were undermined by the preoccupation with the bountiful material goods that resulted from industrialization. This led scientists of the late 1800's to explore the nonrational, unreasonable side of human actions. Scientific discoveries also changed the way in which people looked at themselves and at the universe.

SOCIAL DARWINISM The impact of Darwin's theory of evolution was immediately felt throughout nineteenth-century society. Although Darwin was careful to apply his ideas only to biological science, others quickly adapted the theory to the study of society. Social Darwinists, as they became known, had a great influence upon European thought during the late 1800's and the early 1900's.

One early social Darwinist was Herbert Spencer. Spencer had begun to think of society in evolutionary terms even before the publication of Darwin's ideas. However, Spencer quickly embraced Darwin's theory as an explanation of how society changed. Spencer believed that societies evolved in much the same way as living things. Thus, the concept of natural selection meant to Spencer that the fittest members of society would survive and that society would continually improve. Those who did not survive in society and who remained poor were unfit. Money was the reward for the fittest members of society.

Tragically, social Darwinism was also used as an excuse for the cruel imperialistic and racial policies of some countries during the late 1800's (see Chapter 25). Europeans had begun to look at the world differently. They believed that Europe had a more-civilized way of life and that this way of life must be brought to backward and uncivilized parts of the world. An ugly outgrowth of this point

Charles Darwin developed a theory of evolution to help explain biological development. Social Darwinists, however, applied his ideas to society. A 1902 cartoon satirized the cutthroat practices of big business, which the social Darwinists had readily defended.

of view was racism, the view that the nonwhite peoples of the world were inferior to the white Europeans.

During the twentieth century, social Darwinism came under attack from many directions. Social scientists discredited the theory by showing the complex ways in which societies change. The freedom to think and to choose in a reasonable way undercut the basis of social Darwinism. In addition, such things as the passage of social legislation that eased the lives of the poor and the less fortunate seemed to show that the evolution of society cannot be explained in simple, biological terms.

SCIENCE AND RELIGION The scientists of the nineteenth and early twentieth centuries developed many theories that caused people to question basic religious teachings. For example, in 1795, Scottish geologist James Hutton's book *Theory of the Earth* described the great natural forces that were continually at work forming the earth's surface. Hutton's ideas pointed to the tremendous age of the earth. In 1859, Charles Darwin's theory of evolution added to the growing controversy. In his book *The Descent of Man*, published in 1871, Darwin went even further by attempting to explain human origins. By the end of the century, many new discoveries had led scientists to place human origins far back in prehistory.

Religious groups responded to the discoveries of science in various ways. Some groups reexamined and redefined more broadly their religious beliefs. Other groups held that because religion involved faith, religious concepts could not be completely understood by science. Some religious groups rejected the findings of the scientists. Still other groups came to believe that these discoveries were new ways in which God was being revealed to humans. The leaders of the Roman Catholic Church met the challenge of science by reasserting the church's position in the lives of the faithful. Thus by 1900, many religions and many religious thinkers had, for the time being, reconciled the findings of science with matters of faith.

CHANGING EUROPEAN THOUGHT There were other ways in which science influenced European thought in the late nineteenth century. During the Enlightenment, most thinkers had viewed humans as basically good and reasonable individuals. However, in order to uncover the motives behind human actions, many thinkers of the late nineteenth century looked upon human nature as unreasonable, or nonrational. Perhaps, as some nineteenth-century philosophers wondered, people were neither good nor reasonable. And perhaps people reacted more to emotion and to instinct than they did to reason. By the early 1900's, these ideas began to gain wide acceptance. Eventually, they became characteristic of Western thought during the twentieth century.

One of the foremost thinkers and writers on the nonrational side of human nature was the German philosopher and poet Friedrich Nietzsche [NEE-chuh], who lived from 1844 to 1900. According to Nietzsche, people who achieved control over their emotions were free of all of society's restrictions and codes of behavior. Nietzsche called this type of individual a superman. Nietzsche's ideas were later misinterpreted and twisted to justify the horrible racial and militaristic policies of some European nations during the twentieth century (see Chapter 31).

Nietzsche was not alone in his study of the nonrational side of human behavior. As attitudes toward the nature of human behavior began to change during the late 1800's and the early 1900's, social scientists in many countries attempted to understand the nonrational ways in which people sometimes act.

THE INNER SELF The science of *psychology* —the study of human behavior—emerged as scientists of the late 1800's tried to explain the reasons behind human actions. One branch of psychology—behaviorism—began as experimenters attempted to find out how certain physical and environmental factors influenced behavior. The best-known psychologist in this field was a Russian, Ivan Pavlov (1849–1936). Pavlov showed how the behavior of animals—and, by implication, the actions of humans—could be carefully shaped. His studies led to the startling conclusion that the environment was extremely important in shaping behavior.

Some psychologists, however, felt that the experiments of Pavlov and others did not take into account the part that the unconscious mind played in human actions. These scholars did not completely agree with the notion that behavior could be changed as easily as the behaviorists claimed. A physician from Vienna named Sigmund Freud [FROYD], who lived from 1856 to 1939, pioneered the study of the unconscious mind. Freud's work has greatly influenced twentieth-century thought and culture.

From his observations of patients with mental disorders, Freud concluded that people often behaved according to certain desires and feelings of which they were not aware. He also held that dreams revealed the true inner emotions of people. These feelings were usually repressed, or held in, during waking hours. Freud also developed a treatment for mental disorders—called *psychoanalysis*—in which the patient and doctor probe the unconscious mind of the patient through memories of the patient's past. This was done in an effort to uncover the reasons that might lie behind the patient's behavior.

NEW CONCEPTS OF MATTER, ENERGY, AND THE UNIVERSE As the nineteenth century drew to a close, scientific discoveries changed the way in which scientists interpreted nature. Since the time of Newton, scholars had held fast to a belief in the mechanical nature of the universe. By the early 1800's, scientists also believed that the universe was made up of invisible and indestructible particles of matter, called atoms. During the late 1800's and the early 1900's, however, experiments in electricity and magnetism showed that the atom itself was made up of even tinier, electrically charged particles.

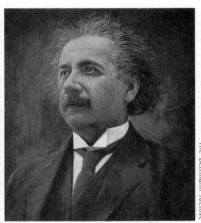

At the turn of the century, Sigmund Freud (left) developed startling theories about human behavior. Marie Curie (center) and Albert Einstein (right) made many discoveries in the physical sciences.

One of the first important discoveries regarding the structure of the atom was made in 1895 when Roentgen discovered X rays. Other developments soon followed Roentgen's experiments. Within a year, the radiation of uranium was first observed by the French scientist Antoine Becquerel. In 1898, Marie and Pierre Curie isolated the radioactive element radium from pitchblende, an ore of uranium. Between 1900 and 1920, further experiments by other scientists showed that atoms were not solid but were made up of even smaller particles. The discoveries of Max Planck (1858–1947), Albert Einstein (1879–1955), and Niels Bohr (1885–1962) showed that matter and energy were not separate substances but were different forms of a single substance. These and other developments helped to explain how an element such as uranium was *radioactive*, or able to give off particles from within the atom at tremendous velocities. The conclusions drawn from these experiments also predicted the incredible amounts of energy that waited to be unleashed in the atom.

Einstein was one of the true geniuses of his time. Besides his work in the field of matter and energy, he also presented a new view of the universe. Einstein believed that time, space, and motion were *relative*—changeable—concepts, not absolute, as Newton had believed. Einstein's work has led to an expanded understanding of how the entire universe works.

QUESTIONS FOR REVIEW

1 *Who were the social Darwinists?*

2 *How did various religious groups respond to the challenge of science in the late nineteenth century?*

3 *Why did Freud believe that dreams were important in the study of the unconscious mind?*

3 CHANGES IN THE ARTS

European cultural development during the first half of the nineteenth century was very different from that of the eighteenth century. The formal approach of the previous century gave way during the early 1800's to emotionalism and fantasy. But by the mid-1800's, a more detached view of society emerged and a new cultural movement developed that pictured life more realistically. Both these views have been important to the development of Western culture to the present day.

ROMANTICISM By the early nineteenth century, European culture had begun to turn away from the reason of the eighteenth-century Enlightenment. Artists, writers, and musicians of a new movement—called *Romanticism*—expressed personal feelings and emotions in their works. Romanticists were idealists who loved freedom, nature, and beauty and who often used legends, fantasies, and folktales in their works. Romanticism was also an escape from the many social problems and the materialism of the Industrial Age.

The beginnings of Romanticism can be traced to the late 1700's and to such writers as Jean Jacques Rousseau, who believed that people had to learn to trust their emotions. In Germany, early Romantic writers included Johann Christoph Friedrich von Schiller (1759–1805) and Johann Wolfgang von Goethe (1749–1832). Goethe's dramatic poem *Faust* was based upon an old German legend about a man who sold his soul to the devil. This poem became a classic of Western literature.

During the early 1800's, Romanticism flourished in Great Britain and in France. The English Romantic poet William Wordsworth (1770–1850) often wrote about nature. But it was not the orderly, mechanical nature of

Newton. Rather, Wordsworth looked at nature as something wonderful and mysterious that was not to be analyzed.

Other British poets were concerned with freedom and showed a rebelliousness and social conscience in their writing. Such concerns reflected the rise of liberalism and of nationalism, so central to the rebellions that swept Europe between 1820 and 1848 (see Chapter 22). Among these poets were John Keats (1795–1821), Percy Bysshe Shelley (1792–1822), and Lord Byron (1788–1824). Byron even joined in the Greek revolt against the Ottomans in 1823. He used his wealth and romantic enthusiasm to fight for the Greeks until his untimely death from a fever.

Romantic historical novels were also popular during the early 1800's. In Scotland, Sir Walter Scott (1771–1832) wrote dramas set in England's medieval past. The historical novel also flourished in France. Romantic

The fanciful novels of Alexandre Dumas—including *The Three Musketeers* and *The Count of Monte Cristo*—were characteristic of the Romantic movement in France.

The Bettmann Archive

French literary figures included Victor Hugo (1802–1885), who wrote about fifteenth-century France in *The Hunchback of Notre Dame*, and Alexandre Dumas (1802–1870), who wrote adventure stories, such as *The Three Musketeers.*

American literature was strongly influenced by Romanticism. Many of the same approaches to romantic writing in Europe can be found in American works. For example, Washington Irving (1783–1859) retold European legends in an American setting in "Rip Van Winkle" and "The Legend of Sleepy Hollow." Mystery, fantasy, and the supernatural were also popular American themes and can be found in the stories of Nathaniel Hawthorne (1804–1864), Edgar Allan Poe (1809–1849), and Herman Melville (1819–1891). A love of nature and of liberty also characterized American Romanticism.

ROMANTICISM IN ART AND ARCHITECTURE The Romanticism of the early nineteenth century also had an impact upon art and architecture. During the late 1700's, painting was dominated by the Classical school, which stressed precise drawing skills and classical poses (see pages 398 and 413). Romantic painters, however, broke away from the traditional themes and forms of the eighteenth-century classicists by relying upon color, emotion, and imagination. Landscapes, legends, and struggles for freedom were common subjects of the Romantic movement in art.

One of the earliest of the Romanticists was the Spanish master painter and political liberal Francisco Goya (1746–1828). His paintings frequently depicted contemporary events, such as the cruelties of Napoleon's repressive occupation of Spain. In France, the Romanticist Eugène Delacroix (1798–1863) often used exotic themes in his paintings that were drawn from a visit to North Africa. The most important Romantic painters in Britain were John Constable (1776–1837) and J.M.W. Turner (1775–1851). Constable also began to create an effect, or impression, of shadow and light in his paintings that was a forerunner of a later movement in art. In general, Romanticists sought to bring out a strong emotional reaction from those who viewed their works.

Architecture of the Romantic period also broke with the architectural traditions of the 1700's, which had been largely based upon Greek and Roman models. During the late 1700's, large public and government buildings in Europe and in the United States often imitated the Greek and Roman past. However, Romanticism revived medieval Gothic architecture in Europe after about 1830. Buildings with spires, towers, and arches were constructed. Among the best examples of Gothic architecture are the Houses of Parliament in London, built between 1840 and 1860.

MUSIC IN THE NINETEENTH CENTURY
Like their counterparts in art, musicians and composers turned away from classicism in the early nineteenth century. Music entered into a period that was characterized by emotion and individualism. Composers began to write music for everyone, not just for the Church or for the privileged upper classes, as they had done in the past. Orchestras, which had been small during the 1700's and chiefly limited to stringed instruments, became much larger, and the piano in particular became an important solo instrument.

The composer who led the movement away from the classical tradition was Ludwig van Beethoven (1770–1827). He wrote music filled with powerful emotions and shocked many of his contemporaries. Many of Beethoven's compositions were written after he began to go deaf in the late 1790's.

Between about 1850 and the early 1900's, the expression of nationalism became an important part of Romantic music, particularly in eastern Europe. Nationalistic composers gave a uniqueness to their music by using in their works folk songs and dances that were native to their lands.

During the early 1800's, the German composer Ludwig van Beethoven revolutionized classical music by writing intensely emotional works.

REALISM During the mid-1800's, critics of Romanticism became more numerous. They felt that Romanticism, with its fanciful subjects and emotions, was an attempt to escape from the problems of everyday life. Romanticism, the critics declared, did not realistically show the serious problems of society. Out of this criticism a new movement called *Realism* emerged. Realists believed that human experiences must be carefully observed and then presented in a relatively unemotional and detached way.

A few writers seemed to be both Romanticists and Realists. Charles Dickens and Victor Hugo were, in many ways, bridges between the two movements. Their writing was intensely emotional yet portrayed the problems of society in a realistic way.

Realism did not become popular in the United States until the last quarter of the nineteenth century. American Realism was characterized by the novels and stories of Samuel Clemens—Mark Twain—who relied upon a biting sense of humor to point out the problems of contemporary society.

Realism also flourished in Russia. Count Lev Tolstoy (1828–1910) wrote the monumental work *War and Peace*. This book, set against the background of the Napoleonic wars, described fundamental relationships between people. Fëdor Dostoevski [DAHS-tuh-YEF-skee] (1821–1881) probed the inner emotions of people in such major works as *Crime and Punishment* and *The Brothers Karamazov*.

By the end of the century, literature had become more probing and psychological. Much of this writing was also pessimistic and filled with symbolism. On the stage, the dramas of the Norwegian playwright Henrik Ibsen (1828–1906) were typical of the changes in literature. Ibsen's plays were deeply critical of middle-class attitudes and morals and often shocked the largely middle-class audiences of the late nineteenth century.

CHANGES IN ART Realism also influenced changes in art. Instead of the exotic scenes of the Romantics, Realist painters used ordinary subjects from everyday life. The Realists neither exaggerated nor idealized their subjects but tried to paint them just as they appeared. The foremost Realist painter was Gustave Courbet [kur-BAY] (1819–1877). His most famous painting is *The Stone Breakers*, in

Le Moulin de la Galette, 1876, EPA/Art Resource/Scala

Beach in Normandy, c. 1869, National Gallery of Art, Washington: Chester Dale Collection

The Church at Auvers, 1890, EPA/Art Resource/Scala

During the 1800's, art flourished as many styles developed in rapid succession. A painting by Gustave Courbet (left) shows how carefully Realists worked to portray everyday subjects. An impressionistic work by Pierre Auguste Renoir (below left) conveys a momentary glimpse of a busy scene. Postimpressionist Vincent van Gogh painted with bold brush strokes (below).

which two workers—one young, one old—toiled with quiet dignity in their jobs.

In Courbet's own lifetime, the invention of the camera offered a serious challenge to realist painting. Whether this development led artists to consciously move away from the realists' exact representations of life is not clear. Nevertheless, during the 1860's and the 1870's, a new school of painting—called *Impressionism*—developed in France. Impressionists used light, especially sunlight, and rich colors to create momentary impressions of scenes before the mind had a chance to analyze the details.

The forerunner of the revolutionary impressionistic style of painting was Édouard Manet [ma-NAY] (1832–1883). It was Claude Monet [moh-NAY] (1840–1926), however, whose painting *Impression: Sunrise* gave the movement its name. Monet used the ideas of Manet to create brilliant outdoor scenes. Meanwhile, the French entertainment world was painted by Pierre Auguste Renoir [REN-WAHR] (1841–1919). Edgar Degas [duh-gah] (1834–1917) carefully studied the movement of the human body and became well-known for his paintings of ballet dancers. The American artist Mary Cassatt [kuh-SAT] (1845–1926) was recognized for her paintings of women and children. The sculptor Rodin [ROH-dan] (1840–1917), while not exactly transferring impressionism to sculpture, was moved by this impressionistic revolution in art. He produced powerful works in bronze—such as *The Thinker*—and in marble.

Biography

Mary Cassatt

The only American painter whose works were exhibited alongside the Impressionists in Paris during the 1870's and the 1880's was Mary Cassatt. She was born in Pennsylvania in 1845. Between 1861 and 1865, Cassatt studied drawing at the Pennsylvania Academy of Fine Arts. At the age of 20, she decided to travel to Europe in order to see firsthand the works of the old masters of European painting. In 1868, after a 3-year tour that took her from Madrid, Spain, to Antwerp, Belgium, Cassatt settled in Paris and became a close friend of the French Impressionist painter Edgar Degas, who greatly admired her work.

Mary Cassatt was principally a figure artist. She was influenced by the style and composition of Degas's works as well as by the style of Édouard Manet. Like Degas, some of Cassatt's best works were done in *pastels*—soft, colored crayons. Cassatt became well-known for her paintings of groups of women and especially of her scenes of women and children together in everyday circumstances and surroundings. During the 1890's, she created several works that showed the influence of Japanese printmakers. These prints rank among her most interesting accomplishments. Her eyesight began to fail after 1900, and she stopped working as an artist around 1914. In 1926, Mary Cassatt died in her home near Paris.

The painting shown below is typical of Mary Cassatt's works, many of which deal with the theme of a mother and her child.

Mother and Child, c. 1890, courtesy of Wichita Art Museum. Roland P. Murdock Collection

By the 1880's, Impressionism began to lose momentum as new approaches to art emerged. A movement known as Post-impressionism developed that was led by the French painters Paul Cézanne (1839–1906) and Georges Seurat (1859–1891) and by the Dutch painter Vincent van Gogh (1853–1890). Color continued to be important to the artists of the late 1800's. But composition and style evolved in the increasingly symbolic and psychological works of the twentieth century.

QUESTIONS FOR REVIEW

1 *What elements were characteristic of Romanticism in literature?*

2 *In what ways did Beethoven's music differ from the music of the 1700's?*

3 *Why, in your opinion, did Realism develop?*

4 GROWING SOCIAL AWARENESS

The late 1800's were years of great promise and opportunity. Industrialization had brought tremendous material progress to many of the nations of western Europe and to the United States. However, this progress was not without great social cost.

During the nineteenth century, an awareness of the rights of women also began to emerge in Europe and in the United States. By the end of the century, the right to vote had become a symbol in the struggle for women's rights. Although women eventually gained the right to vote in most industrial countries, they have continued to fight against other forms of discrimination in the modern world.

SOCIETY IN THE LATE NINETEENTH CENTURY Between 1871 and the early 1900's, the societies of western Europe and the United States changed dramatically. The two most important developments during this period—rapid industrialization and urbanization—had many consequences. On one hand, western industrialized societies produced tremendous quantities of material goods. As a result, manufactured products came within reach of more people than ever before. Moreover, industrialization created large, prospering middle classes in many countries. By the late 1800's, these middle classes were quickly becoming both economically and politically powerful.

However, industrialization also had another side. Little planning had gone into the immense, sprawling industrial cities. As a result, the rapid growth of cities produced vast urban wastelands as housing and sanitation facilities did not keep up with the rate of urbanization. Cramped, crime-ridden slums appeared in nearly every major industrial city on both sides of the Atlantic Ocean.

During the late nineteenth century, concern increased over the social problems brought about by industrial and urban growth. In response, movements arose that aimed at improving society. Governments began to enact social legislation—such as Bismarck's reforms in Germany that provided workers with health, accident, and old-age insurance (see Chapter 24). Factory reforms that improved working conditions in many industrialized countries were also put into effect.

AN INCREASINGLY LITERATE SOCIETY By the late 1800's, the reading public in many of the industrial countries of Europe and North America had rapidly expanded. One reason for this growth was a larger educated middle class, whose members could afford the time and the money to read for recreation. In addition, cheaper ways of making books and newspapers by mechanical means brought inexpensive reading material within reach of most people. For example, the number of newspapers in Europe increased from 6,000 in 1860 to 12,000 in 1900. A wider reading audience also meant that people of all social classes in the industrialized countries were exposed to many of the same attitudes and ideas for the first time.

Along with these developments, education was supported and expanded in many industrial countries. In Great Britain, for example, the percentage of people who could read and write rose from 66 percent in 1870 to 95 percent in 1900. France and Belgium had also reached 95-percent literacy by the turn of the century. In addition, the majority of citizens in Germany, Holland, and the Scandinavian countries were literate. Only eastern European countries lagged behind.

WOMEN IN THE NINETEENTH CENTURY

Among the many reform movements that began in Europe and in the United States during the 1800's was the drive toward greater equality for women. In nineteenth-century society, women had few rights. However, this had not always been true in European society. Between the 1500's and the 1800's, there had been a significant and steady decline in certain rights that women had enjoyed during the Middle Ages. In medieval England, for example, married women could inherit property and participate in business affairs if they chose. By the early 1800's, they could not.

Not only had women lost many traditional rights by the mid-1800's, but the spread of industrialization had also greatly influenced the role of women in society. Labor shortages in the factories of the industrializing countries had led many women to work outside the home. Previously, the economy of western Europe had relied upon the domestic system of production, in which goods were made at home by the entire family. The basic economic change from the domestic system of production to the factory system resulted in the decline of the family as an important part of a country's economy.

Prior to industrialization, most women had typically made many things at home, such as cloth, bread, and soap. Industry, however, provided cheap, factory-made goods that nearly everyone could afford. Fresh produce and meat also became available in urban

During the latter half of the nineteenth century, women for the first time entered the work force of many of the industrializing Western nations. By the late 1880's, telephone service in New York City depended, in part, upon women workers.

Women from all walks of life joined the suffragist movement. In May 1912, suffragists in New York City sponsored one of many marches supporting their cause.

areas as railroads and other forms of transportation improved.

But many women—middle class and working class alike—found that while industry had changed their roles in society, men were still unwilling to accept women as equals. Working conditions were often bad, and wages for women were almost always lower than wages paid to men. Education for women was still limited and entry into professional occupations was nearly impossible. American feminist leader Lucy Stone (1818–1893) wrote about the prospects of working women in the 1830's:

> When I was a girl, . . . I seemed to be shut out of everything I wanted to do. I might teach school . . . I might go out dress-making or tailoring, or trim bonnets, or I might work in a factory or go out to domestic service; there the mights ended and the might nots began.

THE SUFFRAGIST MOVEMENT During the late 1800's and the early 1900's, the struggle of women for greater equality centered on woman *suffrage*—the right to vote. Attitudes in many countries toward the full participation of women in political life changed slowly. The early changes in this attitude

came in frontier lands, where a hard life and a need to attract more settlers tended to blur sharp differences in the rights of each sex. This development led to more equality and greater freedom for women in many parts of the world. One of the first areas in the British Empire to give women the vote was New South Wales, Australia, in 1867.

In Great Britain and in the United States, however, the fight for complete political equality was long and bitter. In 1869, British women householders gained the vote in local elections. In 1870, the first bill that would have granted women the right to vote in parliamentary elections was defeated. The all-male Victorian political tradition was too deeply set to be broken easily. Even Queen Victoria, who supported many social reforms during her long reign, rejected the idea that women had the right to vote. As a result of this opposition, a long, and sometimes bitter, campaign was fought by the *suffragists*, as women who agitated for the vote were known. Among the leaders of the British suffragist movement were Emmeline Pankhurst and her two daughters Christabel and Sylvia. In 1918, women over the age of 30 finally gained the right to vote in all

British elections. In 1928, the vote was extended to all women over the age of 21.

Although the suffragist movement began earlier in the United States—during the late 1840's—it followed a similar pattern. The vote was gained in many local and state elections but not in national elections. The leaders of the American suffragist movement included Lucretia Mott, Elizabeth Cady Stanton, and Susan B. Anthony. A constitutional amendment for woman suffrage was introduced into every session of Congress between 1878 and 1920. Finally, in 1920, the amendment passed, allowing American women to vote in all elections.

Suffrage was not the only issue that attracted the attention and the abilities of women reformers during the 1800's. Throughout the century, particularly in the United States, women worked for many different social reforms. American women worked for the abolition of slavery, the improvement of education, the end of the drinking of alcoholic beverages—called *temperance*—the welfare of the poor, and an end to prostitution. In Great Britain, women were important in the reform movements of the 1830's and the 1840's—the Chartist and the Anti-Corn Law movements—and later were instrumental in the movements for educational and employment reforms.

QUESTIONS FOR REVIEW

1 *What factors led to a wider reading audience in the late 1800's?*

2 *How did industrialization affect working-class women?*

3 *Why do you think that woman suffrage became the focus of the woman's movements in many countries during the late 1800's and the early 1900's?*

CHAPTER SUMMARY

The revolutionary developments in science during the nineteenth century were felt throughout the industrialized world. Achievements were made in the study of mechanical power and electricity, in surgical techniques and the causes and treatment of disease, and in the study of radioactivity. Moreover, in 1859, Charles Darwin put forward a theory of evolution that held that living organisms changed and developed over time. Social scientists quickly adapted Darwin's ideas to the study of society. However, they soon found that the theory of evolution was inadequate to explain many of the social changes taking place around them. Psychology, which applied scientific methods to the study of human behavior, developed in the latter half of the nineteenth century.

Western culture also thrived throughout the century in Europe and in America. Many beautiful works of literature, poetry, art, and music were created. Along with the developments in science and in the arts, the struggle of women for complete equality began at this time.

CHAPTER 26 IN REVIEW

IMPORTANT WORDS, NAMES, AND TERMS

1 Explain, define, or identify each of the following:

On the Origin of Species   psychology   John Constable
Michael Faraday   behaviorism   Ludwig van Beethoven
immunity   Sigmund Freud   Impressionism
Joseph Lister   Albert Einstein   suffrage

FACTS AND IDEAS

2 What was the importance of the laws of thermodynamics?
3 Who developed the germ theory of disease?
4 Who was Friedrich Nietzsche?
5 What is the goal of psychoanalysis?
6 What was the objective of the style of writing known as realism?

ANALYZING VISUAL MATERIAL

7 Study the cartoon on page 504. What do you think the social Darwinist concept of "survival of the fittest" meant to the large industrial producers of the late nineteenth and early twentieth centuries?
8 How does Vincent van Gogh's Postimpressionist painting on page 510 differ from the other paintings of the mid and late 1800's shown on pages 500, 510, and 511?

CONCEPTS AND UNDERSTANDINGS

9 What were the elements of Darwin's theory of evolution?
10 Why did social Darwinism come under attack?
11 In what ways was impressionism a departure from traditional styles of painting?
12 In what ways did the role of women change in Europe between the 1500's and the 1800's?
13 Why, in your opinion, was the suffragist movement unsuccessful in Great Britain and the United States until about 1920?

PROJECTS AND ACTIVITIES

14 The program music of the 1800's attempted to picture events or feelings in music. A well-known piece of program music is Tchaikovsky's "1812 Overture," which was written about Napoleon's invasion of Russia. Obtain a recording of this work and play it for the class. Write a description of what you saw or felt as you listened to this work.
15 Women achieved success in many different fields during the nineteenth century. Among these women were writers (George Sand, George Eliot, and Harriet Beecher Stowe), scientists (Marie Curie), musicians (Clara Schumann), and many others. Based upon library research, prepare a report on the life of a successful nineteenth-century woman.

CHAPTER 27 PRELUDE TO WAR

1 Problems Arise in Europe 2 A Precarious Balance
3 Russia: Reaction and Change 4 A Region in Turmoil

A delicate balance of political, economic, and social forces was formed in Europe between 1871 and 1914. During these years, industrialism spread, and great colonial empires were founded by the nations of Europe. Relations among the European powers were soon strained, however, as large standing armies, secret diplomacy, arms races, and distrust and misunderstanding became commonplace in Europe. At first, the alliance system that developed in Europe during the late 1800's worked to keep peace on the continent. But as tensions among nations increased, alliances divided the continent into two opposing, and well-armed, sides. In the Balkans, fervent nationalism often erupted in open war. In addition to this unrest, the imperial aims of the Great Powers of Europe clashed in the Balkans and focused international attention on the region.

Culver

Kaiser William II of Germany was photographed reviewing his troops. By 1914, the German army was the most powerful army in the world.

1 PROBLEMS ARISE IN EUROPE

During the late 1800's, Europe reached the height of its world influence and power. At the same time, however, competition among Europe's major powers led to growing and ever more-dangerous tensions. By the early 1900's, international cooperation and understanding in Europe had been overturned by ambition, jealousy, suspicion, and fear among Europe's leaders. During the first decades of the twentieth century, these forces undermined the status quo in Europe and drew the nations of Europe into open conflict.

EUROPE IN THE LATE NINETEENTH CENTURY By the end of the 1800's, the nations of Europe dominated world affairs. European industrialization, commerce, and colonization had drawn the world and its people more closely together than ever before. The British Empire stretched around the globe. During the late nineteenth century, British factories still supplied many of the world's manufactured goods. However, other nations, such as Germany and the United States, had joined Britain as industrial leaders by the beginning of the twentieth century. As a result, economic rivalries developed that led to growing tensions among industrialized nations.

In France, the policies of Napoleon III had helped to shape the modern French industrial economy. During the late 1800's, French colonial growth restored some of the national prestige that the French had lost in their unsuccessful war against the Germans in 1871. Colonization also enabled French traders to exploit rich, new markets in Asia and in Africa.

The unification of Germany in 1871 formed a new and rapidly growing military and industrial power in Europe. As a result of its growing power, Germany's influence soon eclipsed that of France on the European continent. The rise of German dominance in Europe greatly affected European relations during the late nineteenth and early twentieth centuries.

Domestic affairs occupied Austria-Hungary and Russia during the last decades of the 1800's. The multiethnic empire of Austria-Hungary was constantly challenged by the demands of nationalists. Industry began to develop rapidly in Russia in the 1880's and

By the end of the nineteenth century, foundries, particularly in the Saar region, placed Germany among the world's industrial leaders.

the 1890's, bringing about many changes. In foreign matters, the decay of the Ottoman Empire drew Austria-Hungary and Russia into the affairs of the Balkans.

By 1914, all of Europe stood on the edge of war. Jealousy and ambition had steadily led the Great Powers—Germany, France, Great Britain, Austria-Hungary, Russia, and Italy—toward open conflict. Traditional ways of dealing with the problems that had arisen among the European powers failed at this time. As cooperation and negotiation broke down, the threat of war rose.

SEEDS OF CONFLICT Historians point out that during the last years of the 1800's and the early years of the 1900's, many factors resulted in the increase of tensions among the Great Powers. These factors included the clash of economic and colonial interests, as well as the growth of militarism, rival alliances, secret diplomacy, and nationalism.

During the last quarter of the nineteenth century, the establishment of colonial empires led to increasing friction among European nations. The spread of industrialization created new demands for raw materials. In addition, new markets were needed for the industrial goods that were being produced in great quantity by industrialized nations. Sharp competition for overseas colonies resulted from these changing conditions in Europe.

Since the late 1400's, a balance of power had defined the relationships between the sovereign states of Europe. In effect, this meant that the status quo in Europe was preserved by a general, but unwritten, agreement that no nation would be allowed by the others to dominate the continent. This was often accomplished by the formation of alliances. However, European nations often fought one another to maintain the balance of power. At times, strong leaders, such as Napoleon, and powerful ideas, such as the democratic ideals of the French Revolution, nearly destroyed the European balance of power.

POLITICAL		SOCIAL AND ECONOMIC
	1869	British debtors' prisons abolished
German Reich founded	1871	
Three Emperors' League formed	1872	
	1876	Short-lived liberal constitution proclaimed in Turkey
Congress of Berlin met	1878	
Triple Alliance of Germany, Austria-Hungary, and Italy formed	1882	
	1883	Bismarck introduced social insurance in Germany
Reinsurance Treaty between Germany and Russia signed	1887	
Bismarck dismissed Triple Alliance renewed	1890	
	1891	Famine spread across Russia
	1895	Roentgen discovered X rays
	1896	First modern Olympics held in Athens
	1901	Trans-Siberian railway reached the Pacific
Entente Cordiale between Britain and France formed	1904	
Russia joined Britain and France in Triple Entente	1907	
Young Turks gained control of Turkish government	1908	
Morocco became French protectorate	1912	S.S. *Titanic* sank after striking an iceberg
Second Balkan War ended	1913	

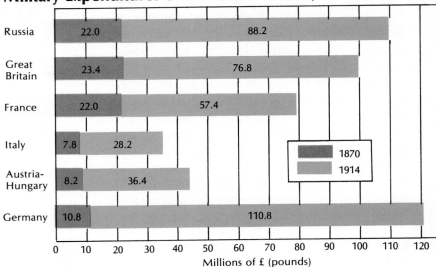

Military Expenditures of the Great Powers, 1870 and 1914

	1870	1914
Russia	22.0	88.2
Great Britain	23.4	76.8
France	22.0	57.4
Italy	7.8	28.2
Austria-Hungary	8.2	36.4
Germany	10.8	110.8

Millions of £ (pounds)

During the late nineteenth and early twentieth centuries, the Great Powers rapidly increased the strength of their armies. Germany, for example, raised its military expenditures by about 1,000 percent over a 44-year period.

THE CHANGING BALANCE OF POWER

After the revolutions of 1848, the balance of power in Europe gradually, but steadily, changed. One of the most important reasons for this change was the rise of a strong Germany. Another important factor was the development and the rapid spread of nationalism.

Nationalism had long been a major force in European affairs. During the mid-1800's, nationalism contributed greatly to the creation of two important European nations— Germany and Italy. Moreover, nationalism often fed the international rivalries that became so serious in the late 1800's. Nationalism also presented a major challenge to Ottoman control of the Balkan Peninsula. Balkan independence movements eventually drew the Great Powers into the region and led to the breakup of the Ottoman Empire. Within the Hapsburg realm, the Hungarians' desire for independence resulted in the formation of the dual monarchy of Austria-Hungary in 1867. For the next 50 years, struggles for independence continued in the Austro-Hungarian Empire.

During the last quarter of the nineteenth century and into the early twentieth century, international rivalries touched off an arms race. Between 1870 and 1914, the yearly military expenses of the Great Powers more than quadrupled. In 1914, Germany spent more than one fourth of the total military outlay of all the European powers (see graph on this page).

Unfortunately, an international body did not exist in Europe at this time to settle the many problems that came about because of growing political tensions. Instead, armies that had been designed for defense soon became powerful tools in international negotiations. Survival became an overriding concern in the dealings of each nation with its neighbors. The international cooperation that had begun at the Congress of Vienna in 1815 dissolved into rival alliances. As a result, the security of all the nations of Europe was threatened.

QUESTIONS FOR REVIEW

1 Which nations had equaled or surpassed the annual industrial production of Britain by the early 1900's?

2 In what ways did the spread of industrialization increase international rivalries?

3 Why was the balance of power important in maintaining the status quo in Europe?

2 A PRECARIOUS BALANCE

The European balance of power was upset with the rise of a strong Germany. Between 1871 and 1890, the foreign dealings of the Germans, under the crafty leadership of Otto von Bismarck, led to a precarious new balance. After Bismarck's fall from power in 1890, however, Europe became increasingly divided into two armed camps, and relations between the Great Powers grew worse.

BISMARCK'S DIPLOMACY The founding of the German Empire in 1871 not only completed the unification of Germany but formed a strong national state as well. The aim of the German chancellor Otto von Bismarck was to maintain the unity and the security of the new nation. Bismarck was responsible for both the domestic and the foreign policies of Germany. But it was Germany's involvement with the other nations that drew the chancellor's greatest interest.

Bismarck has often been characterized as unscrupulous and treacherous in his conduct of German foreign affairs. In many ways, however, Bismarck's policies stemmed from his intense nationalism and from his desire to protect the empire he had helped to build. Also, Bismarck understood European foreign policy better than most of his rivals. He once explained European diplomacy to a Russian ambassador in the following way:

> You forget the importance of being a party of three on the European chess-board. That is the object of all the Cabinets, and above all of mine. Nobody wishes to be in a minority. All politics reduce themselves to this formula: try to be *á trois* [with the three] in a world governed by Five Powers.

After the Franco-Prussian War ended in 1871, Bismarck wanted to isolate France from the other nations of Europe. He believed that France might one day enter into an alliance to oppose Germany in a war of revenge. Although Bismarck did not fear a war with France, he wanted to avoid a two-front war between Germany and a coalition of European states led by France. Eventually, Bismarck tried to accomplish his goals through a network of alliances.

One of Bismarck's first acts in his effort to isolate France was to form a rather vague union that consisted of Russia, Austria-Hungary, and Germany. This was called the *Dreikaiserbund*, or the Three Emperors' League. Basically, this agreement guaranteed that the three nations would not attack each other. The agreement also worked against France, because Bismarck believed that the French would not attack Germany without Russian or Austrian support.

The Three Emperors' League was not without problems, however. By 1878, it had been undermined by Russian and Austrian ambitions in the Balkans. Austria-Hungary's main goal was to maintain the status quo in the Balkans. On the other hand, Russia sought to expand into the region. In 1879, Bismarck made an important decision to form a secret alliance with Austria-Hungary. This partnership formed the basis of German foreign policy for the next three decades.

THE CHESSBOARD OF EUROPE In 1882, Bismarck's policies were expanded to include Italy. Italy barely qualified militarily or economically as a member of Europe's Great Powers. Nevertheless, Bismarck saw that Italy's neutrality was yet another way to isolate France from the rest of Europe. In order to ensure Italian neutrality in any war that might break out between Austria and Russia, Bismarck promised the Italians that they would have Germany's support against any French invasion of Italy. Thus, the *Triple Alliance*—Germany, Austria-Hungary, and Italy—came into being.

In 1885, the pattern of alliances that Bismarck had so carefully built was shaken.

A serious conflict over Bulgaria developed between Austria-Hungary and Russia as the Austro-Hungarians tried to prevent the extension of Russian influence in the Balkans. Mainly as a result of this conflict, Russia refused to renew the Three Emperors' League with Germany and Austria-Hungary. Bismarck then attempted to offset the breakdown of this agreement by separately strengthening Germany's ties with both Austria and Russia. In 1887, Bismarck replaced the Three Emperors' League with a secret nonaggression pact with Russia, called the Reinsurance Treaty. It promised that Germany would remain neutral in a war between Russia and any of the Great Powers except Austria-Hungary. The Germans also recognized certain Russian aims in the Balkans. In return for these promises, Russian neutrality was guaranteed in a war between Germany and any other country except France. In the case of a war between Germany and France, Russia could join either side. The Reinsurance Treaty, which had been signed for only three years, was not renewed.

At the same time that Bismarck was negotiating with Russia, he encouraged and supported the policies of Austria-Hungary. The Austrians were able to negotiate Mediterranean naval agreements with Great Britain, Italy, and Spain. Significantly, France was excluded from these talks. Earlier, Austria-Hungary had also made separate agreements with the Balkan countries of Serbia and Rumania. These agreements were aimed at maintaining Austro-Hungarian influence in the Balkans by keeping Russia out of the region.

CHANGING GERMAN POLICY Bismarck's primary goal of isolating France was nearly achieved in 1890. He had made firm alliances with Austria-Hungary and with Italy. And although Bismarck distrusted the Russians, an agreement had also been reached between Germany and Russia.

Bismarck had not ignored Great Britain.

Although he had not made an alliance with the British, it seemed unlikely to Bismarck during his years in office that they would become allied with the French. For centuries, France and Great Britain had been enemies. Moreover, colonial rivalries between the two old enemies were intense and, in fact, increased during the late 1800's. Moreover, the British were wary of Russian aims in Asia, and it was improbable that Russia and Great Britain would become partners. As long as Bismarck remained in power, it seemed there was little chance of a general European war.

Bismarck was removed from power in 1890, however, when Kaiser William II took personal control of Germany's foreign policy and dismissed his chief minister. Bismarck's successors found it nearly impossible to hold together the web of intricate alliances and diplomatic understandings that had been formed. In fact, the German government did much to dismantle Bismarck's work. For example, the Reinsurance Treaty with Russia was allowed to lapse in 1890. Almost at once, the French began negotiations with the Russians. Within two years, France and Russia concluded a military agreement. During the next 20 years, French financiers made substantial loans to the Russian government and invested heavily in Russian private industry.

Under pressure from the kaiser, German foreign ministers improved relations with Austria-Hungary. In addition, the ominous military buildup that had started under Bismarck was continued and increased. By 1900, Germany had begun an all-out drive to challenge Great Britain for naval supremacy.

ANGLO–GERMAN RIVALRY After 1900, relations between Great Britain and Germany worsened. Germany was not only a military rival to Britain but a commercial rival as well. At the end of the 1800's, Britain's yearly increase in its rate of industrial production was less than half that of Ger-

During the early 1900's, vastly improved warships, such as the *Kaiser Wilhelm* II, which was built in 1901, made Germany's navy a powerful rival to traditional British naval supremacy.

many's. Between 1860 and 1913, the British share of the world's industrial production fell from 25 percent to less than 10 percent. During the same period, Germany's annual rate of industrial production remained constant at about 15 percent of world production. In addition to these challenges, Germany's leaders resolved to build a navy that would directly rival that of Great Britain.

Not surprisingly, Britain's leaders became increasingly alarmed at Germany's growing strength. For more than three centuries, Britain's navy had been an important factor in British foreign policy and commercial growth. The Industrial Revolution had added new importance to Britain's navy. Industrial growth in Great Britain had come largely at the expense of agriculture. As a result, by the late 1800's, the British imported much of their food from other countries. British leaders were determined to protect their lines of supply by maintaining their country's naval dominance.

This determination led British leaders to develop the so-called "two-power standard," by which the British navy would be equal in size and strength to the combined fleets of the next two largest navies. By 1900, however, the German naval leaders had countered this policy by forming the idea of a "risk fleet." This meant that Germany's navy and the next largest European fleet had to be larger than Britain's. In that event, Germany's leaders believed that the British would not risk war.

Theoretically, the race for naval supremacy between Great Britain and Germany had no limit. Each nation could continue enlarging its fleets indefinitely. Realistically, the Germans had several advantages in such a race. First, even though the German fleet was much smaller than Britain's aging navy, fewer German vessels were outdated. Also, construction costs were lower in Germany. Finally, Germany's navy was cheaper to maintain than Britain's because the Germans used a military draft to fill their naval ranks. Britain's navy depended upon costlier volunteer recruits.

ENTENTE CORDIALE During the 1890's, Britain's leaders watched as Europe became increasingly divided into two armed camps. On one side was the Triple Alliance of Germany, Austria-Hungary, and Italy. On the other side was the Russo-French alliance. Great Britain remained the only major European power outside the alliance system, and it was also the only nation that could tip the military balance in either direction.

During the early 1900's, Great Britain's policy of isolation from European affairs ended. In 1898 and again in 1901, British diplomats had approached German leaders about a possible alliance between Great Britain and Germany but had been rebuffed. British security was also threatened by growing German naval strength. As a result, Britain turned to its traditional enemy, France.

The Anglo-French partnership, formed in 1904, became known as the *Entente Cordiale*, or "friendly understanding." Basically, the French recognized the British occupation of

Egypt in return for France's freedom to move into the North African country of Morocco. Differences between the French and the British in other parts of the world were also resolved. Within a decade, this accord hardened into a clear understanding of military cooperation.

In 1907, the Entente Cordiale was expanded to include Russia. The resulting partnership became known as the *Triple Entente*. Thus, the worst fears of the Germans were realized. A coalition of powerful military nations confronted Germany on all sides.

To add to Germany's problems, Italy was an unreliable member of the Triple Alliance. Many Italians still resented Austria's control of several provinces along the Adriatic Sea, including the city of Trieste, that had formerly been Italian. Moreover, by 1902, France had supplied large loans to the Italian government. These two factors resulted in an agreement between Italy and France concerning their territorial aims in North Africa. Thus, it seemed unlikely that the Italians would risk a war with France or with Great Britain. It appeared that Germany's only true ally in Europe was Austria-Hungary.

THE QUESTION OF MOROCCO Between 1905 and 1912, the northwest corner of Africa finally came under European colonial domination. This area included Morocco and Tripoli—in what is today the nation of Libya. The region also became an important testing ground for the alliances that had developed among the major powers of Europe.

The French controlled Algeria to the east of Morocco and French West Africa to the south. Over the years, tribal warfare in Morocco had often spread into these French lands. The French aimed to put an end to this warfare by gaining control of Morocco. As a result, in 1904 France came to an agreement with Spain that gave Spain control of a narrow region of Morocco along the

Royal cousins Kaiser William II of Germany (left) and Czar Nicholas II of Russia (right) were photographed wearing the uniforms of each other's nation, a common courtesy among European royalty during official visits at the turn of the century.

FPG

Strait of Gibraltar. The rest of Morocco would come within the French sphere of influence.

In 1905, the Germans directly challenged the strength of the Entente Cordiale, in which France was a partner, by interceding in Morocco. Kaiser William II visited the city of Tangier on the Mediterranean coast and declared Germany's support for Moroccan independence. The Germans demanded an international conference to consider this issue, a demand with which the French agreed. Germany's gamble failed, as Austria-Hungary was the only European power to support the Germans. Great Britain stood steadfastly by its new friend, France.

In 1911, a civil war in Morocco provided France with a convenient excuse for sending military aid to Morocco. The Germans, however, were not content to sit idly by and allow France to gain a military foothold in Morocco. The Germans sent a warship to Morocco for the questionable purpose of protecting German interests. Great Britain again backed the French position, and Germany was forced to recognize French interests in Morocco. In exchange, Germany received two strips of disputed land in central Africa.

In 1912, Morocco officially became a French protectorate. The area along the Strait of Gibraltar remained under Spanish control. As a result of these clashes with Germany over North Africa, France and Great Britain became firm military allies.

QUESTIONS FOR REVIEW

1 *Who were the members of the Triple Alliance and of the Triple Entente?*

2 *How did Bismarck hope to isolate France from the rest of Europe?*

3 *Why did Germany challenge France's interests in North Africa during the early 1900's?*

3 RUSSIA: REACTION AND CHANGE

During the last two decades of the nineteenth century, Russia's economy underwent a transformation. Industrial production rose rapidly. But this change was also accompanied by growing unrest. The spread of liberal ideas in Russia led to greater demands for political freedom. Various reform movements sprang up, but brutal repression of these radical groups soon followed. During the early 1900's, an unsuccessful war and widespread domestic discontent finally forced the Russian czar to accept a diluted form of constitutional government to avert complete revolution.

RUSSIA IN THE LATE 1800's Rapid social and economic change took place in Russia at the end of the nineteenth century. The reforms of Alexander II, especially the emancipation of the serfs, weakened the power of the upper class in Russia. By 1911, members of the upper class owned only about one half of the land they had held in 1877. Moreover, as industrialization spread in Russia at the end of the nineteenth century, a middle class of traders and entrepreneurs emerged.

Russia's industrial production expanded tremendously between 1880 and 1900. In fact, its annual increase in the rate of industrial production outstripped that of Europe's other Great Powers and reached about 8 percent of the world's production during the 1890's. Railroad construction also boomed during the last decade of the century as the government completed about 15,000 miles (24 000 kilometers) of track. Russia's economic expansion, however, was largely financed by foreign investors, primarily French, German, and British. The Russian government itself borrowed heavily from foreign nations to finance industrial expansion. The plight of the Russian peasants worsened as taxes rose rapidly to meet the country's growing debt.

A trans-Siberian railway was begun in Russia during the 1890's and eventually stretched more than 5,000 miles (8 000 kilometers), linking western Russia with the Pacific Ocean.

It is not surprising that these changes led to discontent and unrest in Russia. While Russia was industrializing, a poor urban working class was also being created in industrial centers, such as St. Petersburg and Moscow. Peasants, who still made up about three quarters of Russia's population in 1897, also grew steadily poorer. Depleted farmland, primitive farming methods, bad harvests, and heavy taxes made many Russian peasants' lives miserable. As a result, a number of radical political movements emerged in Russia.

RUSSIAN REVOLUTIONARY MOVEMENTS AND CZARIST REACTION In the 1860's, Russia became increasingly polarized between a growing radicalism among educated Russians and the harsh reaction of the Russian government. One radical movement that began in the 1860's was known as *nihilism* [NIY-uh-LIZ-uhm]. Nihilists rejected the existing order in Russia and questioned all the old traditions and values of Russian society. Nihilists, however, failed in their initial attempts to bring reform to Russia. As a result, many educated young Russians turned to helping the peasants and went into the countryside as doctors, teachers, laborers, storekeepers, and veterinarians,

hoping to spread their ideas of reform. Bewildered peasants often rejected the outsiders. At the same time, the government moved to crush the movement for reform. Many members of the movement were arrested and were jailed or exiled.

By 1879, the government's persecution, and a growing disillusionment at the failure of peaceful reform, led some radicals to turn to terrorism and assassination. In 1881, Czar Alexander II, who had earlier brought many important reforms to Russia, was assassinated. His son, Alexander III, had none of his father's liberal leanings. Narrow-minded, conservative, and reactionary, Alexander III believed that Russia would be destroyed unless the democratic ideas and liberalism of western Europe were shut out. The czar also believed in a strong autocratic government and an orthodox church. Alexander III used the state secret police to suppress liberal ideas. Strict censorship of the press was part of this policy. Limits were also placed upon university enrollment. Bloody persecutions—called *pogroms*—were organized against Russia's Jews. Exile to Siberia was widely used as a weapon by the government. The czar also tried to promote loyalty and patriotism in multicultural Russia. For example, he declared that only the

Russian language could be used in government, in schools, and in the press. This policy became known as *Russification*.

NEW POLITICAL PARTIES When Alexander III died in 1894, his successor, Nicholas II, took the throne and expanded the government's repressive policies. He also continued to impose Russian culture on the many peoples of the Russian Empire. During Nicholas's reign, however, the liberal and radical movements in Russia were crystallized by the formation of several important political parties.

The most moderate of these parties grew out of a movement for a Russian constitution that emerged during the 1890's. Members of the movement hoped to establish a western-style constitutional monarchy in Russia that would resemble the constitutional monarchy of Great Britain. By 1905, a constitutional party had been formed.

By the early 1900's, two other political parties had been formed by Russian socialists. The first of these was called the Socialist Revolutionary, or SR, party. It was loosely based upon a mixture of liberal ideas and Marxism. The SR's main support was among the peasantry. The second, and more radical, socialist party was the Social Democratic party.

The Social Democrats were committed Marxists and hoped to organize the industrial working class in Russia along Marxist lines. In 1903, the Social Democrats split into two groups over differing views of Russia's future. One group was called the *Bolsheviks*—from the Russian word for majority. They were led by Vladimir Ilyich Ulyanov [ool-YAHN-uhf], who took the name Lenin. The Bolsheviks firmly believed in the violent overthrow of the government. In addition, Lenin taught that a small group of professional, tightly organized, and highly disciplined revolutionaries was needed to control the government. These revolutionaries would establish a dictatorship until the proletariat was ready to assume lead-

Georgi Valentinovich Plekhanov (1856–1918) was the founder of the Russian Marxist movement. After the Russian Marxists split in 1903, he sided with the Mensheviks but worked to reunite the party.

ership. The Bolsheviks believed that they would be the vanguard of the revolution.

On the other side of the split were the *Mensheviks*—from the Russian word for minority. They also accepted the need to overthrow the Czarist government. But after the revolution, they looked forward to more gradual and peaceful change. The Mensheviks advocated a democratic system of government that would bring about peaceful change in Russia.

THE REVOLUTION OF 1905 Amid the growing discontent within Russia, a new problem arose. This new problem—a war with Japan—soon led to increased turmoil in Russia. As you have read, both Russia and Japan had expanded into Chinese Manchuria and Korea during the 1890's (see Chapter 25). However, after the turn of the century the Japanese worked for a diplomatic understanding with the Russians over

On what has become known as Bloody Sunday, Russian workers, demanding government reforms, faced Russian soldiers near the czar's Winter Palace in January 1905. The troops fired on the crowd, killing and wounding hundreds.

spheres of influence in the region. The Japanese overtures were ignored by the Russians, and in 1904 the Japanese attacked Russian forces in Manchuria and in Korea. Within a year, the Japanese had scored several major victories and had destroyed much of the Russian fleet.

The relative ease of Japan's victories over a major European power shocked many Europeans. More than that, the mismanagement of the war and Russia's ultimate defeat discredited the czar's government in the eyes of many Russians. Demonstrations against the Russian government—one of the last absolute monarchies in Europe—increased. In January 1905, a huge demonstration by Russian workers took place in St. Petersburg. The workers and many members of their families gathered at the czar's Winter Palace to ask for government reforms. Government troops responded by attacking the crowd and killing or wounding hundreds of people. This massacre became known as Bloody Sunday and touched off still more strikes and demonstrations.

Throughout the rest of the year, the government of Russia was threatened by growing disorder and by mutinies in the armed forces. In October 1905, a general strike was organized by the industrial workers, and Russia was quickly paralyzed. Czar Nicholas II was forced to accept many of the workers' demands and issued the October Manifesto. In effect, the manifesto declared Russia to be a constitutional monarchy. It granted some civil liberties and created a legislative assembly—the *duma*—which had certain limited powers to make laws. The manifesto also expanded the right to vote.

Russian liberals, however, tended to support the government's attempts at reform far more than did radicals. This division helped to weaken Russia's reform movement. As a result, revolutionary fervor gradually diminished, and order was restored throughout the country. During the summer of 1906, the czar dismissed the first duma. Nicholas and his advisors reasserted much of their former power.

QUESTIONS FOR REVIEW

1 *Who were the nihilists?*

2 *In what important way did the Bolsheviks and the Mensheviks disagree over Russia's future?*

3 *Why did many Russians revolt against Russia's czarist regime in 1905?*

4 A REGION IN TURMOIL

During the early 1900's, the Balkan Peninsula became the scene of bitter rivalries between the major powers of Europe. In addition, Balkan nationalists who sought independence continually attacked the weak Ottoman Empire, which had been forced to yield to many nationalist demands throughout the nineteenth century. Rebellion among the Turks themselves also contributed to the increasing tensions in the region. Moreover, as the imperial ambitions of the leaders of Austria-Hungary and Russia collided in the Balkans, new threats of war loomed.

EUROPEAN AIMS IN THE BALKANS

During the early 1900's, problems in the Balkans steadily drew the Great Powers of Europe into the affairs of the region. The two countries that had the most to gain—or to lose—in the Balkans were Austria-Hungary and Russia.

Throughout the nineteenth century, the weakness of the Ottoman Empire had given hope for independence to the many nationalities that lived under Turkish rule in the Balkans. By 1900, Serbia, Montenegro, Bulgaria, Greece and Rumania had gained varying degrees of independence. But many Slavs still remained under the rule of Austria-Hungary and under Ottoman control. As a result, movements that aimed to unite all southern Slavs into one nation gained momentum among the Balkan peoples, especially in Serbia.

The leaders of Austria-Hungary feared that Slavic nationalism would spread to their empire. Throughout the 1800's, Austria-Hungary, composed of many ethnic groups, had sought to maintain the status quo in the Balkans and had continually tried to suppress nationalist movements. Ominously, however, Slavic nationalism had gained the support of Russia. Gradually, Austrian policy in the Balkans began to concentrate on the need to keep the Russians out of the region.

Russia's interest in the Balkans was twofold. Russia was the only European power that had a large Slavic population that was Eastern Orthodox in religion. As a result, the Russians supported Balkan nationalists and their goal of uniting Balkan Slavs. Self-interest, however, was also an important part of Russian policy. Ice-free ports that would allow a year-round sea trade had long been an objective of Russian foreign policy. Also, the Russians wanted to control the Dardanelles and the Bosporus—the straits that separated the Black Sea from the Mediterranean Sea—in order to permit Russian warships into the Mediterranean.

The decay of the Ottoman Empire made the attainment of the Austrian and the Russian goals a possibility and heightened the competition between the two countries. By the late 1800's, the Turkish government was regarded as weak and ineffective by leaders throughout Europe.

THE SICK MAN OF EUROPE

Reform of the corrupt and weak Ottoman Empire, which was long overdue, had been attempted in 1876. At that time, Turkish liberals persuaded the Ottoman sultan, Abdul-Hamid II, to accept a written constitution. The document, the first of its kind in any Islamic country, established a two-house parliament as a check against the sultan's power. However, since the constitution itself was derived from the sultan's power, the document was ignored by the sultan. Within a year, the first elected parliament in the empire was dismissed and many of the Turkish reformers were exiled or sent to their deaths. From that point on, Abdul-Hamid's regime, supported by an enormous network of spies, became steadily more tyrannical. Censorship was strict, and opposition to the government was ruthlessly and effectively crushed.

(*Text continued on page* 531.)

Life at the Time

Life in the Balkans

The intense nationalism and rebelliousness felt by many southern Slavs during the nineteenth century grew out of centuries of oppression. The Christian peasantry of the region had been ruled, often cruelly, by the Muslim Turks for more than 400 years. As a result, ideas of freedom and independence flourished among the southern Slavs.

In the following excerpt, a British archaeologist, Sir Arthur Evans, writing in a book entitled *Through Bosnia and Hercegovina on Foot*, described the miserable, feudal conditions in which many peasants in the Balkans lived in 1875. It is tragic to note that after the Congress of Berlin gave control of this area to the Austro-Hungarians in 1878, the peasants' life-styles saw little improvement.

"Suffering from his double disability, social and religious, the Christian *kmet*, or tiller of the soil, is worse off than many a serf in our darkest ages, and lies as completely at the mercy of the . . . owner of the soil as if he were a slave. Legally, indeed the [landowner] is bound to enter into a written agreement with the *kmet* as to the dues and labours to be paid him; but as a matter of fact this petty potentate [overlord] haughtily refuses to enter into any such compact; . . . [and] can break the law with impunity [without fear of punishment]. He is thus allowed to treat his *kmet* as a mere chattel [property]: he uses a stick and strikes the *kmet* without pity, in a manner that no one else would use a beast. . . . The ordinary dues, as paid by the *kmet* to the landowner are heavy enough. He has to pay a fourth part of the produce of the ground; to present him with one animal yearly, and a certain quantity of butter and cheese; to carry for him so many loads of wood; and if the [landowner] is building a house, to carry the materials for it; to work for him gratuitously whenever he pleases, and sometimes the [landowner] requisitions one of the *kmet*'s children, who must serve him for nothing; to make a separate plantation of tobacco, cultivate it, and finally warehouse the produce in his master's store; and to plough and sow so many acres of land, the harvest of which he must also carry to his master's barn. Finally, [he has] to lodge the [landowner] in his own house when required, and to provide for his horses and dogs."

Life in the Balkans is filled with long days of hard work. The young Rumanian shepherd shown at the right lives in a country that still raises more sheep than any other kind of livestock.

Carl Mydans, Life Magazine. © 1964, Time, Inc.

Throughout the nineteenth century, the lands of the declining Ottoman Empire had been coveted by the nations of Europe. The weakness of the Ottoman government had enabled Russia and Austria-Hungary to make considerable gains in Ottoman-held Balkan lands at the Congress of Berlin in 1878 (see Chapter 23). By 1900, much of Turkish North Africa had come under the domination of other European powers. In addition, Arab nationalism began to stir for the first time in the Middle Eastern lands ruled by the Turks. Like their Turkish rulers, these peoples were Muslim. However, they were also intensely proud of their own cultures and traditions.

After 1900, opposition to the repressive policies of Abdul-Hamid developed among the Turks themselves. In 1908, revolution finally forced the sultan to accept the principles of a liberal constitution.

THE YOUNG TURK REVOLUTION In July 1908, a group of Ottoman army officers, seeking liberal reforms within the empire, rebelled against Abdul-Hamid's government. These reformers became known as the Young Turks. They forced the sultan, who could no longer depend upon the loyalty of the Ottoman army, to restore the constitution of 1876. But the Young Turks were not prepared to carry the revolution farther than this point. As differences grew over the ways in which the Turkish government might be changed, the Young Turks were faced with the threat of counterrevolution. In order to prevent counterrevolution, the Young Turks deposed the sultan. The constitution was then changed to give the Turkish parliament more control over the government.

Beginning in 1909, the Ottoman Empire, under the Young Turks, underwent many social reforms. The educational system was reorganized and improved. Ottoman law, long based upon Islamic tradition, became more westernized. The position of women in Turkish society was slightly improved. In

In 1908, a group of soldiers known as the Young Turks successfully overthrew the government of Abdul-Hamid II of Turkey. In the years that followed, the Young Turks instituted many reforms.

addition, industrialization was encouraged for the first time.

While changes occurred within Ottoman government and society, other parts of the empire were vulnerable to nationalist agitation and to the aims of European imperialists. In 1908, Austria-Hungary officially annexed the Slavic areas of Bosnia and Herzegovina, effectively cutting off Turkish control of this area. The annexation also ended, for the time being, the Serbian dream of dominating the heart of the Balkan Peninsula. In the same year, the Bulgarians proclaimed their complete independence from Ottoman control. In 1912, Italy gained control of Tripoli, the last Ottoman possession in North Africa. During the next two years, Balkan wars led to the loss by Turkey of most of the remaining Ottoman lands in the region.

TENSIONS GROW IN THE BALKANS The Austrian annexation of Bosnia and Herzegovina in 1908 angered both the Serbians and the Russians. It prevented the landlocked Serbians from gaining a port on the Adriatic Sea. It also halted the Serbian-led movement to unify the southern Slavs. The Russians, on the other hand, had struck a bargain with the Austrians over the region. Russia was willing to recognize the annexation in exchange for the use of the Bosporus and the Dardanelles for Russian warships. However, Austrian leaders annexed the territories before the Russians could gain approval from the other Great Powers for use of the straits. Despite Russian demands, the Austrians refused to back down. Germany firmly backed its ally, Austria, and helped to force the Russians to recognize the Austrian gains.

In 1912, tensions in the Balkans mounted rapidly. Greece, Serbia, Bulgaria, and Montenegro hoped to gain more land for themselves by preying upon the weakness of the Ottomans. As a result, they declared war on the Turks. Although untested, the forces of the Balkan allies fought well. The Greek fleet dominated the Aegean and limited the movement of Turkish troops into Europe to a single route through Istanbul. After several defeats, the Turks asked for peace. The peace settlement, reached in the spring of 1913, gave most of Macedonia to Bulgaria. Smaller shares of the region went to Serbia and Montenegro. A new nation, Albania, was established along the Adriatic. The creation of Albania, which had been backed by Austria-Hungary, also served to keep Serbia landlocked.

THE SECOND BALKAN WAR Serbia and Greece were not happy with the peace settlement of 1913. Both nations felt that they should have received more land for their war efforts. On the other hand, Bulgaria refused to give up any land it had gained. The disagreement soon turned into open warfare, with Serbia and Greece on one side and Bulgaria on the other. The Bulgarians

In the years prior to 1914, the forces of nationalism and imperialism kept the Balkan Peninsula in a state of constant turmoil. The disintegration of the Ottoman Empire and a series of wars created new nations and continually changed national boundaries.

The Balkans in 1913

gained the advantage of surprise by attacking the Greek and Serbian forces in Macedonia, thus beginning the second Balkan war. Montenegro and Rumania quickly sided with Serbia and Greece against Bulgaria. Greece's former enemy, Turkey, also entered the war against Bulgaria.

In a short and bitterly fought war, Bulgaria was defeated. As a result, Serbia and Greece gained most of Macedonia. Greece also gained Crete. Turkey took control of eastern Thrace from Bulgaria.

By the end of 1913, the Balkan wars had increased tensions among the Great Powers. The Austrians were still anxious to prevent the spread of Serbian nationalism and to discourage Russian expansion into the Balkans. Meanwhile, the Russians continued to support the Serbian cause and to seek certain territories in the Balkans. During the early months of 1914, Serbian nationalists began to agitate for the liberation of southern Slavic peoples who were still ruled by Austria-Hungary. By the summer of 1914, this agitation again brought Europe to the brink of war.

QUESTIONS FOR REVIEW

1 *What was the significance of the Bosporus and the Dardanelles to the Russians?*

2 *In what ways did Abdul-Hamid II reassert his autocratic rule after 1876?*

3 *Why did Austria-Hungary follow an anti-Serbian policy during the early twentieth century?*

CHAPTER SUMMARY

Between 1871 and 1914, the balance of power in Europe was reshaped. The rise of Germany forced a reevaluation of the traditional relationships among the nations of Europe. The German chancellor Otto von Bismarck was able to maintain a delicate political balance in Europe through a web of alliances. However, after Bismarck's dismissal, the 1890's and the early 1900's were years of growing tensions between the Great Powers. Bismarck's creation, the Triple Alliance of Germany, Austria-Hungary, and Italy, was opposed by the Triple Entente of Great Britain, France, and Russia.

The period between 1871 and 1914 also was a time of change and growth in Russia. Just before 1900, Russian industrial expansion began to outpace that of the other Great Powers. This rapid change, however, was not without social consequences. Unrest grew among Russia's working classes. In 1905, domestic turmoil forced the czar to accept a constitution that limited his powers. But political reform proved to be short-lived in czarist Russia.

After 1900, the Balkans were in constant turmoil. Slavic nationalists continued to struggle for independence. Austro-Hungarian and Russian imperial ambitions also collided in the region. By the summer of 1914, all of the Great Powers of Europe had been drawn into opposing camps.

CHAPTER 27 IN REVIEW

IMPORTANT WORDS, NAMES, AND TERMS
1 Explain, define, or identify each of the following:

Great Powers	Triple Entente	Bolsheviks
balance of power	Morocco	duma
Reinsurance Treaty	nihilism	Abdul-Hamid II
Entente Cordiale	pogroms	Young Turks

FACTS AND IDEAS
2 What were the factors that contributed to the growing conflicts among the Great Powers between 1871 and 1914?

3 What were the aims of German foreign policy under Otto von Bismarck?

4 In what ways did a powerful Germany present a challenge to Great Britain after 1900?

5 How did Czar Alexander III hope to stifle change and the spread of liberal ideas in Russia during his reign?

6 Why did the decline of the Ottoman Empire lead to open conflict in the Balkans in 1912 and 1913?

ANALYZING VISUAL MATERIAL
7 According to the chart on page 520, which nation increased its military expenditures by the lowest percent between 1870 and 1914?

8 Study the illustration on page 526. Under what kind of conditions were some Russians forced to work in building the railroad across Siberia?

CONCEPTS AND UNDERSTANDINGS
9 In what way did nationalism lead to the breakdown of peace in the Balkans during the early twentieth century?

10 Why did Morocco become, in effect, a testing ground between the Triple Alliance and the Triple Entente?

11 In your opinion, what were the causes of the Russian Revolution of 1905?

12 Why did the leaders of Russia support the Slavic nationalist movements? Why did the leaders of Austria-Hungary oppose these movements?

PROJECTS AND ACTIVITIES
13 Make a series of maps for classroom display that show the various stages of development in the European alliance system after 1871. Try to include on the maps the ever-changing boundaries of the region of the Balkans during these years. A historical atlas will provide the best source for these maps.

14 Prepare a research report for the class on the development of the secret police in czarist Russia. Information on czarist Russia might be found in encyclopedia articles and in other library resources.

CHAPTER 28 THE GREAT WAR

1 Crisis in the Balkans   2 The World at War   3 Revolution in Russia   4 The Versailles Settlement

In the summer of 1914, Europe was prosperous and tranquil. The appearance of peace in Europe was deceiving, however, because it was based on a perilous balance of power among the Great Powers. It took only a minor incident to plunge Europe and the world into war.

By the time peace was restored, the map of Europe had been changed forever. Empires collapsed, and many new nations were established. And in Russia, the czarist regime of the Romanovs was replaced by a group of radical revolutionaries.

Throughout the world, millions thought that they had suffered and fought for some useful purpose. They hoped that the new peace would be permanent and that no one would ever again have to endure such a disastrous war.

Imperial War Museum, London

During World War I, the western front became a vast network of trenches where soldiers of both sides suffered unbelievable hardships.

1 CRISIS IN THE BALKANS

Europe between 1871 and 1914 was a scene of growing tension caused by political, economic, and territorial competition among the continent's major powers. Europe's government leaders were able to maintain a fragile peace through diplomacy. But as crises became more frequent during the early 1900's, the Great Powers edged closer to open conflict. The European powder keg finally exploded in mid-1914, when the murder of Austria's royal heir plunged the world into global war.

THE MARCH TOWARD WAR In early 1914, Europeans could look back over 40 years of relative peace. There had been numerous local clashes, but none of the major powers had fought one another since 1871. As you read in Chapter 27, however, many forces had combined to build international tensions during these years.

Growing nationalistic and imperialistic rivalries among the European powers had helped to spark an armaments race. Supported by massive armies and navies, governments became less willing to settle disputes through compromise and diplomacy and more ready to go to war.

By 1914, Europe was divided into two armed camps. Germany, Austria-Hungary, and Italy, bound by agreements into the Triple Alliance, were in one camp. In the other camp—the Triple Entente—were France, Great Britain, and Russia. Other, less powerful, nations were allied with each group.

These alliances were designed to preserve the balance of power, but in reality, they helped to push Europe toward armed conflict. For these agreements guaranteed that if two major powers went to war, a general war could follow.

ASSASSINATION AT SARAJEVO On June 28, 1914, the heir to the throne of Austria-Hungary, Archduke Francis Ferdinand, paid a state visit to Sarajevo, the capital of the Austrian province of Bosnia. As the Archduke and his wife were driving through the town, a terrorist approached the imperial couple's car and fired two shots. Both Francis Ferdinand and his wife were killed.

The assassin, Gavrilo Princip, was a member of a secret Serbian terrorist organization known as Union or Death or the Black Hand. The Austrians had no proof that the Serbian government was behind the assassination, and Serbia denied any official link with the Black Hand. There was, however, considerable circumstantial evidence indicating that Serbia's leaders had some knowledge of the plot or had actually helped plan the murder. It was also rumored that several prominent Serbian officials belonged to the Black Hand.

For years, relations between Serbia and Austria had been strained. The Serbians wanted to unite the South Slavs into a greater Serbia that would include the Austrian provinces of Bosnia and Herzegovina.

A contemporary drawing depicts the assassination of Archduke Francis Ferdinand and his wife, which triggered the outbreak of World War I.

The Serbians also wanted an outlet on the sea, and the annexation of these Austrian territories would give Serbia some valuable seaports. To promote its objectives, the Serbian government willingly gave asylum to Austrian political refugees and became a center of anti-Austrian propaganda.

The Austrians ruled over many ethnic minorities and feared that an independence movement in the south would cause further insurrections throughout their empire. The Austrians therefore decided to use the assassination as an excuse to punish Serbia.

THE AUSTRIAN ULTIMATUM Serbia had a defensive alliance with Russia, and Austria did not want to risk standing alone in the case of Russian intervention. The Austrian emperor, therefore, dispatched diplomats to Germany to ask the kaiser to support Austria's actions against Serbia. Since the kaiser had been shocked by the assassination at Sarajevo, he willingly agreed to back his Austrian ally. Historians have called this endorsement the "blank check," because it assured Austria of Germany's "faithful support" for whatever actions the Austrian leaders chose to take. Both Austria and Germany accepted the fact that an Austrian move against Serbia might lead to a general war. But both countries hoped that the other Great Powers would view the matter as a local disagreement between Austria and Serbia and would not intervene.

Confident of Germany's support, the Austrians sent an ultimatum to Serbia. The ultimatum demanded that Austrian officials be allowed to enter Serbia for an investigation of the assassination plot. The terms of the ultimatum were so harsh that if they were accepted, Serbia would effectively cease to exist as an independent nation. In fact, the ultimatum was designed to be unacceptable to the Serbians and thus to provide Austria with a reason to invade the tiny country.

The Serbians accepted almost all the Austrian demands, and for a time it looked

POLITICAL		SOCIAL AND ECONOMIC
Imperial Duma created in Russia	~1905~	First regular cinema established
Triple Alliance renewed	~1906~	First French Grand Prix motor race
Anglo-Russian Entente signed	~1907	
Austria-Hungary annexed Bosnia and Herzegovina	~1908	
	1909~	Robert Peary explored North Pole
	1911~	Marie Curie won Nobel prize for chemistry
First Balkan War began	~1912~	*Titanic* sank
Second Balkan War began	~1913~	Albert Camus born
Francis Ferdinand assassinated World War I began	~1914~	James Joyce published *Dubliners*
Lusitania sunk	~1915~	First epic film, *Birth of a Nation*, produced
Battle of Verdun	~1916	
Russian Revolution United States entered World War I	~1917~	Trans-Siberian Railroad completed
Ex-Czar Nicholas II executed End of World War I	~1918~	Worldwide influenza epidemic began
Versailles Peace Conference	~1919~	First nonstop flight across Atlantic
Civil War in Russia ended	~1920	

as if peace might be preserved. When the kaiser heard of Serbia's response, he said, "What an outstanding result, more than ever we hoped for . . . a great moral victory for Austria—now there is no need for war." Only one hour later, on July 28, Austria declared war on Serbia.

EUROPE MOBILIZES Russia responded to the Austrian declaration of war by ordering *mobilization*—full-scale preparation for war, including troop call-ups—against Austria. In response to Russia's actions, Germany quickly mobilized. France responded to German mobilization by also ordering its troops to prepare for war.

On August 1, 1914, Germany declared war on Russia. The following day, when France refused to guarantee its neutrality, Germany declared war on France. By August 2, a general European war had begun. Germany invaded neutral Belgium the next day, after being refused the right to pass through Belgian territory in an attack upon France.

Meanwhile, in Great Britain, two factors influenced the thinking of government leaders. One was that the British had pledged to defend Belgium's right to remain neutral. The other factor was that the British,

through the Triple Entente, had an obligation to aid France in a defensive war. Therefore, the British declared war on Germany on August 4, 1914.

Thus, by the end of the first week of August 1914, all the Great Powers except Italy were at war. In addition, Serbia, Montenegro, Luxembourg, and Belgium were also involved. By the end of August, Japan had entered the war against Germany and Austria. The Ottoman Empire, siding with Germany and Austria, was at war by the end of 1914. Italy attacked Austria, while Bulgaria joined the German side in 1915. By that time, Germany and its allies had become known as the Central Powers, and they were opposed by the Allied Powers (see map on this page).

CAUSES FOR THE BREAKDOWN OF PEACE Historians today hold conflicting views about the question of responsibility for the outbreak of World War I. The Serbian government's anti-Austrian policy, as well as Russia's determination to defend Serbia, was a factor, as was Austria's desire to crush Serbia. Germany's "blank check" support of the Austrian ultimatum, of course, encouraged Austria to take action against Serbia.

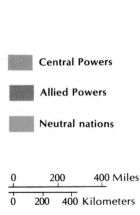

After the outbreak of war in 1914, European nations—both large and small—chose sides in what most Europeans believed would be a short and glorious war. By 1915, almost every European nation was involved in the bloody conflict.

Central Powers

Allied Powers

Neutral nations

0   200   400 Miles

0   200   400 Kilometers

European Alliances in World War I

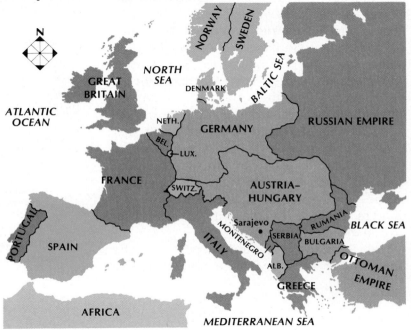

Some believe that the British should have made it clear that they would fight to protect Belgian neutrality. This might have stopped Germany from declaring war on France.

Mobilization is also cited as being responsible for the outbreak of fighting. Each country had plans for getting troops and supplies ready for war. The plans involved exact schedules for calling up reserves, requisitioning supplies, and moving masses of troops into battle position. During mobilization, an entire country's industrial and transportation systems were dedicated to preparing for war in the shortest possible time. It was believed that whichever country mobilized first would be victorious. Cancellation of the mobilization order would throw a country into complete chaos and leave it vulnerable to enemy attack. Therefore, once mobilization was begun, a nation's leaders were very reluctant to call it off. And the issuing of mobilization orders virtually guaranteed that a war would follow.

The outbreak of war in August of 1914 was greeted with massive outpourings of patriotism and enthusiasm throughout Europe. The crowds wildly cheered the troops and fully expected the armies to return victorious by Christmas. Many statesmen and diplomats, however, did not share the public optimism. As the British foreign secretary, Sir Edward Grey, sadly stated: "The lamps are going out all over Europe; we shall not see them lit again in our lifetime."

QUESTIONS FOR REVIEW

1 What was the goal of the Triple Alliance and the Triple Entente?

2 How did Austria's ultimatum threaten Serbia's independence?

3 Why was there a race among the Great Powers to mobilize first?

2 THE WORLD AT WAR

At the outbreak of World War I in August 1914, almost all the European powers had battle plans that they thought would lead them to quick and decisive victory. As the fighting continued, however, it became evident that these plans were not going to work. Since the Franco-Prussian War of 1871, new weapons with immense destructive power had been developed. Machine guns and rapid-firing artillery gave the defense a decisive advantage over the offense. The result was a military stalemate that lasted until 1918.

WAR PLANS When war was declared in August 1914, Germany had the most developed plan of attack. As early as 1895, Alfred von Schlieffen [SHLEE-fuhn], Chief of the German General Staff, had prepared what became known as the Schlieffen Plan. It was based on the idea that Germany would be forced to fight France and Russia at the same time. Schlieffen also assumed that it would take Russia much longer than France to mobilize and begin fighting. The plan therefore called for a quick war against France, which Schlieffen estimated would take from six to eight weeks to win.

Schlieffen thought that the French would begin the war with a drive toward the east. He planned to counter this attack by invading France through neutral Belgium and then encircling the French forces from the rear (see map on page 540). After the defeat of France, the Germans planned to turn on Russia with all their strength. In this way, Germany would actually fight two separate wars rather than a single war on two fronts.

The Schlieffen Plan totally ignored the probability that Britain would honor its commitment to defend neutral Belgium. The plan also required both numerical superiority and an excellent military commander. In

German and French War Plans

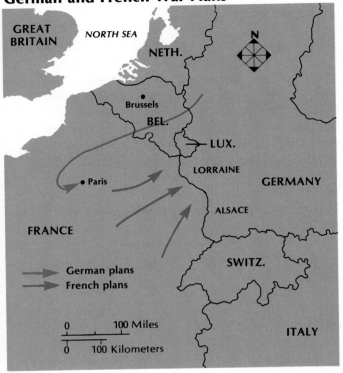

In August 1914, the French and the Germans each had a detailed war strategy that they hoped would guarantee a quick and decisive victory.

1914, the Germans had neither. Schlieffen had retired in 1905 and was replaced by General von Moltke, who proved to be an indecisive leader.

The French and Russian battle plans were far less exact and organized than the Schlieffen Plan. As Schlieffen had predicted, the French planned an offensive eastward into the German-occupied area of Lorraine and Alsace. After conquering those two provinces, the French armies were to continue into Germany and capture the German capital, Berlin.

Of the three major continental powers, Russia had the least developed war plan. The Russians had promised their French allies that they would attack Germany through East Prussia 15 days after mobilization. The Russian army was not at all prepared to launch an offensive that

quickly. Russia's top generals, however, considered it their duty to honor the commitment to their French ally. Thus, the Russians attacked East Prussia on schedule, despite their lack of readiness.

The Russian, French, and German war plans had one thing in common. They all took for granted that the war would be short. A few European leaders had warned of the likelihood of a long struggle, but the strategists chose to ignore those predictions. Consequently, when a long war ensued, there were no alternative plans.

THE OPENING STRUGGLES During the first weeks of August 1914, the Germans advanced through Belgium and into northern France. The rapid German attack met little effective resistance by the French and British forces, and by September, the German armies were within 15 miles (24 kilometers) of Paris. With the enemy literally on its doorstep, the French government fled to Bordeaux in the south of France. At this point, however, General von Moltke, Chief of the German General Staff, failed in his command. First, the Russian attack in East Prussia had forced the Germans to send some divisions, which were badly needed in France, to fight the Russians. Second, instead of allowing the French to advance far into Lorraine, and thus to leave Paris undefended, Moltke permitted his officers to order a strong and effective defense of the area. Thus, there were many more French troops available for a fight near Paris than the Schlieffen Plan had anticipated.

On September 5, 1914, a major confrontation began near the Marne River, north of Paris. The French transportation system was in such disarray that troops had to be moved from Paris to the front in taxis. The combined French and British forces succeeded in halting the German advance in what became known as the miracle of the Marne. By the end of 1914, the western front had turned into a static line of trenches that stretched some 300 miles (483 kilometers) from the North Sea to Switzerland. Offensives were launched, but gains were measured in feet and yards rather than in miles.

On the eastern front, the Russians were beaten decisively by a German army commanded by General Paul von Hindenburg at the Battle of Tannenberg in August 1914. The poorly organized Russian army suffered more than 300,000 casualties and the loss of much valuable equipment. The Battle of Tannenberg was only the first in a series of German victories that, by 1915, had driven the Russian army deep into its own territory.

In the Balkans, the Serbian army was crushed in 1915. The Serbians had successfully repulsed three Austrian invasions in 1914, but they finally lost to larger Austrian and German forces. The tiny country that had figured so prominently in the outbreak of war thus ceased to exist.

A NEW KIND OF WARFARE During the initial battles of World War I, almost everyone was dedicated to outdated ideas and methods of fighting. Massed cavalry still made heroic, saber-swinging charges, and infantry still advanced in regular formations with fixed bayonets. World War I, in contrast, became a war of *attrition*—gradual wearing down of the enemy—because of numerous technological advances made over the preceding 50 years.

The development of heavy, highly accurate artillery and of the rapid-firing machine gun were among these technical advances. A few well-placed artillery pieces or machine guns could effectively destroy a large group of attacking troops. After the Battle of the Marne on the western front, both sides dug trenches to protect themselves from these guns. In front of the trenches, they strung barbed wire barriers that slowed the progress of attacking troops. The wire could be cut through, but in doing so the soldiers exposed themselves to machine-gun fire. Attacks on enemy trenches could thus be made only at tremendous cost in human lives.

At the Battle of the Somme in 1916, the British unveiled a new weapon, the tank, designed to cut a path through barbed wire and trenches. The problem at the Somme was that the British used too few tanks, and those they did send into battle were mechanically unreliable. By the end of the war,

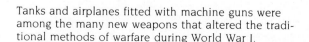

Tanks and airplanes fitted with machine guns were among the many new weapons that altered the traditional methods of warfare during World War I.

however, tanks—along with airplanes—had become effective weapons.

Trench warfare also involved hand-to-hand combat, and new weapons were developed especially for this kind of fighting. Grenades were widely used. Also, the Germans introduced the dreaded flamethrower, which wreaked untold horror and death.

The Germans were also the first to use poison gas. Its first large-scale use came as a surprise to the Allies at the Second Battle of Ypres in Belgium in 1915. The Allies quickly followed the German example, and throughout the war both sides used gas extensively. Soon after Ypres, troops on both sides were issued protective gas masks, and antigas defensive techniques became normal battlefield training.

To produce all the new weapons that were used during World War I required a massive industrial effort on the home front. With so many men in their armies, the nations that were engaged in the war faced constant labor shortages. As a result, women

As nations increased their production of weapons, women, like those shown here in a German ammunition factory, became an important part of the work force.

joined the work force in unprecedented numbers. By 1918, for example, women accounted for one third of the workers in munitions factories in Britain. In the countries that participated in the war, women held many jobs that had traditionally been held by men.

THE WIDENING WAR After the German plans for a quick victory over France failed in 1914, the kaiser replaced Moltke with General von Falkenhayn. Having concentrated his reinforcements on the eastern front in 1915, Falkenhayn decided that the key to victory was a decisive engagement in the west. He therefore devised a plan to attack the heavily fortified French positions at Verdun, near Lorraine. The German commander planned to wage a battle so fierce that it would destroy the French army's morale and force it to surrender. Germany would thus be granted an honorable peace. In fact, the Germans might have been able to win a quick victory, but Falkenhayn wanted a long battle of attrition. The resulting encounter lasted from February until December 1916. The losses on both sides were the worst of any battle in history, with approximately one million casualties. The Battle of Verdun did not, however, achieve Falkenhayn's objective. The French managed to keep control of the forts at Verdun, and the result was actually a moral victory for France and the Allies.

In the East, Russia was effectively cut off from Allied support and supplies when Turkey joined the Central Powers in 1914. The Turks closed the Dardanelles—the entrance to the Black Sea—and thus deprived Russia of its warm-water ports. The Allies briefly tried to capture the strategic Dardanelles at the Battle of Gallipoli, but their efforts failed. After being defeated in East Prussia in 1914, the Russians were never again able to launch offensives against Austria or Germany that threatened to overwhelm the Central Powers. By 1917, moreover, popular unrest in Russia had

Although most navies had experimental submarines, the Germans developed their version of the submarine—the U-boat—into one of the most dreaded and effective weapons of World War I. As early as 1914, the Germans began using their U-boats, which could approach enemy ships undetected, to interrupt Allied shipping. Despite protests from neutral nations whose merchant ships were sunk, the Germans continued to use U-boats throughout the war.

grown to such an extent that the country's war effort had greatly weakened.

The fighting of the First World War was by no means confined to Europe. Japan entered the war on the side of the Allies in 1914 and quickly occupied most of the German colonies in the Pacific.

The conflict also spread to Africa, where Germany controlled outposts in both East and West Africa. The war in Africa was mainly a struggle between Britain and Germany, and each country relied heavily on African troops. By 1918, the British were everywhere triumphant.

THE WAR AT SEA On the seas, there were few naval confrontations. The Germans realized that their fleet was not as strong as Britain's. As a result, the German fleet spent most of the war in its home ports. There was only one major sea battle, the Battle of Jutland, in 1916, but the results were inconclusive.

The British used their powerful navy to blockade Germany in an effort to cut German overseas supply lines. The British blockade effectively deprived Germany of both war goods and essential civilian food supplies.

Germany, in turn, declared a blockade against Britain and the Allies in 1915. The Germans used their submarines—U-boats—to destroy Allied shipping. But the German U-boats failed to choke off the Allied war effort.

As their situation worsened in early 1917, Germany's leaders decided to begin unrestricted submarine warfare. Any ships found in British waters would be sunk without warning. Since the United States was one of the Allies' major overseas suppliers, the new German policy outraged Americans. Thus, the United States declared war on Germany in April 1917.

THE NIGHTMARE ENDS At the beginning of 1918, the western front was still a vast network of trenches where neither side possessed a distinct advantage. The eastern front, however, was completely changed by political events in Russia. In 1917, revolution swept across that country, and the czar was forced to abdicate (see page 546). Russia's new revolutionary government signed a peace treaty with Germany in March 1918.

The Germans were therefore free to concentrate all their forces on the western front. The German high command hoped to win a decisive victory before the Americans had a chance to send in fresh troops. Thus, they mounted a massive attack in March 1918. Once again the Germans achieved early victories, but two major factors contributed to their final defeat. First, the German troops were so exhausted after four years of fighting that they were simply unable to press on to victory. Second, the Americans arrived and reinforced and resupplied the Allied armies much more quickly than anyone had anticipated. By August 1918, the Allies had successfully turned back the German offensives. The remaining months of the war saw the Germans slowly retreating into Belgium.

The other Central Powers fared no better. On September 29, 1918, Bulgaria collapsed. The Ottoman Empire surrendered on October 30, and Austria followed on November 4. Finally, the Germans agreed to an *armistice* —suspension of hostilities—for November 11, 1918.

The war was finally over but at a staggering price. Wartime casualties and financial costs were so vast that numbers can only be estimated. Of the total mobilized forces, 13 million had been killed and 34 million seriously wounded. In financial terms, the totals were equally staggering. The direct cost of the war was placed at about $180 billion, while the indirect cost—property damage and lost farm and factory production—was $150 billion. For years, until World War II brought the world to new levels of bloodshed and destruction, World War I was known simply as the Great War.

QUESTIONS FOR REVIEW

1 *What was the Schlieffen Plan?*

2 *What new techniques and inventions changed the nature of war?*

3 *Why did the last great German offensive of March—July 1918 fail?*

3 REVOLUTION IN RUSSIA

Despite widespread discontent with Romanov rule, the regime of the Russian czar remained in power throughout the early 1900's. During World War I, however, government mismanagement and a growing war-weariness among soldiers and civilians weakened the czar's authority. Finally, in 1917, the Russian people simply stopped obeying the czar. As a result, the cumbersome Romanov government quickly collapsed. A small group of radicals eventually seized power. After a period of chaos and civil war, Russia's new rulers established a cruel and repressive new dictatorship.

THE CONTINUING AUTOCRACY The Revolution of 1905 caused many Russian liberals to hope that a constitutional monarchy could be built in their country (see Chapter 27). The liberals' hopes, however, quickly faded. Czar Nicholas II felt that it was his sacred duty to preserve Russian *autocracy*— government based on the unlimited power of one person. Nicholas therefore worked to abolish the political reforms that he had promised during the revolution.

Nicholas had been forced by the revolution to grant elections for a *duma*—a legislative assembly. As soon as peace was restored, however, Nicholas severely limited the list of those eligible to vote for representatives to the assembly. He also tried to curb the powers of the duma as much as possible. The assembly that finally met in 1906 contained some radicals and revolutionaries, but most of its members were loyal to the czar. Nevertheless, Nicholas viewed the duma as a threat to his power and tried to ignore it as much as possible. Authoritarian government was thus continued, and all opposition was cruelly put down.

The outbreak of World War I in 1914 united the Russian people behind the czar in a flood of patriotism. Many revolutionaries promised to support Nicholas's government and to end—temporarily, at least—their calls for reform.

The spirit of unity brought about by the war, however, did not last long. It was soon clear that Nicholas's government was mismanaging the war effort and that the organization and supply of the Russian armies was no match for that of the Germans. News of military defeats, coupled with economic hardships for the civilian population, created an atmosphere of disillusionment and discontent among the people. Thus, the patriotic enthusiasm felt by most Russians in August 1914 was rapidly replaced by open hostility to the government.

In 1915, the czar took personal command of the army and left Petrograd—the new name for St. Petersburg—for the front. Nicholas entrusted the day-to-day control of the government to his wife, Czarina Alexandra. The czarina was unable to make decisions without the aid of her friend and advisor, a deceitful Siberian holy man named Rasputin. Rasputin and Alexandra became the virtual rulers of Russia while the czar was at the front.

The Russian autocracy was based on the decisions of one person—the czar. If the czar was careful and appointed able ministers to help him rule, the government functioned smoothly. Nicholas II, however, was not that astute. Instead of choosing wise ministers, he gave authority to incompetent favorites.

For the common people, conditions continued to deteriorate. Between 1914 and 1917, the cost of living increased by 700 percent. Basic services, such as communication and transportation, broke down because of government corruption and mismanagement. Economic and social disruption throughout Russia brought about serious food shortages and a growing lack of necessary consumer goods. Strikes and unrest spread throughout the country.

THE MARCH REVOLUTION On March 8, 1917, demonstrations protesting food shortages started in Petrograd. Political agitators quickly took advantage of the situation and turned the peaceful demonstrations into strikes to protest the repressive and corrupt government. By March 9, more than 200,000 Petrograd workers were on strike, and the

Russia's defeats in World War I were often blamed on Czar Nicholas, shown at the left with his family, and the notorious Rasputin, shown above.

capital was paralyzed. Riots broke out, and soldiers were called in to put down the protests. But the army refused to act against the strikers. In fact, some soldiers fired on the police who were trying to put down the riots. Nicholas responded by dissolving the duma, but the deputies ignored his order.

On March 12, the duma appointed a provisional government, which was intended to lead Russia until elections were held for a constituent assembly in January 1918. The assembly was to write a constitution and set up a new government. On the same day a rival government was set up. The government, or *soviet*—a Russian word meaning "council"—was called the Petrograd Soviet of Workers' and Soldiers' Deputies. The Soviet consisted of delegates from Petrograd's factories and from its military garrison.

The breakdown of law and order in Russia and the growing wave of demonstrations against his government forced Czar Nicholas II to abdicate on March 15, 1917. Many historians agree that the czarist government was not overthrown. Rather, it fell because of its loss of authority and its general mismanagement of the country and of its war effort.

THE RIVAL GOVERNMENTS The czarist government was not replaced by a single authority. The provisional government proclaimed itself as the legitimate government of Russia, based on the fact that it had been appointed by the duma. The provisional government proceeded to conduct domestic affairs and continued the war effort as if it were the true government. In reality, however, there were two rival governments—the provisional government and the Petrograd Soviet—that vied for the right to govern the country. Neither government, however, had the organization or the power to assume complete control.

An uneasy peace existed between the two rivals from March through October 1917. The provisional government was recognized by other countries and continued Russia's war effort against Germany. Nevertheless, neither the provisional government nor the Petrograd Soviet was able to claim the support of the majority of Russians. The two rivals appealed to different groups within Russia. The provisional government was made up of liberal elements that favored a constitutional form of government. It was generally supported by the more liberal nobles and the middle classes. The Soviet, on the other hand, was far more radical and consisted mostly of socialists and revolutionaries. The Soviet drew most of its support from the workers.

As a whole, the Russian people were freer during those months of 1917 than ever before. The provisional government acted quickly to guarantee freedom of speech, of the press, and of religion. Despite these swift and sweeping changes, the revolution was initially peaceful. There was relatively little political violence. Some former high czarist officials were imprisoned, and the czar and his family were placed under house arrest. But there were very few political executions.

THE RETURN OF LENIN The provisional government continued to carry on the war against Germany. Thus, the Germans decided to try to create disorder within Russia as a way to weaken the Russian war effort. Accordingly, in April 1917, the German government secretly helped Vladimir Ilyich Lenin, a fiery radical, to return from his exile in Switzerland to Russia. The Germans hoped that Lenin's return would cause further upheaval in Russian society.

Lenin was head of a small, extremely militant Marxist party called the Bolsheviks. The Bolsheviks were dedicated to creating a revolution based on the theories of Karl Marx (see Chapter 22). In March 1917, the Bolsheviks were only one of the many groups that were active in the Petrograd Soviet.

In April 1917, Lenin called for "all power to the soviets." Lenin meant that the sovi-

On November 7, 1917, the Bolsheviks stormed the Winter Palace—the seat of Kerenski's provisional government—in Petrograd and proclaimed a new government.

ets that had been established throughout Russia should be accepted as Russia's new government. Lenin refused to cooperate with the provisional government or with any other group in the Petrograd Soviet.

The Bolsheviks were still a very small minority, and Lenin's ideas were not widely accepted. Gradually, however, the Bolsheviks gained support as the other radical parties and the provisional government failed to win control of Russia.

By the end of July 1917, Russia's war effort had failed. Aleksandr Kerenski, a member of the Petrograd Soviet, became Russia's new prime minister. But the days of the provisional government were numbered, as food shortages and civil unrest increased. Capitalizing on the growing discontent, the Bolsheviks gained control of the Petrograd Soviet in September and called for the overthrow of the provisional government.

THE NOVEMBER REVOLUTION Prior to dawn on November 7, 1917, the Bolsheviks moved to overthrow Kerenski's provisional government. They first occupied strategic points throughout Petrograd, such as power stations, bridges, and telephone exchanges.

That evening, armed Bolsheviks took over the seat of the provisional government, the Winter Palace. They arrested the former ministers of state and proclaimed a new government. Thus, with very little resistance, the Bolsheviks gained control of Petrograd and of the Russian government. They were able to seize power so quickly and quietly because they faced no organized opposition. The provisional government and the other revolutionary parties had no band of dedicated followers. In contrast, the Bolshevik party had specific goals and extremely loyal and dedicated members who were willing to do anything to further their cause.

The Bolsheviks rapidly moved to consolidate their power. Their first decrees called for a quick end to the war and for the immediate distribution of land to the peasants. These actions assured the new government of some popular support.

The Bolsheviks acted quickly to implement their initial decrees. In March 1918, Germany forced the Bolsheviks to sign the Treaty of Brest-Litovsk, which formally withdrew Russia from the war. Under the terms of the treaty, Russia lost 1.3 million square miles (3 380 000 square kilometers) of territory to Germany. But the important point for the Bolshevik rulers was that Russia was finally out of the war.

THE BOLSHEVIK DICTATORSHIP

The new Communist government was quickly set up. A council of Peoples' Commissars—Communist party officials—was appointed to make all political and economic decisions. Lenin became chairman of the council, and all decisions were made by majority vote. However, as the months of 1918 wore on, Lenin consolidated his personal power to such an extent that he became the virtual dictator of Russia.

During the first months of Communist rule, Russia was in a state of almost total chaos. Lenin realized that something must be done quickly to establish order and to safeguard Communist rule. Consequently, he soon set up an extensive secret-police system, known as the Cheka, to seek out counterrevolutionary—anti-Bolshevik—forces. The Cheka became one of the most feared aspects of Communist rule and was responsible for the wholesale slaughter of those suspected of being against the revolution.

THE CIVIL WAR

There was opposition to the Communist takeover from the beginning, but as the months passed, it became more fervent. By the summer of 1918, a full-scale civil war had broken out across Russia.

The Communists, commonly known as the Reds, worked to rebuild the fragmented Russian army. By the end of 1918, the Commissar of War, Leon Trotsky, had built a well-organized and unified army from volunteers, conscripts, and former czarist officers.

The forces against the revolution were called the Whites. The Whites were united in their opposition to the new Communist rule, but they agreed upon little else. In fact, the Whites contained so many different groups that they often hated and distrusted one another as much as they despised the new Communist regime. It was this dissension among the Whites that helped to guarantee their eventual defeat by the Reds.

Both the Whites and the Reds were savage in their pursuit of victory. When either side captured a village or region, anyone suspected of helping the enemy would be killed. Territory was constantly

This drawing done in 1918 captures the savagery of the Russian civil war. The members of the Red army supported the Bolshevik government, while members of the White army opposed it.

changing hands, and the resulting destruction and bloodshed were enormous.

Lenin chose this time to begin the *Red Terror*—an unprecedented reign of terror in Bolshevik-held lands—in order to consolidate Communist power. The Red Terror was intended to permanently remove anti-Bolshevik elements from Russian society. But people taking part in counterrevolutionary activities were not the only ones murdered or imprisoned during the Terror. The mere fact that a person was a member of the middle class or the nobility was often enough to guarantee death without the formality of a court trial. The Terror effectively made Russia a proletarian state because it wiped out the middle and upper classes of Russian society. The former czar and his family were among the victims of the Red Terror. They were murdered in the summer of 1918 to prevent their rescue by the Whites.

By 1920 the civil war was largely over, and the Reds were triumphant. Russia's society and economy, however, were in total disarray. The middle classes had run the businesses and factories of the country during czarist times, and their extermination weakened Russia's economy and society. The Communists, however, ruled as ruthless dictators to rebuild the country into a new kind of society. The czarist regime was thus replaced by an even more brutal form of rule—the Communist dictatorship.

QUESTIONS FOR REVIEW

1 *What were the two governments of Russia after the March Revolution?*

2 *In what way did the Germans help to promote unrest within Russia?*

3 *Why were the Bolsheviks able to take over the Russian government so quickly in November 1917?*

4 THE VERSAILLES SETTLEMENT

The end of World War I in 1918 was greeted with celebration throughout the Allied countries. The leaders of the Allies met at Versailles, France, in 1919 to work out the peace terms. It was soon evident, however, that the Allied leaders disagreed over the nature of the peace that was to be imposed upon the Central Powers. Some wanted a very lenient peace. Others felt that the Central Powers should be forced to accept the entire responsibility—both moral and financial—for the war. Thus, the final peace treaties were compromises between these two viewpoints.

REVENGE VERSUS CONCILIATION World War I ended with the armistice of November 11, 1918. It was up to the victorious Allies to work out the specifics of a peace treaty. The war had proved so devastating that everyone wanted to forge a lasting settlement. But the type of peace to be sought caused major disagreements among the Allied leaders.

In January 1918, the American President, Woodrow Wilson, made a speech outlining his ideas for a peace that would be fair to all sides. He called for a lenient settlement that would remove the motives for future war and would thus guarantee a lasting peace. An important part of Wilson's plan—the Fourteen Points—called for the establishment of an international organization—the League of Nations. The League would consist of representatives from countries around the world, and would mediate disputes between nations in order to prevent the outbreak of war.

Another of Wilson's plans called for the self-determination of nationalities. By this, Wilson meant that international boundaries should be redrawn so that most nationalities would govern themselves. This would require the establishment of new nations in

The Big Four, who represented the leading Allied Powers at the Versailles peace conference, are shown here outside the Palace of Versailles. From left to right, they are David Lloyd George of Great Britain, Vittorio Orlando of Italy, Georges Clemenceau of France, and Woodrow Wilson of the United States.

eastern Europe and the Middle East, where the Austro-Hungarian and Ottoman empires had ruled over ethnic minorities for centuries.

Wilson's declarations were very popular among Europeans. They reasoned that perhaps all the horrors of the war were worthwhile if the final result was a permanent peace based on noble principles. For their part, the Germans signed the armistice in November 1918 with the hope that a peace settlement would be based on the Fourteen Points.

Many of the Allied leaders had doubts about Wilson's plan. Because of the popularity of the program, these diplomats had to publicly favor the concept of a lenient peace, but in private they disagreed with Wilson. These Allied leaders felt that the only way to prevent future wars was to create a new balance of power in favor of the Allies. That is, the diplomats wanted to punish the Central Powers and to weaken them so that they would be unable to take part in another war.

THE BIG FOUR The peace conference convened in the Palace of Versailles, outside Paris, on January 18, 1919. There were 70 delegates from 27 countries present, but there were no representatives from the defeated Central Powers. Whatever the conference decided, it was clear that the result would be a dictated peace. That is, the defeated nations would not be permitted to help frame the settlement. Instead, they would be invited only to sign the final treaties. Russia, too, was not permitted to attend the conference because none of the Allied powers recognized the new Communist government.

Most business of the conference was conducted by a group of government leaders—the Big Four. This group included Georges Clemenceau, premier of France; David Lloyd George, prime minister of Great Britain; Vittorio Orlando, prime minister of Italy; and Woodrow Wilson, President of the United States.

Each of the Big Four had different goals at the peace conference. The French were dedicated to getting back Alsace and Lorraine and forcing the Central Powers to pay massive *reparations*—costs of war. The French also wanted to permanently weaken the Germans so that they could never again invade France. The British prime minister, David Lloyd George, was more moderate, but he believed that he must be responsive to the British people, many of whom called for revenge against defeated Germany. The Italians were determined to gain territories from defeated Austria-Hungary in the area of the South Tirol. The United States had no territorial claims, but President Wilson wanted a peace based on his Fourteen Points. The American President was gradually forced to compromise upon most issues in order to salvage the League of Nations and the self-determination clauses. In the end, the other Allies got Wilson to agree to many harsh peace terms in exchange for their support of those two points.

THE TREATY OF VERSAILLES The delegates to the peace conference drafted separate treaties with each of the defeated Central Powers. In the spring of 1919, the treaty with Germany—the Treaty of Versailles—was finished. On May 7, 1919, a German delegation assembled to hear the terms of what they hoped would be a fair and just peace. What the Germans heard that day so shocked and humiliated them that they refused to sign the treaty. Another German delegation had to be summoned, and the treaty was finally accepted on June 28, 1919.

The terms of the Treaty of Versailles were indeed harsh. Germany lost one tenth of its prewar territory and all its colonial empire in Africa and the Pacific. France received the provinces of Alsace and Lorraine, which had been taken by Germany after the Franco-Prussian War of 1871. In order to replace coal production from mines destroyed during the war, France was to administer Germany's coal-rich Saar Valley for 15 years. At that time a *plebiscite*—election—would be

held to see whether the Saar's inhabitants wished to be reunited with Germany. An area in western Germany, the Rhineland, was to be occupied by Allied military forces for 15 years. This district was on the French-German border, and the French wanted to ensure that Germany would never be able to launch an attack on France from that area. After the Allies withdrew from the Rhineland, Germany was forbidden to have military forces in the area.

One of the newly independent countries established by the Treaty of Versailles was Poland. To give Poland an outlet on the sea, Germany had to give up a strip of territory that cut off the German province of East Prussia from the rest of Germany. At the northern end of this Polish Corridor the German city of Danzig was declared a free city (see map on page 552). That is, Danzig was a part of no country.

To prevent the future buildup of German military power, the German army was limited to 100,000 soldiers. There was to be no air force, and the navy was severely limited in size and strength. The Germans also had to surrender much of their merchant fleet to repay the Allies for ships that had been sunk during the war.

Perhaps the most controversial section of the treaty was Article 231. The article forced the Germans to acknowledge their guilt for the war. Germany and the other Central Powers had to accept responsibility for all the losses and casualties suffered by the Allies. The Germans were also forced to admit that their aggressive actions had caused the war. It logically followed that Germany was also to be held liable for the costs of the war. The treaty therefore assessed heavy reparation payments.

The war had been so disastrous that the cost of the destruction could not be determined before the Germans signed the treaty. Instead, the Allies were given until 1921 to figure the exact amount of reparations that Germany would have to pay. Damages and losses were finally calculated

Post–World War I Europe

In an attempt to follow the principle of self-determination, the victorious Allies redrew the national boundaries of Europe to follow ethnic divisions more accurately. New nations were created at the expense of the former Russian, German, and Austro-Hungarian empires.

at 33 billion dollars. The payment of such a large sum would have crippled the German economy for years to come.

Allied treaties with the other defeated countries were signed separately and contained equally harsh terms. Moreover, these treaties disbanded the Austro-Hungarian and Ottoman empires. Following the idea of self-determination, the two empires were divided into countries that were created along ethnic and nationalistic lines (see map on this page). In many areas, ethnic groups were intermixed. Therefore, it was impossible to draw the new boundaries strictly according to ethnic divisions. Thus, all of the new countries contained minority groups. The presence of these minorities caused problems for many of the new countries in the years after the war. The new map of Europe, however, more clearly followed ethnic lines than had the prewar map of Europe.

THE LEAGUE OF NATIONS Woodrow Wilson agreed to the harsh peace terms in order to ensure that his plan for a League

of Nations would be accepted. Because of these compromises, each treaty also included the Covenant of the League of Nations. This document outlined the structure of the peacekeeping organization. Two other international institutions were also founded. First, the International Court was created to settle legal disputes between countries. Second, the International Labor Office was set up to strive for improved conditions for workers throughout the world.

The League of Nations itself was designed to help settle disagreements anywhere in the world and to pressure countries into accepting peaceful settlements of their differences. The League, however, had no military force, and all compliance with its decisions was voluntary. Therefore, the League had to depend on the cooperation of its members to carry out its decisions. Also, most League actions had to be approved unanimously by its members. It was often difficult, if not impossible, to achieve such agreement.

One of the principal members of the new League was to be the United States. After

World War I, however, many Americans did not want to become involved in European or world politics. The United States Senate refused to approve the Treaty of Versailles. Ironically, the United States, whose President had fought for the establishment of the League, never joined. Nor did the United States sign the Treaty of Versailles.

THE SEEDS OF DISCONTENT Historians still debate the effects of the Versailles settlement on postwar Europe. One effect,

Biography

Woodrow Wilson

Thomas Woodrow Wilson became America's twenty-eighth President in 1912, after a distinguished career as a university professor and president. During World War I, Wilson worked to restore world peace through a program called the Fourteen Points. Wilson's plan was designed to build a lasting peace that ensured the rights of all people. To safeguard world peace, the President called for a League of Nations that would serve as a global peacekeeping organization.

Wilson's proposal was praised by many Europeans, who welcomed the idea of a settlement that would bring permanent peace to Europe. Thus, when Wilson went to Europe to attend the Versailles peace conference, the people greeted him as a hero.

The Allied leaders, however, did not agree with the Fourteen Points. Europe had suffered tremendous death and destruction during the war. And many leaders thought that Wilson, whose country had not suffered as much as the other Allies, had no right to dictate peace terms. Now that the war was over, the Allied leaders wanted to seek revenge against the defeated countries.

As the conference continued, public attitudes toward Wilson's plan changed. The spirit of nationalism was very strong in postwar Europe. When it was revealed that Wilson opposed nationalistic goals, his popularity fell dramatically.

The final peace terms were very harsh. But Wilson hoped that the new League of Nations would prove a powerful peacekeeping instrument.

When Wilson returned to the United States with the treaty, he was confronted with widespread domestic opposition to his plan. The Senate, which had not been consulted by the President during the conference, was strongly isolationist. Thus, Senate leaders were against American membership in the League of Nations.

The President went on a nationwide tour to win public support for the treaty. But Wilson suffered a paralyzing stroke in October 1919, and a few months later the Senate rejected the Treaty of Versailles. The League of Nations never became the true world peacekeeper that Wilson envisioned, because of America's refusal to join.

When Woodrow Wilson arrived in Europe, he was greeted as a hero. Here, a group of French people welcome the American president in 1919.

however, cannot be questioned. The 1919 treaties failed to establish a permanent peace. In fact, the settlement may have acted to promote future global conflict. For within 20 years of the treaties, the world was engulfed in another, even more destructive, war—World War II.

Some historians contend that the Versailles peace so humiliated the Germans that they were forced to seek revenge against the Allies. The Germans lost much territory and were ordered to make tremendous financial payments to the Allies. The terms were a disastrous blow to German national pride. But it was the war-guilt clause that proved unbearable to Germany. The German people felt that they had fought an honorable war. The German army surrendered with the understanding that the peace settlement would be just. The Germans felt betrayed when the harsh terms of Versailles were revealed. Thus, many Germans were willing to follow any leader who promised that the Treaty of Versailles would be avenged. Ultimately, such a leader appeared in the person of Adolf Hitler.

QUESTIONS FOR REVIEW

1 What kind of peace settlement did Woodrow Wilson want?

2 How was the League of Nations to enforce its decisions?

3 Why did the Germans find the Treaty of Versailles unacceptable?

CHAPTER SUMMARY

On June 28, 1914, the heir to the throne of Austria-Hungary was murdered in the Balkans. Austria first issued an ultimatum to Serbia and then declared war when the Serbians did not accept all the terms of the ultimatum. What started as a local conflict rapidly became a world war, as various countries lined up to honor their alliances and agreements.

At the beginning of the war almost everyone predicted a short conflict between the Central Powers and the Allied Powers. Neither side, however, had a distinct advantage. Also, many new weapons totally changed the face of war. Thus, World War I became a long and extremely devastating conflict.

In 1917, Russia's czarist government fell. It was first replaced by two authorities—the provisional government and the Petrograd Soviet—that vied for power in Russia. In November 1917, a small, extremely militant revolutionary group—the Bolsheviks—took over the government. After a bloody civil war, the Bolsheviks, led by Lenin, emerged as the rulers of Russia.

In 1918, the Central Powers surrendered with the hope that they would be accorded a fair peace based on the Fourteen Points of Woodrow Wilson. The peace conference at Versailles, however, wrote a harsh peace that humiliated Germany and the other Central Powers.

CHAPTER 28 IN REVIEW

IMPORTANT WORDS, NAMES, AND TERMS

1 Explain, define, or identify each of the following:

Francis Ferdinand
mobilization
Schlieffen Plan
miracle of the Marne

Verdun
Treaty of Brest-Litovsk
commissars
Cheka

Red Terror
Fourteen Points
League of Nations
reparations

FACTS AND IDEAS

2 What did the Austrians hope to gain by sending a harsh ultimatum to Serbia in 1914?

3 What was unrestricted submarine warfare?

4 Who were the Bolsheviks?

5 What was meant by self-determination of nationalities?

ANALYZING VISUAL MATERIAL

6 Compare the map of Europe in 1914 on page 538 with the map of postwar Europe on page 552. What new European countries were established after the war?

7 Study the painting of aerial warfare on page 541. How do the airplanes in this illustration of World War I combat differ from the airplanes that are being built today?

CONCEPTS AND UNDERSTANDINGS

8 What were some of the factors responsible for the outbreak of World War I?

9 Why did World War I become a totally new type of war?

10 How were the Reds eventually able to triumph over the Whites in the Russian civil war?

11 How did Woodrow Wilson's plans for peace differ from those of the other members of the Big Four?

12 How was the Treaty of Versailles harsh on the Germans?

PROJECTS AND ACTIVITIES

13 The Treaty of Versailles established many new countries in Europe. Choose one of these countries and prepare a report on conditions in that country after the war. You should include facts on geography, government, economics, and social development.

14 World War I was the first time that the airplane was used as a weapon. The pilots became legends for their bravery and daring, and the most successful were called aces. Prepare a bulletin-board display showing some of the airplanes and aces of World War I. Your school or public library should have illustrations available. For each illustration, prepare a short report explaining it.

Using Geography Skills

Graphs are sometimes used with maps to give us more information on a particular subject. For example, from a political map of Europe in World War I we can learn much about the locations of the countries that formed alliances. By adding graphs, we can also learn about the relative stength of each European nation engaged in the war.

World War I saw the mobilization of tremendous armies. Because the war dragged on for more than four years, the resulting casualties reached the millions. Graphic information showing the troop strength and the casualties of each of the European nations has been added to the political map below. The eastern and western fronts of the war are also shown. Study the map, and the graphic information it contains, to answer the following questions:

1 What country had the smallest number of mobilized troops?
2 What country was probably least affected by the war? Why?

3 Compare the map below with the map of postwar Europe on page 552. With the exception of the Balkans, what country lost the largest amount of territory as a result of World War I?
4 In proportion to its total mobilized forces, what country suffered the most casualties during the war?
5 In what ways do you think the number of casualties suffered by the Allied Powers and by the Central Powers affected their postwar recovery and development?
6 What countries probably suffered the most damage to civilian and industrial property? Why?

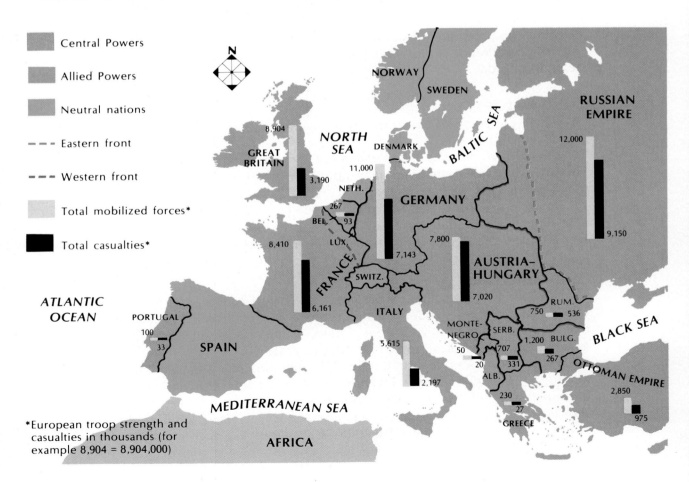

Central Powers

Allied Powers

Neutral nations

– – – Eastern front

– – – Western front

Total mobilized forces*

Total casualties*

*European troop strength and casualties in thousands (for example 8,904 = 8,904,000)

556

UNIT 7 IN REVIEW

CONCEPTS AND UNDERSTANDINGS

1 What laws providing social benefits for workers were passed in France, Germany, Russia, and Britain during the late 1800's?

2 How did the imperialistic ambitions of the Great Powers lead to conflict from 1871 to 1915? Give examples.

3 How did the Chinese view their society and foreigners?

4 What did Charles Darwin mean by the phrase "survival of the fittest"? How were Darwin's theories later applied to the evolution of society?

5 What were some of the new Russian political parties in the late 1800's? What did each party hope to achieve?

6 Why did Lenin institute the Red Terror?

QUESTIONS FOR DISCUSSION

1 The Balkan Peninsula was often referred to as the "Powderkeg of Europe" in the late 1800's and the early 1900's. Do you think this phrase was accurate? Explain your answer.

2 At the end of World War I, many people believed that the war had been the "war to end all wars." Since then, however, there have been many wars. Why do you think this hope for a permanent peace was never realized?

3 During the late 1800's, many Europeans felt that it was their duty to colonize Africa and Asia. In doing so, they thought that they were bringing the benefits of their civilization to other areas of the world. Do you think they were correct in doing so? Why or why not?

4 Patriotism is often praised as a virtue; yet, extreme patriotism—nationalism—is cited as one of the causes for World War I. In your opinion, how do patriotism and nationalism compare or contrast?

SUGGESTED READING

Farr, Naunerle. *Madame Curie—Albert Einstein.* West Haven, Conn.: Pendulum Press, 1979.

Gollwitzer, Hunz. *Europe in the Age of Imperialism: 1880 to 1914.* New York: W.W. Norton and Co., 1979.

Killingray, David. *The Russian Revolution,* eds. Malcolm Yapp, et al. St. Paul: Greenhaven Press, 1980.

Mee, Charles L. *The End of Order: Versailles 1919.* New York: E.P. Dutton, 1980.

O'Connor, Edmund. *Darwin,* eds. Malcolm Yapp, et al. St. Paul: Greenhaven Press, 1980.

Schechter, Betty. *Dreyfus Affair: A National Scandal.* Boston: Houghton-Mifflin Co., 1965.

Taylor, A.J.P., ed. *History of World War I,* compiler S.L. Mayer. London, England: Octopus Books, 1974.

Tuchman, Barbara. *The Proud Tower.* New York: Macmillan Publishing Co., Inc., 1974.

UNIT 8

THE TURBULENT DECADES

1920 to 1960

Hugo Jaeger/LIFE, © Time Inc.

Milt and Joan Mann

The wealthy at ease in Europe in the 1920's   Hitler at a Nazi party rally in Nuremberg

558

T here was unrest throughout most of Europe after World War I as nations tried to return to peacetime conditions. While new countries worked to set up democratic governments, older nations wrestled with other postwar problems. After the collapse of the American economy in 1929, European countries faced even more challenging difficulties.

Political changes affected Asia, Africa, and the Pacific after the war. At that time, large areas of the Middle East came under foreign rule. As European powers failed to respond to the political goals of colonial peoples in the 1920's and 1930's, nationalism began to grow in many colonial lands.

During the 1930's, several dictators rose to power as people became increasingly disillusioned by the outcome of World War I. The turmoil caused by the Great Depression added to the growing unrest, which some dictators exploited. Then in 1939, another world war began. Six years later, this tragic conflict ended, but the world faced new problems as the democratic nations and the Communist world became increasingly antagonistic.

The Mansell Collection

Wreckage of an American tank off the Pacific island of Saipan

ASIA, AFRICA,
AND THE PACIFIC
CHAPTER 29
BETWEEN THE WARS

1 China in Turmoil   2 A Time of Adjustment in Japan
3 Africa and the Middle East   4 Colonialism in Southeast
Asia and the Pacific

Following World War I, there were many important changes in the regions of Asia, Africa, and the Pacific. Political unrest in China brought an end to imperial rule in that country. At the same time, Japan seemed to become more liberal, as new leaders came to power in the 1920's. This liberalization, however, ended in the 1930's, as Japan was affected by the worldwide economic depression.

During the 1920's, European colonial powers strengthened their hold on their African colonies. In addition, many lands in the Middle East came under foreign rule after World War I. And nationalism began to grow in Southeast Asia in the 1920's, as more people became aware of the exploitative nature of colonialism.

Marc Riboud

Peking's Forbidden City contains palaces once used by China's rulers.

1 CHINA IN TURMOIL

China was swept by a new wave of political and social upheaval after the overthrow of the ruling dynasty in 1911. Efforts were made to set up a new government. However, there was much disagreement among the different groups of Chinese who wanted to reform the government. As a result, there was great political confusion in China. By 1916, most of the political power in the country was held by local military leaders.

Within a few years, however, a strong national leader, who worked to unify the country and to curb the power of the local military rulers, had emerged. And by the late 1920's, a fairly stable central government had been set up to deal with the many problems facing China and its people.

THE END OF MANCHU RULE By the early 1900's, the ruling Manchu dynasty of China had grown weak and ineffective. Within China, the Manchus had failed to improve conditions. The life of the average peasant remained one of hard work coupled with the danger of famine and disease. At the same time, the Manchu rulers had been unable to protect China from foreign powers. Other nations seized parts of China and controlled much of China's trade during the late 1800's and early 1900's. These problems led to serious unrest in many areas of China.

A revolt against the Manchus finally broke out in October 1911. As the uprising spread, the leaders of the rebellion met in the city of Nanking and set up the Republic of China. Dr. Sun Yat-sen [SUN-YAHT-SEN], who was an important leader in the movement to overthrow the Manchu government, was chosen as the first president of the new republic (see Biography, page 564).

The Manchu government reacted to the uprising by choosing General Yüan Shih-k'ai [yu-AHN-SHIR-KIY] to put down the rebellion. However, Yüan secretly arranged for a settlement of the revolt. The settlement called for Yüan to replace Sun as the president of the Chinese republic. This agreement ended Manchu rule in China.

After becoming president, however, Yüan began to expand his power and to oppose efforts to reform the Chinese government. Meanwhile, ex-president Sun Yat-sen set up the Nationalist party—the *Kuomintang* [KWOH-min-TANG]—to carry out his revolutionary program. As Yüan continued to expand his power, the Nationalist party began to oppose Yüan's policies. In 1913, a revolt against Yüan was supported by Sun, but this action failed to oust Yüan from office. Sun Yat-sen went into hiding, and Yüan made himself the emperor of China.

In the next three years, opposition to Yüan and his policies grew. Then, in June

While serving as the president of the Chinese republic, Yüan Shih-k'ai increased his power and, in May 1914, he became a virtual dictator of the country.

561

POLITICAL		SOCIAL AND ECONOMIC
Revolt against Man-chus in China	⁓1911	
Egypt made a protec-torate by Great Britain	⁓1914	
Japan's Twenty-One Demands to China	⁓1915	
	1916⁓	National Bank of the Philippines chartered
Balfour Declaration made by the British government	⁓1917	
Provisional government under Kemal set up in Turkey	⁓1920⁓	First imperial census taken in Japan
British protectorate in Egypt ended	⁓1922	
	1923⁓	Devastating earth-quake struck Tokyo
First Kuomintang na-tional congress met	⁓1924	
Universal male suf-frage enacted in Japan	⁓1925⁓	Hebrew University opened in Jerusalem
Nationalists captured Peking	⁓1928	
	1929⁓	Union membership in Japan reached over 300,000 workers
	1930⁓	Chinese-Japanese tariff agreement
Tydings-McDuffie Act passed	⁓1934	
	1935⁓	Railroad bridge across lower Zambezi River in Africa opened

1916, Yüan died and the power of the central government collapsed. The real power passed to local military leaders, who were called warlords. As a result, conditions in China grew worse, and the country became hopelessly divided.

A TIME OF CONFUSION For several years following the death of Yüan, there was no effective government in China. Most foreign powers recognized the warlord-dominated government in Peking as the official government. However, the Kuomintang under Sun Yat-sen had set up another government in the city of Canton. Neither government was able to control the widespread fighting among local warlords. Most of these local leaders used their forces in efforts to enlarge their power. The almost endless fighting caused destruction throughout much of China.

Appalled by the unsettled conditions, Sun worked to build a strong government that could unite China. To achieve this goal, Sun found it necessary to accept help from other countries. In 1923, for example, an agreement was reached between Sun and the Soviet Union. The agreement called for advisers from the Soviet Union to come to China to help organize the Kuomintang and to build popular support for it. At the same time, Chinese Communists were allowed to join the Kuomintang. The Chinese Communist party had been founded in 1921 by a few Chinese intellectuals who were attracted to the ideas of Marx and Lenin. Together, the two parties began a joint effort to defeat the warlords and to strengthen Chinese national pride.

Sun's efforts to unify China were based on a program known as the *Three Principles*. These ideas centered around three broad goals—nationalism, self-government, and livelihood. The first goal was to free China from foreign control. The second was to bring self-government to China. This was to be done over a period of time as the

Fierce fighting took place in China in 1927, as Kuomintang armies fought to dislodge Chinese Communist forces from central China.

Kuomintang slowly trained the people in the ways of democracy. The third goal was to bring economic security and a better way of life to the people of China.

Sun did not live to see the Chinese people reach these goals, for he died in 1925. Sun's work, however, was carried on by his successor and brother-in-law, Chiang Kai-shek [jee-AHNG-KIY-SHEK], who had been an assistant to Sun for several years.

CHINA UNDER CHIANG KAI-SHEK Chiang Kai-shek had been attracted to Sun Yat-sen's ideas when Chiang was a young military student in the early 1900's. Later, after joining Sun, Chiang was sent to the Soviet Union to study military science. Following his return to China, Chiang had been made the head of the Whampoa Military Academy in Canton. This school had been founded by Sun in the early 1920's.

After Sun's death, Chiang set out to consolidate his power and to unify China. In 1926, he undertook a military campaign into northern China against the warlords. The Kuomintang army met scattered opposition and won several important victories.

At the same time, however, Chiang encountered problems within the Kuomintang as dissension grew between different groups. The wealthy merchants, landlords, and bankers who supported Chiang were against having Communists in the Kuomintang. In 1927, Chiang also turned against the Communists. The advisers from the Soviet Union were expelled from China, and the Chinese Communists were forced out of the Kuomintang. Some of the Communists went to rural areas of China, and a few others left the country. During this time, Chiang also set up a government at Nanking. This Nationalist regime came to be recognized by Western powers as the official government of China.

In 1928, Chiang's soldiers captured Peking from a powerful warlord. Then peace was arranged with most of the warlords in northern China. Thus, by 1930, Chiang controlled much of China. The Communists, however, still dominated some rural areas of China. Also scattered throughout China were smaller areas controlled by local warlords.

Many Chinese hoped that Chiang would be able to bring harmony and stability to their country. However, China still faced many problems, such as large foreign debts and lack of industry. In time, some Chinese began to criticize Chiang's government for

Biography

The Father of China

The great political changes that began in China during the early 1900's were due, in large part, to the work of the Chinese revolutionary Dr. Sun Yat-sen. Sun was born in 1866 to a humble farming family in southern China. When he was about 13 years old, Sun went to Hawaii and attended a British school and then an American school. While attending these schools, Sun was first exposed to those Western ideas that later influenced his thinking about China. Sun entered medical school in 1886 and graduated in 1892. Sun, however, was deeply troubled by the way China had been treated over the years by foreign countries. As a result, he decided to give up medicine and to enter politics.

Sun returned to Hawaii in 1894 and set up the *Revive China Society*. This group was the forerunner of later revolutionary groups that Sun founded to bring about the downfall of China's Manchu rulers. After Sun's plan for an uprising in China failed in 1895, he traveled to many other countries for the next 16 years. During these travels, he worked to gain support for the overthrow of the Manchus. Sun also set up revolutionary groups in many of the nations that he visited. However, the Manchu rulers of China wanted to stop Sun's activities. As a result, these rulers appealed to foreign governments to curtail Sun's revolutionary actions, and he was banned from several foreign countries.

In 1911, the Manchus were overthrown, and Sun returned to China to assume leadership of the new government. For several years, however, there was much turmoil and confusion in China as Sun, who was an ambitious person, worked to consolidate his power.

Sun died in 1925, but his work was carried on by his successor, Chiang Kai-shek. By the late 1920's, conditions in China had stabilized. Even though Sun had many enemies during his lifetime, he is revered by most of the people of China today. Sun has been called the Father of China. He had a magnetic personality that attracted many people. However, Sun's un-swerving pursuit of power alienated many of his followers. Sun, who had a vast knowledge of the Western world, wanted to make China a strong nation like the countries of the West. Thus, to many Chinese, Sun was a symbol of the modernization of China.

Chiang Kai-shek (standing) spent several years serving as a military adviser to Dr. Sun Yat-sen (seated).

Historical Pictures Service

its lack of reforms and its failure to help the great mass of Chinese people. As Chiang and the Kuomintang struggled to solve problems within China, there were also problems in dealing with foreign powers.

CHINA AND FOREIGN AFFAIRS IN THE 1920's Since the mid-1800's, parts of China had come under foreign domination through wars and through treaties (see Chapter 25). As a result, by the early 1900's, foreign countries controlled much of China's trade and also held special rights over a number of areas of the country. Some foreign powers also had gained the right of *extraterritoriality*. This privilege allowed many foreigners living in China the privilege of not being subject to Chinese laws. Instead, these foreigners were subject only to the laws of their own countries.

Foreign countries also stationed soldiers in China and placed warships in Chinese waters. These forces were kept in China to protect foreign interests. But many Chinese looked upon these actions and upon the right of extraterritoriality as violations of Chinese sovereignty. From the beginning of foreign intervention, some Chinese had tried to end such meddling in their country. But the weakness of China's government prevented the Chinese from seriously challenging foreign encroachment in China before the 1920's. This situation began to change as the Kuomintang government grew in power.

In 1922, several countries that held special rights in China signed an agreement known as the Nine Power Treaty. These countries agreed to respect China's rights over its lands. They also agreed that they would not take advantage of the generally unstable conditions within China to gain special rights there.

Several years later, the Nationalist government began working to end the unequal treaties that gave special rights to foreign powers. As a result, several countries agreed to give up their right to fix tariffs on trade

Japan's aggressive moves into China in the 1930's were often dramatically portrayed by political cartoonists.

within China. In addition, a number of countries gave up the right of extraterritoriality. China also joined the League of Nations during the 1920's. This act showed the growing importance of China in world affairs.

CHANGING CONDITIONS IN CHINA The 1920's were years of change and growth in China. For example, the number of people who were being educated began to increase. At the same time, most Chinese intellectuals began to urge the use of a simplified written language based on the spoken language, to make reading and writing easier. Some scholars also worked to have one spoken dialect—Mandarin—used throughout the country. The use of one dialect would allow people from all parts of China to be understood when speaking to each other. Such a common language also would help to unify the country.

Chinese society was affected by other changes as well. Some people in the urban areas of China began to dress in Western-style clothing. At the same time, modern conveniences such as telephones, electric lights, and water systems were installed in a few of China's large cities. Many young Chinese from the countryside came to the cities during the 1920's in search of jobs. As these young people found work in the cities, they developed a sense of independence. This independence caused some young Chinese to question many of the traditional, family-oriented ways of Chinese society.

There was some industrial growth in China during the 1920's, but most factories continued to be owned or controlled by foreign investors. The profits from these factories usually went to the foreign investors. As a result, the Chinese people did not benefit from their country's economic growth. In most cases, profits were not put back into the Chinese economy.

Even though China's trade with other countries grew in the 1920's, there were many problems. One of these problems was that local wars hampered trade. Another problem was China's transportation system, which was not well developed. This made it hard to move goods easily throughout the country. Thus, the growth of trade often did not help the common people of China. During the early 1930's, the people of China continued to face an uncertain future.

QUESTIONS FOR REVIEW

1 *For what reasons were advisers from the Soviet Union sent to China in 1923?*

2 *How were Sun Yat-sen's Three Principles designed to help China?*

3 *Why did some scholars work to have one spoken dialect in China?*

2 A TIME OF ADJUSTMENT IN JAPAN

Following World War I, important political changes took place in Japan. At that time, the Japanese government appeared to become more liberal. However, a number of factors prevented Japan from becoming a truly democratic country during the 1920's.

While political changes were taking place, the Japanese economy grew. But by 1930, worldwide economic failures had seriously weakened economic growth in Japan. Meanwhile, in foreign affairs, the Japanese followed a bold policy that was aimed at making Japan the dominant country in Asia.

POLITICAL TRENDS In the years before World War I, the government of Japan was dominated by an *oligarchy*—rule by a few people—of older, aristocratic leaders. After World War I, however, the political situation changed. As the old rulers died, younger leaders came to power. Under these new leaders, several important political changes were made. Some of these changes indicated that the Japanese government was becoming more liberal.

In 1924, a former Japanese diplomat named Kato [kah-toh] became the prime minister. While he was in office, some important reforms were enacted by the government. For example, the right to vote was given to all Japanese men who were 25 years of age or older. Other reforms included a reduction in the size of the government bureaucracy and of the army. The army leaders, however, agreed to accept this reduction only on the condition that a system of military training be set up in Japanese universities and secondary schools. The military leaders were allowed to buy new military equipment with the money that was saved by cutting down the size of the army.

Despite the political reforms that took place in Japan, there were some steps taken to limit political freedom. One example was the Peace Preservation Act, which was passed in 1925. This act provided prison terms for those who favored extreme political or social changes in Japan.

Following Prime Minister Kato's death in early 1926, the leadership of Japan changed several times over the next few years. Under some of these leaders, efforts were made to limit political activities. Thus, even though some reforms were approved during the 1920's, Japan did not become a truly democratic country during those years.

ANTIDEMOCRATIC INFLUENCES Several factors hindered the growth of democracy in Japan in the 1920's. Most Japanese, for example, were not used to the democratic ideas of individual rights and free speech. Above all, most Japanese wanted a unified society ruled by leaders who were very loyal to the state.

Another factor that worked against the growth of democracy in Japan was the great concentration of wealth among a few families that controlled many businesses. These few families used their wealth and power to influence political leaders. As a result, Japan's political parties often neglected the needs of the farmers and the workers in favor of the goals of the wealthy families. Thus, many political parties in Japan did not have wide popular support. Farmers and workers usually did not trust the parties' ties to the wealthy families.

Japan's ancient military tradition and the great respect that many Japanese had for the military also worked against the growth of democratic ideas. Most Japanese were proud of the gains made by their country's armed services. Therefore, the work of liberal Japanese leaders to limit the size and the power of the armed services was often looked upon as an act of disloyalty.

By the 1930's, Japan's growing militarism was apparent, and Japanese youngsters received intensive military training.

UPI

An ancient Japanese tradition of secret societies also served to increase the influence of the military in Japan. Many members of the military belonged to secret groups. During the 1920's, several *ultranationalist*—extremely patriotic—secret societies became active. They tried to stop the growth of liberal ideas and to limit reforms. They felt that such ideas and reforms stood in the way of making Japan a powerful country.

ECONOMIC PROGRESS As Japanese industry grew during the early 1900's, two types of organization emerged. One was the small family-owned workshop with only a few workers. The other was the large factory with thousands of workers. Most of the large factories, as well as many banks, were controlled by giant business combinations known as *zaibatsu* [ziy-BAHT-soo]. These great businesses had developed during the late 1800's.

The Japanese economy expanded dramatically during World War I as Japan became a major supplier of war goods to the Allies. As Japanese factories rushed to fill the orders from the Allies for munitions and for other goods, industrial production soared. At the same time, the Japanese also took over many of the Asian markets that were once controlled by the warring European countries. This economic growth also increased the power of the *zaibatsu*. When the war ended, however, the Japanese economy faltered as munitions contracts were canceled and as European countries again began making goods.

Despite this setback, the Japanese economy recovered. One reason was that the Japanese had been able to retain at least some of the markets that had been gained during the war. Since Japanese factories used modern machines and paid low wages, the cost of making many goods was lower than in other countries. As a result, Japanese producers were able to sell goods at lower prices in the world's markets.

As Japan's industry expanded, labor unions also grew in size and in importance. By 1929, the Japanese Federation of Labor had more than 500 associations, with over 300,000 members. But despite the importance of labor unions, only a few laws to protect the workers were passed after World War I. And since wages generally were low, most workers did not share in the prosperity that came to Japan's industries during those years.

ECONOMIC PROBLEMS Even though industry grew during the 1920's, these years were difficult for some groups in Japanese society. Many farmers found themselves sinking into debt because the prices received for some farm products remained low. As a result, many farmers had to borrow in order to pay their rent and to buy needed supplies.

Another problem affecting the economy was the rapid growth of Japan's population. Between 1920 and 1931, the number of people in the country increased by over 16 percent. This population expansion meant that more jobs would have to be provided to meet the needs of the people.

Japan also lacked many important raw materials—such as coal, iron ore, timber, and petroleum—for its growing industries. Therefore, Japan was very dependent on world trade. Only by selling more and more goods on world markets were the Japanese able to raise the money needed to buy raw materials.

By 1930, however, a worldwide economic collapse (known as the Great Depression in the United States) had severely cut down overseas trade. As world trade dropped, Japan's exports fell sharply. The Japanese faced a serious economic crisis as the lack of trade led to rising unemployment and to cutbacks in production.

Some members of the military felt that Japan's economic problems could be ended through overseas expansion. They believed that such expansion would give Japan

William A. Ireland/The Columbus Dispatch

Married Again

Worldwide hopes for lasting peace were reflected in the political cartoons that were published in 1928, after more than 60 nations signed an agreement to renounce war.

needed raw materials, new markets, and sources of food for the growing population. The result was an increasingly aggressive foreign policy.

FOREIGN AFFAIRS During the early 1900's the Japanese had followed a foreign policy that had helped to make their country a dominant power in Asia. After World War I began in 1914, Japan—an Allied power—declared war on Germany and took over German-held lands in China and German-held islands in the Pacific Ocean.

After gaining these lands, the Japanese moved to increase their power within China. In early 1915, Japan presented China with the infamous Twenty-One Demands. These demands included Japanese control of former German-held lands in China and broader railroad, travel, and business rights

in Manchuria. Other demands were designed to give Japan virtual control over most of China's internal and foreign affairs. Because of the war in Europe, other countries could do little to help China. At the same time, the Chinese were too divided to resist the Japanese demands. As a result, China accepted most of the Twenty-One Demands in May 1915. The nature of these demands seemed to indicate that Japan planned to expand its territories in Asia.

After World War I ended, Japan was allowed to keep the formerly German-held province of Shantung [SHAN-TUHNG] in China and the German-held islands in the Pacific Ocean. In addition, Japan was made one of the five permanent members of the Council of the League of Nations (see Chapter 28). This showed Japan's growing importance in world affairs.

569

As a dominant power in Asia, Japan began to work more closely with other powerful countries. In 1922, for example, Japan agreed to limit the number of its battleships in a fixed ratio with those of the United States and Great Britain. Japan also signed a treaty agreeing to respect China's territorial rights and assenting to other conditions in regard to China (see page 565). Then Japan returned Shantung to China's control. Despite this move, Japan retained special trading rights in the Chinese province.

Japan's policy of cooperation with other countries also resulted in the establishment of diplomatic relations with the Soviet Union in 1925. In addition, several outstanding territorial differences between Japan and the Soviet Union were settled at the same time.

In the late 1920's, however, there was a change in the leadership of Japan, and the government became more conservative. As a result, the Japanese became less cooperative in foreign matters than they had been right after World War I. Throughout the economic turmoil of the 1930's, Japan's foreign policy was less cooperative and more aggressive. This policy was designed to further Japan's growth and security regardless of the views of the United States and the nations of Europe.

QUESTIONS FOR REVIEW

1 *What voting reform was enacted by the Japanese government while Prime Minister Kato was in office?*

2 *How did the worldwide economic collapse affect Japanese trade in the 1930's?*

3 *Why did some members of the military favor overseas expansion in the 1930's as a way of solving Japan's economic problems?*

3 AFRICA AND THE MIDDLE EAST

The European countries that held colonies in Africa strengthened their hold on these lands during the early 1900's. However, many Africans disliked foreign domination because of the unfair policies used by many of the colonial powers.

German-held lands in Africa were turned over to some of the victorious Allied powers after World War I. Similar changes took place in the Middle East as former Ottoman lands came under French and British control. But these changes angered many Arabs, who began working for the independence of Arab lands during the 1920's.

A TIME OF CONSOLIDATION IN AFRICA

By the early 1900's, most of Africa had been divided among the major powers of Europe. These countries, eager to gain wealth, raw materials, and new markets for their goods, worked to organize and to consolidate their African possessions. Formerly unknown areas were mapped, railroads were built, and communications were expanded. In addition, the great mineral wealth of Africa was tapped as diamond, tin, and gold mines were opened. Unfortunately, much of the mineral wealth that was taken out of Africa was used to enrich European investors rather than to benefit Africans.

The European powers that held lands in Africa, however, made some positive contributions during the years of colonial rule. New government bureaus were set up to improve the administration of the colonies. At the same time, efforts were made to stop intertribal warfare in Africa. European governments also worked to expand educational facilities, even though most schools were under the control of missionaries. Public health facilities were improved as clinics and hospitals were set up. Sanitation campaigns were also started to improve public health. Farm experts from Europe showed African farmers how to use new fertilizers and improved seeds. And veterinarians helped Africans learn about new ways of caring for their herds.

Many Africans, however, resented European rule of their lands, since the colonial powers often followed policies that kept the Africans in an inferior role. For example, racial discrimination was often practiced, and Africans were given little chance to take part in important political matters. In addition, the economic development of the colonies was usually designed to enrich the colonial powers rather than to raise the standard of living for the Africans. Thus, many Africans were hopeful that Europe's domination of their lands would change after World War I.

THE MANDATE SYSTEM IN AFRICA Several important changes took place in Africa after World War I. The peace treaty that ended the war stripped Germany of its colonies in Africa. Then the League of Nations (see Chapter 28) set up what was known as the *mandate system*. Under this plan, control of the German-held lands in Africa was *mandated*—entrusted—to several of the Allied powers that won the war. The league also set up a commission to visit the colonies and to evaluate the way that they were governed. Even though the commission had no power, it could publicize any bad conditions that were found.

World reaction to the mandate system was mixed. Some countries, for example, believed that the mandate idea was a positive step in colonial administration.

Mandated Territories in Africa and the Middle East

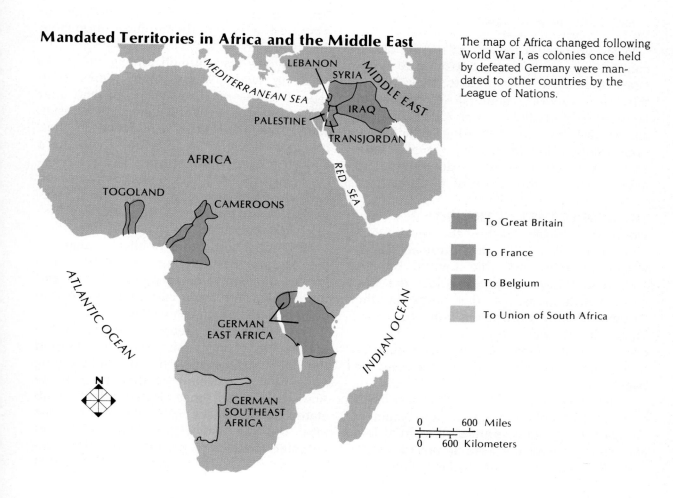

The map of Africa changed following World War I, as colonies once held by defeated Germany were mandated to other countries by the League of Nations.

To Great Britain

To France

To Belgium

To Union of South Africa

0   600 Miles

0   600 Kilometers

Other countries—especially those that were colonial powers—looked upon the mandate idea as an invasion of their right to govern overseas lands.

While the peace agreement that led to the mandate system was being worked out in Paris in 1919, another important meeting was also taking place in Paris. This was the Pan-African Congress, which was made up of black Americans and people from 15 other countries. This group wanted the former German holdings in Africa to be governed by an international agency through the League of Nations. One member of the congress stated that

> ... the natives of Africa must have the right to participate in the government as fast as their [political] development permits, in conformity with the principle that the government exists for the natives, and not the natives for the government.

In the years after the establishment of the mandate system African opposition to European colonialism continued to grow. During this time, African nationalism began to emerge. In part, the rise of African nationalism was due to increasing educational opportunities among a small group of Africans. These people were determined to have a voice in the future of African affairs.

THE MIDDLE EAST IN TRANSITION When World War I began, much of the Middle East was weakly ruled by the Ottoman Turks, who were allied with the Central Powers. The Central Powers, however, lost the war. As a result, most of the lands in the Ottoman Empire were taken from the Turks. These lands were then turned over to France or to Great Britain as mandates under the League of Nations (see map on page 571).

France received the former Ottoman lands of Syria and Lebanon. During the years of French rule, political repression, martial law, and strict censorship were imposed whenever the Lebanese or Syrians failed to

satisfy the French administrators. But the French did build roads and irrigation systems in these lands.

The Middle Eastern lands of Iraq and Palestine were given as mandates to Great Britain. A constitutional monarchy was set up in Iraq, and the country gained full independence in 1930. The British, however, had problems in dealing with Palestine, an area then occupied largely by Arab peoples. Through the *Balfour Declaration* of 1917, the British government had stated that Palestine should become a national home for the Jewish people. But in 1918, the British stated that they recognized the right of the Arabs to rule their lands. The Arabs found the different statements made by the British both confusing and disappointing. Conditions were generally peaceful in Palestine between 1921 and 1929. However, Arab attacks on the Jewish settlers in Palestine increased in 1929 and continued throughout the 1930's.

There was also turmoil among the Turks following World War I. Many Turks were angry because of Turkey's loss of land after being defeated in World War I. As a result, many Turks had little confidence in their country's leaders. In the early 1920's, a Turkish military hero, Mustafa Kemal [moos-tah-FAH kuh-MAL] led a successful revolt and set up a new government. Under Kemal's rule, many reforms to modernize Turkey were instituted.

There were also other political changes in the Middle East during the 1920's. The Pahlavi dynasty came to power in Iran, and the Arabian Peninsula came under the rule of ibn-Saud [IB-uhn-sah-OOD].

The 1920's were years of unrest in the Middle East. Many Arab groups had helped the British against the Ottoman Turks during World War I. In return for their help, these Arabs expected that independent Arab states would be set up in the Middle East after the war. However, when the former Ottoman lands were placed under the mandate system, Arabs in these lands felt that

4 COLONIALISM IN SOUTHEAST ASIA AND THE PACIFIC

By the early 1900's, several areas of Southeast Asia had become colonial possessions of major Western powers. These countries ruled their Asian holdings through very different colonial policies. For example, some colonies were allowed a great amount of self-government to prepare them for the time when they would be independent. But many colonial lands in Southeast Asia were exploited by their foreign rulers.

In time, this unfair treatment led to the growth of nationalistic feelings among the peoples of these colonial lands. As a result, Asian leaders emerged who worked to end foreign domination in their homelands.

Mustafa Kemal worked to westernize and to modernize Turkey through major economic, legal, educational, and religious reforms.

they had been betrayed. Thus, Arab nationalism grew during the 1920's and 1930's, as Arab groups worked to gain independence for their lands.

QUESTIONS FOR REVIEW

1 What African mineral wealth was tapped as mines were opened during the early 1900's?

2 How did colonial powers generally view the mandate system?

3 Why were many Arabs upset by the British statements about Palestine in 1917 and 1918?

THE UNITED STATES AND THE PHILIPPINES The Philippine Islands came under the control of the United States in the late 1800's following the defeat of Spain in the Spanish American War. After subduing Filipino resistance to American rule, the United States worked to help the Philippine people become independent. To train the people for self-government, schools were built, and teachers were sent from the United States. At the same time, the United States also built hospitals and sanitation systems to improve public health.

In 1916, the United States Congress passed the Jones Act. This law promised independence to the Philippines as soon as a stable government was set up in the islands. The law also provided for a Philippine legislative body made up of a senate and a house of representatives. This gave the people of the Philippines greater control of political affairs in the islands.

During the 1920's, however, there was a change in American policy toward the Philippines. Some Filipino business leaders were found to have engaged in corrupt business practices. As a result, the United

States tightened its control over Philippine internal affairs. But the new policy unified Filipino nationalists, who became increasingly anxious to win Philippine independence.

In 1934, a new law—the Tydings-McDuffie Act—was passed by the American Congress. This law gave the Filipinos the power to draft a constitution. In addition, the law provided for a ten-year transition period while the Filipinos gained complete independence. During this time, the United States was responsible for Philippine foreign relations and for the defense of the islands.

While the United States worked toward independence for the Philippines, other countries tried to develop effective policies for their colonies in Southeast Asia. These policies were often much different from those followed by the United States.

EUROPEAN AND JAPANESE POSSESSIONS

By the early 1900's, much of South and Southeast Asia was controlled by three major European countries (see map on page 575). Britain governed India, Ceylon, Burma, and Malaya. France dominated Indochina—present-day Vietnam, Kampuchea, and Laos—and the Dutch held the East Indies.

Great Britain allowed some people in the colonies to hold government jobs. But these jobs were usually less important positions that did not involve policymaking. The right to vote was given to all adults in Ceylon in 1931. But in Burma, there were frequent clashes between the British authorities and Burmese nationalist groups. In Malaya, the British allowed few political changes or freedoms, although native Malays benefited to some degree from economic growth during the 1920's.

In ruling Indochina, the French taxed the people heavily and used the country as a market for French goods. The French also took natural resources from Indochina with no regard for conservation. Similarly, strict policies were followed by the Dutch in their East Indian colonies. These policies did not permit the people of the East Indies to be involved in government affairs.

Japan gained control of the Mariana, Marshall, and Caroline islands in the Pacific Ocean during World War I (see map on page 575). Following the war, these islands were given to Japan by the League of Nations under the mandate system. The Japanese made no effort to develop a policy for self-government, since they wanted these islands for military purposes only.

Thus, the colonial policies of European powers and of Japan differed greatly from those of the United States. Since many of the colonial powers failed to involve the

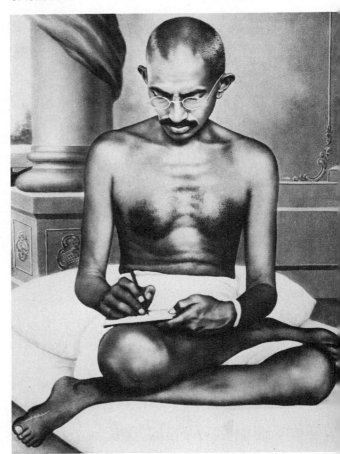

During the years that India was struggling to free itself from Great Britain, Mohandas Gandhi became the unchallenged leader of the movement for independence. The appeal of his magnetic personality drew millions of followers.

Ewing Galloway

574

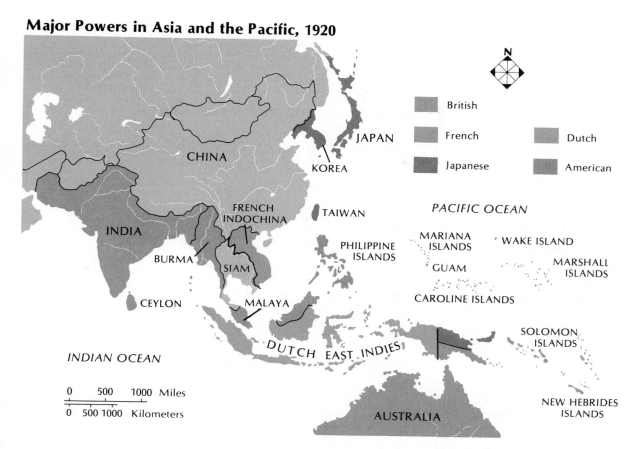

Major Powers in Asia and the Pacific, 1920

Legend:
- British
- French
- Japanese
- Dutch
- American

CHINA
JAPAN
KOREA
INDIA
FRENCH INDOCHINA
TAIWAN
BURMA
SIAM
CEYLON
MALAYA
DUTCH EAST INDIES
PHILIPPINE ISLANDS
MARIANA ISLANDS
GUAM
CAROLINE ISLANDS
WAKE ISLAND
MARSHALL ISLANDS
SOLOMON ISLANDS
NEW HEBRIDES ISLANDS
AUSTRALIA
PACIFIC OCEAN
INDIAN OCEAN

0 500 1000 Miles
0 500 1000 Kilometers

During the 1920's, much of Southeast Asia was governed by colonial powers, such as Great Britain, France, and the Netherlands.

people that they ruled in government decisions, nationalism began to grow during the 1920's and 1930's.

NATIONALISM IN SOUTHEAST ASIA The Allied victory in World War I greatly stimulated nationalism in Southeast Asia. Many Asians who were ruled by foreign countries felt that the war had been fought, in part, for the right of *self-determination*. This was the idea that all people had the right to govern their countries without interference from other countries.

Another factor that influenced the development of nationalism was the growth in educational opportunities for Southeast Asians in the 1920's and 1930's. Many people who lived in colonial lands did not like foreign rule. They also did not like the discriminatory practices followed by some colonial officers. But as more people in these lands were exposed to new ideas through education, they began to realize that they were being exploited by the colonial powers. In addition, education further exposed the discriminatory practices used by some colonial officers. Thus, small groups of well-educated Southeast Asians began to set up nationalistic political parties to work for the end of foreign rule.

The effectiveness of these groups, however, depended on the way that the colonial powers ruled their overseas lands. In general, the demands for independence from nationalistic groups in the British colonies varied according to how much self-government the British allowed in these lands. But the French gave the people that they ruled little chance for self-government. Consequently, nationalistic groups became very active in the French colonies.

In Indochina, for example, the Communists under Ho Chi Minh [HOH-CHEE-MIN] were well organized in parts of the country during the 1920's. Even though the French tried to suppress nationalistic groups in Indochina, these groups continued to work for self-rule. Many of the groups that worked for Indochina's independence were *underground*—secret—organizations. This was because such groups were generally outlawed by the French.

Thus, nationalism was a growing influence in Southeast Asia in the 1920's and 1930's. The leaders of the nationalistic movements believed that their activities would, in time, bring an end to the foreign domination of their lands.

QUESTIONS FOR REVIEW

1 *For what reason did the United States tighten its control over Philippine internal affairs in the 1920's?*

2 *How did the Japanese plan to use the Pacific islands that they gained during World War I?*

3 *Why was education an important factor in the development of nationalism in Southeast Asia in the 1920's and 1930's?*

CHAPTER SUMMARY

During the early 1900's, the ruling dynasty of China was overthrown. A republic was set up with Dr. Sun Yat-sen as the president, but there was much unrest in the country. In 1916, the power of the central government collapsed, and warlords took control of different parts of the country. Despite the unsettled conditions, Sun continued working for a unified China. After Sun died in 1925, he was succeeded by Chiang Kai-shek, who established a stable government by the late 1920's.

As new leaders came to power in Japan during the 1920's, several important reforms were enacted. But despite the apparent liberal trend, there were factors that hindered the growth of democracy in Japan.

There was also economic growth in Japan during the 1920's, accompanied by many economic problems. In foreign affairs, Japan gained land as a result of World War I.

In Africa, European powers worked to consolidate their colonial holdings during the 1920's. And in the Middle East, many parts of the Ottoman Empire were turned over to European countries under the mandate system after World War I.

In Southeast Asia, the United States controlled the Philippine Islands, while several European powers held other lands in the area. These countries followed different policies in ruling their Asian colonies.

CHAPTER 29 IN REVIEW

IMPORTANT WORDS, NAMES, AND TERMS

1 Explain, define, or identify each of the following:

Sun Yat-sen	ultranationalists	Balfour Declaration
Kuomintang	*zaibatsu*	Mustafa Kemal
Three Principles	Twenty-One Demands	Tydings-McDuffie Act
extraterritoriality	mandate system	Ho Chi Minh

FACTS AND IDEAS

2 From what country did Sun Yat-sen accept aid in 1923?

3 For what reason did the Japanese economy expand greatly during World War I?

4 What was the purpose of the Pan-African Congress?

5 What right was given to all adults in Ceylon by the British in 1931?

ANALYZING VISUAL MATERIAL

6 Study the political cartoon on page 569. To what event do you think the artist was referring in the small sign that reads "Divorced in 1914," drawn at the bottom of the steps?

7 Look at the map on page 575. According to the map, which European country controlled the most land in Asia in 1920?

CONCEPTS AND UNDERSTANDINGS

8 Why did the industrial growth that took place in China in the 1920's do little to help the people of China?

9 What did the ultranationalist groups that were active in Japan in the 1920's hope to achieve?

10 Why did many Arab groups expect that independent Arab states would be set up in the Middle East after World War I?

11 How did the Jones Act give the Philippine people greater control of political affairs in their country?

PROJECTS AND ACTIVITIES

12 Japanese industrial development increased greatly during the early 1900's. Several students might compile a list of Japanese goods that are sold in the United States today. Some students might look for pictures of different Japanese products used today to display in the class.

13 Following World War I, many different areas of the world were mandated to other nations through the League of Nations. Some students might do some research to learn more about the mandate system. Information about the lands that were included and about how the mandate system worked might be found in encyclopedias and in books about the League of Nations. After the information has been presented, have the class discuss the value of the mandate system.

CHAPTER 30 EUROPE AFTER WORLD WAR I

1 Postwar Conditions in Europe   2 Political Changes in Europe After the War   3 Worldwide Economic Collapse

The end of World War I brought many problems and changes to Europe. For example, new economic conditions made the return to peace difficult. At the same time, people everywhere hoped that world leaders could find some way to prevent another world war.

There was also much political unrest in Europe after the war as new countries, as well as older nations, worked to solve their postwar problems. Some of the new nations faced many problems, since they were working to set up democratic governments but had no tradition of democracy. Then in 1929, an economic collapse in the United States spread to many of the major countries of Europe. As a result, the world faced an uncertain future as economic problems continued during the early 1930's.

Imperial War Museum/painting by Sir William Orpen

The Hall of Mirrors in the Palace of Versailles provided the background for the signing of the treaty ending World War I.

1 POSTWAR CONDITIONS IN EUROPE

European countries faced many challenges in the years after World War I. The war had upset most European economies. Thus, countries faced many problems in returning to peacetime economic conditions. Moreover, countries set up after the war had to deal with new political conditions, while the Allies had huge war debts to pay.

After the war, there was a great outpouring of antiwar feeling around the world. As a result, world leaders tried to find ways to prevent future wars. And the newly formed League of Nations also worked to preserve world peace.

ECONOMIC CONSEQUENCES OF THE WAR

The years immediately following World War I were a time of readjustment, as European countries worked to return to peacetime conditions. Despite the peace settlements at Versailles, the economic effects of the war continued to affect most European countries. The fighting had taken millions of lives. In addition, there was considerable damage to property—especially in France, where villages, factories, farms, and railways were devastated by the fighting.

Another problem that hampered the return to prewar economic conditions concerned the new countries that were set up under the treaties made following the war. During the 1920's, many of these countries passed high tariffs to protect their home industries from foreign competition. But high tariffs tended to limit trade, since other countries passed similar laws to keep out foreign goods.

European nations also faced the problem of finding jobs for returning soldiers. There were fewer jobs available in most of Europe's industrialized countries because they had lost a large share of the world's markets. During the war, such countries as Great Britain and Germany had concentrated on building war matériel. They had also stopped shipping many goods overseas. As a result, the United States, Japan, and some Latin American countries began selling to nations that once had bought goods from Europe. After the war ended, many countries continued to buy from the United States, Japan, and Latin America rather than from European countries. Thus, production fell and unemployment rose in such countries as Great Britain and Germany as the demand for goods failed to return to prewar levels.

Wages were another problem after the war. The pay of workers had risen considerably during the war. When the war ended, workers were determined not to give up these wage gains despite pressures from factory owners to do so. This led to rising tension between workers and employers during the 1920's.

Thus, the end of the war brought new problems to the people of Europe. In addition, there were also problems caused by the formation of new countries in Eastern Europe after the war.

As inflation in postwar Germany intensified, the government was forced to print paper money in million-mark and billion-mark denominations to keep pace with soaring prices.

Currency courtesy of Joachim R. Schneider; Don Antoszkiewicz

579

POLITICAL		SOCIAL AND ECONOMIC
Weimar Constitution adopted by Germany	~ 1919	
Danzig placed under protection of League of Nations	~ 1920	
Washington disarmament conference held	~ 1921 ~	1 million unemployed in Great Britain
March on Rome by Mussolini and the Fascists	~ 1922 ~	German economy collapsed
French and Belgians occupied the Ruhr	~ 1923	
France and Britain recognized the Soviet Union	~ 1924 ~	Dawes Plan accepted by Germany
Hindenburg elected president of Germany	~ 1925	
	1926 ~	General strike in Great Britain
Kellogg-Briand Pact signed in Paris	~ 1928	
Lateran Accord signed by the Papacy and the Italian government	~ 1929 ~	Young Plan reduced German war debt Stock market collapsed in the United States
London naval conference held	~ 1930 ~	French government enacted workers' insurance
	1931 ~	Moratorium on war debts and reparations
Soviet Union joined the League of Nations	~ 1934	

THE PROBLEMS OF NEW NATIONS The map of eastern Europe was changed considerably by the peace agreements after World War I. For example, the new nations of Finland, Estonia, Latvia, Lithuania, and Poland were established along the Baltic Sea. Czechoslovakia, Austria, Hungary, and the Kingdom of the Serbs, Croats, and Slovenes —later named Yugoslavia—were set up on lands that had been part of Austria-Hungary. In addition, the port city of Danzig and surrounding lands in East Prussia were made an independent city-state under the League of Nations (see map on page 581).

The populations in many of the new countries were very diverse. For example, more than 3 million Germans lived in the area of Czechoslovakia called the Sudetenland. About 750,000 Hungarians also lived in Czechoslovakia. There were also minority ethnic groups in many of the other new countries of eastern Europe.

The different groups in some of the new nations were often divided by language and by religion. As a result, many of these groups did not get along with one another. There were also border controversies between some of the new countries, since they had gained land after the war at the expense of neighboring countries. While the new countries of eastern Europe struggled with their problems, the Allies faced problems caused by war debts and reparations.

WAR DEBTS AND REPARATIONS The major European Allied powers were deeply in debt after World War I. These countries had borrowed from one another and from the United States to pay their war costs. Some of the Allies believed that the war debts among them should be canceled, since they had worked together to win the war. The European Allies were willing to cancel the debts to one another if the United States canceled the debts owed by these Allies. However, the United States looked upon the Allied war debts as legal obligations and refused to cancel them.

Territorial Adjustments After World War I

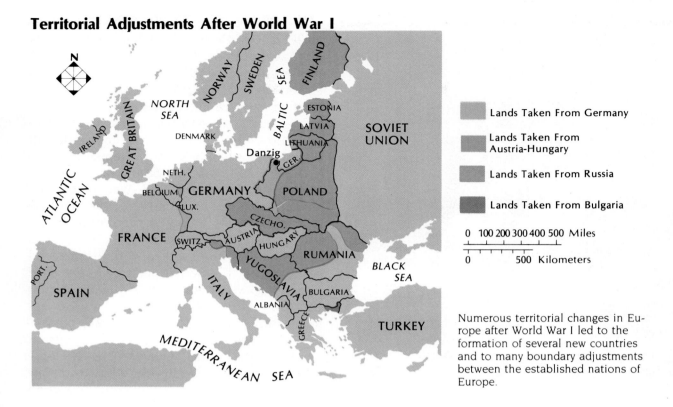

Numerous territorial changes in Europe after World War I led to the formation of several new countries and to many boundary adjustments between the established nations of Europe.

Then in 1922, a compromise on the debt question was reached. At that time, the United States agreed to spread the Allies' debt payments over many years and to lower the interest rate. However, the United States still refused to cancel the remaining war debts.

The Allies argued that they could not pay their debts to the United States unless Germany fulfilled its obligation to pay *reparations*. These were payments that Germany was to make to the Allies for war damages. The total due for these damages had been set at about 32 billion dollars. But it was difficult for Germany to pay such a huge debt, since the country's economy had been weakened by the war.

The Treaty of Versailles provided that Germany could pay some of its reparations in raw materials. But in 1923, Germany fell behind in the delivery of raw materials to France. The French occupied the German industrial region called the Ruhr Valley and demanded that workers there supply raw materials to the French. The German government, however, urged Germans in the Ruhr not to work for the French. As a result, production in the Ruhr dropped sharply, and the Germans stopped making reparations payments.

To solve the crisis, a group of financial experts headed by Charles G. Dawes of the United States worked out the Dawes Plan. Under this plan, the German debt payments were lowered. In addition, an American loan of about 200 million dollars was made to bolster the German economy. After the plan went into effect, Germany again made reparations payments, and France withdrew from the Ruhr.

In 1929, a new plan for reparations called the Young Plan lowered the total German reparations debt to about 8 billion dollars plus interest. Germany was also given more than 50 years to pay this debt. Thus, by reducing the German debt, the Young Plan finally brought reparations within Germany's ability to pay.

Many French cities and towns, such as the ancient city of Ypres, were completely devastated by the furious fighting that took place in western Europe during World War I.

EFFORTS FOR PEACE One important outcome of World War I was an outpouring of antiwar feeling around the world after the war. People in all countries fervently hoped that there would never be another world war. In response to this desire for peace, world leaders worked during the 1920's to find ways to limit armaments and to outlaw warfare.

An important naval-disarmament conference was held in Washington, D.C., in 1921 and 1922. Following intense negotiations, the United States, Great Britain, Japan, Italy, and France agreed to limit the number of large warships that each country could build. These nations also agreed not to build large warships for ten years. Even though many kinds of warships were not included in the Washington agreement, it was looked upon as a positive step toward disarmament.

In 1925, representatives from Great Britain, France, Germany, Belgium, and Italy met at Locarno, Switzerland. After almost two weeks of meetings, these countries signed several treaties. In one of these treaties, the five nations agreed not to go to war against one another unless they were attacked. They also agreed to settle all disputes peacefully among themselves.

One of the most important peace agreements signed after World War I was the Kellogg-Briand Pact of 1928. The nations that signed this treaty agreed not to use war as part of their national policy. These countries also promised to work for peaceful settlements of international disputes. The one great weakness of the Kellogg-Briand Pact was its failure to set up a way to enforce the agreement. Despite this serious defect, however, the treaty was a significant step toward world peace. The Kellogg-Briand Pact was a worldwide effort to outlaw war, since most countries eventually signed the agreement.

In 1930, another naval-disarmament agreement was reached between Great Britain, Japan, and the United States. Under this treaty, these countries agreed to further limits on the size and number of warships in their fleets.

Thus, the 1920's were years when the countries of the world tried to find ways to preserve peace. During this time, the League of Nations also worked to improve conditions in the world.

THE WORK OF THE LEAGUE The League of Nations settled a number of territorial disputes that arose in the world during the 1920's. For example, the league helped to settle a dispute between Finland and Sweden over control of the Åland [OH-LAHND] Islands in 1921. The league solved the problem by giving Finland control of the islands. However, the people of the islands, who were mainly Swedes, were allowed to control local matters. Border disputes between Germany and Poland and between Albania and the country that became

known as Yugoslavia were also successfully resolved by the league during the early 1920's.

A serious problem arose in 1923, when some Italian members of an international border commission were killed on Greek land. The Italian government made certain demands on Greece and landed soldiers on the Greek island of Corfu, west of Greece. Instead of giving in to the Italian demands, the Greek government asked the League of Nations for help. Italy, however, stated that it would not be bound by any action taken by the league. To avoid this challenge, the league asked a group of ambassadors to settle the dispute. This group decided that Greece should pay a large fine to Italy. Following this decision, Italy withdrew its soldiers from Corfu. But the action of the Italian government showed that the league was powerless if its members chose not to cooperate.

The League of Nations was more successful in dealing with other problems during the 1920's. For example, the league arranged for the exchange of prisoners between countries after World War I. The league also raised loans to help Austria, Bulgaria, and Hungary recover from the war. And the league worked with governments to solve health problems around the world.

Thus, the League of Nations worked in many different ways to preserve world peace. The league was not always successful in solving world problems. But it did help many countries recover from the effects of World War I.

QUESTIONS FOR REVIEW

1 What new nations along the Baltic Sea were set up after World War I?

2 How did world leaders react to the worldwide outpouring of antiwar feeling after World War I?

3 Why did the settlement of the dispute between Greece and Italy by the League of Nations in 1923 show the weakness of the league?

2 POLITICAL CHANGES IN EUROPE AFTER THE WAR

The new countries of eastern Europe faced many problems after World War I. The unsettled conditions during the 1920's led to the rise of dictators in many of these countries.

At the time in western Europe, the French faced the job of rebuilding their war-torn country, while unemployment was a serious problem for British leaders. Germany's new democratic government faced public hostility as the country's leaders worked to solve national problems. And a new leader came to power in Italy a few years after the war. Within a short time, this ruler ended democratic government and became the dictator of the country.

NEW NATIONS IN EASTERN EUROPE The new countries set up in eastern Europe after World War I faced the problem of forming workable governments. All of these nations hoped to be democratic. However, minority problems and lack of experience in democratic rule soon led to the rise of dictators in many of these countries.

One country that became a successful democracy after the war was Finland. The Finns had declared their independence from Russia in 1917. After a civil war had raged for a few years, a democratic republic based on adult suffrage was set up. Conditions improved during the 1920's as the Finns worked to solve problems within the country.

Finland's neighbors—Estonia, Latvia, and Lithuania—started out as democracies. But they soon came under the rule of nationalistic dictators. This happened, in part, because of the danger of being taken over by the Soviet Union.

Poland also began as a democratic republic. But political instability led to the rise of a dictatorial government in 1926. However, this government kept some features of democracy.

The new country of Czechoslovakia was more fortunate after the war. Despite many

problems, the Czechs had economic wealth and capable leaders. As a result, Czechoslovakia maintained a workable and a popular democratic government throughout the 1920's.

Some of the other new countries, however, were not so fortunate. For example, Austria struggled through the 1920's with little enthusiasm for democracy. Hungary was ruled for a short time by a Communist government. But it was replaced by an anti-Communist dictatorship in 1919. The Kingdom of the Serbs, Croats, and Slovenes was ruled by a king. However, there were minority problems within the country. The lack of unity among the different groups led the king to set up a dictatorship in 1929. The country then became known as Yugoslavia.

As the new countries of eastern Europe worked to set up governments and to deal with their internal problems, there were also problems in western Europe. The powerful countries of France and Great Britain faced many difficulties as they worked to return to peacetime conditions.

PROBLEMS IN FRANCE AND GREAT BRITAIN France was one of the major Allied powers that suffered greatly from World War I. For example, more than 1 million French soldiers were killed in the war. Property damage totaled more than 20 billion dollars. French leaders were determined that the cost of rebuilding and of debt payments would be paid by Germany through its reparations to France.

The French also wanted to make certain that Germany would never again attack France. Therefore, the French government signed a number of defense agreements with other countries in Europe during the

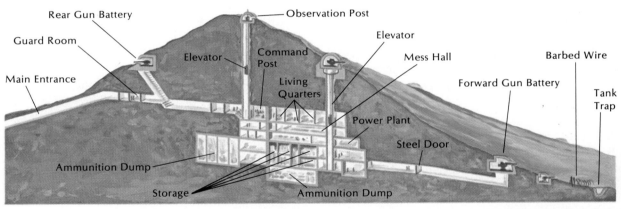

Rear Gun Battery

Guard Room

Main Entrance

Observation Post

Elevator

Command Post

Elevator

Mess Hall

Barbed Wire

Living Quarters

Forward Gun Battery

Tank Trap

Power Plant

Ammunition Dump

Steel Door

Storage

Ammunition Dump

The cross section of the Maginot Line—the line of forts and gun emplacements designed to protect France from a German invasion—shows the underground world where French soldiers lived and worked. Gun emplacements had special seals and elaborate air-pressure systems to protect their crews from poison-gas attacks.

1920's. In addition, the French built a very elaborate underground defense system called the *Maginot* [MAZH-uh-NOH] *Line* to protect the eastern border of France from German invaders.

There was much political turmoil in France during the 1920's. Since there were so many political parties, no single party had enough support to govern without help from the other parties. As a result, France was often ruled by a *coalition*—a group of parties. But the different parties seldom agreed on what policies to follow. Thus, there were many changes in government leadership.

The British faced the problem of chronic unemployment during the 1920's as the demand for British goods remained low. Britain's foreign trade did not return to prewar levels because of the loss of markets to other countries during the war. In addition, many European countries were so poor after the war that they could not buy British goods.

An important political development in the 1920's was the emergence of the Labour—or Socialist—party. Socialists hoped to introduce *socialism*—government ownership of the major industries—into Great Britain within the framework of democracy. The other major party in Britain—the Conservative party—believed that the role of the government in the economy should be limited.

During most of the 1920's, the Conservatives were in control of the British government. They faced a serious problem in 1926, when a strike by coal miners over wage cuts developed into a general strike. But the strike failed when volunteers kept most of the essential services of the nation in operation. While France and Britain struggled with their problems, Germany was also working to return to peacetime conditions.

THE GERMAN DEMOCRATIC EXPERIENCE

After Germany's defeat, a new government was set up in 1919 under a democratic constitution written in the city of Weimar [VIY-MAHR]. This new government was called the Weimar Republic. The Allies had demanded that there was to be no kaiser, so the constitution provided for a president chosen by the people. The president appointed the chancellor, who was in charge of all government policies. The constitution also called for a legislative body —the *Reichstag* [RIYKS-TAHK]—chosen by the people.

Many Germans, however, hated the Weimar government. They blamed it for Germany's defeat in the war. The Weimar government was also blamed for the peace terms that forced Germany to pay reparations and to accept responsibility for the war.

In addition to public dislike, the Weimar government also faced serious economic problems. Factories were closed, foreign trade had disappeared, unemployment was widespread, and Germany owed a huge reparations bill. To meet its financial needs, the Weimar government began printing more paper money rather than raising taxes. But since there was no gold to back this paper money, it became worthless. Merchants constantly raised the price of goods. Thus, the money declined in value and Germany was struck by runaway inflation. German leaders realized that quick action was needed to save the country's economy. The German government met with the Allies and arranged for loans and for a new way of paying reparations. As a result, the German economy began to improve, and many Germans began to accept the Weimar regime.

There were, however, a number of weaknesses in the German democracy. The German people had lived under authoritarian rule since the late 1800's. Under this rule, the state was looked upon as being more important than the individual. Thus, the German people had no democratic tradition nor any experience with the workings of democracy.

The many political parties in Germany after the war added to the weakness of German democracy. The country was often ruled by a coalition. But there were times when a coalition could not agree on government policies. This sometimes led to political unrest. At such times, the president was allowed to rule through emergency decrees. This action, however, bypassed the legislative branch of government and made the normal procedures of democracy seem unnecessary. Because of these weaknesses, the German democracy faced an uncertain future in the late 1920's. At the same time, important governmental changes were taking place in Italy.

TURMOIL IN ITALY   There was much unrest in Italy after World War I, as the country was plagued by strikes, food shortages, and inflation. But efforts by the Italian government to solve these problems were weak and ineffective. As a result, discontent grew and radical groups constantly worked for change.

Many Italians were greatly disappointed by the peace treaty that ended World War I. Even though Italy had been one of the Allies, it had gained only a little land and a small share of the reparations payments. But half a million Italian soldiers had been killed, and Italy owed a huge war debt. Thus, many Italians felt that their country had given much but had gained very little from taking part in the war.

The discontent within Italy led to frequent changes in the leadership of the country between 1919 and 1922. These changes reflected the inability of the leaders to solve the country's problems. As the government became increasingly ineffective, there were growing demands for a strong leader who could save the country.

In the midst of the growing chaos, a political leader emerged who, in time, became the ruler of Italy. This leader was Benito Mussolini, who had served in the Italian Army in World War I. After the war, Mussolini had organized groups of veterans into what became known as the Fascist party. This name came from a symbol of authority in ancient Rome—the *fasces* [FAS-EEZ]—a bundle of rods with the blade of an ax projecting from them. The main purpose for which the Fascists were formed was to fight the Communists, who were constantly fomenting discontent among Italian workers.

In 1921, the Fascists won several seats in the Italian parliament. Then, in October 1922, Mussolini organized a march on Rome by his black-shirted Fascist followers. Despite the danger posed by this march, the Italian king refused to allow the government to use force against the Fascists. As a result, the premier resigned, and the Fascists entered Rome without opposition. Mussolini was asked by the king to become the premier and was given wide powers to restore order in the country. By 1930, however, Mussolini had destroyed democracy in Italy and had made himself the master of the country.

ITALY UNDER MUSSOLINI   After coming to power, Mussolini, who was known as Il *Duce*—the leader—moved to consolidate his power and to eliminate all opposition. Within a few years, most aspects of life in Italy came under government control. For example, newspapers could not print a story without government approval. A special court was set up to punish anyone who did not conform to Fascist beliefs. Teachers were fired if they failed to instill Fascist ideas in their students. Any person or group who opposed Mussolini and his policies could be arrested and imprisoned by the secret police.

To control the country's economic life, Mussolini set up what was known as the corporate state. Under this plan, *syndicates*—groups—representing workers, employers, and professional people were formed. Each syndicate was headed by a Fascist-party member. Thus, the government had direct control over workers and employers.

Mussolini wanted to impress the world with the accomplishments of fascism. Therefore, he ordered the construction of great public buildings as well as a system of highways. These projects gave jobs to thousands of unemployed workers. Consequently, Mussolini boasted that fascism had ended unemployment in Italy.

The Italian ruler believed that military power was very important. Thus, boys in Italy began military training at the age of 6, and at the age of 21, all Italian men were required to

The military aspects of Italian fascism were apparent whenever Mussolini appeared in public. In addition, Italian children were given military training at an early age.

join the armed forces. In keeping with his belief in military power, Mussolini once wrote

> ... War alone brings up to its highest tension all human energy and puts the stamp of nobility upon the peoples who have the courage to meet it. ...

In 1929, Mussolini settled a long-standing dispute with the Roman Catholic Church over the relationship between the Church and the Italian government. Under an agreement called the Lateran Accord, Vatican City in Rome was recognized as an independent country ruled by the pope. In addition, the Roman Catholic Church was recognized as the national religion of Italy.

In spite of the seeming accomplishments of Mussolini's Fascist government, there were still problems in Italy. For example, many people lived in great poverty. Taxes were in-creased to pay for the huge building projects ordered by Il Duce. But the greatest tragedy for Italy was the disappearance of democracy. By the 1930's, the Italian people were living under a government that held limitless power over their lives.

QUESTIONS FOR REVIEW

1 By what name was the Kingdom of the Serbs, Croats, and Slovenes known after 1929?

2 After World War I, how did the French try to make certain that Germany would never again attack France?

3 Why did many Germans hate the Weimar government?

587

3 WORLDWIDE ECONOMIC COLLAPSE

Following World War I, the United States enjoyed generally prosperous times, even though there were some problems. But in 1929, a combination of factors led to the collapse of the American economy. The effects of this breakdown quickly reached Europe and led to serious problems in many countries. As a result, the leaders of the major European powers worked to solve the growing economic crisis.

AMERICAN ECONOMIC PROBLEMS Following World War I, the United States was the most prosperous nation in the world. But this prosperity was deceiving, for there were a number of disturbing problems in the American economy.

Farmers, for example, did not share in the prosperity of the 1920's. Prices for farm goods dropped sharply after the war as the overseas demand for food products fell. At the same time, the prices of farm equipment and supplies remained high. Thus, American farmers had to pay high prices for goods while their income was dropping.

Another problem in the American economy during the 1920's was the continuing rise in stock prices. Many Americans hoped to take advantage of this situation to gain quick riches through stock-market *speculation*. This meant that people bought stocks when prices were rising in hopes of selling at higher prices. Such a scheme, however, was entirely dependent on a never-ending rise in stock prices. Unfortunately, such increases would not go on indefinitely.

The dream of quick wealth ended in October 1929, when a wave of selling hit the American stock market. As prices tumbled, people rushed to sell their stocks in an effort to keep from losing money. But this panic selling only drove prices down more. This, in turn, led to more selling. As stock prices fell dramatically, millions of Americans lost the money they had invested in stocks.

Many banks had also purchased stocks. As prices dropped, some banks began calling in their loans to cover their stock-market losses. But when borrowers could not pay, these banks closed. As the news of bank closings spread, people rushed to withdraw their money from banks. The flood of withdrawals, however, forced many banks to go broke. As more banks failed, business activity was affected. At the same time, factories began to close, since people had little money to spend on goods. Thus, more

The Great Depression deeply affected American society. Crowds of people often waited anxiously outside their local banks to withdraw their savings. This bank closed in 1931. Such closings were common during the depression as depositors rushed to withdraw their money.

Wide World

people lost their jobs, since the demand for goods kept dropping.

By the early 1930's, the United States was affected by the Great Depression—the worst economic disaster in American history. Eventually the decline in business activity and the resulting unemployment in the United States affected the economies of many other countries.

THE WORLDWIDE EFFECTS OF THE DEPRESSION As economic conditions in the United States grew worse, there was a decline in the demand for manufactured goods from Europe. Thus, factory output dropped and unemployment increased as the depression reached Europe. The *gross national product* (GNP)—the total value of all goods and services produced within a country in a given year—of European countries began to drop. By 1932, for example, the GNP of Germany had fallen 20 percent from what it had been before the depression. A year later, union leaders in Germany estimated that more than 40 percent of their union members were unemployed. At the same time, about 25 percent of the workers in Great Britain were out of work.

The growing unemployment lowered the standard of living of millions in the United States and Europe. Since people had little or no money, they could not pay for food and for other necessities. To help these people, government agencies and private charities set up public kitchens that gave food to the needy.

Some government leaders believed that industrial output could be revived and unemployment ended by raising tariffs again. They believed this would limit imports and help businesses by reducing foreign competition. Such measures, however, only made economic recovery more difficult, since the higher tariffs further limited international trade. Between 1929 and 1933, the value of goods exchanged in world trade declined by about 65 percent.

The depression also affected the payment of war debts and reparations. In 1931, President Hoover of the United States proposed a postponement of one year on all payments between governments. By the end of the year, however, the question of war debts and reparations had become less important as the depression continued.

REACTION TO THE DEPRESSION France was the one major European country that was not as deeply affected by the depression as were some of the other European

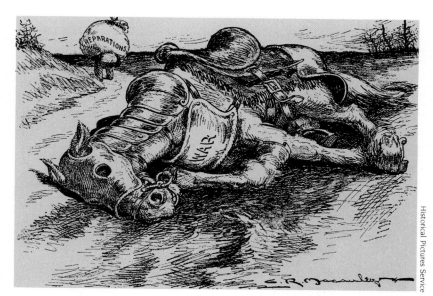

After World War I, most Americans wanted the United States to avoid any future involvement in European affairs. Americans also expected European countries to pay their war debts. However, the artist who drew this cartoon apparently sympathized with Germany because of the burden of reparations payments imposed on the Germans under the harsh terms of the Treaty of Versailles.

Historical Pictures Service

countries. But there was political instability as the different political parties argued over how to deal with the problem. Socialist Léon Blum came to power in 1936 and worked for reforms to help French workers. But Blum left office a year later, and the political squabbling continued.

Over 2 million people were out of work in Great Britain in 1931, when a Conservative-dominated coalition came to power. This

Life at the Time

The Great Depression

One of the most serious aspects of the Great Depression was the widespread unemployment that it caused among industrial workers. As the depression grew worse, more people lost their jobs, and those already unemployed were unable to find work. The continuing lack of job opportunities greatly influenced people's outlook on life. The experiences and feelings of three people in Great Britain who were affected by the depression are quoted below:

"My chief trouble is the monotony of a long spell of unemployment—monotonous and insufficient food and having nothing to do all day . . . kill all a man's interest in life. . . . There is no substitute for work. . . . There is nothing I can do to keep myself efficient; odd repairs in a house are no substitute for . . . work on a steam engine." [A skilled worker—aged 49]

"Any long spell of unemployment leaves you with little to be proud of and much to be ashamed of. Our child is still too young to realize that it is her mother who works. We carefully keep her from knowing it." [A skilled worker—aged 32]

"My husband is a good man and he does a lot for me in the house. . . . But he is a changed man these last two years. He never complains, but I wish he would. It makes me unhappy to find him becoming quieter and quieter, when I know what he must be feeling. If I had someone to talk to about my troubles I should feel much better. But having to keep them to myself, as my husband does, makes everything so much worse. We quarrel far more now than we have ever done in our lives before. We would both rather be dead than go on like this. . . . He has been out of work so long now that I do not think that he will get his Old Age Pension when he is sixty-five, for he will not have enough stamps on his Health Insurance Cards. . . . That will be our greatest disappointment." [A miner's wife—aged 66]

These statements reveal a deep sense of hopelessness and frustration. Clearly, the Great Depression profoundly affected the lives of many workers in Great Britain during the 1930's.

The Great Depression affected workers around the world. Unemployed British workers sometimes demonstrated to emphasize the need for jobs.

Wide World

government worked to improve the economy by raising tariffs and by cutting government spending. The government also launched a campaign to stimulate the sale of goods within the country by asking people to buy only British-made goods. And by the late 1930's, economic conditions in Britain had improved.

The depression greatly affected Germany, which had enjoyed general prosperity between 1924 and 1929. As world trade declined, German exports stopped, and the demand for German goods went down. As a result, factories closed, and more than 6 million Germans were out of work by 1932. The Weimar government tried to deal with the growing economic crisis. But many Germans felt a sense of futility and of despair over the conditions in their country. Thus, the German people were ready to follow any new leader who promised to improve the situation.

QUESTIONS FOR REVIEW

1 *What group in the United States did not share in the economic prosperity of the 1920's?*

2 *How did the depression affect the standard of living of people in the United States and in Europe?*

3 *By the early 1930's, why were many Germans willing to follow any new leader?*

CHAPTER SUMMARY

After World War I, European countries faced the task of rebuilding and of providing jobs for returning soldiers. Returning to peacetime conditions was not easy because of changes brought by the war. Moreover, a great outpouring of antiwar sentiment led world leaders to look for ways to prevent future wars.

Some new countries set up in Europe after the war established democratic governments, while in other new European countries, dictators rose to power. The French wanted Germany to pay the cost of rebuilding their war-torn country. In Britain, the Labour party became an important political force. In addition, different British leaders worked to overcome the chronic unemployment that affected the country during the 1920's. A democratic government was set up in Germany after the war. But this government faced public hostility as well as the problems of inflation and reparations. Benito Mussolini came to power in Italy in the early 1920's after a time of unrest. Within a short time, democracy in Italy was destroyed, as Mussolini became the dictator of the country.

During the 1920's, economic conditions in the United States were prosperous. But in 1929, these conditions changed as the American economy was gripped by a shattering depression. This economic catastrophe spread to Europe and crippled the economics of many countries during the early 1930's.

CHAPTER 30 IN REVIEW

IMPORTANT WORDS, NAMES, AND TERMS

1 Explain, define, or identify each of the following:

reparations	Maginot Line	Reichstag
the Ruhr Valley	coalition	corporate state
Dawes Plan	socialism	speculation
Kellogg-Briand Pact	Weimar Republic	Great Depression

FACTS AND IDEAS

2 For what reason did the French occupy the Ruhr Valley of Germany in 1923?

3 How did French leaders plan to pay the cost of rebuilding in France and of debt payments after World War I?

4 What were some of the weaknesses in the democratic government of Germany after World War I?

5 How did the Conservative-dominated coalition work to improve the British economy in the early 1930's?

ANALYZING VISUAL MATERIAL

6 Study the map on page 581. How was Germany affected by the territorial adjustments after World War I?

7 Look at the diagram on page 584. How effective do you think a system like the Maginot Line might be in protecting a nation from an enemy attack today?

CONCEPTS AND UNDERSTANDINGS

8 Why did many of the industrialized countries of Europe lose a large share of the world's markets after World War I?

9 Why was the Kellogg-Briand Pact a significant step toward world peace?

10 Why were many Italians disappointed by the peace treaty that ended World War I?

11 How was Germany affected by the depression?

PROJECTS AND ACTIVITIES

12 Inflation was a serious problem in many European countries after World War I. Several students might make a list of items that they frequently purchase. Then, these students might make a chart to display in class showing the effect of inflation on the price of these items during the last five years.

13 After World War I, disarmament was an important topic among world leaders. Several students might do some research to learn about disarmament. Information might be found in encyclopedias and in books on disarmament. After the information has been presented, have the class discuss the disarmament plans of today.

CHAPTER 31 THE RISE OF TOTALITARIANISM

1 Hitler and the Nazi Regime 2 The Soviet Union Under Stalin 3 The Spread of Totalitarianism 4 The Rise of Militarism in Japan

The economic disorder caused by the worldwide depression that began in 1929 led to political unrest in Germany. As a result, Adolf Hitler was able to gain power in Germany during the early 1930's. Hitler quickly set up an all-powerful dictatorship over the German people.

A new leader also emerged in the Soviet Union several years after Lenin's death in 1924. This person was Joseph Stalin, who introduced ambitious economic programs to build Soviet industries. Unfortunately, Stalin's plans brought great hardship to the Soviet people.

During the 1930's, the Italian dictator Benito Mussolini took over lands in Africa. At the same time, a bloody civil war in Spain led to the rise of a dictator in that country.

In Japan, the people turned to military leaders when the depression upset the Japanese economy. These leaders believed that Japan should take over other lands in Asia. As a result, Japan followed an aggressive foreign policy during the 1930's.

The Bettmann Archive

German military leaders and high party officials accompany Hitler at a Nazi party rally in Nuremberg.

1 HITLER AND THE NAZI REGIME

Adolf Hitler rose to power in Germany amid the economic chaos of the Great Depression. Germany's aggressive new leader aimed to restore his country's greatness and power. Hitler worked to rearm Germany and to bring all aspects of life under government control. At the same time, Hitler's opponents were jailed, and certain minority groups were persecuted. By the late 1930's, Hitler had succeeded in making Germany the most powerful country in Europe.

ADOLF HITLER AND THE NAZI PARTY A new political leader emerged in Germany during the early 1930's. This leader—Adolf Hitler—was born in 1889 in a small Austrian town near the German border. Although he was Austrian by birth, Hitler greatly admired German culture and history. Thus, when World War I began, he joined the German army and served on the western front.

Germany's defeat in the war was a bitter disappointment to Hitler. He returned to Munich, Germany, in 1919 and secured a job with the army. This job involved checking on the activities of radical political groups, such as the German Workers' party.

Hitler joined this group in September 1919. He was attracted to the party because of its opposition to democracy and to communism. Moreover, the anti-Jewish ideas of the German Workers' party also appealed to Hitler. He became an officer in the party, and the name of the group was changed to National Socialist German Workers' party— the Nazi party. Like the Fascists of Italy, the Nazis glorified war and stressed extreme patriotism. The Nazis also believed that service to Germany and to the party was an individual's most important duty. Both the Nazis and the Fascists used emblems, uniforms, special salutes, and their own armies.

In 1923, Hitler helped lead a *putsch* [PUCH]—revolt—against the local government in Munich. But the revolt failed and Hitler was sent to prison, where he wrote a book called *Mein Kampf* (*My Struggle*). In this book, Hitler told about his life and about his plans for Germany. He also outlined his anti-Jewish feelings and his belief that the individual should work for the good of the party and for the state.

After serving only eight months of a five-year sentence, Hitler was released from prison. He immediately began working to build the party, for he was determined to become the leader of the German people.

Hitler used the party newspaper and his persuasive speaking ability to convince Germans to become Nazis. Soon a few military leaders were attracted to the Nazi movement, since Hitler promised to rearm Germany. A number of industrialists favored the party because the Nazis opposed communism, which business leaders feared. In time, many Germans joined the Nazi movement because of Hitler's promise to restore German greatness by renouncing the Treaty of Versailles.

GERMANY UNDER HITLER Adolf Hitler rose to become chancellor of Germany as the country's economy was collapsing from the effects of the Great Depression in the early 1930's. Millions of Germans were out of work, and there were frequent clashes between unemployed workers and police and soldiers. Fear and insecurity gripped the country, but the Weimar government was unable to control the disorder.

Hitler took advantage of the situation to promote himself for leadership of the country. Through well-developed propaganda campaigns, Hitler told the people that he was the only person who could save Germany from economic ruin or a Communist takeover. At huge party rallies, uniformed Nazis marched in torchlight parades under the glare of powerful searchlights. Money for these party spectacles came from members' dues and from contributions by wealthy business leaders. At these rallies, Hitler would step forward and speak emotionally of restoring German power and prosperity. Through such tactics, the Nazi party had become the largest single party in Germany by 1932. However, the Nazis were never supported by a majority of the German people. After a series of crises in the government in 1933, the president of the German republic, former field marshal Paul von Hindenburg, called on Hitler to become the chancellor.

Hitler's appointment as chancellor ended democratic rule in Germany. He was given power to rule by decree by the Reichstag in March 1933, and thus became the dictator of the country. All political parties except the Nazi party were banned. Enemies of the party were jailed by the secret police—the *Gestapo*. Nazi party leader and propaganda specialist Dr. Joseph Goebbels was put in charge of all publications, radio broadcasts, plays, and musical and artistic works to control people's thinking.

When President Hindenburg died in 1934, Hitler gained more power by taking over the duties of the president. He became known as *der Führer* [FYUR-uhr]—the leader—and named the new regime the Third *Reich* [RIYK]. The first German Reich—empire—had been the Holy Roman Empire of the Middle Ages. The second Reich lasted from 1871 until 1918, when Kaiser Wilhelm II abdicated.

Under the Third Reich, all economic, social, and political aspects of German life were controlled by the government. For example, young people were expected to join youth groups to serve the country. In these groups, boys were prepared for military service and girls were taught to serve in the home. Teachers were trained in Nazi ideas, and textbooks were rewritten to reflect the Nazi party's views. Religious groups were treated with contempt, for the Nazis hated any philosophy based on compassion. Thus, Hitler and the Nazi party controlled the lives of all Germans.

POLITICAL		SOCIAL AND ECONOMIC
Civil war in the Soviet Union ended	~1920~	Unemployment insurance introduced in Great Britain and Austria
	1921~	NEP launched in Soviet Union
Hitler's unsuccessful Beer Hall Putsch staged	~1923~	Union membership in Germany reached over 9 million
Death of Lenin	~1924	
Pilsudski became dictator of Poland	~1926	
	1929~	First Five Year Plan began in the Soviet Union
Hitler became chancellor of Germany	~1933~	First concentration camp set up in Germany
Italian forces invaded Ethiopia	~1935~	Germany reintroduced compulsory military service
German troops occupied the Rhineland	~1936~	Olympic Games held in Berlin
Japan invaded China	~1937~	First jet engine built
Germany occupied the Sudetenland	~1938~	Anti-Jewish laws passed in Italy
German-Soviet non-aggression pact signed Germany occupied remainder of Czechoslovakia	~1939~	Conscription adopted in Great Britain

THE NAZI ECONOMY Under Nazi rule, the German economy was rigidly controlled by the government. For example, manufacturers were told what to make, where to sell, and what prices to charge for goods. Despite government controls, however, giant businesses made huge profits, in part because of the great rearmament program started by the Nazis during the mid-1930's.

Rearmament and public works were two of the main activities used to end unemployment in Nazi Germany. A network of superhighways was built to connect German cities. At the same time, factories poured out tanks, guns, airplanes, and warships to equip the growing German military machine. But even though there were plenty of jobs, German workers had few individual rights. Strikes, for example, were banned, and all relations between workers and employers were controlled by the government. Labor unions were replaced by an agency of the Nazi party called the Labor Front. The purpose of this arm of the party was to see that workers performed the maximum amount of work.

Joblessness among young men was lowered by requiring them to spend six months working for the Labor Service, which was independent of the Labor Front. The Labor Service took young men out of the job market and put them to work on farms and on conservation projects. After 1935, joblessness was further reduced because all German youths were drafted into the army when they reached the age of 18. Between the ages of 10 and 18, German boys belonged to the Hitler Youth.

Hitler hoped to make Germany a self-sufficient country. But this was not easy to do, since Germany lacked many important natural resources. German scientists were told to develop *synthetic*—substitute—resources in an attempt to overcome dependence on other countries for resources. Thus, efforts were undertaken to make synthetic rubber, synthetic cloth, and other artificial goods. However, the synthetics were generally more expensive to make and of poorer quality than the natural resources that they were meant to replace. Thus, the use of synthetics was actually a burden on the German economy.

Under Hitler, the German economy was slowly prepared for war. The dictator believed that Germany would have to go to war with other countries within a few years to gain land and natural resources. At the same time, the Nazis followed some peculiar racial ideas that led to the persecution of many groups in Nazi Germany.

NAZISM AND RACE Nazi racial policies were based on a strange mixture of ideas that stressed the superiority of a so-called Aryan race. According to Nazi thinking, the Germans were the best examples of the "Aryans," while "non-Aryan" peoples were viewed as enemies of the "Aryan" Germans. In writing of the "Aryans," Hitler stated, "All the human culture, all the results of art, science and technology that we see before us today, are almost exclusively the creative product of the Aryan. . . ."

During their rise to power, the Nazis kept repeating the idea that the Jewish people were the cause of all of Germany's problems. According to the Nazis, the Jewish people wanted to dominate the world. The Nazis felt that their racial policies were the only way to keep the Jewish people from reaching the imagined goal of world domination. Thus, the Jewish people, who made up about one percent of the population, were blamed for causing Germany to lose World War I. After gaining power, the Nazis began a planned campaign of *anti-Semitism* —anti-Jewish measures. This anti-Semitism aimed at keeping Jewish people from taking part in everyday life in Germany. For example, Jewish people could not hold government jobs or practice medicine or law. Jewish actors and musicians could not perform in public. In 1935, laws were passed that took away the citizenship of Jewish people in Germany. As a result, some

Jewish people left Germany to escape the growing anti-Semitism of the Nazis.

The Jewish people who stayed in Germany, however, faced even greater cruelty. By the mid-1930's, Jewish people were being taken from their homes and imprisoned in concentration camps. Most of these camps—and later others in German-held lands—became extermination centers. Between about 1942 and 1945, millions of Jewish people were put to death in these camps. Hitler and some high Nazi officials had decided to eliminate the Jewish people in what became known as the final solution.

Even though the Jewish people were the main victims of Nazi racial ideas, other groups also suffered. For example, members of both Catholic and Protestant religious groups were sent to concentration camps and put to death. Moreover, Hitler persecuted Gypsies and other ethnic minorities within Germany. Mentally and physically disabled Germans were also singled out for persecution by the Nazis.

The strange Nazi philosophy was used to justify the killing of millions of defenseless people. At the same time, Hitler followed a bold foreign policy, by which he hoped to gain land for Germany without actually going to war.

NAZI FOREIGN POLICY Hitler's foreign policy was based on the idea that Germany needed *lebensraum* [LAY-buhnz-ROWM]—living space. The German leader was determined to gain land either by diplomacy or by force.

In 1935, Hitler ordered compulsory military training for German youths. This move violated the Treaty of Versailles, and Great Britain and France made weak protests against the German move. They failed, however, to back their protests with action. As a result, Hitler continued to build Germany's military power. Moreover, Hitler showed his dislike for international cooperation by taking Germany out of the League of Nations.

In March 1936, German soldiers were sent

Military training was an important part of the instruction given to members of the Hitler Youth.

into the Rhineland in violation of the Treaty of Versailles (see map on page 598). Hitler correctly judged that Britain and France would be unable to agree on what steps to take against Germany. Once again, the two countries protested the German move but failed to act.

As Germany's power grew, Hitler drew closer to the Italian dictator, Benito Mussolini. In October 1936, for example, Germany and Italy signed a treaty of friendship. A month later, Germany and Japan signed an anti-Communist treaty. The following year Italy also joined in this agreement, thus forming an alliance known as the Rome-Berlin-Tokyo Axis.

HITLER'S DIPLOMATIC VICTORIES In the spring of 1938, Hitler made his next move by using diplomatic pressure to force Austria to unite with Germany. Later the same year, he threatened to unleash a war unless the Sudetenland area of Czechoslovakia was

597

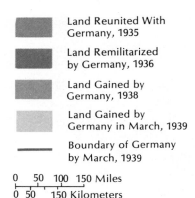

Land Reunited With
Germany, 1935

Land Remilitarized
by Germany, 1936

Land Gained by
Germany, 1938

Land Gained by
Germany in March, 1939

Boundary of Germany
by March, 1939

0   50   100   150 Miles
0   50   150 Kilometers

Hitler successfully expanded German power in Europe in the years immediately prior to World War II. The military occupation of the Rhineland and the acquisition of Austria and Czechoslovakia were diplomatic triumphs that bolstered Hitler's popularity.

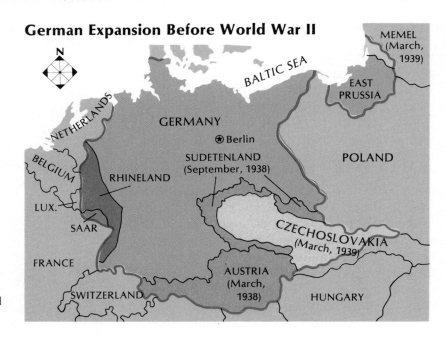

German Expansion Before World War II

MEMEL (March, 1939)

BALTIC SEA

EAST PRUSSIA

NETHERLANDS

GERMANY

⊛ Berlin

POLAND

BELGIUM

RHINELAND

SUDETENLAND (September, 1938)

LUX.

SAAR

CZECHOSLOVAKIA (March, 1939)

FRANCE

AUSTRIA (March, 1938)

SWITZERLAND

HUNGARY

given to Germany (see map on this page). The Sudetenland, which was once part of Germany, had been given to the newly formed country of Czechoslovakia under the Treaty of Versailles. For several tense days, the world waited. Then a settlement was reached through the frantic efforts of Britain's prime minister, Neville Chamberlain. Both Britain and France were involved in the talks with Hitler, since these countries were allies of Czechoslovakia. The Soviet Union also offered to support Czechoslovakia if the French would resist Germany. But the French refused unless the British agreed to take action. Chamberlain, however, believed that by *appeasing* Hitler—that is, by making concessions to him for the sake of maintaining peace—war would be avoided. This belief was based on Hitler's promise that he would make no further territorial demands in Europe. Thus, the Sudetenland was given to Germany. Chamberlain, unfortunately, was tragically mistaken, for in March 1939, Hitler ordered German soldiers to take over the rest of Czechoslovakia.

Later the same year, the world was stunned when Hitler signed a nonaggression treaty with Germany's enemy—the Soviet Union. Under a secret section of this treaty, Germany and the Soviet Union agreed to divide eastern Europe into German and Soviet spheres of influence. This agreement allowed Hitler to turn to his next target—Poland—without fear of Soviet opposition. The German-Soviet treaty also meant that Hitler would not have to face enemies on two fronts—eastern and western.

By the late 1930's, Europe's fragile peace was crumbling. As Hitler's plans to dominate the continent were revealed, Great Britain and France moved to strengthen their armies and to resist any further demands by the German ruler. Hitler could no longer expect to gain land in Europe without using force.

QUESTIONS FOR REVIEW

1   What was the purpose for putting Dr. Joseph Goebbels in charge of all publications, plays, and musical and artistic works in Nazi Germany?

2   How did Hitler hope to overcome Germany's lack of natural resources?

3   Why was the German-Soviet nonaggression treaty of 1939 important to Hitler's plans to dominate Europe?

Myths and Realities

Opposition to Hitler

Many people believe that under Hitler, Nazi Germany was a completely controlled society where no person dared to oppose the dictator or the Nazi party. However, there were some groups that opposed Hitler and Nazism.

German opposition to the Nazis existed in spite of the work of the secret police and the efforts of the government-run media to control thinking. Most Germans, however, enthusiastically favored Hitler because of his economic and foreign successes gained during the middle and late 1930's. Nevertheless, some Germans— including a few powerful military, political, and religious leaders—resisted Hitler and his dangerously twisted plans for Germany.

Among those who opposed Hitler were some officers in the German army. In 1938, for example, General Ludwig Beck, Chief of the German General Staff, wrote several memoranda in opposition to Hitler's plan to invade Czechoslovakia. In his statements, General Beck warned other German officers of the dangers of such a war.

". . . So we are faced with the fact that military action by Germany against Czechoslovakia will automatically lead to a European or a world war. I need not enlarge upon the fact that such a war will in all probability end not only in a military but also in a general catastrophe for Germany. . . .

"Final decisions involving the existence of the nation are at stake here. History will charge our present leaders [of the army] with having committed a capital crime if they do not act according to their professional and political knowledge and conscience. Their obedience as soldiers has a limit at which their knowledge, their consciences and their sense of responsibility forbid the carrying out of an order.

"If their advice and warnings are not heeded in such a situation, they have the right and the duty to their people and to history to resign their commands. If they all act in unison, it will be impossible to carry out an act of war. They will thereby have preserved their fatherland from the worst that could happen—its downfall."

Beck's ideas were rejected by the Commander-in-Chief of the army—General Brauchitsch. As a result, Beck resigned in August 1938. Later, other opposition groups were formed in Germany. These groups worked to find ways to destroy the Nazi regime. There were even attempts to assassinate Hitler, but these efforts failed.

Thus, as the Nazi government continued in power, there were isolated groups in German society that opposed the government. These groups believed that they could help their country by working against the leader and the party that they felt were destroying Germany.

An attempt to kill Hitler with a time bomb, in July 1944, injured him slightly and damaged his headquarters in East Prussia. The arrow and circle, drawn by Hitler, show the location of the bomb before the explosion.

2 THE SOVIET UNION UNDER STALIN

After gaining power, Lenin introduced an economic plan designed to help the Soviet economy by allowing some private enterprise. Following Lenin's death in 1924, a bitter struggle for leadership took place within the Soviet Union. In time, Joseph Stalin emerged as the new ruler. Stalin worked to eliminate his enemies. He also forced the Soviet people to make great sacrifices to build their country's industrial power. In 1939, the Soviet ruler signed a treaty with Nazi Germany. But few people believed that this seeming friendship would last, for Nazism and communism were implacable enemies.

CONDITIONS IN POSTWAR RUSSIA The end of the Russian civil war in 1920 brought about a new era of national adjustment under Lenin's leadership. Organized resistance to the Communist takeover had been crushed with the defeat of the anti-Communist White armies and the withdrawal of Allied troops. But Russia and its people were exhausted by the long years of war and civil strife. Economic growth had come to a standstill, society was badly disrupted, and conditions throughout the country were chaotic.

Russia's Communist leaders were unable to agree on how to restore peace and order in the country. Many Communist leaders realized that the harsh economic measures of wartime communism had turned peasants and factory workers against the Communist regime. These leaders pointed to sharp declines in Russian farm and factory output as proof of widespread dissatisfaction. Almost 40 percent less land was farmed in Russia in 1920, for example, than had been cultivated in 1914. Steel production was down to about 200,000 tons (181 400 metric tons) in 1920, which was less than 5 percent

of 1913 levels. Food, clothing, and other needs were extremely scarce. Transportation and communication had broken down throughout the country. And Russia's currency was worthless, for the economy was in the grip of runaway inflation.

During the first months of 1921, Red Army soldiers, peasants, and factory workers began to demonstrate against the government. The naval base at Kronstadt, once a center of Communist support, erupted in revolt. These sailors called for a socialist government free of Communist influence. Strikes, although outlawed by the Communists, were called throughout the country. At the same time, a major peasant uprising against the Communists spread through the countryside. Thus, by early 1921, Lenin and his Communist followers faced a serious challenge to their government.

THE NEW ECONOMIC POLICY The Communist party was in grave danger when the Tenth Party Congress met in March 1921. Workers and soldiers who had backed the party during the dark days of the civil war now called for an end to communism in Russia.

During secret party meetings, Lenin admitted that he had tried to achieve the goals of Marxism too quickly. Thus, Lenin introduced a plan that temporarily set aside some of the Communists' more extreme economic aims. In fact, Lenin's plan—called the New Economic Policy, or NEP—was a return to some of the ideas of capitalism.

The NEP did away with the government food requisitions that had led to widespread peasant unrest and hardship. Under the new plan, the peasants now paid heavy taxes in food and other farm goods. However, under the NEP the peasants were allowed to sell the remainder of their harvests to the state or to private buyers. Thus, the NEP encouraged higher farm production by restoring the concept of profit to Russian farming.

Factory and business owners and individ-

Stalin (behind Lenin) sought to portray a close association with Lenin by ordering Soviet artists to show the two leaders together.

THE SECOND SOVIET DICTATOR The Communist dictatorship in the Soviet Union faced a new crisis in 1924, when its founder, Lenin, died. While he lived, Lenin's prestige did much to calm disputes within the party. Following his death, however, the Soviet Union moved into a period of transition, since there was no clear successor to take Lenin's place. As a result, several high-ranking party members openly competed for leadership of the country for the next few years.

By 1925, two major rivals had emerged in the struggle for power in the Soviet Union. Leon Trotsky, the leader of the Red Army during the revolution, was one contender for leadership. Even though Trotsky was a fine speaker and scholar, he was disliked by many party members because of his air of self-importance. Trotsky's rival, Joseph Stalin, was less of an intellectual but very shrewd. Stalin's real name was Joseph Dzhugashvili [JOO-guhsh-VEE-lee], but he took the name Stalin—meaning man of steel—in 1913. Stalin had taken part in radical political activities for many years before the 1917 revolution brought the Communists to power.

In 1922, Stalin became the general secretary of the Communist party and assumed direct control of the party's bureaucracy. Despite Stalin's party rank, Lenin did not want Stalin to become the ruler of the Soviet Union. Lenin felt that Stalin was too overbearing and narrow-minded in dealing with other party members. But Lenin died before he could remove Stalin from his post within the party.

The main difference between Trotsky and Stalin concerned their ideas about how to reach the goals of Soviet and world communism. Trotsky believed in the permanent world revolution, which meant starting Communist revolutions throughout the world. But Stalin fanatically maintained that the Soviet Union should strengthen itself before promoting Communist revolutions in other countries.

ual workers also gained greater economic freedom under the NEP. The state maintained control over such major industries as steel and energy production, transportation, overseas trade, and banking. But smaller industries and businesses were no longer under strict government control. Control of most trade within Russia was decentralized as well. Moreover, the government's role as overall economic planner was greatly reduced.

Farm and factory output quickly recovered under the NEP, although production did not return to prewar levels until the late 1920's. At the same time, the Communist leaders of Russia—called the Union of Soviet Socialist Republics after 1922—tried to speed industrial growth. By improving economic conditions within the country, the Communists were able to consolidate their power over the new Soviet Union.

The debate between the two party leaders continued during the mid-1920's. Since Stalin controlled the administration of the Communist party, he carefully filled important party posts with people who favored his views. As a result, Stalin became so powerful that he was able to arrange for Trotsky to be expelled from the party in 1927. With Trotsky deported to Siberia, Stalin was able to strengthen his power within the Soviet Union.

STALIN AS RULER Both Lenin and Stalin believed that the Soviet Union should be ruled by an elite group of dedicated Communist party members. The two leaders felt that the function of the great majority of party members was to carry out the orders of the elite group, which was made up of the members of the *Politburo* [PAHL-uht-BYUR-oh]. Stalin also believed that the Politburo should be controlled by one all-powerful leader—the general secretary of the party. This post was held by Stalin.

Between 1934 and 1938, the Soviet dictator ruthlessly *purged*—removed—government and party officials that Stalin believed to be his enemies. The victims of these purges included many who had taken part in the 1917 revolution, high army officers, government workers, and even members of the secret police. During public trials, these people were accused of such charges as plotting Stalin's death or conspiring with the enemies of the Soviet Union. Many people were not brought to trial, but were privately condemned to death or imprisonment by the tyrannical Soviet ruler. These purges consolidated Stalin's power and eliminated the possibility of future conspiracies against the cruel dictator.

At the same time that the purges were taking place, a new constitution for the Soviet Union was passed. This document, which appeared in 1936, had many seemingly democratic features. For example, all citizens over the age of 18 were given the right to vote. In addition, freedom of speech, press, assembly, and worship was apparently guaranteed by the new constitution.

Despite these features, however, little was

Communist party leaders, purged from the party by Stalin for so-called crimes against the state, listen intently to the court proceedings during their trial. All of these defendants pleaded guilty and were sentenced to prison terms ranging from five to ten years.

changed for the people of the Soviet Union. The real power in the government was still held by the general secretary of the Communist party—Stalin—through the Politburo. In addition, the rights set down in the constitution were generally meaningless. This was because these rights could be limited or taken away any time that the government felt that it was necessary for the security of the country. And when elections were held, there was actually little choice of candidates, since only the Communist party was allowed to run its members for office.

STALIN AND THE ECONOMY Stalin wanted to make the Soviet Union a great industrial power in an attempt to bring the country up to the level of other industrialized nations. He abandoned Lenin's NEP and launched an ambitious economic program called the Five Year Plan. Under this plan, which began in 1929, Soviet industry was to be strengthened. At the same time, farm output was to be raised.

The first Five Year Plan emphasized the buildup of heavy industries, such as mining, steel mills, and railroads. Consumer needs were largely ignored, since these goods were not looked upon as important to the country's industrial development.

To raise farm output, Stalin ordered all farmlands to be *collectivized*. Small plots of farmland owned by poor peasants were to be joined with lands taken from the well-to-do peasants—the *kulaks*. These *collectives* then would be run by a cooperative association of peasants, who would share the farm tools and the land.

Most peasants, however, were strongly opposed to the idea of giving up their land to the collectives. As a result, many peasants, especially the kulaks, refused to follow the government's orders. Some kulaks killed their cattle and destroyed their crops rather than turn them over to the collective farms. Thousands of kulaks were jailed or put to death for resisting collectivization. Then in 1931 and 1932, famine swept across the Soviet Union, and millions of people starved to death. The government did nothing to aid these people, since the famine helped to wipe out resistance to collectivization.

There were also other problems during the first Five Year Plan. There were few managers and workers with the skills needed to carry out the government's plans. Thus, production goals were sometimes not reached. In addition, the crop failures of 1931 and 1932 lowered farm output. Thus, the Soviets had fewer farm products to export to help pay for imported machines.

Despite these problems, however, the first Five Year Plan was partly successful. For example, a railroad across Siberia was completed a year ahead of schedule, and a huge hydroelectric dam across the Dnieper River was built. A second Five Year Plan, begun in 1933, was designed to raise the quality of industrial goods and to make more consumer goods available. The goal of the third Five Year Plan, which began in 1938, was to improve the country's defenses. However, World War II broke out before this plan was completed.

SOVIET SOCIETY While Stalin was in power, the Soviet government made many changes that affected the way the people lived. The major goal of these changes was to increase government control over the people. Women were encouraged to take jobs that were once held only by men. This made more workers available to help meet the goals of the Five Year Plans. At the same time, the government set up state-run nurseries to care for children of working mothers.

Another change in Soviet life concerned public health. As new hospitals were built, more people, including many women, were trained to become doctors. In addition, efforts were made to wipe out such diseases as typhus, malaria, and cholera.

One of Stalin's major goals was to end illiteracy in the Soviet Union and to indoc-

To meet the ambitious economic goals that Stalin sought to achieve through the different Five Year Plans, women in the Soviet Union were actively encouraged to become part of the nation's labor force. These women worked with farm machinery on a collective farm in the North Caucasus region of the country.

trinate the people in the values of communism. Thus, the purpose of education was not to help the people, but rather to teach loyalty and obedience to the state. As a result, facts and interpretations were often slanted to glorify the Soviet system and to promote communism. Moreover, students had little freedom in choosing their fields of study.

Government influence also extended to music, literature, and art. Composers were expected to write music that would lead to devotion to the Soviet Union. All newspapers, magazines, and books were published by the government in an attempt to control thinking.

Living standards in the Soviet Union were also very low. For example, there was a housing shortage, and the housing that was available was poorly built. There were also few consumer goods made or sold. The goods that were found in the shops were of very poor quality. Thus, Soviet society under Stalin was characterized by tight government control, hard work, and poor living conditions.

SOVIET FOREIGN POLICY The Soviet Union was not trusted by many countries after the Communists came to power in 1917. This suspicion was justified, for in 1919, Lenin founded the *Comintern*, an organization that called on Communists around the world to join against capitalism. Thus, capitalist countries became fearful of Soviet efforts to spread Communist revolutions around the world. During the 1920's, however, the Soviet government was involved with problems within the country. Consequently, Soviet leaders were forced to change their plans for spreading communism. As the danger of Communist revolutions seemed to lessen, there was a relaxation of tensions between the Soviet Union and many other countries. By 1924, all of the major powers of Europe had recognized the Soviet regime. However, many countries were still suspicious of Soviet intentions. The United States did not recognize the Soviet government until 1933.

Stalin believed that the rise of Hitler's Germany during the 1930's posed a serious and growing threat to the Soviet Union.

Hitler had often said that communism was one of Germany's greatest enemies. Hitler also declared that he hoped one day to bring much of the Soviet Union under Nazi rule. Reacting to the growing Nazi menace, the Comintern softened its revolutionary and anticapitalist activities in the mid-1930's. This was done in the hope that capitalist countries would join with the Soviet Union against Nazism.

Stalin feared German power even more after Hitler's demands for the Sudetenland were met in 1938. Thus, in March 1939, the Soviet Union began negotiating with Great Britain and France for an alliance to oppose the growing power of Germany. However, these negotiations failed, since neither the British nor the French trusted the Soviet leader.

Then in August 1939, the Soviet Union shocked the world by announcing that it had signed a nonaggression treaty with Nazi Germany. The Germans and the Soviets promised not to attack each other and to remain neutral if one of them went to war. However, Hitler and Stalin were using this agreement as an opportunity. Both rulers knew that in time, their nations would go to war. The treaty gave Hitler a free hand in Poland and in western Europe. The pact gave the Soviet Union time to prepare its defenses for the inevitable attack by Nazi Germany. Thus, the two cynical rulers played a deadly waiting game.

QUESTIONS FOR REVIEW

1 *Who founded the Communist dictatorship in the Soviet Union?*

2 *How did Trotsky and Stalin differ in their ideas about the goals of Soviet and world communism?*

3 *Why was the 1936 Soviet constitution generally meaningless?*

3 THE SPREAD OF TOTALITARIANISM

The rise of dictatorships in southern and eastern Europe was common in the years after World War I. Italy, under Benito Mussolini's leadership, began a campaign of aggressive expansion in Africa during the 1930's. The League of Nations failed to stop this aggression. Meanwhile, political, social, and economic unrest led to bloodshed in Spain. In time, the disputes among opposing Spanish political groups led to the outbreak of civil war in 1936. The conflict ended in 1939, when a dictatorship was set up in Spain. By that time, many of the countries of eastern Europe had also come under the control of dictators.

ITALIAN AGGRESSION The Italian dictator, Benito Mussolini, believed that Italy should follow an aggressive foreign policy. According to Mussolini, Italy needed to gain more land for its growing population. In addition, overseas expansion would help to realize Mussolini's dream of restoring Italy to the greatness of the Roman Empire.

To carry out his ideas, Mussolini turned to Ethiopia—one of the few African countries that had not come under European domination. In 1934, there was a clash along the border dividing Ethiopia from Italian Somaliland (see map on page 606). Mussolini accused Ethiopia of causing the fighting and demanded an apology and reparations from the Ethiopian government. But instead of giving in to the Italian demands, Emperor Haile Selassie [HIY-lee-suh-LAS-ee] of Ethiopia asked the League of Nations to help settle the dispute.

Mussolini, however, was in no mood to compromise, for he was determined to annex Ethiopia. After a lengthy military buildup, Italian planes and tanks attacked Ethiopian forces in October 1935. The League of Nations declared Italy an aggressor nation. The league also imposed

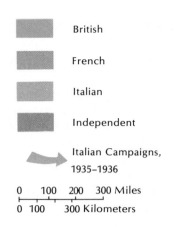

British

French

Italian

Independent

Italian Campaigns, 1935–1936

0   100   200   300 Miles

0 100   300 Kilometers

Conquest of Ethiopia, 1935–1936

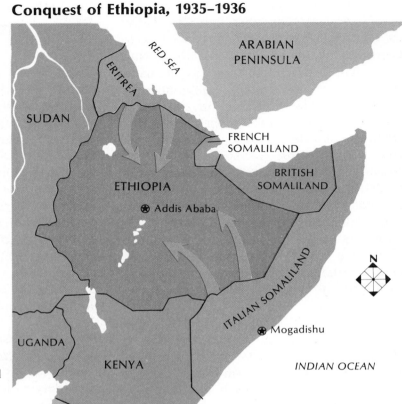

RED SEA

ARABIAN PENINSULA

ERITREA

SUDAN

FRENCH SOMALILAND

BRITISH SOMALILAND

ETHIOPIA

⊛ Addis Ababa

ITALIAN SOMALILAND

UGANDA

KENYA

⊛ Mogadishu

INDIAN OCEAN

N

The ambitious Italian dictator Mussolini hoped that the attack launched against Ethiopia from Italian Somaliland in 1935 would help make Italy a great and powerful nation.

sanctions on Italy. This meant that members of the league were not to sell arms or certain raw materials to Italy. But the sanctions were meaningless because the raw materials that were not to be sold to Italy did not include oil, coal, steel, or iron. Oil was important to Italy in its war against Ethiopia, since the Italian army needed oil for its tanks and planes. The sanctions were also ineffective because neither the United States nor Germany belonged to the league. Thus, neither of these countries was obligated to follow the league sanctions.

Within a few months, Ethiopia was defeated, since its forces were no match for the well-equipped Italian army. After crushing the Ethiopian defenses, Italian soldiers entered the capital of Addis Ababa in May 1936, and the country was annexed by Italy. Emperor Haile Selassie fled to Great Britain, where he lived in exile.

The conquest of Ethiopia showed the ineffectiveness of the League of Nations. Mussolini's aggression in Ethiopia also proved that some European dictators would stop at nothing to gain their objectives.

UNREST IN SPAIN Political disorder and violence in Spain added to the tensions in Europe during the 1930's. Throughout World War I, Spain had remained neutral. But Spain profited by selling food and other materials to the countries that were fighting. After the war, however, prosperity ended as the demand for Spanish goods went down. As Spain's international trade declined, unemployment rose. The result was growing disorder in Spain.

In 1923, Spain's constitutional monarch, King Alfonso XIII, supported a military takeover of the government by General Primo de Rivera in an attempt to bring stability to the country. Rivera set up a dictatorship, but his leadership was unpopular because he dissolved the Spanish parliament and censored the press. Public reaction finally forced Rivera to resign in 1930. King Alfonso then reestablished a constitutional government and allowed elections to be held. The election results showed widespread support for the establishment of a republic. King Alfonso left Spain and a republican government was formed. King Alfonso refused to abdicate and give up his claim to the Spanish throne. The republican government then took his property and ordered the king never to return.

A new constitution was adopted in December 1931. The new government, made up of a parliament and a president, was set up. It lasted for only a few years.

The new republican government took steps to improve conditions in Spain. Large estates were divided among the peasants. The power of the Roman Catholic Church in the government was limited. In addition, many high-ranking army officers were removed, since they had been promoted because of their influence rather than for their ability. Despite these changes, political unrest in Spain grew. Right-wing groups of army officers and church leaders were opposed by leftist socialists, Communists, and trade-union leaders. These extremist groups argued with one another over the policies that the government should follow. By 1936, the country was hopelessly divided. Members of the extremist groups—leftists and rightists alike—attacked and killed one another and destroyed much property. The moderate supporters of the government were attacked by both sides.

In this atmosphere of unrest, new elections were held early in 1936, but this only led to more violence. The leftist parties gained control of the government through the election. But it was immediately clear that this situation was opposed by the army. Conditions were right for a civil war in Spain.

THE SPANISH CIVIL WAR The disorder in Spain finally erupted into a civil war in July 1936. The war began in North Africa when army units in Spanish Morocco revolted against the government. The uprising quickly spread to Spain, where General Francisco Franco was chosen to lead those who opposed the republican government. The rebels were known as Nationalists or Insurgents, while those who supported the republican government were called Loyalists. The Insurgents were backed by the army, the clergy, the wealthy, and many big businesses. The Loyalists had the support of some military units, many leftist groups—including the Communists—and most of the poorer Spanish people.

Both sides expected the war to end quickly. The conflict, however, lasted for almost three years and became a bloody contest between the Insurgents and the Loyalists. Neither side showed mercy toward captured enemies, who were looked upon as traitors.

As the war went on, many countries promised to remain neutral. But only Great Britain, France, and the United States followed this policy. Fascist Italy and Nazi Germany sent soldiers and war equipment to aid Franco and the Insurgents. The Soviet Union sent help to the Loyalists. In addition, the Loyalists received some help from private volunteers from Poland, Austria, Great Britain, and the United States.

The equipment and soldiers from Italy and Germany eventually helped Franco to defeat the Loyalists. In March 1939, Franco captured Madrid, Spain's capital, and Loyalist opposition ended. Franco then set up a dictatorship, with the parliament serving just as an advisory group. Only one political party—Franco's—was allowed to exist.

The costly civil war greatly weakened Spain. Over 1 million Spanish soldiers and civilians lost their lives in the long and bitter struggle. In addition, many Spanish cities and towns were destroyed by the fighting.

In 1938, Hitler succeeded in gaining the Sudetenland from Czechoslovakia. As German soldiers entered the Warnsdorf district of the Sudetenland, they were greeted by crowds of people.

On the eve of World War II, Spain, like Italy and Germany, had become an absolute dictatorship. By 1939, dictatorships had become a common form of government in many other countries in Europe as well.

TOTALITARIANISM IN EASTERN EUROPE

In the years immediately following World War I, most of the countries of eastern Europe worked to set up democratic governments. But the lack of a democratic tradition, illiteracy, economic problems, and problems of unrest from disunited ethnic minorities made survival difficult for these new democracies. Thus, during the two decades that followed World War I, most of the countries of eastern Europe fell under dictatorial rule.

In 1925, the tiny country of Albania became a republic. But three years later, the first Albanian president made himself king and ruled as a dictator. As in Albania, a moderate government came to power in Bulgaria in 1926. This regime worked to improve the economy. However, unrest within the country led to the establishment of a dictatorship in the 1930's.

In Poland, Marshal Pilsudski ruled as a dictator between 1926 and 1935. After his death, a new constitution was adopted. This document was unusual in that it contained elements of fascism and of democracy. However, the president still remained all-powerful under the new constitution.

Poland's neighbor, Rumania, was a parliamentary monarchy during the 1920's. Then in the early 1930's, King Carol II made himself dictator. Later, the king abolished the constitution.

Conditions in Hungary and in Austria were similar to those in Poland and Rumania after World War I. Hungary was ruled by a dictator, Admiral Horthy, who came to power in the 1920's. Under his leadership, Hungary followed a policy of friendship toward Germany and Italy. Later, Hungary gained lands in eastern Europe as a result of its alliance with Nazi Germany. Austria came under dictatorial control during the early years of the Great Depression in the 1930's.

In contrast, Czechoslovakia was the only country in eastern Europe that remained a democracy during most of the 1930's. The first Czechoslovak president, Tomáš Masaryk [MAHS-uh-rik], was succeeded in 1935 by another capable leader, Eduard Beneš [BEN-esh]. The democratic government of Czechoslovakia opposed dictatorships, protected minority groups, worked for land reform, and strongly supported the League of Nations. Of the new nations formed after World War I, only Czechoslovakia remained a democracy by 1938.

The end of Czech freedom began in 1938 when Germany gained the Sudetenland. The Munich agreement stripped Czechoslovakia of most of the lands that had formed a buffer between Czechoslovakia and Germany. The importance of the Sudetenland became clear the following year. In 1939, the last remaining democracy in eastern Europe came to an end when Hitler's troops moved into what was left of Czechoslovakia.

QUESTIONS FOR REVIEW

1 *What steps were taken by the League of Nations in response to the Italian attack on Ethiopia in 1935?*

2 *How were Fascist Italy and Nazi Germany important to the Insurgents during the Spanish civil war?*

3 *Why did many of the democratic governments in eastern Europe fail to survive after World War I?*

4 THE RISE OF MILITARISM IN JAPAN

Japan emerged as an important industrial and military power during World War I. The depression of the 1930's, however, temporarily ended Japan's prosperity. High unemployment and agricultural unrest affected the country as the general downturn in world trade ended demands for Japanese goods.

As discontent increased, Japan's leaders searched for answers to their country's problems. Some of these leaders felt that overseas expansion was the answer to Japan's survival as an economic power. If necessary, this land would be gained by force. As a result, the power of the military leaders grew, and the Japanese worked to make their country the most powerful military force in Asia.

UNREST IN JAPAN Many Western nations were surprised to find that by the end of World War I, Japan was the most powerful industrial country in Asia. Japan's prosperity, however, depended on world trade. With limited natural resources, the Japanese sold manufactured goods to other countries to make money to buy raw materials needed in Japan. As countries throughout the world began to experience the Great Depression, the demand for Japan's goods declined. Japan's exports fell by about 50 percent between 1929 and 1931. As fewer Japanese goods were sold, factories closed and workers lost their jobs. High unemployment and worker discontent became serious problems in Japan during the early 1930's.

Manufacturers were not alone in their distress. Japanese farmers—especially those who raised silkworms—were also affected by the depression as the demand for silk fell drastically around the world. The way of life for many Japanese farmers fell to the subsistence level. Within a short time, rural discontent grew. The government seemed unable or unwilling to improve conditions.

There was also great resentment among both farmers and unemployed factory workers toward the *zaibatsu*. These giant business combinations controlled most of Japan's industries and financial institutions. Many Japanese blamed these firms for the country's economic problems. Blame was also directed toward Japan's political leaders, who had close ties with some of the *zaibatsu* companies.

THE MILITARY IN THE GOVERNMENT As discontent in Japan grew, certain military leaders began to build their power. Traditionally, members of the Japanese military services were respected by the people. Members of the military were praised for their devotion to their country and to the emperor. Not surprisingly, the people who criticized the politicians and the *zaibatsu* began to look to military leaders for solutions to Japan's problems. Understandably, many Japanese military leaders encouraged this trend.

Military leaders responded with the suggestion that Japan's economic problems could be solved. The answer, according to the military leaders, was that Japan should take over other lands in Asia. This expansion would give Japan the raw materials it needed. Expansion would also open new lands for Japan's rapidly growing population.

Many of Japan's military leaders belonged to ultranationalistic groups that were devoted to making Japan the greatest power in Asia. These groups disliked the influence that Western ideas had had upon Japan. These alien ideas were looked upon as enemies of Japanese traditions. The *zaibatsu* companies were often blamed for bringing Western influences to Japan through the industrialization of the country. Differences between business leaders and military leaders also existed over the growth of the army. Many business leaders opposed such growth because the cost had to be paid through higher taxes.

The gulf between the military and the

Japan's friendship with Germany and Italy was evident as the flags of the three countries were flown together in Japanese cities in the 1930's.

Kodansha International

government widened when Japan signed an agreement in 1930 that limited the size of Japan's navy. Many military officers pointed out that this treaty showed that civilian leaders could not be trusted. Several ultranationalistic groups decided to take action against the country's civilian leaders. Several officials who argued for peace and who objected to Japan's overseas expansion were marked for assassination. Meanwhile, a number of military leaders worked to gain control of the government. At the same time, the army took steps to bring Manchuria under Japanese control.

THE OCCUPATION OF MANCHURIA The Japanese had been interested in dominating the part of China called Manchuria ever since Japan's defeat of China in 1895 and of Russia in 1905. Over the years, the Japanese had worked to build their influence in the Chinese province through force and diplomacy. By 1930, these actions had borne fruit. Japan gained control of the major transportation link in Manchuria—the South Manchurian Railway. In addition, the Japanese also controlled the main seaport—the city of Port Arthur—and much of the mineral wealth of Manchuria.

The Chinese, however, resented Japan's presence in Manchuria. But China's military was weak. About the only way that the Chinese could protest Japan's action was by boycotting Japanese goods. As a result, Manchuria remained a source of friction between Japan and China.

The friction increased in September 1931, when a section of the South Manchurian Railway was slightly damaged by an explosion. Japan blamed China for the incident. Japan's army quickly occupied all of Manchuria. A puppet government under Japanese control was set up in 1932. Manchuria was renamed Manchukuo.

Japan's occupation of Manchuria, however, violated the covenant of the League of Nations. Since both nations were members of the league, the Chinese asked the league to intervene. A commission was set up by the league to look into the matter. After an investigation, the commission reported that Japan had acted without cause. The league then voted to condemn Japan's aggression. The Japanese reacted angrily by giving notice that their country would withdraw from the league, which it did several years later.

Even though the League of Nations condemned Japan's aggression, no other action was taken. None of the major powers were willing to risk a war to force Japan out of Manchuria. Nor did any country want to use economic pressure to get the Japanese to withdraw, since the worldwide depression had already upset world trade. The league's failure to act encouraged Japan's military leaders in their plans for expansion.

The following year, 1933, the Japanese army moved into northern China. Since the

As Japanese troops moved into Manchuria in 1932, there was little that China's government could do. Chinese forces were no match for the well-equipped Japanese armies.

Japan's full-scale invasion of China in 1937 was marked by bitter fighting. Here, Japanese soldiers advance toward Peking while inflicting heavy casualties on the defending Chinese troops.

Chinese were having problems within their country, they were not able to resist the Japanese move. A year later, China signed a truce with Japan. Under this agreement, China accepted the Japanese conquest of Manchuria and also agreed to Japan's take-over of parts of northern China. But this truce lasted only a few years. Japan, determined to conquer all of China, began a full-scale invasion in 1937.

WAR WITH CHINA In 1936, the two main political groups in China—the Communists and the Nationalists—formed a common front to stop Japan's aggression toward their country. Many of Japan's military leaders were disturbed by this action. These leaders believed that Japan should strike China before the Chinese were unified and organized well enough to resist further Japanese action.

The chance for Japan to move came in mid-1937, when there was a clash between Japanese and Chinese soldiers near Peking. Japan blamed the Chinese for the incident, and the Japanese launched a full-scale war against China. Once again the League of Nations condemned Japan, but this had no effect.

The next year Japan announced that it was working for a "New Order" in eastern Asia as part of its war plans. These plans included the destruction of Chiang Kai-shek's government in China and the ending of all Western influences in eastern Asia. The Japanese also said that they would set up a self-sufficient economic bloc in Asia made up of China, Manchuria, and Japan.

By the end of 1938, the major coastal cities of China were under Japanese control. However, the Chinese army had not collapsed as the Japanese had expected. Instead, as Chinese soldiers retreated deep within the country, they destroyed everything that the invading Japanese might use. Thus, before the Japanese could establish their control over captured lands, they had to rebuild bridges, roads, railroads, and other facilities.

As the war against China continued into 1939, the Japanese tried to stop outside aid from reaching the Chinese. The Japanese advised Great Britain and France not to allow supplies for China to pass through British and French lands in Asia. This effort met with some success, since the British and the French were preoccupied with problems in Europe. Neither Britain nor France wanted a confrontation with Japan. The Japanese also began pressuring the Dutch to supply more oil to Japan from the Dutch East Indies. Shortly after, Germany invaded Poland and World War II began.

By 1940, Japan's involvement in China had become very costly. The fighting involved over a million Japanese soldiers and cost billions of dollars. Despite the cost, however, the Japanese were determined to carry out their plans to conquer China and to build a "New Order" in eastern Asia.

QUESTIONS FOR REVIEW

1 *For what reason did Japanese prosperity depend on world trade?*

2 *How did Japanese military leaders think that their country's economic problems could be solved?*

3 *Why did Japan's military leaders decide to invade China?*

CHAPTER SUMMARY

The 1920's and 1930's were a time of political and economic change. Dictatorships arose and the Great Depression spread throughout the world. In Germany, Hitler gained power and began a campaign to bring other European countries under German control.

There was a power struggle in the Soviet Union following Lenin's death. But in the late 1920's Joseph Stalin emerged as the nation's dictator.

In the mid-1930's, Italy took over the African nation of Ethiopia as Mussolini worked to build Italian power. The League of Nations made a feeble effort to stop Italy's aggression, but was not successful. A civil war erupted in Spain in 1936, and General Francisco Franco became the dictator of that country. Other dictators were in power in many of the countries of eastern Europe by the 1930's.

The depression greatly affected Japan's economy. Some people blamed the *zaibatsu* companies and Japanese politicians for the poor economic conditions. Thus, many Japanese people supported the outspoken military leaders who favored overseas expansion to solve Japan's problems. As a result, Japan took over Manchuria in 1931 and six years later went to war with China.

CHAPTER 31 IN REVIEW

IMPORTANT WORDS, NAMES, AND TERMS

1 Explain, define, or identify each of the following:

Mein Kampf	Neville Chamberlain	sanctions
der Führer	NEP	Loyalists
final solution	collectivized	Tomáš Masaryk
lebensraum	Haile Selassie	Manchukuo

FACTS AND IDEAS

2 How did Hitler build the strength of the Nazi party?

3 With what country did Germany sign a nonaggression treaty in 1939?

4 How did Stalin eliminate his enemies in the 1930's?

5 What changes were made to improve conditions in Spain after a republican government was set up in the early 1930's?

6 How did the Japanese ultranationalistic groups look upon the *zaibatsu* companies?

ANALYZING VISUAL MATERIAL

7 Study the map on page 598. In what areas did the greatest expansion of German power take place prior to the outbreak of World War II?

8 Look at the picture on page 601. Why do you think that the Soviet dictator Stalin wanted to be pictured as a close associate of Lenin?

CONCEPTS AND UNDERSTANDINGS

9 How were the Nazis and the Fascists alike?

10 Why did many countries distrust the Soviet Union after the Communists came to power in 1917?

11 Why were the sanctions imposed on Italy by the League of Nations after the invasion of Ethiopia largely meaningless?

12 How did some Japanese military leaders react when the Chinese Communists and Nationalists formed a common front in 1936?

PROJECTS AND ACTIVITIES

13 During the purge trials of the 1930's, no effort was made to protect the rights of the accused Soviet officials. You and several other students might prepare a bulletin-board display showing how an accused person is protected under the American judicial system.

14 The anti-Semitic campaign waged by the Nazis brought suffering and death to millions of innocent people in Europe. You might do research into what was known as the Holocaust. Information can be found in books about Nazi Germany and in books about the Holocaust. After you have presented this information to the class, lead a discussion on how government persecution of one group in a country poses a danger for all of society.

32 WORLD WAR II AND ITS AFTERMATH

1 The Onset of War   2 World War II and the United States   3 Postwar Recovery in Europe and Asia   4 The World Divided

Many people throughout the world became bitter and disillusioned in the years after the end of World War I. There was a growing belief among the peoples of the world that the long and costly war had solved nothing. Worldwide discontent was further increased by rising political and economic tensions in the 1920's and 1930's.

Aggressive dictators used the postwar unrest to rise to power in several countries of central and eastern Europe. The belligerent policies of some of these leaders slowly pushed the world toward another war, which began in 1939. For almost six years, the most destructive war in history raged in Europe and Asia. With the return of peace in 1945, war-weary people around the world struggled to rebuild their devastated countries. But political differences between the Western democracies and the Communist world led to new tensions that threatened world peace.

Leo de Wys Inc.

This war memorial in Washington, D.C., commemorates an American victory on the island of Iwo Jima in the South Pacific during World War II.

1 THE ONSET OF WAR

As the years passed after World War I, people around the world realized that the war had solved nothing. Americans were angered by the results of the war and wanted to isolate themselves from the affairs of Europe. At the same time, the League of Nations was ineffective in preserving world peace.

The failure of the policy of appeasement was tragically apparent when German armies attacked Poland in September 1939, thus starting World War II. By the spring of 1941, Germany and its allies had conquered much of western Europe. Hitler then turned eastward and attacked the Soviet Union. The Germans won many victories, but the Soviets regained their strength and counterattacked. By mid-1943, Hitler's plan to conquer the Soviet Union had been smashed.

CONDITIONS ON THE EVE OF WORLD WAR II There was a growing sense of disillusionment around the world in the years after World War I. People hoped that there would never be another war, but worldwide political conditions grew worse. At the same time, the United States entered a period of isolationism. The American people were disgusted with the jealous bickering of the Allies during the peace talks at Versailles. Thus, Americans wanted their country to stay out of the affairs of other countries. The Senate's refusal to approve the Treaty of Versailles kept the United States out of the League of Nations. This lack of action was the beginning of America's isolation.

The rejection of the League of Nations by the United States played a major part in the league's inability to preserve world peace after World War I. The league's ineffectiveness was shown when it failed to stop Italy's aggression in Ethiopia and Japan's moves against China in the 1930's.

The growth of intense nationalism also characterized the years between the two world wars. Hitler's demands that Germans in the Sudetenland be ruled by Germany led to a policy of appeasement. The terrible failure of the appeasement policy quickly became apparent as the Fascist dictators of Germany and Italy pursued their goal—the domination of Europe.

On the eve of World War II, Hitler had achieved several of his goals through threats and diplomacy. In 1938, Austria had been forced to unite with Germany under Hitler's rule. During the September 1938 talks in Munich over the annexation of the Sudetenland, Hitler announced, "It is the last territorial demand I have to make in Europe." Eleven months later, however, Hitler broke his word by ordering German forces to take the remainder of Czechoslovakia.

A nonaggression pact with the Soviet Union completed Hitler's goal of protecting Germany in the east and making the invasion of Poland possible. Great Britain and France slowly began the task of rearming as the two European democracies awakened to the growing danger.

THE POLISH CRISIS In March 1939, Hitler demanded that the independent city of Danzig—governed by the League of Nations—be given to Germany. Hitler also demanded that a German-controlled railroad and highway be built across the land known as the Polish Corridor. This land separated the German state of East Prussia from Germany (see map on page 618). Poland, bolstered by promises of aid from Great Britain and France, refused to meet the German demands. The German government then mounted a propaganda campaign against Poland, accusing that country of mistreating the Germans living in Poland. In late August 1939, Hitler gave the Polish government a list of demands that were to be accepted immediately. When the Poles failed to meet these demands, Hitler ordered an attack on Poland on September 1, 1939. Two days later, Poland's allies, Great Britain and France, declared war on Germany. Thus, World War II had begun.

The Polish army was no match for the well-equipped German forces. Columns of German armor and mechanized infantry raced across Poland in a *blitzkrieg*—lightning war. While the Germans attacked from the west, the Soviet Union, in accordance with secret terms of its nonaggression treaty with Germany, invaded Poland from the east. Caught between two powerful armies, the Poles surrendered in late September 1939. Germany annexed several of Poland's western provinces and made the remainder of western Poland a German protectorate. The Soviets took the eastern half of the country. Neither Great Britain nor France had been able to give much help to Poland during its war with Germany. The British and French were not yet prepared to attack Germany from the west.

While Germany and the Soviet Union were destroying Poland, the Soviets were also adding to their power in other lands of eastern Europe. In the fall of 1939, the Soviet Union forced the Baltic countries of Latvia, Lithuania, and Estonia to allow Soviet military bases on their lands. Several months later, these three countries were annexed by the Soviet Union. The Soviets also demanded land and military bases from Finland in 1939. When the Finns refused to meet these demands, the Soviet Union attacked Finland. The Finns fought bravely, and their small army won stunning victories, exposing the weakness of the Soviet armed forces. Finally overwhelmed by the vast numbers of Soviet troops, the Finns surrendered in March 1940. Finland was forced to give up some of its land and to grant rail-transit rights across Finnish soil to the Soviet Union.

While the Soviets marched into Finland and the Baltic, Hitler prepared to turn the German military machine against the French and the British. By March 1940, Hitler was

POLITICAL		SOCIAL AND ECONOMIC
World War II began with German attack on Poland	~1939~	Radar developed by British
Dunkirk evacuated	~1940~	Penicillin developed
Japanese attacked United States at Pearl Harbor	~1941~	Intensive atomic research began in United States
Americans won Battle of the Coral Sea	~1942~	Gasoline rationed in United States
Germans surrendered at Stalingrad	~1943~	Shoes and meat rationed in United States
Invasion of Normandy by Allies	~1944~	First nonstop flight from London to Canada
Germany and Japan surrendered	~1945~	Woman's suffrage legalized in France
UN General Assembly held first session	~1946~	Xerography invented
	1947~	British coal industry nationalized
Israel established Berlin blockade began	~1948~	British railroads nationalized
NATO established	~1949~	
North Korea invaded South Korea	~1950~	Population of world reached 2.3 billion
	1951~	Heart-lung machine developed for heart operations
End of Korean War	~1953	
	1955~	Death of Albert Einstein
Soviet Union crushed revolt in Hungary	~1956~	Oral polio vaccine developed

World War II in Europe

Allied Advances 1942–1943
Allied Advances 1944–1945
Allies
Axis Powers
Neutral Countries
Greatest Extent of Axis Expansion

During World War II, the Allied leaders devised a careful plan that was designed to crush the Axis in Europe and the Middle East by engaging them on several different fronts.

ready. Germany's eastern borders were now secure, since Poland had been destroyed and Germany had a nonaggression pact with the Soviet Union. Thus, Germany could attack western Europe without fear of being struck from the east.

THE WAR IN WESTERN EUROPE During the early months of the war, there was little fighting in western Europe. As a result, the war in the west became known as the *phony war*. For about six months neither side launched an offensive. Then, in April 1940, German forces attacked and swiftly conquered Denmark and Norway. In the following month, Germany launched its major offensive by invading the Netherlands, Belgium, and Luxembourg. After defeating these countries, German forces ripped into northern France and trapped British and French forces at the port of Dunkirk (see map on this page). The Germans hoped to surround and destroy the British and the

French. But through a daring naval operation, the British soldiers and some of the French troops were rescued from the German trap.

While the Germans raced through France, Italy declared war on the Allies and attacked France from the south. Faced with two attacking armies, the French surrendered in June 1940, and most of France was occupied by the Germans. However, many patriotic French people refused to accept their country's defeat. These people rallied around General Charles de Gaulle, who organized French resistance forces outside of France.

After defeating France, Hitler turned on Great Britain. German planes bombed Britain day and night to force the British to surrender. But the courageous defense of the island by the British Royal Air Force forced the Germans to give up their daytime raids. Great Britain's situation, however, became desperate as many of the ships that brought supplies to the embattled British Isles were sunk by German submarines. Only massive American aid enabled Great Britain to continue fighting the Axis.

During the fighting that took place in 1939 and 1940, the United States, under the leadership of President Franklin D. Roosevelt, maintained its neutrality. Despite this policy, the American government increasingly supported the Allies with war matériel and food. In August 1941, President Roosevelt met with Prime Minister Winston Churchill of Great Britain. The two leaders drew up a document called the *Atlantic Charter*. This charter provided a general statement of the aims for which the Allies were fighting. To many observers, it was clear by mid-1941 that America would side with the Allies if the United States should be drawn into the war.

NORTH AFRICA AND THE BALKANS
While German armies were conquering much of western Europe, Hitler's ally Mussolini was trying desperately to seize land in Africa and the Balkans. The Italians invaded Egypt in September 1940, after taking lightly-defended British and French lands in northeastern Africa. However, in Egypt the Italian forces made little progress and were driven back by British counterattacks.

In the Balkans, Mussolini first seized Albania and then tried to move into Greece. Italian armies attacked Greece in the fall of 1940. But the Italians met unexpected resistance and were driven back into Albania.

The collapse of Mussolini's offensives in 1941 forced Hitler to send German forces to aid the faltering Italians in North Africa and the Balkans. Earlier, the Germans had pressured the Balkan countries of Bulgaria, Rumania, and Hungary to join the Axis cause. German forces along the borders of these countries poured into Yugoslavia and Greece on April 6, 1941, and quickly conquered the two nations. At the same time,

General Rommel stayed close to the front when his Afrika Korps was fighting the Allies in North Africa.

special German forces trained for desert fighting were sent to North Africa. Under the aggressive leadership of General Erwin Rommel, the "Desert Fox," the Germans mounted a powerful attack and forced the British to retreat. By late May 1941, Rommel's famed Afrika Korps had reached the Egyptian border.

Thus, by the spring of 1941, the German and Italian armies held much land in western Europe, North Africa, and the Balkans. Great Britain was the only major power that continued to resist the Axis onslaught, despite Hitler's efforts to bomb the British into submission. Delayed by the need to help Mussolini's armies in the Balkans and in Africa, Hitler had postponed his plan to complete the conquest of Europe. But in June 1941, Hitler put his plan into effect. On June 22, three huge German armies launched a surprise invasion of the Soviet Union.

ATTACK ON THE SOVIET UNION
Despite Germany's nonaggression pact with the Soviet Union, Hitler had never abandoned his

long-standing dream of bringing Soviet land under German domination. The Nazi leader had often spoken of how such a move would strengthen Germany. Hitler wanted Germany to control the grain of the Ukraine, the oil of the Caucasus, and the mines of the Ural Mountains.

Before the attack, however, Hitler looked for an excuse to invade the Soviet Union. Therefore, the Germans began to accuse the Soviets of threatening Germany by stationing many soldiers along the boundary between the two countries. The Germans also complained that the Soviet government was following an anti-German foreign policy.

The German attack on the Soviet Union began on June 22, 1941, without warning and without a declaration of war. More than 3 million Axis soldiers poured into Soviet lands along a 2,000 mile [3 219 kilometer] front. The attacking armies included not only German soldiers but also troops from Finland, Hungary, Italy, and Rumania. These countries had decided to join Germany in its attack on the Soviet Union.

The Axis invasion moved rapidly across the open land of the Soviet Union. Axis forces, using tanks and dive-bombers and the now familiar blitzkrieg tactics, moved deep into Soviet territory. Within a few months, the great city of Leningrad in the north had been surrounded and besieged. At the same time, the Axis armies reached the outer defenses of Moscow, the Soviet capital. As the Axis armies advanced, they captured more than 1 million Soviet prisoners and huge quantities of fighting equipment. By the fall of 1941, the military situation for the Soviet Union was bleak. Most military observers felt that the fall of the Soviet Union could come at any time.

DEFENSE OF THE SOVIET UNION Shortly after the invasion, the Soviet government adopted a defensive policy that would give them time to rebuild their forces. This policy came to be known as the *scorched-earth policy.* As the Soviet armies retreated, everything that could not be moved was destroyed. Most important industrial plants and machinery were uprooted and moved eastward beyond Moscow. Farms, crops, cities, bridges, railroad yards, and power stations were blown

German forces fighting in the Soviet Union had to contend not only with fierce resistance but also with severe winter conditions. Soviet soldiers were accustomed to the harsh weather. The Germans, however, were unprepared for the bitter cold and heavy snowfall that they encountered.

up or burned. The Axis armies found nothing but destruction and desolation as they moved into the Soviet Union.

As the Germans and their allies scored victory after victory, Hitler boasted that the power of the Soviet Union had been broken. But the Soviets were not defeated. They had merely traded their land for the time needed to prepare a counteroffensive. In addition, as the Soviets retreated, they drew the invading forces deeper into their land. This caused problems for the Axis as supply lines grew longer and more vulnerable to attack by Soviet *partisans*—guerrilla forces that fought behind enemy lines. The Germans and their allies were also not prepared for the harsh Soviet winters. Soviet forces, however, were accustomed to fighting under the severe winter conditions. In 1941, the winter came earlier than usual. Beset first by rain that turned roads into thick mud and then by a sharp drop in temperature and by snow, the German offensive ground to a halt. Moscow was in sight, but beyond the reach of the invading armies.

Then in December 1941 and again in January 1942, the Soviets counterattacked in several places along the immense battle line. Huge numbers of Soviet tanks, supported by massive artillery barrages and well-equipped infantry, attacked the surprised German armies. The Germans and their allies were pushed back and some land was retaken. Moscow remained in Soviet hands.

Awaiting their chance, the Germans launched a new offensive in the summer of 1942 toward the oil-rich Caucasus region. This attack brought the Axis invaders to Stalingrad, on the Volga River (see map on page 618). There, in a bitter and decisive struggle that lasted for several months, the Soviet defenders held out against furious Axis attacks. Once again the Soviets counterattacked, and they succeeded in surrounding the German forces. By early 1943, the German situation in Stalingrad was hopeless. Despite Hitler's orders not to surrender, the Germans finally gave up. Thus, Hitler's dream of conquest in the east was shattered. The Battle of Stalingrad was the turning point of the war against the Soviet Union.

QUESTIONS FOR REVIEW

1 *For what reasons did the United States enter a period of isolationism after World War I?*

2 *How did the German nonaggression pact with the Soviet Union further Hitler's plans to attack western Europe?*

3 *Why was the scorched-earth policy an important part of the defense of the Soviet Union?*

2 WORLD WAR II AND THE UNITED STATES

Despite strong isolationist feelings, many Americans favored the Allies in World War II. After the defeat of France, the United States began taking steps to help Great Britain and to strengthen America's defenses. At the same time, the United States worked to stop Japan's aggressive moves in Asia.

The Japanese, however, were determined to expand their power in Asia. After the Japanese attacked Hawaii in December 1941, the United States entered World War II on the side of the Allies.

The Allied nations decided to defeat Germany first and then Japan. After years of bloody conflict, the Germans surrendered in the spring of 1945. A few months later, Japan surrendered after the first atomic bombs were dropped on two Japanese cities.

AMERICA'S DRIFT TOWARD WAR When the war in Europe began in 1939, most Americans sympathized with the Allies. But isolationist feelings were very strong throughout the United States, and many Americans wanted their country to stay out of the fighting. As the war went on and as Hitler's armies continued to win many victories, public opinion in the United States about the war began to change. After the fall of France in 1940, the American government moved quickly to help Great Britain, which at that time was the only major country still fighting Germany.

In September 1940, the United States gave the British 50 destroyers to help them in their battle with German submarines. In return, Great Britain gave America the right to build air bases in certain British possessions. The United States also began a program to build up the American navy. In addition, the Selective Service Act was passed as a step to bolster America's defenses. This act allowed the government to strengthen the armed forces by drafting men into the military services. A year later, the Lend-Lease Act was passed. This act helped Great Britain, which was having difficulty paying for war goods. Under the law, the President could supply war matériel to any country whose defense was thought to be vital to the United States. After the Soviet Union was attacked by Germany in June 1941, American supplies were also sent to that country under the Lend-Lease Act.

While America's involvement in Europe was growing, relations between the United States and Japan were becoming increasingly strained. Since the early 1930's, Japan had been following a policy of expansion. The aim of this policy was to gain new sources of raw materials—such as oil, rubber, iron, and farm goods—for the island nation. But Japan's aggression in Asia made the United States uneasy about Japanese intentions. In September 1940, Japan began to occupy French Indochina. The same month, Japan signed a second treaty with Nazi Germany and Fascist Italy. This treaty included promises of mutual aid if any of the partners became involved in a war with a country not yet at war. In April 1941, Japan and the Soviet Union signed a non-aggression pact. Thus, Japan did not become involved in the Axis' war against the Soviet Union.

During the fall of 1941, the United States and Japan tried to settle their growing differences through diplomacy. But the takeover of French Indochina indicated that the Japanese were in no mood to compromise on their expansionist plans. Following Japan's occupation of Indochina, the United States placed an embargo on the shipment of petroleum, steel, and scrap iron to Japan. Several months later, the American government froze all Japanese assets in the United States. These moves greatly angered the Japanese. By late 1941, relations between the two countries were so strained that there seemed to be little chance of avoiding war.

A NEW ALLIED POWER Changes in the Japanese government in October 1941 virtually doomed any chance for peace with the United States. At that time, General Hideki Tojo, a military leader and a supporter of Japanese expansion, became the premier of Japan. Tojo was determined that no country should stand in the way of Japan's territorial aims in Asia. The United States, however, had been working to stop Japanese aggression in Asia. Specifically, the United States had called for Japan's withdrawal from Indochina and for peace between Japan and China. When diplomatic talks between the United States and Japan stalled in late 1941, Japanese leaders decided that their only alternative was war.

On the morning of December 7, 1941, the Japanese struck American military bases at Pearl Harbor in Hawaii. The Japanese attacked without warning and without a declaration of war. As a result, the United States suffered serious losses. Eighteen ships were

The Japanese attack on Pearl Harbor on December 7, 1941, caught the American forces completely off guard. As a result, many American warships were either sunk or seriously damaged. There were also many casualties, since the attack came early in the morning and American military personnel were unwarned and unprepared.

sunk or damaged, and over 3,000 American military personnel were killed or wounded. America's Pacific Fleet was seriously damaged, but it was not destroyed. Fortunately, none of the American aircraft carriers were in Pearl Harbor on the day of the attack.

The Japanese sneak attack shocked the American people and united them in their resolve to defeat Japan. On December 8, 1941, President Roosevelt went before Congress and asked for a declaration of war:

> Yesterday, December 7, 1941—a date which will live in infamy—the United States of America was suddenly and deliberately attacked by naval and air forces of the Empire of Japan.
>
> The United States was at peace with that nation and, at the solicitation [request] of Japan, was still in conversation with its Government and its Emperor looking toward the maintenance of peace in the Pacific. . . .

Three days after the United States declared war on Japan, Germany and Italy declared war on the United States. Thus, the war became a global conflict. The major Axis countries—Germany, Italy, and Japan—were opposed by the Allied powers, led by the United States, Great Britain, and the Soviet Union. By the end of 1941, 26 Allied nations had joined forces against the Axis.

On January 1, 1942, the Allied powers met in Washington, D.C., to agree on a coordinated war strategy. These nations issued the *Declaration of the United Nations*, in which they promised to work together for the defeat of the Axis. In addition, the Allied countries pledged that they would seek peace on the basis of the aims of the Atlantic Charter.

Despite the unity of the Allied countries, the war was far from over. By 1942, the Axis powers had won many victories, and they dominated large portions of the world. The Allies' task was first to stop Axis advances and then to launch counteroffensives that would take the war to the Axis countries.

THE DEFEAT OF GERMANY After the United States entered the war in 1941, the leaders of the major Allied powers met to plan Allied war strategy. The Big Three—Roosevelt, Churchill, and Stalin—decided that the Allies should defeat Germany first and then concentrate on defeating Japan. These leaders agreed, however, that Allied forces should maintain military pressure against the Axis on all fronts. In the months that followed, the Allies mounted their major effort in Europe and Africa, while they carried on the war in the Pacific on a somewhat limited basis.

An important Allied push against the Axis began in November 1942, when American and British forces invaded North Africa. After a relentless campaign, the German and Italian troops in Africa were defeated in May 1943. The Allies then invaded Sicily and pushed into Italy. The Italian government surrendered to the Allies in September 1943. But this did not end the fighting, for the Germans moved into Italy and blocked the Allied armies. As a result, the costly struggle for Italy did not end until Germany collapsed.

While the Americans and the British were fighting Axis forces in Africa and Italy, Soviet armies were pushing the Germans out of the Soviet Union. During 1943, the Soviets succeeded in retaking much of the land that had been captured earlier by the Axis. By early 1944, Soviet armies had forced the Germans back to the borders of prewar Poland.

As early as 1942, the British and the Americans had been asked by Stalin to relieve the German pressure on the Soviet Union by invading western Europe and establishing a second front. However, this invasion was not possible until June 6, 1944. On D day, Allied armies under General Dwight D. Eisenhower of the United States stormed the beaches of Normandy in German-held France (see map on page 618). The opening of this second front in western Europe caught Germany between powerful armies attacking from two directions. The Americans, the British, and the French pushed toward Germany from the Atlantic coast, while Soviet forces attacked from the east.

By April 1945, the German military machine was smashed. The Americans, the British, and the French were in Germany, and the Soviets were in Berlin. Faced with certain defeat, Hitler was determined not to be captured. The Nazi dictator took his own life in late April 1945. Following Hitler's death, German resistance collapsed and Germany surrendered unconditionally. The leaders of the United States and Great Britain proclaimed victory in Europe on May 8, 1945—VE Day. Unfortunately, President Franklin D. Roosevelt did not live to see the Allied victory, for he died the month before the German surrender. He was succeeded in office by Vice-President Harry S Truman, who then faced the task of defeating Japan.

THE WAR AGAINST JAPAN After the attack on Pearl Harbor in December 1941, the Japanese had quickly overrun Burma, Malaya, the Philippine Islands, the Dutch East Indies, and many islands in the South Pacific (see map on page 625). At the time, Britain was fighting for its life in Europe, and the United States could do little to support its scattered and outnumbered forces in the Pacific. The United States was also working to rebuild its damaged Pacific Fleet. As a result, the Japanese advances went unchecked for the first few months of the war.

In the spring of 1942, however, Japan suffered two major naval setbacks. The first was in the Coral Sea, where the Americans turned back an advancing Japanese fleet. The opposing surface ships did not fire at each other in this battle, for each side attacked the other with carrier-based aircraft. The second Japanese defeat came a month later, when the Japanese navy suffered heavy damage, including the loss of four aircraft carriers, in the decisive Battle of Midway Island.

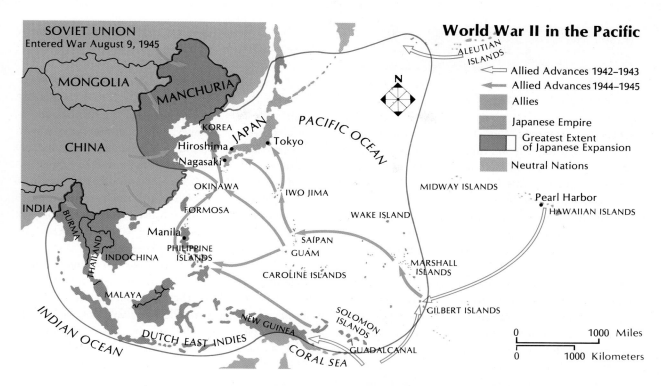

World War II in the Pacific

SOVIET UNION
Entered War August 9, 1945

MONGOLIA

MANCHURIA

CHINA

KOREA

JAPAN

PACIFIC OCEAN

Hiroshima
Nagasaki
Tokyo

OKINAWA

IWO JIMA

MIDWAY ISLANDS

FORMOSA

WAKE ISLAND

Pearl Harbor
HAWAIIAN ISLANDS

INDIA

BURMA

THAILAND

INDOCHINA

Manila
PHILIPPINE
ISLANDS

SAIPAN
GUAM

CAROLINE ISLANDS

MARSHALL
ISLANDS

MALAYA

INDIAN OCEAN

DUTCH EAST INDIES

NEW GUINEA

SOLOMON
ISLANDS

GILBERT ISLANDS

GUADALCANAL

CORAL SEA

ALEUTIAN
ISLANDS

N

Allied Advances 1942–1943
Allied Advances 1944–1945
Allies
Japanese Empire
Greatest Extent
of Japanese Expansion
Neutral Nations

0   1000 Miles
0   1000 Kilometers

The Allies' Pacific strategy called for moving to within striking distance of Japan by capturing Japanese-held islands.

The American victories in the Coral Sea and at Midway Island destroyed the offensive power of the Japanese navy. But in 1942, an Allied invasion of the strongly-defended home islands of Japan was not possible. With few Pacific bases from which to launch an attack, the Allies faced overwhelming supply problems. Moreover, powerful Japanese forces stationed on captured Pacific islands posed an ever-present threat to the Allies.

In mid-1942, the Allies decided to follow a plan of *island hopping*. This meant that the Allies would attack important Japanese-held islands in the Pacific and bypass less-important enemy bases. During the next two years, the Gilbert, Marshall, Caroline, Mariana, and Philippine islands were retaken by the Allies. These victories brought Allied forces within striking distance of Japan. But Japanese resistance to the Allied campaign was furious, especially on the islands of Tarawa, Saipan, Iwo Jima, and Okinawa. As a result, Allied and Japanese casualties in the Pacific were very high.

FINAL VICTORY Following Germany's defeat, American and British troops prepared to invade Japan during the summer of 1945. The Allies knew that an invasion would be costly in terms of casualties. President Truman then made a fateful decision on July 24, 1945, that ended the war and ushered in the atomic age. During a conference with British and Soviet leaders, President Truman authorized the dropping of the first atomic bomb.

On August 6, 1945, an atomic bomb destroyed the city of Hiroshima. Three days later, another Japanese city—Nagasaki—was wiped out by a second atomic bomb. At the same time, the Soviet Union declared war on Japan and invaded Japanese-occupied Manchuria. Japan now faced total destruction. Emperor Hirohito and the Japanese

(*Text continued on page* 627.)

Contributions

Science and the War

Even though World War II caused great destruction and loss of life, several important scientific gains resulted from the war. For example, radar—the electronic instrument used to detect and locate objects—was improved and was widely used during the war. Allied radar could detect incoming enemy aircraft long before these planes reached their target. Thus, Allied fighter planes and antiaircraft gun crews were prepared when attacking planes arrived. Radar also provided accurate weather information for Allied aircraft crews. In addition, Allied scientists found ways to make enemy radar ineffective.

Radar can determine the speed of moving objects, as well as their direction and distance. Radar is used today to provide weather information and to aid aircraft navigation. This electronic wonder is very important in helping planes land and take off in bad weather. Radar can work very well in rain, fog, snow and at night.

Important medical gains were also made during the war. For example, scientists found ways to make large amounts of penicillin—a drug used to cure many diseases. Scientists made insecticides to fight jungle insects that caused sickness. Sulfa drugs were made and used to fight infections. The use of *blood plasma*—the liquid part of blood—helped save the lives of many soldiers badly wounded in battle.

The development of the atomic bomb during World War II led to research that resulted in the peaceful use of nuclear power. For example, ways were found to use nuclear reactors to make electricity and to power submarines and other ships. In recent years, nuclear radiation has been used to treat certain illnesses and to aid in certain industrial processes.

Other important gains during the war included the invention of the first successful jet-propelled aircraft and the use of guided missiles. Both of these devices were developed by German scientists.

Thus, in spite of the death and destruction caused by the war, many important scientific gains were made. Many of these advances have been further improved since 1945.

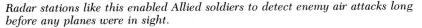

Radar stations like this enabled Allied soldiers to detect enemy air attacks long before any planes were in sight.

Brown Bros.

government accepted the terms for unconditional surrender outlined by Allied leaders. On September 2, 1945, Japan's formal surrender to the Allied powers took place in Tokyo Bay on board the American battleship *Missouri*. The worst conflict in history finally came to an end.

QUESTIONS FOR REVIEW

1 *What was the only major country still fighting Germany after the fall of France in 1940?*

2 *How did a change in the Japanese government in October 1941 doom the chances for peace with the United States?*

3 *Why was an Allied invasion of the Japanese home islands not possible in 1942?*

3 POSTWAR RECOVERY IN EUROPE AND ASIA

The people of the world shared a deep hope for lasting peace after World War II. War-weary Europeans and Asians faced the huge task of rebuilding their devastated countries. The establishment of the United Nations seemed to indicate that world leaders were determined to prevent another world war. But growing distrust between countries soon led to new tensions.

War-torn Germany was divided into zones of occupation by the Allies after the war. However, differences between the occupying powers led to the permanent division of Germany into two countries. American aid poured into Europe after the war to help war-ravaged countries revive their economies. At the same time, the United States helped the Japanese set up a democratic government and rebuild their damaged industries.

EFFORTS FOR PEACE One of the major wartime goals of the Allies was to find a way to maintain lasting peace after the war ended. Throughout the war years, Allied leaders often discussed the idea of setting up a world organization to preserve peace.

In February 1945, the Big Three suggested that a meeting of nations be called to form such an organization. As a result, the representatives of 50 countries met in San Francisco in April 1945. After two months of talks, these nations approved the Charter of the United Nations. The charter contained the four major goals for which the United Nations—the UN—was set up. According to the charter, the UN was to maintain world peace, promote friendship between nations, foster international cooperation, and help nations reach these goals.

The charter set up a number of major bodies within the UN to help the organization carry out its work. One group was the General Assembly, which was composed of representatives from all member nations. Each nation had one vote. This body discussed important questions and recommended action to other UN bodies. A second body of the UN was the Security Council, which had five permanent members—the United States, Great Britain, the Soviet Union, China, and France. Ten other members of the Security Council were elected by the General Assembly for two-year terms. The Security Council handled disputes that endangered world peace. The Council had the power to recommend settlements, but only if all five permanent members agreed. Thus, any one of the five permanent members could veto the Security Council's actions. Another UN body—the Secretariat—carried out the administrative work of the UN. Other important UN agencies were set up to raise living standards around the world, handle international legal questions, and govern lands held in trust by the UN.

The UN faced many problems after the war. At times, the UN helped keep disputes between countries from growing into larger wars. But the UN was not as effective as its founders hoped that it would be. One reason was that the peacekeeping powers of the UN were limited, since the world organization depended on the cooperation of its members to maintain peace. In addition, the UN had little power to force members to accept UN decisions. Despite drawbacks, however, the UN has provided a place where member countries could air their grievances and try to solve their differences. One of the first tasks facing the UN after the war was to punish those who carried out the cruel Nazi racial policies.

NAZI GENOCIDE During the last few months of the war, while the Allies were planning the UN organization, the full extent of the Nazis' barbarism was revealed. As Soviet troops moved through lands once held by Germany, they discovered special concentration camps where the Nazis had murdered great numbers of Jewish people. American and British forces moving into Germany from the west found similar camps where people had been imprisoned and put to death. These camps exposed the true nature of Hitler's anti-Semitic policies.

Hitler had harbored an intense hatred for the Jewish people ever since he was a young man. After gaining power, he tried to remove all Jewish influences from German life through harsh laws. To escape Nazi persecution, some Jewish people left Germany and migrated to Palestine—today the country of Israel.

After German armies overran most of Europe, millions of Jewish people came under German control. To deal with what he called the Jewish problem, Hitler and high Nazi officers worked out a plan to kill the Jewish people of Europe. This *genocide*—the planned destruction of an entire race—was carried out in death camps run by the SS—a Nazi political police organization.

One of the most notorious of these camps was in Poland, at a place called Auschwitz [OWSH-VITS]. Freight trains rolled into this camp each day, bringing thousands of prisoners, mainly Jews from German-occupied areas of Europe. Upon their arrival, the prisoners were separated according to whether or not they were fit to work as

Conditions in the Nazi concentration camps were so harsh that only a few prisoners survived. Here, the gaunt inmates of the camp at Buchenwald await medical aid after being freed from the Nazi terror by the advancing Allied armies.

628

slave laborers. Those chosen to work were made to labor under miserable conditions. The people found unfit for work—women, children, and old people—were crowded into sealed rooms, where they were killed with poison gas. The bodies of these people were then burned in special ovens. As many as 12,000 people were killed each day at Auschwitz. Those who were not immediately killed lived under horrible conditions. Little food was provided, clothing was scarce, and medical care was virtually nonexistent. Housing consisted of damp, unheated barracks, and beatings by guards were commonplace. Many thousands died from the inhuman living and working conditions found in the camps.

Between 1 million and 4 million people are estimated to have been killed at Auschwitz alone. The total number of Jewish people killed by the Nazis in what is known as the *holocaust* is thought to be about 6 million.

As the extent of Nazi cruelty became known at the end of the war, there were angry demands from around the world that the Nazis be punished. Thus, many former Nazis were brought to trial after the war.

WAR–CRIMES TRIALS The cruel treatment of the Jewish people was one of the many atrocities and crimes for which Axis leaders were brought to trial after the war. Early in the war, the Allies declared that they would punish those found guilty of war crimes. Thus, in 1943, the United Nations War Crimes Commission was set up. The purpose of this commission was to gather evidence and to make a list of Axis war criminals to be tried after the war.

In August 1945, the United States, Great Britain, the Soviet Union, and France signed an agreement establishing an international military *tribunal*—court. The first meeting of this court took place in Berlin in October 1945. At that time, 24 German leaders—most of whom were Nazis—were charged with crimes against peace, war crimes, and crimes against humanity. The actual trials of the accused Germans began in November 1945 and were held in Nuremberg, Germany. The United States, Great Britain, the Soviet Union, and France were each represented at these trials.

During the trials, one defendant killed himself, and another was found to be too sick to be prosecuted. After more than ten months, the trials ended. Three of the former German officials were set free. Twelve Nazis were sentenced to death, and the rest were given varying prison terms.

The International Military Tribunal for the Far East was set up in early 1946. This court was also made up of representatives from each major Allied power. The tribunal heard cases involving Japanese civilian and military leaders who were charged with crimes against peace and humanity. Two of the accused died during the trials. The tribunal met for more than two years. When it ended in mid-1948, seven Japanese defendants had been sentenced to death, and the others had received prison terms. Other war-crimes trials were held in different countries as the people who suffered under the Axis conquests sought to punish those responsible for the war.

POSTWAR GERMANY While the Allied powers were dealing with war criminals, they also faced the problems of setting up an administration in devastated postwar Germany. During an important Allied meeting at Yalta in February 1945, Roosevelt, Churchill, and Stalin agreed on a plan for the joint occupation of Germany. Another Allied meeting was held in the summer of 1945 at Potsdam, near Berlin. The United States was represented by President Truman. The new British prime minister, Clement Atlee, replaced Churchill. Only Stalin remained of the original Big Three, and he represented the Soviet Union. During the conference, the three leaders agreed to divide Germany into four separate zones of occupation—American, British, French and

Soviet. The city of Berlin, in the Soviet zone, was also to be divided and occupied by the four powers.

Within a short time, however, disputes arose between the Soviet Union and the other Allied powers. The Soviets balked at any plan to join the zones of occupation into a united Germany. Nevertheless, the other Allies gradually merged their zones. In 1949, after a new constitution was written, West Germany—officially known as the Federal Republic of Germany—was set up in the former American, British, and French zones. Konrad Adenauer [AD-uhn-OWR] was chosen as chancellor of the new West German republic, and Bonn became the country's capital.

The Soviets were angered by the Allied action. In retaliation, the Soviets set up a Communist regime—the German Democratic Republic—in their zone of occupation in 1949. The new East German government, however, was controlled by the Soviet Union. Even after the German Democratic Republic supposedly became independent of Soviet control in the 1950's, Soviet soldiers remained in the country.

THE BERLIN BLOCKADE The Soviets clashed with the other Allies over Berlin even before Germany was permanently divided. The presence of the three democracies in a city within Communist-held land was a source of irritation to the Soviets. Therefore, the Soviet Union tried a new tactic in 1948 in an attempt to force the other Allies out of Berlin. The Soviets arrogantly cut all railroad, highway, and water access to the city. By depriving the other Allies of these surface routes, the Soviets hoped to drive the United States, Great Britain, and France out of Berlin. The Soviets did not think that the other Allies would risk a war over the blockade.

The three Allies, however, outsmarted the Soviets. They began to supply their zones in Berlin by air. For more than a year, a huge airlift of food, fuel, and other goods poured into the city. When the Soviets realized that the other Allies would not leave, the Berlin blockade was lifted in 1949.

In the opinion of many people, the Soviets suffered a loss of prestige, since their plans were thwarted by the determination of the other Allies. While the United States, Great Britain, and France argued with the Soviet Union, the Allies also faced the task of helping European nations recover from the war.

During the Soviet blockade of Berlin in the late 1940's, the 2.5 million people of West Berlin depended on the Allied airlift for food, fuel, medicine, and other necessities. The people of the beleaguered city watched anxiously as the incoming aircraft flew into the city with vital supplies.

The Bettmann Archive

ECONOMIC RECOVERY A major goal of the Allies after the war was the restoration of European economic life. The destruction caused by the war was staggering. Burned-out cities, gutted factories, flooded mines, damaged railroads, and uncultivated fields were the result of almost six years of fighting. About 40 percent of the prewar housing in Germany was damaged or destroyed. Relief and reconstruction were urgently needed in much of Europe.

Relief came through the United Nations Relief and Rehabilitation Administration—UNRRA—which distributed food, clothing, and medicine to needy countries. In 1945 and 1946, over 1 billion dollars was spent by UNRRA. Most of the money for the supplies was provided by the United States.

At the urging of Secretary of State George C. Marshall, the United States launched a massive aid plan in 1948 to speed European economic recovery. Under the European Recovery Program (ERP)—generally called the Marshall Plan—the United States offered to match the money that devastated countries spent for economic recovery. American dollars helped pay for the rebuilding of European railroads, highways, and ports and for fertilizer and equipment for European farms. More than 11 billion dollars was spent on economic aid under the ERP between 1948 and 1951.

All of the war-ravaged countries of Europe were invited to share in the aid offered by the ERP. But the Soviet Union apparently feared American influence and refused to take part. The Soviets also made Communist-dominated governments in Eastern Europe reject American help.

As European recovery continued, a trend toward greater economic cooperation began. In 1947, Belgium, the Netherlands, and Luxembourg formed *Benelux*—a customs alliance that allowed goods to be shipped between the three countries without import duties. Further progress toward economic union took place in 1951. Realizing the importance of economic cooperation, France,

Germany, Italy, and the Benelux countries set up the European Coal and Steel Community—ECSC. Tariffs and quotas on iron ore, coal, coke, and steel shipped between these countries were ended under the ECSC.

The trend toward greater economic cooperation in Western Europe went on throughout the 1950's. At the same time, European economic recovery was also achieved. By 1952, industrial production in 16 Western European countries had surpassed prewar levels.

JAPAN AFTER THE WAR While Europe was recovering from the war, defeated Japan also faced many challenges. In 1945, Japan was a battered country facing a bleak future. Several million Japanese had died in the war, and many of the country's cities were in ruins.

The original Allied plan for postwar Japan called for the occupation of the country under an Allied commission. This group was to set occupation policies and to guide the military commander chosen to carry out these policies. But differences quickly arose with the Soviet Union over the role of the commission. As a result, the United States took over the major responsibility for the occupation of Japan. An American leader, General Douglas MacArthur, became the supreme commander for the occupation.

MacArthur's first goal was to bring democracy to Japan. Thus, when the Japanese seemed reluctant to write a new constitution, MacArthur had members of his office write the document. The constitution, which was accepted by the Japanese in 1946, brought democratic reforms to the tradition-bound country.

DEMOCRACY IN JAPAN The new constitution dramatically altered the Japanese government. Traditionally, the Japanese emperor had been looked upon as divine. Under the new constitution, however, the emperor became merely a national symbol. For the first time in history, Japanese women were given the right to vote, to own property, and to decide whom they would marry. A bill of rights guaranteed freedom of speech, the press, assembly, and religion.

One of the most important changes undertaken by General MacArthur was land reform. Despite opposition from rich landowners, the *Diet*—Japan's lawmaking body—passed laws that helped farmers buy land at low prices. Also, the right to unionize was gained by Japanese workers under American occupation. Unionization was so popular that by 1948, over 5 million Japanese workers belonged to unions.

The occupation authorities also tried to break up the giant *zaibatsu*—family-owned monopolies—which were looked upon as undemocratic. Laws were passed to make these companies sell some of their holdings. *Zaibatsu* members were not allowed to take part in businesses that their families had once held. But by careful maneuvering, *zaibatsu* leaders were able to avoid many of the new legal restrictions. As time passed, the unique aspects of the *zaibatsu* were seen as important to Japan's economy. Thus, efforts to destroy these giant companies declined, especially after the occupation officially ended in 1952. By that time, economic recovery in Japan was well under way. The astonishing growth of Japan's industries continued throughout the 1950's.

QUESTIONS FOR REVIEW

1 *What was the purpose of the Security Council of the United Nations?*

2 *How did the occupation of Japan differ from the occupation of Germany after World War II?*

3 *Why was the new constitution of 1946 a dramatic change for the Japanese people?*

4 THE WORLD DIVIDED

The wartime friendship between the Western democracies and the Communist world faded after the war. Europe was increasingly divided into two hostile groups of nations as the Soviet Union failed to keep its wartime promises. A period of transition in the Soviet Union followed Stalin's death in 1953. In time, a new leader emerged, who initiated policies that were very different from Stalin's practices. When these changes reached the Soviet satellites, the underlying discontent in many of the Communist countries of Eastern Europe was revealed.

After the war, many new countries were set up in the colonial lands once held by European powers. These countries faced many problems. At the same time, the new countries worked to avoid the ideological struggle that raged between the Western democracies and the Communist world.

COLD WAR TENSIONS Differences between the major Western democracies and the Communist world had arisen even before the end of World War II. These ideological disputes ushered in a postwar era of world tension known as the *cold war*.

A major cause of the cold war was the Soviet Union's expansion in Eastern Europe. At the Yalta conference of 1945, the Soviets had promised to allow free elections and democratic governments in the countries taken from the Germans by Soviet armies. But after the war, the Soviets broke their pledges in the hope of spreading communism throughout Eastern Europe. The countries that the Soviets had occupied —Hungary, Rumania, Bulgaria, Poland, Yugoslavia, and Czechoslovakia—fell to communism through deceit and violence. In the years that followed, only Communist Yugoslavia refused to follow the orders of the Soviet leadership. In effect, most of Eastern

Europe became a collection of satellites—countries under Soviet domination.

In 1946, Britain's wartime prime minister, Winston Churchill, warned that Europe was being divided into two hostile groups of countries separated by an *iron curtain*. According to the former British leader, this division was a threat to future world peace.

Then in 1947, the United States took steps to stop the spread of communism. At that time Communist guerrillas threatened Greece, and the Soviet Union menaced Turkey. President Truman announced that the United States would give military and economic aid to Greece and Turkey. Aid would also be given to any country that resisted internal or external threats of a Communist takeover. This policy of containment—the *Truman Doctrine*—was aimed at halting further Soviet efforts to take over countries.

Prompted by the growing Soviet menace, the United States, Canada, and several countries in Western Europe set up the North Atlantic Treaty Organization—NATO—in 1949. Under the NATO agreement, each country looked upon an attack on any partner in the alliance as an attack on all the members. The NATO treaty also provided that American soldiers and weapons would be stationed in Western Europe to discourage a Soviet attack.

A storm of Soviet criticism greeted the establishment of NATO. Members of NATO were accused of trying to cause another world war, and the United States was accused of working to dominate Western Europe. However, six years later, the Soviet Union formed a defensive alliance—the Warsaw Pact—with its Eastern European satellites. Thus, the Soviet leadership followed the same course that it had so severely criticized the United States and the democracies of Western Europe for developing.

THE KOREAN WAR The important changes in Europe after the war tended to over-shadow events in other areas of the world. But in 1950, attention shifted to Asia, where Communist aggression led to the outbreak of a major new conflict.

At the end of World War II, the formerly Japanese-held land of Korea was divided into two zones. The part of the country north of the thirty-eighth parallel was held by the Soviet Union. Below this line, the United States was the occupying power. Despite efforts to unite the two zones, the United States and the Soviets could not agree on a workable plan of government. In 1948, the United States and the Soviet Union withdrew from Korea after setting up separate governments in the former occupation zones. The North Korean government was Communist dominated, while in South Korea a somewhat autocratic regime under President Syngman Rhee was established. The South Korean government was supported by the United States and its allies.

On June 25, 1950, North Korean armies suddenly invaded South Korea and quickly

American financial and material aid to Europe was an important factor that prevented some of the nations in Western Europe from turning to communism after World War II.

"Step on it, Doc!"

moved southward. The United Nations immediately declared North Korea an aggressor and demanded its withdrawal from South Korea. Then President Truman, with the backing of the UN, ordered American troops in Japan to aid the embattled South Koreans. The UN also called on its members to unite in a collective police action to repel the North Korean invaders. As a result, several UN member nations sent troops to help South Korea.

During the first months of the war, the North Koreans almost defeated the UN armies. But after reorganizing, the UN forces under General Douglas MacArthur counterattacked and pushed the North Koreans back across the thirty-eighth parallel. Then in late 1950, Communist Chinese "volunteers" intervened and helped the North Koreans force the UN armies back to the thirty-eighth parallel. The war became a bloody and drawn-out conflict in which the UN forces made only limited gains. Finally, after months of heated negotiations, a truce was arranged in 1953, and the fighting ended. But ill feelings between Communist-backed North Korea and South Korea and its Western allies remained a major source of world tension.

CHANGES WITHIN THE SOVIET UNION
Four months before the Korean War ended, Joseph Stalin, the Soviet dictator, died. For about six months, the Soviet Union was ruled by the collective leadership of former associates of Stalin. But dissension soon arose among these leaders. Finally, a shrewd but little-known Communist party leader, Nikita Khrushchev [krush-AWF] emerged as the new ruler of the Soviet Union.

Khrushchev made several important changes that affected Soviet life. For example, he gave regional councils some power to make economic plans, rather than having all economic plans made by government ministries in Moscow. This change, however, did not lead to any great improvement in either industrial or farm output in the Soviet Union.

Khrushchev shocked the Communist world in a speech given at the Twentieth Party Congress in 1956. Speaking boldly, Khrushchev stated that Joseph Stalin had been a ruthless tyrant whose leadership mistakes had brought great suffering to the Soviet people. This statement began the official program of *destalinization* that was intended to downgrade Stalin's place in Soviet history. Pictures and statues of Stalin were removed from public places. At the same time, some of the people imprisoned by Stalin were set free from labor camps. There was even limited public criticism of Stalin by Soviet writers.

Khrushchev also launched a new foreign policy known as *peaceful coexistence*. According to Khrushchev, the Communist world and the democratic-capitalistic countries could avoid war by competing in peaceful ways in such fields as science and economics. But while Khrushchev was in power, the Communist world was far from peaceful.

UPRISINGS IN EASTERN EUROPE Within three months after Stalin's death, trouble erupted in Soviet-dominated Eastern Europe. Violence broke out when workers in East Berlin demanded better working conditions. Students joined the workers, and fighting spread throughout East Germany. Frantically, the puppet East German government called on its Soviet masters for help. For several days, the Soviet army ruthlessly suppressed the workers' and students' groups, and the rebellion ended.

The smoldering unrest within the Soviet satellites again came to the surface after Khrushchev's destalinization speech in 1956. In the summer of that year, workers in Poznan, Poland, protested for better working conditions and for higher pay. The demonstrations grew into a general revolt against the Communist government of Poland. After a few days of rioting, the revolt was quelled by units of the Soviet and Polish armies.

Photoreporters

Patriotic Hungarians patrol a city street during the unsuccessful revolt against communism that occurred in 1956.

A few months later, huge demonstrations took place in Warsaw over the political repression that had occurred in Poland while Stalin ruled the Soviet empire. These protests led to a change in the leadership of Poland and to some economic and political liberalization.

Encouraged by events in Poland, anti-government demonstrations began in Hungary in October 1956. The Hungarians were protesting the civil rights abuses by the Hungarian Communist party and the secret police. But Hungarian authorities over-reacted to these protests, and trouble spread throughout the country. Thus, the protest became a national revolt against communism in Hungary.

At first, the Hungarian uprising seemed successful, and Soviet forces left the country. The leader of Hungary then stated that his country was withdrawing from the Warsaw Pact alliance and would become a neutral nation.

This statement brought Soviet forces pouring into Hungary. In bloody clashes between the poorly-equipped Hungarians and Soviet tanks, the uprising was brutally put down. Many of the people involved in the revolt were sentenced to prison. Over 200,000 Hungarians fled their homeland. Following these uprisings, conditions in Soviet-dominated Eastern Europe became even more repressive.

EMERGENCE OF THE THIRD WORLD
While the Communist world was racked by unrest, many important changes were taking place in other areas of the world. At the end of World War II, the war-weary colonial powers of Western Europe were in no position to regain control of the colonial empires they held before the war. Slowly, new countries emerged from former European colonies in Asia, Africa, and the Middle East. These new countries were often very poor. They also lacked trained government leaders and skilled technical and professional workers.

The new developing nations of the post-war world were viewed with apprehension

635

by Europe's former colonial powers. At the same time, critics in the developing countries spoke harshly of the militarism and materialism of the Western democracies. These people also criticized the aggressive foreign policies and the totalitarian societies of Communist countries. Many leaders in the developing countries believed that the cold war was unimportant and disruptive to their future progress. These *third world* nations—not aligned with either the democratic world or the Communist bloc—wanted to solve their problems without outside interference.

The United States and the Soviet Union, however, were eager to gain the resources and the markets of third world nations. Economic, technical, and military aid pro-grams to help third world countries were set up by the Americans and the Soviets. Even though many third world countries wanted this aid, they did not want to accept the political ideas fostered by either the democracies or the Communist world.

QUESTIONS FOR REVIEW

1 *What was the purpose of the Truman Doctrine?*

2 *How did the UN react to the invasion of South Korea in 1950?*

3 *Why were nations of the third world reluctant to accept aid from either the United States or the Soviet Union?*

CHAPTER SUMMARY

Many people around the world believed that World War I had been fought in vain. Americans, embittered by the outcome of the war, retreated into isolationism. The League of Nations was unable to preserve the peace after the war. At the same time, the aggressive policies of Germany and Italy pushed the world closer to war, which began in Europe with the German invasion of Poland in 1939. Axis armies overran much of western and eastern Europe and North Africa. Hitler's armies then attacked the Soviet Union in the summer of 1941.

While Great Britain and the Soviet Union were battling the Axis powers, the United States moved toward involvement in the war. Differences with Japan over its expansionist policies in Asia led to a Japanese attack on American bases in Hawaii. With the Japanese overrunning many areas of Asia and the Pacific, the United States joined the Allied powers. After years of fighting, the Axis countries surrendered in 1945.

Following the war, the UN tried to maintain the peace, but its success was limited. As Germany was divided and occupied by the Allies, the country faced major problems during the postwar years. But Japan recovered quickly under the guidance of the United States.

A cold war developed between the Western democracies and the Communist world after the war. But third world countries worked to avoid involvement in this ideological conflict.

CHAPTER 32 IN REVIEW

IMPORTANT WORDS, NAMES, AND TERMS

1 Explain, define, or identify each of the following:

isolationism	Big Three	Truman Doctrine
blitzkrieg	holocaust	destalinization
Atlantic Charter	Marshall Plan	peaceful coexistence
scorched-earth policy	cold war	third world

FACTS AND IDEAS

2 How was America's distrust of Europe shown in the 1920's and 1930's?

3 How did the Lend-Lease Act help Great Britain in the early days of World War II?

4 Why did the Soviets cut all surface routes to Berlin in 1948?

5 How was American and Soviet aid a problem for third world countries?

ANALYZING VISUAL MATERIAL

6 Study the map on page 618. In what areas did most of the major Allied advances of 1942–1943 take place?

7 Look at the picture on page 628. How does this picture reflect the attitude of the Nazis toward the prisoners held in the concentration camps?

CONCEPTS AND UNDERSTANDINGS

8 How did the Soviets add to their power in eastern Europe in the fall of 1939?

9 Why did Adolf Hitler believe that a German attack on the Soviet Union would strengthen Germany?

10 How did the conditions at Auschwitz reveal the extent of Nazi cruelty toward the Jewish people?

11 How did conditions in the Soviet Union change under the destalinization program of Khrushchev?

PROJECTS AND ACTIVITIES

12 The United Nations has worked to alleviate hardship and suffering in many of the underdeveloped areas of the world. You might look for pictures of UN agencies at work around the world since the end of World War II. These pictures might be displayed for the class.

13 The struggle between the Soviet Union and Germany during World War II involved some of the most bitter fighting in world history. You might research battles such as the siege of Leningrad, the Battle of Stalingrad, and the great tank engagement at Kursk. Information can be found in books about the fighting in the Soviet Union during the war. Report your findings to the class. Then discuss why Soviet resistance to the German invaders was so intense.

Using Geography Skills

Political maps can provide important information about national and international problems. For example, political maps can help us to understand some of Germany's postwar problems.

After World War II, Germany was divided into four *sectors*—zones—of occupation. France, Great Britain, the United States, and the Soviet Union each controlled one zone. The city of Berlin, in the Soviet sector, was also divided into similar zones. In 1948, the Soviets tried to force the Western Allies out of Berlin by closing all land routes into their zones. The blockade was broken in 1949, after the Western Allies used planes to bring in supplies.

During the same year, the Western Allies joined their zones of Germany into one country, which was called the Federal Republic of Germany—West Germany. Similarly, the Soviets set up a new country in their zone of Germany. This country was called the German Democratic Republic—East Germany.

In 1961, the Soviets and the East Germans built a wall between the former Soviet zone of Berlin—East Berlin—and the former zones of the Western Allies—West Berlin.

The two political maps below show the division of Germany and of Berlin after the war. Study the two maps carefully. Then answer the following questions:

1 According to Map A, the smallest sector of occupation was held by what country?

2 Why were the Soviets able to halt the flow of supplies from Schönefeld airfield to West Berlin during the blockade of 1948–1949?

3 According to Map B, why, in your opinion, was Tempelhof airfield better suited to receive incoming supplies than other airfields?

4 Why do you think that people attempting to flee from East Berlin to West Germany did not go around the Berlin wall to reach West Berlin?

5 After studying the two maps, why do you think the Soviets believed that they could use a blockade to force the Allies out of West Berlin? Why did the Allies decide to use an airlift to supply West Berlin?

6 For what reasons might the Soviets have considered the presence of the Western Allies in West Berlin to be a threat to Soviet domination in East Germany?

Map A

Map B

UNIT 8 IN REVIEW

CONCEPTS AND UNDERSTANDINGS

1 What were some of the factors that hindered the growth of democracy in Japan in the 1920's?

2 How did the British Labour party differ from the Conservative party during the 1920's?

3 How did Hitler use the economic conditions in Germany to promote himself for leadership of the country?

4 What was the true purpose of education in the Soviet Union under Stalin?

5 What was the aim of the American foreign policy that was initiated by the Truman Doctrine?

QUESTIONS FOR DISCUSSION

1 Why, in your opinion, was the right of extraterritoriality humiliating to China?

2 To what extent would you agree or disagree with the following statement: "A depression in the United States today would have little effect on the world."

3 What, in your opinion, are the evils of a dictatorship such as the one that existed in Germany under Adolf Hitler?

4 The war-crimes trials held after World War II were criticized because some people felt that the victorious nations were merely trying to punish the defeated countries. How do you think that the problem of war criminals should have been handled?

5 The use of atomic bombs against Japan during World War II has been criticized in recent years as inhuman. But the use of these weapons has also been defended, since dropping the bombs helped to end the war. Is the use of such devastating weapons ever justified? Explain your answer.

SUGGESTED READING

Douglas, Roy. *In the Year of Munich*. New York: St. Martin's Press, Inc., 1978.

Elson, Robert, et. al. *Prelude to War*. Alexandria, Virginia: Time-Life Books Inc., 1976.

Fehrenbach, T.R. *Crossroads in Korea*. New York: MacMillan Publishing Co., Inc., 1968.

Gilbert, Martin. *Churchill*. Garden City, New York: Doubleday and Co., Inc., 1980.

Kurland, Gerald. *The Cold War: 1945–63*. Charlotteville, New York: SamHar Press, 1973.

Rawcliffe, Michael. *The Roosevelt File*. North Pomfret, Vermont: David and Charles, Inc., 1980.

Salisbury, Harrison. *The 900 Days: The Siege of Leningrad*. New York: Avon Books, 1970.

Shirer, William L. *The Rise and Fall of the Third Reich*. New York: Simon and Schuster, Inc., 1981.

UNIT 9

A CHANGING WORLD
1960 to the Present

33 Europe and the Americas **34** Changing Times in Asia
35 Africa and the Middle East **36** Epilogue: Past, Present, and Future

FPG

Photri

The Chinese people celebrating a national holiday in Peking   Oil-refining equipment in Nigeria

Since the end of World War II, important changes have affected all regions of the world. European countries have moved toward greater economic and political cooperation, while Latin American nations have worked to further their economic development against a background of social and political turmoil. In Asia, China has come under the control of a powerful Communist government, and Japan has become one of the world's great industrial powers. Other areas of Asia have been the scene of much instability as nations have achieved independence. The independence movement has also brought problems to Africa, and conflict in the Middle East has been a continuing threat to world peace.

Today, the world faces many serious problems, and there will be new challenges facing the world in the years ahead. But in spite of these problems and challenges, human resourcefulness offers the hope of solutions that may lead to a better world in the future.

Photri

A view of the earth from outer space

CHAPTER **33** EUROPE AND
THE AMERICAS

1 The Rise of a New European Community   2 A Changing
World Order   3 Problems and Goals in Modern Latin America

In the aftermath of World War II, the countries of Western Europe slowly moved toward economic integration. A number of important organizations were set up between the late 1940's and the mid-1970's to encourage cooperation and unity. At the same time, some progress was made toward the development of closer economic ties between Eastern and Western Europe, even though political differences divided the two areas. As Europe moved toward greater economic cooperation, many important political changes also took place.

In recent years, Latin America was also affected by political and economic changes that caused many problems. For example, the rising power of communism in some parts of Latin America was viewed with alarm by many government leaders. Lack of economic growth and the large gulf that continued to divide the wealthy from the poor led to growing calls for reform in many Latin American countries. Thus, world leaders faced many new challenges in the remaining years of the twentieth century.

A conference of Western nations to promote international cooperation led to the signing of the Helsinki Agreement in April 1975.

1 THE RISE OF A NEW EUROPEAN COMMUNITY

The countries of Western Europe shared several major aims in the years after World War II. One of the most important of these goals was the common desire to build economic prosperity and political strength through international cooperation.

The Soviet Union and its satellites also worked to build a unified economic bloc in Eastern Europe. At the same time, trade and commerce between Eastern and Western Europe slowly expanded.

The signing of the Helsinki Agreement in 1975 led to new hopes for greater international understanding. But deep political divisions continued to separate Eastern and Western Europe.

STEPS TOWARD UNITY A trend toward economic and political unity began to grow among the countries of Western Europe after World War II. Several organizations were set up to promote Western European unity and cooperation. Many of these groups continue to function at the present time.

The Council of Europe was set up in 1949 to encourage economic and social progress through cooperation among member governments. The council, however, had no real power and acted only to advise member nations on economic, social, legal, and scientific matters. Today, 21 countries belong to the Council of Europe.

An important European economic organization—the European Free Trade Association (EFTA)—was set up in 1959. The original members included Great Britain, the Scandinavian countries, Austria, Switzerland, and Portugal. The members of EFTA worked to promote *free trade*—the exchange of goods without the payment of tariffs—in Western Europe. To reach this goal, EFTA countries ended most tariffs and other restrictions on manufactured goods shipped among associ-

ation members. The standard of living in these countries rose appreciably, largely as a result of greater economic cooperation among them. In 1972, however, Great Britain and Denmark left EFTA. The next year, both countries joined the largest economic group in Western Europe—the European Economic Community.

THE EUROPEAN ECONOMIC COMMUNITY

The goal of economic unity in Western Europe became a reality during the late 1950's. In 1957, a group of leading European economic powers—including France, Belgium, Italy, the Netherlands, Luxembourg, and West Germany—formed the European Economic Community—the EEC.

The purpose of the EEC—often called the Common Market—was to set up a huge international market for the free flow of goods, people, and services among the member countries. Partners in the community agreed that they would slowly end all import quotas and tariffs on goods shipped within the EEC. EEC members also decided to set uniform tariffs on goods that were imported by Common Market countries from nations outside the organization. This would prevent a member country from trying to gain an unfair advantage by having goods enter the country at a lower tariff than goods entering the other member countries.

The establishment of the Common Market was a major factor in the startling economic growth of Western Europe after the mid-1950's. Between 1958 and 1972, for example, trade among the EEC's six original members grew by over 720 percent. After Denmark, Great Britain, and Ireland became members in 1973, the Common Market surpassed the United States in the production of steel and of automobiles.

By the early 1980's, however, the growth of the Common Market had slowed, in part because of worldwide inflation. At the same time, unemployment in the EEC countries began to rise. Thus, by the mid-1980's, the EEC faced serious problems.

POLITICAL		SOCIAL AND ECONOMIC
Castro came to power in Cuba	~1959~	European Free Trade Association set up
Kennedy elected President of United States	~1960~	First American weather satellite launched
	1961~	Gagarin of Soviet Union orbited earth
Cuban missile crisis	~1962	
Hot line between United States and Soviet Union set up	~1963	
Khrushchev replaced by Brezhnev and Kosygin in Soviet Union	~1964~	Longest suspension bridge in world opened in New York
Soviets and other Warsaw Pact nations invaded Czechoslovakia	~1968	
	1971~	Willy Brandt of West Germany given Nobel peace prize
	1973~	Denmark, Great Britain, and Ireland joined Common Market
Helsinki Agreement signed	~1975	
	1978~	World's population reached about 4.4 billion
Margaret Thatcher became prime minister of Great Britain	~1979	
Mitterand elected president of France	~1981~	Terrorists kidnapped American general James L. Dozier
Crisis between Argentina and Great Britain over Falkland Islands	~1982~	Violence between Catholics and Protestants in Northern Ireland continued

COMECON AND EAST–WEST TRADE A few years after the end of World War II, the Soviet Union and its Eastern European satellites were also working toward economic cooperation. In 1949, the Council for Mutual Economic Aid—COMECON—was set up by the Soviet Union, Poland, Czechoslovakia, Hungary, Rumania, and Bulgaria. Other Communist countries that joined COMECON were Albania, East Germany, the Mongolian People's Republic, and Cuba. Albania, however, broke away from the Soviet-dominated council in 1961.

By the early 1970's, COMECON members had begun to exchange trade goods and to provide financial aid and technical help to each other. Serious economic problems and labor troubles in Poland in 1981, however, kept that country from delivering goods and raw materials to other COMECON countries. As a result, the long-range plans of COMECON were disrupted.

There was also a trend toward increasing trade between Eastern and Western Europe and the United States in recent years. For example, the Soviet Union purchased computers and electronic technology from the United States and Western Europe in the 1970's. The Soviets also bought large amounts of grain from Western countries as a result of recent poor harvests. In 1980, however, President Jimmy Carter of the United States stopped the sale of grain and suspended the sale of high-technology equipment to the Soviets. These steps were taken in retaliation for the Soviet invasion of Afghanistan in late 1979. The grain embargo was lifted in 1982 by President Reagan.

The growth of economic involvement between Eastern and Western Europe was shown in 1981, when West Germany signed an agreement to buy natural gas from the Soviet Union. The gas was to be supplied through a new Soviet-built pipeline from Siberia to Czechoslovakia. The gas would then be distributed by other pipelines to West Germany and to many other countries in Western Europe. The joint project was strongly opposed by the United States, which felt that Western Europe would become too dependent on the Soviets for energy. In 1982, President Reagan banned the sale of oil and gas equipment and placed further restrictions on the sale of computer technology to the Soviet Union. The President was fearful that the Soviets might use such equipment and technology for military purposes. The President's actions, however, were widely criticized by many Western European leaders.

THE HELSINKI AGREEMENT Political differences and conflicting aims have slowed the growth of economic cooperation between Eastern and Western Europe in recent years. Some progress toward closer ties—diplomatic as well as economic—has been made, however. An important agreement designed to reduce the tensions that resulted from World War II and the cold war was signed in Helsinki, Finland, on August 1, 1975.

The countries that signed the Helsinki Agreement—including the United States and the Soviet Union—agreed to work for economic cooperation. The treaty also called for greater cultural and educational cooperation between countries. In addition, the boundaries set up between European countries after World War II were accepted as official by the governments that signed the treaty.

An important part of the Helsinki accord stated the need to protect human rights. Among the most important of these rights were freedom of conscience and freedom of religion. Some intellectuals in the Soviet Union and in Eastern Europe spoke against their governments for failing to protect human rights, even though these Communist countries signed the treaty. At the same time, President Jimmy Carter of the United States was criticized by Communist leaders because of his strong support for human rights. Many Communist countries, led by

In recent years, the Soviets have built natural-gas pipelines from Siberia to other areas of the Soviet Union and to Eastern Europe.

the Soviet Union, felt that President Carter was interfering in the affairs of other countries by pointing out human rights violations in Communist countries.

The Helsinki accord stated that regular meetings would be held to review the agreement. However, there was much disagreement over the issue of human rights.

EUROPEAN PROBLEMS TODAY While cooperation between European nations expanded in recent years, these countries also faced new problems. One of the most serious problems was the spread of terrorism throughout Europe. In 1972, for example, Arab terrorists of the Black September group disrupted the Olympic Games in Munich, Germany. After two Israeli athletes were killed, nine other Israelis were taken hostage. The Israeli hostages and five terrorists were killed when German police stopped the group from leaving Germany.

American army bases in Europe and American officials were also the targets of terrorist attacks. In December 1981, for example, an American military officer attached to NATO—General James L. Dozier—was kidnapped by members of the Italian Red Brigades terrorist group. Fortunately, Dozier was later rescued by the Italian police.

The goals of these terrorist groups varied from country to country. In general, most terrorist organizations worked to destroy established governments. In addition, the terrorists believed that violence was the only way to bring about the radical changes that they felt were necessary.

The growth of terrorism led several countries to work together to fight these violent groups. In 1978, Canada, Japan, the United States, France, Great Britain, Italy, and West Germany agreed to boycott any nation that refused to return terrorists who hijacked airplanes from these countries. They also agreed not to meet any demand made by terrorists.

Another problem in Western Europe was the growing power of Eurocommunism. This was a movement by Western European Communists to gain political power by being voted into office rather than by revolution. Eurocommunist leaders stated that they believed in the democratic process, universal suffrage, and human rights. In addition, Eurocommunists stressed that they were independent of the Soviet Union. As a result, Eurocommunism was denounced by the Communist leaders of the Soviet Union. At the same time, Western European and American leaders were alarmed by the success of Eurocommunism. In 1976, for example, Italian Communists gained 34 percent of the vote in elections that year. However, the popularity of communism in Italy declined quickly in the next few years. There were demands that Italian Communists give up Eurocommunism and again align themselves with the Soviet Union. But the leader of Eurocommunism in Italy rejected this idea and pushed for cooperation with the Socialists in Italy and in other European countries.

More than 50 people were killed in April 1983 when a terrorist bomb exploded outside the American embassy in Beirut, Lebanon.

Black Star

QUESTIONS FOR REVIEW

1 What was the purpose for which the European Economic Community was set up?

2 How did the United States react to the Soviet invasion of Afghanistan in 1979?

3 Why was President Jimmy Carter's support for human rights under the Helsinki Agreement criticized by Communist countries?

2 A CHANGING WORLD ORDER

Many changes have affected Europe in recent years. For example, Great Britain moved toward socialism after the Labour party gained power in 1945.

Both Great Britain and France granted independence to many of their former colonies during the 1950's. But this change led to problems for the former colonial powers and for the newly independent countries.

After Charles de Gaulle became the head of the French government, he worked to make France a strong power in Europe. German leaders faced the problem of tension between the two Germanys.

The end of Nikita Khrushchev's leadership of the Soviet Union in 1964 brought new leaders to power in that country. These leaders faced growing economic problems at home as well as tensions with other countries.

GREAT BRITAIN Several important changes took place in Great Britain after the Labour party came to power in 1945. The new government passed many laws that indicated a growing trend toward socialism. Great Britain became a *welfare state* as social benefits were broadened and as the government began to provide many basic services to the people. For example, free milk and orange juice were made available to school children. At the same time, health-care costs, unemployment income, and old-age pensions were already provided by the government through taxes collected from workers and employers.

The Labour government also *nationalized* most important industries in Britain. This meant that the government bought railways, coal mines, trucking firms, and iron and steel plants from private owners. The leaders of the Labour party felt that nationalization allowed the government to regulate key industries and to provide basic goods and services at low cost. However, government-owned industries that lost money placed a burden on the government and the people, since losses were made up out of tax revenue.

By the time the Conservatives returned to power in 1951, the British economy was thriving. This prosperity continued into the early 1960's. But conditions changed in mid decade, as Britain began to import more goods than it exported. Paying for foreign goods and raw materials drained the country's finances and forced Britain to borrow to pay its debts. At the same time, the high cost of the many social programs further strained Britain's economy.

In 1979, the Conservatives again gained control of the government after being out of power since 1974. Margaret Thatcher became the new prime minister—the first woman in British history to hold that office.

Prime Minister Thatcher wanted to reduce the government's control over the British economy. Therefore, she asked that the

Britain's Prime Minister Margaret Thatcher discussed important world problems with American leaders during a visit to the United States in 1980.

647

government sell some of the businesses that had been nationalized. In addition, the British leader worked to control inflation by lowering government spending.

Despite these moves, the British economy did not improve appreciably. Some Conservatives, as well as members of the Labour party, advocated higher government spending to revive the faltering economy. While British leaders tried to revitalize the sagging economy, they also faced problems within Britain's empire.

BRITAIN'S EMPIRE Great Britain began to grant independence to many of its overseas lands even before World War II. For example, Canada, Australia, New Zealand, South Africa, and several other possessions were given their independence in the early 1930's. However, these countries still maintained loose ties with Great Britain under what was called the *Commonwealth of Nations*. Members of the Commonwealth continued to follow Britain's lead in matters relating to trade, culture, and defense.

After World War II, Britain's Asian and African colonies increasingly demanded their independence. As a result, India, Pakistan, and Ceylon—today called Sri Lanka—gained their independence by 1948.

While the British Empire slowly dissolved after World War II, serious conflicts broke out in Northern Ireland. The trouble dated back to the English conquest of Ireland centuries ago. Moreover, deep religious differences divided the Catholics of Northern Ireland from their Protestant neighbors.

Many Irish Catholics disliked the fact that Ireland was divided into two areas (see map this page). The southern part of the island, where most Catholics lived, was an independent country—the Republic of Ireland. But a small area—Northern Ireland—was still part of Great Britain. Here, the Catholics were a minority. The Catholics of Northern Ireland believed that they were often discriminated against in jobs and housing by the Protestant majority. As a result, bloody clashes between the Catholics and the Protestants broke out in the 1960's.

Many lives were lost as the violence continued throughout the 1970's and into the 1980's. The British government sent soldiers to stop the fighting. But these efforts, as well as calls by religious leaders for peace, failed to end the violence.

THE FRENCH EMPIRE While the British worked to solve problems within their empire, the French also faced difficulties in their overseas lands. After suffering heavy losses during years of fighting to hold their lands in Indochina, the French finally withdrew from Southeast Asia in 1954. Most French African colonies also became independent in the 1950's.

The French colony of Algeria in North Africa, however, presented a serious problem. A revolt began there in 1954, and after four years of fighting most French people felt that Algeria should be independent.

Northern Ireland is ruled by Great Britain, whereas the rest of Ireland is an independent nation.

Great Britain and Ireland

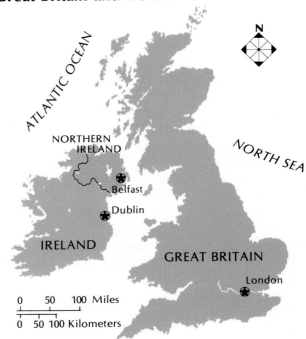

However, French settlers in Algeria, as well as some army leaders, opposed this move. These people revolted and, in turn, threatened to overthrow the French government.

In the midst of this turmoil, political leaders in France turned to the former World War II resistance leader General Charles de Gaulle. He was asked to become France's prime minister and was given emergency powers to rule by the French Parliament. After agreeing to lead the country, de Gaulle had a new constitution written that gave the president greater authority while reducing the power of Parliament. The new constitution was approved by French voters in 1958, and de Gaulle was elected president in December of that year.

A STRONG LEADER At the time of his election, the new French president had agreed to continue the war in Algeria. But de Gaulle realized that the only way to end the fighting was to give the Algerians their independence. Thus, in spite of bitter resistance by many French people in Algeria and by some French army officers, Algeria became an independent country in 1962. This move, however, touched off a wave of terrorist attacks in France and Algeria. A secret organization of army leaders even plotted to kill de Gaulle. But the violence subsided, and these officers were brought to trial and sentenced to prison.

De Gaulle's growing power offended some French political leaders, who felt that de Gaulle was too dictatorial. Efforts to limit the president's powers, however, were unsuccessful. De Gaulle was elected to a second term in 1962, which showed that he was very popular.

The aggressive French leader embarked on a plan to make France a dominant power in Western Europe. De Gaulle wanted France to be free of both American and Soviet influence. As a result, de Gaulle ordered scientists to develop nuclear weapons for France and took French soldiers out of NATO. He also demanded that NATO bases and soldiers be removed from France.

After the Common Market was set up in the late 1950's, de Gaulle hoped to use the organization to promote French influence. De Gaulle successfully blocked a British move to join the Common Market in 1963, since he felt that Britain would be a rival of France.

By the late 1960's, however, French dissatisfaction with de Gaulle's leadership had become more widespread. Student protests and worker strikes in opposition to the government led to battles with police. The strikes and violence hurt the French economy, and many people feared the outbreak of civil war. However, de Gaulle was able to quiet the unrest, and in the election of June 1968 his supporters won more than 70 percent of the seats in Parliament. De Gaulle's position as an effective leader, however, had been damaged by the turmoil. In April 1969, following the defeat of some minor constitutional reforms, de Gaulle resigned.

FRANCE AFTER DE GAULLE Charles de Gaulle's resignation brought about the election of Georges Pompidou [PAHM-pi-DOO] as president of France in June 1969. Pompidou had served loyally under de Gaulle. But the new leader disagreed with his former chief over matters of foreign policy. President Pompidou's foreign policy was designed to improve relations with the United States and Great Britain. As a result, France did not oppose Britain's entrance into the Common Market in 1973.

While Pompidou was in office, France faced serious economic problems. For example, prices and unemployment rose, while industrial growth slowed. France was also affected by sharp rises in the price of oil in the early 1970's.

After Pompidou's death in the spring of 1974, a new French president—Valery Giscard d'Estaing [zhis-kahr-des-ten]—was elected in May 1974. During Giscard d'Estaing's time in office, old-age pensions were raised, and the voting age was lowered from 21 to 18.

In 1981, François Mitterand [MEE-ter-ahn], a Socialist, was elected president of France. The Socialist party also won a majority of the seats in Parliament. After coming to power, the Socialists promised to increase the government's role in business.

Two important problems facing the new French president were unemployment and inflation. Mitterand announced plans to train young people for jobs and to give aid to French businesses that hired young people. There were also plans for higher taxes on the wealthy to provide jobs for the unemployed and to raise pensions for the needy. Thus, the French worked to adapt to the changing conditions of the 1980's.

WEST GERMANY Since its formation in 1949, West Germany—like the other countries of Western Europe—has faced many challenges. Under the leadership of Chancellor Konrad Adenauer during the 1950's,

West Germany rapidly recovered from the destruction of World War II. Adenauer also helped Germany to once again become an important part of the international community.

Following Adenauer's retirement in 1963, West Germany was led first by Ludwig Erhard (1963–1966) and then by Kurt Kiesinger (1966–1969). In 1969, the former mayor of West Berlin—Willy Brandt—became West Germany's fourth chancellor. He soon gained a reputation as an outspoken peacemaker. Brandt worked tirelessly to reduce tensions between Communist and non-Communist countries in Europe. For these efforts, Chancellor Brandt was given the Nobel peace prize in 1971. Brandt also arranged for nonaggression treaties between West Germany and the Soviet Union and other Eastern European countries. In addition, Brandt worked to ease relations between East and West Germany.

Chancellor Brandt was forced to resign from office in 1974, after it was revealed that one of his aides was an East German

Dr. Konrad Adenauer was West Germany's first chancellor after the Federal Republic was set up in 1949. Under his guidance, the West German economy made a remarkable recovery from the effects of World War II. Today, West Germany plays an important role in the affairs of Western Europe.

Wide World

spy. Helmut Schmidt then became West Germany's chancellor. Schmidt, who was known for his expertise in economic matters, worked for greater economic cooperation in Western Europe. He was re-elected in 1976 and again in 1980.

The trend toward cooperation between the two Germanys' continued during the late 1970's, although progress was often slow. Both countries agreed to build a highway joining West Berlin with Hamburg, West Germany. However, East Germany enforced its requirement that travelers between the two Germanys cross only at designated places called checkpoints.

In recent years, West Germany, like many other European countries, has faced growing economic problems. A slowdown in business activity, coupled with rising prices, has led to a general economic slump. West German unemployment in the early 1980's was between 3 and 4 percent.

West Germany's relations with the United States became strained in the late 1970's because of differences over defense and economic policies. Relations remained strained in the early 1980's, when President Reagan opposed West Germany's plans to buy natural gas from the Soviet Union. At the same time, Schmidt's government appeared to be losing favor within West Germany. This was because the two major parties in the coalition government increasingly differed over Schmidt's budget and energy policies. Schmidt was replaced by Helmut Kohl after a parliamentary vote of no confidence on October 1, 1982. Kohl promised to work to pull West Germany out of a growing economic slump.

CHANGES IN THE SOVIET UNION The leaders of the Soviet Union continued to build their country's military and political power in recent years. Under Premier Nikita Khrushchev, relations between the Western democracies and the Soviet Union generally improved, despite mutual suspicion and hostility. In 1963, the United States agreed to hold only underground tests for the development of nuclear weapons. A *hot line* —a direct communications link—between Moscow and Washington was also set up in 1963. This line provided quick and personal access between the leaders of the world's two superpowers as a means of preventing misunderstandings that might lead to war.

While there were some improvements in Soviet foreign relations, Khrushchev's domestic programs were far from successful. Crop failures, droughts, inefficiency, and other farm problems in the early 1960's forced the Soviets to buy grain from Western countries. Moreover, industrial output failed to grow as planned. As a result, Khrushchev was forced to retire in 1964. He was replaced by Leonid Brezhnev [BREZH-NEFF], who became secretary of the Communist party. Aleksei Kosygin [kuh-SEE-guhn] was named the new premier of the Soviet Union.

The new leaders worked to improve the overall Soviet economy and to correct the industrial and farm failures that had taken place under Khrushchev. Thus, supervision of factories was again placed under central control through the Council of Ministers in Moscow.

A policy of *détente* [day-tahnt] was followed by Brezhnev and Kosygin in dealing with other countries. This policy, which was the outgrowth of the ideas of several world leaders, was aimed at reducing tensions between the Soviet Union and the Western democracies.

One problem that strained Soviet relations with other countries involved the government's policy toward Soviet Jewish people. In recent years, many Jewish people wanted to leave the Soviet Union and move to Israel. While some Jewish people were allowed to leave, many thousands were forced to remain in the country.

At the same time, some Soviet intellectuals complained about their government's suppression of individual rights, such as freedom of speech and of the press. To silence these people, the Soviet government either imprisoned them or sent them to mental hospitals on the pretext that they were mentally unbalanced.

Brezhnev's power as party secretary grew in the late 1970's as Premier Kosygin's health declined. By the time that Kosygin died in 1980, Brezhnev had complete control of the Soviet government. But in the early 1980's Brezhnev's health began to fail. He died in November 1982, and a high communist party official, Yuri Andropov, became the leader of the Soviet Union.

SOVIET INVASION OF CZECHOSLOVAKIA

Brezhnev and Kosygin faced a serious challenge to Soviet domination in Eastern Europe in 1968. Early that year, the government of Czechoslovakia introduced a number of changes after a liberal Communist—Alexander Dubček [DOOB-chek]—became the head of the party. Censorship was ended, and the press, radio, and television began to comment freely about political matters. At the same time, conservative Communists were removed from the party and from the government.

These liberal moves were deeply disturbing to the Soviet Union, for they threatened Soviet control of the satellite countries. As a result, the Soviets arranged for the Warsaw Pact satellites to hold military maneuvers inside Czechoslovakia (see chart on page 653). This action was taken to frighten the Czechs and to show that the Soviets would not permit liberal changes in any country under Soviet domination. The Soviet government demanded that press censorship again be used in Czechoslovakia. The Soviets also urged Czech Communists to remove liberal party members.

In late July 1968, talks were held between the Czechs and high Soviet officers. A few days later, Warsaw Pact leaders met with Czech leaders. These talks seemed to show some tolerance among the satellite countries for the changes in Czechoslovakia.

Then in mid-August 1968, Soviet troops and forces from other Warsaw Pact countries invaded Czechoslovakia. The Soviets justified their move by claiming that antiliberal Czech leaders had asked for Soviet help in overturning the Dubček reforms. The Czech government, however, denied this statement. Dubček and other liberal Czech leaders were sent to Moscow under unofficial arrest. They were released only after the Soviets had taken control of the country.

Dubček was replaced by a hard-line Communist in 1969. Most of the reforms started under Dubček's leadership were ended. Thus, the Soviet Union once again suppressed a move for greater freedom in one of its satellite countries. Since the 1970's, the Czech Communist government has maintained tight control over its people.

RECENT SOVIET FOREIGN PROBLEMS

Soviet leaders have faced many foreign problems in recent years. For example, relations with China—a leading Communist power since 1949—grew hostile in the 1960's. The Chinese leaders scorned Khrushchev's policy of peaceful coexistence with the democratic world. The Chinese felt that war with the democracies was inevitable and that Khrushchev's ideas were not in keeping with the true goals of communism. As tension grew between the two countries, the Soviet Union stopped sending technical aid to China.

Relations became even more strained in 1963 when the Soviet Union signed a nuclear test ban treaty with the United States and Great Britain. The Chinese angrily accused the Soviets of joining the Western countries in a plot against China. The gulf between the two Communist powers continued to widen. In the late 1960's Chinese and Soviet forces clashed along a disputed border on the Amur River in northeastern China. Despite the fighting, both sides were reluctant to launch a full-scale war, and tensions slowly eased. In recent years, the two countries have tried to settle their differences, but with little success.

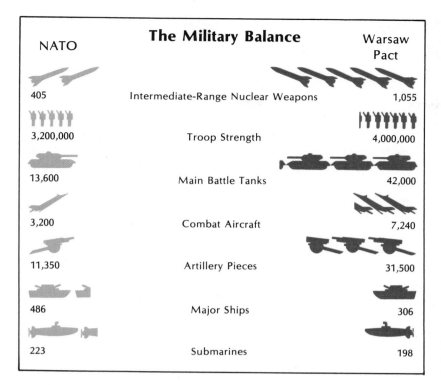

The Military Balance

NATO		Warsaw Pact
405	Intermediate-Range Nuclear Weapons	1,055
3,200,000	Troop Strength	4,000,000
13,600	Main Battle Tanks	42,000
3,200	Combat Aircraft	7,240
11,350	Artillery Pieces	31,500
486	Major Ships	306
223	Submarines	198

In the early 1980's, NATO countries were reevaluating their military strength as the power of the Warsaw Pact nations continued to grow. According to this chart, the Warsaw Pact countries were substantially more powerful in many categories of weapons than were the NATO countries.

In view of the growing differences with China, the Soviet leadership worked to build friendlier ties with the United States. In 1969, the two countries began to hold Strategic Arms Limitation Talks (SALT) that were aimed at controlling the development of nuclear weapons. A treaty to limit such weapons was signed in 1972 when President Richard M. Nixon visited the Soviet Union. At that time, agreements that provided for cooperation between the two countries in space exploration and in other fields were also signed. The United States, moreover, agreed to sell grain to the Soviet Union after Soviet farmers had experienced several disastrous crop failures.

A second agreement to limit nuclear arms was reached under President Jimmy Carter in 1979. However, this agreement was opposed by many American senators, and their approval was needed before the treaty could take effect. The Soviet invasion of Afghanistan in late 1979 destroyed any chance for Senate approval of the treaty. After President Reagan took office in 1981, American-Soviet relations became less friendly, as the new President was wary of Soviet military power. Nevertheless, new talks—called the Strategic Arms Reduction Talks (START)—were held by the two countries. Thus, the United States and the Soviet Union worked to limit the danger of nuclear war.

QUESTIONS FOR REVIEW

1 What happened to many of the important industries in Great Britain after the Labour party came to power in 1945?

2 How did the foreign policy of President Pompidou of France differ from that of President de Gaulle?

3 Why was Alexander Dubček's leadership of the Czech Communist party in the late 1960's a challenge to Soviet domination of Eastern Europe?

Contributions

THE TGV TRAIN

A popular way to travel in Europe today is by train. All of the major urban centers of Europe are linked by fast, clean, and efficient trains. Many high-speed trains, pulled by electric engines, carry thousands of passengers each day. Such trains neither pollute the air nor burn scarce fuels.

Planners for the government-owned French railroads recently introduced new trains known as *Très Grande Vitesse* [tre grahnd vee-tess]—very high speed—trains. These trains are built to run at speeds of over 160 miles (267.4 kilometers) per hour.

Instead of devising new ways of moving and suspending these trains, French railroad designers worked to improve existing railway technology. Thus, by refining present train suspension systems and roadbeds, French designers have been able to achieve both stability and low wind drag at high speeds. The weight of the TGV trains is spread evenly over the length of the train among several sets of powered and unpowered wheels. In addition, the number of wheels carrying the train has been reduced, thus cutting wheel-to-rail friction. As a result, the TGV trains cruise at over 160 miles (267.4 kilometers) per hour with the same

power plant that propels other French trains at only 120 miles (193 kilometers) per hour.

The new trains run on tracks used by passenger trains only. These tracks have specially sloped curves designed to balance the centrifugal force encountered by the trains at high speeds. All seats on the TGV trains are reserved, so there will be no standees.

The TGV trains now run between Paris and Lyons in south-eastern France. The distance between these cities is 280 miles (550.6 kilometers). The trip takes about 2 hours and 40 minutes. On the initial run of the TGV train, speeds of over 236 miles (380 kilometers) per hour were reached. This speed broke the previous world's speed record for trains, which was 205 miles (330 kilometers) per hour. By improving existing railway technology, the French have contributed to better mass transit.

The French TGV train represents one of the most recent advances in high-speed rail travel. On the right, travelers enjoy a meal while speeding to their destinations.

French National Railroads

Liaison

3 PROBLEMS AND GOALS IN MODERN LATIN AMERICA

The political scene in much of Latin America has been characterized by turmoil and change in recent years. For example, Cuba became a Communist country and worked to further communism throughout Latin America. New treaties affecting control of the Panama Canal were signed. A leftist political leader rose to power in Chile, which led to unrest in parts of South America.

Far-reaching economic changes accompanied Latin America's political developments in the years after 1950. Several Latin American countries underwent rapid economic growth. At the same time, the United States worked to find an effective policy for dealing with the changing conditions in Latin America.

THE PROBLEM OF CUBA In 1959, a young lawyer named Fidel Castro led a successful revolt to overthrow the oppressive government of Fulgencio Batista in the island country of Cuba. Shortly after taking power, Castro alienated the United States by taking over American-owned cattle ranches and sugar plantations on the island. Relations grew worse when Castro set up a Communist government and turned to the Soviet Union for military and economic aid. At the same time, Castro also began working to spread communism throughout Latin America.

Formal diplomatic ties between the United States and Cuba ended in 1961, after the Castro government took over all remaining American businesses in Cuba. Hostility between the two countries continued to grow after anti-Castro Cubans tried to invade the island in 1961. The invading forces landed at the Bay of Pigs, on Cuba's southwestern coast, but were quickly crushed by Castro's Soviet-armed soldiers. The American government had known of the

Since gaining power in 1959, Cuban leader Fidel Castro has worked to spread the influence of communism throughout Latin America.

invasion and had promised to aid the invaders. But when the attack took place, President Kennedy refused to send military aid, thus breaking the American promise.

An even more serious crisis arose in 1962. Convinced that the United States was going to attack Cuba, Castro asked for more military aid from the Soviet Union. The Soviets responded by sending missiles and launching equipment to Cuba. When the American government learned that Soviet missiles were in Cuba, President Kennedy ordered a naval blockade of the island. The president also demanded that the Soviet missiles be removed from Cuba. Finally, the Soviet premier, Nikita Khrushchev, agreed to take the missiles out of Cuba on the condition that the United States promise not to attack Cuba.

Under Castro, Cuba continued to be the center of Communist-inspired unrest in Latin America. Throughout the 1970's, the Cuban economy remained weak. With little industrial capacity, the country's main exports were farm goods, such as sugar and tobacco. Moreover, Cuba had to buy needed manufactured goods from the Soviet Union and other Communist countries.

In the early 1980's, Castro indicated that he would like to improve relations with the United States. But the American government was wary of such a move in view of Castro's continuing efforts to spread Communist revolts in Latin America. Thus, the situation between the United States and Cuba remained generally unfriendly into the 1980's.

PANAMA Political turmoil in Panama in recent years greatly affected that country's relations with the United States. During the 1950's and 1960's, anti-American riots and demonstrations broke out in Panama. Panamanians were resentful of America's control of the Panama Canal and of the Canal Zone—the land around the Canal (see map on this page). As a result of the growing unrest in Panama, President Lyndon Johnson agreed in late 1964 to hold talks for new treaties relating to control of the Canal. Such agreements would replace the 1903 agreement, which had given the United States unrestricted control of both the Canal and the Canal Zone.

While these talks were underway, important domestic political changes took place in Panama. General Omar Torrijos Herrera [tawr-EE-hohs uh-RER-uh], commander of the National Guard, became the dictator of Panama in 1968. Torrijos openly agitated for a new and more favorable canal treaty with the United States. Finally, after years of negotiation, agreements between the two countries were reached in 1977. The new treaties set down the terms under which the Canal would operate until the end of 1999, when Panama would take over

Under agreements signed in 1978 between the United States and Panama, control of the Panama Canal was to be given to Panama in 1999.

Panama and the Canal Zone

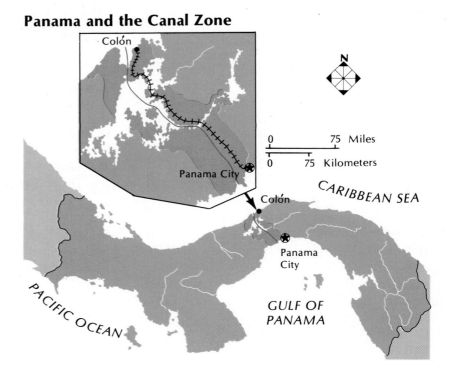

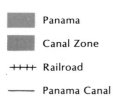

- Panama
- Canal Zone
- ++++ Railroad
- —— Panama Canal

the Canal. The treaties also provided that the Canal Zone was to be turned over to Panama in 1979.

Within a few months, the two treaties were approved by Panama's government. There was, however, strong opposition to the treaties in the United States, where Senate approval was needed. Finally, after much work by President Carter to gain senatorial approval, the new treaties were ratified in April 1978.

Later in 1978, General Torrijos turned over control of the Panamanian government to Aristides Royo, a civilian. However, as head of Panama's National Guard, Torrijos was still the most powerful person in Panama. Then, in July 1981, Torrijos was killed in a plane crash. Although President Royo remained in office, there was growing speculation over who would take Torrijos's place as head of the National Guard.

Other problems also arose after the death of Torrijos. A new oil pipeline across Panama and a new rail line across southern Mexico were expected to affect the amount of ship traffic through the Canal. At the same time, there was the problem of training Panamanians to maintain and run the Canal once it was turned over to Panama. Thus, Panama's leaders faced many challenges.

TURBULENCE IN CHILE Another Latin American country that was plagued by political unrest in recent years was Chile. During the 1960's, Chile's leaders worked to solve such problems as inflation, industrial expansion, poverty, and land reform.

Then, in 1970, the Chilean political scene changed drastically. At that time, Salvador Allende Gossens [ah-YEN-day-GAW-sens], a Marxist supported by the Communists and the Socialists, became the president of Chile. Allende was the first Marxist chosen democratically to lead a country in Latin America.

Under Allende's leadership, Chile's banks and copper mines were taken over by the government. In addition, Allende also worked to redistribute the nation's farmland so that poor farmers owned their land. Many conservative and wealthy Chileans were deeply disturbed by Allende's election and his plans to make Chile a socialist country. Wealthy Chileans were afraid that Allende's plans would ruin the country's economy.

While Allende was in office, Chileans were divided in their support for him. But in general, there was growing opposition to Allende's policies. For example, there were many strikes in 1972 to protest inflation and food shortages.

By 1973, conditions in Chile were chaotic. Workers, business leaders, and professional people demanded that Allende stop his program of socialism. The Chilean president, however, refused to change his policies. After weeks of strikes and economic upheaval, a group of military officers decided to act. In September 1973, a violent revolt took place as the Allende government was overthrown. The Chilean leader was reported to have taken his own life rather than surrender to the rebels. The new military government suppressed all political opposition, banned political parties, broke up the country's largest labor organization, and censored the press.

By the early 1980's, the military government of Chile was working to encourage foreign investments by emphasizing Chile's stability. At the same time, government leaders stated that the country would remain firmly anti-Communist. While the government promised to restore democracy, many Chileans complained about the repressive rule of the military regime. By the mid-1980's, much remained to be done by Chile's leaders to end the social and economic inequalities in their country.

CHANGES IN BRAZIL The largest country in Latin America—Brazil—has suffered from considerable political unrest and thus has had many different leaders in recent years. Even though the Brazilian leadership has changed often, the country's military establishment has been the real power behind the government.

Military rule in Brazil continued throughout the 1970's. In recent years, however, some Brazilians have called for an end to the military's involvement in the government in the hope that the country might become more democratic. There seemed to be a slight move in that direction in 1981, as the country's leader favored a program calling for a slow return to free elections and to civilian control of the government. Although some people felt that military rule was necessary to insure stability in Brazil, most business leaders and church leaders favored moving toward democracy.

In spite of political unrest in Brazil, the country's economy has grown rapidly in recent years. By the early 1980's, Brazil was exporting goods worth about 24.5 billion dollars. In addition, the country had become an important shipbuilding nation. Among the products being made in Brazil were automobiles, auto parts, airplanes, and armaments. Brazil also exported agricultural products.

High prices and a widening gap between the country's rich people and poor people were two serious problems faced by Brazilians during the 1980's. At the same time, crime was growing in many of Brazil's cities. Despite these difficulties, and the lack of a democratic government, Brazilians looked forward to continued economic growth.

DEVELOPMENTS IN MEXICO Mexico was another Latin American country that made great economic gains in recent years. Automobiles, clothing, electrical appliances, cement, and chemicals were some of the goods being made in Mexico. The country's growing tourist trade also helped the Mexican economy. In the 1970's, new petroleum deposits were found in Mexico. As a result, the country's income from petroleum production rose. Natural gas output also increased greatly.

Rapid economic growth and higher national income, however, added to Mexico's problems. While prosperity grew, most Mexicans failed to share in the country's rising income, since many of Mexico's industries were held by the wealthy. Thus, the gap between the rich and poor widened. Mexicans in farming villages and in the overcrowded city slums continued to live amid poor housing, schooling, and nutrition. In addition, Mexico's rapidly growing population added to the poor and overcrowded living conditions.

In the early 1980's, a drop in world oil prices and in the demand for petroleum products lowered Mexico's oil income. At the same time, inflation and foreign debts were serious problems.

There were also changes in Mexico's relations with other countries. During the early 1970's, for example, the American government opposed Mexico's efforts to improve its ties with the leftist governments of Cuba and Chile. Illegal immigration and growing drug traffic from Mexico into the United States also caused tension between the two countries. Some Americans and Mexicans hoped that relations would improve following the election of Miguel de la Madrid in 1982, as Mexico's new president.

UNREST IN ARGENTINA The Latin American country of Argentina—like its neighbor to the north, Brazil—suffered from growing political unrest during recent years. Throughout the early 1950's, different groups became increasingly dissatisfied with the leadership of dictator Juan Perón. Perón's repressive government angered many Argentineans, including members of the middle and upper classes and leaders of the Church. As a result, the Perón regime was overthrown in September 1955.

Perón's overthrow, however, did little to bring stability to Argentina. A series of military and civilian governments followed the revolt. Unrest continued during the 1960's and early 1970's. Argentineans often

Southern Latin America

A dispute over the ownership of the Falkland Islands in the South Atlantic Ocean led to warfare between Argentina and Great Britain in April 1982. Here, Argentinean soldiers watch as the British bombard the settlement of Port Stanley. A short time after the hostilities began, Argentinean forces on the Falklands surrendered.

protested to show their anger over the leadership's failure to solve the nation's problems.

Perón came back to Argentina in 1973 and again returned to power as president. However, he died the next year and was succeeded by his third wife, Isabel, who ruled until her overthrow by the army in 1976. Military leaders again took over the government and set to work to end the labor trouble and to check inflation.

Argentina faced a serious international crisis in 1982. For many years, Argentina had disputed the ownership of the British-held Falkland Islands—known in Argentina as the Islas Malvinas—in the South Atlantic (see map on this page). In April 1982, Argentine soldiers moved into the Falklands. The Argentine government then declared that

the Falklands belonged to Argentina. After efforts to end the crisis through diplomacy failed, Great Britain invaded the Falklands and retook them from Argentina.

The humiliating defeat of Argentine soldiers by a smaller British force led to yet another change in Argentina's government. General Reynaldo Bignone was chosen by the country's military leaders to be the new president. Public anger over Argentina's defeat led to growing pressure for more democracy and for an end to military rule.

THE UNITED STATES AND LATIN AMERICA The policies of the United States toward Latin American countries has undergone many changes during the twentieth century. During the first half of the century, the United States was often accused of being too ready to interfere in Latin American matters. Since the end of World War II, the United States has been criticized for overlooking social injustice while helping Latin American governments that were anti-Communist.

In 1961, the United States tried to improve its image by starting a new plan to help Latin America. Under this plan—the Alliance for Progress—the United States and Latin American governments worked together to pay for projects to aid in Latin America's economic growth.

The Alliance for Progress, however, failed to solve the problems of unemployment, overpopulation, and illiteracy in Latin America. As a result, the United States began working to increase its trade with Latin America as a way to build Latin American economies.

Despite moves to improve ties with Latin America, the United States was again accused of interfering in Latin American affairs in the 1980's. At that time, the United States was very concerned by the activities of Communist-backed leftists in Central America. As a result, the United States sent military and financial aid to such countries as El Salvador and Honduras to help fight the leftists. However, many people in the United States and in Latin America opposed this aid as undue interference.

QUESTIONS FOR REVIEW

1 *Who became the ruler of Cuba after leading a successful revolt in 1959?*

2 *How has recent economic growth added to Mexico's problems?*

3 *Why did the Falkland Island crisis cause a change in the leadership of Argentina in 1982?*

CHAPTER SUMMARY

A growing trend toward economic cooperation has brought closer ties among the industrialized countries of Western Europe since the late 1940's. A move toward the development of greater trade between Eastern and Western Europe also emerged in the 1970's.

While Europeans moved toward greater economic integration, many important political changes took place. After the Labour party came to power in Great Britain, many industries were taken over by the government. The French leader Charles de Gaulle worked to build French influence in Western Europe. German leaders faced the problem of dealing with two Germanys—democratic West Germany and Communist East Germany. New leaders came to power in the Soviet Union in the 1960's.

In recent years, Latin America has been affected by important political changes, the rising influence of communism, and greater economic growth. At the same time, the United States followed new policies in dealing with Latin America.

CHAPTER 33 IN REVIEW

IMPORTANT WORDS, NAMES, AND TERMS
1 Explain, define, or identify each of the following:

EEC	Helmut Schmidt	Alexander Dubček
Helsinki Agreement	hot line	Juan D. Perón
Eurocommunism	Leonid Brezhnev	Islas Malvinas
nationalized	détente	Alliance for Progress

FACTS AND IDEAS
2 Why did President Jimmy Carter stop the sale of grain and suspend the sale of high-technology equipment to the Soviet Union in 1980?

3 What steps were taken by Canada, Japan, the United States, France, Great Britain, Italy, and West Germany in 1978 to discourage terrorists?

4 For what reasons did the British Labour party feel that nationalization of important industries was necessary?

5 Why did Chinese leaders criticize Khrushchev's policy of peaceful coexistence in the 1960's?

6 How did President Kennedy react when Soviet missiles were discovered in Cuba in 1962?

ANALYZING VISUAL MATERIAL
7 Study the chart on page 653. In what categories are the NATO countries stronger than the Warsaw Pact nations? According to the chart, which of the two military alliances seems to be the more powerful?

8 Look at the picture on page 654. What do you think are the advantages of using electrically powered trains?

CONCEPTS AND UNDERSTANDINGS
9 Why did a proposed gas pipeline across the Soviet Union to Czechoslovakia in the early 1980's strain relations between the United States and Western European countries?

10 How have religious differences been the cause of serious problems in Northern Ireland since the 1960's?

11 Why has the United States often been criticized for its policies toward Latin America?

PROJECTS AND ACTIVITIES
12 The European Economic Community—the Common Market—is a powerful economic force in today's industrialized world. You and several other students might look for pictures of goods made in EEC countries. Make a bulletin-board display on these pictures.

13 The second wife of the Argentine dictator Juan Perón was extremely powerful. Do some research on the life of Eva Perón. Information can be found in books on Juan and Eva Perón and in other reference books. Report your findings to the class. Then discuss whether the wife of a political leader should take part in government affairs.

CHAPTER **34** CHANGING TIMES IN ASIA

1 The Evolution of Communist China 2 Japan: Modern Industrial Giant 3 India: Making Democracy Work 4 Southeast Asia: Problems and Conflict

The struggle between China's Nationalists and Communists had emerged during the 1930's. The two groups had cooperated, to some extent, against the Japanese during World War II. But large-scale fighting between the Nationalists and the Communists erupted soon after the war. In 1949, the Communists took control of China.

Japan's leaders faced the problems caused by rapid economic recovery and growth after World War II. In spite of the prosperity that came to Japan, many Japanese were concerned about the long-term effects of continued economic expansion.

The people of India worked to industrialize after their country gained its independence in the late 1940's. But population growth, religious differences, and border problems caused many difficulties for the new nation and its people.

In 1954, four independent countries—Laos, Cambodia (Kampuchea), North Vietnam, and South Vietnam—were set up after France lost the colony of Indochina in Southeast Asia. After the United States withdrew from the area in the early 1970's, Communist influence increased. But violence and unrest continued to threaten Southeast Asia in the 1980's.

Joachim Schneider

The crowded and dynamic city of Hong Kong illustrates the growing economic importance of Asia in today's world.

1 THE EVOLUTION OF COMMUNIST CHINA

Nationalist efforts to destroy China's Communist party in the late 1920's and early 1930's failed. But the Nationalists, under Chiang Kai-shek, forced the Communists to retreat deep into China. There, Communist leaders built up the party by gaining the support of Chinese peasants.

During the 1930's, China's Communists and Nationalists worked together to stop Japanese aggression in China. But after Japan's defeat in 1945, civil war returned to China. After four years of struggle, the Communists defeated the Nationalists and set up a new government in China. But by the 1980's, China faced new tensions caused by changing leadership and worldwide economic problems.

THE LONG MARCH As you read in Chapter 29, the fragile alliance between Chiang Kai-shek's Nationalists and the Chinese Communists ended in 1927. At that time, Chiang launched a campaign in Shanghai and in other major Chinese cities to destroy the Communist party. Suspected Communists were killed or captured in a devastating sweep that shattered the party's power.

A few Communists escaped and fled to the hills of southern China, beyond the reach of the Nationalists. There, a young Communist leader named Mao Tse-tung [MOW-zuh-DUNG] began building a strong Communist army. Mao stressed the importance of using guerrilla warfare to gain power. He believed that a powerful enemy could be worn down through repeated surprise attacks and quick withdrawals. But guerrilla armies needed information, supplies, and recruits. Since these needs could be provided by local peasants, Mao worked to win the peasants' support by calling for the redistribution of land from large landowners to the peasants.

In the early 1930's, the Nationalists tried four times to destroy the remaining Communists in China and were defeated each time. But in 1934, aided by German military advisers, Chiang and his armies surrounded the Communists in their southern stronghold. In a desperate move to escape, the Communists broke through the blockade at a weak point. After escaping from the Nationalist trap, the Communist leaders decided to move their soldiers deep into the interior of China. During the next year, 100,000 Communist troops struggled across snow-covered mountain passes and dangerous marshes in what was called the *Long March*. Eventually, less than 10,000 of these soldiers reached the mountainous and forbidding interior of China, where they were safe from Nationalist attacks.

THE UNITED FRONT Chiang Kai-shek was still determined to destroy the Communists even though they had marched beyond the reach of the Nationalist forces. However, the Japanese invasion of China in the 1930's forced a change in Chiang's plans. At that time, the Communists suggested a *United Front*—a Nationalist-Communist alliance to fight the Japanese. However, the Communists insisted on the control of their own areas of China and of their own army. This insistence caused Chiang to fear that the Communists were a greater danger to China than the Japanese. But some of Chiang's military officers did not agree with him. In 1936, Chiang was taken prisoner by some of his officers and held for two weeks. He was finally released after agreeing to end the campaign against the Communists.

Between 1936 and 1945, the Chinese Nationalists and the Communists appeared to settle their differences as they worked to fight Japan. Behind the scenes, however, both groups maneuvered for power. For example, the Nationalists used some of their best troops to watch the Communists rather than fight the Japanese. Then, when the war turned against Japan, Chiang began

POLITICAL		SOCIAL AND ECONOMIC
United States tried to mediate dispute between Chinese Nationalists and Communists	~1945	
Communist People's Republic proclaimed under Mao Tse-tung	~1949	
	1950~	Population of Tokyo reached 5.3 million
	1951~	Food needs forced India to buy wheat from United States
War in Korea ended	~1953~	Mount Everest climbed for first time
Japan and United States signed defense agreement	~1954	
Japan admitted to UN	~1956	
War in Vietnam intensified	~1964	
	1966~	Red Guards demonstrated in China
Nixon elected President of United States	~1968	
	1969~	Protests in United States against Vietnam involvement
	1970~	Japanese passed laws to curb pollution
Communist China admitted to UN	~1971	
Nixon visited China	~1972	
Cease-fire signed in Vietnam	~1973~	Poor harvests forced India to buy wheat from abroad
	1976~	Fertilizer plants built in China, India, Pakistan, and South Korea
Diplomatic relations established between United States and Communist China	~1978	
	1979~	Drought destroyed much of India's grain harvest
Nakasone became prime minister of Japan	~1982~	Population of China reached over 1 billion Northern India affected by drought

holding back his soldiers to use against the Communists once the war with Japan was over.

The Nationalists and the Communists often fought fiercely against the Japanese. These efforts, however, sometimes appeared halfhearted because the Nationalists and the Communists did not trust each other. While the two groups fought the Japanese, the Communists expanded their influence behind the battle lines into rural China. There they worked to turn the peasants against the Japanese, the rich landlords, and the Nationalists. Between 1936 and 1945, membership in the Chinese Communist party grew from fewer than 1 million to over 7 million members.

THE TRIUMPH OF COMMUNISM A few months after Japan surrendered in 1945, President Truman sent General George C. Marshall to help the Chinese Nationalists and the Communists settle their differences. Both sides agreed to a cease-fire while discussing the possibility of forming a coalition government. But this delicate peacemaking effort collapsed as fighting broke out again in mid-1946.

At first the Nationalists seemed successful, for they took control of many of China's large cities. However, the Communists held most of the lands around these cities. In addition, many Nationalist soldiers became demoralized by the fact that they were fighting their own people.

In contrast to the Nationalists, the Communists were dedicated and well organized. As the Communist armies gained more land in rural China, they freed the peasants from the high fees charged by landlords and moneylenders. Thus, to many Chinese peasants, the Communists seemed to be helping the people.

In July 1947, the war turned against the Nationalists, as the Communist armies attacked on several fronts in the north of China. In the last great battle of the war, Chiang Kai-shek's army lost 200,000 soldiers.

During the late 1950's, rice yields in China were raised through the efforts of workers like these from Kwangtung Province.

The Chinese leader also lost the main supply route to his armies farther north. Following the surrender of Peking (Beijing),* Mao Tse-tung proclaimed the establishment of the People's Republic of China on October 1, 1949. Chiang and some of his troops fled to the island of Taiwan—Formosa—off the southeastern coast of China. After setting up a government, he vowed to continue the fight against communism.

CHINA UNDER COMMUNISM The new leaders of China were determined to use communism to reshape their country. As head of the Communist party, Mao Tse-tung was also the head of the government. An associate named Chou En-lai (Zhou Enlai) was made the premier, or chief administrative official. All important decisions were

* Beijing is the spelling of Peking in the Pinyin system of westernizing Chinese words that was recently adopted by the Chinese. To avoid confusion, traditional spellings of historical Chinese names and places have been used in this text. Pinyin is introduced here to familiarize the reader with the new system.

made by the highest government leaders, most of whom were Communists.

By 1952, China's war-damaged factories and railways were again operating, and inflation had been brought under control. At the same time, a program of land redistribution was also carried out. Many landlords and rich peasants were executed, and their lands were divided among the peasants.

In 1953, China embarked on the first ambitious plan of economic development—the Five Year Plan. The Soviet Union helped China at this time by training Chinese technicians and by sending machinery and Soviet experts to China.

Most of the money needed to pay for China's economic growth came from agriculture, which was still the basis of the Chinese economy. A plan was undertaken to replace the existing small, individually owned farms with government-owned collective farms, where land, labor, and tools were shared by the peasants.

By the time the Five Year Plan ended,

665

agriculture had been reorganized, and the government was in firm control of industry. Moreover, production goals for iron, coal, and steel had been exceeded.

THE GREAT LEAP FORWARD In 1958, Mao announced a plan called the Great Leap Forward. Under this plan, China's people were mobilized to raise the country's economic output. High goals were set for steel and iron production. At the same time, collective farms were joined into huge *communes*, where thousands of peasants lived and worked together on government lands under the government's supervision. The production and distribution of all farm goods was handled by the communes. To provide for the peasants' needs, schools, hospitals, child-care centers, dining halls, and centers for the aged were set up on each commune.

Through the Great Leap Forward, the Chinese people were involved in a common effort to make China strong. But the plan failed to reach the ambitious goals that had been set by the government.

By 1960, China's leaders realized that the Great Leap Forward had failed. As a result, the government ended many of the unpopular features of the plan. New policies were adopted that allowed the peasants in the communes to work in small groups rather than in large production teams. The new policies also allowed the peasants to have small, private plots of land, which they could farm on their own time for their own use. The failure of the Great Leap Forward was a major setback for the Communists.

A CHANGING SOCIETY Daily life in China also underwent many changes as the country's Communist leaders tried to reshape the Chinese society. The Communists, for example, attempted to alter religious beliefs among the people by proclaiming that religion had no place in a modern society. In addition, the traditional pattern of family life was attacked as young people were encouraged to join party-sponsored communal organizations as a way of having the party take the place of parents.

Under communist rule, the Chinese people had little opportunity for free expression. No group could oppose the government, and the press was closely censored. Throughout China, creativity was thwarted as literature and art were allowed only as ways to gain public acceptance of communist ideas and policies.

The failure of the Great Leap Forward had led to criticism of Mao Tse-tung's leadership. To counter this criticism, Mao announced a new program—the *Cultural Revolution*—which began in 1966. This plan was designed to bring the party in touch with the people and to rekindle the revolutionary spirit in China. Groups of young Chinese Communists—called Red Guards—were sent to live among the people to arouse enthusiasm for Mao and his ideas. However, the Red Guards often went too far and publicly criticized other Communist officials. At times, there were open battles between the Red Guards and other Communist groups who opposed the Guards.

Eventually, some order was restored after the regular Chinese army was used against the Red Guards, as Mao realized that they had gone too far. But as order returned, conflict continued among different groups within the Chinese Communist party.

FOREIGN RELATIONS After the Communists came to power in 1949, many countries, including the Soviet Union and several Western European nations, recognized the Communist regime as China's official government. However, the Nationalists on Taiwan still claimed to be the only legal government of China. For many years, the United States continued to recognize only Chiang Kai-shek's government on Taiwan.

When the Korean War broke out in 1950, relations between the United States and Communist China grew worse (see Chapter 32). China sent soldiers to help Communist

North Korea, while the United States and other UN members aided South Korea. After the war ended in 1953, Chinese-American relations remained hostile.

In the mid-1950's, Communist China's friendship with the Soviet Union began to cool. The two countries disagreed over how communist revolutions should be carried out. As relations grew more strained, Soviet aid to China was stopped. Relations grew worse after Soviet Premier Nikita Khrushchev came to power, for the Chinese felt that the Soviet leader failed to pursue the true goals of communism. In the late 1960's, fighting broke out between China and the Soviet Union over disputed land along the Amur River in Asia. Although peace was soon restored, the Chinese and the Soviets continued to distrust each other.

China's relations with the United States, however, began to improve. In 1971, the United States dropped its opposition to Communist China's bid to join the UN. As a result, the People's Republic of China was admitted to the UN in October 1971. The next year, President Richard M. Nixon visited China and met with Chinese leaders. Seven years later, under President Jimmy Carter, the United States formally recognized the People's Republic of China. Since that time, relations between China and the United States have remained cautious but generally friendly.

CHINA SINCE MAO Under the leadership of Mao Tse-tung and Premier Chou En-lai, the Chinese people made some important gains. Health care, for example, was improved, illiteracy was greatly reduced, and famine was less common. In addition, Chinese women had gained equal status with men. But these accomplishments were made at great cost, for many people who opposed the Communist takeover of China were executed during the years that Mao ruled China.

Then, in 1976, both Mao and Chou died. Following their deaths there was a struggle

The historic meeting in 1972 between President Richard Nixon of the United States and Mao Tse-tung, the leader of Communist China, marked the beginning of friendlier relations between the two countries. Formal diplomatic relations between the two nations were reestablished in 1978.

among different groups of Chinese Communists for leadership of the country. For a short time, Mao's wife, Chiang Ch'ing (Jiang Qing) and three other radical Communists sought to control the government. But in October 1976, the four radicals—known as the Gang of Four—were arrested for treason and were expelled from the government. The next year, a moderate Communist, Teng Hsiao-p'ing (Deng Xiaoping), emerged as the dominant political figure in China.

Under Teng's leadership, many changes took place in China. For example, the development of agriculture, industry, defense, and science was stressed, while Communist party doctrine was played down. Plans were made to build more iron and steel plants, to expand coal mining and railway lines, and to improve harbor facilities. China increasingly turned to Western countries and to Japan for technological aid and for financial help to reach these goals.

By the early 1980's, however, China's leaders realized that their country could not afford to pay for many of the ambitious economic improvements suggested in the late 1970's. As a result, the country's economic plans were significantly trimmed. Despite this change, large loans and credits were made available to China from international sources. Thus, in the final decades of the twentieth century, China's leaders were still hoping to make their country a modern industrial power by the year 2000.

QUESTIONS FOR REVIEW

1 *What kind of warfare did Mao Tse-tung believe would be most effective in defeating a powerful enemy?*

2 *How did Mao Tse-tung hope that the Great Leap Forward would benefit China?*

3 *Why did Soviet-Chinese relations change in the mid-1950's?*

2 JAPAN: MODERN INDUSTRIAL GIANT

Japan's industrial power has continued to grow in recent years. Japanese factories have turned out many different goods that are sold worldwide. However, there were also many problems as Japan's economy expanded.

Since World War II, Japan has been governed by conservative leaders. But many different groups have opposed the policies of the government. In international relations, Japan has worked to promote nuclear disarmament. The worldwide marketing of Japanese goods has caused problems with other countries in recent years. During this period, many Japanese have questioned the wisdom of continued economic growth within their country.

AN EXPANDING ECONOMY The rapid economic recovery of Japan after World War II was matched by continued economic growth in recent years. During the 1950's, the Japanese concentrated on building up their heavy industry. As a result, in the 1950's Japan became the world's leading shipbuilder and the third largest maker of iron and steel. After heavy industry was well established, the Japanese moved into the manufacture of computers and electronics. In addition, Japanese factories turned out huge quantities of cars, television sets, and cameras, which were sold all over the world. By the 1960's, Japan's gross national product—GNP—was increasing by more than 11 percent a year.

To support the growing manufacturing operations, new kinds of business groupings emerged in Japan. Instead of the family-centered *zaibatsu*, the Japanese developed large enterprise groups that included banks and insurance companies, real estate firms, and clusters of companies engaged in many different businesses. These organizations

Air and water pollution have become increasingly serious problems in Japan in recent years. On the left, industrial wastes are carried along a river near Tokyo, and above, Tokyo is shrouded in thick smog.

became so powerful that by the mid-1970's, 175 centralized companies held over 21 percent of all capital in Japan.

Overseas trade was of vital importance to Japan's economic growth. The Japanese made far more goods than could be used in the home islands. By selling goods all over the world, the Japanese earned money to buy the raw materials and food that their country lacked. By the early 1980's, however, some industrialized countries charged that their domestic markets were being flooded with Japanese goods. This led to calls for the Japanese to voluntarily limit their exports, especially the exportation of automobiles.

JAPAN'S ECONOMIC PROBLEMS Even though Japan's economy has grown in recent years, there have been some serious problems. Between 1974 and 1976, for example, there was a severe recession in Japan. Consequently, the government was forced to stimulate employment by spending money for public works.

The Japanese faced other problems because of the country's growing population. These people lived in a land area about the size of California. Almost 60 percent of Japan's 120 million people lived in only 4 major urban areas. This concentration of people caused housing and sanitation problems. In addition, as the population grew, there was an increase in automobile ownership and in traffic. Thus, huge traffic jams often clogged the streets of Japanese cities.

Air and water pollution were additional problems that were caused by economic growth. The great industrial area along the eastern—or Pacific—coast of Japan was one of the most polluted regions in the country. At times, the capital city of Tokyo was covered by thick smog caused by car and factory fumes. Some Japanese factories poured their wastes into inland waters and into the ocean. This practice harmed food supplies, since fish from inland and coastal waters were sometimes poisoned by these wastes. At first, the Japanese government was slow in taking steps to stop pollution.

669

But by the 1980's, strict laws had been passed to protect the environment.

Another economic problem centered on Japan's lack of raw materials and of farmland. For example, between 95 and 100 percent of the oil, iron ore, wheat, cotton, sugar, and soybeans used by the Japanese was imported from other countries. In 1973, oil-producing countries cut their shipments of oil to many industrialized countries because of war in the Middle East. Japan was hurt by this move, since its industries depended heavily upon energy from oil. This oil embargo showed Japan's vulnerability because of its dependence on foreign oil.

THE POLITICAL SCENE   Prime Minister Yoshida [yoh-shi-dah] dominated Japanese politics for several years after World War II. Under his leadership, the Japanese government followed domestic policies that favored business and economic growth. In 1950, the American occupation authorities allowed Yoshida to set up the National Police Reserve to handle internal security in Japan. Over the next few years, the police reserve became the basis of Japan's Self-Defense Forces.

During the 1950's, Japan's major political party—the Liberal Democratic party, or LDP—was formed. This group was set up when two conservative groups, the Liberal party and the Democratic party, joined forces. Since the 1950's, the major opposition to the LDP has been from socialist groups, Communists, and other less powerful parties. These opposition groups were generally too divided to seriously challenge the power of the LDP.

During the 1960's, Japan was led in turn by Prime Ministers Ikeda and Sato. While Sato was in office, the government worked closely with business leaders at home and with the United States on foreign-policy questions. During the 1970's, Prime Minister Miki came to power. He was a popular leader because of his efforts to control pollution and the power of big business.

In the early 1980's, a political leader named Suzuki became the prime minister of Japan. In 1981, Suzuki visited the United States and a number of countries in Western Europe and Southeast Asia to discuss economic and political problems. Prime Minister Suzuki resigned in late 1982, and the nation faced the challenge of finding a new leader.

FOREIGN RELATIONS   Since World War II, Japan has worked to promote world peace in dealing with other countries. The great suffering caused by the war deeply affected the Japanese people. In the 1946 constitution, the Japanese government renounced war as a means of settling international disputes.

In keeping with this policy, Japan joined the UN in 1956. Since that time, Japan has worked through the UN to help settle disputes and to prevent armed conflict among countries. In addition, the Japanese have tried to promote worldwide nuclear disarmament.

Japan and the United States have worked together on many international issues since the end of the Allied occupation in 1952. An indication of this friendship was shown between the 1950's and the 1970's, when the United States returned several islands taken from Japan during World War II. The United States and Japan have also signed a Treaty of Mutual Cooperation and Security. In addition, close trade ties have developed between the two countries. By the early 1980's, however, there was growing concern over the influx of Japanese goods into the United States. As a result, the Japanese agreed to voluntarily limit the export of cars to the United States for three years.

In 1956, Japan and the Soviet Union signed a document that ended the state of war between the two countries and set up diplomatic relations. However, no peace treaty was ever signed between Japan and the Soviets. One reason for this was the question of Soviet control of four of the

Kuril Islands, portions of which Japan also claimed. In 1981, the two countries agreed to hold talks on outstanding questions, including the control of the disputed islands.

Japan and China set up diplomatic relations after meetings in 1972. Since that time, relations between these two Asian countries have continued to develop.

JAPAN TODAY Japan has become an important world power as its economy has continued to grow. Recently, however, the economy has been growing at a slower rate than in the 1960's. Efforts have been undertaken to increase trade between Japan and Southeast Asia. In this way, the Japanese hope to reduce their country's dependence on trade with the United States.

Some Japanese leaders have suggested that continued economic growth has brought more harm than good to Japan. These leaders have pointed out that Japan's environment has deteriorated because of the damage caused by industrial air and water pollution. According to these critics, the government should work to improve housing and social services, rather than concentrate on economic growth. But other leaders have stated that economic growth is needed to make it possible to pay for improvements without raising taxes. Thus, as Japan moved into the 1980's, the country faced new and complex social, economic, and political challenges.

QUESTIONS FOR REVIEW

1 *What kind of industry was greatly expanded by the Japanese during the 1950's?*

2 *How has overseas trade been of vital importance to Japan's economic growth?*

3 *Why have some Japanese leaders suggested that continued economic growth has harmed Japan?*

3 INDIA: MAKING DEMOCRACY WORK

After a long struggle, India gained its independence from Great Britain in the mid-1940's. Under Prime Minister Nehru, moves were made to improve India's economy, educational system, and public health. At the same time, the Indian government tried to avoid involvement in the cold war.

In recent years, Prime Minister Indira Gandhi faced internal unrest and political opposition. But in spite of these and other problems, many economic and social gains have been achieved by the Indian people.

THE INDEPENDENCE MOVEMENT During the 1920's, Mohandas K. Gandhi [GAHN-dee] emerged as the leader of India's movement for independence from Great Britain (see Biography on page 673). As head of an important political group—the India National Congress—Gandhi urged a policy of nonviolent civil disobedience toward the British. This disobedience involved such things as refusal to pay taxes, to attend British schools, or to obey laws that were considered unjust.

As efforts for independence grew, however, there was fear among India's Muslims that they would be treated unfairly by the country's Hindu majority when India became free from British rule. As a result, the Muslim leader Muhammad Ali Jinnah urged that a separate country be set up for India's Muslims.

When World War II began, India took part in the war effort against Germany and Japan. After the war, British leaders decided to grant independence to India. However, in 1946, before India became independent, fighting broke out between Hindus and Muslims. In an effort to stop the bloodshed, British and Indian leaders agreed to create a separate Muslim nation. Thus, when India became independent in 1947, Pakistan was set up as the national home for India's

India's vast population has often been used to provide the labor needed to complete the many economic projects carried out under India's five-year plans, which were begun in 1951. Here, Indian workers, using only essential heavy construction equipment, work to finish a hydroelectric dam on one of the country's many rivers.

Muslim people. Pakistan itself consisted of two regions—East Pakistan and West Pakistan.

The division of India, however, led to many problems. Millions fled their homes to avoid the threat of religious persecution. Thus, Hindus in Pakistan went to India, while Muslims in India moved to Pakistan.

The year after India became independent, the great nationalist leader Mohandas Gandhi was killed. He was shot by a Hindu who hated the Indian leader for his tolerance toward Muslims. After Gandhi's death, Jawaharlal Nehru [NER-oo] became the prime minister of India.

EFFORTS TOWARD DEVELOPMENT A major objective of Prime Minister Nehru's was to improve the Indian economy. Under his leadership, the first of several five year plans designed to raise economic output was launched in 1951. The goals of this plan were to expand industry and to raise living standards. The plan focused on agriculture, irrigation, and transportation. Railroad tracks and equipment were repaired or replaced, and irrigation and hydroelectric projects were undertaken. There was some improvement in agricultural yields. But even with an increase in food grain production, India had to buy about 4 million tons (3.6 million metric tons) of wheat from the United States in 1951.

Under the second five year plan, food grain production was raised again. Coal production was also raised, and the country's industries also began making machine tools, diesel engines, and even bicycles. A third five year plan, introduced in the 1960's, led to higher outputs of steel, electricity, cement, and fertilizer. To aid the Indians' efforts to improve their country's economy, technical and financial help was provided by several industrialized countries. Further steps to raise India's industrial and agricultural output were undertaken in five year plans launched in the 1970's. By raising industrial output and food production, the Indian government hoped to generate jobs and to improve nutrition for the Indian people.

(Text continued on page 674.)

Biography

India's Great Soul

In 1869, India's great leader, Mohandas K. Gandhi, was born to a deeply religious Hindu family. As a young man, he was sent to London to study law. After completing his studies, Gandhi returned to India in 1891. But his law practice in India was not successful. Two years later, Gandhi went to South Africa to follow a legal career. At that time, South Africa, like India, was controlled by Great Britain. While living in South Africa, Gandhi struggled to end the discriminatory practices often used against Indian workers in that country. During this struggle he developed the idea of using nonviolent civil disobedience to draw attention to unfair and discriminatory laws. Even though he was arrested many times, Gandhi continued working to end the discrimination against Indian workers. Eventually, some reforms were enacted by the British in South Africa.

Gandhi returned to India in 1915, and within a few years he became the leader of the movement for India's independence from Great Britain. Gandhi worked tirelessly to draw attention to the discriminatory measures used by the British in India. As part of the nonviolent resistance, Gandhi urged Indians to boycott the courts, withdraw from schools and colleges, refuse to serve in the army, and refuse to run for elective office. Gandhi was jailed many times, but he believed that there was honor in being jailed for a just cause.

After India gained its independence in 1947, Gandhi was disappointed by the fighting that took place between Hindus and Muslims. He sincerely wanted India to be a united country, where all Indian peoples could live in peace. In 1948, Gandhi began fasting to stress his desire for an end to the bloodshed among Hindus, Muslims, and other groups. After religious leaders promised to halt the fighting, Gandhi ended his fast. But a few days later, Gandhi was killed by a Hindu who opposed Gandhi's tolerance of other religious beliefs.

During his lifetime, Gandhi was known as *Mahatma*—Great Soul—by the millions of Indians who respected his leadership. Today, Gandhi is honored by the Indian people for his efforts in behalf of India's independence. Gandhi is also respected throughout the world for his tolerance and concern for others as well as for his ideas of using nonviolent resistance to bring about social change.

As part of his nonviolent resistance to British policies in India, the popular leader Mohandas K. Gandhi often fasted in the hope of forcing British officials to change their policies. Here, the great leader dictates a letter to a secretary after ending a five-day fast.

Magnum

Important gains were also made in improving India's educational system, despite a lack of teachers, books, and school buildings. By the mid-1970's, over 100 million students of all ages were being educated in the country's 648,000 schools. As a result, literacy in India reached a national average of over 30 percent. The government also took steps to improve public health in India. Malaria, cholera, and smallpox, for example, were sharply reduced. In addition, many new hospitals and clinics were built. The improvements in health care and in nutrition raised average life expectancy in India to more than 50 years by the early 1980's.

INDIA'S FOREIGN RELATIONS India also faced serious problems in dealing with other countries after gaining independence. Under Prime Minister Nehru, the Indian government tried to follow a policy of *nonalignment*—neutrality—in the cold war between the Western democracies and the Communist world. Nehru felt that the internal problems facing India were far more important than the cold-war confrontation between East and West. India also strongly supported the UN.

During the late 1950's and early 1960's, fighting broke out between Communist China and India over disputed border lands in northeastern India. In 1962, Indian forces moved into lands that India felt were wrongly held by China. But Chinese armies repulsed the Indian troops and then moved across India's northeastern frontier. After a short time, the Chinese withdrew. India's defeat, however, partially shattered the policy of nonalignment, as American and British military aid was sent to help India fight the Chinese.

India was involved in another war in 1965. At that time, fighting broke out along the India-Pakistan border over the disputed land called Kashmir. After India's armies scored impressive gains, a cease-fire was arranged by the UN. The Soviet Union then mediated the dispute by arranging for both sides to withdraw.

In 1971, a civil war erupted in Pakistan. During the fighting, millions of people living in East Pakistan fled to India. India supported East Pakistan in its efforts to form an independent nation separate from West Pakistan. After a short but bloody conflict, West Pakistan was defeated. East Pakistan became the independent country of Bangladesh. By March 1972, most of the 9 million refugees who had fled to India returned to Bangladesh. In addition, over 50 countries had recognized the People's Republic of Bangladesh as an independent nation.

In the early 1980's, India and China improved their relations. At that time, a high-ranking Chinese official visited India for the first time since the two countries fought along their border in 1962. In late 1981, Chinese and Indian officials met in China to discuss ways to settle their border dispute. Although these talks have settled nothing, the two countries have continued meeting in the hope of reaching an agreement.

POLITICAL CHANGES IN INDIA While India's leaders worked to deal with foreign problems, many important political changes took place within the country. In May 1964, Prime Minister Nehru died. Following the death of this popular leader, Lal Bahadur Shastri [SHAHS-tree]—a member of Nehru's cabinet—became India's second prime minister. However, he died suddenly less than two years later.

After Shastri's death, there was a bitter struggle for leadership between Indira Gandhi—Nehru's daughter—and Morarji Desai [de-SIY]. Indira Gandhi represented the liberal wing of the Congress party, while Desai represented the conservative branch of the party. Even though she had little administrative experience, Indira Gandhi had enough support to be the first woman chosen as India's prime minister.

Prime Minister Gandhi faced growing public unrest over food shortages and unemployment after coming to power. Dissension also grew within the Congress party. In the election of 1967, the Congress party received only 40 percent of the popular vote. By 1969, the party was hopelessly split between those who favored Gandhi and those who opposed her leadership. Despite this split, Gandhi's branch of the Congress party won a stunning victory in the election of 1971 by capturing a large majority of the seats in Parliament.

Four years later, however, Prime Minister Gandhi faced a serious challenge after being found guilty of campaign fraud during her 1971 election campaign. Even though there were public protests and demands for her resignation, the prime minister refused to give up her office. Using the excuse of a national emergency, the elite Central Reserve Police arrested hundreds of the prime minister's political enemies. At the same time, all civil rights were suspended, and the press was censored.

As the tension eased, conditions began to return to normal over the next two years. Then in March 1977, Indira Gandhi was defeated in her bid for reelection to Parliament and her branch of the Congress party lost control of the government. As a result, Morarji Desai, supported by a coalition of groups opposed to Gandhi, became the new prime minister.

In 1979, a split developed within the coalition. Desai resigned and new elections were held early in 1980. Indira Gandhi's party—now called the Congress-I party—won the election, and she regained her seat in Parliament and became India's prime minister for a second time.

INDIA TODAY As the leader of the world's most populous democracy, Prime Minister Gandhi has faced serious problems in recent years. India's population, for example, has continued to grow rapidly. By the early 1980's, almost 700 million people were living in India. Providing food for this immense population has been a constant problem. Through the use of chemical fertilizers, high-yield grains, and irrigation projects, farm output has been raised. Indian farmers, however, still have not been able to grow enough food to keep up with the population growth.

Another serious problem for India in recent years has been soaring inflation. By mid-1981, the rate of inflation had reached over 20 percent a year. The rising cost of goods caused much hardship for the Indian people, most of whom were very poor. For example, the average income per person in India was only 80 dollars a year in 1981.

Internal problems over religion, language, and the caste system also caused unrest. The constitution of 1950 outlawed discrimination against members of India's lowest caste—the untouchables. But many Indians still looked upon the untouchables as inferior and unworthy of equal treatment.

Since 1955, the Indian government has launched several extensive campaigns to eliminate caste discrimination throughout the country.

Prime Minister Indira Gandhi (left) accompanied Britain's Prime Minister Margaret Thatcher during a recent tour of India by the British leader.

4 SOUTHEAST ASIA: PROBLEMS AND CONFLICT

Much of Southeast Asia was wracked by warfare and instability after 1945. Immediately after World War II, France tried to reestablish its control over Indochina. But the French were ousted from their former colony by nationalist and Communist groups. Then in the 1960's and 1970's the United States became entangled in a long and costly war in Southeast Asia, as American leaders tried to halt communist expansion.

Following America's withdrawal from Southeast Asia, the Communists gained control of several countries. But differences among these Communists led to more fighting. Thus, by the 1980's, Southeast Asia was still an area of turmoil.

In spite of these problems, much progress has been made in India in recent years. For example, the role of women in India's society has increased greatly. As a result, women have entered government service and the professions in growing numbers. The fact that India's government was headed by a woman showed the growing importance of women in India. Although many problems remained, the Indian people looked forward to continued progress in the 1980's.

QUESTIONS FOR REVIEW

1 Who became the leader of the movement for independence in India in the 1920's?

2 How did Prime Minister Nehru's attitude about the cold war affect India's foreign policy?

3 Why was there a serious government crisis in India in the mid-1970's?

FRANCE AND INDOCHINA The area of Southeast Asia known as Indochina—present-day Vietnam, Laos, and Cambodia (Kampuchea)—became a French colony in the late 1800's. During World War II, these lands came under Japanese rule. After Japan's defeat in 1945, the French government moved to reestablish its control over Indochina. However, in Vietnam, the Communist leader, Ho Chi Minh, had set up an independent government under the *Vietminh*—a nationalist group. The French and the Vietminh tried to settle their differences, but the French refused to grant complete independence to Vietnam. Ultimately, negotiations broke down, and in 1946, the French became embroiled in a bitter conflict with the Vietminh for control of Vietnam.

Under the shrewd leadership of Ho Chi Minh, the Vietminh waged a guerrilla war against the French. By enlisting the help of Vietnamese peasants, the Vietminh was able to gain control of the rural areas of Vietnam, while the French held the cities.

Using guerrilla tactics, the Vietminh slowly wore down French resistance. By the early 1950's, the French had lost their will to fight. Then in 1954, the French stronghold at Dien Bien Phu in northeastern Vietnam fell to the Vietminh after a 55-day siege. Following this humiliating defeat, arrangements were made for peace talks between the French and the Vietminh.

French and Vietminh officials met in Geneva, Switzerland, to work out a peace settlement. Under the terms of the agreement, Laos and Cambodia became independent countries. Vietnam was temporarily divided into two countries until elections to unite the country could be held. The Communist Vietminh under Ho Chi Minh was given control of North Vietnam. South Vietnam became an independent republic. Thus, with the signing of the Geneva agreement, French rule in Southeast Asia was ended.

THE VIETNAMESE WAR Following the withdrawal of France from Southeast Asia, the United States became increasingly involved in the affairs of South Vietnam. The American government was anxious to stop the spread of communism in Southeast Asia.

Even though the Geneva agreement called for elections in Vietnam to unite the country under one government, the leaders of the north and the south could not agree on how these elections should be conducted, and Vietnam remained divided into two countries. North Vietnam's Ho Chi Minh, however, was determined to bring South Vietnam under communist control. As a result, North Vietnamese soldiers moved into South Vietnam and worked to gain support in the rural areas of the country. In addition, the *Vietcong*—South Vietnamese Communists—began attacking areas of South Vietnam in the late 1950's.

As the fighting intensified, American military advisers and equipment were sent to aid South Vietnam. At the same time, the Vietcong received aid from the Soviet Union and Communist China, as well as from North Vietnam.

As the United States became increasingly involved in the war in Vietnam in the 1960's, American soldiers often aided South Vietnamese forces in looking for Vietcong guerrillas. Here, two Vietcong captives are closely questioned by South Vietnamese and American soldiers about possible hideouts used by other members of the Vietcong.

Photo Trends

677

Although American forces began withdrawing from South Vietnam in 1969, fighting between the two Vietnams continued for several years. After the collapse of South Vietnam's government in 1975, the North Vietnamese quickly took control of South Vietnam. Here, Vietcong tanks move into the South Vietnamese capital of Saigon on the morning of April 30, 1975.

The war continued to escalate in the mid-1960's. The North Vietnamese army increasingly supported the Vietcong, while thousands of American troops aided South Vietnam's forces. Over half a million Americans were serving in South Vietnam by the late 1960's.

While the fighting increased, the government of South Vietnam changed several times, as different leaders tried to win the war and to solve the country's problems. But despite the changes in leadership, there was little popular support for the war from many of the people of South Vietnam.

THE END OF THE WAR The late 1960's were a time of growing anxiety in the United States over America's role in the war. Despite thousands of American battle casualties and billions of dollars spent in war costs, the Vietcong and the North Vietnamese did not surrender. Americans increasingly wondered about their country's involvement in the war. As discontent grew, antiwar protests spread throughout the United States.

In response to the growing antiwar sentiment, President Richard M. Nixon began taking American forces out of South Vietnam in 1969. Efforts toward peace were renewed as talks between the United States and South Vietnam on the one hand and North Vietnam and the Vietcong on the other were begun. Finally, after years of negotiations a cease-fire agreement was signed in January 1973.

The United States quickly withdrew its forces from South Vietnam. But fighting continued between the two Vietnams. Then, in early 1975, the North Vietnamese mounted a major invasion of South Vietnam, in clear violation of the peace accord of 1973. As the military situation grew worse, the government of South Vietnam disintegrated. The war ended abruptly in April 1975, when South Vietnam surrendered to the northern Communists. The next year, North Vietnam and South Vietnam were joined into the single country of Vietnam.

OTHER PROBLEMS IN SOUTHEAST ASIA
The end of the war in Vietnam did not bring

peace to Southeast Asia. At first much of the fighting was confined to border clashes between rival Communist groups in Cambodia (Kampuchea) and Vietnam. Then, in 1977, the Vietnamese invaded Cambodia and seized control of the country. A Vietnamese-backed government was set up in 1979, and two years later, rigidly controlled elections were held.

The fighting in Southeast Asia has left a tragic legacy of suffering. Thousands of refugees from Cambodia, Vietnam, and Laos—also under Communist rule—have fled from their homes to escape the warfare and the oppressive Communist governments. Some refugees, known as *boat people*, sailed in small vessels, hoping to find a welcome in other lands. But many of the other Asian countries refused to admit these refugees.

As the sad story of the refugees became known, the UN and other international relief groups joined together to help these people. But relief efforts have often bogged down. As a result, the suffering caused by the turmoil in Southeast Asia has continued.

QUESTIONS FOR REVIEW

1 *What Communist leader directed the Vietminh guerrilla war against the French?*

2 *How did the Vietminh gain control of the rural areas of Vietnam?*

3 *Why did antiwar protests spread throughout America in the late 1960's?*

CHAPTER SUMMARY

After years of civil war, China fell under the control of Mao Tse-tung and the Communist party. China's new leaders worked to modernize their country and to organize it along communist lines. However, growing tensions between the Chinese and the Soviet Union led China to move toward closer relations with the United States and the Western world.

Following World War II, Japan's postwar economy expanded tremendously, and by the 1970's, the country had become a great economic power. But rapid economic growth has led to many problems in Japan in recent years.

During the postwar period, India gained its independence from Great Britain. Since then, India's leaders have tried to avoid involvement in the cold war, working instead for economic and social growth. In recent years, India made considerable progress, despite major internal problems.

Throughout Southeast Asia, Communist leaders worked to dominate the region after French moves to regain their colonies in Indochina failed. After a long struggle to stop communist expansion in Vietnam, the United States withdrew from the region. Violence and upheaval continued, however, as opposing Communist groups fought for control of Southeast Asia's emerging countries.

CHAPTER 34 IN REVIEW

IMPORTANT WORDS, NAMES, AND TERMS
1 Explain, define, or identify each of the following:

Long March
United Front
Taiwan
Great Leap Forward

communes
Prime Minister Suzuki
Mohandas K. Gandhi
civil disobedience

nonalignment
Vietminh
Vietcong
boat people

FACTS AND IDEAS
2 How was the Cultural Revolution designed to bring the Communist party close to the people of China?

3 What new kinds of business groupings emerged in Japan after World War II to support Japan's industrial growth?

4 Why did relations between India and China change in the 1980's?

5 Why did the United States become increasingly involved in South Vietnam after the withdrawal of France from Southeast Asia?

ANALYZING VISUAL MATERIAL
6 Study the pictures on page 669. How do you think that the different kinds of pollution shown might affect the quality of life of the Japanese people?

7 Look at the picture on page 678. Describe how the people of Saigon seem to be reacting to the arrival of Vietcong military forces as they move into the city.

CONCEPTS AND UNDERSTANDINGS
8 What was Mao Tse-tung's strategy regarding China's peasants during his struggle against the Nationalists?

9 How has a rapid expansion of Japan's population caused problems for the Japanese people?

10 Why did Prime Minister Nehru believe that India should follow a policy of nonalignment in the cold war?

11 What was the result of the American withdrawal from Vietnam?

PROJECTS AND ACTIVITIES
12 Japan has become one of the most industrialized countries in the world. You and several other students might conduct a survey among the members of the class to determine the number and kind of Japanese products found in the students' homes today. Compile a list of these goods and share your findings with the class to demonstrate the impact of Japanese trade on the American economy.

13 Since 1949 the Chinese Nationalists have been in control of Taiwan. Investigate the government and economy of Taiwan. Also find out how relations between the United States and Taiwan have changed in recent years. Present your findings to the class. Then discuss how the differences between Taiwan and Communist China might be resolved.

35 AFRICA AND THE MIDDLE EAST

1 Emerging Nations in Africa 2 The Middle East and Southwestern Asia 3 A Region of Continuing Conflict

Many changes took place in Africa after World War II. New nations were set up in lands once held by European powers. Some of these new countries adjusted to independence with little difficulty, but in several of the new nations, independence brought many problems.

Important changes also took place in the Middle East after World War II. The establishment of the Jewish state of Israel in 1948 led to violence as Arab countries refused to recognize Israel's right to exist. The Soviet Union took advantage of the unstable conditions in the Middle East to further Soviet influence.

Throughout the 1960's and the 1970's, the continuing Arab-Israeli conflict erupted into warfare several times. Even though Egypt and Israel settled some of their major differences in 1979, the Middle East remained a volatile region into the 1980's.

Leo de Wys Inc.

These colorfully dressed women of Namibia represent one facet of the great diversity of Africa, which is a continent of many cultures.

1 EMERGING NATIONS IN AFRICA

After World War II, colonialism in Africa ended as European powers granted independence to their colonies. But the change to independence was difficult because of many problems.

Several of the new African countries made great progress in improving living standards for their people. In foreign affairs, most of the new countries of Africa tried to stay out of the cold war. Nevertheless, Communist and non-Communist countries worked to build their influence in Africa.

THE PROBLEMS OF INDEPENDENCE As you read in Chapter 29, most of Africa was controlled by several European nations before World War II. After the war, however, the pressure for independence increased. As a result, colonialism faded, and over 50 independent nations were set up in Africa between the late 1940's and the 1980's.

These new countries faced many challenges. For example, the people in many of the new African states had not been allowed to take part in government during the years of colonial rule. Thus, few Africans were prepared for national self-government.

Another problem was the lack of unity in some of the new African countries. When the European powers set up their African colonies, borders were drawn without regard for the lands held by local tribal groups. Therefore, several tribes were ruled under a single colonial government. After colonialism ended, these tribes often felt no common loyalty to their new national government. Thus, some of the new African countries faced the problem of unifying different and frequently hostile tribal peoples.

Another obstacle to unity involved the conflict that emerged between traditional ways of life and European ways of life. During the years of colonial rule, some Africans began to reject African customs and to follow European ways of life. Other Africans, however, clung to traditional customs. These people were looked upon as backward by the Africans who eagerly accepted European ways. The differing attitudes toward European customs only added to the lack of unity.

An additional problem was the lack of education among the African peoples. Under European rule, few Africans had been allowed to gain an education. As a result, most citizens of the new African countries could neither read nor write. Even among those Africans who had gained an education, few were trained well enough to staff the different departments within each new government.

Since gaining power in 1965, Mobutu Sese Seko has worked to build a strong government in Zaire.

These problems added to the difficulties facing many of the new African nations. As a result, there was often instability while the African peoples were adjusting to their newly gained independence.

ZAIRE The transition to independence was an especially tragic experience for the people of the Belgian colony called the Belgian Congo. After demands for independence had resulted in violence, the Belgians decided to grant independence to the Belgian Congo in June 1960. But the people were not prepared for self-government. Violence erupted immediately. Tribal groups fought, the army rebelled, and fighting broke out between Africans and Europeans. In addition, the mineral-rich province of Katanga [kuh-TAHNG-guh] broke away from Congo, in part because of the encouragement of Western business interests.

The violence continued for a number of years, but finally, through the efforts of the UN, an uneasy peace was established and the country was reunited. In 1965, General Joseph Mobutu took control of Congo and set up a dictatorship. He changed his name to Mobutu Sese Seko, and the country was renamed Zaire [ZIYR]. These changes were part of Mobutu's plan to eliminate European influence in the former Belgian colony.

After coming to power, Mobutu worked to improve Zaire's economy. However, a worldwide recession, as well as inflation, reduced the demand for copper, one of the country's main sources of revenue. In 1977, attempts were made by rebels who had been living outside Zaire to again separate Katanga— which had been renamed Shaba—from the country. But the government defeated the rebels with the aid of Western countries. By the 1980's, Mobutu was still working to improve Zaire's economy.

NIGERIA There was also turmoil in Nigeria after that former British colony became independent in 1960. The difficulty began in 1966, when army officers belonging to the

POLITICAL		SOCIAL AND ECONOMIC
Nasser became ruler of Egypt	~1954	
Belgian Congo granted independence	~1960	
	1961~	UN condemned policy of apartheid
Independent republic of Zambia set up	~1964~	Sierra Leone launched program to develop rubber industry
	1965~	Construction began on hydroelectric project on Tana River in Kenya
Six-day war between Israel and Arab nations	~1967	
	1968~	Aswan High Dam in Egypt completed
Golda Meir became prime minister of Israel	~1969	
President Nasser died and was succeeded by President Sadat	~1970	
	1973~	Arab oil embargo
	1975~	Suez canal reopened after being closed in 1967 during Arab-Israeli war
Civil war in Angola	~1976	
Menachem Begin became prime minister of Israel	~1977	
	1978~	World population reached an estimated 4.4 billion
Camp David Accords signed		
Khomeini regime came to power in Iran	~1979	
President Sadat assassinated	~1981	Organization of Petroleum Exporting Countries—OPEC— announced cut in oil production
	1982~	
American embassy in Beirut bombed	~1983	

Ibo [EE-boh] tribe revolted and took over the government. The unrest continued as the Ibo leaders were forced out of power. The next year, the Ibo leaders tried to secede from Nigeria and set up the independent state of Biafra [bee-AF-ruh] in eastern Nigeria. For more than two years, the country seethed with conflict, and a million people died from the fighting and from starvation as the war raged. Finally, Biafra surrendered in January 1970.

The military leaders of Nigeria then began working to rebuild the country. Since Nigeria had large oil resources, money from the sale of oil was used to improve living conditions in the nation. New factories and schools were built, and transportation facilities were improved. Then, in 1979, a civilian government came to power. The new government worked to develop Nigeria's industries while making the nation less dependent upon imports—particularly food.

RACIAL TURMOIL The transition to independence in much of Africa was marked by racial conflict. South Africa, for example, followed an official policy of *apartheid* [uh-PAHR-TAYT]—strict separation of the races—even before severing all ties with Britain in 1961. Under apartheid, blacks and people of mixed racial background were forced to live apart from white South Africans. Segregation was strictly enforced. Blacks and those of mixed race could not go to the same schools or use the same beaches, theaters, or even park benches as whites. Blacks and those of mixed race also could not travel without carrying special pass books, which contained detailed information about each person. Any black or person of mixed race who was found without a pass book could be arrested and held by the police.

One of the leaders in the struggle for black rights in South Africa was Chief Albert Luthuli [lu-TOO-lee]. He urged that black Africans use nonviolent methods to gain equality. In 1960, Luthuli was awarded the Nobel peace prize for his support of nonviolence to gain rights for black South

The policy of strict separation of races—apartheid—that is followed in South Africa is reflected in this sign reserving a beach for the use of white people only. Many nations have openly criticized South Africa for its discriminatory racial policies. In addition, many of these nations have worked to influence the South African government to ease its harsh racial practices.

Jacob Sutton/Photo Trends

Africans. During his acceptance speech, Luthuli criticized the South African government when he stated that in South Africa,

> all skilled and highly paid jobs are for whites only, . . . all universities of any academic merit are an exclusive preserve of whites, . . . and . . . almost one million Africans a year are arrested and jailed or fined for breaches of innumerable pass and permit laws which do not apply to whites.

The same year, South Africa was torn by violence when some blacks, convinced that peaceful methods were not working, protested against the pass-book laws. The police fired on a crowd of protesters in Sharpeville, and 69 Africans were killed and 180 were wounded.

In 1979, the South African government removed some of the racial restrictions. But few meaningful changes were made, since black South Africans could still not work or live where whites lived and worked. The situation remained largely unchanged into the 1980's. Blacks could not serve in Parliament or vote for members of Parliament.

There were also problems in the former British colony of Rhodesia during the 1970's as the white minority there worked to keep black Africans from taking part in government affairs. After several years of turmoil, however, black Africans gained control of the government in the late 1970's. In 1980, the name of the country was changed to Zimbabwe.

AFRICAN ACHIEVEMENTS Although the new countries of Africa faced many problems during the early years of their independence, important gains were made that improved life for many Africans. Education, for example, was a prime goal, as new nations worked to make certain that their people could read and write. Universities provided training for future lawyers, doctors, and teachers, while special skills programs were used to train technicians. The number of schools in African countries increased after they gained independence. Today, these schools are striving to train enough professionals and technicians to meet the growing needs of the new African countries.

Since the 1960's, efforts have been made to improve public health. African peoples have been taught about nutrition, cleanliness, and infant care in an effort to prevent illnesses. Many African countries have taken part in research projects designed to find the causes of sicknesses that are common in Africa. Some countries have started vaccination programs to stop the spread of diseases.

Improved living conditions have also developed as many of the new African governments have worked to raise farm output through loans and technical help to farmers. Transportation and communications have been improved and hydroelectric power projects have been undertaken to help African industries grow. The Organization of African Unity (OAU) was set up in 1963 to further economic and political cooperation between African countries.

Unfortunately, the presence of valuable natural resources in many of the new African countries has led to interference in African affairs by other countries. Many of these resources were important to the world's industrialized nations. Although African governments wanted to sell their resources, they did not want the industrialized countries to interfere in African affairs to gain these resources. Such interference—frequently called *neocolonialism*—led to instability in some of the new African states as non-African governments worked to influence the policies of African governments. Neocolonialism also led to African distrust of some of the industrialized countries.

The cold war made neocolonialism a problem for the newly independent countries of Africa. These nations needed financial and technical aid from advanced countries, such as the United States and the Soviet Union. However, many Africans did not want to accept any aid if they had to

The unrest caused by the civil war in Angola in the 1970's was apparent as refugees awaited transportation out of the troubled nation.

take part in the cold-war struggle between the Western democracies and the Communist world. As a result, most African countries tried to follow a policy of nonalignment in the hope of avoiding involvement in the cold war.

FOREIGN INFLUENCES IN AFRICA Even though African countries tried to stay out of the cold war, the Soviet Union and its ally Cuba became deeply involved in African affairs as both nations worked to expand their influence. Communist China was also involved in Africa in the 1960's and the 1970's. China lent money to African countries for agricultural and economic development and helped build a railroad in eastern Africa. However, the Chinese became increasingly concerned about their own economic development. As a result, China reduced its foreign-aid programs and became less involved in Africa in the 1980's.

Soviet and Cuban involvement in Africa centered around military aid to African leftists. The Soviet Union and Cuba, for example, helped a leftist government gain power in the former Portuguese colony of Angola. The Soviets and the Cubans continued aiding the Angolan government in its fight against moves to overthrow the leftists during the late 1970's. In addition, Soviet weapons were being supplied by Angola's leftist government to an African nationalist group called the South West Africa People's Organization (SWAPO). SWAPO was helping Namibia, in southwestern Africa, in its struggle for independence from South Africa.

The Soviet Union and Cuba also supported Ethiopia's leftist government in the late 1970's as it battled rebel groups and fought with neighboring Somalia over disputed lands. Between December 1976 and October 1977, the Soviets supplied Ethiopia with 500 million to 800 million dollars worth of military aid. By November 1977, Cuba had sent about 400 military advisers to Ethiopia.

In the early 1980's, however, growing resentment at the continuing Communist presence in Africa developed among many African leaders. In 1981, Liberia asked the Soviet Union to reduce its diplomatic staff by more than half. Moreover, Soviet military advisers had been either expelled from or asked to leave several African countries. Although sizable Cuban forces remained in Angola and Ethiopia, in general, Communist groups faced difficult times in Africa in the early 1980's. Thus, the future of Communist involvement in Africa was becoming increasingly uncertain.

The United States was also involved in Africa in the early 1980's. Under President Reagan, the United States encouraged American businesses to invest in Africa. In addition, the American government appeared to favor the rebels in Angola, who were fighting against that country's leftist government. In 1981, steps were taken to allow American military aid to be sent to the Angolan rebels. However, there was considerable opposition to this move within the United States. In the years ahead the Communist countries and the democratic nations are expected to continue their efforts to influence affairs within Africa.

QUESTIONS FOR REVIEW

1 *For what reason did the newly independent nations of Africa find it difficult to find trained people to administer government affairs?*

2 *How did Nigeria's military leaders use the country's oil resources to improve living conditions for Nigerians?*

3 *Why did Soviet and Cuban efforts to spread communism in Africa become increasingly difficult in the early 1980's?*

2 THE MIDDLE EAST AND SOUTHWESTERN ASIA

Other areas in which there has been turmoil since the end of World War II are the Middle East and southwestern Asia. The establishment of the Jewish state of Israel in 1948 led to disputes and wars between Israel and the surrounding Middle Eastern countries. At the same time, there was much unrest within many Middle Eastern countries as they tried to solve domestic problems. The Soviet Union invaded Afghanistan in late 1979. But the Soviets were unable to establish firm control over the country.

THE ESTABLISHMENT OF ISRAEL After World War I, the Middle Eastern land of Palestine had been turned over to Great Britain under a mandate from the League of Nations. During the 1930's, the Jewish population of Palestine increased as Jewish people left Europe to escape Nazi persecution. But this influx of refugees only led to growing Arab resentment against the Jewish people for living in Palestine—land that the Arabs felt belonged to them. Thus, when World War II ended, the British turned to the UN for a solution to the problem of Palestine.

Over the years, several Jewish leaders had suggested that a national homeland for the Jewish people be set up. In the 1890's, a movement called Zionism had been started in Europe by Theodor Herzl. Zionists wanted Palestine to be made a Jewish national homeland. After the Palestine question was turned over to the UN in 1947, Zionist leaders urged the world body to make Palestine a Jewish homeland. But Arab leaders argued against this idea by pointing out that Palestine had been under Arab control for centuries and that its population was predominantly Arab.

After listening to both Jewish and Arab leaders, the UN decided that Palestine

After World War II, survivors of the cruel anti-Jewish policies of the Nazis in Europe hoped to emigrate to Palestine to begin a new life.

should be divided into a Jewish state and an Arab state. Jewish leaders quickly accepted the plan. Thus, in May 1948, the new Jewish homeland—called Israel—was set up in Palestine. The Arabs, however, did not accept the UN plan and refused to recognize Israel. As a result, no Arab state was set up in Palestine.

The day after Israel was established, armies from five Arab nations attacked the new country. Even though the Israelis were outnumbered and poorly armed, they defeated the Arabs and gained control of additional land. A cease-fire was arranged by the UN in January 1949. The war settled nothing, however, for the Arab countries still refused to recognize Israel's right to exist.

The Arab-Israeli war also left an enormous refugee problem. Hundreds of thousands of Palestinian Arabs had left Israel to escape the fighting and to avoid living under Jewish rule. These people lived in other Arab countries in squalid camps amid great hardships. Arab leaders felt that the refugees had a right to return to their homes in Palestine. Jewish leaders, however, wanted the Arab refugees to be resettled in Arab countries.

EGYPT Another country that has been beset by problems in recent years is Egypt. Egypt gained its independence from Great Britain in 1922. The British, however, retained special rights in Egypt, especially in the area of the Suez Canal, which was owned by British and French interests. During World War II, Britain maintained armed forces in Egypt to protect the Suez Canal and the important sea routes to the oil-rich Middle East.

After the war ended, there was growing public discontent in Egypt over the continuing presence of British soldiers around the canal. Egyptians were also angered by the corruption within their government and by Egypt's defeat in the 1948 Arab-Israeli war. Growing dissension led a group of Egyptian army officers to seize the government in 1952. After a time of instability, Colonel Gamal Abdel Nasser emerged as

688

Egypt's prime minister in 1954. Later he was also chosen president of Egypt.

One of Nasser's first goals was to improve Egypt's economy. Through the programs started by Nasser, the output of autos, cement, steel, and chemicals was expanded. In addition, cooperatives were set up to help Egyptian farmers get seeds and tools at reasonable prices.

Nasser kept pressing the British to remove their soldiers from the Suez Canal Zone. Britain finally agreed to have all of its soldiers out of Egypt by mid-1956. Then Nasser began working to strengthen Egypt's military power. After several Western countries refused to sell arms to Egypt, Nasser signed an agreement in 1955 to buy military goods from Czechoslovakia. The growing ties between Egypt and the Communist bloc disturbed the United States and Great Britain. The two democracies withdrew an offer to help Egypt build a dam across the Nile River near Aswan.

In response to the American and British action, Nasser ordered the seizure of the Suez Canal in July 1956. He asserted that the tolls on ships passing through the canal would be used to build the Aswan dam, although Egypt later turned to the Soviet Union for help with the dam. Egypt then closed the Suez Canal to Israeli ships and stopped ships going to and from Israel.

Relations between Israel and Egypt continued to deteriorate. In addition, Eqyptian military power grew stronger as the Soviet Union supplied weapons to Eqypt. Fearing an Egyptian move, Israeli armies attacked Egypt in October 1956, and occupied most of the Sinai Peninsula. Israel's allies, Britain and France, entered the war by bombing Egyptian bases and landing soldiers in the Suez Canal Zone. Following an emergency meeting of the UN, the United States, the Soviet Union, and other nations demanded that Britain, France, and Israel withdraw immediately from Egypt. The three countries agreed, and a 10-nation peacekeeping force was sent by the UN to patrol the border between Egypt and Israel. Although the fighting had ended, the tensions that had caused the war still remained.

IRAQ AND JORDAN Unrest has been a major factor in Middle Eastern affairs for many years. During World War II, for example, some army officers in Iraq tried to bring their country into the war on the side of the Axis powers. Britain, however, sent troops into Iraq under a 1930 treaty, and the pro-Axis leaders were ousted.

In 1948, Iraq joined several other Arab countries in a war against the new Jewish state of Israel. The defeat of the Arab powers in this war led to uprisings in Iraq in 1948 and in 1952. Order was finally restored with the help of the army. But in 1958, Iraqi army officers revolted and set up a new government. Despite this change, unrest in Iraq continued, especially as the minority Kurdish people agitated for self-rule. In 1980, war broke out between Iraq and its neighbor Iran. By 1982, the Iraqis had been forced out of Iran, but they had stopped Iranian moves to push deep into Iraq.

Transjordan was another Arab country that took part in the war against Israel in 1948. After the fighting ended, Transjordan held about half of Jerusalem and most of the land on the west bank of the Jordan River. This land became part of Transjordan, which in 1949 became known as Jordan.

The land that Jordan gained was inhabited by many Palestinian Arabs. In addition, many more Palestinians had fled from Israeli-held land to Jordan. Most of these refugees resented the establishment of Israel. As a result, some Palestinians formed guerrilla groups that attacked Israeli towns and military bases. One important group was the Palestine Liberation Organization (PLO), which was dedicated to the establishment of an independent country for the Palestinians. The frequent raids led Israel to attack guerrilla bases in Jordan.

After another Arab-Israeli war in 1967,

In the rugged mountains of Afghanistan, guerrilla fighters opposed the invading Soviet forces. By using guerrilla warfare, the Afghan rebels were able to prevent the Soviet armies from gaining a firm hold on the rural areas of the isolated southwestern Asian country.

Jordan lost its sector of Jerusalem and its territory on the west bank of the Jordan River. Seven years later, King Hussein gave up Jordan's claim to these lands. The Jordanian ruler stated that if the Israelis withdrew, the west bank lands should become part of an independent Palestinian state. Throughout the early 1980's, King Hussein was successful in keeping his country out of further involvement in the Arab-Israeli conflict and in building Jordan's economy.

AFGHANISTAN Unrest has continued in Afghanistan since that southwestern Asian country gained its independence from Great Britain in 1919. During the 1920's, tribal and religious groups opposed the sweeping reforms that were introduced by the Afghan government. As a result, several leadership changes took place between 1929 and 1933, and efforts toward reform moved ahead slowly. During World War II, change continued at a slow pace as Afghanistan was affected by economic hardship and inflation.

In 1953, a new ruler came to power, who followed a policy of neutrality in the cold-war struggle between the democratic world and the Communist bloc. Since Afghanistan was a nonaligned country, the Afghan government accepted aid from both the United States and the Soviet Union. This aid enabled the Afghans to begin building irrigation systems, schools, roads, and factories.

In 1964, a new constitution was approved that provided for a democratic government in Afghanistan. But there were disputes among the nation's leaders over reform programs. In addition, there was little support for the new government from the Afghan people. Thus, democracy failed to gain a foothold.

In 1973, Afghan military leaders revolted and took over the government. Five years later, a pro-Communist government was set up after a revolt by leftist military leaders. While coming to power, the leftists had been given military and financial help by the Soviet Union. Many Afghans resented the growing influence of the Soviet Union in their country. In many cases, the people disliked the new leftist regime because its policies often conflicted with the Islamic laws that were followed in Afghanistan. The antigovernment feelings intensified, and a revolt erupted shortly after the leftists came to power in 1978. Fighting between government forces and the rebels quickly spread throughout the country.

In December 1979, the Soviet Union invaded Afghanistan to aid the leftist government in its fight against the rebels. The invasion was condemned by most nations and by the UN. However, the Soviet Union continued to attack rebel strongholds.

As the war went on, the Afghans used guerrilla tactics to harass the Soviet forces. Throughout the early 1980's, the Soviets continued to attack Afghan towns and villages. Some diplomats speculated that the Soviet Union was trying to cripple the guerrillas through these attacks in the hope of reaching a negotiated settlement of the war.

UNREST IN TURKEY Since the end of World War II, Turkey has also experienced unstable conditions. After the war ended, the Soviet Union demanded land in eastern Turkey and the right to build military bases along the straits leading from the Black Sea into the Mediterranean Sea. However, the United States, in accordance with the Truman Doctrine, which was announced in 1947, gave Turkey vast amounts of military and economic aid. This aid enabled the Turks to resist the Soviet threats.

During the 1950's, the Turkish government encouraged foreign investments in the country and favored less government control of the economy. These policies led to dissatisfaction, especially among Turkish military leaders. These leaders seized control of the Turkish government in 1960, and in the following year a new constitution was adopted. Free elections were held and the country returned slowly to civilian rule during the 1960's.

An age-old dispute led to a serious crisis in the 1960's between Turkey and Greece over the Mediterranean island of Cyprus. After fighting broke out between the Greeks and the less numerous Turks living on the island, both Turkey and Greece threatened to intervene. Peace was restored, but trouble flared again in 1974, when Greek military leaders on Cyprus overthrew the president of Cyprus. The Turks then invaded the island and threatened to set up a separate state in that part of Cyprus held by the Turks. Since that time, Cyprus has continued to be a point of contention between Turkey and Greece.

Aside from external problems, the Turkish government also had to handle certain internal problems. Unrest over high taxes and inflation in the late 1960's led to growing terrorist activity against the Turkish government. In the years that followed, various civilian governments were unable to resolve Turkey's problems, and conditions remained unstable. In 1980, to halt the growing disorder, army leaders again stepped in and took over the government. The military leaders acted swiftly to reduce terrorism.

Although the new leaders of Turkey promised to restore parliamentary government when conditions improved, progress toward the restoration of civilian rule was slow. The lack of a definite program to bring Turkey under civilian rule led the Common Market to delay a 650-million-dollar aid plan for Turkey. This money was to have been used to improve the Turkish economy. Thus, the people of Turkey faced continuing hardships as the chances for economic improvement seemed bleak.

QUESTIONS FOR REVIEW

1 *What was the goal of Zionism?*

2 *How did President Nasser of Egypt react when the United States and Great Britain withdrew their offer to help Egypt build the Aswan dam?*

3 *Why did many Afghans dislike the pro-Communist government that was set up in their country in 1978?*

3 A REGION OF CONTINUING CONFLICT

Unrest in the Middle East continued to intensify throughout the 1960's and the 1970's. The government of Iran was overthrown in 1979. Hostility between Arab countries and Israel led to several wars. But the chances for peace brightened in 1979, as Israel and Egypt signed new peace agreements.

Continuing problems, however, threatened the peace in other areas of the Middle East. Religious differences resulted in violence in Lebanon. Israel invaded Lebanon in 1982. Thus, the continuing turmoil in the Middle East remained a major threat to world peace.

TURMOIL IN IRAN The Middle Eastern country of Iran began to emerge as a modern nation after Riza Khan Pahlavi became the *shah*—ruler—in 1925. Under his leadership, industry was encouraged, transportation was improved, and new legal codes were enacted.

During World War II, British and Soviet forces moved into Iran to protect its oil fields and transportation facilities. The shah resigned in protest and his son, Mohammed Riza Pahlavi, became the new shah.

After World War II ended, many Iranian nationalists urged an end to all foreign influence in Iran. The growing nationalism among Iranians eventually led to the seizure of the British-controlled Anglo-Iranian Oil Company by the Iranian government in 1951. However, two years later, the demand for oil on world markets declined and Iran's oil production virtually stopped. After suffering heavy losses, Iran arranged to have foreign companies sell its oil. Oil production and sales rose. The increased revenue from the sale of oil enabled the Iranian government to undertake internal improvements.

As Iran's wealth grew, Shah Mohammed Pahlavi began a series of reforms. In 1963, the shah began a program of land reform to distribute land to the people. In addition, women were given the right to vote. But these and other reforms led some conservative Iranians to criticize the shah for changing Iranian society. In addition, liberal critics felt that the shah's government was too dictatorial. These people pointed out that there was little political freedom in Iran and that the dreaded secret police was used in attempts to silence all opposition to the shah.

In 1978, riots swept through Iranian cities as liberals, religious groups, and landowners joined to overthrow the shah. One of the most important opposition leaders was a powerful *ayatollah* [AH-yuh-TOHL-uh]—Muslim religious leader—named Ruhollah Khomeini [koh-MAY-nee]. As strikes and demonstrations against the government spread, the shah fled into exile, and in February 1979, the revolutionaries took over the government.

Although a civilian government was officially in charge of Iran, the Ayatollah Khomeini held the real power. He declared that Iran would become an Islamic republic based on Islamic laws. Not all Iranians, however, supported the new government.

In October 1979, the shah was allowed to come to the United States for medical treatment. This move enraged many Iranians. A group of Khomeini's followers seized the American embassy in Teheran, and over 50 Americans were taken hostage. The Iranians demanded that the shah be returned to Iran for trial, but the United States refused to meet this demand. The hostages were set free in early 1981 after lengthy negotiations.

Iran made some economic progress in 1981 by resuming oil exports and overseas trade. As the war with Iraq that had begun in 1980 dragged on, however, the nation's economic recovery was affected. At the same time, unrest within Iran continued as opposition to the Khomeini regime mounted.

THE CONTINUING ARAB–ISRAELI CONFLICT

While Iranians worked to solve their internal problems, Arab-Israeli differences continued to keep the Middle East in turmoil. After the 1956 Arab-Israeli war, an uneasy peace existed between Israel and its Arab neighbors for about 10 years. During these years, however, Arab and Israeli forces along Israel's borders clashed.

In the spring of 1967, the Egyptians closed the Strait of Tiran to prevent Israeli ships from reaching the Red Sea. Israel looked upon the closing of the strait as an act of war. Thus, the third war between the Arabs and the Israelis broke out in June 1967. Within a few days, Israel's forces had inflicted heavy losses on the Arabs, and the UN arranged a cease-fire. By that time, Israeli forces had taken the Gaza Strip, the Sinai Peninsula, and the land on the west bank of the Jordan River. Although the fighting had ended, the war had settled nothing. Israel refused to leave the land it had occupied, and the Arabs refused to recognize Israel's right to exist until the Israelis withdrew.

Sporadic border fighting between Israel and Arab countries continued during the early 1970's. Then, in October 1973, war erupted again as Egyptian and Syrian forces attacked Israel. The UN helped to arrange new cease-fire agreements, and most of the fighting had ended by May 1974.

In 1978, there was a major breakthrough toward peace in the Middle East. At that time, President Jimmy Carter of the United States held talks with Prime Minister Begin of Israel and President Sadat of Egypt to discuss an end to the Egyptian-Israeli conflict. Sadat had succeeded Nasser as Egypt's leader. In 1979, after lengthy negotiations, agreements—the Camp David Accords—were reached that called for a gradual Israeli withdrawal from the Sinai Peninsula, the Gaza Strip, and the land west of the Jordan River. Many Arab leaders, however, criticized Sadat for signing these agreements and refused to recognize the Camp David Accords. Then, in October 1981, worldwide apprehension about the chances for peace in the Middle East increased after

(*Text continued on page 695.*)

President Carter (center), President Sadat (left) of Egypt, and Prime Minister Begin (right) of Israel shake hands in a display of friendship during the signing of the Camp David Accords in 1979. Many people hoped that the Camp David Accords would lead to other agreements, which would further reduce tensions in the Middle East.

Robert Rathe/Alpha

693

Life at the Time

Iran Under Khomeini

After the overthrow of the shah of Iran in 1979, the country came under the control of Ayatollah Ruhollah Khomeini. His rule greatly affected life in Iran, as was indicated by a report made by an American magazine correspondent who visited the country in the early 1980's.

"Food shortages abound. The economy teeters on the brink of chaos. Inflation runs at between 25 and 28 percent. . . .

"Although Iran once was one of the world's richest oil nations, men and women stand in line for hours to buy kerosene. Meat is more precious than caviar. . . .

"After three years, Teheran's skyline, against the backdrop of the snow-covered Elburz Mountains, remains starkly unchanged —scores of partly completed high-rise apartment buildings topped by rusting cranes that have not moved since the day the Shah left. . . .

"The city's drivers are as reckless as ever. But traffic has been cut . . . by a rule banning private vehicles downtown. Parts [for cars] are hard to find, and cars are abandoned as they wear out. Few Iranians can afford the black-market price of $25,000 for a new auto or $200 for a new tire.

"Beef and dairy products such as milk and cheese are luxury items. Imports of meat have dwindled, and Iranian cattle are being slaughtered to make up the loss. . . .

"Teheran today is not the bustling city it once was. The mood is one of depression. Fuel conservation has dimmed the lights at night as power cuts of up to 3 hours are ordered. Through the winter, lines for kerosene have lengthened along with those for meat, rice and other staples. . . .

"Some Iranians try to leave. . . . One businessman says he is willing to pay $25,000 or more for an exit visa that would allow him to join his wife and children in Florida. . . ."

Thus, life in Iran in the early 1980's was filled with shortages and problems. Khomeini's power, however, remained strong because of the support of those who shared his religious ideas. But opposition to the Khomeini government was growing among those who belonged to Iran's educated upper class.

Surrounded by Revolutionary Guards, the Ayatollah Khomeini looks sternly at those attending his weekly meeting with the public.

Alfred/Gamma

President Sadat was assassinated. However, his successor—Hosni Mubarak [moo-BAHR-ek]—promised to continue working for peace with Israel.

Although Israel's relations with Egypt improved, relations with other Arab states remained hostile. Much of the Arab opposition to Israel centered around the Palestine Liberation Organization (PLO), which continued to threaten Israeli settlements from bases in Arab countries. Israeli leaders were determined to protect their country by destroying the PLO.

PROBLEMS IN LEBANON The PLO was especially strong in Lebanon, Israel's northern neighbor. Lebanon had been a center of turmoil in the Middle East since gaining its independence in the 1940's. Disputes between Christian and Muslim factions in Lebanon finally led to American intervention in the country in the late 1950's. This intervention enabled the Lebanese government to restore order, and the Americans withdrew.

The unrest in Lebanon continued during the 1960's. Muslims and other groups felt that their economic and political influence was not equal to that of Lebanon's Christians. The country's stability was further threatened by the presence of more than 300,000 Palestinian refugees. Palestinian guerrilla groups sometimes raided Israeli settlements from bases in Lebanon. In retaliation, the Israelis frequently attacked these camps.

In 1975, a civil war erupted in Lebanon as Christians and Muslims fought again. There was great destruction, and thousands of Lebanese were killed. Even though most of the fighting ended in late 1976, sporadic clashes between Muslims and Christians continued.

The presence of PLO bases in southern Lebanon further complicated the situation in the Middle East. Repeated PLO raids into Israel and Israeli raids into Lebanon led the UN to send a peacekeeping force into the area in the late 1970's. Despite this move, fighting between the PLO and the Israelis continued.

In June 1982, Israel moved into southern Lebanon. After bitter fighting that led to many civilian casualties, the remaining PLO members were surrounded in Beirut. With the help of American diplomats, an agreement was reached that called for the evacuation of the PLO to other Arab countries. But the assassination of Lebanon's new president and the massacre of Palestinian refugees in September 1982, during the Israeli occupation, heightened tensions in war-torn Lebanon. By late 1983, Israel was under growing pressure to leave Lebanon. There was also increasing opposition within Israel to the continuing occupation of Lebanon. Thus, the situation in Lebanon remained explosive.

THE IMPACT OF TURMOIL IN THE MIDDLE EAST By the early 1980's, the continuing turbulence in the Middle East was of growing concern to world leaders. Many leaders were aware that the Arab-Israeli conflict was a serious threat to world peace. In addition, American and Soviet involvement in the Middle East only added to the complexity of the situation. The United States was a strong supporter of Israel, and the Soviet Union supported some Arab nations. As fighting erupted at different times in the Middle East, there was a real danger of direct involvement by the United States and the Soviet Union. Because of its tremendous oil reserves the Middle East remained important to both the Communist and the free nations of the world.

The importance of the Middle East was apparent in the oil embargo of 1973. For years the Arab countries had reacted angrily to America's support for Israel. Then, when war erupted between Israel and Egypt and Syria in 1973, many Arab countries stopped shipping oil to the United States and to the Netherlands. This step was taken in retaliation for American and Dutch support for

Israel. An oil shortage developed and prices soared. The oil embargo showed that the Arab-Israeli conflict could directly affect economic activity in nations throughout the world.

An important issue in the continuing Middle Eastern conflict involved the right of the Palestinians to have an independent homeland. This idea was strongly supported by Arab countries, but the proposal was rejected by Israel. However, in recent years there has been growing pressure on Israel to accept the idea of a Palestinian homeland.

An additional factor that added to instability in the Middle East was Israel's invasion of Lebanon in June 1982. This move led to worldwide criticism of the Israelis and to strained relations between the United States and Israel. American leaders worked to find a diplomatic solution that would persuade Israel to withdraw from Lebanon. However, some Israeli leaders looked upon the American efforts as meddlesome.

The future of the Middle East remained unclear in the early 1980's. Many people hoped that some gains toward solving the Arab-Israeli conflict might be made through meetings of the countries involved in the disputes. Most diplomats, however, felt that Arab-Israeli hostility would continue until both sides showed greater willingness to compromise.

QUESTIONS FOR REVIEW

1 *For what reasons did some Iranian liberals criticize their government in the 1960's?*

2 *How did the government of Iran change in 1979?*

3 *Why was there much unrest in Lebanon in the 1960's and the 1970's?*

CHAPTER SUMMARY

After World War II, many colonies in Africa gained their independence from European countries. But the people of these lands, in general, were not prepared for self-government. As a result, there was frequent unrest in many of the new African nations. Although most of the new countries tried to avoid the cold war, Communist and non-Communist nations often worked to further their influence in Africa.

In the Middle East, the establishment of Israel in 1948 led to many problems. Since Arab countries opposed the new Jewish state, the Middle East was the scene of constant fighting. The presence of thousands of refugees from the lands now held by Israel added to the unrest in the Middle East.

In 1979, the Soviet Union invaded Afghanistan. In the same year the government of the shah of Iran was overthrown and a government based on Islamic law was set up. Adding to the turmoil was Israel's invasion of Lebanon in 1982. Despite some moves toward peace by Egypt and Israel, the Middle East remained a major trouble spot in the world well into the 1980's.

CHAPTER 35 IN REVIEW

IMPORTANT WORDS, NAMES, AND TERMS

1 Explain, define, or identify each of the following:

Biafra	neocolonialism	shah
apartheid	SWAPO	ayatollah
Albert Luthuli	Zionism	Ruhollah Khomeini
OAU	PLO	Hosni Mubarak

FACTS AND IDEAS

2 What were some of the restrictions placed on black South Africans under the policy of apartheid?

3 Why did Communist China reduce its involvement in Africa in the early 1980's?

4 Why did the Soviet Union invade Afghanistan in 1979?

5 For what reason was the American embassy in Teheran seized by Iranian revolutionaries in October 1979?

ANALYZING VISUAL MATERIAL

6 Look at the picture on page 686. How does this picture indicate that the people are planning to leave the country permanently?

7 Study the picture on page 690. What kinds of problems would a conventional army face in this kind of terrain? Why might this rugged country be suited for guerrilla fighting?

CONCEPTS AND UNDERSTANDINGS

8 Why was there a lack of unity in many of the African countries that became independent after World War II?

9 How has the Palestinian-refugee problem intensified hostilities between the Israelis and the Arabs?

10 Why was the continuing turmoil in the Middle East a serious threat to world peace in the early 1980's?

PROJECTS AND ACTIVITIES

11 Since most of the European colonies in Africa have become independent nations, you and other members of the class might prepare a map showing the countries of Africa today. Include on your map the locations of Africa's natural resources. Discuss how these resources might affect international relations. Display your map for the class.

12 The Israeli invasion of Lebanon in 1982 was extremely controversial. Investigate the reasons for the Israeli move and the effects of the invasion both on the Arab world and on Israel. Information might be found in news magazines and in newspaper articles. Present your findings to the class. Suggest possible solutions to the Arab-Israeli conflict.

CHAPTER 36 EPILOGUE: PAST, PRESENT, AND FUTURE

1 Meeting the Challenges of Today   2 The World of Tomorrow

The importance of history has often been considered by historians. More than 2,000 years ago, the Roman orator Cicero said, "Not to know what has been transacted in former times is to be always a child. If no use is made of the labors of past ages, the world must remain always in the infancy of knowledge." Thus, history helps make the world intelligible by showing us how our present situation came to be what it is.

Today, air travel and rapid communication have brought all peoples into closer contact with different ways of life. As a result, people in the developing countries want the same kind of life as that enjoyed by the people living in the developed countries. Thus, the world's peoples are becoming interlinked by common desires as human society becomes more global.

The world faces challenges today that few people would have imagined possible 50 years ago. At the same time, the great achievements made in the twentieth century have improved life for many people around the world. But continued human progress will depend largely on the ability of humankind to solve the challenges it faces today.

Nuclear power-stations such as this one in West Germany have been built in recent years to meet the world's growing energy needs.

1 MEETING THE CHALLENGES OF TODAY

The world faces many challenges in the 1980's. As the world's population grows, there is a need for more food. Energy needs are also rising. These and other problems have added to worldwide unrest in recent years.

THE MEANING OF HISTORY India's first prime minister, Jawaharlal Nehru, once wrote, "Everything changes continually. What is history, indeed, but a record of change." He continued by saying, "And if there had been very few changes in the past, there would have been little of history to write."

As you have learned throughout this book, the history of humankind has indeed been a story of change. But human history has also been marked by adaptation. From the time of the Ice Age to the present, people around the world have learned to live with changing conditions. Two great revolutions—the Agricultural Revolution and the Industrial Revolution—reshaped human life. Each revolution brought challenges and changes. But adapting to new conditions led to additional changes.

Some of the major challenges that threaten the peace and stability of our world today are population growth, the need for food, the energy crisis, and the dangers of pollution. Several possible future challenges are discussed in the second section of this chapter. But first it is important that we look at the challenges that the world faces today.

THE WORLD'S GROWING POPULATION One important challenge that the world faces in the 1980's is the continuing growth in the world's population. Many experts have predicted that by the year 2000, there will be over 6 billion people in the world.

The problem of population growth is complicated by the fact that the largest

This scene in Rio de Janeiro, Brazil, reflects the growing problems of poverty and of urban overcrowding in Latin America.

increases are taking place in the developing nations of the world. The United Nations Fund for Population Activities has predicted that by 2110, the population of the industrialized nations will be only about 13 percent of the world's population. The remaining 87 percent of the world's people will be living in the nonindustrialized and developing nations of Asia, Africa, and Latin America.

Many of these countries are finding it difficult to provide food and work for their people today. For example, in 1982, the World Bank estimated that 1.5 billion people were living in conditions characterized by malnutrition, illiteracy, and disease. In addition, 750 million people were estimated to be living in conditions only slightly

Global Population Expansion

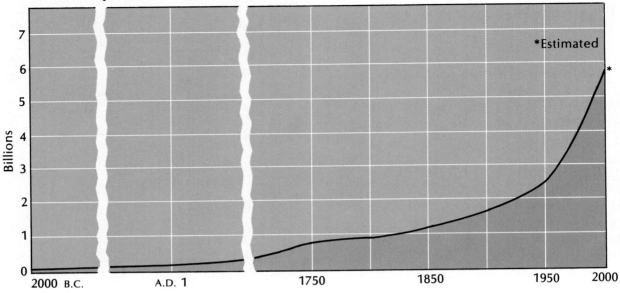

In spite of the rapid growth of the world's population, recent trends indicate a decline in the population growth rate in many nations.

above this level. A conservative estimate is that more than 40,000 children die each day because of poor health or poor living conditions found in the world.

World leaders are increasingly concerned about the earth's ability to support its expanding population. Some experts have pointed out that the resources of the world are limited. While the world's population is growing, the amount of usable land per person is declining. In the early 1980's, about 23 percent of the land on the earth was desert. But an additional 25,000 square miles (64 750 square kilometers) each year is becoming desert through the depletion of land in many parts of the world.

A few experts are hopeful that the earth can support its growing population for many years through better farming methods and improved distribution of resources. Most observers, however, believe that unless population growth is controlled, the world faces increasingly serious problems.

MEETING THE WORLD'S FOOD NEEDS

As the world's population has continued to grow, food production has become more important. Unfortunately, the output of food in the developing countries has failed to keep pace with their population growth. Today, about 75 percent of the world's people live in the nations of Asia, Africa, and Latin America. But these countries produce only about 50 percent of the world's food.

Some worldwide improvement in the output of wheat and rice did take place during the 1950's and the 1960's. At that time, farmers in the developing countries used improved farming methods and high-yield grains to raise their production. This development—called the *Green Revolution*—involved the use of irrigation, fertilizers, and special seeds to raise crop output. But the Green Revolution had its limitations, for many farmers could not afford the supplies required to make the Green Revolution work. In addition, the use of irrigation, fertilizers, and high-yield seeds made growing crops more costly. As a result, food prices rose in those countries where the people were already very poor.

Food shortages have brought extreme suffering to many people in different regions of Africa.

During the early 1980's, several international meetings were held to discuss the world's continuing food problems. Even though food production rose in China and in Latin America in 1981, there were still many countries that were short of food. Today, famine continues to affect parts of Africa and Asia. In 1981, India was forced to import food for the first time in several years, and poor harvests led the Soviet Union to buy wheat from the United States and Canada.

THE WORLD'S GROWING ENERGY NEEDS Another important world problem today concerns the ever-growing demands for energy. The worldwide increase in the use of energy has threatened to exhaust some of the world's resources. For example, the extensive reliance on petroleum has led experts to predict that world petroleum reserves will be gone by the early 2000's. Natural gas reserves are also being rapidly depleted. However, coal reserves are still plentiful, and experts estimate that the world has enough coal to last for another 300 or 400 years.

There are several reasons for the increase in the use of energy around the world. The growth in population has led to a corresponding increase in the world's work force. As more people get jobs, especially in the industrialized countries, more energy is needed to transport workers, to run machines, and to provide light and heat for factories. And as more people earn money from their jobs, they buy energy-using goods, such as cars and electrical appliances. At the same time, there has been an increase in the use of such materials as plastics, fertilizers, and synthetic fabrics, which are made from petroleum. This has led to ever-growing demands for petroleum.

The tremendous growth in the use of energy has taken place mainly in the industrialized countries. As a result, only a small portion of the world's people are using a vast amount of energy. For example, in the early 1980's, Europe, Japan, and the United States contained about 25 percent of the world's population. But the Europeans, the Japanese, and the Americans were using about 75 percent of the world's energy.

The problem of energy has gained worldwide attention. Experts have begun looking for new sources of energy, for ways to make energy more efficiently, and for ways to conserve energy.

THE POLLUTION PROBLEM The world also faces the growing problem of environmental pollution. The air, the water, and the soil in many areas of the world are increasingly being affected by pollutants. The main causes of the air and water pollution are car exhausts and factory fumes and wastes. Other sources of pollution are chemical fertilizers and pesticides, which are harming the soil in many parts of the world.

Eliminating the causes of pollution, however, may create a dilemma for people. Even though cars pollute the air, they are needed for transportation. Factories that pour their wastes into the air and the water also provide jobs for millions of workers.

Fertilizers and pesticides are important in raising farm output for the world's growing population. Thus, finding ways to limit pollution without affecting economic growth is difficult.

The effects of pollution are varied and far-reaching. Air pollution, for example, is linked to lung and breathing disorders. Air pollution is also known to cause rapid deterioration of metal and concrete. Water pollution kills fish and makes water unsafe for drinking. Chemical fertilizers break down the ability of soils to make their own nutrients, and some pesticides destroy organisms needed to make soils fertile.

Pollution has become a major problem because of the accelerated industrialization of the world. Today, the air, the water, and the soil in the most heavily industrialized countries has been damaged by pollutants. However, concerned people in many countries have begun to realize that uncontrolled pollution is a serious threat to the environment. As a result, many governments have been forced to pass laws to control pollution. In some countries, for example, cars cannot be sold unless they are equipped with pollution-control devices.

Despite these measures, pollution is still a problem. Continuing technological change and the resulting increase in pollution have made pollution control difficult. Thus, protecting the environment remains a challenging task.

WORLD TENSIONS In the past few years, unrest has been common in many areas of the world. Much of the tension has been caused by hostility between countries. It has been estimated that over 250 wars of varying intensity have been fought since 1945.

Worldwide terrorist activities have also added to the unrest of recent years. The actions of terrorists have been denounced by most nations. However, this criticism has

Growing concern over the long-range effects of pollution has led to increasing media attention to the problem.

"I knew there'd be a catch in it when they said the meek would inherit the earth."

not stopped terrorist groups from continuing their violent attacks.

The expanding nuclear arms race is another factor causing worldwide unrest. Antinuclear rallies have taken place in many countries as people have become increasingly concerned about the danger of a nuclear war. In the early 1980's, the nations of the world were spending over one million dollars a minute on armaments, including nuclear weapons. This staggering expenditure has continued even though millions of people are living in desperate poverty. In spite of moves toward disarmament, many world leaders are reluctant to weaken their country's defenses by cutting military spending.

Unrest has also increased as the gap between rich and poor nations has continued to grow. About 75 percent of the world's people are living in the developing countries of Asia, Africa, and Latin America. But these nations have less than 20 percent of the world's income. In a recent year, for example, hundreds of millions of people in countries where the gross national product per person was less than 200 dollars a year lived on 30 cents a day or less. In comparison, the GNP per person in the advanced countries was over 9,000 dollars a year.

Today, many poor countries look to the developed countries for economic aid. But these developed nations also have problems to solve and are often unable to provide much help to the poor countries.

QUESTIONS FOR REVIEW

1 *In what parts of the world are the greatest increases in population occurring today?*

2 *How might eliminating the causes of pollution cause a dilemma for people?*

3 *Why has there been growing opposition around the world to the nuclear arms race?*

2 THE WORLD OF TOMORROW

In the years ahead, the people of the world will face ever-changing conditions. New ideas and products will influence all aspects of human life. There will also be new problems to solve. But throughout history, the world's peoples have repeatedly shown that they have the resourcefulness to meet the problems that have challenged their abilities.

THE TECHNOLOGICAL REVOLUTION In the years ahead, rapid technological change will continue to be an important characteristic of life in much of the world. New products and new manufacturing methods will constantly influence people's lives.

One important technological change today is the growing use of robots in factory jobs. Experts predict that by 1990 about 32,000 robots will be in use in automobile assembly plants around the world. Robots are used for such jobs as loading hot metal into stamping machines and welding automobile bodies. In addition, the field of *robotics* — the study of the use of robots — is expanding.

Another important change brought about by the technological revolution is the ever-expanding use of computers. These amazing devices are being used for an endless variety of jobs. For example, computers store information for banks, control robots in factories, record airline reservations, and speed checkouts in supermarkets. In addition, computers are being used in schools to help students learn.

In the future, the role of technology is expected to continue expanding. For example, computers for controlling farm machines and for monitoring crops so that they are properly fertilized may be developed within a few years. In the years ahead, people may use home computers to pay bills and to check their bank accounts.

Scientists also hope to develop computers that can "see" and "hear." Such computers could drive cars or control mobile robots to deliver mail. Robots controlled by "seeing" computers could differentiate between parts on an assembly line and increase the usefulness of robots. Scientists are even working on computers that talk, reason, learn, translate, and answer questions. With such computers, a plant manager could increase production merely by giving an order to the computer that controlled the plant robots.

ADVANCES IN MEDICINE Many important medical advances have been made in recent years. Diseases that were once widespread have been brought under control or eliminated through vaccinations and new medicines. A vaccine to prevent polio, for example, was developed in the 1950's by an American, Dr. Jonas E. Salk.

In recent years, electronic machines have been widely used by doctors for such tasks as checking the vital signs of seriously ill hospital patients. In addition, small devices called *cardiac pacemakers* are being implanted in heart patients to help keep their heartbeat steady. Computer-operated scanning machines are helping doctors learn about

disorders within the body. A mechanical heart has successfully been placed in a person suffering from heart trouble.

There are promising signs of even greater medical gains in the years ahead. Doctors are working to make synthetic blood for use in emergencies when natural blood is not available. Experiments are being carried out to find successful cures for all types of cancer through new drugs and new methods of radiation. An American doctor has found that a new kind of radiation treatment is 40 percent more effective in killing cancer cells than regular X rays. Dentists hope to develop a vaccine that will prevent tooth decay. In the years ahead, people can look forward to other gains that will bring improvements in health care.

NEW SOURCES OF ENERGY Finding new sources of energy has become increasingly important in recent years as the world's petroleum supplies continue to dwindle. Almost half of the world's energy was coming from petroleum in the early 1980's. Another 30 percent of the world's energy needs were being supplied by coal, while natural gas and water were other sources of energy.

In recent years, nuclear fission has been

This truck assembly plant in Michigan uses robots to weld truck bodies together. Unlike human workers, who are often bored by repeating the same work, robots are unaffected by such routine. As a result, the quality of the goods that are assembled by robots is usually quite high.

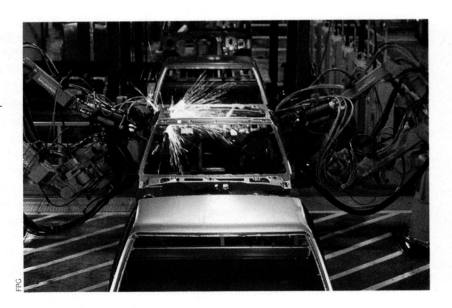

FPG

used on an ever-widening scale to make electricity. Nuclear fission power stations need only small amounts of fuel, and they do not pollute the air as do coal-burning power plants. But the use of this nuclear power source has several disadvantages. Plants using nuclear fission need complicated cooling systems and produce huge amounts of radioactive wastes that remain dangerous for years. Disposing of these wastes is difficult. There is also the danger of an accident, which might release radioactive contamination into the air around the nuclear plant. Because of these dangers, some people have become apprehensive about the risks involved in using nuclear power. As a result, protests against the development of nuclear plants have been becoming more numerous in recent years.

Within a few years, scientists hope to utilize another nuclear process, called fusion. Fusion is a complicated process that uses hydrogen to generate energy. The process has advantages over other ways of producing energy with nuclear fuels. Fusion leaves almost no waste. In addition, there is plenty of hydrogen available from the sea.

Scientists are working on many other new ideas to provide energy for the world in the future. Since the world's coal reserves are huge, researchers are working to find ways of making gas and oil from coal. Projects to generate electricity by wind-driven machines are being studied. Danish scientists have built one such windmill, which produces 4 million kilowatt-hours of electricity a year.

THE WORLD OF TRANSPORTATION In recent years, important changes have taken place in the ways people travel. The automobile is still the major means of transportation in many areas of the world. However, the automobile has increasingly been criticized for using too much fuel and for polluting the air. In addition, the use of the automobile in the developed countries is a major factor in the continuing depletion

Experiments with wind-driven generators may help to solve some of the world's growing energy problems.

of world petroleum supplies. As a result, people in these countries have been urged to use public transportation, which is more fuel efficient than cars. Carmakers are now building cars that use less fuel and cause less air pollution.

Many countries have been working in recent years to improve their intercity passenger-train service, since trains use less fuel per passenger than do planes, cars, or buses. The Japanese are operating a fleet of high-speed trains—the *Bullet trains*—that run at speeds of 135 miles per hour (217 kilometers per hour). The French are using trains that run even faster.

Experiments to raise the speed of trains further are continuing. The French, the Japanese, and the Germans, for example, are testing trains that use magnetic force to hold the cars a few inches above a guide rail.

Other improvements in transportation in the future may permit planes to fly and land by themselves by using on-board computers. Air travel may also be made safer

Julie Houck

The Japanese Bullet trains operate at speeds of well over 100 miles (160.9 kilometers) per hour.

future. Dealing with population growth, nutritional needs, technological change, energy needs, arms control, and pollution will challenge human ingenuity.

People will also continue working to improve the quality of life. In recent years, steps have been taken to ensure that the rights of all peoples be respected. Efforts to gain equal rights for women, to promote education, and to combat racism have also been made. But much remains to be done to overcome social injustice.

Throughout the centuries, the needs of people have remained the same. No matter the age in which people lived, they have sought food, shelter, work, and a sense of meaning in their lives. At times, securing these goals has been difficult. But throughout recorded time, people have used their intellectual and material resources to overcome the challenges facing them.

by having on-board computers alert pilots to possible dangers and suggest ways to correct problems. Within a few years, electric cars that can travel long distances without being recharged may be developed. It is hoped that these and other ideas will make travel safer, easier, and faster in the years ahead.

MEETING CHALLENGES OF THE FUTURE
The world will face many difficulties in the

QUESTIONS FOR REVIEW

1 *What are some of the jobs for which computers are being used today?*

2 *How have electronic machines been used by doctors in recent years?*

3 *Why has the automobile been increasingly criticized in recent years as a means of transportation?*

CHAPTER SUMMARY

The people of the world face many problems. As the world's population expands, there is a growing need for food. Finding new sources of energy and controlling pollution are other concerns today. At the same time, terrorism and the nuclear arms race have contributed to worldwide unrest.

Recent developments in technology, medicine, energy, and transportation have improved life in many ways. Even though problems will continue, the world's peoples are confident that they can overcome the challenges they will face in the future.

CHAPTER 36 IN REVIEW

IMPORTANT WORDS, NAMES, AND TERMS

1 Explain, define, or identify each of the following:

Green Revolution	robots	petroleum
coal reserves	robotics	fusion
pollution	computers	Bullet trains
nuclear arms race	cardiac pacemakers	electric cars

FACTS AND IDEAS

2 According to some experts, what will the population of the world be by the year 2000?

3 How much of the world's energy was being used by the people of Europe, Japan, and the United States in the early 1980's?

4 What are some of the far-reaching effects of air pollution?

5 What are the advantages of nuclear fusion?

ANALYZING VISUAL MATERIAL

6 Study the picture on page 699. What do you think might be some of the problems that could result from the overcrowded conditions that are shown? What difficulties might a government face in trying to solve such overcrowding?

7 Look at the cartoon on page 702. Why do you think that such a cartoon might be a more effective antipollution statement than a newspaper article about the effects of pollution?

CONCEPTS AND UNDERSTANDINGS

8 Why are some world leaders concerned about the earth's ability to support its expanding population?

9 How might the development of computers that "see" and "hear" expand the usefulness of these devices?

10 Why are some countries working to improve their intercity passenger-train service in the 1980's?

PROJECTS AND ACTIVITIES

11 Population experts have become increasingly concerned about the world's expanding population. You and several other students might make a chart showing population expansion in the world from 1850 to the present. Display your chart for the class.

12 Computers are being used for an ever-widening variety of jobs. Do some research into the development of computers, their use today, and their possible uses in the future. Information can be found in books on computers as well as in encyclopedias. Report your findings to the class. Then hold a class discussion on how society might be affected in the future by the growing use of computers.

Using Geography Skills

Maps are very helpful in learning about the world and its people. For example, demographic maps are used to present information on population. Some demographic maps show population density—the number of people living within a certain area. Other demographic maps show the rates of population growth around the world.

One of the serious problems that the world faces today is the continuing expansion of the world's population. The number of people in the world will probably reach 10 billion to 12 billion by the year 2100.

Unfortunately, the most rapid increase in population is taking place in areas of the world that do not have the ability to support large numbers of people. As a result, the people in these lands are forced to live in poor conditions.

The demographic map below shows the rates of population growth in different parts of the world. The higher the rate of population growth, the more quickly a country's population will double. For example, a country that has an annual growth rate of 3.5 percent will double its population in 20 years. A lower growth rate means that doubling the population will take longer.

This map also shows several cities around the world that are growing rapidly. By the year 2000, the population of each of these cities, except Mexico City, will exceed 10 million. Mexico City, however, may contain over 30 million people by the year 2000.

Study this map carefully. Then answer the following questions:

1 According to the map, the slowest rate of population growth is occurring in what areas of the world?
2 What areas of the world show population growth rates that will lead to a doubling of the population within the shortest time?
3 In what areas of the world are the rapidly expanding cities located?
4 After studying this map, to what extent would you agree or disagree with the following statement? "Rapid population growth is a problem in only a few regions of the world." Use the map to support your answer.
5 How might rapid population growth in some areas of the world affect areas where population growth is taking place more slowly?

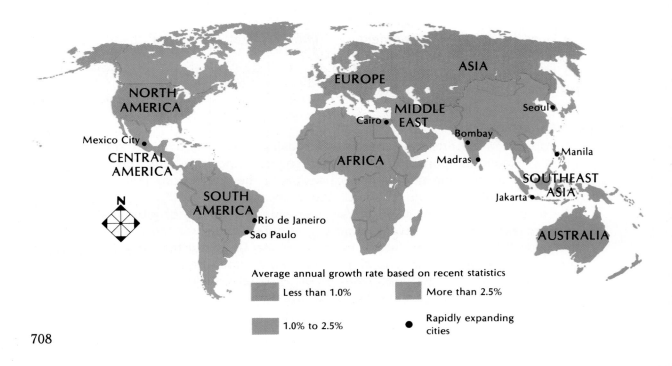

Average annual growth rate based on recent statistics

- Less than 1.0%
- More than 2.5%
- 1.0% to 2.5%
- ● Rapidly expanding cities

UNIT 9 IN REVIEW

CONCEPTS AND UNDERSTANDINGS

1 How was the Helsinki Agreement designed to reduce the international tensions that resulted from World War II and from the cold war?

2 Why did anti-American riots break out in Panama in the 1950's and the 1960's?

3 How did China's Communist leaders work to reshape Chinese society after coming to power in 1949?

4 Why do you think South African blacks and South Africans of mixed races opposed the policy of apartheid?

5 Why was the nuclear arms race of growing concern to many people in the 1980's?

QUESTIONS FOR DISCUSSION

1 Why, in your opinion, is the protection of human rights, as provided in the Helsinki Agreement, such a controversial issue between governments?

2 Why, in your opinion, might the Soviet Union view Eurocommunism as a threat?

3 How would you respond to the following statement? "Gandhi's policy of nonviolent civil disobedience was generally ineffective." Explain your answer.

4 The Arab-Israeli conflict in the Middle East has caused suffering for thousands of displaced Palestinians. How do you think that the problem of these displaced people might be solved?

5 The growing use of robots has led to much speculation about the effects of these machines. How, in your opinion, will robots influence employment in the future?

SUGGESTED READING

Carras, Mary C. *Indira Gandhi in the Crucible of Leadership*. Boston: Beacon Press, Inc., 1980.

Carter, Gwendolen M. *Which Way Is South Africa Going?* Bloomington, Ind.: Indiana University Press, 1980.

Dornberg, John. *Eastern Europe: A Communist Kaleidoscope*. New York: Dial Press, 1980.

Fraser, Nicholas, and Marysa Navarro. *Eva Perón*. New York: W.W. Norton & Co., Inc., 1979.

Rachleff, Owen S. *Young Israel: A History of the Modern Nation the First 20 Years*. New York: Lion Books, 1981.

Santoli, Al. *Everything We Had: An Oral History of the Vietnam War as Told by 33 American Soldiers Who Fought It*. New York: Random House, Inc., 1981.

Thornton, Richard C. *China: A Political History, 1917–1980*. Boulder, Colo.: Westview Press, 1981.

Urwin, W. *Western Europe Since 1945: A Short Political History*. New York: Longman, Inc., 1982.

MAP ATLAS

Europe

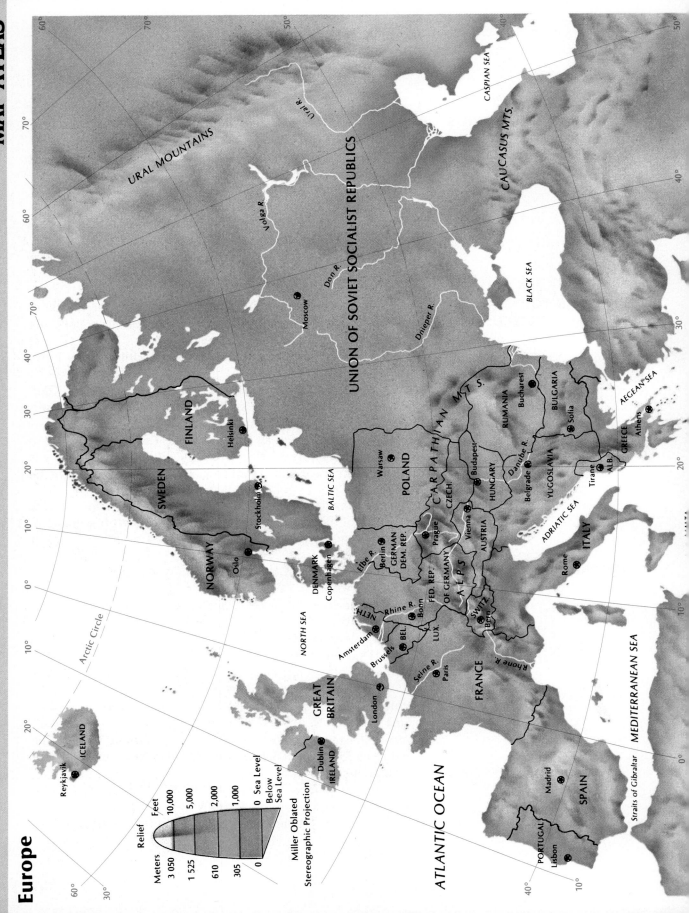

Relief

Meters | Feet
3 050 — 10,000
1 525 — 5,000
610 — 2,000
305 — 1,000
0 — Sea Level
— Below Sea Level

Miller Oblated Stereographic Projection

URAL MOUNTAINS

CASPIAN SEA

CAUCASUS MTS.

BLACK SEA

UNION OF SOVIET SOCIALIST REPUBLICS

Ural R.

Volga R.

Don R.

Dnieper R.

Moscow

FINLAND

Helsinki

SWEDEN

Stockholm

BALTIC SEA

Warsaw

POLAND

CARPATHIAN MTS.

RUMANIA

Bucharest

BULGARIA

Sofia

AEGEAN SEA

GREECE

Athens

Danube R.

Budapest

HUNGARY

YUGOSLAVIA

Belgrade

ADRIATIC SEA

Tirane

ALB.

CZECH.

Prague

Vienna

AUSTRIA

ITALY

Rome

NORWAY

Oslo

DENMARK

Copenhagen

Elbe R.

Berlin

GERMAN DEM. REP.

FED. REP. OF GERMANY

ALPS

SWITZ.

Bern

Rhine R.

Bonn

NETH.

Amsterdam

BEL.

Brussels

LUX.

NORTH SEA

Seine R.

Paris

FRANCE

Rhone R.

GREAT BRITAIN

London

Dublin

IRELAND

Arctic Circle

ICELAND

Reykjavik

ATLANTIC OCEAN

MEDITERRANEAN SEA

Straits of Gibraltar

SPAIN

Madrid

PORTUGAL

Lisbon

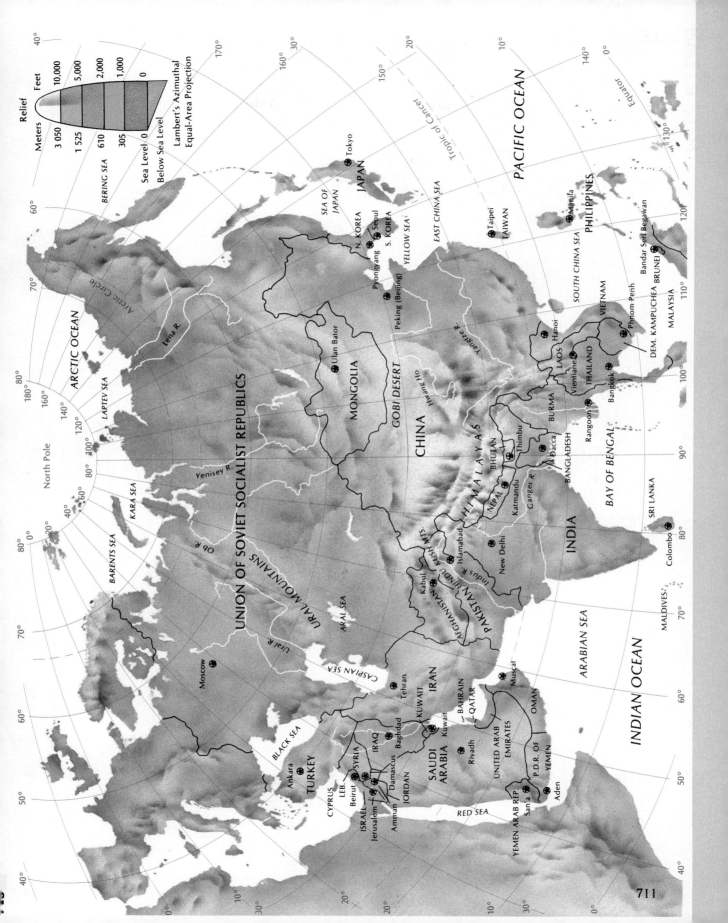

Relief

Meters	Feet
3 050	10,000
1 525	5,000
610	2,000
305	1,000
Sea Level 0	0
	Below Sea Level

Lambert's Azimuthal
Equal-Area Projection

40°
170°
160°
30°
150°
20°
140°
10°
0°
130°
120°
110°

Tropic of Cancer

PACIFIC OCEAN

BERING SEA

Equator

Tokyo
● JAPAN

SEA OF JAPAN

N. KOREA
Seoul ●
● Pyongyang
S. KOREA

EAST CHINA SEA

Taipei ●
TAIWAN

Manila ●
PHILIPPINES

60°

Bandar Seri Begawan ●
BRUNEI

Peking (Beijing) ●

YELLOW SEA

SOUTH CHINA SEA

MALAYSIA

70°

ARCTIC OCEAN

Arctic Circle

LAPTEV SEA

Ulan Bator ●

MONGOLIA

GOBI DESERT

CHINA

Hwang Ho

Yangtze R.

Hanoi ●
LAOS
VIETNAM

DEM. KAMPUCHEA

Phnom Penh ●

80°
180°
160°
140°
120°
100°
80°
60°
40°
20°
0°
20°

Lena R.

UNION OF SOVIET SOCIALIST REPUBLICS

Vientiane ●
THAILAND
Bangkok ●

BURMA

North Pole

Yenisey R.

HIMALAYAS

BHUTAN
Thimbu ●

Rangoon ●

BANGLADESH
Dacca ●

BAY OF BENGAL

KARA SEA

NEPAL
Katmandu ●

Ganges R.

70°

BARENTS SEA

Ob R.

URAL MOUNTAINS

HINDU KUSH MTS.

Islamabad ●
● New Delhi

INDIA

SRI LANKA
Colombo ●

ARAL SEA

AFGHANISTAN

PAKISTAN

Indus R.

Kabul ●

MALDIVES

80°
20°
0°
40°

CASPIAN SEA

ARABIAN SEA

INDIAN OCEAN

Moscow ●

Tehran ●

IRAN

Muscat ●

BLACK SEA

KUWAIT
BAHRAIN
QATAR

OMAN

60°

Ankara ●

Baghdad ●
IRAQ
Kuwait ●

UNITED ARAB EMIRATES

TURKEY

SYRIA
Damascus ●

SAUDI ARABIA
Riyadh ●

P.D.R. OF YEMEN

CYPRUS
LEB.
Beirut ●
ISRAEL
Jerusalem ●
Amman ●
JORDAN

Aden ●

50°

RED SEA

YEMEN ARAB REP.
Sana ●

711

Africa

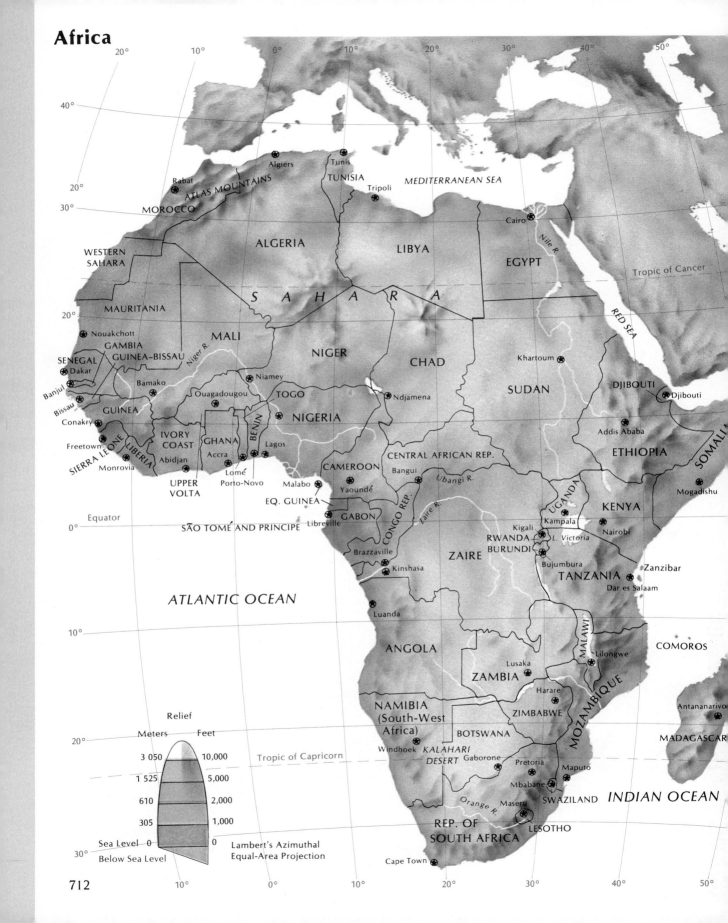

20° 10° 0° 10° 20° 30° 40° 50°

40°

20°

30°

Algiers   Tunis
Rabat
ATLAS MOUNTAINS   TUNISIA
MOROCCO   Tripoli   MEDITERRANEAN SEA

Cairo

MEDITERRANEAN SEA

WESTERN
SAHARA   ALGERIA   LIBYA   EGYPT

Nile R.

20°   Tropic of Cancer

MAURITANIA   S   A   H   A   R   A   RED SEA

Nouakchott
GAMBIA   MALI   NIGER   CHAD   Khartoum
SENEGAL   GUINEA-BISSAU   DJIBOUTI
Dakar   Bamako   Niger R.   Niamey   SUDAN   Djibouti
Banjul   Ouagadougou   TOGO   Ndjamena
Bissau   GUINEA   NIGERIA   Addis Ababa
Conakry   IVORY   GHANA   BENIN   Lagos   CENTRAL AFRICAN REP.   ETHIOPIA
Freetown   COAST   Accra   CAMEROON   Bangui   SOMALIA
SIERRA LEONE   LIBERIA   Abidjan   Lomé   Malabo   Ubangi R.   KENYA
Monrovia   UPPER   Porto-Novo   Yaoundé   Mogadishu
VOLTA   EQ. GUINEA   CONGO REP.   UGANDA
Equator   SÃO TOMÉ AND PRINCIPE   Libreville   GABON   Zaire R.   Kampala   Nairobi
0°   Kigali   L. Victoria
RWANDA   BURUNDI
Brazzaville   ZAIRE   Bujumbura
Kinshasa   TANZANIA   Zanzibar
Dar es Salaam

ATLANTIC OCEAN

10°   Luanda

ANGOLA   MALAWI   COMOROS
ZAMBIA   Lusaka   Lilongwe
NAMIBIA   Harare   Antananarivo
(South-West   ZIMBABWE   MADAGASCAR
Africa)   BOTSWANA   MOZAMBIQUE

Relief

Meters   Feet
20°   Tropic of Capricorn
Windhoek   KALAHARI
3 050   10,000   DESERT   Gaborone
Pretoria   Maputo
1 525   5,000   Mbabane
Orange R.   Maseru   SWAZILAND   INDIAN OCEAN
610   2,000   Cape Town   REP. OF   LESOTHO
SOUTH AFRICA
305   1,000

Sea Level   0   0   Lambert's Azimuthal
Below Sea Level   Equal-Area Projection

712

10°   0°   10°   20°   30°   40°   50°

Australia and the South Pacific

170° 0° 10° 20° 180° 30° 40°

Equator

FIJI
Suva

New Hebrides Is.

New Caledonia I.

PACIFIC OCEAN

NEW ZEALAND

Wellington

SOLOMON IS.
Honiara

CORAL SEA

NEW GUINEA

PAPUA
Port Moresby

INDONESIA

SINGAPORE

Jakarta

INDIAN OCEAN

Tropic of Capricorn

GREAT DIVIDING RANGE

Darling R.

Murray R.

Canberra

AUSTRALIA

GREAT SANDY DESERT

GIBSON DESERT

GREAT VICTORIA DESERT

Tasmania

160° 150° 140° 130° 120° 110° 100° 90°

Relief

Feet	Meters
10,000	3 050
5,000	1 525
2,000	610
1,000	305
0	305
Sea Level	Sea Level
	Below Sea Level

Lambert's Azimuthal Equal-Area Projection

North America

ARCTIC OCEAN

North Pole

BERING SEA

Greenland

Alaska

Arctic Circle

PACIFIC OCEAN

ROCKY MOUNTAINS

Columbia R.

HUDSON BAY

CANADA

Missouri R.

Mississippi R.

Ottawa

Ohio R.

APPALACHIAN MTS.

Washington, D.C.

**UNITED STATES
OF AMERICA**

Colorado R.

Bermuda

ATLANTIC OCEAN

Rio Grande

Tropic of Cancer

MEXICO

GULF OF MEXICO

BAHAMAS

Nassau

Havana

Mexico City

CUBA

Puerto Rico

Santo
Domingo

HAITI

JAMAICA

DOM. R

Kingston

Port-au-Prince

Belmopan

BELIZE

CARIBBEAN SEA

Guatemala City

HONDURAS

Tegucigalpa

GUATEMALA

San Salvador

NICARAGUA

EL SALVADOR

Managua

San José

PANAMA

COSTA RICA

Panama City

Relief

Meters	Feet
3 050	10,000
1 525	5,000
610	2,000
305	1,000
Sea Level 0	0

Lambert's Azimuthal Equal-Area Projection

South America

CARIBBEAN SEA

BARBADOS

Port of Spain
Caracas ⊙
TRINIDAD AND TOBAGO

VENEZUELA

Orinoco R.

Georgetown
Bogotá ⊙
COLOMBIA
GUYANA
SURINAM
Paramaribo

Fr. Guiana

Equator

Quito ⊙
ECUADOR

Amazon R.

PERU

BRAZIL

São Francisco R.

Lima ⊙

ANDES
La Paz
⊙ BOLIVIA

Brasília ⊙

MOUNTAINS

PARAGUAY

CHILE

Tropic of Capricorn

Asunción ⊙

PACIFIC OCEAN

URUGUAY

Santiago ⊙
Buenos Aires ⊙
⊙ Montevideo

ARGENTINA

ATLANTIC OCEAN

Relief

Meters		Feet
3 050		10,000
1 525		5,000
610		2,000
305		1,000
Sea Level 0		0

Falkland Is.

Strait of Magellan

Lambert's Azimuthal Equal-Area Projection

PRONUNCIATION GUIDES

General Pronunciation Guide

When certain words are used for the first time in this book, they are respelled in a special way to help the reader pronounce them. The respelling of a word appears in brackets.

When a word has two or more syllables, the syllables are not usually given equal stress. In the respelling of a word, the syllable or syllables with primary stress are printed in large capital letters. Syllables with secondary stress are printed in small capital letters. Syllables that are not stressed are printed in small letters. Words that have only one syllable are printed in small capital letters.

Below is a list of special letters and letter combinations used for the respelling of words. A description of the way the letter or letters are pronounced and an example of a respelled word follow each letter or letter combination.

a	*a* in *trap* [TRAP]		oo	*oo* in *food* [FOOD]
ah	*a* in *far* [FAHR]			*u* in *rule* [ROOL]
	o in *hot* [HAHT]		ow	*ou* in *out* [OWT]
aw	*a* in *all* [AWL]		oy	*oi* in *voice* [VOYS]
	o in *order* [AWRD-uhr]		th	*th* in *thin* [THIN]
ay	*a* in *face* [FAYS]		th̲	*th* in *that* [TH̲AT]
e	*e* in *let* [LET]		u	*u* in *put* [PUT]
	a in *care* [KER]			*oo* in *foot* [FUT]
ee	*e* in *equal* [EE-kwuhl]		uh	*u* in *cup* [KUHP]
	i in *ski* [SKEE]			*a* in *asleep* [uh-SLEEP]
i	*i* in *trip* [TRIP]			*e* in *term* [TUHRM]
	e in *erase* [i-RAYS]			*i* in *bird* [BUHRD]
iy	*i* in *kite* [KIYT]			*o* in *word* [WUHRD]
	y in *sky* [SKIY]		z	*s* in *atoms* [AT-uhmz]
oh	*o* in *rodeo* [ROHD-ee-OH]		zh	*s* in *measure* [MEZH-uhr]
	ow in *slow* [SLOH]			*z* in *azure* [AZH-uhr]

Pinyin Pronunciation Guide

On January 1, 1979, the government of the People's Republic of China adopted a new system for spelling Chinese place-names and personal names. The new system is called Pinyin for the Chinese word meaning "to spell phonetically." The following is a guide to the new system. It should be noted that traditional names for people and places are used throughout most of this text for easy reference. However, Pinyin is used in the spelling of the names of current Chinese political leaders, since this spelling is now commonly used in newspapers and magazines.

Pinyin Alphabet	Former Spelling System(s)	Standard American Pronunciation	Pinyin Alphabet	Former Spelling System(s)	Standard American Pronunciation
a	(a)	*a* in *far*	o	(o)	*aw* in *law*
b	(p)	*b* in *be*	p	(p')	*p* in *part*
c	(ts)	*ts* in *its*	q	(ch')	*ch* in *cheek*
ch	(ch')	*ch* in *church*	r	(j)	*r* in *right*; *z* in *azure*
d	(t)	*d* in *do*	s	(s, ss, sz)	*s* in *sister*
e	(e)	*e* in *her*	sh	(ch)	*sh* in *shore*
f	(f)	*f* in *foot*	t	(t')	*t* in *top*
g	(g, k)	*g* in *good*	u	(u; ü)	*oo* in *too*; *ü* in German *für*
i	(i; u)	*ea* in *eat*; *i* in *sir* (after *c, ch, r, s, sh, z,* and *zh*)	v	——	*v* in *very* (used for foreign words)
j	(ch, j)	*j* in *jeep*	w	(w)	*w* in *want*
k	(k)	*k* in *kind*	x	(hs)	*sh* in *she*
l	(l)	*l* in *land*	y	(y)	*y* in *yet*
m	(m)	*m* in *me*	z	(ts, tz)	*z* in *zero*
n	(n)	*n* in *no*	zh	(ch)	*j* in *joke*

Special Letter Combinations

In addition to the letters of the alphabet and their sounds, there are special letter combinations that have special sounds in Chinese, depending on where the letter combinations are used in a word. These include:

Pinyin Spelling	Former Spelling System(s)	Standard American Pronunciation	Pinyin Spelling	Former Spelling System(s)	Standard American Pronunciation
ai	(ai)	*i* in *hi*	en	(en)	*un* in *under*
an	(an)	*o* in *on*	ian	(ian)	*yen* in *yen*
ao	(au)	*ow* in *how*	ie, ye	(ieh, yeh)	*ye* in *yes*
ei	(ei)	*ei* in *eight*	ou	(ou)	*o* in *go*

Pinyin also uses an apostrophe (') to indicate that certain vowel combinations should not be pronounced as a single combination but should be separated into two sounds and pronounced in more than one syllable. For example, Xian is pronounced [SHYEN], but Xi'an is pronounced [SHEE-AHN]. (In former spelling systems, however, an apostrophe after a letter meant that the letter should be pronounced with a strong *h* sound.)

INDEX

Key to Index Abbreviations: *c.* = *chart*; *cart.* = *cartoon*; *exc.* = *excerpt*; *g.* = *graph*; *ill.* = *illustration*; *q.* = *quotation*

Hardenberg, Prince von, 434
Hargreaves, James, 423, *ill.* 423
Harsha (India), 156–157
Harvey, William, 315, 389
Hastings, Battle of, 232
Hawthorne, Nathaniel, 508
Hay, John, 484
Haydn, Franz Joseph, 395
Hebrews, 57, 58, 59
Hegel, Georg, 432
Hegira, 196
Hellenic Age, 103–107
Hellenistic world, 122–128, *ill.* 127, *m.* 123
Hellespont, 101
Helots, 105
Helsinki Agreement, 645, *ill.* 642
Henry the Fowler, 231, 234, 246, *ill.* 231
Henry the Navigator, 317
Henry Tudor, 243
Henry II (England), 241, 242
Henry III (England), 242
Henry IV (France), 339, 340
Henry IV (Holy Roman Empire), 249, 464, *q.* 249
Henry V (England), 245
Henry VII (England), 342, 343
Henry VIII (England), 314, 332, 342, 343
Heraclius, 191
Herodotus, 113
Herod the Great, 143
Hertz, Heinrich, 502
Herzegovina, 454, 455, 530, 532, 536
Hieroglyphics, 51
Himalaya, 63, 78
Hindenburg, General Paul von, 541, 595
Hinduism, 70–71, 154–155, 200, 284, 491, *ill.* 70, 71, 155
Hipparchus, 125
Hippocrates, 122, *q.* 112
Hirohito, 625
Hiroshima, 625
Hispaniola, 415, *m.* 417
History: dating of, *c.* 74; meaning of, 699
Hitler, Adolf, 554, 594–598, 616, 617, 624, *ill.* 558–559, 593, 599, *q.* 616

Hittite Empire, 56, 67, *m.* 57
Hobbes, Thomas, 392
Ho Chi Minh, 576, 676
Hohenzollerns, 348–350
Holbein, Hans (the Younger), 314, *ill.* 314
Holland, 359–360, 481, 574
Holocaust, 629
Holy Land, 247, 248
Holy Roman Empire, 231, 246–247, 249, 347–350, *m.* 232, 349, 350
Homer, 101, 109, 112
Homo erectus, 30
Homo habilis, 30
Homo sapiens, 30
Honduras, 416, 660
Hong Kong, 477, 483, *ill.* 662
Hoover, Herbert, 589
Horace, 150
Horthy, Miklós von Nagybánya, 609
House of Commons. See Parliament.
Hsüan Tsang, 156
Huaris, 186
Hugo, Victor, 508, 509
Huguenots, 339, 340, 341
Hui Tsung, 289
Humanism, 307–309, 311–316
Hundred Years' War, 244–245, 338, *ill.* 245, *m.* 244
Hungary, 280, 442, 580, 584, 608, 609, 619, 632, 635, *ill.* 635. *See also* Austria-Hungary.
Huns, 146
Hunting, 180–181, 184, *ill.* 181
Huss, John, 251, 325–326
Hussein (Jordan), 630
Hussites, 251
Hutton, James, 388, 405
Hyksos, 47, 48

I

Iberian Peninsula, 245–246
Ibn-Saud, 572
Ibsen, Henrik, 510
Ice Age, 31–32, *m.* 32
Ikeda, Hayato, 670

Imperialism: 441–444, 466, 471–472, 476–478; in Africa, 492–498; in China, 482–484; in India, 489–492; in Japan, 487–488
Incas, 186, 371–372
India: 671–676, *m.* 62; agriculture in, 63, *ill.* 38; ancient, 62–75, *m.* 66; art in, 154–155, 286, *ill.* 64, 68, 70, 72, 74, 152, 155, 156; caste system in, 284, 675, *ill.* 675; and Communist China, 674; Delhi sultanate, 284–285; development of, 672, 674, *ill.* 672; and Europe, 361–362; free enterprise in, 490; and Great Britain, 362, 477, 489–492, 574, *m.* 489, *ill.* 490; Gupta Empire, 153–156; independence of, 671–672; *jizya* in, 284; Kushan Empire, 75; literacy in, 674; Maurya Empire, 73–74; middle class in, 491; Mogul Empire, 489; and Muslim conquest, 284–287, *m.* 284; and Muslim League, 491; nationalism in, 491; population of, 491, 675; *purdah* in, 286; and Rajputs, 157; religion in, 69–71, 154, 155, *ill.* 155, 157, 286–287, 491, 671–672; science and mathematics in, 155–156; Sepoy Rebellion, 489–490; social structure of, 69–70; Taj Mahal, *ill.* 286; Urdu in, 286; women in, 70, 676
Indians, American, 182–186, 368–374, *ill.* 185, *m.* 183, 184, 369. *See also specific tribes and civilizations.*
Indo-Aryan culture, 66, 67–68
Indochina, 471, 481, 574, 576, 648
Indo-Europeans, 67
Indonesia, 360, 362
Indus River Valley, 57, 62, 63, 66, 73, 121, *m.* 66
Industrial Revolution: 385, 421, 426–427, 699, *ill.* 425, *q.* 427; in Belgium, 425; child labor, 428, *ill.* 428; factory system, 424, 426–427; in France, 425; in

Mazarin, Cardinal, 341

Mecca, 195, 196, 279

Medicine: in Egypt, 51; in Europe, 388–389, 502–503; in future, 704; in Middle Ages, 259; in Renaissance, 311

Medina, 196, 279

Mein Kampf (Hitler), 594

Memphis, 46, 48

Mendel, Gregor, 501

Menes, 46

Mentuhotep II (Egypt), 47

Mercantilism, 381–385, 403. *See also* Commercial Revolution.

Merici, Angela, 333

Meroë, 173

Merovingians, 209

Mesopotamia, 42, 52–54, 191, *m.* 52

Messana (Messina), 136

Methodius, 193, 275

Metternich, Prince von, 434, 435, 441, 445

Mexico: 42, 181–182, 416–417, 658, *m.* 417; civil war, 416; constitution of, 416

Michael VIII (Byzantium), 276

Michelangelo Buonarroti, 310, *ill.* 311

Middle Ages in Europe: 222–225, *ill.* 221, 238, 239, 240; Age of Faith, 247; agriculture in, 206, 218, 226, 227, 228, 230, *ill.* 208; art in, 258–259, *ill.* 204, 207, 208, 213, 216, 217, 222, 228, 229, 230, 252, 253, 254, 255, 257, 259; banking in, 255–256, *ill.* 255; decline of, 206, 241; early, 205–207; education in, 207, 258; guilds in, 253–254, 255, *ill.* 253; High Middle Ages, 247; landholding in, 217, 219, 227–229; lawlessness in, 206, 217, 218; literature in, 258; mutual protection, 217, *ill.* 217; science in, 259–260; towns in, 252–253, 256–257, *ill.* 238–239, 252, 276; trade in, 206, 252, 256; universities, 258; women in, 255, *ill.* 254. *See also* Feudalism; Manorialism; *individual countries.*

Middle East: 47, 54, 56, 195, 688–690, 693–696; American and Soviet involvement, 695; and Greece, 99; and League of Nations, 571, *m.* 571; oil embargo, 695; oil reserves, 695; and Ottoman Turks, 572; and Roman Empire, 189. *See also individual countries.*

Migrations: in Africa, 177–178; in America, 180, *ill.* 183; Indo-Aryan, 67; in Italy, 131

Miki, Takeo, 670

Milan, 246, 256, 306

Milton, John, 258

Minamoto, Yoritomo, 296–297

Ming dynasty, 292–293, 481

Minoan civilization, 99, 100, *ill.* 97, 101

Missi dominici, 210

Mitterand, François, 650

Mobutu Sese Seko, 683, *ill.* 683

Mochicas, 186

Mogadishu, 179

Mohenjo-Daro, 64–65, *ill.* 61

Molière, 393

Moltke, General Helmuth von, 540

Moluccas, 358, *m.* 358

Mombasa, 179

Monasticism, 215–216

Monet, Claude, 511

Money: 206, 316, 334, *ill.* 110, 334; in China, 90–91; in Middle Ages, 255–256, *ill.* 255; in Rome, 141, 145, 149. *See also* Banks and banking.

Mongol Empire, 270–272, *m.* 270, *q.* 270

Mongols, 267, 278–279

Monomotapa, 178

Monotheism, 57, 58, 59, 143, 195

Montenegro, 454, 455, 529, 532, 533

Montesquieu, Baron de, 391, 402, 403

Monteverdi, Claudio, 393

Montezuma II (Aztec), 370

Moors, 245–246

More, Sir Thomas, 315

Morelos, Father José, 416

Morocco, 365–366, 496, 524–525

Morse, Samuel, 426

Moscow, 269, 271–272, 526, 620, *m.* 262, 271

Moses, 58

Mo Ti, 88

Mott, Lucretia, 515

Mozambique, 368

Mozart, Wolfgang Amadeus, 395

Mubarak, Hosni, 695

Muhammad, 195–196, *ill.* 196

Muhammad II (Ottoman Empire), 279, *q.* 279

Muhammad, Askia, 364, 365

Munich, 616, 645–646

Music, 393–395, 509

Muslims: 195, 206, 491; and Byzantine Empire, 191; crusades against, 247–249; expansion of, *m.* 236; and Gaul, 210; and Ghana, 174; and Mediterranean, 211, 218; and Songhai, 364. *See also* Moors.

Mussolini, Benito, 586–587, 605–606, 619, *ill.* 587, *q.* 587

Mustafa Kemal, 572, *ill.* 573

Mycenaean civilization, 99, 101

Myths and Realities: The Charge of the Light Brigade, 452; The Code of Chivalry, 224; Dating the Mysterious Past, 39; Early Chinese Technology, 161; The Invincible Armada, 346; Opposition to Hitler, 599

N

Nachtigal, Gustav, 466, 496

Nagasaki, 625

Namibia, 686, *ill.* 681

Nantes, Edict of, 339, 341

Napoleon III (France), 437, 442–443, 445, 446, 447, 449, 451, 467, 518

Napoleon Bonaparte, 411–415, *ill.* 379, 413

Napoleonic Empire, 411–415, *m.* 414

Nasser, Gamal Abdel, 688

Nationalism: in Austria-Hungary, 518–519; in Balkans, 520, 529,

Peru, 185, 417
Peters, Carl, 496
Peter the Great (Russia), 351
Peter III (Russia), 354
Petrarca, Francesco, 308
Philip (Macedonia), 107
Philip II (France), 243, 343, 359
Philip II (Macedonia), 117–118
Philip IV (France), 243, 250, 323–324
Philip V (Macedonia), 137
Philip VI (France), 244
Philippines, 362, 573, 574, 625
Philosophes, 390–391
Phoenicia, 48
Pilsudski, Marshal, 608
Pindar, 113
Pisan, Christine de, 255
Pisistratus, 105
Pius IX (pope), 464–465
Pizarro, Francisco, 372
Plague, 243, 257, ill. 257
Planck, Max, 507
Plato, 111, 112, 202
Plekhanov, George, ill. 527
Plutarch, 150
Poe, Edgar Allan, 508
Poland, 267, 355, 436, 551, 580, 583, 608, 616, 632, 634–635
Polish Corridor, 551, 616
Pollution, 699, 701–702, cart. 702
Polo, Marco. See Marco Polo.
Pompey, 139
Pompidou, Georges, 649
Pope, Alexander, 388, 393, q. 388
Population, 24–25, 699–700, c. 700, ill. 25, m. 24
Portugal, 179, 245–246, 317–319, 358–359, 415, 435, 481
Potsdam, 629
Primo de Rivera, General, 606, 607
Prince Henry. See Henry the Navigator.
Princip, Gavrilo, 536
Proletariat, 432–433, 527
Protestantism, 331–332, ill. 322. See also Reformation.
Protestant Reformation. See Reformation.
Prussia, 348–350, 441, 448, 449, 450, 451, m. 350

Ptolemaic Empire, 122, 124
Punic Wars, 136–137
Puritans, 344
Pyramids, 51, ill. 44, 47
Pythagoras, 112

R

Rabelais, François, 315
Railroads: in France, 645; in Germany, 441, 463; in Great Britain, 426; in Italy, 448; in Japan, 487, ill. 487; in Russia, 525, 603
Ramayana, 68, 154, ill. 68
Rasputin, 545, ill. 545
Reagan, Ronald, 644, 645, 653, 687
Reformation, 251, 322–335, 339
Reign of Terror, 409–411
Religion: in Age of Faith, 247; in Age of Reason, 391–392; in ancient Egypt, 48–50; in ancient Greece, 109, 110, ill. 116; in ancient Rome, 142; in Byzantine Empire, 193; and Calvin, 330–331; in China, 81; and colonialism, 491, 493, 498; in England, 343, 344–345; and government, 331, 338; in India, 70–71, 74, ill. 70; and Luther, 326, 328, ill. 328; in Middle Ages, 213–216, ill. 213, 214; in Middle East, 58, 193, 195–197; in Persian Empire, 57; and warfare, 328; and Zwingli, 330. See also individual religions and countries.
Renaissance, 304–321, ill. 304, 307, 309, 310, 312, 314, 317, 334
Renoir, Pierre Auguste, 511, ill. 510
Republic of Ireland, 648, m. 648
Rhàzes, 200
Rhee, Syngman, 633
Rhodes, Cecil, 477–478, 494, cart. 495
Rhodesia, 478, 494, 685. See also Zimbabwe.
Richard III (England), 243
Richard the Lion-Hearted, 248
Richelieu, Cardinal de, 340–341

Rig-Veda, 67
Roads and highways: in ancient China, 154, m. 158; in Roman Empire, 150
Robespierre, Maximilien, 409
Rodin, 511
Roentgen, Conrad, 503
Roman Catholic Church: 193, 213–216, 265, 323–326, ill. 213, 214; and Carolingians, 210; decline of power, 241, 243–244, 247–251, 323–326; and education, 207, 216, ill. 216; and Franks, 209; and Great Schism, 324; and Holy Roman Empire, 249–250; and land, 323; and lay investiture, 249; and political order, 216; and primogeniture, 325; and reform movements, 325–326; and simony, 249, 325; and tithes, 323, ill. 323. See also Reformation.
Roman Empire: 75, 141–145, 166, 188, m. 138; agriculture in, 142; army, 145; civil war, 145; decline of, 145–150, 205; division of, m. 146; Eastern Empire, 145, 189–191; extensions of, 137, 141; government of, 141, 145, 149; industry in, 142, 145; invasions of, 189, m. 148; life in, 142; roads of, 141; trade in, 141, 145; Western Empire, 145, 189
Romanovs (Russia), 351–355
Romanticism, 507–508
Rome, 124, 131–138, 141–148, 149–150, ill. 130, 134, 140, 149. See also Roman Empire.
Rome-Berlin-Tokyo Axis, 597
Rommel, Erwin, 619, ill. 619
Roosevelt, Franklin D., 619, 623, 624, 629, q. 623
Roosevelt, Theodore, 488, ill. 488
Rosetta Stone, 51, 64, 412, ill. 51
Rousseau, Jean Jacques, 392, 403, 415, 507
Routes, trade and travel, 100, 101, 122, 123, 136, 141, 171, 267, 316–317, m. 104. See also Trade.

Westphalia, Peace of, 348, *m.* 348
Whitney, Eli, 424, 425
William the Conqueror, 232, 233, 234, 241
William I (Prussia), 448, 451
William II (Germany), 466–467, 522, 525, 537–538, *cart.* 467, *ill.* 524, *q.* 538
Wilson, Woodrow, 549, 550, 553, *ill.* 554
Women: 513–514; in Byzantine Empire, 190; in Egypt, 50–51; in feudal society, 225–226, *ill.* 225; in Germany, *ill.* 542; in Great Britain, 428, 430; in Greece, 105, 109; in the Middle Ages, 235, *ill.* 254; in Soviet Union, 603, *ill.* 604; suffragists, 514–515, *ill.* 514; in Sumer, 54. *See also individual countries.*
World Bank, 699
World War I: 535–554, *ill.* 535, *m.* 538; in Africa, 543; aftermath, 549–554; Allied Powers, 538; armistice, 543, 544, *ill.* 460; assassination at Sarajevo, 536–537; battles, 540, 541, 542, 543; causes, 519, 538–539; Central Powers, 538; crisis in Balkans, 535–539; debts and reparations, 580–581, *ill.* 589; destruction, *ill.* 582; and Japan, 543; mobilization, 538; pre-war period, 517–533, *cart.* 517; and Russian Revolution, 543, 547; at sea, 543, *ill.* 543; and Turkey, 542; and United States, 518, 543–544, 588, 616, 621, 622; warfare, 541, 542, *ill.* 541; and war plans, 539, 540, *m.* 540; women in, 542, *ill.* 542. *See also individual countries.*
World War II: 616–621, *ill.* 559, 620; aftermath, 643; Allied powers, 623; Axis powers, 623; and Big Three, 624; D day, 624; defeat of Germany, 623–624; in Europe, 616–624, *m.* 618; Iwo Jima monument, *ill.* 615; and Japan, 624–625, 627, *m.* 625; in North Africa, 619, 624; in Pacific, 624–627, *m.* 625; and United States, 616, 619, 621–627, *ill.* 615, 623, 626, *m.* 625; VE Day, 624; war crimes, 629; in Western Europe, 618–619, *m.* 618. *See also individual countries.*
Worms, Diet of, 328, *ill.* 328
Worms, Edict of, 328
Writing, 29, 49, 51, 53, 54, 63–64, 78, 81, 91, 133, 160, 171, 174, 184, 193, 195, 211, 216, 565, *ill.* 51, 55, 81, 216
Wu Ti, 157, 159
Wycliffe, John, 251, 325–326, *ill.* 251

X

Xerxes, 105
X rays, 503

Y

Yalta conference, 632
Yang Chien, 163
Yang Ti, 164
Yangtze River, 38, 78–79
Yaroslav, 268–269, *ill.* 268
Yellow River, 38, 42, 78, 80
Yoshida, Shigeru, 670
Young Plan, 581
Ypres, *ill.* 582
Yüan Shih-k'ai, 561, 562, *ill.* 561
Yugoslavia, 580, 584, 619, 632

Z

Zacharias (pope), 210
Zaibatsu, 568
Zaire, 683
Zambezi River, 171, 178
Zanzibar, 495
Zeno, 127
Ziggurat, 53, *ill.* 27
Zimbabwe, 178, 685
Zionism, 687
Zola, Émile, 470–471
Zollverein, 441, 448
Zoroastrianism, 57
Zwingli, Huldreich, 330

(Acknowledgments continued from page 4.)

Historical Association, 1960./Pages 232–233: from *Chronicle of the Kings of England*, Book III. Translated by J. Sharpe. George Bell and Sons, 1876./Page 254: from *Medieval People* by Eileen Power. Harper & Row, Publishers, Inc, 1965./Page 270: from *A History of Russia* by N.V. Riasanovsky. Oxford University Press, 1969./Page 291: from *The Travels of Marco Polo* by Cottie A. Berland. McGraw-Hill Book Company. Reprinted by permission of Anton Schroll & Co., 1970./Page 292: from *The Forbidden City* by Roderick MacFarquhar. Newsweek Books, 1972./Page 312: from *The Book of the Courtier* by Count Baldesar Castiglione. Translated by L.E. Opdycke. Charles Scribner's Sons, 1903./Page 327: from *Martin Luther*, edited by E.G. Rupp and Benjamin Drewery. St. Martin's Press, 1970./Page 328: from *Institutes of the Christian Religion*, Vol. II, by John Calvin, translated by Henry Beveridge. William B. Eerdmans Publishing Company, 1957./Page 328: from *The Reformation of the Sixteenth Century* by R.H. Bainton, Beacon Press, 1952./Page 331: from *The Lawes and Statutes of GENEVA*. Courtesy of The Newberry Library, Chicago./Page 366: from *A Short History of West Africa: A.D. 1000 to the Present* by T.A. Osae, S.N. Nwabara, and A.T.O. Odunsi. Copyright © 1975, Farrar, Straus & Giroux, Inc./Page 370: from *The Discovery and Conquest of Mexico* by Bernal Diaz del Castillo. Copyright © 1970, Farrar, Straus & Giroux, Inc./Page 385: from *The Wealth of Nations: Inquiry Into the Nature and Causes of the Wealth of Nations* by Adam Smith. Random House, Inc., 1937./Page 388: from *The Complete Poetical Works of Pope* (Cambridge Edition). Houghton Mifflin Company, 1931./Page 410: Reprinted by permission of G.P. Putnam's Sons from *The French Revolution* by Georges Pernoud and Sabine Flaissier, trans. by Richard Graves. Copyright © 1960 by Martin Secker & Warburg, LTD./Page 427: from *The Condition of the Working-Class in England in 1844* by Frederick Engels. Reprinted by permission of Allen and Unwin, Inc., 1952./Pages 428 and 429: from *Hard Times* by Charles Dickens. Holt, Rinehart, and Winston, 1958./Page 429: from *A Reader's Guide to Charles Dickens* by Philip Hobsbaum. Farrar, Straus & Giroux, Inc./Page 465: from *Economic Development of Modern Europe* by Frederic A. Ogg and Walter R. Sharpe. (Copyright 1917 by Macmillan Publishing Company, renewed 1945 by Frederic A. Ogg. Copyright 1926 by Macmillan Publishing Company, renewed 1954 by First National Bank of Madison and Walter Sharpe.)/Page 475: from *The Edwardians* by Paul Thompson. Indiana University Press and Weidenfeld and Nicolson, Ltd./Page 482: from *Annals and Memoirs of the Court of Peking* by E. Blackhouse and J.O.P. Bland. Houghton Mifflin Company, 1914./Page 497: from *Art in Africa* by Tibor Bodrogi. McGraw-Hill Book Company, 1968./Page 530: from *The Road to Sarajevo* by Vladimer Dedijer. Copyright © 1966 by Vladimer Dedijer. Reprinted by permission of Simon & Schuster, a division of Gulf & Western Corporation./Page 572: from *The World and Africa* by W.E.B. DuBois, International Publishers, New York, Copyright © 1965./Page 587: from "The Political and Social Doctrine of Fascism" by Benito Mussolini. *Political Quarterly*, July–September 1933./Page 590: from *Full Employment in a Free Society* by William Beveridge. Reprinted by permission of George Allen & Unwin (Publishers) Ltd., 1945./Page 596: from *Mein Kampf* by Adolf Hitler, translated by Ralph Manheim. Coypright 1943 and © renewed 1971 by Houghton Mifflin Company. Reprinted by permission of the publisher./Page 599: from Walther Hofer—*Der Nationalsozialismus: Dokumente 1933–45*, an excerpt of 18 lines. © Fischer Bücherei KG, Frankfurt am Main 1957. Mit Genehmigung der Fischer Taschenbuch Verlag GmbH, Frankfurt/Main./Page 694: from "Iran: A Land of Hardship and Hatred," *U.S. News & World Report*, April 12, 1982. Copyright © 1982, *U.S. News & World Report*. Reprinted with permission.

ACHIEVEMENTS
THROUGH
THE
AGES

John A. Mears
Associate Professor of History
Southern Methodist University
Dallas, Texas

Joachim R. Schneider
Social Studies Resource Teacher
Leyden Township High School
Franklin Park, Illinois

LAIDLAW BROTHERS · PUBLISHERS

A Division of Doubleday & Company, Inc.

RIVER FOREST, ILLINOIS

Irvine, California   Chamblee, Georgia   Dallas, Texas   Toronto, Canada